THE ARCHAEOLOGY OF GREEK AND ROMAN TROY

The Archaeology of Greek and Roman Troy provides a synthetic overview of all excavations that have been conducted at Troy, from the nineteenth century through the latest discoveries between 1988 and the present. Charles Brian Rose traces the social and economic development of the city and related sites in the Troad, as well as the development of its civic and religious centers from the Bronze Age through the early Christian period, with a focus on the settlements of Greek and Roman date. Along the way, he reconsiders the circumstances of the Trojan War and chronicles Troy's gradual development into a Homeric tourist destination and the adoption of Trojan ancestry by most nation-states in medieval Europe.

Charles Brian Rose is James B. Pritchard Professor of Mediterranean Archaeology in the Department of Classical Studies at the University of Pennsylvania and Curator-in-Charge of the Mediterranean Section of the Penn Museum. Between 1988 and 2012 he was Head of Post–Bronze Age excavations at Troy and English-language editor of *Studia Troica*, the annual journal of the Troy excavations. He is currently director of the Gordion Excavation Project in central Turkey. He has served as an Academic Trustee and the First Vice-President and President of the Archaeological Institute of America and as the Deputy Director of the Penn Museum. He has received grants from the National Endowment for the Humanities, the Rome Prize of the American Academy in Rome, the Berlin Prize of the American Academy in Berlin, the American Council of Learned Societies, the American Research Institute in Turkey, and the Samuel H. Kress Foundation. He is the author of *Commemoration and Imperial Portraiture in the Julio-Claudian Period* (Cambridge University Press, 1997) and the co-editor (with Gareth Darbyshire) of *The New Chronology of Iron Age Gordion* (2011).

THE ARCHAEOLOGY
OF GREEK AND
ROMAN TROY

CHARLES BRIAN ROSE

University of Pennsylvania

CAMBRIDGE
UNIVERSITY PRESS

CAMBRIDGE
UNIVERSITY PRESS

32 Avenue of the Americas, New York, NY 10013-2473, USA

Cambridge University Press is part of the University of Cambridge.

It furthers the University's mission by disseminating knowledge in the pursuit of
education, learning, and research at the highest international levels of excellence.

www.cambridge.org
Information on this title: www.cambridge.org/9780521762076

First published 2014

A catalog record for this publication is available from the British Library.

Library of Congress Cataloging in Publication data
Rose, Charles Brian.
The archaeology of Greek and Roman Troy / Charles Brian Rose.
pages   cm.
Includes bibliographical references and index.
ISBN 978-0-521-76207-6 (hardback)
1. Troy (Extinct city)   2. Excavations (Archaeology) – Turkey – Troy
(Extinct city)   3. Turkey – Antiquities.   I. Title.
DF221.T8R67 2013
939′21–dc23   2013023925

ISBN 978-0-521-76207-6 Hardback

CONTENTS

LIST OF ILLUSTRATIONS

FIGURES

PLATES

Plates follow page xvi

ACKNOWLEDGMENTS

When Manfred Korfmann, Getzel Cohen, Stella Miller-Collett, and I inaugurated the Troy Excavation Project in 1988 we founded an annual excavation journal (*Studia Troica*) that featured interdisciplinary studies dealing with every aspect of the Troad – archaeological, historical, philological, and scientific – as well as virtually every period of habitation. Nineteen volumes have been published thus far, and six synthetic monographs on specialized topics are nearly complete.[1] There was still a need for a single book that joined the latest discoveries to those made in the late nineteenth and early twentieth centuries, in a format that would be accessible to students, scholars, and the public, and this monograph is an attempt to fill that need.

Manfred Korfmann's name appears throughout the pages of this book, and I will always regret that he did not live to see its completion. I had the privilege of working with him for eighteen years at Troy, where I learned something new every day as a consequence of our interaction. What impressed me in particular was his determination to focus on all phases of habitation at the site, from the Early Bronze Age through the Ottoman. That is the approach that I have followed here, although the periods between 1000 B.C. and A.D. 300 receive the majority of the emphasis.

In the course of twenty-five seasons of fieldwork at Troy I have incurred a heavy debt to a large number of scholars, but I would like to single out several of them who have been especially helpful during the preparation of this book: Meg Andrews, Nurettin Arslan, Carolyn Aslan, Cem Aslan, Rüstem Aslan, William Aylward, Christoph Bachhuber, Barbara Barletta, Maureen Basedow, George Bass, Andrea Berlin, Phil Betancourt, Gebhard Bieg, Debby Boedeker, Ann Brownlee, Rick Bullard, Barbara Burrell, Nick Cahill, Richard Catling, Caryn Chow, John Clarke, Eric Cline, Getzel Cohen, Jack Davis, Jennifer Davis, Donald Easton, Andrew Erskine, Marian Fabiş, Joe Farrell, Lisa French, Nadine Frey, Lynn Grant, Crawford Greenewalt Jr., Lothar Haselberger, Christoph Haussner, Sebastian Heath, Brian and Darlene Heidke, Pavol Hnila, Sam Holzman, Friedmund Hueber, Jeffrey Hurwit, Peter Jablonka, Christopher Jones, Henrike Kiesewetter, Manfred Klinkott, Ömer

Koç, Reyhan and Funda Körpe, Ann Kuttner, Mark Lawall, Kathleen Lynch, Dietrich Mannsperger, Jeremy McInerney, Tim McNiven, Andrew Meadows, Blanche Menadier, Zora Miklikova, Stella Miller-Collett, Moni Möck, Sarah Morris, Penelope Mountjoy, Jenifer Neils, Jim Ottaway, Bob Ousterhout, Mehmet Özdoğan, Coşkun Özgünel, John Papadopoulos, Holt Parker, Peter Pavuk, Ernst Pernicka, Felix Pirson, Gabriel Pizzorno, Gianni Ponti, Cemal Pulak, Kurt Raaflaub, Chris Ratté, Louise Rice, Brunilde Ridgway, Kent Rigsby, Elizabeth Riorden, Peter Rockwell, Chris Roosevelt, Steven Rosen, Eva Rosenstock, Elmar Schwertheim, Nurten Sevinç, Alan Shapiro, Julia Shear, Elizabeth Simpson, Bert Smith, Marcello Spanu, Shari Stocker, Donna Strahan, Turan Takaoğlu, Kurtis Tanaka, Tom Tartaron, Billur Tekkök, Mikhail Treister, Jim Tucker, Hans-Peter and Marguerite Uerpmann, Lut Vandeput, Peter van Minnen, Mary Voigt, John Wallrodt, Bonna Wescoat, Malcolm Wiener, Charles Williams, Susan Wise, Fatih Yavuz, and Fikret Yegül.

Without Stella Miller-Collett's guidance and support, the post–Bronze Age excavations could not have continued as long as they did, and without Billur Tekkök's careful dating of the pottery, our chronology would be very fragmented. I owe a special debt to Gebhard Bieg, Sebastian Heath, and Linda Meiberg, who examined the entire manuscript with great care and saved me from a host of errors. Beatrice Rehl at Cambridge University Press shepherded the manuscript through the publication process with her customary speed and expertise, and John Wallrodt, Gabriel Pizzorno, and Henry Bernberg handled the preparation of the photos, maps, plans, and reconstructions. Gabriel Pizzorno, in particular, seems to have devoted nearly as much time to this book as I did, and I am indebted to him, as always, for his perspicacity, creativity, and guidance.

I began this book when I was still a faculty member at the University of Cincinnati, and I acknowledge a heavy debt to librarians Jean Wellington, Jacqui Riley, and Michael Braunlin, who never tired of helping me locate an unusually large number of arcane publications. The remainder of the research was conducted in the library of the American Academy in Rome and the Rhys Carpenter Library at Bryn Mawr College, and I owe tremendous thanks to their directors, Christine Huemer and Camilla MacKay, respectively.

An equally large debt is owed to the staff of the Çanakkale Archaeological Museum, who have provided much hospitality to us over the years, especially during the period in which we were working together on the publication of the tombs from the Granicus River Valley. Nurten Sevinç, Reyhan and Funda Körpe, Ömer Özden, Candan Kozanlı, and Musa Tombul all deserve our thanks, as does the Turkish Ministry of Culture and Tourism, which granted us permission to conduct fieldwork at Troy and served as an unending source of support for us.

Financial support was generously supplied by the Louise Taft Semple Fund of the University of Cincinnati Classics Department, and I will always be grateful to the trustees of the Fund, especially Margo Tytus, for their encouragement. Additional financial support was provided by the Center for Hellenic Studies, the National Endowment for the Humanities, the American Council of Learned Societies, the American Academy in Berlin, the American Academy in Rome, and the George B. Storer Foundation. I am grateful to all of them for their assistance, and to my family, Patricia and Molly Rose, Marta and Charles Dabezies, and Bob Ousterhout, for their unflagging support.

C.B.R.

Plate 1. Annotated view of the coast of Western Turkey, photographed from the International Space Station. Courtesy of the Image Science and Analysis Laboratory, NASA-Johnson Space Center (ISS028-E-18561).

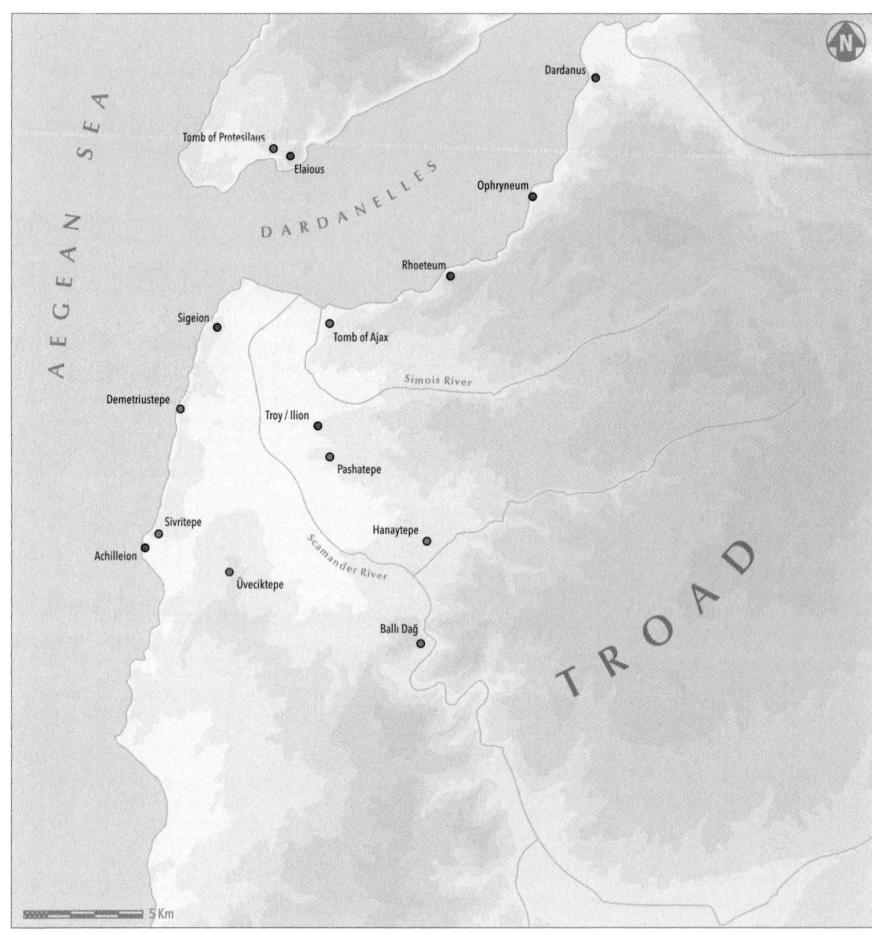

Plate 2. Map of the "Homeric" tumuli of the Troad, prepared by Gabriel Pizzorno.

Plate 3. Aerial view of the citadel mound of Troy with the Dardanelles and the Gallipoli peninsula visible to the north. Troia slide 23964.

Plate 4. Map of the Aegean and Asia Minor during the Early Bronze Age, prepared by Gabriel Pizzorno.

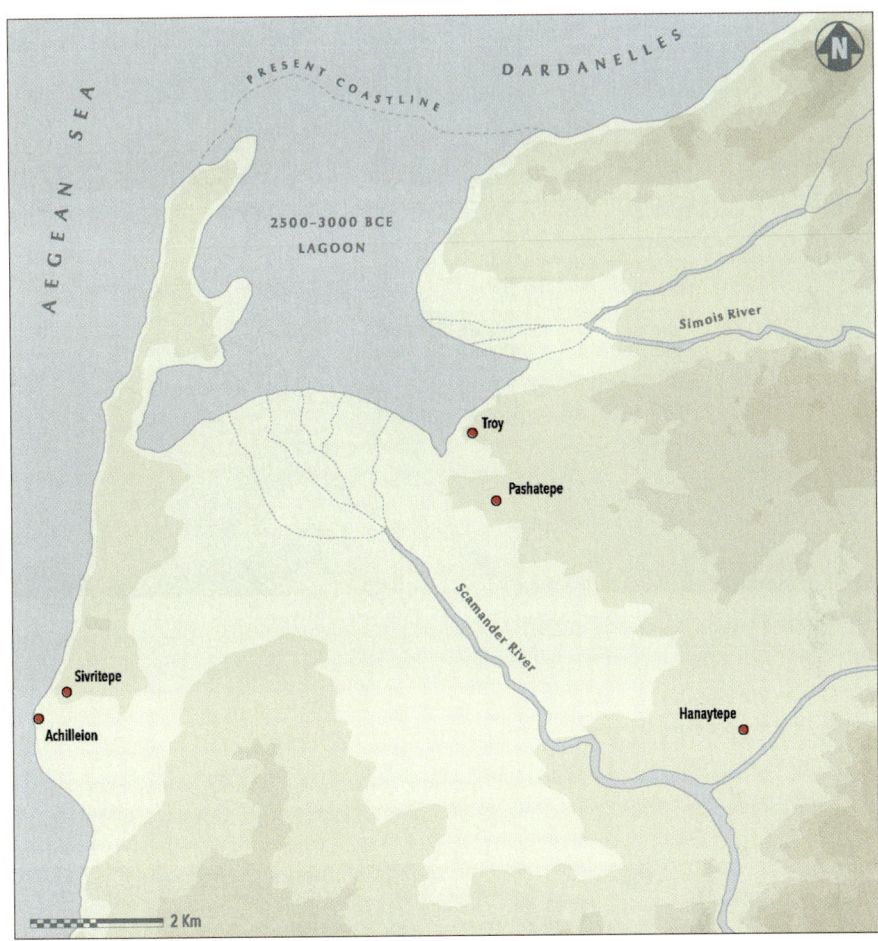

Plate 5. Map of the coastline of the southwest Hellespont during the early third millennium, prepared by Gabriel Pizzorno, based on Kraft et al. 2003.

Plate 6. Aerial view of the citadel mound and the Lower City. Troia slide 1581A.

Plate 7. Aerial view of the citadel mound. Troia slide 5007.

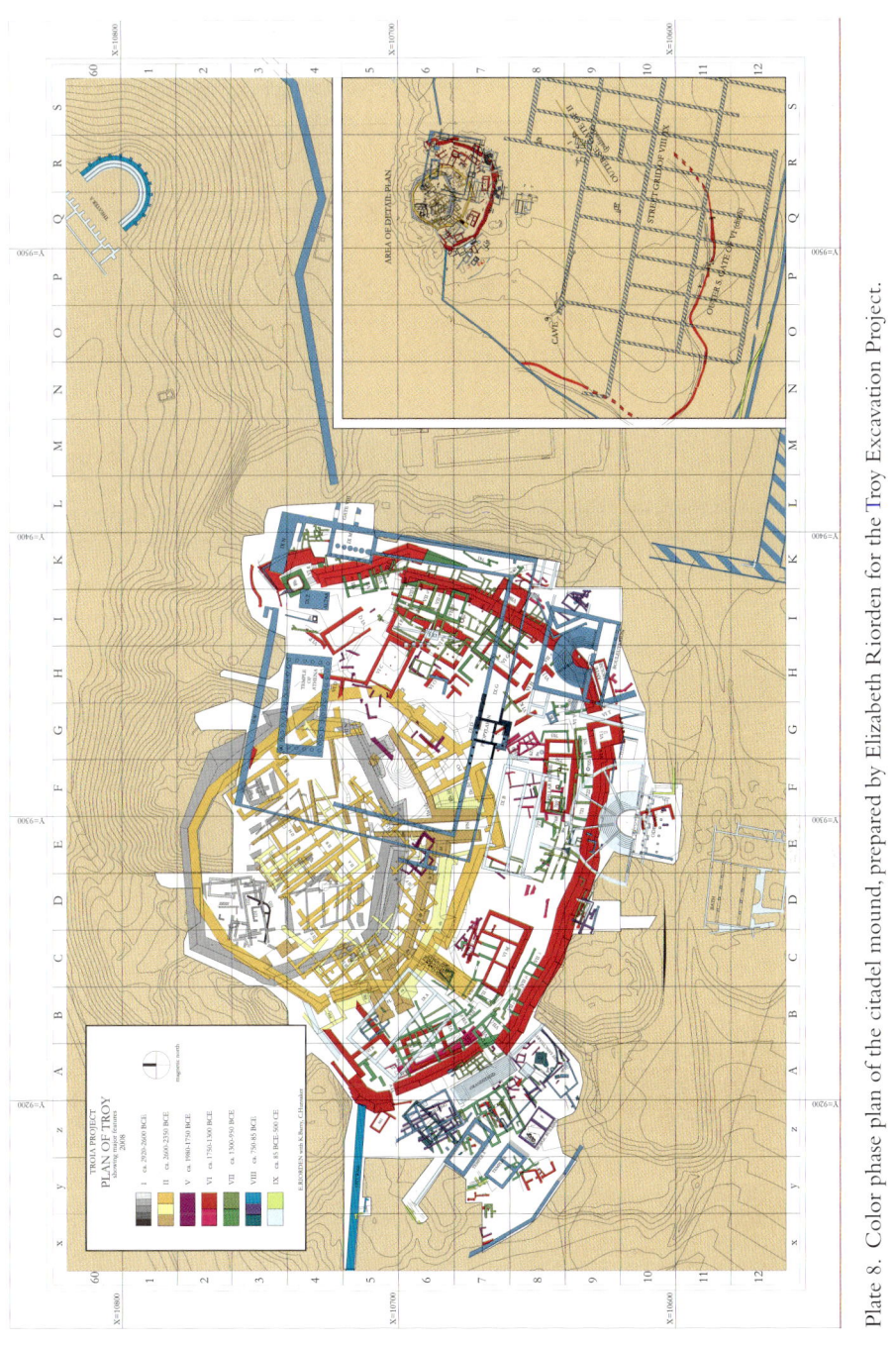

Plate 8. Color phase plan of the citadel mound, prepared by Elizabeth Riorden for the Troy Excavation Project.

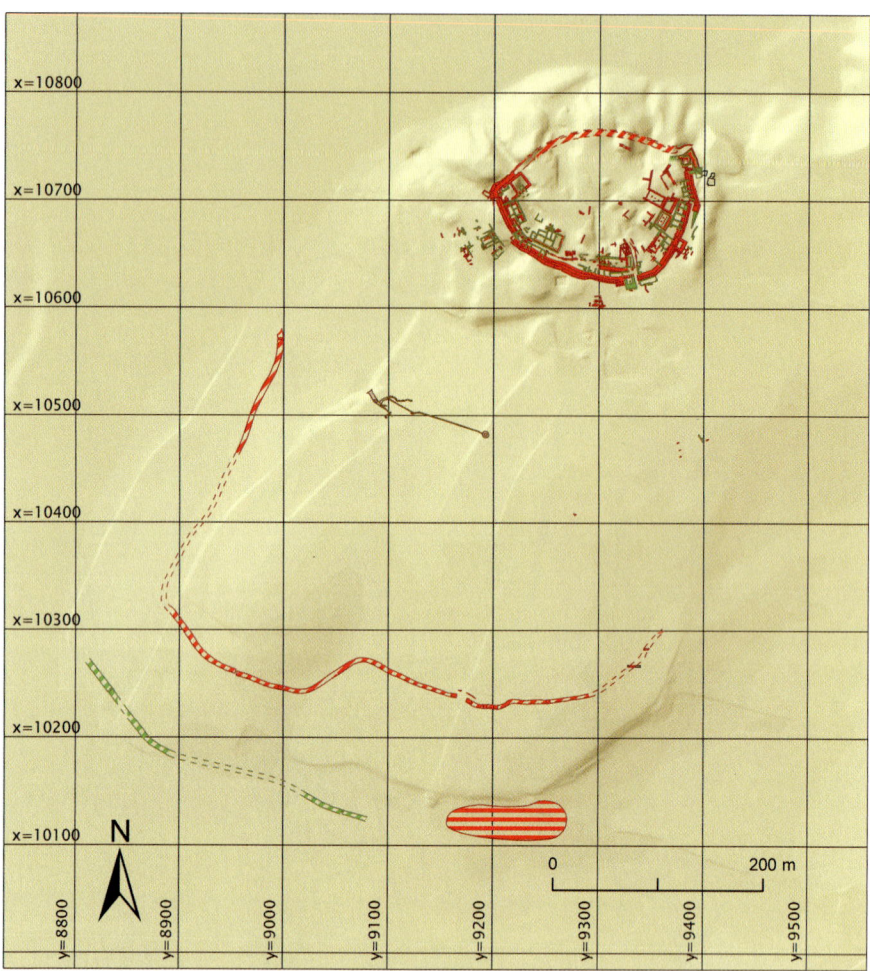

x=10800

x=10700

x=10600

x=10500

x=10400

x=10300

x=10200

x=10100

N

y=8800
y=8900
y=9000
y=9100
y=9200
y=9300
y=9400
y=9500

0   200 m

Plate 9. Plan of the rock-cut ditch in the Lower City, Troy VI, prepared by Gebhard Bieg for the Troy Excavation Project.

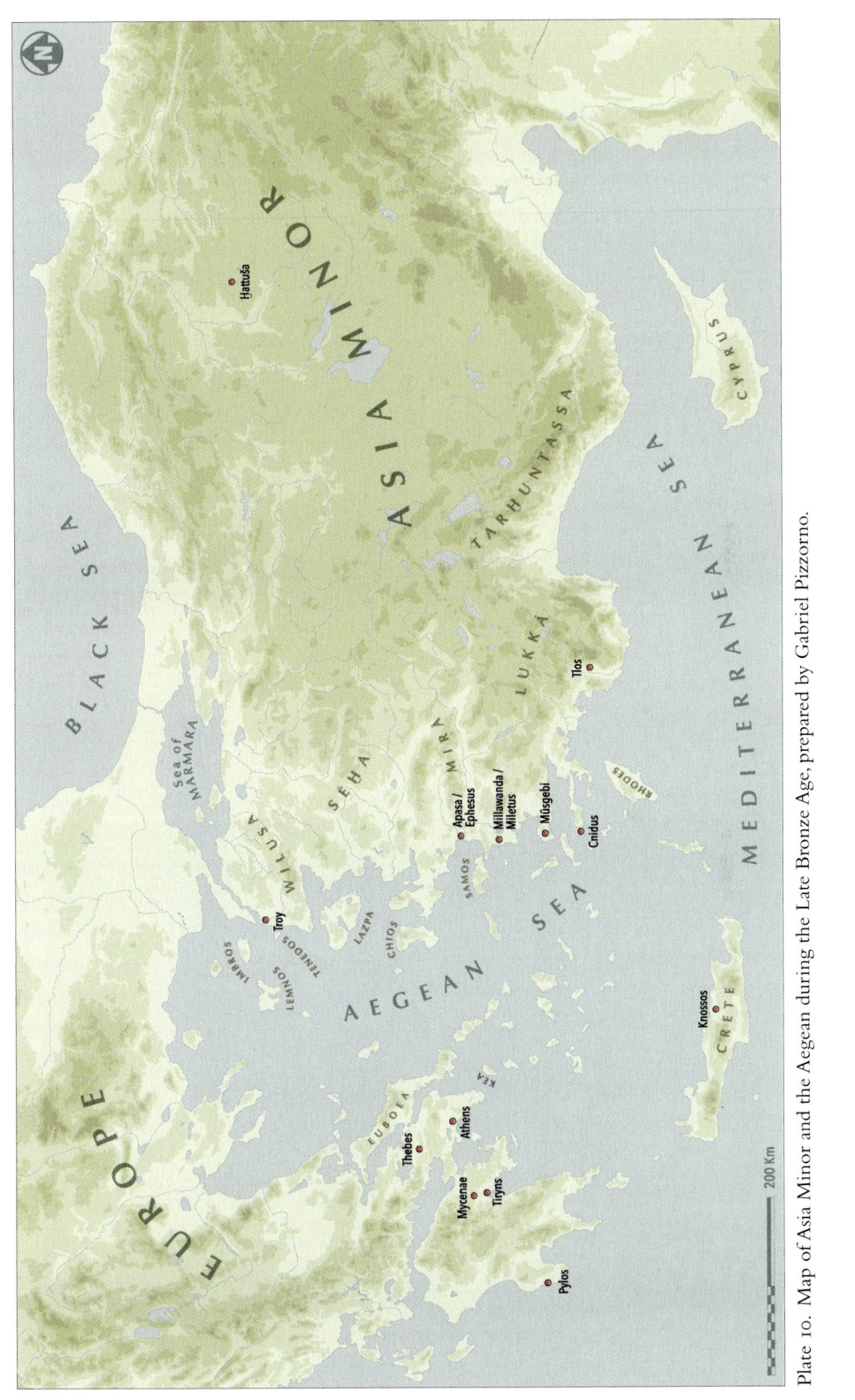

Plate 10. Map of Asia Minor and the Aegean during the Late Bronze Age, prepared by Gabriel Pizzorno.

Plate II. Map of the Aegean during the Archaic Period, prepared by Gabriel Pizzorno.

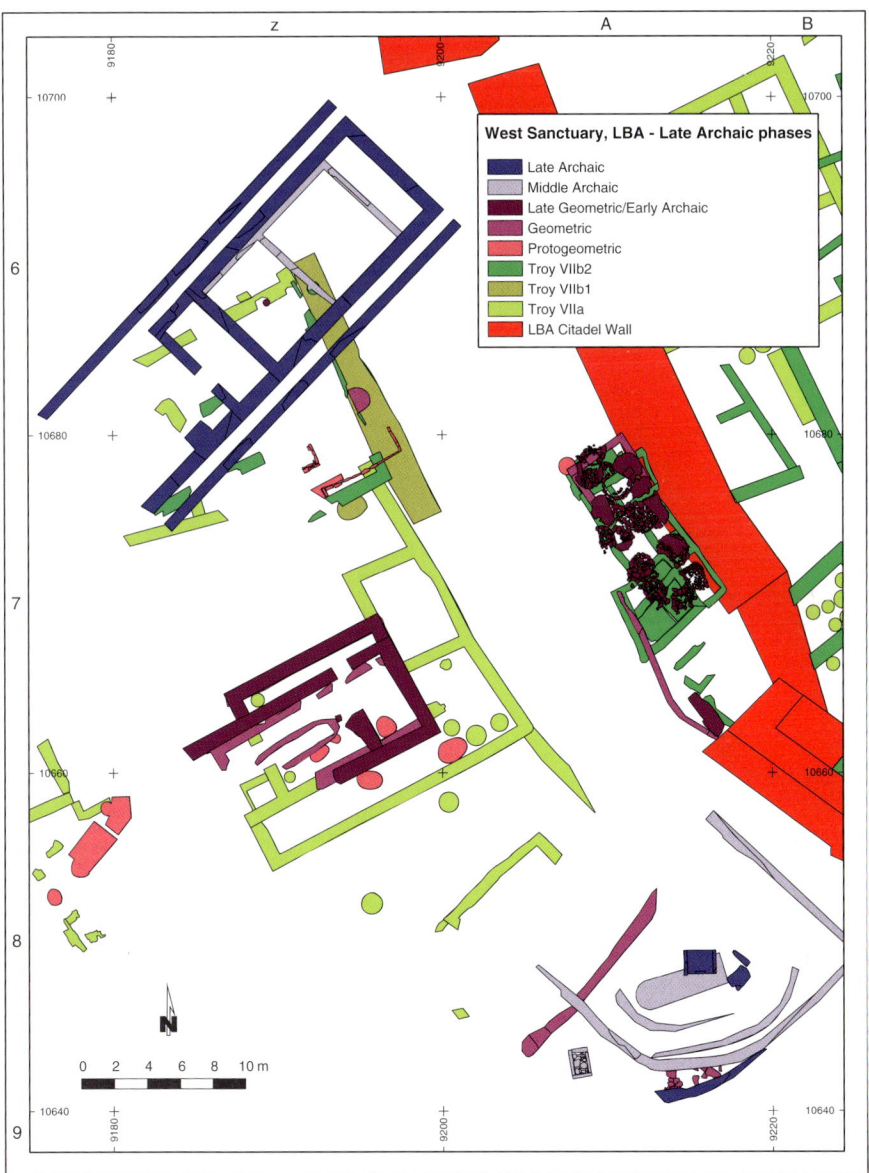

Plate 12. Plan of the West Sanctuary during the Late Bronze Age and Archaic Period, prepared by Pavol Hnila for the Troy Excavation Project.

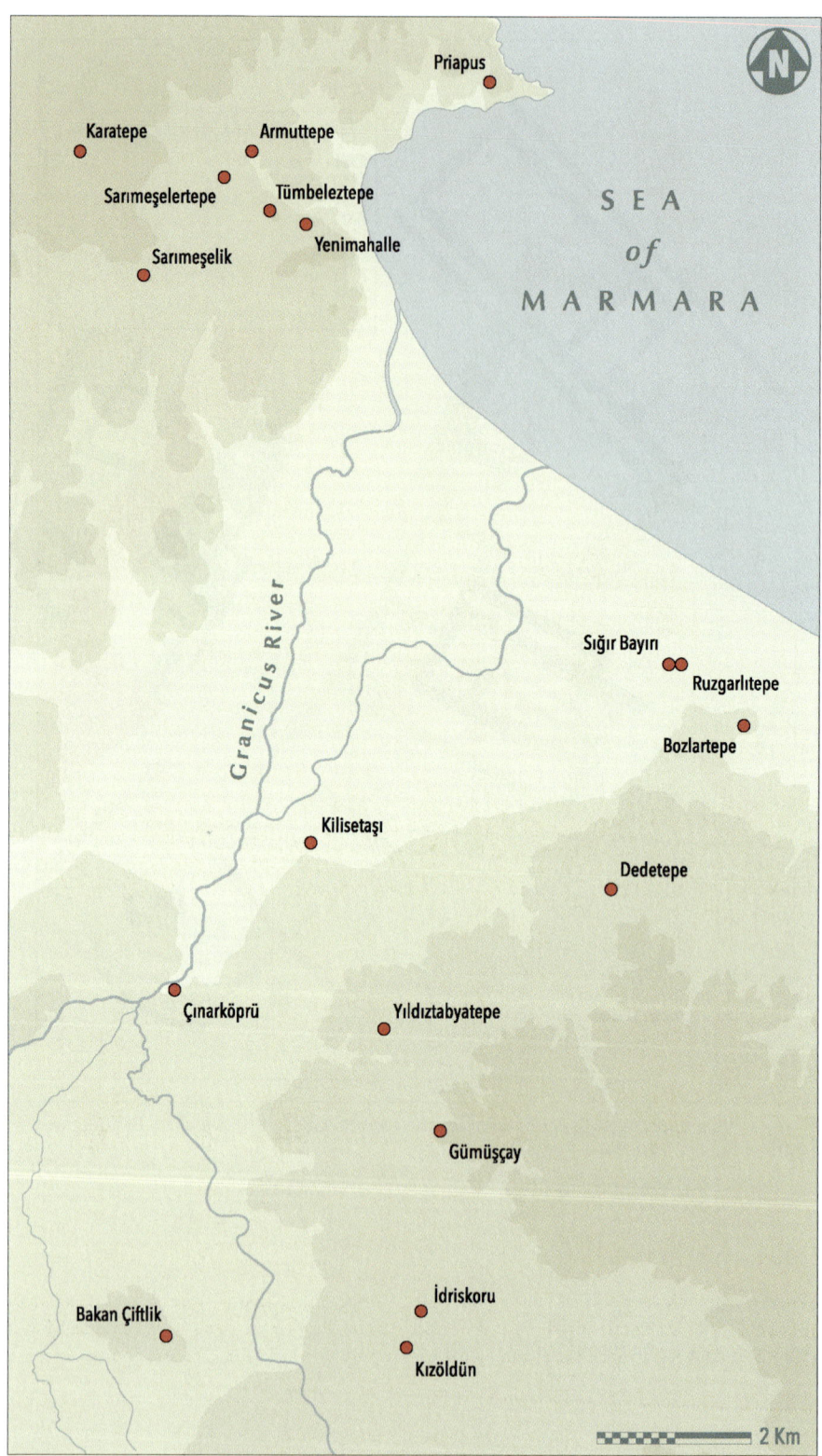

Plate 13. Map of the tumuli in the Granicus River Valley, prepared by Gabriel Pizzorno.

Plate 14. (A) Gold necklace with glass beads from the Child's Sarcophagus. Çanakkale Archaeological Museum. Troy Excavation Project photo. (B) Detail of pendants and glass beads of gold necklace. Çanakkale Archaeological Museum. Troy Excavation Project photo.

Plate 15. Interior view of the Dedetepe tomb chamber. Troy Excavation Project photo.

Plate 16. Detail of the west kline leg, Dedetepe tomb chamber. Troia slide 32747.

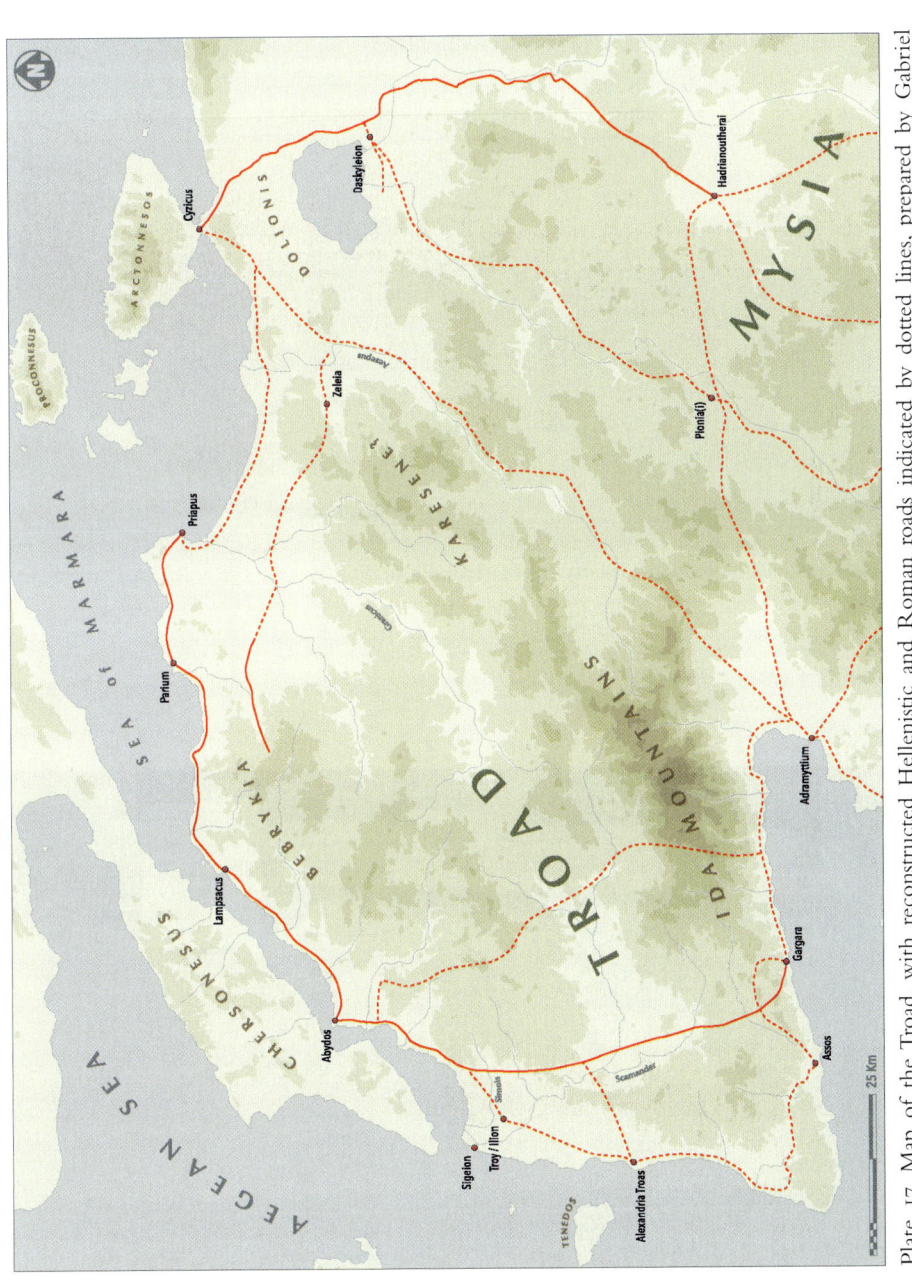

Plate 17. Map of the Troad, with reconstructed Hellenistic and Roman roads indicated by dotted lines, prepared by Gabriel Pizzorno.

Plate 18. Reconstructed elevation of the Çan Sarcophagus with lid, by Gabriel Pizzorno, based on an original by Robert Hagerty for the Troy Excavation Project. Çanakkale Archaeological Museum.

Plate 19. The front of the Çan Sarcophagus, with stag hunt at left and boar hunt at right. Çanakkale Archaeological Museum. Photo by the author.

Plate 20. Detail of the boar hunt on the Çan Sarcophagus. Çanakkale Archaeological Museum. Troy Excavation Project photo.

Plate 21. Detail of the boar and dog on the Çan Sarcophagus. Çanakkale Archaeological Museum. Troy Excavation Project photo.

Plate 22. Detail of the rider in the stag hunt. Çanakkale Archaeological Museum. Troy Excavation Project photo.

Plate 23. The battle scene on the short side. Çanakkale Archaeological Museum. Troy Excavation Project photo.

Plate 24. Detail of the rider in the battle scene. Çanakkale Archaeological Museum. Troy
Excavation Project photo.

Plate 25. Hypothetical reconstruction of the Trojan horse in the Sanctuary of Artemis Brauronia on the Athenian Acropolis, prepared by Henry M. Bernberg.

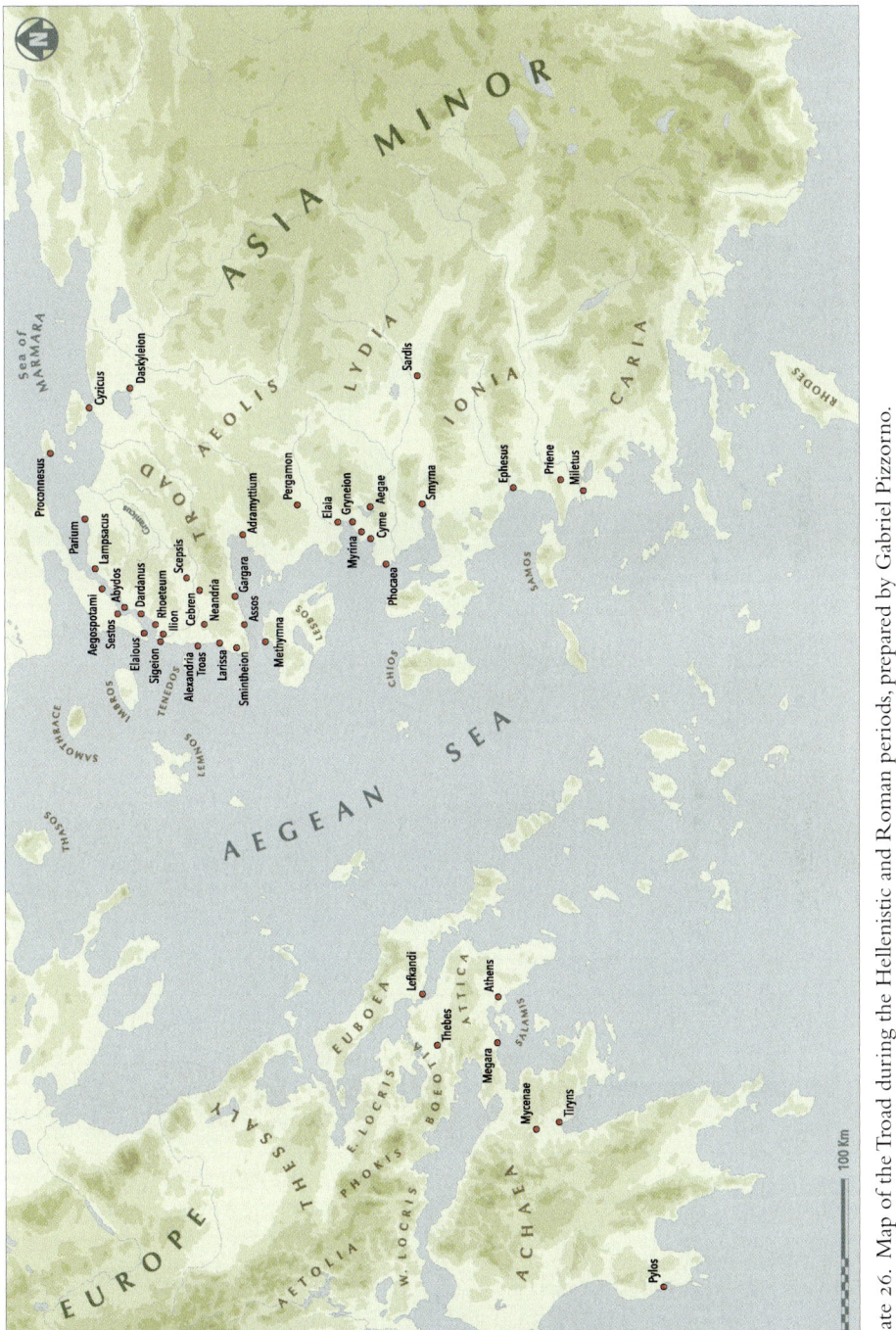

Plate 26. Map of the Troad during the Hellenistic and Roman periods, prepared by Gabriel Pizzorno.

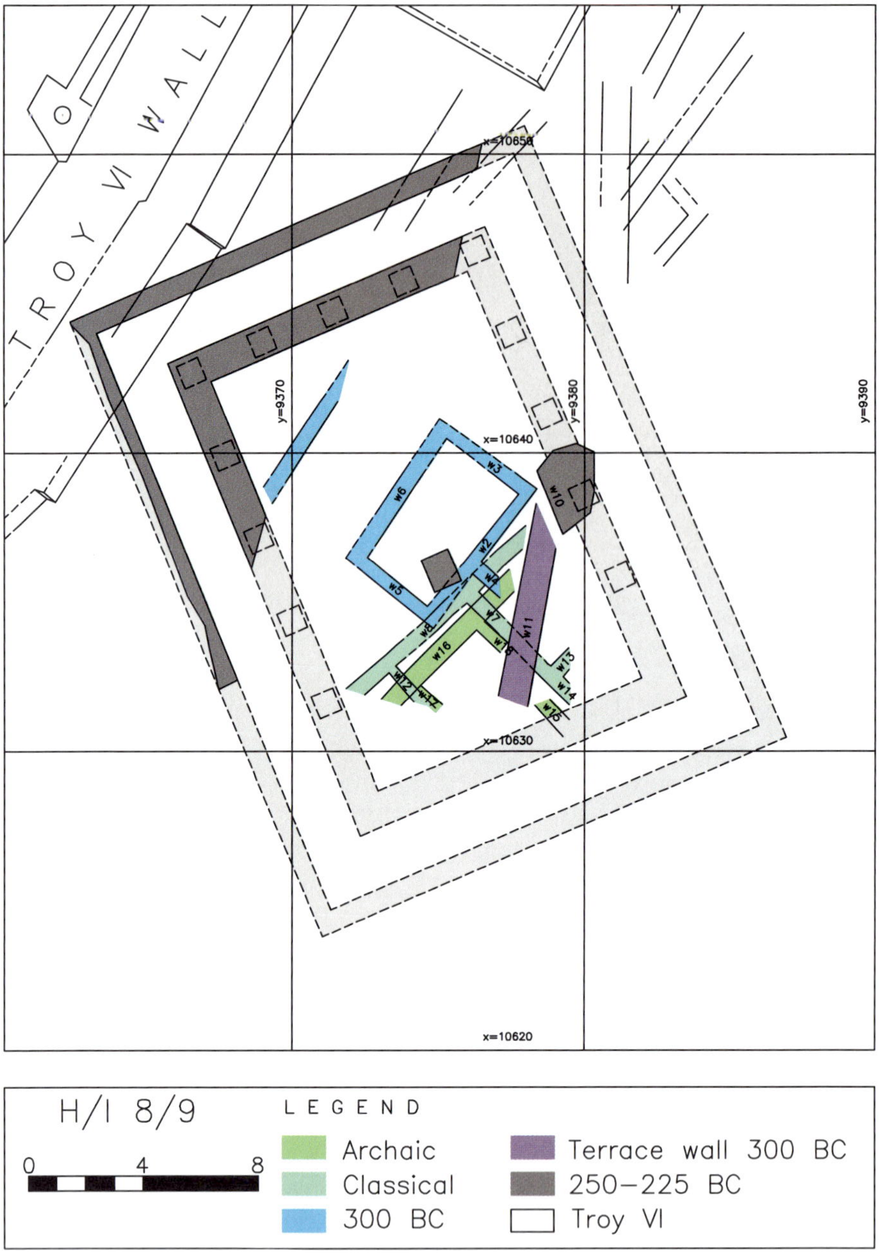

TROY VI WALL

x=10658
y=9370
y=9380
y=9390
x=10640
x=10630
x=10620

W3, W6, W2, W5, W8, W10, W11, W7, W16, W12, W13, W14, W15

LEGEND
H/I 8/9
0   4   8

Archaic
Classical
300 BC

Terrace wall 300 BC
250—225 BC
Troy VI

Plate 27. Phase plan of the Bouleuteria, prepared by Elizabeth Riorden for the Troy Excavation Project.

Plate 28. Painted plaster wall decoration from the Mosaic Building. Troy Excavation Project photo.

Plate 29. Plan of the citadel mound and the Lower City, prepared by Gebhard Bieg for the Troy Excavation Project.

INTRODUCTION

Excavations in and around Troy have occurred over the course of nearly forty-five years, beginning in 1855 and continuing sporadically until the present day, which means that the history of fieldwork there is nearly as fascinating as the archaeological discoveries themselves. Within that 150-year period there have been three major campaigns, those of Heinrich Schliemann and Wilhelm Dörpfeld (1870–94), Carl Blegen (University of Cincinnati, 1932–8), and Manfred Korfmann and me (Universities of Cincinnati and Tübingen, 1988–2012).[1] The critics of Schliemann's publications were vociferous in their objections, and divergent opinions about Troy's significance have surrounded every field project that has explored the site. The most recent campaign was no exception: many of the interpretations we advanced during the last twenty-five years were controversial, thereby prompting the publication of a large number of increasingly specialized publications that required of the reader an advanced understanding of the site.

Consequently, I felt that there was a need for a synthetic overview of all of the excavations and research that have been conducted at Troy, with the nineteenth and early twentieth century finds joined to those that were discovered between 1988 and the present. The sphere of activity for which I was responsible involved Greek, Roman, and Byzantine material culture, or "post–Bronze Age," whereas the Bronze Age excavations were conducted by Prof. Korfmann, who served as overall director of the site.[2] From the inception of the project, however, the work of the post–Bronze Age group was inextricably intertwined with that of Prof. Korfmann, and the narrative that I present here is very much influenced by and indebted to his excavations and research.[3]

When I began researching this book, I planned to concentrate on the Greek and Roman periods, since the Trojan material of that date had never been synthesized. I quickly realized, however, that such an analysis had to be framed by an overview of the Bronze Age settlements as well as by an assessment of the manipulation of the Trojan tradition in post-antique Europe and Asia. As a result, the material presented in these chapters encompasses over five millennia of history and ranges from Britain to Afghanistan, even though the core focus remains on the Trojan settlements of Greek and Roman date.

Post–Bronze Age excavations in the surroundings of Troy actually began nearly a century before Schliemann, and the initial attractions were the monumental burial mounds, or tumuli, that had become linked to the Homeric heroes over the course of several millennia (Plates 1 and 2). Count Choiseul-Gouffier, French ambassador to the Ottoman Empire, sponsored excavations in 1787 at the "Tomb of Achilles" north of Yenişehir, 6 km from Troy; he also inspected the "Tomb of Ajax" and identified the cliffs around the village of Yeniköy as the rocks of Hesione, the sister of Priam, who was rescued from a sea monster by Herakles.[4]

Excavation would not recur until the winter of 1855–6, when a British railroad engineer named John Brunton began exploring areas around the mound that probably coincide with the Agora and Lower City (Plate 8), reportedly finding the ruins of a Corinthian temple and a house with a mosaic floor featuring a boar hunt.[5] Also excavating in that area in the 1850s was Frank Calvert, a British expatriate and American Consul who ultimately bought the eastern half of the mound of Hisarlık with the expectation that it encompassed the ruins of Troy.[6] In 1855, he excavated the tumuli of Priam and Patroclus, after which he began to conduct fieldwork on and around the citadel mound itself.

These were the first excavations of the Temple of Athena and the Hellenistic City Wall, which continued to be explored by Heinrich Schliemann in the 1870s and 1880s.[7] In the course of his seven campaigns, Schliemann also extended his fieldwork to the large theater on the northeast side of the mound, the Spring Cave in the Lower City, and probably a part of the Agora. Following the model of Choiseul-Gouffier and Calvert, Schliemann also excavated several of the "Homeric" mounds that had been investigated by his predecessors, including those of Achilles and Patroclus, as well as Beşik-Sivritepe, identified in this book as the "Tomb of Achilles" that was visited by Alexander the Great.

Schliemann's broader sphere of exploration allowed him to offer the first solid overview of Hellenistic and Roman habitation at Troy, which was placed on an even firmer footing by the fieldwork and publications of his successor, Wilhelm Dörpfeld, who unearthed substantial parts of the Agora, including the Bouleuterion and Odeion.[8] He also exposed the west side of the citadel, dominated by Building IXA (Plate 8), and proposed a plausible reconstruction of the City Wall's circuit based on several strategically situated trenches in the Lower City. Neither Schliemann nor Dörpfeld had a firm grasp of the Iron Age, Archaic, or Classical periods at the site, but the architectural remains and small finds, including coins and inscriptions, were chronicled for the first time, and Dörpfeld's color phase plan of the nine known settlements would serve as one of the principal foundations for diachronic research on Trojan habitation for the next century.[9]

Although Carl Blegen's primary purpose in restarting the Troy Excavations was to refine the chronology of Bronze Age habitation at the site and search for prehistoric cemeteries, he uncovered several important complexes dating to the Greek and Roman periods.[10] These included two baths, one of which lay in the agora, a likely Early Christian Church paved in mosaics, and more of the Odeion, which had first been explored by Dörpfeld. His most significant post–Bronze Age discovery, however, was a large religious complex on the southwest side of the mound, generally referred to as the West Sanctuary.[11] Blegen began investigations there in an attempt to ascertain the nature of habitation on the outer face of the Late Bronze Age (Troy VI) fortification wall, in an area that also coincided with the projected line of the Early Bronze Age (Troy II) stone ramp further to the west. What he found was the best evidence that had ever been uncovered for the later Iron Age and Archaic period at Troy, as well as an unusually rich assemblage of material relating to local cults during those periods.

Carl Blegen noted in his final Troy report that there was much more of interest to explore at the site, but he was ending the project in order to leave as many opportunities as possible for the next generation of archaeologists who would be equipped with more advanced tools and techniques than he possessed – a decision I would also make sixty years later.[12] Although Blegen subsequently moved on to even more impressive discoveries at Pylos, in southwestern Greece, he did not neglect the publications of the material produced by his excavations at Troy: four volumes of the Bronze and Iron Age discoveries appeared during the course of the 1950s, with the coins and terracotta figurines each receiving monographic treatment in the early 1960s.[13]

After a fifty-year hiatus, new excavations were launched by Manfred Korfmann. In 1987, after he had secured permission from the Turkish Ministry of Culture to inaugurate a new project at Troy, Korfmann approached the University of Cincinnati with the offer of a joint excavation, wherein Tübingen would be responsible for the Bronze Age investigations, and Cincinnati for the post–Bronze Age. The intent was that the new Troy project would be different from the earlier campaigns: the team would focus on all phases of habitation at the site, from the Early Bronze Age through the Ottoman, treating the remains of each with the same respect so that a complete diachronic reconstruction could be produced for the first time.[14]

We were fortunate in that much of Lower City had already been subjected to magnetic prospection, and we had a good idea of the size of the Roman residential district.[15] The prospection results were splendid, in large part because the Lower City was essentially flat, not heavily wooded, and the ruins – at least the Roman ruins – were only a few centimeters below the surface. The use of magnetometry was not unprecedented on archaeological sites – it had been used at Gordion already in the mid-1960s – but it was not a common technique, especially on Greek and Roman excavations, and it enabled us to gain an understanding of post–Bronze Age habitation in the Lower City much more rapidly than would otherwise have been the case.

Within the Lower City, much of the post–Bronze Age excavations was ultimately tied to Bronze Age research goals: the Hellenistic and Roman houses at the southern edge of the Lower City were found during the exploration of the Troy VI defensive ditch, and the excavations in and around the Spring Cave were launched because Manfred Korfmann hoped to demonstrate a link between the cave and Kaskal.kur, "the god of the underground water-course," who was mentioned with Wilusa, the Hittite name for Ilion, in a Late Bronze Age treaty.[16] These trenches allowed us to reconstruct Hellenistic occupation in the Lower City for the first time, and clarified the water systems as well.

In addition to the Lower City, the West Sanctuary emerged as the primary focus of fieldwork for nearly the entire duration of the project. More than any other area, the West Sanctuary excavations allowed us to construct a ceramic chronology spanning the entire first millennium B.C. They also demonstrated that there was much less of a gulf between the end of the Bronze Age and the beginning of the Greek period than we had expected at the outset of the project. The first Archaic monumental architecture to have been uncovered at the site gradually appeared during excavations in the Sanctuary, as did our first evidence for Ilion's "great recovery," as Strabo called it, during the second century B.C.[17]

The eastern part of the Troad also became a target for research, survey, and publication beginning in 1994. This was a period during which the looting of tumuli became increasingly common, especially in the vicinity of the Granicus River, between the modern towns of Biga and Karabiga. Subsequent rescue excavations by the Çanakkale Museum yielded three extraordinary sarcophagi and a tomb chamber with painted *klinai*, after which we launched a four-year survey of tombs in the area.[18] The material retrieved from the Granicus tombs was essential to our understanding of the Troad during the late Archaic and

Classical periods, in that material of this date was rarely discovered at Ilion or, for that matter, in most of the coastal cities of western Asia Minor.[19]

What binds together these different campaigns spanning more than 220 years is the interface of archaeology and the Homeric tradition. When Choiseul-Gouffier began his excavations in 1787, he targeted the "Tumulus of Achilles," and other Homeric tumuli were subsequently explored by Calvert, Schliemann, Manfred Korfmann, and me. Excavations were driven by a desire to assess the historicity of the Trojan War as well as the validity of its connection to the mound of Hisarlık.

To an extent, that interface still prevails, in that many of our discoveries, especially those of Bronze Age date, are viewed against the backdrop of the *Iliad*. Scholars have, in fact, occasionally voiced concerns that we have allowed the Homeric tradition to play too prominent a role in our fieldwork, research, publications, and exhibits. The origins of these accusations are probably tied to the discovery of the Late Bronze Age rock-cut ditch in 1993, immediately interpreted as a fortification component, which propelled the issue of the Trojan War to the forefront of archaeological discussions.[20] Such ditch fortifications were referred to several times in the *Iliad*, albeit in association with the Greek camp near Troy, and the *Iliad* passages were noted in connection with the ditch in several articles in *Studia Troica*.[21]

The discovery of a thirteenth-century B.C. bronze seal inscribed with Luwian hieroglyphics, a script used by the Hittite kingdom in the second millennium B.C., prompted a more extensive discussion of the potential link between the topographical names "Ilion" and "Wilusa," as well as an inclination to bring the Hittite references to Wilusa into the broader discussion of the Trojan War (Fig. 1.16, below).[22] Homer also began to be viewed in a more Anatolian perspective than had earlier been the case.[23]

Perhaps the most direct link forged between site and epic appeared in Korfmann's 1999 excavation report, where he noted, "I regard Homer as a 'contemporary witness,' reporting on whatever the condition of Ilios was in about 700 B.C."[24] This meant that physical features associated with Troy in the *Iliad* could conceivably be identified in the Late Geometric or Archaic levels of the site, and the Spring Cave was cited as a potential case in point.

Such attempts to assess the historicity of Homer have always been controversial, and they form part of a very long intellectual tradition that has been operating as least since the fifth century B.C. Herodotus registered his disbelief in the story of Helen's departure for Troy, while Strabo and his primary source, Demetrius of Scepsis, cast doubt on the claim of Ilion's inhabitants that they were living above the ruins of Priam's citadel.[25] The archaeologists had their critics too: Ernst Bötticher, a member of the German Society for Anthropology, Ethnography, and Prehistory, wrote several long critiques of

Schliemann's conclusions, especially regarding Schliemann's interpretation of Troy II and the Trojan War. This prompted Schliemann to assemble an international group of scholars in 1889 and 1890 (the "Hisarlık Conference") to discuss the excavation results.[26]

The Hisarlık Conference model was also employed by Manfred Korfmann, although it did not prevent the appearance of a level of criticism nearly as pronounced as what had been directed toward Schliemann.[27] The question of the size of the Bronze Age Lower City and, indeed, the prominence of Troy in the Late Bronze Age would become a major issue in 2001, when a new Troy Exhibit ("Troia: Traum und Wirklichkeit") opened in Germany. Included in the exhibit and the catalogue was a hypothetical reconstruction of the Lower City during the Late Bronze Age, which showed the district as densely inhabited.[28] Our evidence for this reconstruction was limited because we had excavated approximately 2 percent of the Lower City, and a surface survey of the area had not yet taken place, but since the reconstruction was presented as conjectural, no one at the time considered that it would become as controversial as it subsequently did.

The leader of the critics was Korfmann's colleague, Frank Kolb, who also taught at the University of Tübingen, although in a different department. He pointed out that the evidence for such dense occupation in the Late Bronze Age was absent, as was the proof that Troy was a major mercantile center at that time.[29] Some of his arguments picked up on the criticisms made by Eberhard Zangger in 1994, and those written by Dieter Hertel in a series of publications during the last decade.[30] This scholarly dispute developed into a kind of intellectual war marked by strikes and counterstrikes, with scholars assembling on either side of a Kolb–Korfmann line.[31] The post–Bronze Age excavation results were also brought into the discussion from time to time, especially regarding the question of an Aeolian migration and the issue of settlement continuity between the Bronze and Iron Ages, both of which were tied to the composition and dissemination of the *Iliad*.[32] All of these issues will be treated in greater detail in Chapters 1 and 2, as will the question of a Trojan War.

Whether or not the current excavation team interfaced too closely with the Homeric tradition is something that historiographers of the future will undoubtedly be in a better position to clarify, but that tradition unquestionably constituted the dominating element in the site's history throughout the Greek and Roman periods. This is a theme that surfaces continually throughout these chapters, as I attempt to investigate the ways in which Ilion's alleged Homeric heritage was approached, manipulated, and aggrandized over the course of its history, as far as the twentieth century.

Throughout the book, the reader will notice the intersection of Bronze Age and post–Bronze Age investigations, which is a reflection of the collaborative nature of the project. Each year I attempted to ensure that the post–Bronze

Age team's goals were compatible with the developing Bronze Age excavation strategy, which meant reshaping my own strategic plan to take advantage of Manfred Korfmann's new (and often unexpected) areas of exploration. This was not easy to do, either for me or for Korfmann, but in the end the project was mutually advantageous, yielding results far broader than expected and far more intellectually satisfying, as I hope the following chapters will demonstrate.

ONE

TROY IN THE BRONZE AGE

We usually speak of the Troad, the peninsular section of northwestern Asia Minor in which Troy is located, as if it were a relatively homogeneous zone, but the geography of the region varies considerably (Plates 1 and 2). The most dominant feature is the Ida mountain range that crosses the southern part of the peninsula in a roughly east-west direction and serves as the source for the three principal rivers that cross the Troad: the Scamander (modern Kara Menderes), which flows west and north, emptying into the Dardanelles north of Troy; the Aesepus (modern Gönen Çay), which terminates at the central southern coast of the Sea of Marmara and, according to Homer, forms the eastern boundary of the Troad; and the Granicus (modern Biga Çay), which lies between them and flows in a meandering northeast direction to the Sea of Marmara.[1]

Nearly the entire coast of the Troad is ringed by sections of the Ida range, which meant there was often a separation in communication between coast and interior. Since larger settlements tended to be established along the coast, the interior was reserved primarily for farming and shepherding. Geologically, the center of the Troad lies near the North Anatolian Fault, at the intersection of the Rhodope and Menderes Blocks, thereby making the entire area extremely prone to earthquakes throughout its history.[2] Raw materials suitable for a variety of industries were easily available, including gold, copper, and iron, as well as plentiful clay beds and pine tree forests on Mt. Ida.[3] Aristotle notes that the mollusks on the coast near Troy were ideal for purple dye production, and such dyers appear to be attested on the nearby island of Lesbos during the Late Bronze Age.[4]

Seven of Troy's nine settlements date to the Bronze Age and span a period of two millennia, from ca. 3000 B.C. to 1000 B.C. Three of those settlements have typically attracted more attention than the others: one from the Early Bronze Age (Troy II, 2550–2300 B.C.), because of the multiplicity of precious-metal assemblages or "treasures" with which it has been associated, and two from the Late Bronze Age (VI and VIIa, 1800–1180 B.C.), due to their alleged links to the Homeric tradition. All three are discussed extensively in this chapter since their impact on the site's subsequent history was so significant, although I situate them within a complete diachronic overview of prehistoric habitation in and around Troy, beginning with the earliest evidence for habitation.

Reconstructing occupation in this area prior to the Bronze Age is not easy, but the surveys of Mehmet Özdoğan in Thrace have made it possible for us to sketch its development in broad outline.[5] In the interior of the Troad (the Çan–Yenice–Pazarköy region) there is evidence for occupation beginning in the Upper Paleolithic (late Stone Age), which had extended to the coast of the Troad, the Gallipoli peninsula, and the island of Imbros in the seventh and sixth millennia.[6]

In the immediate region around Troy, however, the first signs of habitation do not appear before ca. 5000 B.C., and the best evidence comes from the site of Kumtepe, which lies 5 km northwest of Troy and 2 km south of the Dardanelles.[7] Only small sections of the settlement have been excavated, but the houses seem to have been rectangular and freestanding, with stone foundations and mud-brick walls. Similar settlements in the general vicinity were established at more or less the same time: Beşik-Sivritepe (which would ultimately become the site of Achilleion), Gülpınar (the Smintheion), Hanaytepe, Alacalıgöl, approximately 5 km to the west of Troy, and Işıldaktepe altı, on the coast of the Dardanelles.[8] All of these sites were in communication with each other, judging by the pottery, and they clearly formed part of a broad-based exchange network that linked the Troad with the eastern Aegean and southeastern Europe.[9] Already by the fifth millennium B.C., then, boats were sailing from the Troad across the Dardanelles and into the Aegean.[10]

For some reason, still undetermined, habitation in the region was interrupted around the middle of the fifth millennium B.C. and commenced again only ca. 3300 B.C., at which point there was new occupation at Kumtepe (Ib) and Karaağaçtepe, among others.[11] The end of the fourth millennium witnessed the foundation of Troy, which appears to have absorbed the inhabitants from the other sites in the area (Plates 3–8, Figs. 1.1 and 1.2), although another small settlement was simultaneously established a few kilometers away, on the Aegean coast (Beşik-Yassıtepe).[12] At that point in time the topography of the area was very different, as one can see from the results of core sampling or

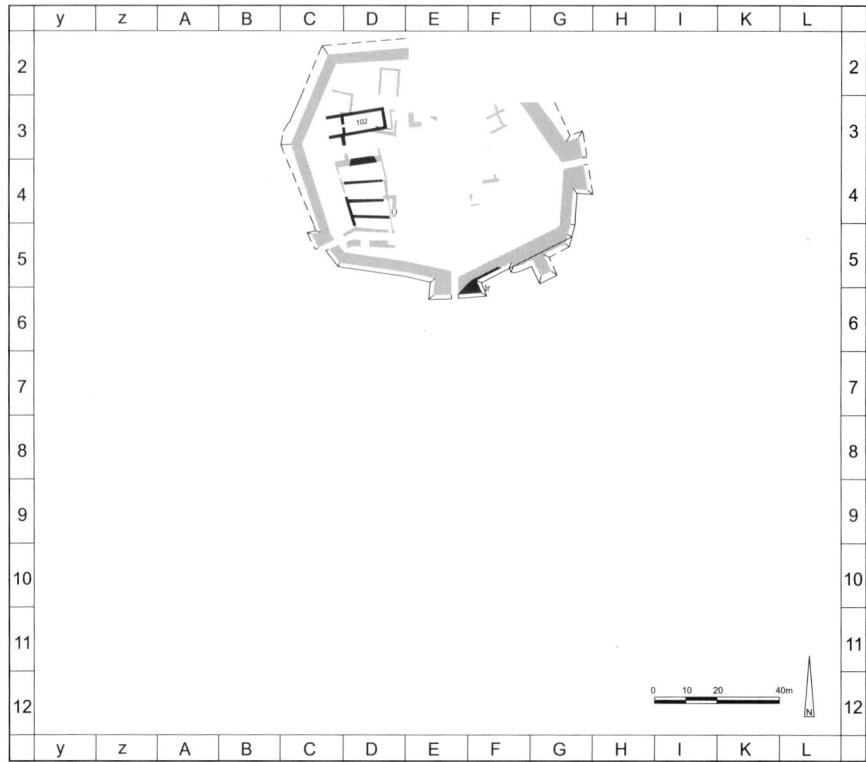

1.1. Plan of Troy I, prepared by Elizabeth Riorden for the Troy Excavation Project.

explorative drilling in the plains to the north of Troy. Such sampling provides a diachronic perspective on the movement of the coastline over several millennia and has revealed that a lagoon originally extended approximately 6 km inland from the Dardanelles at the time in which Troy was founded, thereby essentially transforming the northwest corner of the Troad into a peninsula (Plate 5). Troy's location on the eastern side of this lagoon afforded easy access to the Dardanelles as well as protection from its winds and currents.[13]

Such strategic locations are often tied to security concerns, and this may explain why Troy was always an unusually well-fortified settlement. The citadel of Troy I measured only ca. 85 × 95 m, and was therefore small by comparison to the subsequent settlements, yet dramatically different from what had existed at Kumtepe and Beşiktepe. The limestone fortification walls were continually strengthened, gradually increasingly from a thickness of 2.5 m to 3 m, and with a height of more than 3.5 m (Plate 8, Figs. 1.1, 1.2). The first walls were founded on bedrock and featured a 2 m wide gate flanked by towers. Several of the buildings they protected were of megaron shape, with a vestibule leading into a large room with central hearth, and one of them was conspicuously larger than the others, measuring nearly 19 × 7 m. Determining the city plan is difficult, since so much of it is covered by later settlements, but the houses, in general, are parallel to the fortification wall at the south.[14]

1.2. The fortification wall of Troy I in sector F6, looking north. The relief in Figure 1.3 was found at its base. Photo courtesy of the University of Cincinnati Classics Department, Troy Archives.

Although Troy appears to have been the best-fortified site in northwestern Turkey at the advent of the Bronze Age, it was one of several fortified settlements along or near the western coast of Asia Minor, such as Limantepe near Izmir, Emporio on Chios, and Poliochni on Lemnos (Plate 4).[15] Similar megaron types are attested in Thessaly and southeastern Europe, and the imported pottery that has been found in Troy I habitation levels comes, in general, from the Aegean rather than central Anatolia.[16] Also worth noting within the Troy I settlement is a monumental stone stele carved with a human face and what appears to be a weapon at its side (Fig. 1.3). This is the earliest stone relief to have been found in western Anatolia, and only one other such armed warrior stele has been discovered thus far in the Aegean during the early third millennium B.C., on the island of Thasos.[17] All of these parallels led Manfred Korfmann to label this phase and the two that follow it (Troy I–III) as a "Maritime Culture," focused more on the north Aegean and the Greek mainland than on settlements lying further to the east within Anatolia.[18]

There is no evidence for a cultural break after Troy I was destroyed by fire, although Troy II was a very different kind of settlement (Figs. 1.4 and 1.5).[19] By this point Troy had developed into a major commercial center within a trade network that extended from the Aegean to central Asia.[20] There was also cross-Aegean maritime traffic during this period as well as movement across

1.3. Stone warrior relief, Troy I. Photo courtesy of the University of Cincinnati Classics Department, Troy Archives.

the Dardanelles into Thrace, and the land routes extended at least as far as Afghanistan's Hindu Kush mountains.

The pottery of Troy II (ca. 2550–2300 B.C.) included wheel-made vessels, for the first time, and the newly reconstructed citadel was approximately 25 percent larger than its predecessor, measuring roughly 100 m in diameter. The citadel's fortification walls were also much more massive, with a thickness of more than 4 m and a height of more than 5 m, lined with projecting towers at regular intervals (Fig. 1.5). There is evidence for at least two entrances, at southwest and southeast; the latter (FO) appears to have been the primary gate into the citadel, while the former (FM) was entered via a stone-paved ramp more than 21 m long and 7.5 m wide.[21]

By the middle of the Troy II period, the citadel was divided into two precincts: the inner one featured a colonnade framing at least five megarons, the largest of which (IIA) was at least 35 m long with a central room measuring more than 20 × 10 m and a central hearth 4 m in diameter (Fig. 1.5).[22] This megaron was aligned with the colonnade's propylon, which, in turn, was set at a slightly oblique angle with respect to the main citadel gate (FO). In other words, the city plan of Troy II was far more complex than that of its predecessor, in that a chain of carefully coordinated architectural spaces would have progressively contracted and expanded the viewers' sense of space as they were

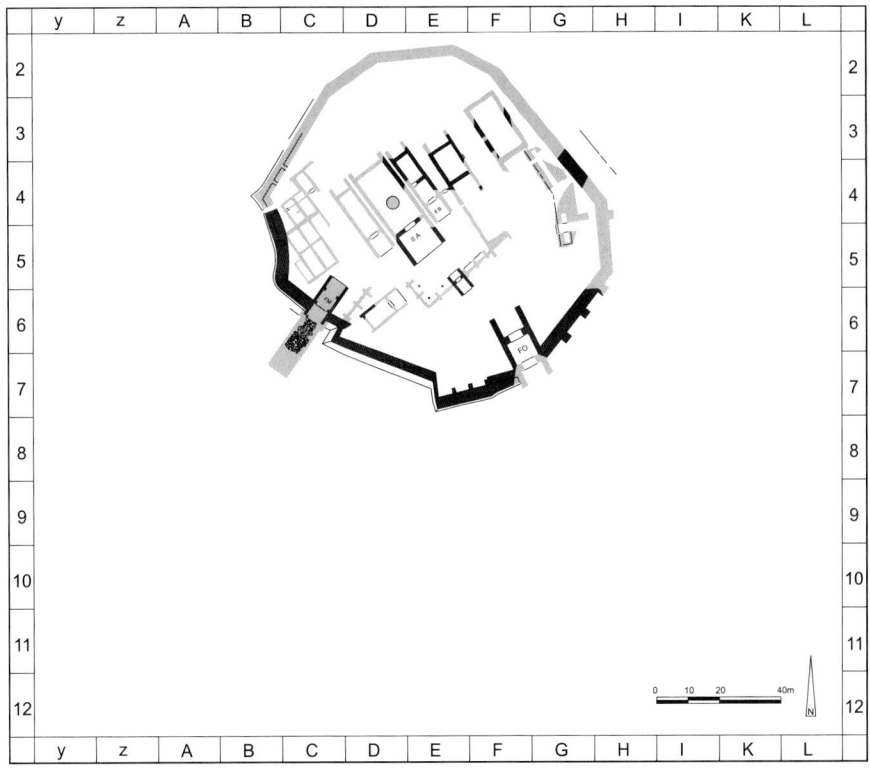

1.4. Plan of the Troy II citadel, prepared by Elizabeth Riorden for the Troy Excavation Project.

led toward the principal megaron. This suggests a more intricate socio-political stratification than what one would have found in Troy I, and it was almost certainly tied to ceremony and ritual. Little evidence for the latter has been uncovered in the Second Settlement, although the megaron in sector G6 adjacent to the Main Gate yielded a clay cult vessel with anthropomorphic handles in a pose of adoration (Fig. 1.6).[23] The architectural layout itself may also be relevant here: as some scholars have emphasized, the Second Settlement was not so large that it required two monumental entrances, and one of them, FM, may have been primarily ceremonial.[24]

The city plan was not static: at some point in the late Troy II period (ca. 2350 B.C.) a fire swept through the site and the citadel became crowded with smaller houses of irregular plan – a phenomenon that would occur again a millennium later, after an earthquake of ca. 1300 B.C.[25] The citadel wall at the southwest was enlarged, but the monumental Megaron IIA burned down and went out of use, while Gate FM at the top of the stone paved ramp was now blocked.[26] Adjacent to it rose a new building, called "the House of the City King" by Schliemann, which measured at least 8 × 15 m and contained five rooms, some of which were filled with storage vessels ca. 1.5 m high (Fig. 1.4).[27] Such a radical change in city planning has been linked to an equally radical shift in local politics and society, but whatever the case, Troy had now

1.5. (A) Conjectural reconstruction of the Troy II citadel, prepared by Christoph Haussner for the Troy Excavation Project. (B) The southwest ramp of Troy II. Troia slide 9297.

developed into a rather loosely planned city like Lemnian Poliochni rather than the hierarchically structured citadel of a century earlier.[28]

The construction of such massive fortifications, stone ramps, and large megarons was not unique; one could have found similar features in cities

1.6. Anthropomorphic vessel from the Troy II megaron in sector G6. Çanakkale Archaeological Museum. Troia slide 36622.

on the north Aegean islands (Lesbos, Lemnos, Thasos) or at Liman Tepe on the west coast of Asia Minor, although Megaron IIA seems to have been the largest building of its kind on either side of the Aegean – at least 10 m larger than the massive and only slightly earlier House of Tiles at Lerna in mainland Greece.[29]

What does appear to have been unique at Troy during the Early Bronze Age was a residential district in the Lower City that was protected by a wooden palisade (Fig. 1.7). The Lower City or "Unterstadt" is an area south, east, and west of the citadel where extensive remote sensing has occurred during most of the last twenty-five years. Excavation approximately 200 m to the south of the citadel revealed a series of cuttings in the bedrock for a wooden palisade with interior buttresses and columns that recall the construction technique of the inner colonnade within the Troy II citadel.[30] The palisade's width was nearly 3 m, and a 2 m wide opening in its circuit must have connected to a road that led directly to the main citadel gate. The size of the area under protection is still unclear: only 40 m of the palisade's length have been uncovered and it clearly continued further, possibly joining the citadel walls at east and west, but the complete line of its circuit cannot be ascertained by remote sensing alone since bedrock in this area lies more than 3 m below ground level.

The discovery of a dual defense network – wooden palisade and stone citadel fortifications – represents a major advance in our understanding of Early

(A)

(B)

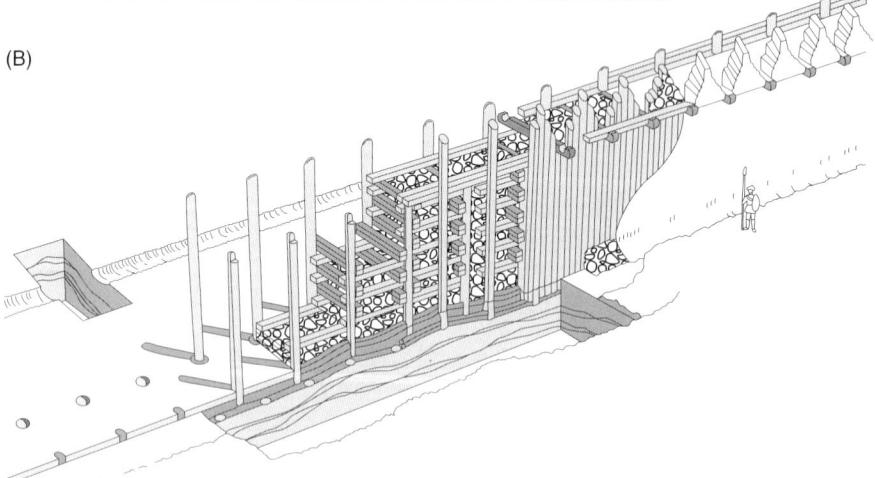

1.7. (A) The Troy II palisade cuttings in the Lower City, looking northeast. Troia slide 35308. (B) Conjectural reconstruction of the building of the Troy II palisade by Kate Clayton, based on an original by Friedmund Hueber. Troy Excavation Project.

Bronze Age Troy, and it is worth noting that no other such wooden palisades of Early Bronze Age date have been discovered in Anatolia, Greece, or the Aegean.[31] Indeed, when it was discovered in the 1990s, there was a disinclination to believe that such a palisade could have been installed in the third millennium B.C., and it was initially placed in the Late Bronze Age.[32]

Why was such a sophisticated system of fortifications considered essential by the inhabitants of the settlement? There was clearly a heightened concern with security installations at several sites within and around the northern Aegean at this time, prompted at least in part by the increased demand and possession of prestige goods in precious metals. "Treasures" of Early Bronze Age date have been uncovered at Ur, in southern Mesopotamia; at Alaca Höyük and Eskiyapar in central Anatolia; and at Poliochni on Lemnos, among others.[33] The Ur and Alaca Höyük assemblages were recovered from tombs; others, such as those from Poliochni, were buried in or near public buildings and never retrieved after a period of destruction at the site.

The latter situation appears to apply to the examples from Troy, which comprise as many as twenty-one "treasures" of objects in precious metal, although Schliemann's questionable recording methods at the time of excavation have made it difficult to determine the precise number.[34] The treasures span a period of 400 or 500 years, with the earliest assemblages deposited around Megaron IIA, and most of the later ones around the "House of the City King." Ironically, the most impressive treasures dated to the later period, when the irregularly planned houses had been added to the citadel.

The most elaborate of these was Treasure A, christened "Priam's Treasure" by Schliemann, which appears to have been discovered a few meters to the west of the "City King" house but within the citadel walls.[35] The assemblage had been set into a cist-like enclosure in the ground, either for safekeeping or as a ritual deposit.[36] Within this group were nineteen gold, electrum, silver, and bronze vessels, including a bronze serving platter and gold sauceboat; six silver ingots; thirty-five bronze spearheads, daggers, and axes; and a silver jar filled with gold jewelry, among which were diadems, bracelets, torques, and earrings (Fig. 1.8A).[37]

Another treasure discovered beside it (Treasure B) contained silver vessels, and 13 m to the north was Treasure J, in which lay another cache of gold jewelry. On the eastern side of the citadel Schliemann uncovered Treasure L, with four stone axes, one of which was made of lapis lazuli (Fig. 1.8B); six pommels of rock crystal, possibly once attached to scepters, swords, or daggers; beads of carnelian and amber that figure among the oldest amber objects known in Asia Minor; and half of an iron pommel, one of the oldest iron artifacts in the world.[38]

Especially remarkable are the stylistic and technical similarities among the assemblages from Ur, Troy, and Poliochni, which have prompted speculation that

(A)

(B)

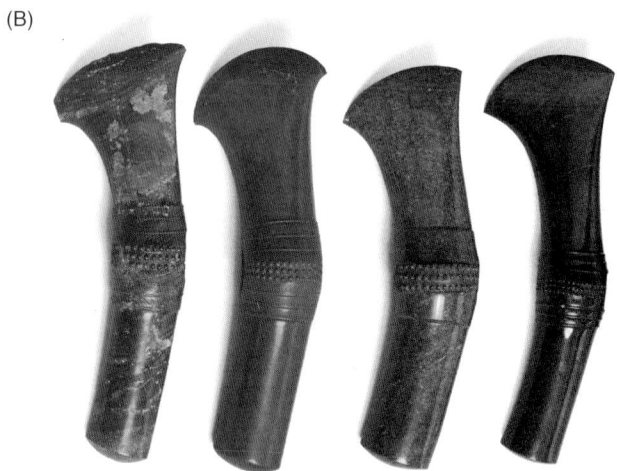

1.8. (A) Gold diadem from Treasure A, Troy II. Pushkin Museum, Moscow. Photo by the author. (B) Stone axes from Treasure L, Troy II. Pushkin Museum, Moscow. Troia slide 32437.

there were teams of itinerant jewelers traveling across the Near East and making gold and silver objects for elite patrons within a growing network of aristocratic competition.[39] In the case of Troy and Poliochni, Mikhail Treister has suggested that "there are grounds for supposing that individual finds from [these two sites] were manufactured in the same workshops by the same nomadic masters."[40]

The objects were intended for a variety of uses: two of the axes were gilded and therefore undoubtedly ceremonial; the drinking and serving vessels were intended for elite dining and/or ritual; and the rock crystal "lenses" may have been used for magnification by local jewelers experimenting with filigree and granulation, which would fit with the large amount of metalworking equipment discovered at the site.[41] The stylistic parallels for the jewelry, the weapons, and several of the vessels cover a wide area: mainland Greece, the Aegean, and the Near East, including Ur. The amber must have been imported from the

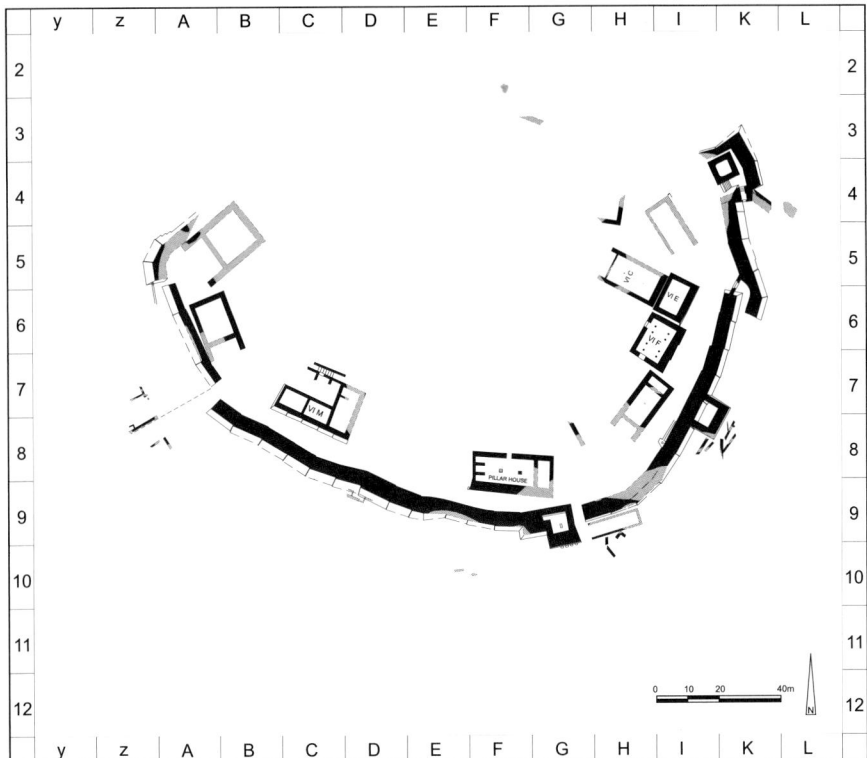

1.9. Plan of Troy VI, prepared by Elizabeth Riorden for the Troy Excavation Project.

Baltic, the carnelian from the Indus Valley, and the lapis from Badakhshan in northeastern Afghanistan.[42]

Another fire occurred at the end of the Troy II period (ca. 2300 B.C.), although there is no conclusive sign of enemy attack or of a significant death toll – only one adult skull was found in the destruction debris, so it looks as if the population escaped either before the conflagration began or at its outset.[43] Nevertheless, the residents were apparently unable to return and retrieve the aforementioned treasures, or the returnees refrained from extensive searching in the destruction level.

Either way, there is no sign of a cultural break in Troy III when the site was resettled, nor in the succeeding phases of IV and V, which encompassed a period of 550 years altogether (ca. 2300–1750 B.C.). Our knowledge of these three periods is still very limited, largely because Schliemann removed so much of the relevant evidence, although Blegen noted that a fortification wall was function-ing during each of the phases, and domed ovens appear to have been introduced during the period of Troy IV.[44] The houses of Troy V were damaged around the middle of the eighteenth century B.C., again with no sign of attack or fire.[45]

With Troy VI (1750–1300 B.C.) and VII (1300–1050 B.C.), however, we encounter the strongest of Troy's prehistoric citadels as well as the Homeric

1.10. (A) The fortification walls of Troy VI, looking northwest. Photo by the author. (B) Reconstruction of the Troy VI city walls by Christoph Haussner. Troia slide 48855.

tradition that has been wrapped around them continually during the last century. The area of the citadel protected by fortification walls now reached 2 hectares, or 20,000 m², which was more than twice the size of the fortified Early Bronze Age citadels that had preceded it (Plate 8, Fig. 1.10).[46] Also increasing in size were the fortification walls, now 4–5 m thick and approximately 10 m high, with five gates leading into the citadel. The changes did not come overnight, of course: when the earliest fortification walls of the Sixth Settlement began to rise in the seventeenth century, they had a thickness of only 1.20 m; the construction of the monumental fortifications with walls nearly 5 m thick did not commence until the fifteenth century, and the building program continued into the fourteenth century.[47]

The masonry technique of the walls is difficult to parallel. Although the basic format of a battered stone wall with vertical superstructure and mudbrick capping is reminiscent of its Troy II predecessor, several features had not appeared before.[48] One is a line of vertical offsets in the masonry, usually 0.10–0.15 m in depth, that occur every 9 or 10 m. Such offsets also appear in Mycenaean palaces and fortifications, although there they seem to be tied to sections of construction.[49] None of the offsets at Troy is associated with the joints of the stones, nor are they confined to the defensive walls, and they may be primarily decorative.[50] Another distinctive feature is the carefully cut ashlar masonry, wherein the closely fitting ashlars have been used for the entire wall rather than only as the face of a rubble core. Comparable construction techniques do not appear in mainland Greek or Hittite Empire architecture, nor do the Trojan fortifications feature the figural sculpture that decorated defensive walls at Mycenae and Hattuşa.

The construction of the monumental fortification walls appears to have occurred in tandem with the cutting of a defensive ditch that surrounded the residential district (the Lower City) south of the citadel (Plate 9, Figs. 1.11 and 1.12). This is arguably the most important discovery within the last twenty-five years of excavation at Troy and its presence was detected through magnetic prospection, a technique that records magnetic variations and so allows mapping of subsurface features. The ditch was cut directly from the bedrock and measures 4 m in width and between 1 and 2 m in depth, with at least two gateways leading through it.[51] The southern edge is located 400 m south of the citadel, and the area it encompassed must have ranged between 250,000 and 350,000 m² (25–35 hectares), which would be slightly larger than that of Mycenae.[52]

How the ditch intersected with the citadel's fortification walls is still unclear, as is the format of a defensive wall on the ditch's inner side. It seems likely that the stone excavated from the ditch would have been used to create a defensive wall behind it, which was the usual technique, although no such wall has appeared during excavation. What we do have, in the trench that revealed one of the gateways, are two long cuts in the bedrock that run parallel to the ditch, 5 m behind it. These cuts are not especially deep (0.20–0.25 m) or wide (0.40–0.50 m) but they could conceivably have been intended for a wooden wall backed by earth and stone, which is how they have been graphically reconstructed (Fig. 1.12).[53] It is also worth noting that the original Late

1.11. View of the Troy VI rock-cut ditch in the Lower City (sector y28/29), looking southeast. The area between the ditches served as a gateway during the Late Bronze Age, although the stone walls visible there are Hellenistic additions. Troy Excavation Project photo.

Bronze Age surface would have been 1.5–2 m higher than it is now due to extensive erosion in the area, so the original appearance of the wall may never be known.

In any event, Troy VI, like Troy II, clearly benefited from a dual system of defense with inner and outer fortifications. This is a configuration that would actually have a long history in the ancient Near East, especially in the Late Bronze Age and early Iron Age, as one sees at Hattuşa, Kanesh, and Zincirli in Asia Minor.[54] Similar defensive ditches have appeared in Anatolia (Gordion, Carchemish), Syria (Qatna, Ebla, Kadesh), and Palestine (Hazor, Lachish, Ashkelon), among others, so the presence of such a feature at Troy is not surprising.[55] By this point, the coastline was ca. 2 km away from the site

1.12. Conjectural reconstruction of the Troy VI rock-cut ditch in Figure 1.11, including gate and defensive wall. Prepared by Gebhard Bieg and Peter Jablonka for the Troy Excavation Project.

due to a lower water level of the Dardanelles, and the area north and west of the site had subsequently become marshy. This meant that the bay of Beşik, ca. 8 km west of the citadel, must have been used by any ships harboring in the region.[56]

The extent of occupation in the Lower City during the Late Bronze Age has been one of the most controversial subjects in recent discussions of Trojan archaeology. Reconstructions of Bronze Age Troy created for a 2001 exhibition ("Troia: Traum und Wirklichkeit") showed the Lower City as a densely occupied district, although the image was presented as hypothetical due to the fact that only 2–3 percent of this district has been excavated.[57]

There is still insufficient evidence to support such a reconstruction, and we may not be able to make much more progress: Bronze Age building materials were subsequently reused in Hellenistic and Roman construction, and extensive erosion over the last three millennia has significantly disrupted most of the Bronze Age strata, which is why the bedrock ditch was found less than 1 m below modern ground level.[58] Nevertheless, we have found the remnants of huts and stone pavements of Late Bronze Age date throughout the Lower City, together with threshing floors, *pithoi* (storage containers), heaps of murex shells probably used for the production of purple dye, and evidence of metalworking.[59] Consequently, it looks as if the area was used for industrial purposes

1.13. Stone stelae positioned at the left of the Troy VI South Gate. One of the stone supports of "Pillar House" can be seen at upper left. Photo by the author.

in the late second millennium B.C., as would be the case again during the Hellenistic and Roman periods.

Reconstructing the center of the Troy VI citadel is no longer possible because the Late Bronze Age remains were shaved off the mound when the Sanctuary of Athena was constructed during the Hellenistic period, but the buildings around the perimeter of the citadel wall are still relatively well preserved. Within the citadel were a series of freestanding buildings erected on rising terraces, including a two-story structure supported by stone pillars (hence "Pillar House") that was apparently intended for weaving activities.[60] The primary entrance to the citadel, now and for the remainder of antiquity, was the South Gate (VIT), 3.30 m wide. Located next to it was a long narrow building ("Anta House") in which animal bones and areas of burning were discovered, along with pottery that is not particularly characteristic of domestic assemblages. The building was probably connected to cult, as were a series of stone stelae that were installed on the opposite side of this gate as well as the east and west entrances to the citadel (Fig. 1.13).[61]

Near the latter gate was a large megaron-type house with side rooms in which an unusually rich assemblage of small finds was discovered, including a Mycenaean seal, a terracotta rhyton (drinking vessel) in the shape of a bull, several gold fragments, an ivory spindle with whorl still attached, one or two miniature stone axes, and the bronze figurine of a striding male that may represent a worshipper (Fig. 1.14).[62] This building may also have been related to cult, and it would later develop into one of Troy's principal sites for ritual, probably connected to hero cult.

The sophisticated town planning and the distinctive features of the fortification walls were not the only innovations –
the horse now figured in the life of Troy for the first time,
as did new ceramic shapes made in a burnished gray fabric
("Anatolian Gray Ware").[63] Blegen believed that such significant changes in material culture must indicate the arrival of
a completely new group of settlers, probably Greek speakers
from the north.[64] This was a bold statement that, surprisingly,
has prompted little subsequent discussion, and it requires an
examination of Troy within the larger sphere of western Asia
Minor, where recent research has transformed our understanding of settlement patterns and inter-state relations during the Middle and Late Bronze Ages.

TROY, THE AEGEAN, AND CENTRAL ANATOLIA DURING THE SECOND MILLENNIUM

The early second millennium B.C. witnessed an intensifi-
cation of contact between Crete and western Asia Minor,
as recent fieldwork at Miletus has made abundantly clear
(Plate 10). Excavations there have revealed a wealth of
Minoan components in the site's material culture, includ-

1.14. Copper alloy statuette
from the West Sanctuary, Troy
VIIa. Çanakkale Archaeological
Museum. Troia slide 26239.

ing Minoan-style wall painting, ceramics, and Linear A inscriptions – the only
such inscriptions in Asia Minor.[65] Minoan objects have also been found in the
northeast Aegean, such as Samothrace, Lemnos, and Troy itself, where Minoan
imports would continue into the fourteenth century B.C.[66]

The ceramic assemblages of early Troy VI suggest increased contact with
mainland Greece as well: the Anatolian Gray Ware referenced above has long
been discussed in conjunction with Middle Helladic Gray Minyan Ware that
began several centuries earlier, and renewed study of the gray ware at Troy has
demonstrated that most of the earliest shapes are Aegean – goblets, cups, and
possibly kantharoi and small amphoriskoi. In other words, the new Aegean-
inspired gray ware vessels at Troy were intended primarily for drinking activities, and were used in conjunction with wheel-made Anatolian shapes such as
bead-rim bowls.[67] These Aegean shapes lasted for only two or three generations, however; by ca. 1700 B.C. (LHI) they had been replaced by Anatolian
shapes (Troy VIb/c).

It therefore looks as if there was contact between mainland Greece, probably Boeotia/Thessaly, and several settlements on the western coast of Asia
Minor during the second half of the eighteenth century B.C. (Troy VIa). The
inhabitants of Troy subsequently began producing drinking vessels modeled
on the shapes and wares that were used by their Aegean contacts. These were

locally made products, not imports, and it is tempting to link them to drinking activities that would have involved both groups. Roughly fifty years after their introduction, the Aegean-influenced gray ware vessels disappear, which probably indicates they were intended for special occasions that were no longer occurring. In any event, the vessels do not provide evidence for a new element in the population, although the Sixth Settlement was clearly developing into a more multifaceted community than any settlement that had preceded it.

By the first half of the sixteenth century B.C. (LH IIA/Troy VId), Mycenaean shapes and decorative motifs begin to enter the ceramic assemblages of Troy, followed by Lemnos and Lesbos a century later.[68] At this point much of the Mycenaean pottery appears to have been imported, although recent neutron activation analysis (NAA) has yielded somewhat ambiguous results, in that the chemical configuration of the clays at Troy and in the Argolid are similar.[69] Since none of the local gray and tan wares at Troy was made of the same clay as that of the early Mycenaean specimens, it seems likely that the latter was imported, but further testing could alter this picture.

Either way, the Mycenaean pottery in Troy's sixteenth- and fifteenth-century B.C. assemblages represents only a very small percentage of the vessels in circulation (roughly 1%). This would not change until the second half of the fourteenth century B.C. (LH IIIA2/VIh), when the percentages rise considerably (3–5%).[70] Even then, the numbers are miniscule by comparison with Miletus, where approximately 95 percent of the fourteenth- and early thirteenth-century B.C. ceramics are of Mycenaean type.[71] Whether the imports derived from trade with the Mycenaeans themselves or via other western Asia Minor cities such as Miletus is still unclear, but some of the early and middle Troy VI ceramics suggest a Dodecanese origin, and there must have been regular commercial interaction between Troy and the coastal cities.[72]

This raises the issue of the extent of Troy's involvement in long-range commerce. During the last decade some scholars have argued that Troy occupied a position of limited importance in Late Bronze Age trade networks, while others have proposed that the wealth of the city was largely tied to the site's strategic location at the western end of the Hellespont, which meant that it lay at one of the easiest crossing points between continental Europe and Asia, and at the entrance to the primary waterway linking the Aegean with the Black Sea.[73]

Our best evidence for the broader geopolitical significance of Troy VI comes from the texts preserved in the Hittite capital of Hattuša (Boğazköy), which effectively enable us to reconstruct the history of western Asia Minor during the Late Bronze Age (Plate 10).[74] Several of the texts refer to a region named Wilusa, which lay in the general vicinity of the island of Lazpa (Lesbos) and adjacent to the "Seha River Land." Already in 1924, the land of Wilusa was equated with the Troad, with "Wilusa" or "Wilios" viewed as the Hittite version of "Ilios." Although this suggestion was consistently viewed by the archaeological community as highly likely, the equation of Wilusa and the Troad was not firmly established until the late 1990s, as a consequence of the pioneering work of Frank Starke and David Hawkins.[75]

In one of the texts, "Wilusa" is tied to the geographical designation "Taruisa," which has often been regarded as a reference to the citadel of Troy itself, within the larger region of Wilusa.[76] This identification has also been more readily embraced in the wake of the "Wilusa–Troad" linkage, although not everyone has been convinced. Regardless of how one translates "Taruisa," Troy was the only fortified settlement in the Troad during the second millennium B.C., and it must have served as the region's center of power.[77] Therefore, by combining the textual descriptions of Wilusa's historical events with the archaeological evidence from the site, we can situate Troy's topographical development within a broad sphere of political and military initiatives during the late fifteenth, fourteenth, and thirteenth centuries B.C.

The first reference to Wilusa, and thus to the realm of Troy, occurs already in the sixteenth century B.C., in a fragmentary song connected to the Hittite cult center of Istanuwa. Written in Luwian, only one fragment of the song is preserved, but it contains the line "when they came from steep Wilusa..." Calvert Watkins has suggested that this fragment may have formed part of an epic song – a "Wilusiad" of sorts; and although this can be regarded as no more than a suggestion, it does show that Troy was already known to the Hittites by that time, which would have been approximately a century after the earliest fortification walls of Troy VI had been built.[78] Moreover, its inclusion in what appears to be a ritual song indicates that Troy's status in the sixteenth century B.C. was not an insignificant one, at least to the Hittites. This was also the period in which, judging by the pottery, Troy was in contact with the inhabitants of mainland Greece over the course of several generations.

Toward the end of the fifteenth century B.C., and for the next 200 years, there are several critically important references to Troy in the Hittite documents. Around 1400 B.C., during the reign of the Hittite king Tudhaliyas II, Troy had joined with other vassal states in western Asia Minor in a confederation referred to in the king's annals as "Assuwa," often considered an early version of "Asia." Twenty-two members of this confederation opposing the Hittites are listed, the last two of which are Wilusa and Taruisa, which would indicate that the group included Troy. The confederation was resoundingly defeated by Tudhaliyas, after which 10,000 of the rebellious soldiers were taken to Hattuşa along with 600 teams of horses for chariots.[79]

A bronze sword recently discovered at Hattuşa probably bears witness to this victory. The sword itself is similar in style and technique to those manufactured in the Aegean during the sixteenth and fifteenth centuries B.C., and along its blade is a complete Akkadian inscription: "as Tudhaliyas the Great shattered the Assuwa country, he dedicated these swords to the storm god, his lord."[80] A later treaty between Wilusa and the Hittites notes that Tudhaliyas did not enter Wilusa during the campaign, so there is no reason to expect signs of destruction at Troy at this time; and there is, in fact, no such evidence.[81] Nevertheless, the Assuwa revolt would have been roughly contemporary with the new construction project that included a defensive ditch and significantly enlarged citadel walls, so it seems likely that the two developments are related. It is worth noting that the building of Troy's enlarged fortifications would have begun roughly half a century after those of Hattuşa, and half a century before those of Mycenae.[82]

The reference in the Assuwa inscription to Troy's interface with other city states in western Anatolia also fits well with the configuration of the site's contemporary ceramic assemblages, which display clear Mycenaean influence and include likely imports from southwest Anatolia.[83] Consequently, it seems reasonable to conclude that the origins of the Assuwan confederation lay in a network of partners in trade.

AHHIYAWA

Into this political configuration came another significant player named "Ahhiyawa," with whom the Hittites were often in conflict. Ahhiyawa had a great king whose power was analogous to that of the Hittite king, and his realm clearly lay somewhere to the west of Asia Minor, across the water.[84] The association of the Ahhiyawans with the Achaeans, or Mycenaean Greeks, is becoming increasingly difficult to dispute.[85] The Hittite texts clearly indicate that Ahhiyawa was not located on the Anatolian mainland but was reachable by ship from there. Moreover, at least during the thirteenth century B.C., Miletus was under the protection of Ahhiyawa, and the Late Bronze Age remains from that site reveal extensive Mycenaean acculturation, especially the ceramics.[86] This fact, coupled with the discovery of Mycenaean chamber tombs there, has led Wolf-Dietrich Niemeier to conclude that Miletus was actually a Mycenaean colony during the Late Bronze Age. The settlements on the adjacent islands do not appear to have been colonies per se, although they, like Miletus, also evince a high level of Mycenaean acculturation.

As several scholars have noted, if Ahhiyawa does not refer to mainland Greece or to these Mycenaean-affiliated areas, then we have to assume (1) that the Hittites did not mention the Mycenaeans in their documents – which would be very surprising considering the new evidence from Miletus – and (2) that the kingdom of Ahhiyawa to which the texts *do* refer has thus far remained undetected in the archaeological record.[87] Whether Ahhiyawa consisted of a group of Aegean islands, sites on the Greek mainland, or both cannot at this point be determined, but it must refer to a center of Mycenaean culture.[88]

Ahhiyawa appears to have entered into the political affairs of western Anatolia even before the Assuwa revolt, that is, during the late fifteenth century B.C.[89] An Ahhiyawan ruler received islands – unnamed, but presumably off the western Asia Minor coast – from the king of Assuwa in what may have been part of a gift exchange linked to a dynastic marriage.[90] The date of the gift is not provided, but it occurred at a time when there was still a king of Assuwa, which would have ended with the Hittite suppression of the revolt, ca. 1400 B.C. Consequently, the gift of the islands to Ahhiyawa must have occurred in the same general period as the Assuwan rebellion, possibly during its preparations.

Ultimately, a change in the political configuration of western Asia Minor occurred. During the late fourteenth and thirteenth centuries B.C., the area formed part of the district of Arzawa, which was subdivided into four vassal states: Wilusa, which occupied the Troad; Mira, which encompassed Ionia; the Seha River Land, which lay between them, extending from Adramyttium to Smyrna and including Lazpa (Lesbos); and Hapalla, which encompassed parts of Pisidia and Phrygia (Plate 10).[91] The inhabitants of Arzawa were sometimes allies of the Hittites but were not considered of equal status or as part of the same social group, as the Hittite laws unearthed in Bogazköy demonstrate. This zone was continually a locus of struggle between the Hittites and Ahhiyawa, with Miletus (Millawanda) often serving as an ally of the latter.[92]

Ahhiyawan attacks on western Anatolia had certainly begun by the early fourteenth century B.C., when a commander named Attarissiya, who had 100 chariots at his disposal, conducted raids in western Anatolia and Cyprus.[93] Toward the end of that century, during the reign of Mursili II (1321–1295 B.C.), Arzawa and Miletus formed an alliance with Ahhiyawa against the Hittites, which prompted Hittite military intervention in Arzawa.[94] The documents indicate that Miletus was subsequently destroyed by Mursili's troops, and a destruction level at Miletus dating to the late fourteenth century B.C. attests to the validity of that statement.[95] The loyalties of the Seha River Land were also clearly changeable, and they alternated at various times among Arzawa, Ahhiyawa, and the Hittites. Troy's relations with the Hittites during this period, however, were peaceful. An early thirteenth century B.C. letter praising Troy's consistent loyalty to the Hittites notes that Kukkunni, the ruler of Troy during the later fourteenth century B.C., refrained from joining any of the western Anatolian revolts against Hattuša.[96]

Most of the preserved correspondence between the Hittite and Ahhiyawan kings related to military conflicts, but there were exceptions. At one point in his reign, Mursili II was ailing, possibly from a minor stroke, and asked for images of the deities of Ahhiyawa and Lazpa (Lesbos) to be brought to him, which they were.[97] This passage also indicates that figural sculpture formed part of the settlements of Lesbos ca. 1300 B.C., as it did of Hattuša, although no such sculpture appears to have decorated Troy at that time.

The Arzawan conflicts during the reign of Mursili II were not the only sources of hardship in western Asia Minor. A plague had broken out in Hittite lands, and the preserved prayers of Mursili indicate its severity.[98] The precise length of the plague is unclear, as is the extent to which it traveled to the west, but about the same time Troy was struck by a crippling earthquake that damaged the citadel walls. This earthquake, which signals the division between Troy VI and VII, seems to have caused no widespread burning at the site, nor is there evidence of human casualties. Everyone apparently evacuated the city in time, or the bodies of those who died were pulled from the wreckage.[99]

There was no change in population or in diet, but the appearance of the settlement now changed substantially, as did the city plan. Many of the damaged walls and houses were repaired with blocks dislodged by the earthquake, and new buildings, some of which had party walls, were inserted into the passageways between the houses. The floors of these houses were filled with pithoi, many of which were between 1.75 and 2 m high, and one house had as many as twenty-three of them (Fig. 1.15).[100] It seems indisputable that there was now a larger population living on the citadel, which may have developed into a secure redistribution center for the surrounding villages. The trade network in which Troy was involved also appears to have changed: virtually all of the Mycenaean-style pottery was now locally produced, although Anatolian Gray Ware was still being exported to both Cyprus and the Levant.[101]

Throughout the settlement there is also evidence for heightened security. A new tower was added at the South Gate; the entry to the East Gate was lengthened, presumably to allow for better defense; and Gate VIU at the west was blocked altogether – an act that the inhabitants would repeat after the late Roman earthquakes in the early sixth century A.D.[102] The rock-cut ditch at the southern edge of the Lower City had gradually filled up with earth during the Troy VI period, so a new rock-cut ditch at least 3 m wide and 3 m deep was now dug approximately 100–150 m to the south of the first one, thereby increasing the size of the protected area south of the citadel.[103] This was clearly a time of increased concern over security, which prompted more of the inhabitants to seek shelter within the citadel walls, even though it meant living in unusually crowded conditions.

The earthquake itself would not have been the only stimulus for such dramatic changes. The first half of the thirteenth century B.C. witnessed a series of raids throughout western Asia Minor by a power broker named Piyamaradu, who was possibly a descendant of one of the kings of Arzawa.[104] He successfully undermined the authority of three Hittite kings: Muwatalli II (1295–1272), Urhi-Tesub (1272–1267), and Hattusili III (1267–1237), and his exploits sparked a continual animosity between Ahhiyawa and the Hittites that would continue for much of the thirteenth century. As noted above, there is evidence for shifts in the western Anatolian trade networks during

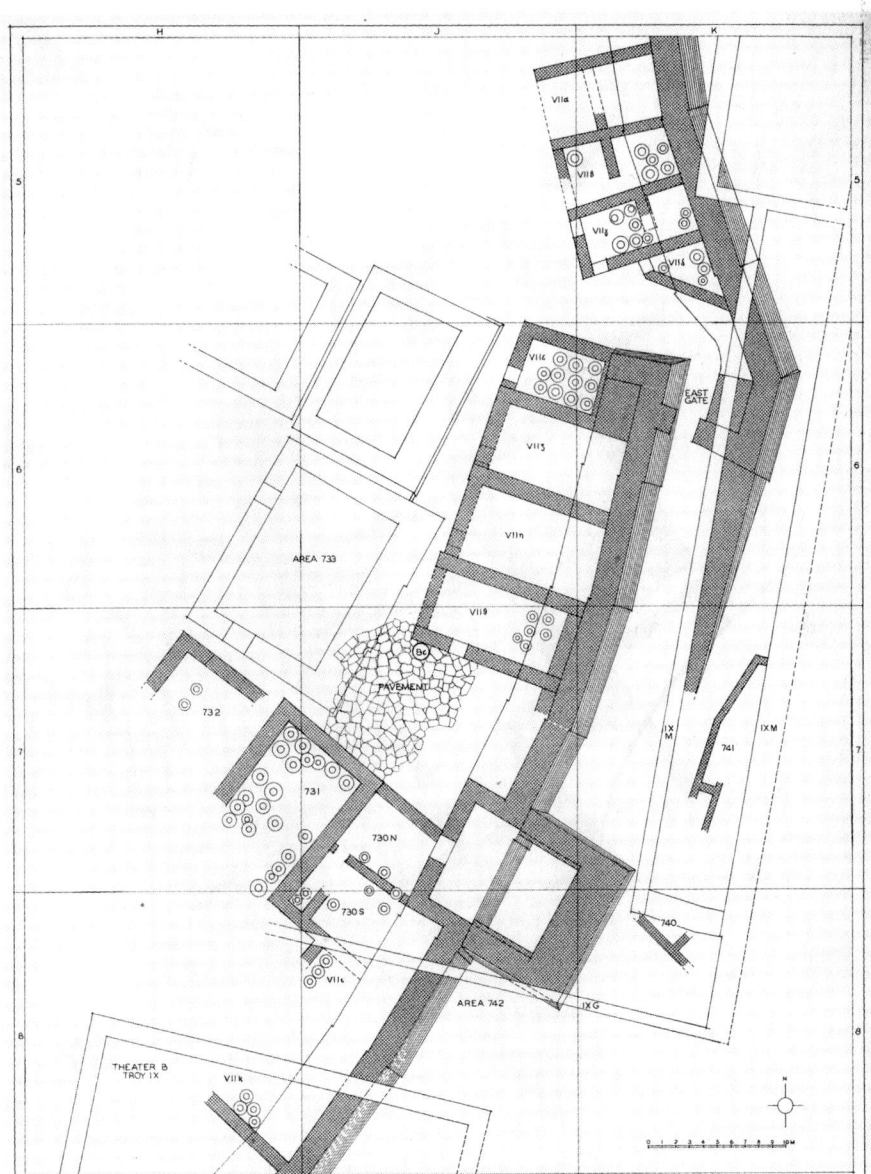

1.15. Plan of Troy VIIa house with pithoi embedded in the floor. Photo courtesy of the University of Cincinnati Classics Department, Troy Archives.

the thirteenth century, and Piyamaradu's raids may well have been one of the causes.

His request for a vassal kingship during the reign of Muwatalli was denied, after which he began a series of attacks that spanned the entire western coast. He had a reliable base of power in Miletus, now under the control of Ahhiyawa and ruled by a man who had married Piyamaradu's daughter. His attacks in the first quarter of the century were directed toward the northwest: Wilusa,

Lesbos, and the Seha River Land.[105] He and his army successfully seized Wilusa and raided Lesbos, which prompted the Hittite king to dispatch an army to Wilusa to oust him. There is no indication in the Hittite documents of the size of Piyamaradu's army, but in his later raids on Lycia he reportedly carried off 7,000 captives, which suggests a sizable force.[106]

Whether Piyamaradu occupied the citadel of Troy during this campaign is not clear, nor is it certain that his forces actually battled the Hittite army within the borders of Wilusa. There is no sign of combat or burning on or around the citadel at this time, so if there was a battle, it did not take place at Troy. It is, of course, possible that the residents fled prior to Piyamaradu's arrival at the citadel, as one sees with the Hittite occupation of Arzawa during the reign of Mursili II.[107] In any event, one can easily see why the residents would have been concerned about safety: two opposing armies had entered Wilusan territory shortly after an earthquake had compromised the security of the settlement.

The Hittite documents continually refer to Piyamaradu's escape to safety in Ahhiyawa following his raids or to the Ahhiyawan protectorate of Miletus. Such a situation understandably increased the tension between the Hittites and Ahhiyawa, as one can see very clearly in the so-called Tawagalawa letter, ca. 1250 B.C., written by an obviously frustrated Hattusili III to the Ahhiyawan king regarding Piyamaradu's attacks.[108] One section of that letter contains a fragmentary line that has attracted considerable attention, and has been restored as "about the matter of the land of Wilusa, concerning which he and I [the kings of the Hittites and Ahhiyawa] were hostile to one another..."[109] This has been viewed as a kind of Homeric smoking gun – the conclusive evidence for a war between Greeks and Anatolians at Troy that so many have sought. There is no reason to cast it in that kind of light, but it does highlight Wilusa's tenuous position during the period of Piyamaradu's raids in the area.

We know the name of Troy's ruler during this period – Alaksandu – since a treaty between him and the Hittite king Muwatalli II survives intact.[110] His name has attracted as much attention as the "hostility" quote from the Tawagalawa letter due to the fact that "Alaksandu" is the Hittite version of "Alexandros," the alternate name for Paris in the *Iliad*. "Alaksandu, ruler of Wilusa" has therefore been interpreted as "Paris, king of Troy." What is of central importance here is the political context of the treaty: Alaksandu's territory had just experienced both natural disaster and military intervention, and a stronger alliance with the Hittites must have seemed like the most prudent course of action. This would also have allowed Muwatalli to secure the northwest flank of his empire prior to his battle with the Egyptians at Kadesh in northern Syria.[111] The Alaksandu Treaty includes a brief history on Trojan–Hittite relations, noting that with the exception of Troy's involvement in the Assuwa revolt ca.

1430 B.C., the inhabitants had consistently maintained peaceful relations with Hattuša. If this is, in fact, accurate, then it seems unlikely that the leaders of Troy had sided with Piyamaradu during his campaign in Wilusa.

In spite of this treaty and other diplomatic overtures, the second half of the thirteenth century B.C. was marked by military conflict throughout western Anatolia, especially during the reign of Tudhaliyas IV (1237–1209 B.C.). A new rebellion by the Seha River Land, supported by Ahhiyawa, was crushed by the Hittites, while Miletus, which had served as an Ahhiyawan outpost for nearly two centuries, was brought under Hittite control, thereby ending the influence of Ahhiyawa in the affairs of Anatolia.[112] Shortly thereafter, a letter by Tuhaliyas IV to the king of Amurru, in northern Syria, mandated a ban on trade between Ahhiyawa and Assyria, with whom the Hittites were then at war.[113] Especially noteworthy in the last document is the erasure of the name of the king of Ahhiyawa, which was perhaps carried out after the attack on Miletus.[114]

Troy is represented in the Hittite documents from this period as well. In a letter to the new ruler of Miletus, Tudhaliyas wrote that Walmu, king of Troy, had fled to the king of Mira after having been deposed.[115] Tudhaliyas notes that Walmu's investiture tablets are still intact, and asks that the exiled king be sent to Hattuša so that the king can assist in Walmu's reinstatement as ruler of Troy. From this we learn that civil unrest at Troy during the later thirteenth century B.C. resulted in a significant change in political authority. Based on Tudhaliyas' reaction to the incident, it seems clear that Walmu had been pursuing a decidedly pro-Hittite policy, but there is no way to determine whether that was the cause of the unrest. In any event, there are no indications that he ever regained the throne.

There is one other body of evidence that is sometimes cited in connection with Ahhiyawan raids along the west coast of Asia Minor, and this takes us to the years around 1200 B.C. The evidence is in the form of Linear B tablets from Pylos that record the groups of slave women who worked in the palace textile industry.[116] Some of these women are listed by the cities from which they were presumably seized, and a substantial number of these lie on or near the western coast of Asia Minor, including Miletus, Cnidus, Halicarnassus, Didyma, Chios, Karpathos, Lemnos, and possibly Imbros. The first five encompass the southwestern region of Asia Minor, which was the predominant center of Mycenaean power and culture in Anatolia, but Lemnos is in the northeast Aegean, as is Imbros, and they have been connected to an additional ethnic that appears in the text as To-ro-ja, often linked to Troy. Thomas Palaima has shown that the latter equation is unlikely – Tlos, in Lycia, is a more probable candidate – but the reference to Lemnos reveals that at least some of the raids occurred not far from the Troad.[117]

1.16. Bronze bi-convex seal of thirteenth century B.C. date. Çanakkale Archaeological Museum. Troy Excavation Project photo.

WRITING AND COMMERCE

The tablets of Pylos and the aforementioned letter of Tudhaliyas IV raise the vexed problem of writing at Troy or, rather, the issue of why so little writing has been found.[118] There are, to my knowledge, three indications of writing at Troy during the Late Bronze Age. One of them is the set of investiture tablets – referred to in Tudhaliyas' letter as wooden – that had been made for Walmu by the king and retrieved by a Hittite envoy.[119] The second is the Alaksandu Treaty, which was copied by Muwatalli II and given to Alaksandu with the provision that he read it publicly three times a year. The medium is unspecified. The third is a bronze bi-convex seal of thirteenth century B.C. date that represents the only actual Bronze Age writing that has ever been discovered at Troy (Fig. 1.16). The script is hieroglyphic Luwian, and features the name of a man identified as a scribe on one side, and the name of a woman, perhaps his wife, on the other.[120]

Given the history of Troy's relationship with the Hittites, one would expect that copies of other correspondence, similar to the Alaksandu Treaty, were kept in an archive there, although such a collection has never been found. There are probably two reasons for this, and neither gives us much hope of ever finding such an archive. One can imagine that the building that housed the documents was on the citadel, and probably served as one of the more important buildings of the settlement. All of these structures were pushed over the northern side of the citadel in the later third century B.C. when the Temple of Athena was constructed, and Schliemann deposited tens of meters of excavation dump on top of them in the late nineteenth century.

Even if we were able to remove the dump and uncover the remains of the purported Late Bronze Age archive, it is not clear that anything would remain.

Tudhaliyas' letter notes that Walmu's investiture tablets were wooden, undoubtedly of the type that was found in the Uluburun shipwreck of late fourteenth century B.C. date and also mentioned in the *Iliad*.[121] There was, in fact, a separate group of scribes entrusted with producing wooden documents – the "Writing Board Scribes" – who were fewer in number than the "Clay Tablet Scribes."[122] If this material were representative of that of the other documents, then they would not have survived in the climate of northwestern Turkey.

There has always been the expectation that such documents would clarify the nature of the long-distance commerce in which Troy was engaged during the Sixth and Seventh Settlements, on which, as I mentioned earlier, there have been sharply divergent opinions.[123] The treasures of Early Bronze Age date found at Troy, Poliochni, and Alaca Höyük have revealed the trade networks to which those settlements were linked, but no such assemblages exist for Late Bronze Age Troy, nor do the textual references to Wilusa cited above provide much information about the area's commercial activities.

In this case we have to depend on the assorted small finds and ceramics that have been excavated in strata associated with the Sixth Settlement of Troy. The finds include faience, ostrich egg fragments, carnelian, ivory, and alabaster, some of which is Cretan. Gold and silver have also been found, as has imported pottery from Mycenae, Crete, Cyprus, and the Levant, although none of the pottery, except the Mycenaean, has appeared at Troy in significant numbers.[124]

Especially striking is the absence of Hittite pottery at the site in light of the political alliance between Troy and Hattuşa after the Alaksandu Treaty. There are only two small finds from Troy to which one can point as potential indications of interaction. One is the Luwian seal mentioned above (Fig. 1.16), although Luwian was the primary language of much of central and western Asia Minor during the Late Bronze Age, and therefore not in itself indicative of contact.[125] The other is a copper alloy figurine of a striding male, 10 cm in height, that dates to around 1200 B.C. and conforms to the "smiting god" type known from Syria and central Anatolia, including Boğazköy (Fig. 1.14).[126] Although its style is somewhat idiosyncratic, this is the only bronze sculpture ever to have been in Troy's Late Bronze Age levels, and it may have been an import.

There is no indication that the Trojan–Hittite treaty prompted a corresponding increase in commerce between the two areas.[127] It is possible, of course, that the items of exchange did not leave traces in the archaeological record, as would have been the case for timber, slaves, textiles, and animals, and new textual evidence may one day elucidate the issue. In the meantime, it is clear that during phases VI and VII, Troy formed part of a commercial network that encompassed both the Aegean and the Eastern Mediterranean, even if the volume of that trade and its fluctuations remain to be determined.[128]

The situation would be clearer if we could assess the extent to which Troy's geographic location, at the crossroads of Europe and Asia as well as the Aegean and Black Seas, was a critical component in maritime trade during the Late Bronze Age. Manfred Korfmann believed that Troy's wealth at this time was partially related to its ability to provide safe harbor for ships waiting for the appropriate winds and currents to sail into the Black Sea, and even today small ships have difficulty negotiating the formidable winds of the straits;[129] but such a thesis rests on the assumption that the Black Sea was open to Aegean maritime traffic during the Bronze Age, and there is currently insufficient evidence for such shipping prior to the eighth century B.C.[130] No traces of Bronze Age settlements have been found along the coastal areas of the Black Sea, other than Bulgaria, nor any Mycenaean pottery, while the stone anchors found off the eastern coast of Bulgaria, which have been compared with Aegean types, cannot be dated.

This is not as simplistic a scenario as one might think, however, since the Black Sea has risen considerably since ca. 1000 B.C. Several submerged Bronze Age sites have been discovered along the Bulgarian coast, which has led Turkish archaeologist Mehmet Özdoğan to propose that the Black Sea, during the Bronze Age, was at least 12 m below the current level. This suggests that we are not yet in a position to answer the question of trade between the Aegean and the Black Seas, which means that Troy's role in such a network must remain uncertain at present.[131]

THE TWELFTH CENTURY B.C.

The waves of destructions that characterized the beginning of the twelfth century B.C. spanned much of Greece and Asia Minor, though not all can be attributed to the same cause.[132] There is an abundance of evidence for political and economic problems throughout the region, and the civil unrest at Troy toward the end of the thirteenth century B.C. has already been mentioned. Cilicia was experiencing a famine, alleviated by the king of Ugarit, to whom the ruler of Alasiya (Cyprus) appealed when his cities were under attack ca. 1200 B.C.[133] The king replied that his troops were in Hatti (Hattuşa) and his fleet in Lycia, which suggests that there were additional disturbances in those areas that required intervention.[134] Ugarit was subsequently destroyed, as was Hattuşa and several of the palaces in mainland Greece, including Mycenae, Tiryns, and Thebes, although an earthquake in the Argolid appears to have been a contributing factor.[135] Much of the responsibility for these destructions has been linked to the Sea Peoples, whose marauding forces comprising a variety of ethnicities are described in the inscriptions of the pharaohs Merneptah (1213–1204 B.C.) and Ramesses III (1185–1154 B.C.).[136]

The same sort of destruction is attested at Troy in the early twelfth century B.C. Carl Blegen found traces of fires throughout the site and up to a meter of blackened debris in some areas, including two fragmentary human skulls and assorted bones inside the South Gate, a human mandible near the East Gate, and a complete human skeleton outside the fortification wall at the west.[137] In the excavations of the last twenty-five years, the best evidence for this destruction has been discovered in what would become the West Sanctuary, near the western entrance to the Bronze Age citadel (Plate 12). Within that destruction deposit were several bronze arrowheads and three piles of stones that may have been intended for slingshots.[138] The assembled evidence suggests armed combat, although there is no way of determining who the attackers might have been or even whether the conflict might have stemmed from internal unrest that followed the deposing of Walmu.

Manfred Korfmann continually expressed the opinion that the nature of the conflict would be clearer if an elite cemetery datable to the period of VIIa could be identified and excavated, but no such cemetery has been pinpointed in spite of extensive magnetic prospection throughout the region. Late Bronze Age adult burials have, however, been uncovered in three areas in and around Troy: in the West Sanctuary, directly outside the southwest gate (VIU) of the citadel; at the southern edge of the Lower City, roughly 500 m south of the citadel; and at Beşik Tepe, 6 km west of Troy near the later settlement of Achilleion. One of the Sanctuary graves contained the skeleton of a man between twenty-five and thirty-five years of age who had been inhumed in the seventeenth century B.C., during the earliest phase of Troy VI (VIa).[139] His skull exhibited evidence for cranial surgery (trephination), which suggests an elevated status, although he appears to have died during the operation.

All of the graves in the cemetery at the southern edge of the Lower City date to the end of Troy VI, immediately prior to the earthquake, and all were cremations.[140] These had been extensively disrupted by the construction of the Hellenistic City Wall and by World War I trenches, but twenty-one cinerary urns were recovered, and Blegen estimated that there were originally more than 200 of them. Based on the sample that was recovered, there were twice as many children as adults, which highlights the high rate of infant mortality at Troy during the Bronze Age.[141] A few of the graves contained bronze rings and drinking vessels, but this was clearly not the elite cemetery for which Blegen and his colleagues had been searching.

The third cemetery, at Beşiktepe, also dates to the late Troy VI period (fourteenth century B.C.), and features a mix of cremations and inhumations, although the majority are inhumations in *pithoi*, many of which held more than one burial.[142] Several of the graves contained bronze jewelry and weapons, including a knife and sword, as well as five stone seals, two of which were Mycenaean imports.[143] These were presumably tied to the settlement where ships trading with Troy would have anchored during the Late Bronze Age, although habitation does not appear to have continued there after the earthquake.[144] These burials provide a wealth of information concerning the inhabitants of the Sixth Settlement, but an array of questions still remain to be answered. Where are the cemeteries that preceded and followed those of Troy VI, and if elite cemeteries of Late Bronze Age date did exist, as they must have, why has remote sensing failed to identify them?

SETTLEMENT VIIB (1180–1050 B.C.)

The phase that follows the destruction, VIIb1 (1180–1130 B.C.), is actually not as clear-cut as the earlier publications indicate.[145] There are few pure VIIb1 deposits that can be distinguished in the archaeological record, but from what we can judge, there was certainly a decrease in the population. A few of the houses were rebuilt after the attack, but only on the citadel, and the East Gate (VIS) was blocked.[146] Wheel-made table wares continued to be produced, although handmade burnished coarse wares now began to be used, and *pithoi* disappeared.[147] Since Handmade Coarse Ware appears to have been restricted to shapes used for cooking and storage, Carolyn Aslan and Pavol Hnila have suggested that a change in diet had occurred, possibly prompted by coordinate changes in the environment.[148] Determining the existence or extent of cultural change is not easy, since so few VIIb1 contexts have been uncovered, but there are no overt signs of a shift in the inhabitants.

Troy VIIb2 (ca. 1130–1050 B.C.), however, is a different case. In these levels Carl Blegen recorded striking changes in the assemblages he discovered, including a preference for stone orthostats in house construction, and molds for tools and weapons that can be paralleled in southeastern Europe. There are also changes in the ceramic record, in that Handmade Burnished Ware was now employed for both cooking and table wares.[149] The shapes and decoration of the handmade vessels find their best parallels in Thrace and the eastern Balkans, as do the molds for the weapons and tools. Blegen therefore concluded that they signaled a new element in the local population, while noting that there appears to have been no attack, and most of the wares and shapes used in VIIb1 did, in fact, continue.[150]

Indeed, the handmade wares are found in domestic contexts with local wheelmade Gray and Tan Ware, and the shapes in both categories are functionally similar; in other words, there are wheel-made and handmade cups and pitchers, although the forms are not identical.[151] The percentage of these handmade wares in VIIb2 assemblages is not consistent over time: they comprise between one-quarter and one-third in the trenches of Blegen, and between 50 and 60 percent in recent excavations of VIIb2.[152] By the Protogeometric period (VIIb3), the percentage of handmade wares reaches a level as high as 70 percent in some areas.[153]

Handmade Burnished Ware is found at a large number of Mediterranean sites in the twelfth century B.C., and its appearance has been ascribed to the movement of slaves, merchants, mercenaries, and guest workers.[154] It seems likely that Trojan Handmade Ware was locally produced in VIIb2 by migrants who arrived there from Thrace, and recent neutron activation analysis has verified its local origins.[155] But within the area of northwestern Asia Minor, these wares were traveling only to the vicinity of Troy and Daskyleion; the recent surveys of Mehmet Özdoğan have shown that handmade wares are notably absent from the southern and eastern Marmara region, as well as other sites on the Gallipoli peninsula with the exception of Eceabat, on the northern side of the entry to the Dardanelles.[156]

The other VIIb2 feature traditionally regarded as a sign of foreign occupation, orthostat construction, is also not as straightforward as one might expect. No parallels in the Balkans have been identified, although M. Pienazek-Sikora has suggested that several sites in the northwest Pontic area may supply relevant comparanda.[157] In his final publication, Blegen noted that orthostats were used in earlier construction at Troy, even if not as extensively as in VIIb2, and we should not rule out a local development.[158] The situation would undoubtedly be clearer if we could assess changes in mortuary customs among phases VIIa, VIIb1, and VIIb2, but no cemeteries of those periods have yet been identified.

Nevertheless, a few conclusions do emerge from the evidence that can be assembled. The collapse of the Hittite Empire seems to have prompted the opening of a commercial corridor stretching from southeastern Europe to central Anatolia, thereby facilitating contact between Thrace and Troy.[159] The Handmade Burnished Wares may have been one of the by-products of this new network, which increased in scale during phases VIIb2 and 3 (ca. 1130–900 B.C.) and may ultimately have involved a demographic change.[160] Migrants do tend to settle in regions with which they are already familiar, often due to pre-existing trade links with their homelands, so such a reconstruction seems logical.[161]

It is worth noting that the demographic shift posited for Troy during the twelfth century B.C. does appear to have occurred at Gordion. To quote Robert Hendrickson and Mary Voigt:

> There is no stratigraphic break to indicate a significant hiatus in settlement at Gordion after the fall of the Hittites, so that time alone cannot account for the observed changes in architecture, domestic features, ceramics, and animal remains between the Late Bronze and the Early Iron Age. These ceramic data do not support a gradual transition from the Late Bronze Age into the Early Iron Age. Instead, the archaeological evidence strongly suggests a population change at this time, rather than simply a shift in political and economic organization.[162]

Based on the ceramic, architectural, and artifactual evidence from Gordion, it looks as if the new inhabitants there, who would eventually be called Phrygians, came from the same general Thracian/Balkan region as those who settled at Troy. Whether the immigrants entered Asia Minor via the Dardanelles or the Bosphoros is uncertain, but it is worth recalling Strabo's statement that "the Phrygians crossed over from Thrace and slew a ruler of Troy and of the country near it. Those people took up their abode there."[163] We cannot assess the validity of this statement, but the replacement of a Trojan ruler with a Thracian one during the late twelfth century B.C. is by no means inconceivable given the substantial evidence for cultural change.

THE HISTORICITY OF THE WAR

Carl Blegen ended his analysis of the archaeological remains of Late Bronze Age Troy with a consideration of the site's relationship to Homer and the *Iliad*, which is a topic into which most of Troy's excavators have been drawn. As an archaeologist specializing in post–Bronze Age Troy, I have been able to avoid discussion of this subject in most situations, but since Ilion's identification as Homeric Troy became the engine for the site's development from the Archaic through the Roman periods, a few comments on this increasingly contentious controversy are in order here.

Blegen regarded the issue as relatively straightforward: the *Iliad* concerns a fortified citadel in the Troad that was destroyed in an attack by the Greeks.[164] The hill of Hisarlik contains the only fortified citadel of Late Bronze Age date in the Troad, which was severely damaged in an armed attack following a period of heightened security measures. The date that he proposed for the attack – ca. 1240 B.C. – coincided with a period of strength and prosperity of the Mycenaean palaces, which would have had the ability to mount a unified offense.

Continued research involving Troy, Homer, and Aegean Bronze Age archaeology since the publications of Blegen have brought the issues into sharper focus, even if a host of questions remain unanswered. That the war described in the *Iliad* is set in the Troad is clear from the topographical references to Samothrace, Lesbos, Mt. Ida, and the strong winds of the Dardanelles.[165] Even if we were to exclude those labels from consideration, no other Late Bronze Age site in western Anatolia features such a distinctive geographical setting, and both excavation and survey within the Troad have determined that Troy is the only major citadel of second millennium B.C. date in the region.[166]

An examination of the Hittite records reveals that western Asia Minor was indeed a contested periphery with claims staked by both the Hittites and the Ahhiyawans, who are probably to be linked to mainland Greece.[167] Mycenaean and Hittite involvement in military conflict during the fourteenth and thirteenth centuries B.C. does, in fact, appear to be attested in the Hittite documents at Hattuşa, although there is no indication that soldiers from mainland Greece actually fought in any of the western Anatolian battles. Some of the names associated with this period of Asia Minor politics even appear in the

Iliad, if our translations are correct: Alaksandu, ruler of Wilusa/Paris, ruler of Troy; Tawagalawa/Eteocles, brother of the king of Ahhiyawa; and, just possibly, Attarisiya/Atreus.[168]

It is also true that cities and citadels along the western coast of Asia Minor were damaged in raids during the thirteenth centuries B.C. The Ahhiyawan stronghold of Miletus seems to have been attacked twice, both times by the Hittites, and Piyamaradu's raids occurred continually over several decades. An examination of the Linear B tablets reveals that women were apparently seized from the west coast of Asia Minor during the late thirteenth century B.C. and deployed as workers in Mycenaean palaces, although there is no indication that the reverse was true, that is, that women were taken from mainland Greece to western Asia Minor, nor that the seizures involved members of a city's ruling class.

The conflicts referenced above also included the Troad, where, at some point in the early thirteenth century B.C., Piyamaradu established a base of power that prompted an invasion by the Hittites, even if there is no evidence for an actual battle or for any damage to Troy at that time. The one occasion when there is relatively secure evidence for armed conflict at Troy, at the end of Troy VIIa, occurred after the Mycenaean palaces, and Hattuša itself, had already been destroyed. The generally accepted date of that conflict today, ca. 1180 B.C., is sixty years later than the one proposed by Blegen, which completely changes the foundations of his suggested linkage between Troy and the *Iliad*.[169] Even in the case of the VIIa destruction, we have no secure evidence that allows us to identify the city's attackers. In other words, there were battles in the Late Bronze Age in which both sides of the Aegean appear to have played a role, but we cannot say that Troy was one of the casualties of this conflict.

Although it has often been said, we have to keep in mind that the *Iliad* was not a history book; it presents a collection of cultures that span a period from the Late Bronze through the Iron Age, and most of those periods are represented in one way or another in the epic.[170] Most of the equipment of war described in the *Iliad* belongs squarely in the second millennium B.C.: the boar tusk helmets, the tower shields, silver-studded swords, and the weapons in general, nearly all of which are bronze rather than iron.[171] The Catalogue of Ships in Book 2 appears to be a collection of actual Bronze Age sites, primarily in mainland Greece, many of which are not attested after the Bronze Age.[172] Even the protective ditch around the Greek camp finds a parallel in the rock-cut ditches of the Lower City of Troy VI and VII which occur as well in a series of Anatolian and Leventine citadels.[173]

Nevertheless, there are no references to the Hittites or to Miletus, even though the role played by the latter city in Late Bronze Age east-west politics was more significant than that of any other coastal settlement in Asia Minor.[174] The references to the importance of Delphi and Phrygia are equally telling in that neither acquired its importance until the end of the Iron Age. Phrygia reached the pinnacle of its power in the second half of the eighth century B.C., during the reign of King Midas, and Midas was probably on the Phrygian throne at the time in which the *Iliad* was composed.[175] The casting of Priam's wife Hecuba as a Phrygian also makes sense only as an eighth century B.C. reference, since there were no Phrygians per se in the Late Bronze Age.

Similarly, the concept of a collective expedition of Greek soldiers, all of whom were united by a common language, seems to reflect a period of growing Panhellenism, which would again point to a date in the later Iron Age.[176] This holds true also for the *Iliad*'s descriptions of the allies of the Trojans, who are said to have spoken a variety of languages. Such linguistic diversity does not really match what one would have experienced in western Asia Minor during the Late Bronze Age, when Luwian would have been the primary language, but it is a good fit for the area during the eighth century B.C., when one would have heard Lydian, Phrygian, and Luwian in addition to Greek.[177]

At what time the story of an east-west conflict was first linked to the topography of Troy is unclear, but the ruined citadel walls were continuously visible through the seventh century A.D., and probably until the end of the Late Byzantine period. These were almost certainly the best-preserved ruins of a Late Bronze Age palace along the western coast of Asia Minor, so if one were looking for a citadel to link to a war between Greece and a coastal Anatolian stronghold, Troy would have been the logical choice. That choice must have been made by the eighth century B.C., and the resulting connections among site, legend, and epic have never really faded since then.

The remainder of this book focuses on the ramifications of this identification for the inhabitants of Greek and Roman Ilion, but it is worth asking, before leaving the subject, whether there is any hope of casting additional light on the archaeology of Homeric Troy and its world. Further excavation in the Bronze Age levels of Miletus would furnish the most potentially significant evidence, since the material in those levels would relate to both the Hittites and the Ahhiyawans. The identification and excavation of the capitals of the Arzawan kingdoms will also undoubtedly answer a range of questions concerning the political configuration of Asia Minor in the thirteenth century B.C., and partial fulfillment of that goal may be imminent: it looks as if remote sensing in Gölmarmara, approximately 40 km east of Manisa, has pinpointed the location of the citadel that controlled the Seha River Land, and it is four times the size of the Trojan citadel.[178]

Equally important are the remains of the city center of Late Bronze Age Troy, which still lie buried under Schliemann's dump at the northern edge of the Trojan mound. Even though, as previously mentioned, the documents contained within these buildings may have been wooden and would subsequently have deteriorated, some of the associated cultural material is probably

still there awaiting retrieval, and could clarify the character of public life during the Sixth and Seventh Settlements. We attempted this project in 1996, but
the work became too dangerous and had to be abandoned, with only a small
part of Schliemann's dump having been removed.[179] The renewed excavation
of this ancient dump, and the analysis of the material contained within it, will
probably have to await the arrival of a new team armed with more sophisticated tools and techniques than those currently available. Just as Blegen pinned
his hopes on the next generation of archaeologists, so must we.

TWO

TROY DURING THE ARCHAIC PERIOD

Reconstructing occupation at Troy during the first half of the first millennium B.C. has never been easy, primarily because sealed strata dating to the Iron Age and Archaic period are preserved in only a few areas of the site. Troy's center of habitation during this period was almost certainly the citadel, but all pre-Hellenistic levels were cleared away during the construction of the Athena Sanctuary in the third century B.C., so there is no way to be certain. The only areas where substantial deposits dating to ca. 1000–500 B.C. have been found are in the northern part of the West Sanctuary and in a network of terraces on the south side of the mound (sector D9), neither of which was extensively excavated until the 1990s (Plate 8).

Since the excavations conducted in the late nineteenth and early twentieth centuries yielded no clear archaeological evidence for continuous habitation between the Bronze and Iron Ages, it was assumed that there must have been a long hiatus in habitation following the end of the Bronze Age. Carl Blegen argued that the hiatus extended for nearly 400 years (ca. 1100–700 B.C.), ending only with the beginning of the Archaic period, and this has long remained a dominant viewpoint in scholarship.[1]

When the Troy project began, our understanding of the first millennium B.C. was not so different from that of our predecessors. Manfred Korfmann and I initially assumed that the division between our respective areas of exploration would be relatively easy to determine, since deposits dating between the Late Bronze Age and the Early Hellenistic period were generally absent from every trench. By 1993, however, we realized how wrong we were, and the prospect of a long hiatus in habitation at the site seemed highly unlikely as increasing numbers of Iron Age deposits began to appear.

The pottery in those deposits clarified the commercial networks operating in the Troad during the tenth, ninth, and eighth centuries B.C., and we found ourselves in a better position to assess long-held theories of a widespread Greek colonization of the Troad during the Iron Age, usually referred to as the "Aeolian Migration." That migration, in effect, provides the frame for this chapter. After a review of the relevant literary accounts, I present the archaeological evidence that bears on the migration's historicity, focusing on the new Trojan discoveries of Iron Age and Archaic date but situating them in the broader context of Greek and Anatolian interaction. Such an analysis elucidates the extent to which the migration stories are borne out by the archaeological record, while simultaneously illustrating the political dimensions of Troy's evolving Homeric identity.

There is no uniformity in the ancient sources that deal with the Aeolian Migration, but the narratives generally focus on colonists from mainland Greece who crossed the Aegean after the Trojan War and founded settlements throughout northwestern Asia Minor, including the Troad, Lesbos, and Tenedos (plate 11).[2] One of the fullest accounts of the migration is provided by Strabo, who proposed that Greek immigrants departed from Aulis in Boeotia, like the forces of Agamemnon, and proceeded to Thrace, under Orestes' son Penthilus; then to Daskyleion, under his grandson Archelaus or Echelas; and finally to the Troad and Lesbos, under his great-grandson Gras, after whom the Granicus River is named.[3] As one can easily see from Strabo's summary, the royal family of Mycenae, and especially Orestes, play a particularly prominent role in these narratives.[4]

This feature of early Greek history has become widely accepted, and nearly every archaeologist who has written about Troy during the last century has attempted to tie the Iron Age and Archaic discoveries at the site to the stories of the Aeolian Migration.[5] Not surprisingly, this ambiguous evidence has prompted a wide variety of viewpoints on both the migration and the early phases of post–Bronze Age Troy, which means that the nature of the settlement during the period in which the Homeric epics were composed has always been elusive. A host of historical questions still remain to be answered, even with the addition of so much new and well-stratified evidence, but we are finally in a position to diagram the principal developments at the site during the first five centuries of the first millennium B.C.

THE PROTOGEOMETRIC AND GEOMETRIC PERIODS (VIIB3/EARLY VIII, CA. 1050–650 B.C.)

The VIIb2 phase ended with a destruction (ca. 1050 B.C.), and judging by the tumbled stones covering nearly all of the occupation areas, there may have

2.1. Protogeometric amphora from the West Sanctuary. Çanakkale Archaeological Museum. Troia slide 23684.

been an earthquake.[6] Most of the houses of this phase had been abandoned and cleared out before the destruction, and we have been unable to determine exactly where the survivors subsequently lived; their houses may have been cleared away by Schliemann when he removed the center of the citadel mound. It is during this post-destruction phase, often referred to as Protogeometric or VIIb3, that a new type of wheel-made pottery painted with concentric circles begins to be found, but otherwise there is no substantive change in the ceramic assemblages (Fig. 2.1).[7]

The earliest painted Protogeometric pottery (Group 1) belongs to neck-handled amphoras, and although these sherds comprise only 3 percent of the tenth century B.C. assemblages, they have received an usual amount of attention during the last twenty years. The amphoras were originally thought to have been produced somewhere in mainland Greece – either coastal Locris or southeast Thessaly – but recent neutron activation analysis has demonstrated that virtually all of them were locally made, thereby requiring a shift in our earlier interpretations.[8] Similar neck-handled amphoras, also of tenth century B.C. date and also locally made, have been found at Torone in Macedonia, and others have recently been discovered at Lemnos and Clazomenae.[9] At the same time, there are discernible similarities between ceramics in the Troad and those on mainland Greece: an Early Protogeometric cup from Troy is a Gray Ware imitation of a type found in the Thessalo-Euboean area, and there are wheel-made Gray Wares in Protogeometric levels at Euboean Lefkandi that feature the same decorative schemes as those originating in Troy.[10]

What exactly does all of this evidence tell us about the character of the Protogeometric settlement at Troy and about the site's role in cross-Aegean trade during that period? In spite of the lack of house walls of Protogeometric date, there must have been a settlement with functional kilns that were producing a specialized type of pottery undoubtedly intended for an equally specialized product, probably wine or oil. The settlement was clearly not an isolated one: the stylistic and technical similarities among contemporary pottery from western Asia Minor, Macedonia, and Euboea, cited above, strongly suggest that Troy was in contact with other centers of ceramic production during the tenth century B.C. There is no way of determining whether that contact was confined to the North Aegean or extended all the way to Euboea, although the limited number of potential Euboean imports at Troy may indicate that the influence was indirect rather than direct. Itinerant potters working in and moving around the North Aegean may also have played a role in the development of Troy's new Protogeometric amphoras, but the pottery that they produced appears to have been made of local clay.[11]

Not surprisingly, the presence of these sherds in Troy's Protogeometric levels has been linked to the Aeolian Migration – originally by Walter Leaf, who interpreted the pottery as a sign of Greek colonization at Troy, and more recently by Dieter Hertel, who believed that the Protogeometric sherds should be connected to the subjugation of Troy by Aeolian settlers.[12] The ceramics in these levels, however, do not support such an interpretation: as I mentioned above, only one shape, the neck-handled amphora, is represented. The amphoras may have been components of an exchange system involving both sides of the Aegean, but they supply no proof of a massive migration from west to east.[13]

Although no new buildings can be dated to this period, there are signs of activity in and around one of the ruined structures in the West Sanctuary – the "Terrace House" (Plate 12 and Fig. 2.2).[14] This building, which had been constructed in the thirteenth century B.C. (Troy VIIa), featured a large central room (9 × 6 m) with a hearth, a pithos storage area, and two smaller rooms. A wealth of small finds, probably dedications, were found inside the structure and suggest the existence of cult activity at least by the early twelfth century B.C.[15]

The Terrace House had been destroyed at the end of VIIa (ca. 1180 B.C.) and appears to have been unused during the following 130 years, during the VIIb phase. It would now, once again, be a locus for activity within the complex, and judging by the material in a series of pits both within and around the building, that activity was almost certainly associated with cult. The contents included burned animal bones, amphoras, large kraters and cups, cooking pots, and three fenestrated stands that must have functioned as thymiateria, or incense burners.[16] In one of the pits was a nearly complete neck-handle amphora with post-firing incised signs that may relate to commerce (Fig. 2.1); another pit yielded a relatively well-preserved thymiaterion that is unique within contemporary votive assemblages: it had a height of nearly 0.33 m, and featured four zones of cross-hatched triangles above a frieze of animals (Fig. 2.3).[17]

Based on the nature of the assemblages, it looks as if the activity in the building involved food preparation, feasting, and drinking, coupled with the burning of incense. That in itself is not surprising; what is noteworthy, however, is that the Terrace House shows no signs of repair or reconstruction dating to this time. Whatever rituals and offerings occurred there will have been conducted in the midst of a ruined building of Late Bronze Age date. It is especially striking that there was a hiatus of nearly 130 years between the two main periods

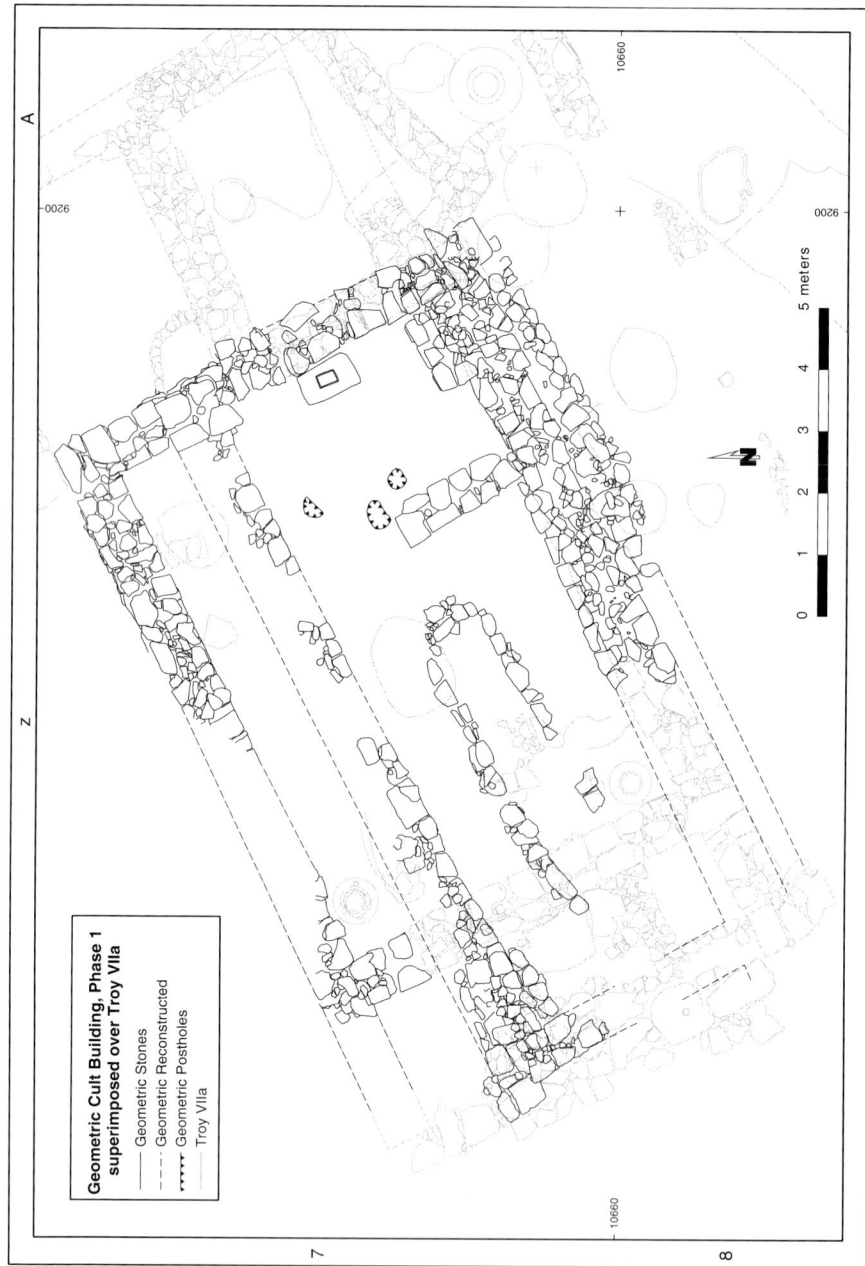

2.2. Plan of the Terrace House with apsidal altar, prepared by Pavol Hnila for the Troy Excavation Project.

2.3. Fenestrated thymiaterion from the West Sanctuary. Troia slide 31402.

of cult activity in the building, with a new group of Thracian settlers arriving at the site midway through the hiatus. We cannot exclude the possibility that the memory of the Terrace House as a locus of sanctity was maintained during this period, and the renewed cult activity may indicate an attempt to re-engage with the Late Bronze Age settlement.

The latter proposition is rendered more likely by the discovery of a contemporary ceramic assemblage adjacent to the Troy VI citadel wall, which can be reconstructed as a small drinking set with a krater, jug, and cups.[18] Here too there appears to have been ritual activity, although, again, no signs of new architecture are apparent. None of this is surprising if one looks at the broader Aegean context: the application of sanctity to a citadel destroyed or abandoned at the end of the Bronze Age can be found at Knossos, Mycenae, and Tiryns, all of which received new cult buildings in the Early Iron Age, even though the citadels per se were abandoned.[19] A particularly relevant comparandum is supplied by the Iron Age settlement on the island of Kea, where a ruined Bronze Age temple continued to serve as a locus of cult activity in the eighth century

B.C., with new benches and a base supporting the head of a terracotta statue of Bronze Age date.[20]

During the Early Geometric period, in the late ninth or early eighth century B.C., the Terrace House was rebuilt and three of the old Bronze Age walls were incorporated into the new construction.[21] The old structure had featured several rooms with a central hall measuring 9 × 6 m; the new one contained one principal room (4.0 × 11.3 m) with a narrow corridor along the north side (Fig. 2.2). Situated along the central axis were a long apsidal altar and a mortised base that were separated by a wall or partition.[22] The base was clearly intended for the insertion of an object related to the cult, and the size of the mortise, 0.33 × 0.22 m, suggests that the object was both large and heavy.[23] The complete skeleton of a sheep or goat had been buried under a rectangular patch of stones during the construction of the mortised base, and may relate to a sacrifice at the time of the building's dedication.[24]

The altar (5.6 × 1.8 m) was filled with ash and burned animal bones, primarily sheep or goat, with cattle and pig represented in smaller numbers.[25] None of the altar stones showed signs of burning, which suggests that the animal bones were deposited here after the sacrifice. Offerings made in or near the altar include four bronze fibulae, two bronze rings, and a bronze spearhead.[26] There is some evidence for benches or seating within the building as well as along the southern exterior side, so the cult activity was clearly communal.[27]

During the later Geometric period (late eighth century B.C.), we begin to find more evidence for occupation at Troy: a house with hearth and oven was constructed in front of the Troy VI fortification wall on the south side of the mound, in sector D9, and the Terrace House in the West Sanctuary was restored once again.[28] This involved extending the length of the building by at least 1.4 m, reinforcing another wall, and removing the cult base at the back of the main hall, which was replaced by a line of stones that may have supported a bench.[29]

The apsidal altar appears to have been covered and put out of use by a higher floor level, but around the same time, ca. 700 B.C., a series of stone paved circles were constructed ca. 20 m toward the east, along the Troy VI fortification wall. Blegen found twenty-eight such circles in all, with an average diameter of 2 m, although not all of them were contemporary (Fig. 2.4).[30] Some were surrounded by orthostats, and each was clearly the locus of a fire judging by the layer of black earth on top of them. The ceramic assemblages associated with these circles suggest feasting (cups, dinoi [mixing bowls], kraters, etc.), which, given the location, was probably associated with the site's Bronze Age heritage.[31] The circles were situated on a terrace, ca. 3 m high, and framed by the adjacent Troy VI fortification wall. The actual feasting, then, must have been extraordinarily theatrical, with fires blazing on a surrogate

2.4. Stone-paved circles in the West Sanctuary. Photo courtesy of the University of Cincinnati Classics Department, Troy Archives.

stage situated against the backdrop of a monumental citadel wall that had been constructed 700 years earlier. Whether the circles were intended as a kind of replacement for the abandoned apsidal altar in the Terrace House cannot be determined, but it seems highly likely that some sort of hero cult had been established by this point.

Hero cult has also been identified in an area 80–90 m northwest of the citadel, to which Carl Blegen gave the title "Place of Burning." It was so called due to the discovery of burned human bones with perhaps as many as fifty cinerary urns of Late Bronze Age date.[32] Set within this area around 700 B.C. was a large oval structure measuring 10 × 5.5 m, around which were unusually large numbers of cups and cooking pots, including dinoi, kraters, and amphoras.[33] Feasting must have occurred here in the Late Geometric/Early Archaic period, and it may have been related to the Bronze Age cemetery that lay beneath it.

The installation of these cultic facilities coincided with several literary, religious, and political landmarks. One was the composition of the *Iliad*, at which time one witnesses the acceleration of hero cult on both sides of the Aegean, especially at sites such as Mycenae and Tiryns that were framed by ruined monumental buildings of Bronze Age date.[34] There is no proof that Troy's new cult facilities were tied to specific Homeric heroes when they were first installed, but such an association would certainly have settled in place during the course of the seventh century B.C.

Another landmark was the dominance in Asia Minor of the Phrygian kingdom, which reached the pinnacle of its power in the second half of the eighth century B.C. This period coincided with the reign of King Midas, who was probably on the Phrygian throne at the time in which the *Iliad* was composed, and this may explain why Phrygia was described as such a prosperous kingdom in the epic. One of the stories in the *Lives of Homer* even included the claim that Homer was commissioned to write an epigram for Midas, which was reportedly inscribed on a stele and set up at his tomb.[35]

There has been speculation that the entire region of northwestern Asia Minor was under Phrygian control during this period, primarily due to the discovery of several Phrygian inscriptions at Daskyleion, approximately 175 km east of Troy. Also cited as evidence for such control are a number of legends that mention a link between northwest Asia Minor and Phrygia: Midas reportedly married the daughter of Cyme's king, and Ilus, son of Dardanus, entered a wrestling match hosted by the king of Phrygia, ultimately winning a cow that led him to the hill of Hisarlık.[36] A few Geometric sherds at Troy are decorated with stamped circles and triangles set in alternating rows, which one also finds at Gordion, although the forms at each site are different, and there may be no direct link between them.[37] It seems more likely that the Phrygian inscriptions from Daskyleion signal local emulation of a dominant culture rather than outright political control.[38]

By the beginning of the seventh century B.C., however, it looks as if all or part of the Troad had come under the control of the Lydians. Strabo and Nicholas of Damascus make this statement outright, and the Milesians reportedly needed the permission of the Lydian king Gyges to found a colony at Abydos, near the modern city of Çanakkale.[39] The settlement of Daskyleion, which would later become the Persian regional capital of northwest Asia Minor, was named after Daskylus, the father of Gyges, and royal hunts were staged for the Lydian kings near Zeleia (modern Gönen), as they would be later for the satraps of Persia.[40] There is no way of determining when Lydian control over the western Troad began and ended, but Croesus, the last of the Lydian kings, had the power to forbid construction of new fortifications at the Troad town of Sidene after he destroyed it, and the city of Adramyttium (Edremit) at the southeast corner of the Troad was named after his brother.[41] Consequently, it seems likely that Lydia held control of most of the Troad for nearly 150 years.[42] It is therefore striking that only a few sherds of Lydian pottery have been found at Troy, although this parallels the situation at the site during the Late Bronze Age when Troy's political alliance with the Hittites was not reflected in the material record.[43]

It is not as easy as one might think to compare the evidence for Archaic habitation at Troy with neighboring sites, since Lesbos is the only other area where a discernible amount of Iron Age material has been found. Bronze Age Lesbos clearly lay within the cultural orbit of the Troad and western Asia Minor, and this appears to have been true for the Iron Age as well. During the tenth and ninth centuries B.C. there is evidence for habitation at several sites on Lesbos: apsidal buildings have been excavated at Mytilene and Antissa, and occupation is attested at Methymna and Pyrrha as well.[44] On Lesbos, as at Troy, there is no substantive change in the Gray Ware vessels from the Bronze to the Iron Age, and the Iron Age pottery of Lesbos, like that of Troy, has more parallels in the eastern Aegean and in Anatolia than in mainland Greece, at least through the eighth century B.C.[45]

With the beginning of the seventh century B.C., there is a distinctive type of pottery produced at Troy that begins to be used at other sites in the North Aegean. This is a fine painted ware usually named G2/3 after the sector at Troy that has furnished a large number of examples. G2/3 Ware was especially popular for drinking sets – cups and small jugs – and the usual decoration features vertical zigzags, step patterns, and hooked spirals.[46] Recent neutron activation analysis has demonstrated that Troy was the source of this pottery, and it has been found in early habitation levels at Thasos, Samothrace, Lesbos, Tenedos, and Lemnos. All of these regions may have formed part of a commercial maritime network with Troy by the beginning of the Archaic period, as they had during the Early Bronze Age.[47]

In assessing the nature of habitation in the northeast Aegean during the Iron Age and Early Archaic period, we would probably be on firmer ground if the evidence for burial customs in the region were more substantial. The one relevant grave at Troy, dating probably to the Late Geometric period, is the poorest of the group, with a contracted skeleton covered by a large pithos sherd.[48] Adult Geometric burials on Lesbos tend to be inhumations in cists or large jars, although in the Archaic period clay sarcophagi began to be used on Lesbos, as at western Asia Minor coastal sites further to the south, with earthen tumuli and ring walls often set above them.[49] The eighth/seventh century B.C. graves on Tenedos are stone-lined pits featuring both cremation and inhumation, with children inhumed in amphoras.[50]

The material recovered from all of these graves, primarily pottery and fibulae, can be paralleled most easily in western Asia Minor and on the eastern Aegean islands, especially Lemnos and Rhodes. The fibulae in the Lesbos tombs, in particular, find their closest stylistic parallels with those from Anatolia (Gordion, Alişar, Cilicia), and several of the tomb gifts from Tenedos maintain a distinct Anatolian iconography as late as the sixth century B.C.[51] None of this is particularly reminiscent of contemporary burial practices in mainland Greece, although we are, of course, dealing with a limited number of settlements and varying levels of wealth at the sites in question.

THE ARCHAIC PERIOD: CA. 650–480 B.C.

Habitation at Troy and, indeed, throughout the Troad, moved in new directions during the second half of the seventh century B.C. Around the middle of the century Troy experienced some sort of disaster: layers of tumbled stones have been found on the western, southern, and eastern sides of the mound; the stone circles in the West Sanctuary go out of use, as does the Terrace House, and the production of G2/3 Ware comes to an end.[52] Although this could, in theory, have been either an attack or an earthquake, the similarity in destruction throughout the site coupled with the site's seismic history makes the latter explanation seem more likely.

It is conceivable that there was a short period of either abandonment or at least a decrease in population after the event, which would fit with Strabo's description of the Troad during the seventh century B.C. He mentions that all the stones of Troy were taken to rebuild other towns in the area, particularly the new Lesbian settlement of Sigeion.[53] Sigeion appears to have been established at some point between ca. 650 and 625 B.C., shortly after the proposed earthquake at Troy, which meant that an extensive supply of loose stones would have been readily available, especially considering that the two towns were separated by only 6 km.

When construction began again at Troy, ca. 625 B.C., there were clear signs of a change. A new limestone cult building (the "Early Archaic Cult Building") was constructed in the northern part of the West Sanctuary – the first building at the site to have been constructed entirely of stone in approximately 500 years. It contained at least two rooms of nearly equal size, one measuring 6 × 4.6 m, the other, 6 × 5.3 m; there may also have been a third room, possibly a porch, at the west (Fig. 2.5).[54] Terrace walls are situated only 1.5 m from the main building, and in light of their proximity, they may have supported a wooden colonnade.[55]

The orientation differs from that of the older buildings in the complex, although it may have been influenced by an earlier wooden structure directly beneath the cult building that has left only a minimal trace in the archaeological record.[56] In the fill above the floor was a large burnished Gray Ware krater, nearly twice the normal size, with molded ridges and knobbed ends that clearly imitate metalwork (Fig. 2.6). It looks as if this structure may have absorbed the ritual drinking activities that had earlier occurred in the Terrace House or around the stone circles.[57]

Shortly after the completion of the new Early Archaic Cult Building, two altars were constructed further to the south, in the precincts that have usually been labeled the "Upper" and "Lower" Sanctuaries (Plate 12 and Figs. 2.2 and 2.7).[58] Both are separated by only 4 m, but a precinct wall existed between them, and they differ significantly in terms of shape and function. The former (Altar A), which faced toward the southeast, was apsidal or J-shaped; next to it stood a stone offering table around which were blackened earth and burned bones, but few if any votive dedications. The Lower Sanctuary altar (Altar B) was rectangular and oriented to the northeast. No evidence of sacrifice was found, although a wealth of votive dedications were uncovered, most of which represent females.[59] The two altars were clearly intended to serve different

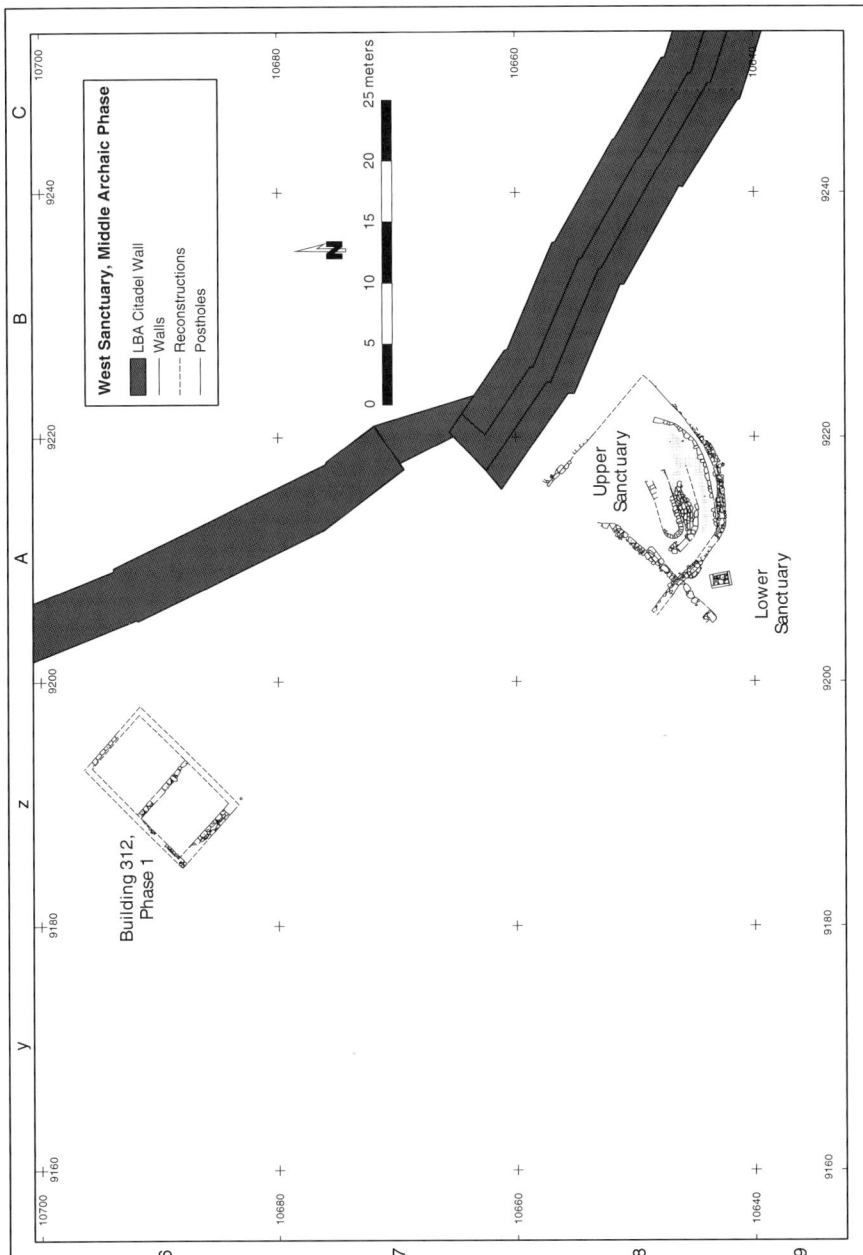

2.5. Plan of Early Archaic Cult Building in the West Sanctuary, prepared by Pavol Hnila for the Troy Excavation Project.

2.6. Gray Ware thymiaterion from the West Sanctuary. Troia slide 26272.

purposes within the complex – one focused on sacrifice, the other on dedications – and we should perhaps therefore refer to Altar B as a table or platform
rather than an altar per se.[60]

The pottery deposited throughout the West Sanctuary during this period
also represented a change from earlier assemblages. Attic and Corinthian pottery now began to appear, as did Ionian cups and the "Wild Goat Style," thereby
attesting to Troy's connection with a much wider East Greek world.[61] Many
of the cups were decorated with painted swans, giving rise to the label "Swan
Style" to describe the new vessels, which would eventually comprise nearly
half of the total assemblage around the altar in the Lower Sanctuary.[62] Faunal
deposits from the same period have yielded an abundance of fallow deer bones,
including antlers, as well as lion bones that may have formed part of skins that
decorated the walls or were worn during ritual activities.[63]

A considerable number of dedications were discovered in close proximity to
the altar in the Lower Sanctuary, and several of the most significant include a
faience scarab with lion decoration, two fibulae of spectacle type – one bone
and one bronze – and a polychrome spindle whorl with horizontal stripes on
the cone and a floral design on the base.[64] Other undecorated spindle whorls
and loom weights had also been deposited here, along with beads, rings, and
arrows.[65] Blegen found several terracotta figurines of Archaic date by the altar,
and we uncovered terracotta heads of swans and geese as well as female heads
and standing women, one of which featured a cylindrical body, wedge-shaped
arms, a pinched face, and a polos, or tall, cylindrical headdress (Fig. 2.8).[66]

2.7. View of the Upper and Lower Sanctuaries in the West Sanctuary. The Lower Sanctuary, with the nearly square Altar B, appears at left; the apsidal altar of the Upper Sanctuary is at right. Troy Excavation Project photo.

All of the evidence suggests that worship was focused on a female deity linked to swans and wild animals, especially lion and deer.[67] The presence of two adjacent altars may point to the co-existence of different cults, although they may also relate to two different functions within a single cult. It is also possible that there was continuity in cultic activity between the new altar precincts and the old Terrace House: the apsidal form of the Upper Sanctuary altar is reminiscent of its predecessor in the earlier building, and Altar B compares well with the rectangular base at the back of that building.[68] The distance between the altar and base in the Terrace Building is also approximately the same as that between the two altars in the Upper/Lower Sanctuaries, with a partition wall used to separate altar from base in both cases.

The only problem with this scenario is that by the time at which the new building in the Upper/Lower Sanctuaries occurred, the Terrace House would probably have been hidden from view for several decades, and perhaps close to a century. The earlier structure would therefore not have been visually accessible as a model for the later ones, although memory of the earlier layout may have played a role here. Even if we assume continuity in cult, however, the changes were dramatic: a new stone temple and altars, ceramic imports from a wider area, and probably a new deity, or at least a deity whose patterns of worship had shifted significantly from the Geometric version.

2.8. Archaic terracotta figurine from the West Sanctuary. Troia slide 18817.

What could have prompted such striking innovations? Surely, part of the explanation lies in the increase in the number of colonies throughout the Troad, in particular, as well as Asia Minor and the Black Sea, in general, during the eighth, seventh, and early years of the sixth century B.C. Judging by the pottery from Cyme, from which Hesiod's father had reportedly come, a settlement already existed there by the middle of the eighth century B.C.[69] Within the sphere of the Troad, Miletus founded colonies at Cyzicus, Proconnesus, Abydos, and Lampsacus, as well as at least ten colonies in the Black Sea, including Panticapaeum, Histria, Sinop, and Olbia. By the end of the seventh century B.C., Athens had established colonies at Sigeion and Elaious, near the mouth of the Hellespont, and Lesbian Methymna had founded Assos, on the southwestern side of the Troad.[70] It is only in the early sixth century B.C., however, that we begin to find evidence for written Greek in the Troad, initially in the form of graffiti on vessels, and then on coinage and stone inscriptions.[71]

For the purposes of Troy, the most important of these sites was Sigeion, the first Athenian colony in the eastern Aegean, which lay on the Aegean coast only a few kilometers northwest of Troy (Plate 11).[72] This had been an area under Lesbian control during much of the seventh century B.C., but it was won by Athens ca. 625 B.C. following a battle in which the poet Alcaeus lost his armor.[73] Herodotus reports on the competing territorial claims of Athens and Lesbos, in which each region's involvement with the Homeric tradition played a significant role. By this point, the rulers of Lesbos had already traced their descent from the royal family of Mycenae, and Orestes in particular.[74] Athens, in turn, argued that any of the mainland Greek cities providing aid to Menelaus during the Trojan War had as much right to the territory as Lesbos.[75] In the end, the conflict was reportedly settled by Periander, tyrant of Corinth, who allowed Athens to keep Sigeion, while Lesbos continued its control of the small town of Achilleion, 9 km to the south.

Judging by the quantities of Attic pottery in the late seventh century B.C. deposits at Troy, the settlement enjoyed frequent interaction with Sigeion, and the time in which the Cult Building in Troy's West Sanctuary was constructed coincides with the establishment of the Athenian colony.[76] This coincidence is difficult to ignore, and it is tempting to link Athenian activity in Sigeion with the construction of the Cult Building, which would not have been inexpensive to build.

The other significant bond between the two cities was that they both honored Athena as their principal goddess, although those temples of Athena are not easy to reconstruct. In his description of the battle over Sigeion between Athens and Lesbos, Herodotus notes that the armor of Alcaeus was installed in Sigeion's temple of Athena as an Athenian war trophy. The location of the Sigeion temple is unknown and the date of its erection cannot be deduced from any ancient source, but it was presumably built shortly after the victory over Lesbos and the foundation of the colony, so sometime in the late seventh century B.C.[77] Athena's temple at Troy was also probably standing by this point, but all of its stones were most likely reused in the Hellenistic Athenaion, and its precise location on the citadel has never been ascertained.[78]

On the south side of Troy's citadel, however, there is evidence for new terracing during the last quarter of the seventh century B.C., which suggests a broader program of construction on the citadel itself, where the Athena temple must have stood.[79] In later periods, the fills in these terraces contain debris from the Sanctuary of Athena, and the terrace deposits dating to 625–600/575 B.C. probably derive from the same source.[80] It is conceivable that the Athena temples at Troy and Sigeion were under construction at more or less the same time in the later seventh century B.C., in which case there may have been reciprocal influence on both cult and architecture, although in the absence of more tangible evidence, we can do no more than speculate.

The only surviving component of the Archaic temple precinct is a well (Bh), located at the base of a flight of steps that led down from the temenos (Fig. 2.9).[81] We have no direct evidence for the construction date of the stairs, but rainwater would have continually run down a slope this steep, and the construction of a stone walkway would have been highly desirable from the beginning of the well's use. The employment of the Troy VI Northeast Bastion as one of the sides of the staircase made its construction a relatively simple undertaking, while simultaneously supplying a symbolic link between the Bronze Age and Archaic settlements.

That linkage would also have been apparent in one other unique tradition, that of the "Locrian Maidens," which casts additional light on the early history of the Athena temple at Troy and, indirectly, the Athenian colony of Sigeion. These maidens were the daughters of the aristocratic families of East Locris in mainland Greece who emerged as the principal players in one of Troy's most important traditions. Locris was the homeland of Ajax, son of Oileus ("the Lesser"), who had raped Cassandra in Troy's Temple of Athena at the end of

2.9. Northeast Bastion. The steps are probably Archaic; the battered fortification wall dates to Troy VI. Troia slide 41707.

the Trojan War. In atonement for the rape, the Locrian nobility were required to send two maidens each year to live in and clean the Sanctuary of Athena Ilias. The maidens arrived at Rhoeteum, near the burial mound associated with Ajax the Greater, and secretly made their way by night to the Sanctuary of Athena where they lived in servitude to the goddess for a year, entering the temple only at night so that they would not be seen by the goddess' statue.[82]

The rather large number of ancient historians who comment on this custom agree in general on the basic form of the tribute but disagree on the date when it originated, with some placing it shortly after the Trojan War, and one, Demetrius of Scepsis, in the period of Persian domination.[83] The most specific account was written by Polybius, who describes the "Hundred Families" of the aristocracy: "these 'hundred families' are those who were identified by the Locrians, before embarking on their colonization, as the ones from which the virgins were sent to Troy, in accordance with the orders of the oracle."[84] The colony in question was Locri Epizephyri in southern Italy, which was founded, according to Eusebius, in the 670s B.C., although the earliest archaeological evidence for the colony is not as clear as one would like.[85] In any event, the custom appears to have been established in the seventh century B.C., which would indicate that the temple of Athena must have been founded by then.[86] If it had been built prior to 650, we should probably assume its destruction in the midcentury earthquake and a reconstruction ca. 625 when building

2.10. Sivritepe, usually identified as the Tumulus of Achilles. Troia slide 37279.

at Troy began again. Such a sequence would fit well with the evidence for new citadel terracing in the later seventh century B.C.

This examination of the chronology of the Locrian Maidens suggests that Ilion had been identified as Homeric Troy by the seventh century B.C., a date that is in harmony with the appearance of the *Iliad* itself. Whether one dates the epic to the later eighth or the early seventh century B.C., it is the Troad that has been used as the setting for the narrative, which means that the link between legendary Troy and historical Ilion must have occurred by ca. 700 B.C. at the latest.[87] The inhabitants of the city would not intensively publicize that identification until the third century B.C., but the process appears to have begun approximately four centuries earlier, and it must have been well enough established by the seventh century that the Locrians decided to send their maidens there.

Occurring at approximately the same time, in all likelihood, was the identification of the monumental mounds in the surrounding landscape as the tombs of Homeric heroes (Plate 2). The majority of these are settlement mounds, not burials, which date between the later Neolithic period and the Bronze Age. Two of the most famous examples are the mound of Sivritepe, 4 km from Troy, and Karaağaçtepe, often identified as the tomb of Protesilaus, at the end of the Gallipoli peninsula (Figs. 2.10 and 2.11); Hanaytepe and Paşatepe are also cases in point.[88]

The reconfiguring of these prehistoric settlement mounds as burial sites of Homeric characters is not surprising: the *Iliad* and *Odyssey* contain several references to the construction of large-scale tumuli for both Greek and

2.11. Karaağaçtepe, usually identified as the tumulus of Protesilaus. Troy Excavation Project photo.

Trojan heroes in the vicinity of Troy, and the identification of Ilion's mounds as "Homeric" burials was a logical assumption once the equation between legendary Troy and Ilion had been established.[89] The ancient sources attest to ten of them in the vicinity of Ilion, evenly divided between the Greeks and Trojans. The most famous include Achilles, Patroclus, Ajax, and Protesilaus, although Hector, Hecuba, Aisyetes, Batieia (wife of Dardanus) or Myrina (queen of the Amazons), Ilus, and Antilochus were also featured.[90]

It is conceivable that some of these "Homeric" tombs were adorned with marble decoration, although the evidence is very slight: sometime around 1892, in Rhoeteum, a large marble anthemion stele was discovered and passed into the collection of Frank Calvert.[91] The stele was reportedly found near the tumulus of Ajax, and the palmette decoration suggests a date around 500 B.C. Since there are no other tumuli in the immediate area, it is likely to have come from the tomb of Ajax, which would have held an unusually prominent position in the landscape.[92] Rhoeteum was the harbor at which the Locrian Maidens arrived and they probably visited the tomb prior to their trip to Troy, even though this was the tomb of Ajax, son of Telamon ("Ajax the Greater"), and they were atoning for the sin of their ancestor Ajax, son of Oileus ("Ajax the Lesser"). The Ajax tomb was admittedly a special case in that it was linked to a continual ritual as the other tombs were not, but paths to the other tumuli of note must have been constructed by this time, and they probably received some sort of decoration, even if it was only a terminal stone.

At some point during the Archaic period the residents of Ilion appear to have created a treasury of Trojan War relics within the Temple of Athena. Our primary sources for this are Hellenistic and tantalizingly brief: in the course of their descriptions of Alexander's visit to Ilion, both Arrian and Diodorus note that he deposited his armor in the temple as a dedication to Athena and withdrew from the temple the finest armor and a shield remaining from the Trojan War, which he subsequently wore into battle.[93]

The passages make it clear that Alexander chose from among several suits of Trojan armor and shields that were kept in the temple, and he was also asked if he wanted to see the lyre of Paris, which may have been another one of the relics.[94] None of the authors mention that the treasury had been installed during the Archaic period, but there was very little activity at the site between the early fifth century B.C. and Alexander's visit in 334, so a date in the sixth century B.C. for the treasury's inauguration seems likely. Since the temple was reportedly small, even in Alexander's time, the treasury probably did not occupy much space.

The creation of this treasury would also have tied the temples at Sigeion and Troy closer together, in that the former contained the armor lost by Alcaeus during the war with Lesbos.[95] Whether Troy was copying Sigeion or vice versa cannot be determined since the time of origin of the Trojan treasury is unknown, but they would probably have been the only temples in the Troad to feature prizes of armor.

The sources of the treasure were most likely local. A considerable amount of building had occurred on and around the citadel mound during the seventh and sixth centuries B.C., and artifacts of Bronze Age date would no doubt have been unearthed in the course of construction, some of which may well have been of gold or silver. These could easily have been marketed as Homeric, although the source of the armor, and the lyre, remains a mystery. A comparable example of this phenomenon can be found on the island of Kea, where the terracotta head of a goddess, discovered in the ruins of the Bronze Age temple, was subsequently set up on a base within the temple as a locus of cult.[96] In both cases, objects of great antiquity unearthed at the site were used to foster a temporal link to and shared identity with the earlier inhabitants.

CO-OPTING TROY

At the same time in which the Troad was solidifying its connection to the *Iliad*, a considerable number of new Greek settlements were being established in western and northern Asia Minor as well as the Black Sea. The Milesian colonies in the Hellespont, the southern shore of the Propontis, and the northern and southern coasts of the Black Sea constituted components of a formidable commercial network, and the Megarian settlements in or around the Bosphorus – at Chalcedon, Selymbria, and Byzantium – were undoubtedly competitive responses to those establishments.[97] As this competition among the new colonizers gathered momentum, one of the by-products was the construction of increasingly distinctive identities, in which charter myths articulated the city-states' heroic heritage and justified their territorial expansion.[98] This was the beginning of a trend that would not really end until the early Renaissance, and would ultimately involve virtually all of the nation-states in Europe and the Near East.

Many of these myths involve the Trojan War and, by extension, the settlement of Troy itself. An excellent case in point is supplied by the aforementioned custom of the Locrian Maidens, which proved mutually beneficial to both Opountian Locris and Troy. One of the most intriguing features of the Locrian custom was that the maidens could be attacked, even killed, by the Trojans if they were caught outside the confines of the Athena Sanctuary.[99] In light of the fact that Troy was hardly a military force at this time (or at any time in the future), one has to ask why the Locrians would have allowed two of their aristocratic children to be subjected to such mistreatment annually on the opposite side of the Aegean. The only sensible explanation is that Locris was simultaneously promoting a link to the Homeric tradition that Troy now embodied, and to their local hero, Ajax, by making the custom a fixed component of their civic identity.[100] The later construction in Locris of a temple to Athena Ilias endowed the custom with a kind of bilateral symmetry, and it conferred upon the Locrians a level of prestige far more potent than wealth.[101]

At this point it is worth revisiting the Athenians' decision to establish a colony at Sigeion ca. 625 B.C. On the one hand, such a location provided a way station of strategic importance for maritime trade between the Aegean and the Black Sea, which was a commercial corridor of increasing interest to the city-states in Greece and Asia Minor. The plethora of Milesian colonies in the Hellespont, on the southern shore of the Propontis, and on the northern and southern coasts of the Black Sea have already been noted. With the foundation of Sigeion and Elaious shortly thereafter, Athenian colonies flanked the entrance to a maritime corridor critically important to grain exports from the area of the northern Black Sea.[102]

But there was another clear advantage to this location: it allowed Athens, in effect, to co-opt the Homeric heritage of Troy, which was a heritage to which it otherwise had only a questionable connection. Sigeion lay in the midst of a series of tumuli identified as the burials of the Homeric heroes, and establishing a colony there allowed Athens, through her colonists, to exercise greater control of Troy and its legendary associations than any other city.[103]

The foundation of this particular colony should also be viewed in conjunction with contemporary politics in and around Attica. Toward the end of the seventh century B.C., Athens and Megara disputed the ownership of Salamis, and in the course of the argument both cities exploited their connection to Telamonian Ajax, king of Salamis.[104] The foundation of Sigeion should probably be considered a complementary development, in that it brought Athens into a geographic sphere staked out by Megara several decades earlier with its colonies on the Bosphorus.[105]

Athenian presence in the Troad did not go unchallenged during the Archaic period. Although it appears that Sigeion was still Attic in the second quarter of the sixth century B.C., Herodotus mentions that Peisistratus had to retake the city from Lesbos, probably sometime in the 530s B.C., which indicates that Lesbos had managed to seize it again sometime around the mid-sixth century B.C.[106] The Peisistratid victory at Sigeion and Athens' subsequent re-entry into the affairs of the Troad nicely complemented the tyrants' incorporation of the Homeric epics into the Athenian Panathenaea, and the two should probably be viewed as components of the same political program.[107]

Another component of that program may have been the Athenian colony at Elaious, on the European side of the Hellespont, which had been established at least by around 550 B.C.[108] Although no buildings datable to the Archaic period have been discovered there, the nearby mound often identified as the tomb of Protesilaus still survives, as do several literary accounts that describe its original appearance (Fig. 2.11). Some of these heroic tumuli were attached to shrines – those connected to Achilles and Ajax are cases in point – but the mound of Protesilaus was the only one that housed its own oracle. Adjacent to the latter mound during the Late Archaic period was a precinct dedicated to Protesilaus with its own treasury of gold, silver, and bronze, undoubtedly gifts to the oracle similar to what one would have found at Delphi.[109] Such an oracular shrine wrapped in a Homeric mantle would have significantly increased the status of Elaious, and it was probably the proximity of the Protesilaus tomb that determined the colony's location.[110]

ILION AND ASSOS IN THE LATE ARCHAIC PERIOD

At approximately the same time in which Sigeion was retaken by the Athenians there was renewed construction in Troy's West Sanctuary, directly above the Early Archaic Cult Building. The new structure, almost certainly a temple, had a length of nearly 18 m and a width of 8 m, and contained a large rectangular room with vestibule, probably the cella and pronaos (Fig. 2.12).[111] The overall measurements are about three-quarters the size of the slightly earlier temple at Neandria and the roughly contemporary temple of Athena at Assos.[112] Each of the foundation blocks on the north side contains two projecting bosses, similar to those on the Assos temple, and the superstructure was formed by finely finished ashlar limestone in pseudo-isodomic technique.[113]

The architectural order was Aeolic, which is characterized by capitals with vertically rising volutes set above a leaf echinus, probably resting on wooden columns with stone bases.[114] Only one Aeolic capital was found during

66

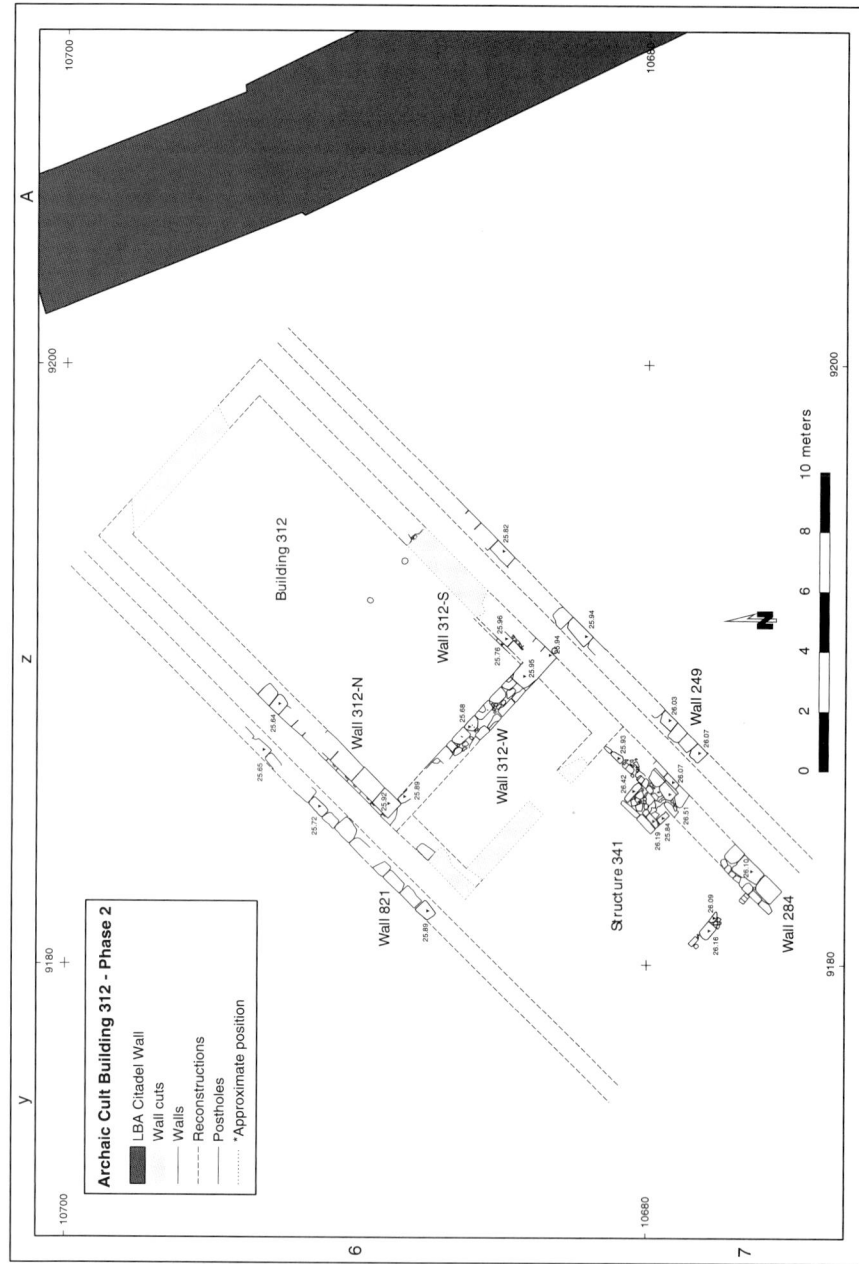

2.12. Plan of the Late Archaic temple in the West Sanctuary, prepared by Pavol Hnila for the Troy Excavation Project.

2.13. Aeolic capital from the West Sanctuary. Troia slide 19321.

excavation, but originally there must have been at least two at the entrance; judging by the size of the extant capital, the height of the building would have been somewhere between 8 and 11 m (Fig. 2.13).[115] Within the cella there would probably have been a cult image of which no trace survives, but the excavation of the temple yielded a mortised statue base that must have stood either in or around the building. The mortise is in the shape of an oval, similar in size to the mortised bases used in the Late Archaic Geneleos monument at Samos, which suggests a roughly life-size wooden or limestone statue of columnar shape.[116]

The altar in front of the temple originally measured ca. 1 m square, although it would be continually modified and expanded over the course of the next three centuries and would ultimately reach a length of nearly 8 m (Plate 12).[117] The altar was perpendicular to the building and faced southeast, like the apsidal altar in the Upper Sanctuary, but the two were not precisely parallel to each other.

There are several points of interest here. The building of the Late Archaic temple was contemporary with Peisistratus' recapture of Sigeion, just as the Early Archaic Cult Building's construction had coincided with Sigeion's initial foundation by Athens nearly 100 years earlier. These two synchronisms may be simply coincidental, but it seems likely, at the very least, that the Athenian entry and re-entry into the region stimulated the local economy and facilitated a higher level of construction, of which Troy's Late Archaic temple was a case in point.

The temple's other noteworthy feature was the incorporation of the Aeolic order, which began to be used in the public buildings of northwestern Asia Minor toward the end of the seventh century B.C. The earliest examples come from Smyrna and Larisa, but by the sixth century B.C. the style had spread

2.14. The temple of Athena at Assos. Photo by the author.

to Neandria, Lesbos, Troy, and Ainos.[118] Based on the surviving evidence, it looks as if Ionia followed a similar model shortly thereafter when the Ionic order began to characterize temples in the region, beginning with Samos and Ephesus.[119] In other words, architectural style became a device by which the settlements of northwestern Asia Minor projected a particular identity for themselves, distinct from that of other regions.

A parallel development is the formation of an Aeolian league, a political and cultural association that was intended to promote a sense of regional identity and cohesion.[120] The league initially included only the cities between Pergamon and Smyrna along or near the coast, but eventually it embraced the entire western Troad.[121] The foundation and early development of the league was probably stimulated by a variety of factors, but among them would have been the extraordinary ethnic and linguistic diversity of western Asia Minor during the Archaic period, which would have included Lydian, Phrygian, Aramaic, and perhaps a derivative of Luwian, in addition to Greek.[122] Conflict with Lydia, which controlled both Aeolian and Ionian areas during the seventh and early sixth centuries B.C., was no doubt also a contributing factor, as was the advent of Persian control in Asia Minor after the mid-sixth century B.C.[123]

One site within the region that stands apart from the aforementioned Aeolic identity is Assos, at the southwestern corner of the Troad, which had reportedly been founded by colonists from Methymna on Lesbos.[124] During the third quarter of the sixth century B.C., at roughly the same time in which Ilion's Late Archaic temple was being planned, the inhabitants of Assos began constructing an andesite Doric temple to Athena that is still regarded as one of the most idiosyncratic structures in the ancient Mediterranean (Fig. 2.14).[125] The temple measured 30 × 14 m, which made it the Troad's largest building, and its location on the acropolis, directly above the Gulf of Adramyttium, turned it into the most prominent component of the surrounding skyline.

The temple is remarkable for both its sculpture and architecture, but one can easily single out three especially important innovations: it was, as far as we know, one of only two Doric temples in the Troad, the other being the temple of Athena at Sigeion.[126] It is also the only temple of Archaic date to have featured both carved Doric metopes and a carved Ionic frieze, and the only building in western Asia Minor to have included Herakles in the architectural decoration, although he was prominently featured in mainland Greece, especially within the Archaic pediments of the temples on the Athenian acropolis.[127]

It is difficult to read such an idiosyncratic choice of order and decoration as anything other than a deliberate statement of civic identity, which, in turn, needs to be viewed against the political configuration of the period in which the temple was constructed. The third quarter of the sixth century B.C. witnessed the Athenian victory over the Mytileneans and the reoccupation of Sigeion, while the Lydian empire that had once extended throughout the Troad now fell to the Persians, who ruled from the satrapal capital at Daskyleion.[128] In other words, this was a political climate that continually led to a re-examination of one's identity and allegiances. It looks as if Assos intended to signal its links with Sigeion, and Athens by extension, rather than Lesbos, and used the most conspicuous landmark in the city as a symbol of those links.

Sometime between 520 and 480 B.C., a major earthquake appears to have brought down the Assos temple, and it probably caused significant damage throughout the western Troad, including at Troy. The Late Archaic temple in Troy's West Sanctuary was not nearly as solidly built as the Assos temple, so it probably collapsed then as well, and the same fate may have befallen Troy's temple of Athena and the public buildings in other coastal cities of the Troad.[129] When Xerxes arrived in the area with his army in 480 B.C., he was probably greeted by a long stretch of ruins.

THE AEOLIAN MIGRATION

If we now return to the issue of the Aeolian Migration with which this chapter began, two different but interrelated sets of conclusions emerge: one archaeological, the other related to intellectual history.[130] An examination of both sides of the Late Bronze Age Aegean demonstrates the commercial and political links between the two areas, with Miletus perhaps functioning as a Mycenaean colony in the thirteenth century B.C. Whether or not we associate the Ahhiyawans in the Hittite texts with the Mycenaean Greeks, it is clear that western Asia Minor functioned as a peripheral region contested by forces associated with both the Hittites and the Aegean.

The twelfth-century B.C. deposits at Troy indicate substantial interaction with Thrace, which probably led to an influx of Thracian immigrants into Asia Minor ca. 1130 B.C. A trading network involving Troy and Thessaly/Locris appears to have developed during the Iron Age, and the custom of the Locrian Maidens may have emerged as a by-product of that relationship once the site of Troy had been linked to the Homeric tradition. By the seventh century B.C., Lesbos had established a claim to part of the Troad, as had Lydia, although the vast majority of colonies in Aeolia were Milesian, none of which dates earlier than the mid-seventh century B.C. At no time during the early first millennium B.C. do we have evidence at Troy for attacks, for the arrival of a new population group, or for any substantive change in ceramic production.[131] The ceramic assemblages, in fact, remained remarkably consistent, with very few imports until the sixth century B.C., when Greek also begins to appear in inscriptions.

Throughout the Iron Age and Archaic period, there would have been centuries of interaction between Greek-speaking communities and the native settlements of Asia Minor in which trade, intermarriage, and territorial conflict played a part;[132] but the culture in most of the western Asia Minor cities would have been a continually changing blend of Luwian, Lydian, Phrygian, and Greek. One witnesses the same kind of gradual acculturation in the western and southern Mediterranean during the Roman Republic, where Punic, Nuragic, and Berber traditions, among others, co-existed with those of Rome.[133] In other words, the process by which Troy became Greek probably involved the gradual adoption of a new identity by the local inhabitants, rather than the arrival of a new wave of immigrants to the site.

If we examine again the ancient literary accounts of the Aeolian Migration in conjunction with the archaeological evidence from the Troad, there are several points of correspondence. The accounts, taken as a whole, stress the roles played in the migrations by Mycenae, Thessaly, Euboea, Locris, Thrace, and Lesbos. As the archaeological record demonstrates, all of these regions interacted commercially and/or politically with western Asia Minor at various points during the Late Bronze and Iron Ages, which probably explains why so many different groups were featured in the migration accounts, but it is clear that no one area played a dominant role in colonizing Aeolis, nor is such a widespread colonization supported by the material record.

It does seem certain, however, that such stories acquired considerable momentum following the Persian Wars, when the promotion of these migration accounts was politically expedient for both Greece and Asia Minor.

Mainland Greek cities fortified their allegedly ancestral connection to western Asia Minor, while the cities of western Asia Minor strengthened their political ties to the principal opponents of the Persians, who still controlled most of this area from their provincial capital at Daskyleion.[134] Many of the authors shaped their migration narratives in accordance with their own political agenda: thus, Pindar writes that Orestes traveled directly to Tenedos, since the author's ode that describes the migration was intended to honor a Tenedian; Hellanicus of Lesbos, on the other hand, gives his own island pride of place in the migration.

With such a clear corpus of evidence arguing against a widespread Aeolian migration, it seems somewhat surprising that it has been so readily embraced in scholarship, but here too one needs to examine the political context. Archaeologists began to work in northwestern Turkey during the second half of the nineteenth century, and the colonialist outlook of the time, coupled with the waning of the Ottoman empire, created an intellectual climate wherein stories of the west colonizing the east were easy to accept at face value, as was the assumption that cultural advances on the eastern side of the Aegean, after the Bronze Age, must have been dependent on some agency from the west.[135] One can find a similar bias in early surveys of the Iron Age and Archaic period, where "Orientalizing" influence on Greece was either denied, disputed, or undervalued.[136]

We may never have enough evidence to judge the existence or extent of cultural convergence in the Troad during the Iron Age, but more progress can be made if archaeologists working in Greece and Turkey increase their level of collaboration. Analyses of ancient settlements on both sides of the Aegean are surprisingly rare, and they have become even rarer in the wake of the 1974 separation of Cyprus into Greek and Turkish zones. Dismantling these political barriers to intellectual discourse is essential to achieving a more balanced diagram of cultural interaction in the early Aegean, as is the acknowledgment that cultural change rarely proceeds along a one-way street.

THREE

THE TOMBS OF THE GRANICUS RIVER VALLEY: THE POLYXENA SARCOPHAGUS

After 546 B.C., when northwestern Asia Minor became part of the Persian Empire, a new center of power in the Troad was created at Daskyleion, approximately 175 km east of Ilion on the southeastern shore of Lake Daskylitis (Manyas Göl)(Plate 11).[1] Daskyleion had earlier served the Phrygians and the Lydians, having drawn its name from the father of Gyges, but the extent and duration of their control of the Troad is still unclear. The newly Persian Daskyleion, however, would maintain its hold over nearly the entire Troad for more than 200 years, and was surrounded by local Anatolian aristocrats who were allied with the court.

The beginning of Persian domination appears to have been an unusually prosperous one judging by the recent results of the Granicus River Survey Project (2004–7). The surface pottery collected between the Granicus and Aesepus Rivers constituted 41 percent of the assemblages, as opposed to less than 1 percent for the Bronze Age and only 5 percent for the Hellenistic period.[2] The percentages suggest a substantial increase in settlement in the interior areas of the region, many of which had not witnessed activity since the Early Bronze Age.[3] The range of pottery imports was equally rich, judging by the renewed fieldwork at Daskyleion, which is the only site in the area to have been systematically excavated. Attic black figure has been discovered in abundance, especially after 525, as has Lydian, and Ionian products reached the satrapal capital through the Milesian colonies on the Marmara coast.[4]

Several imposing marble buildings were constructed at Daskyleion, while a number of major construction projects were inaugurated at a variety of sites in and around the Troad, including Neandria, Larisa, Aegae, and Mytilene and Klopedi on Lesbos.[5] The appearance of the temples in the vicinity of the Granicus and Aesepus Rivers is still an open question, although two marble columns discovered in Biga and belonging to a Late Archaic naiskos give us some idea of how richly appointed they must have been.[6]

The cultural and commercial environment of the area had also become distinctly multicultural. The bullae from Daskyleion are in Aramaic, as are several of the funerary stelai; Phrygian is also found, including a bilingual inscription in Phrygian and Greek. Given the length of time in which the Lydian kings exercised control over the area, it seems likely that Lydian would have been spoken as well.[7]

The extent of the wealth centered in and around Daskyleion has recently become clearer as a consequence of the salvage excavations undertaken by the Çanakkale Museum in response to an increase in looting throughout the Troad. Most of these excavations have occurred along the Granicus River, which lies midway between Troy and Daskyleion and flows for more than 60 km from the Ida Mountains to the Sea of Marmara (Plates 11 and 13).[8] The area did not assume strategic significance until after the Persian conquest, and was most widely known as the site of Alexander's victory over the Persians in 334.[9] Scattered throughout this area, according to Xenophon, were *paradeisoi*, or aristocratic hunting grounds, although the only one that appears to have survived in the modern landscape is the Kuş Cenneti on Lake Manyas, near Daskyleion, which is now a wildlife preserve.[10]

The countryside was controlled by local Anatolian landowners who contributed a part of their income to the satrap and sent their sons to him for training in hunting and warfare.[11] None of their houses has been discovered, primarily because they were constructed from mud brick rather than stone, but the monumental burial mounds or tumuli on their estates have occasionally survived intact.[12] These tumuli served as territorial markers of the estates on which they were built, and their number and size also served as an index of the wealth of the Hellespontine Phrygian elite.[13] By virtue of their size they also functioned as observation platforms and were used as such in times of war: Anatolians as well as Greek mercenaries watched the Macedonian army from some of these tumuli during the Battle of Granicus, as well as during earlier battles.[14]

Consequently, the tombs were often set on high ridges, such as Kızöldün (Fig. 3.1), or in the vicinity of major waterways, such as Dedetepe (Fig. 5.1). From a distance it would sometimes have been difficult to see whether the tumulus was a natural or artificial feature in the landscape, and they were therefore topped by stone balls in square bases, often referred to as "phalloi," or terminal stones, which clearly designated the mounds as aristocratic burials

3.1. The tumulus of Kızöldün. Troy Excavation Project photo.

3.2. Tumulus terminal stones in the museum of Bandırma. Photo author.

(Fig. 3.2). Occasionally, the status of the decedent was signaled by the number of terminal stones adorning the tumulus, with as many as five of them used for King Alyattes' tomb at Sardis.[15]

The area near the battlefield of Granicus was clearly one of the most important Late Archaic and Classical aristocratic burial grounds in northwestern Turkey, with a large number of tumuli situated along or near the Granicus River. Looting has occurred in and around many of these tombs during the last few decades, thereby necessitating salvage excavations that were undertaken in 1994 and 1998 by the Çanakkale Museum. These, in turn, have yielded an extraordinary series of elite burials dating between 500 and 375 B.C., which include a marble chamber with painted banqueting couches, or klinai (Fig. 5.6), and three Proconnesian marble sarcophagi, one of which preserves its original paint (Fig. 6.2).[16]

Two of the sarcophagi were discovered in the mound of Kızöldün, which was constructed on a ridge on the eastern side of the Granicus River, 1.7 km southeast of Gümüşçay (Dimetoka), ancient Didymateiche (Plate 13, Figs. 3.1 and 3.3). With a diameter of approximately 38 m, it is one of the largest tumuli in the area, and from the summit, 54 m above sea level, one can see the mound of Dedetepe. The earlier and more elaborate sarcophagus, now generally referred to as the "Polyxena Sarcophagus," was located 6 m below the summit and dates to ca. 500 B.C. or shortly thereafter (Fig. 3.4).[17] It measures 3.32 m in length, 1.60 m in width, and 1.78 m in height and is the earliest stone sarcophagus with figural scenes ever to have been discovered in Asia Minor. A simpler one, without reliefs but no less valuable, was found only 3 m away from it, and was probably set in the tumulus fifty years later (Fig. 4.1).[18] This second sarcophagus, generally referred to as the "Child's Sarcophagus," will be discussed in Chapter 4.

Looters began digging into the Kızöldün mound in 1994, and their trench miraculously came down directly on the gabled lid of the Polyxena Sarcophagus.[19] Seeing the hole that had been cut into the lid by robbers in antiquity, the modern looters abandoned the mound with no further digging, and it was subsequently excavated by the Çanakkale Museum under the direction of Nurten Sevinç. The reliefs of the sarcophagus were covered by terracotta pan tiles at the time of burial, and uncovered only during the excavation in 1994 (Fig. 3.3).[20] No tomb chamber existed, nor was the sarcophagus deposited on any kind of special base; only the tiles separated the sarcophagus from the surrounding earth. The bones inside the sarcophagus had been jumbled together in the course of the robbery, but they clearly belonged to a man, roughly forty years in age. He clearly suffered from lumbar vertebral ankylosis, which would have caused stiffness of the joints and a rigidity or fusion of the vertebrae.[21]

Leaning against the west side of the sarcophagus were the remains of two wheels, one on top of the other, of which both the wooden frame and its iron nails have survived in part. Next to them were several bronze elements that included a circlet and two shafts with decorative orbs at each end, the function of which is unclear. All of these elements belong to the cart that would have transported the decedent to the mound. Additional examples can be found on

3.3. Excavation of the Kızöldün tumulus. The Polyxena Sarcophagus is in the foreground; the Child's Sarcophagus at the back. Troy Excavation Project photo.

the funerary stelae from Daskyleion, the wall paintings of the Karaburun tomb, and the Mourning Women Sarcophagus from the royal necropolis at Sidon.[22] The dismantlement and ceremonial burial of the hearse next to the tomb was probably standard practice and is attested also at Balıkesir and Sardis.[23] Although such hearses were regularly buried in the tumuli, not every decedent was interred with one: Xenophon notes that after the death of Abradatus, ruler of Susa, his wife, Panthea, used her own carriage to transport the body of her husband to the burial site.[24]

At the time of its excavation, the Polyxena Sarcophagus was the largest example of pre-Roman date ever to have been uncovered, and its length would be exceeded only by the giant Sidamara sarcophagi of the third century A.D.[25] Its size has now been superseded by the Hecatomnid Sarcophagus of early fourth century B.C. date found beneath the Temple of Zeus at Mylasa (Milas). The Polyxena Sarcophagus is longer, but the footprint of the Mylasa Sarcophagus is larger.[26] The ratio of length to width on the Polyxena Sarcophagus is nearly 2:1, which corresponds to that of some of the sixth century B.C. sarcophagi from Samos, several of the Sidonian sarcophagi, and the Alexander Sarcophagus.[27] The length to height ratio, which is slightly less than 2:1, deviates slightly from the usual scheme (approximately 1.5:1), but the extensive length of the Polyxena Sarcophagus precluded a greater height.[28]

The sculptors were unable to complete the carving of this sarcophagus prior to burial: one of the figures in the relief is half finished (Fig. 3.14), and sections of the gabled roof have been only roughed out with a point chisel, including

3.4. The Polyxena Sarcophagus. Çanakkale Archaeological Museum. Troy Excavation Project photo.

the blocks for the antefixes (Fig. 3.4). The architectural decoration on the lid, however, is unusually elaborate, featuring an ovolo course at top and bottom with a bead and reel directly below the upper ovolo, followed by a course of dentils (Figs. 3.5 and 3.6). Relief palmettes appear on each of the corner eggs, although the lower ovolo course is noticeably larger than the upper one: the width of an egg and its two flanking darts on the upper level is roughly equal to the width of a single egg below.[29] The upper section of the body includes a band of two fasciae that echoes the two-stepped base on which the figures stand, while the top of the lid imitates pan and cover roof tiles of the same type as those that had been set against the reliefs as protection in the mound.[30]

None of these features can be easily paralleled in sculpture or architecture on either side of the Aegean. An ovolo course with bead and reel below was not unusual in Greek sarcophagi, as evinced, for example, by tombs from both Lycia and Sidon, but they were never, as far as we know, directly juxtaposed with an additional ovolo and dentil course.[31] Also unusual is the pseudo-tiled roof format, which would not be repeated until the fourth century B.C., and it would

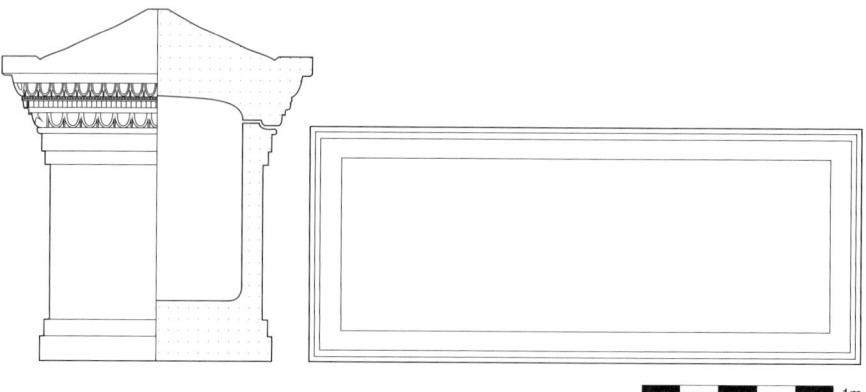

3.5. Elevation drawing of the Polyxena Sarcophagus, by Kate Clayton, based on an original by Nurten Sevinç. Çanakkale Archaeological Museum. Troy Excavation Project drawing.

3.6. Detail of the architectural decoration of the Polyxena Sarcophagus. Çanakkale Archaeological Museum. Troy Excavation Project photo.

never become common in Greek sarcophagus design.[32] The closest parallel occurs in the monumental architecture of Daskyleion, specifically, the cornices of the "Early Classical Building," which featured ovolo courses at top and bottom, below each of which was a bead-and-reel with a dentil course between.[33]

The dentils on the lid are among the earliest for which we have evidence, and these too would not surface again on sarcophagus lids until the fourth century B.C. Slightly earlier examples have been found at Labraunda and Daskyleion (the "Early Classical Building"), and dentils decorated the satrapal palace complex at Daskyleion as well as the tomb of Darius I at Naqsh-i-Rustam.[34] The height and depth of the sarcophagus dentils are equal, as on the Daskyleion examples, but at Kızöldün, the sculptors used "dentil stops" at each of the corners. In other words, at the points where the dentils intersect at right angles, much of the stone has been left in place between them and incised with three vertical lines on each side.[35] This gives the corner stones the appearance of tassels, thereby distinguishing them from the flanking dentils while echoing the lines of the bead and reel course above (Fig. 3.6). At two of the corners the dentils were carved as separate, removable pieces, which allowed for easier moving and maneuvering of the lid during the burial process.[36] Another dentil stop in the form of an Ionic capital was used on a Late Archaic cornice from Daskyleion, and since this is the only region in which they occur, we should probably regard them as indigenous to the western part of Hellespontine Phrygia.[37]

The Polyxena Sarcophagus and its manner of burial reflect a variety of traditions, most of which can be traced to western Asia Minor or the eastern Aegean islands, although their amalgamation here is unique. Stone sarcophagi, usually constructed of limestone, were employed at several sites on either side of the Aegean, some of which were fashioned in the form of a building with gabled roofs and architectural decoration along the sides.[38] These are very much in the spirit of the Polyxena Sarcophagus, whose lid decoration is intended to suggest that of an elite building, even though its architectural format is very different.

What is especially unusual is the use of figural reliefs on each side of the sarcophagus. The decoration of a tomb with stone reliefs was certainly not unprecedented in Asia Minor: already in the late sixth century B.C. the tomb chambers of Lycia had been set on pillars and surrounded by reliefs, but these were not sarcophagi per se, nor did the Lycian chambers appear in the form of a building until the fourth century B.C.[39] The Kızöldün sculptors appear to have employed elements of both traditions, Aegean and Lycian, which, in turn, prefigured the production of the elaborate Late Classical stone sarcophagi of Sidon and Lycia.

The four reliefs that decorate the body of the sarcophagus can be divided into two very different themes, each of which encompasses a long and a short side: one is mythological in nature and deals with the final events in the Trojan War; the other features a celebration with gift presentation, conversation, music, and dancing. There is no obvious link between the two themes, although at the end of this discussion I suggest a potential relationship.

SIDE A: THE SACRIFICE OF POLYXENA

The mythological sides (A and B) focus on the sacrifice of Polyxena, the daughter of Priam, by Neoptolemus, son of Achilles, next to the tumulus of his father.[40] The long relief (side A) includes twelve figures divided compositionally into two groups, with the right half devoted to the sacrifice of Polyxena,

3.7. Side A of the Polyxena Sarcophagus: the sacrifice of Polyxena. Çanakkale Archaeological Museum. Troia slide 19937.

3.8. Drawing of side A of the Polyxena Sarcophagus, by Kate Clayton, based on an original by Nurten Sevinç. The circles represent small drill holes. Çanakkale Archaeological Museum. Troy Excavation Project drawing.

and the left to the Trojan women who mourn her death (Figs. 3.7–3.10). The two sides of the war have been marked by gender: all of the men are Greek; all of the women, Trojan. The women outnumber the men by a factor of 2:1 (eight women, four men), although the men exercise complete control in the narrative. Three landscape elements are clustered together at the intersection of sides A and B: a tree, a tripod, and the tumulus of Achilles, whose half-oval shape was common during this period.[41]

Polyxena's body is held horizontally by three Greek soldiers clad in short, light tunics, while Neoptolemus holds her hair with his left hand and plunges his dagger into her throat with his right (Fig. 3.9).[42] An empty scabbard hangs from the strap around the shoulders of Neoptolemus, whose head has been set low to accommodate the bent right arm with the dagger; nevertheless, the sculptor miscalculated the amount of necessary space and had to cut into

3.9. Detail of Polyxena and Neoptolemus, side A, Polyxena Sarcophagus. Çanakkale Archaeological Museum. Troy Excavation Project photo.

3.10. Detail of the mourning women, side A, Polyxena Sarcophagus. Çanakkale Archaeological Museum. Troia slide 19939.

the lower fascia in order to render the elbow. Only Neoptolemus gazes at Polyxena; the two central men look toward each other, while the man at the left holding her ankles (no. 8) looks away from the scene toward the mourning Trojan women. The hairstyles of three of the four men are characterized by two or three rows of snail curls that leave their ears exposed; the figure who holds Polyxena's legs (no. 9) has long spiral curls that overlap the ears. All of their torsos have been shown frontally, with their heads and legs in profile, and the modeled musculature on the knees and legs highlights the men's power.

A nearly identical version of the Polyxena story, with identifying inscriptions, appears on a Tyrrhenian amphora by the Timiades Painter (ca. 560 B.C.). This enables us to identity the three men holding her body as, from left to right, Ajax, son of Oileus (no. 8), Antiphates (no. 9), and Amphilochus (no. 10), although the men are armed on the amphora and wear only tunics on the sarcophagus.[43] The sacrificial component of the scene on the Tyrrhenian amphora is particularly prominent in that Polyxena is killed directly above the tumulus of Achilles, which was surmounted by a lighted altar. A very different treatment appears on the Polyxena Sarcophagus, where the tumulus is crowned with a terminal stone, thereby replicating the form and decoration of the mound in which the sarcophagus was actually placed.[44]

In Euripides' *Hecuba*, which provides our best literary description of this sacrifice, Polyxena willingly accepted her death, and restraints were unnecessary.[45] The sculptors of the sarcophagus, however, have presented a very different scene in which Polyxena actively resists her fate: her hands have been crossed in front of her, as if they were tied, formally echoing the loose strands of hair held by Neoptolemus. No raised lines indicate the existence of a rope, but if the sarcophagus had been finished prior to burial, some sort of cord would almost certainly have been painted on her wrists. Paint was probably also planned for the three incisions on her neck which mark the sword's point of entry. The Greek soldier farthest to the left (no. 8) has pulled Polyxena's right leg over her left, further restricting her movement, and grasps each of her ankles with his hands. Since the ankles are held separately, one in each hand, and at different levels, one has the impression that she is kicking, thereby fortifying the appearance of resistance.

The sculptor has attempted to show the body of Polyxena in a twisted pose but lacked the expertise to do so. Drawing the right leg over the left would actually raise the hip and increase the size of the abdomen, at least from the viewer's perspective. Instead, the abdomen has been decreased in size, although it appears less awkward than one would expect due to the fulcrum-like intersection of three pairs of hands on and around her hips.[46] The drooping breast and left sleeve, which are handled with great care, also pull one's attention away from the awkwardness of the body's torsion.

The seven remaining figures in the relief are Trojan woman. Ajax, son of Oileus, looks to the left at a slightly shorter woman with long, loose hair that falls down her back (Fig. 3.10). She is clad in a chiton and himation and raises her thumb and forefinger to her nostrils while holding a tall walking stick that rises to the level of her breasts. A walking stick of the same type and size is held by the aged Hecuba on the short side of the sarcophagus (Figs. 3.10–3.12), and it was undoubtedly intended to indicate age, even though this figure does not have the incised crow's feet around her eyes, as Hecuba does (Fig. 3.13).[47]

There has been some confusion regarding the gender of this figure, but the iconography clearly indicates a female: an aged male would surely have been shown with a beard and without such long unbound hair.[48] The gesture of the fingers raised to the nose is not common in Archaic and Classical Greek art, but there are enough examples to connect it with lamentation, and she must therefore belong to the group of Trojan mourners.[49] She alone among the women wears no earrings, which suggests that she is of lower station than they, and therefore almost certainly a servant.[50] If we combine all of these iconographic clues, the evidence points to her identification as Hecuba's aged handmaid, who was reportedly in attendance at the sacrifice of her daughter.[51] Such an identification would also make sense in terms of the composition of the scene. If one views the long and short sides (A and B) as one continuous scene, which seems certain, then Hecuba and her handmaid flank the sacrifice of Polyxena at left and right, with their walking sticks providing a frame for the scene.

The handmaid and Ajax, upon whom she gazes, mark the center of the relief; the variance in iconography between them, which encompasses age, gender, gesture, dress, and attributes, effectively indicates the division between the Greek and Trojan sides. Six additional women, some standing, some kneeling, gesture toward Polyxena and/or pull at their loose hair. The women are singing the *goos* (lament for the dead) typically sung by the kin of the deceased, which suggests that figures 1 to 6 are Polyxena's sisters.[52]

All of the Trojan women wear the loose chiton; nos. 2–5 also wear a short mantle, the last three of which are sleeveless, and nos. 1 and 6 wear the himation (Fig. 3.10). Their gestures are relatively common in Archaic mainland Greek funerary iconography except for the lifting of the fists to the chin, as on figure 2, who is also the only one in this relief to wear the sakkos, or soft woven cap. The same gesture, however, is paralleled on the roughly contemporary Harpy Tomb in Xanthos, where it was used to evoke the mourning of a servant.[53] One might be inclined to assign servile status to this woman, too, since she is kneeling, but she has been shown with earrings, which suggests that her station is as high as that of the other women.

Mourners appear in no other extant scenes of Polyxena's sacrifice, although the combination of women's lamentation with the violent act of sacrifice at the end of the Trojan War is a common theme in Attic vase painting, especially during the second half of the sixth century B.C. Pinakes, or votive panels depicting wailing women, were actually tied to Attic tombs during the Late Archaic period, so the inclusion of scenes of lamentation on the sarcophagus

3.11. Side B of the Polyxena Sarcophagus: Hecuba and mourners. Çanakkale Archaeological Museum. Troy Excavation Project photo.

3.12. Drawing of side B of the Polyxena Sarcophagus, by Kate Clayton, based on an original by Nurten Sevinç. The enlarged circles represent small drill holes. Çanakkale Archaeological Museum. Troy Excavation Project drawing.

can be viewed as a complementary expression of a well-established Attic tradition.[54] But the episode selected for representation is particularly striking in that the precise moment of death has been depicted rather than a scene immediately preceding or following the sacrifice; the same moment appears on the Tyrrhenian amphora and possibly another fragmentary Protoattic vase of late seventh century B.C. date.[55]

3.13 Detail of Hecuba, side B, Polyxena Sarcophagus. Çanakkale Archaeological Museum. Troy Excavation Project photo.

Such scenes of ritual killing were extremely rare: in spite of the similarities between the stories of Iphigenia and Polyxena, the former was never shown at the moment of death.[56] During the Archaic period, in fact, Polyxena seems to have been the only woman shown at the transitional point between life and death.[57] The same habit was followed in scenes of animal sacrifice, both Greek and Roman, which tend to focus on the procession to the altar or, less frequently, the cooking of the meat following the sacrifice.[58] This is not unlike Greek tragedy, where murders or suicides were never shown on stage, nor is the phenomenon at all surprising: showing the transitional point between life and death meant representing the moment when human and supernatural spheres intersected.[59]

Even more noteworthy is the manner of Polyxena's death: Neoptolemus plunges the dagger into her neck, thereby severing the carotid artery, which was the method proscribed for the sacrifice of animals in antiquity as well as in the contemporary Near East.[60] The same iconographic configuration was used for Polyxena on the earlier Tyrrhenian amphora, and both stem directly from the literary tradition in which Polyxena was compared to a sacrificial animal, with her death presented as a sacrifice to the spirit of Achilles.[61] Slightly more than a century later, a similar format would be used in Italy for scenes of Achilles slaying Trojan prisoners next to the tumulus of Patroclus, but it would never again by employed for the execution of women.[62]

A particularly powerful evocation of the assimilation between Polyxena and a sacrificial animal appears in Euripides' *Hecuba*: "Like the young of a wild beast of the mountain, a miserable calf, you [Hecuba] in your misery ... shall see me torn from your arms, and sent down with throat cut to Hades, to the darkness of the earth."[63] This line between human and animal sacrifice is further blurred by the manner in which Polyxena is carried to Achilles' tumulus: the grasping of a woman's ankles is unique in Greek iconography, although this was a common way of holding the legs of recalcitrant animals immediately prior to sacrifice.[64]

Polyxena's head is almost completely horizontal and directly beneath that of Neoptolemus, whose arms create a triangular frame around their two heads and heighten their connection. This is an unusual configuration in that the operative metaphor is animal sacrifice, and in such scenes the animal's head is generally turned down so that the blood flows directly on the ground or the altar.[65] On the Tyrrhenian amphora by the Timiades Painter, Polyxena's head is in fact turned down so that the blood from her neck directly strikes the pyre of Achilles beneath her. The literary tradition follows the same model, which is evident in Aeschylus' powerful narrative of Iphigenia's sacrifice in the *Agamemnon*: "enrapped in her robes, she lay fallen forward...like a goat, high above the altar."[66]

By turning Polyxena's head so that she and Neoptolemus look directly toward each other, with their lips separated by only a few centimeters, the sculptor has introduced an erotic element into the scene. This brings the iconography closer to depictions of Achilles and Penthesilea, *erastes/eromenoi*, or Eros and Psyche, where a similar juxtaposition of heads was employed to connote passion.[67] The issue of sex is not completely out of place in the story of Polyxena in that she was sacrificed so that her spirit could join that of Achilles, whose passion for her had led to his death. As far as we know, however, that passion involved only Achilles, not his son, and the romantic version of Achilles and Polyxena is not attested in literature until the Hellenistic period.[68] She is referred to only as a sacrificial victim in Euripides' *Hecuba*, with no suggestion of sexual passion.

Greek vases with scenes of mythology and romance were clearly prized by the residents within the political sphere of Daskyleion, and the artists were probably aware of the erotic meaning that such a composition would have introduced. It is, in fact, conceivable that the iconography was influenced by scenes of Achilles and Penthesilea, which also involved a woman on the side of Troy who was slain by a Greek commander toward the end of the war. The use of such a model incorporated a narrative element into the story that might strike modern audiences as somewhat jarring, but the movement of iconographic elements among different subjects was much more fluid in this group of artists than it would later be in Hellenistic Greece or imperial Rome. The painted sarcophagus from Çan, discussed in Chapter 6, is an interesting case in point in that the sculptors used hunting iconography to render a battle scene, even though the peripheral figures and manner of death cannot easily be transferred between the two themes (Plate 23). One should therefore not exclude the possibility that the stories of Polyxena and Penthesilea had intersected in some areas of the Aegean during the Archaic period, with an erotic gloss applied to both of them.

All of the figures so far discussed are human; the only possible reference to the realm of the divine on this side is the tripod in front of the tumulus of Achilles, which presumably refers to Apollo (Figs. 3.7 and 3.8). The tumulus has been carved so that its outline completely overlaps the tripod, the rings of which echo the curved form of the terminal stone, and a link between tumulus and tripod is therefore clear. The most likely explanation for their juxtaposition is as a narrative allusion to Apollo's role in the death of Achilles, which was already current by the time of the *Iliad*.[69] By the Roman period, the connection between the two had grown even stronger, with the slaying of Achilles situated in the Sanctuary of Apollo Thymbraios.[70] If viewed in this light, the tripod essentially functions as an iconographic counterbalance to the adjacent scene of sacrifice: the slaying of Polyxena by Neoptolemus is retribution for his father's death at the hand of Apollo, and the tumulus is the conjunction for both episodes. In other words, the viewer is provided with a narrative that one might label temporally chiastic.[71]

The tripod may also have had an additional significance: in Euripides' *Hecuba*, the ghost of Achilles appears above his tomb to ask for the sacrifice of Polyxena as a prize of honor.[72] Tripods figured prominently in the corpus of such honorific prizes, and its presence here may have been intended to situate Polyxena's sacrifice in such a context. As with most images as polyvalent as this one, each viewer would have brought a different range of experience to the viewing process, and all of the above associations may have registered in their minds.

SIDE B: THE MOURNING OF HECUBA

This sacrifice scene continues on the right side of the sarcophagus, where Polyxena's mother, Hecuba, squats beneath a leafless tree as two more women continue the lamentation (Figs. 3.11–3.14). Her arm is raised to her head in lamentation, like several of the other mourning women, and she wears a long veil that overlaps most of her earring. Hecuba carries the same type of walking stick as the figure in the sacrifice scene on the long side of the sarcophagus (no. 7), and her advanced age has been indicated by three incised lines at the corner of her eye.[73] She gazes toward the left in the direction of the tumulus of Achilles, which actually extends into her space, and one is again reminded of the scene in Euripides' *Hecuba* where she sinks to the ground with her head covered as Polyxena is led off to sacrifice.[74] It seems reasonable to regard the two sides as representing a single moment in the narrative, with the tree marking a division between two different spaces, as in the hunting scenes on the Çan Sarcophagus.[75] A somewhat similar depiction featuring the sacrifice of Polyxena and a squatting Hecuba appears on a Campanian amphora dated to the early fifth century B.C., but otherwise Hecuba tends to be shown with Priam.[76] That she is shown sitting on the ground rather than standing

3.14. Detail of mourner, side B, Polyxena Sarcophagus. Çanakkale Archaeological Museum. Troy Excavation Project photo.

or enthroned is in itself interesting as it highlights the disintegration of the authority that she once possessed.[77]

Even more unusual is the representation of advanced age, which is otherwise unprecedented in Late Archaic relief sculpture (Fig. 3.13). The only other roughly contemporary examples that come to mind are the seer on the west pediment of the Temple of Zeus at Olympia and the old woman on the "Boston Throne," whose authenticity has been continually debated.[78] In those examples, however, age has been conveyed through the incision of lines on the checks and forehead, not around the eyes.[79]

The animated gestures of her two companions nearly duplicate those of figures 3 and 5 in the main scene of sacrifice, thereby tying the two sides together and reinforcing one's sense of their contemporaneity. Both of the women wear chitons, sleeveless mantles, and earrings, but the right figure has a sakkos whereas the central one is veiled. The right arm of the central figure (no. 13) is unfinished: the hand has been merely blocked with a point chisel, and the arm was finished only with a tooth chisel (Fig. 3.14). In other words, the carving of the sarcophagus had not yet been completed when it was covered by the tiles and buried in the tumulus.

The unfinished arm of the central figure extends into the tree at the left, the branches of which echo the gestures of the lamenting women on both sides of the sarcophagus, just as the dead tree in the Alexander Mosaic mimics the form of Darius and his charioteer. Whether the tree was intended to have a deeper significance within the narrative is unclear: palm trees and tripods occasionally appear in scenes of slaying at the end of the Trojan War, but they are usually

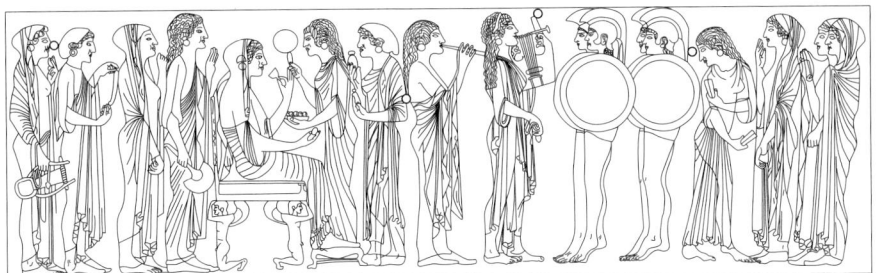

3.15. Drawing of side C of the Polyxena Sarcophagus, by Kate Clayton, based on an original by Nurten Sevinç. The circles outlined in black represent small drill holes. Çanakkale Archaeological Museum. Troy Excavation Project drawing.

intended to indicate the setting as a sanctuary of Apollo. That cannot be the setting here, nor is the tree in question a palm.[80]

Since the discovery of the sarcophagus, scholars have consistently looked on sides A and B for Cassandra and Andromache, who were Hecuba's companions in Euripides' *Trojan Women*, and they have recently been identified as the two standing women on side B.[81] Although such groups appear nowhere else in Archaic or Classical imagery, anyone familiar with the tragedy would probably have interpreted the figures in that way.[82] If we label one of the women on side B as Cassandra, then the tree could have been intended as a laurel, but a laurel can be identified only by its leaves, which were typically not added to trees prior to the Hellenistic period, so one can do no more than speculate about its genus and significance.[83]

SIDE C: THE CELEBRATION

The remaining two sides of the sarcophagus are devoted to a celebration composed primarily of women, with gift giving, music, dancing, and conversation. The scene on the long side seems rather crowded in that it contains seventeen figures (as opposed to twelve on side A), only four of whom are male (Figs. 3.15 and 3.16). As with the scene depicting the sacrifice of Polyxena, the composition can easily be divided into two groups: a gift presentation on the left with seven figures occupies slightly less than half of the side's length; to their right are a group of musicians and dancers, ten in total, although the four dancers and two of the women are presented in groups with conjoined profiles, so the left and right sides strike one as relatively balanced.

The dominant focus in the gift presentation at the left is a young seated woman with veil and earrings, sniffing a flower in her left hand and holding an egg in her right. She is the only woman on this side to be depicted seated on a throne, which is supported by youthful male caryatids, nude and winged, who face opposite directions (Fig. 3.16).[84] The seated woman is flanked by

3.16. Detail of seated woman, side C, Polyxena Sarcophagus. Çanakkale Archaeological Museum. Troy Excavation Project photo.

six attendants, two in front and four behind, most of whom bring her gifts: no. 16 carries a lyre with attached plectrum and an egg positioned close to her mouth; no. 17 holds a fillet, probably recently dyed in Tyrian purple; no. 19 brings a fan.[85] The attendant directly in front of the seated woman (no. 21) offers a plate of eggs in her left hand, one of which the seated woman has taken, and a mirror in her right. The woman behind this figure (no. 22) brings two alabastra.[86] The two figures flanking the enthroned woman wear nothing on their heads; the others are either veiled or wear a sakkos.

The alabastra carrier (no. 22) stands back to back with a female aulos player, who is the first figure in the group of musician and dancers on the right side of this relief. All of the women look toward four Pyrrhic dancers who appear in groups of two and are shown on tiptoe to indicate that they are dancing.[87] Each wears a short tunic with a Chalcidian helmet and carries a round shield. They gaze toward the two female musicians at the left (nos. 23 and 24) who play the aulos and kithara with attached plectrum.[88] The kithara player is the tallest of the musicians and only she wears a fillet, which probably indicates her role as band-leader, as it were. Percussion is supplied by the *krotala* (castanet) player (no. 29), whose twisting body establishes that she too is dancing.[89] The final three women (nos. 30–32), all of whom are veiled, do nothing but observe: each raises her right hand, echoing the gestures of the women on the left side of the scene, and one clutches her cloak in front of her.

The amalgamation of activities of this side of the sarcophagus, featuring music, dancing, and gift presentation, is not per se duplicated anywhere else in ancient art. The combination of aulos, kithara, and castanets can be found in Attic vase painting, especially in Dionysiac scenes, but in none of them are all of the musicians women.[90] The range of contexts in which Pyrrhic dancers appear is quite broad, and includes funerals, weddings, symposia, and divine festivals, such as those to Athena and Artemis. Here it is conceivable that the Pyrrhic dancers were intended as a reference to the Polyxena scene on the principal side, in that Achilles reportedly danced in armor at the tomb of Patroclus, and the custom of Pyrrhic dancing was believed by some ancient authors to have been invented by Neoptolemus, also called Pyrrhus.[91]

The throne on the left side of the relief cannot be paralleled anywhere else in ancient art, although the use of figural supports for chairs or stools has a long history in the ancient Near East, especially on Lycian funerary monuments and

Achaemenid tombs in Persia.[92] Wings were used for both gods and mythical animals to indicate superhuman status, especially in Persian or Graeco-Persian imagery.[93] The sniffing of the lotus, usually by a woman, is also a feature of Near Eastern tradition, and it appears continually in the funerary monuments of western Asia Minor during the Late Archaic period.[94]

SIDE D: THE CELEBRATION CONTINUES

The final scene on the second short side continues the female-focused celebratory iconography, and it is the only scene on the sarcophagus that takes place in an interior setting (Figs. 3.17 and 3.18). Five women, either veiled or wearing sakkoi, congregate on or around a kline with two mattresses, a pillow, and a footstool. The largest figure in the group also occupies the center of the composition, and her right hand is nearly twice the size of that of the other figures. She is seated at the head of the kline with both feet resting on the stool and gestures elaborately to her two associates at the left. Her dress and hairstyle are identical to those of the seated woman on side C.

One of her associates shares the kline with her and raises both hands (no. 34), one of which is wrapped in a mantle.[95] She, in turn, is embraced by a woman with raised left hand who wears a sakkos and a nearly diaphanous chiton (no. 33). The two central women are clearly engaged in animated conversation, and their overlapping legs and feet indicate their closeness. On the right side of the scene is a woman dressed in garb identical to that of the woman at the left (no. 37); she brings gifts, as does the veiled woman at her side (no. 36). The first carries a pitcher and a wine strainer that bears a curved handle terminating in an animal head; the other offers an egg and a cosmetics pyxis with lid.[96] Unlike the celebration scene on side C, all of the women have bare feet, which is appropriate to the interior setting.[97]

Comparable scenes of women sharing a kline are not easy to find. Women appear together in an interior setting in at least one of the reliefs from Daskyleion, although they are seated on stools rather than on a kline, and nothing comparable in Etruria has come to light.[98] The best comparandum is a fragmentary red-figure hydria from Athens depicting two women sharing a kline, probably in connection with a wedding, but there are no precise parallels for this iconography anywhere else.[99] Nor does one find such animated gestures to indicate conversation in other female-focused scenes, although they are sometimes used to indicate discussions between male and female deities, such as on the frieze of the Siphnian treasury.[100]

One notable feature regarding the women's presentation lies in their earrings: although a few are adorned only with simple disks, the majority wear disks attached to ear caps, including Polyxena, the enthroned women on sides C and D, and the musicians, among others.[101] The appearance of these elaborate

3.17. Side D of the Polyxena Sarcophagus: the celebration continues. Çanakkale Archaeological Museum. Troy Excavation Project photo.

3.18. Drawing of side D of the Polyxena Sarcophagus, by Kate Clayton, based on an original by Nurten Sevinç. The circle outlined in black represents a small drill hole. Çanakkale Archaeological Museum. Troy Excavation Project drawing.

3.19. Harpy Monument, Xanthos, ca. 480 B.C., British Museum. Photo courtesy Cast Collection, Ashmolean Museum.

earrings on three sides of the sarcophagus (A, C, and D) succeeds in linking the legendary scenes with contemporary ones. Even when some of the women are veiled, the ear caps are shown bulging beneath the drapery, which indicates the status that must have been attached to them.[102] None of these has survived in the archaeological record, but very similar earrings are worn by women engaging in religious rituals in the frescoes from the roughly contemporary "Painted House" at Gordion.[103]

The composition of these last two sides is unique in sarcophagus design and, indeed, in ancient art. Especially remarkable is its extensive focus on women, who dominate the celebration and comprise more than three-quarters of the figures. The inclusion of dancers and musicians in the celebration recalls the entertainment of a symposium, but there is no feasting or drinking of wine here, and symposium iconography per se is clearly not the basis for the composition.[104]

The ultimate source is probably to be found in Achaemenid reliefs featuring the presentation of gifts to the ruler, such as the tribute reliefs from Persepolis, and one can imagine similar presentation scenes in painted form on the walls of the satrap's palace.[105] The closest iconographic parallel is the Harpy Tomb at Xanthos, carved only a few years later than the Kızöldün sarcophagus, wherein seated men and women receive gifts from associates of the same gender, such as eggs, poppies, pomegranates, and armor, again with no discernible symposium iconography (Fig. 3.19). One of the enthroned women in the Harpy Tomb even holds a lotus to her nose, in the same manner as her counterpart at Kızöldün, as her companions bring a range of offerings.[106]

A similar scene, both compositionally and iconographically, also appears on a recently discovered stele at Daskyleion, where the gestures of the two central women suggest lively conversation while gifts are brought by associates on either side.[107] The main figure appears to sit on a stool rather than a kline, but most, if not all of the participants are women, as in the relief from the Harpy Tomb. It looks, in fact, as if female-focused public funerary memorials were introduced in western Asia Minor at least fifty years before their counterparts in mainland Greece. What distinguishes the Kızöldün scene from the foregoing examples is the unusual combination of a kline gathering with no men, as well as Pyrrhic dancers with an all-women band, neither of which one finds duplicated in either mainland Greek or Persian iconography.[108]

Carola Reinsberg has recently proposed that the entire scene should be interpreted as a wedding celebration, intended to honor the decedent who died before her own marriage could occur, but the iconography does not support such a thesis.[109] The range of gifts presented in Greek wedding iconography is very different from what we have here.[110] One would expect kalathoi (or baskets for wool working), lekanai (large household bowls), wedding vases, jewelry chests, and alabastra, and only the latter of these appear in the Kızöldün reliefs. Eggs were funerary offerings and would certainly not have formed part of a wedding procession. Reinsberg re-identifies them as fruit, but they are, in fact, eggs, as on the Daskyleion and Harpy Tomb reliefs.[111]

For the Pyrrhic dancers to be appropriately placed in a wedding context, they would have to be female, which is what Reinsberg argues, noting that the *perizomai* (shorts) would be unusual on men, but the sculptors of the Polyxena Sarcophagus have used different types of hairstyles to distinguish gender: those of the men are combed down on their foreheads, whereas those of the women are pulled to their sides. The Pyrrhic dancers belong to the former group, as their hair falls to the bases of their necks, like that of the Greek soldiers at the sacrifice of Polyxena. When female Pyrrhics do appear in art, their bodies tend to be turned in the opposite direction from their heads, so that the shields do not hide their torsos.[112] Attitudes toward nudity, of course, vary widely by region, which may be the reason that the *perizoma* is worn here, and it is worth noting that male nudity does not figure prominently in the Daskyleion reliefs or in Achaemenid art in general.[113]

The Polyxena Sarcophagus is often discussed under the "Graeco-Persian" rubric, and we should assess whether specific elements can be identified as characteristically Greek or Achaemenid. On first glance at the sarcophagus, one is left with the sense that this is a distinctly Greek product, linked far more to Ionian than Achaemenid sources, and certainly this is true for the style. If one compares the sarcophagus with roughly contemporary reliefs from Daskyleion, the variation in style is striking, even though they shared the same sources of marble. This is especially apparent in regard to anatomical details, drapery rendering, gestures, and attempts at perspective, such as the turned bodies of the castanet player or the prone Polyxena.[114] The chosen style is probably representative of the type of sculpture produced by the nearby Milesian colonies on the coast, such as Cyzicus, Parium, and Lampsacus, although there are few contemporary reliefs from these areas that make it possible for one to judge with certainty.

The iconography, however, points in a different direction. Although the mourners on the sarcophagus are comparable to funerary scenes in mainland Greece, nearly every other component of the composition can be found at Achaemenid-period sites in western Anatolia. This includes the use of figural scenes on stone sarcophagi, the architectural decoration, the gift presentation scenes with eggs included among the offerings, and the prominence of women and Pyrrhic dancers in a funerary context.[115]

The juxtaposition of sacrifice and celebration can also be paralleled in Asia Minor monuments: the Lycian tomb at Kızılbel, for example, features scenes of the deceased at a symposium coupled with the slaying of Troilus by Achilles.[116] Thus, the style of the sarcophagus as well as its iconography stem from different traditions, and the sarcophagus as a whole reflects the kind of intersection of Greek and Persian models that one would expect in an area that embraced both cultures but chose to be identified exclusively with neither. In other words, we should consider the funerary monuments from this area as distinctly Anatolian rather than Greek or Persian, and the same is true for Persian-period memorials from Lydia, Lycia, and Caria.

Part of the power of the depictions lies in the gender contrasts. Only eight men appear on the sarcophagus, four on each of the long sides, but the two groups are diametrically opposed in terms of their function within the narrative. On side A, all of the power – specifically, the power to decide life or death – resides with the men, while on side C, the men are relegated to the status of entertainers, whose movements follow the rhythms produced by female musicians. Within the Polyxena scene, the contrast between the men and women is especially compelling in that the men are athletic with carefully coiffed short hair, and all of them grip different parts of the body of Polyxena, whereas the adjacent women, characterized by long, disheveled hair, signal their servile status through animated gesture. Body torsion has also been used quite effectively: the contorted body of Polyxena at the moment of her death contrasts with the twisting body of the castanet player on the opposite side, dancing to the lively rhythms that she creates.

The Relationship between Patron and Iconography

The bones inside the Polyxena Sarcophagus are unquestionably those of a middle-aged man, and there are no indications that anyone else was buried within it. How, then, can we reconcile the sex of the decedent with such an emphatically female-focused iconography? I have often been asked why we should even attempt to do so. In other words, couldn't such scenes of sacrifice and celebration have been chosen by a man as easily as a woman in 500

B.C.? A few scholars, arguing that we've missed the point of the two themes, have even proposed that the emphasis is really on the exploits of Achilles and Neoptolemus rather than the death of Polyxena, which would make the mythical scenes eminently more suitable for a male decedent.[117]

The only way to clarify this enigma is to view the iconography of the sarcophagus in a larger Anatolian context. Hellespontine Phrygia was admittedly a multicultural area, with Lydian, Aramaic, and Greek probably spoken at the time in which the sarcophagus was made, and patrons could have selected from a wide variety of stylistic and iconographic options when commissioning monuments or tombs.[118] It is, of course, possible that elite men chose as decoration for their tombs a variety of subjects that they found appealing, with no deeper symbolism at play, but this seems unlikely. There are epitaphs, monumental tombs, and sarcophagi from western Asia Minor in which we can determine which scenes were prized by aristocratic men: battles were certainly popular, as were hunts, and the protagonists were typically male.[119]

A case in point is the Çan Sarcophagus, found in a tumulus approximately 25 km south of Kızöldün and carved between 400 and 375 B.C. (Fig. 6.2 and Plates 18–24). It was decorated with both battle and hunt scenes, and judging by the skeletal remains of the young man buried within it, he probably sustained a fall during one of those endeavors. We can be even more certain of the connection between decoration and decedent in the case of the Mourning Woman Sarcophagus, ca. 360–340 B.C. A band of hunting scenes surrounded the base of the sarcophagus, and placed inside it were an adult male and seven of his hunting dogs.[120] Demonstrated skills in hunt and battle were integral components of a man's virtue, and one would expect to find these two themes in particular highlighted on his tomb, as a kind of visual eulogy. By the same token, a deceased man might be offered a helmet in a funerary scene, as on the Harpy Tomb at Xanthos, but never alabastra or mirrors.

Consequently, it seems to me unlikely that an aristocratic male would have chosen scenes of Polyxena's sacrifice and female celebrations for the decoration of his sarcophagus. If the left half of the sacrifice relief had been filled with Greek soldiers, the Achilles interpretation might make more sense, but the compositional focus is, in fact, on Polyxena's death and the attendant female lamentation, while all of the other scenes are populated primarily by women. One is therefore led to the conclusion that the decorative program of the sarcophagus must have been designed for a woman, even though the ultimate occupant was a man.

The only way I can make sense of the iconography is by viewing it in tandem with Persian-period sarcophagus production, which was a nascent industry at the time in which the Polyxena Sarcophagus was carved. Bereaved families in the Roman Empire had the luxury of selecting nearly complete examples from local showrooms shortly before the death of a family member.

During the Late Archaic period, however, sarcophagi were made to order and had to be commissioned well in advance of the death, especially if they were large and reliefs were involved. Once finished, these elaborate sarcophagi were displayed in patrons' homes as prestige items, thereby creating an environment somewhat akin to that of Trimalchio's party in the *Satyricon*.[121]

But death often comes unexpectedly, before a sarcophagus could be ordered or finished, and there must have been occasions among the elite when a sarcophagus ordered for one person had to be used for another who had died suddenly, prior to the production of his or her own tomb. Such an explanation has been proposed for the Iron Age Tumulus P at Gordion, in central Turkey, and the practice was probably more common than we think.[122] Identifying actual cases in point is not easy, however, since the skeletal material found in sarcophagi is rarely preserved or published, thereby forcing us to guess about the relationship between tomb decoration and the sex or social position of the decedent.

In the case of the Polyxena Sarcophagus, it seems likely that we have an excellent example of the scenario outlined above. The sarcophagus was designed for a young woman, which would explain why the imagery was so female-focused on each side of the sarcophagus and why all of the gifts are presented by and to women. The sarcophagus was nearly finished when a middle-aged man in the family died unexpectedly, or without having ordered a suitable sarcophagus in time.[123] The Polyxena Sarcophagus was subsequently reassigned to him, although there was not enough time to complete the carving of the lid and the reliefs, to paint them, and to fashion a platform to support the sarcophagus.[124] The original (female) patron then presumably commissioned a new sarcophagus that still lies undiscovered in one of the neighboring tumuli.

Assuming, then, that the iconographic program was designed for a woman, should we expect her appearance in the reliefs? There was unquestionably a strong biographical component in the funerary iconography of western Asia Minor, in which several scenes from the life of the decedents were intended to signal their achievements in standard aristocratic activities. This tradition, probably stimulated by biographical narratives in royal Persian iconography, began to appear in elite funerary monuments of Asia Minor several decades after the beginning of Persian domination, and it remained popular until the Early Christian period.[125] One finds such a biographical tradition in the decoration of western Asia Minor tombs of fifth century B.C. date, such as the Harpy Tomb at Xanthos or the Karaburun Tomb in Lycia, both of which feature gift presentations to images of the deceased.[126] Therefore, it seems likely that the enthroned figure on side C was intended as a representation of the young woman for whom the sarcophagus was commissioned.[127]

Could the central seated figure on side D depict the same woman in an additional episode of the celebration (Figs. 3.17 and 3.18)? The two women share the same dress and coiffure, and both receive an array of gifts while seated, although the variation in furniture indicates that the setting is different, as is, presumably, the moment represented. The presence of the same person at two different moments in time was not uncommon in Graeco-Persian sculpture, as evinced by the Lycian Karaburun Tomb, the Çan Sarcophagus, and the Nereid Monument at Xanthos, among others. Moreover, the painted biographical scenes in the tombs of Kızılbel and Karaburun demonstrate that such narrative devices were already being employed in Late Archaic Asia Minor.[128] A link between the two women should therefore not be excluded from consideration, although there are admittedly strong similarities in costume among all of the women on the sarcophagus.

It is worth noting that most of the gifts offered to or handled by these women were almost certainly intended to have been deposited in the tomb at the time of burial, as indicated by the fillet-tied alabastra and pyxis found at Dedetepe and in the Kızöldün Child's Sarcophagus (Fig. 4.3).[129] The same is true for the eggs, both real and imitation, and the discovery of stringed instruments in the tombs at Dedetepe and Dardanus strongly suggests that local funerals also included musicians who deposited their instruments in the tomb at the conclusion of the ceremony.[130] Pyrrhic dancers would have performed at these funerals, moving to the music played by attendant aulos and castanet players, and the gestures of lamentation would also presumably have replicated the actual mourning activities.[131]

In the end, however, this burial ceremony was probably intended to commemorate the life of a man rather than a woman, which means that most of the depicted gifts would not have been used. We should therefore imagine a range of offerings very different from those that appear in the reliefs, such as sabers or knives, as in the Cypriot Palaepaphus Sarcophagus described below. The Hellenistic robbers' removal of all of these objects from the sarcophagus unfortunately prevents us from speculating any further.

I have not yet commented on the inclusion of mythical scenes in the design, which leads us to the question of whether we should regard the choice of the Polyxena scene as a symbolic one, possibly linked to the gender of the deceased. I should begin by noting that the insertion of a myth into the decorative program of a fifth century B.C. sarcophagus is unusual in itself. Myths do appear sporadically in Persian-period sarcophagi from Lycia, Sidon, and Cyprus, but they are usually absent in the extant pre-Roman examples, or they are placed in a subordinate position if they do appear.[132]

The mythical scenes in Lycian monuments tended to include local heroes such as Bellerophon, Chrysaor, and Pegasus, who functioned as visual references to the legendary history of the region in which the tomb was located. The same may be true for the Polyxena Sarcophagus: Ilion had probably been identified as the site of the Trojan War by the seventh century B.C., and within the vicinity of Kızöldün there were sites highlighted by the local guides as the "Tomb of Memnon" and the spot from which Zeus was said to have snatched Ganymede.[133] The myth of Polyxena may have been chosen, at least in part, because it was suited to the Trojan character of the landscape.

We should also consider the possibility of symbolic parallelism: if the sarcophagus was originally intended to hold the body of a young woman, then one could read the inclusion of the Polyxena story as a mythological evocation of her life – supplying a Homeric reference to another young woman who died an untimely death prior to marriage. This takes us into a larger discussion regarding the function of mythological scenes in Anatolian funerary decoration, and the situation is not as straightforward as one might expect.

Only a few tombs or sarcophagi dating to the fifth and fourth centuries B.C. were decorated with mythical scenes, although excavation has admittedly yielded only a handful of figural sarcophagi dating to that period. The "Lycian Sarcophagus" is the only one from Sidon to incorporate myth into the decoration, with two long hunting scenes coupled with two centaur scenes, one of which features Kaineus. In this case the myth has no clear connection to a larger biographical narrative, and none of the sarcophagi from Lycia features any myths at all.[134] The Heroon at Lycian Trysa, however, falls into a different sphere: the juxtaposition of real and mythical hunt and battle scenes on the precinct walls appear to have been intended as complementary themes designed to lend greater prominence to the exposition of the decedent's achievements.[135]

Two Cypriot sarcophagi also seem to incorporate myths within a larger narrative framework. The Golgoi Sarcophagus (ca. 475–460 B.C.) depicts sympotic and hunting scenes flanked by the story of Perseus and Medusa on one short side and a portrait of the deceased man in a chariot on the other.[136] A link between hero and decedent may therefore have been intended, as in the Heroon at Trysa. A more compelling example is provided by a recently discovered painted sarcophagus from Cypriot Palaepaphus that is roughly contemporary with the Polyxena Sarcophagus. No human bones were discovered, but the associated gifts (saber, arrowheads, knife, and strigil) strongly suggest that the decedent was male.

Three of the four sides of the Palaepaphus Sarcophagus were decorated with scenes influenced by the *Iliad* and *Odyssey*, with Odysseus figuring prominently in two of them, and a modified Pasquino Group, probably Ajax carrying the dead Achilles from the Trojan battlefield, on the third side.[137] Given the number of weapons in the tomb, the Homeric scenes were likely intended as a mythical complement to the decedent's life, even though his portrait does not figure in the decoration. In viewing all of these examples together, it certainly seems conceivable that the Polyxena scene was intended as a mythical reference to the life of the young woman for whom the sarcophagus was originally planned, although again, the corpus of relevant comparanda is rather limited.

The Sculptural Workshop

Since no pottery was found in the sarcophagus, the dating relies completely on stylistic analysis, which is highly problematic: the best stylistic parallels come from Attica, and there are no securely dated Late Archaic sculptures from the Granicus region that provide assistance.[138] The relatively short hair and snail curls of the men, the rendering of the bodies, and the swallowtail folds of the drapery would be in harmony with a date between 500 and 490 B.C. The drapery of figures 2 and 23, in particular, can be paralleled on the standing Athena from the west pediment at Aegina (ca. 490–480 B.C.), while the heads and hairstyles of the men are not far from those on the Kouros Base in Athens (ca. 500 B.C.).[139]

Most of the female heads tend to be defined by a long diagonal line curving slightly from nose to forehead, with almond eyes and a half-oval shape used for the back of the head. The latter is a western Asia Minor feature paralleled also in the Kızılbel tombs, as are the eyes and profiles.[140] A similar style appears in Late Archaic coinage from Phocaea, a marble sphinx from Biga, which was certainly carved in this region, and even the Painted House at Gordion, ca. 500–490 B.C. [141] Especially distinctive are the long, mannered hands of the women, although those appear in Late Archaic funerary imagery on both sides of the Aegean.[142] A few of the features, such as the aged eyes of Hecuba or the winged caryatid throne supports, appear to be unique in Late Archaic and Classical sculpture. What is needed most are additional products from the sculptural workshops in this region, especially elite contexts in Daskyleion and Cyzicus, which would enable us to assess the form and development of a regional style in sculpture more effectively.

Even with the minimal evidence at our disposal, however, some features of the workshops and the aristocrats who patronized them are clear. All of the marble used in the elite tombs was quarried on the island of Proconnesus, which was of extraordinary quality and relatively easy to import due to the close geographic proximity of the quarries.[143] It is also noteworthy that such extensive use of marble is not found in other known tumuli of Archaic or Classical date. At Sardis, only the Tomb of Alyattes, father of Croesus, was con-structed of marble – clearly as a mark of royalty. Otherwise, marble was either eschewed in favor of limestone or used only for selected features, such as the door and interior furniture of the Naip Tumulus near Tekirdağ.[144]

We know very little about early activity in the Proconnesian marble quar-ries since the evidence from the island itself is not as full as one would like. None of the unfinished sculptures or inscriptions from the quarries dates earlier than the Roman period, although a number of literary sources coupled with recent isotopic analysis allow us to reconstruct broadly the beginning of the quarry's operations.[145] According to Vitruvius, Proconnesian marble was among the types of stones considered for the construction of the Temple of Artemis at Ephesus, which indicates that the quality of the marble had already been recognized during the period of Lydian domination in the Troad.[146] Isotopic analysis of a stele from Sigeion, dated to 550–540 B.C., shows that Proconnesian marble had begun to be used for sculpture at least by the third quarter of the sixth century B.C., and the new discoveries along the Granicus River demonstrate its continued use throughout the Late Archaic and Classical period.[147]

Proconnesian marble was used consistently in the construction of the new satrapal center at Daskyleion, and it is tempting to link the first exploitation of the quarries to the tyrant Metrodorus, who ruled the island during the reign of Darius.[148] In other words, the advent of Persian domination in western Asia Minor probably stimulated large-scale quarrying of Proconnesian marble, which quickly became the favored building material for tombs, at least in the Granicus Valley, as aristocratic competition among the landowners increased. Judging by the strong similarities between the decorated lid of the Polyxena Sarcophagus and the "Early Classical Building" at Daskyleion, it also seems likely that the carving of marble architecture and sculpture was handled by the same men.[149]

Of the cities in the vicinity of Proconnesus, the largest and most powerful was Cyzicus, which would seize control of the island in the fourth century B.C. Both were also Milesian colonies, and Strabo notes the widespread use of Proconnesian marble in the buildings of Cyzicus.[150] At least some of the sculptors responsible for the Granicus Valley tombs were probably associated with Cyzicus, and systematic excavation at the latter site should succeed in verifying this hypothesis.[151]

In 500 B.C. stone sarcophagi with figural scenes were only beginning to be produced, and this is the first stone sarcophagus with figural decoration for which we have evidence. Since it involved such a complicated composition, one would expect a few signs of difficulty in the carving process, and they do in fact appear. The artists had not planned enough space for the raised elbow of Neoptolemus, the tumulus of Achilles, or the helmets of the Pyrrhic dancers, and all of them extend beyond the rectangular frame.

There is, in addition, a network of small drill holes on each side of the sarcophagus, most of which have been placed next to the elbows, knees, and noses of the figures (cf. the circles in Figs. 3.8, 3.12, 3.15, and 3.18). It seems likely that these were cut into the surface of the sarcophagus once the design had been established but before the carving had begun. I initially thought that these holes could have supplied the artists with a general organizational guide for what was an extraordinarily complex composition, rather like the technique of pouncing in Renaissance painting. Several modern sculptors whom I consulted, however, thought it highly unlikely that such a system would have been employed, so the function of the holes is still unknown.

The greatest number of holes appears on the side with Polyxena (A), where there are twelve (Fig. 3.8); four appear in the main celebration scene (C) (Fig. 3.15); two in the Hecuba panel (B) (Fig. 3.12), and one in the kline conversation scene (D) (Fig. 3.18). In some cases, the rationale for positioning the holes in a particular part of the relief seems clear: on the left side of the first panel (A), three of the holes are vertically aligned along the back of mourner no. 3, behind her head, buttocks, and calf. Five of the holes cluster around the head and hands of mourner no. 5, whose pose is one of the most complex on this side, while the hole in the kline conversation scene is exactly centered between the left and right sides. In other cases, however, the placement does not seem as systematic as one would expect: there is none, for example, around Neoptolemus, the Tomb of Achilles, or the upper body of Polyxena, nor around any of the branches of the tree. Two adjacent holes appear in front of the nose of the Greek holding the ankles of Polyxena (no. 8), and again in front of Hecuba's nose, even though one would have been enough to determine placement.

Some of the original holes may have been cut away as carving progressed, but it is also conceivable that different sculptors were responsible for different sides, and varying systems were used to lay out the composition. Judging by the differences in the treatment of hair and drapery among the panels, the probability that these are the product of several sculptors, presumably working simultaneously, seems high. One of the Late Archaic reliefs from Cyzicus also features drill holes at strategic points in the composition, and the practice may have been more widespread than we think, especially in the case of the earlier reliefs carved in the vicinity of Proconnesus.[152]

Historical Context

We should, as a final note, consider the historical context of the area during the general period when the sarcophagus was carved, since it was as dramatic as some of the scenes on the sarcophagus. The men who owned and operated these estates, as well as those in Persian-controlled cities, were required to serve in the king's army if the need arose, even if, as during the Persian Wars, this required them to fight men of the same ethnicity.[153] At several points between the late sixth and the early fourth centuries B.C., the settlements in north-western Turkey sustained significant damage as a consequence of these wars. In 512, after Darius' campaign against the Scythians, he burned the Hellespontine towns through which he passed so that their resources could not be used by the enemy. Later, in the course of the Ionian revolt, Darius' son-in-law, Daurises, sacked the rebellious Hellespontine and Marmara cities, from Dardanus almost to Parion, while the Phoenician fleet attacked Proconessus.[154] The settlements on Tenedos, Lesbos, and Chios were burned, the boys castrated, and the women prepared for deportation to Persepolis.[155]

From the point of view of the Persians and their affiliates, the satrapy of Sardis had been sacked in defiance of their control of western Asia Minor, and the same could conceivably happen to the other satrapal centers, including Daskyleion, if the rebellion were not quelled. In short, battles would have encompassed the entire Troad during the period in which the sarcophagus was produced. Whether the attacks and their consequences influenced the design of the war scenes on sides A and B can never be determined, but a similar kind of carnage, and lamentation, would have been very much within the recent memory of the inhabitants of the region.

FOUR

THE TOMBS OF THE GRANICUS RIVER VALLEY II: THE CHILD'S SARCOPHAGUS

The mounds that lined the Granicus River Valley were assembled in clusters that belonged to specific families. Two bodies were often buried within a single stone tomb chamber, as one finds in the nearby Dedetepe tumulus and in some of the tombs of Lydia, but rarely does one find two sarcophagi of different dates buried within the same tumulus, as in the case of Kızöldün.[1] Unlike the Polyxena Sarcophagus, the "Child's Sarcophagus" had surprisingly escaped the attention of robbers in both antiquity and the modern period; consequently, the original funerary assemblage was still intact when the sarcophagus was excavated, and points toward a date of around 450 B.C. for the burial. The tomb gifts, which encompass objects made of terracotta, alabaster, silver, gold, glass, and wood, complement the offerings depicted in the reliefs of the Polyxena Sarcophagus, thereby enabling us to assess both the appearance and ritual use of a discrete group of objects used by a specific family over the course of forty to fifty years.

The sarcophagus was buried on the north slope of the tumulus, 3 m to the north of the Polyxena Sarcophagus, with its top located only 0.50 m beneath the surface of the mound (Fig. 3.3).[2] No pieces of a hearse were discovered during the excavation, and since there were no signs that the sarcophagus had been disturbed after the burial, it seems likely that the hearse continued in use. The sarcophagus was not surrounded by tiles or provided with any special protection, but since it features no exterior reliefs, this is not unexpected.[3]

4.1. The Child's Sarcophagus from the Kızöldün tumulus. Çanakkale Archaeological Museum. Troy Excavation Project photo.

Like the other sarcophagi in the Granicus River Valley it is carved of Proconnesian marble and is approximately two-thirds the size of the Polyxena Sarcophagus (Fig. 4.1).[4] The lid imitates a gabled roof but no tiles have been rendered nor were any figural reliefs used for decoration: the finish consists only of a narrow tooth-chiseled margin around the borders of each side. The finish contrasts dramatically with that of the Polyxena Sarcophagus, although this kind of simple surface treatment was not uncommon during the Archaic and Classical periods, even for members of the aristocracy.[5]

When the sarcophagus was opened, we found that it contained the body of a child between the ages of eight and nine. The body was interred so that the head lay at the north, facing southeast, with the arms along the sides of the body and the hands over the pelvis. The child's gender could not be determined on the basis of osteological analysis alone, but the nature of the gifts, viewed as an assemblage, points decisively toward a girl. Such a gender attribution is striking in light of the local name for the tumulus, which is Kızöldün, or "dead girl." Considering that the child's tomb was not disturbed or seen between the time of burial (ca. 450 B.C.) and the excavation in 1994, the name may supply evidence for a very long oral tradition within the region that has lasted for nearly 2500 years.

On the child's skull there was evidence of cribra orbitalia (porotic hyperostosis), a syndrome that results in porosity in the bone above the eye socket. This condition is caused by some kind of stress that is nutritionally or disease-induced, or by anemia brought on by malaria.[6] There are signs of the same

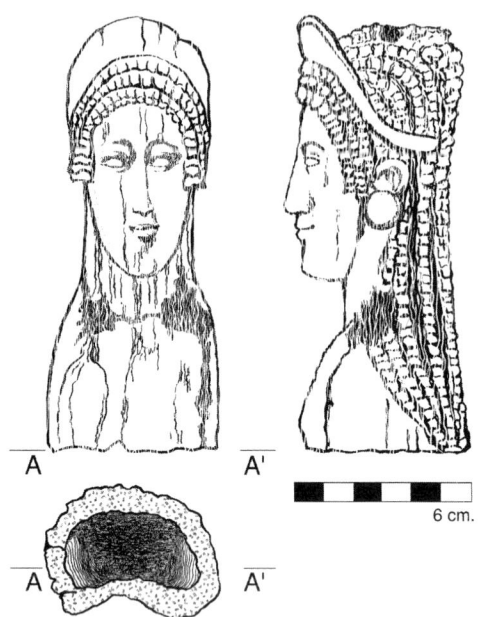

A   A'

A   A'

6 cm.

4.2. Drawing of wooden female protome from the Child's Sarcophagus, by Nurten Sevinç and Robert Hagerty for the Troy Excavation Project. Çanakkale Archaeological Museum. Troy Excavation Project drawing.

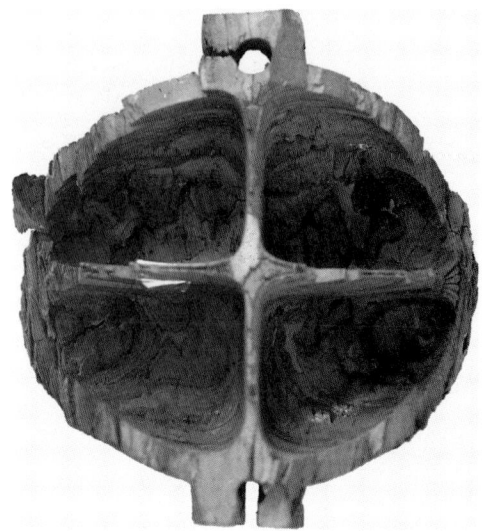

4.3. The lid of the wooden pyxis from the Child's Sarcophagus. Çanakkale Archaeological Museum. Troy Excavation Project photo.

condition on nearly all of the children buried in the Archaic/Classical cemetery at Assos, which suggests that these health problems spanned much of the Troad.[7]

Both the Kızöldün and Assos regions were extremely marshy in the fifth century B.C., so malaria may have been the most likely cause.

Much of the skeleton, including the hands, had disintegrated and was partially immersed in a white substance – probably an alkaline mixture of water, dissolved marble, and organic remains. None of the grave goods was totally immersed in the white substance, and the form of all of them could be distinguished. The gifts included a wooden female protome to the left of the skull (Fig. 4.2), a wooden pyxis next to the shoulder (Fig. 4.3), a glass aryballos (Fig. 4.4), a single-handled flask in pieces at the northern corner of the sarcophagus, and a terracotta alabastron above the skull. An unusual amount of gold was interred with the body, including two necklaces fastened around the neck (Fig. 4.5 and Plate 14), eight identical gold earrings (Fig. 4.6), four on either side of the skull, and a gold bracelet on each arm (Fig. 4.7).

Her finger bones had disintegrated, but a silver ladle and phiale were found on the pelvis where the hands would have been (Fig. 4.8).[8] These must have been positioned in her hands, as if she were ready for sympotic activity. The bowl, stem, and loop of the ladle were hammered from one piece of silver, and the loop terminates in an Achaemenid-style calf's head with chased beard, eyes, nose, and ears.[9] Such ladles were common in Asia Minor, often in conjunction with silver phialai, wine strainers, and other sympotic equipment, although this

4.4. Glass aryballos from the Child's Sarcophagus. Çanakkale Archaeological Museum. Troy Excavation Project photo.

is the first instance in which ladle and phiale have been found directly on the body of the deceased.[10]

By her feet were four black-glazed alabastra with lug handles, between 0.13 and 0.18 m high.[11] Similar alabastra are held by one of the figures on the Polyxena Sarcophagus (Figs. 3.15 and 3.16), and they are comparable in form to those from the nearby and nearly contemporary tomb within Dedetepe.[12] Those from the latter tomb, however, contain streaks of Tyrian purple, probably remnants of freshly dyed ribbons, which are not in evidence here.[13]

Positioned somewhere on her body was a complete spherical glass aryballos, on which were traces of a thin cloth that undoubtedly reflects the weave of the shroud (Fig. 4.4).[14] Over time the alkaline solution in the sarcophagus degraded the original textile and etched the glass surface, leaving behind an exact impression of the fabric. The opaque navy blue ground with opaque yellow and turquoise decoration belongs to Group I of Mediterranean Core-Formed Bottles, usually dated to the late sixth or fifth century B.C.[15] One of the exciting features of this aryballos is the small amount of sediment that was still preserved at the bottom, and our hope was that the chemical composition

(a)

(b)

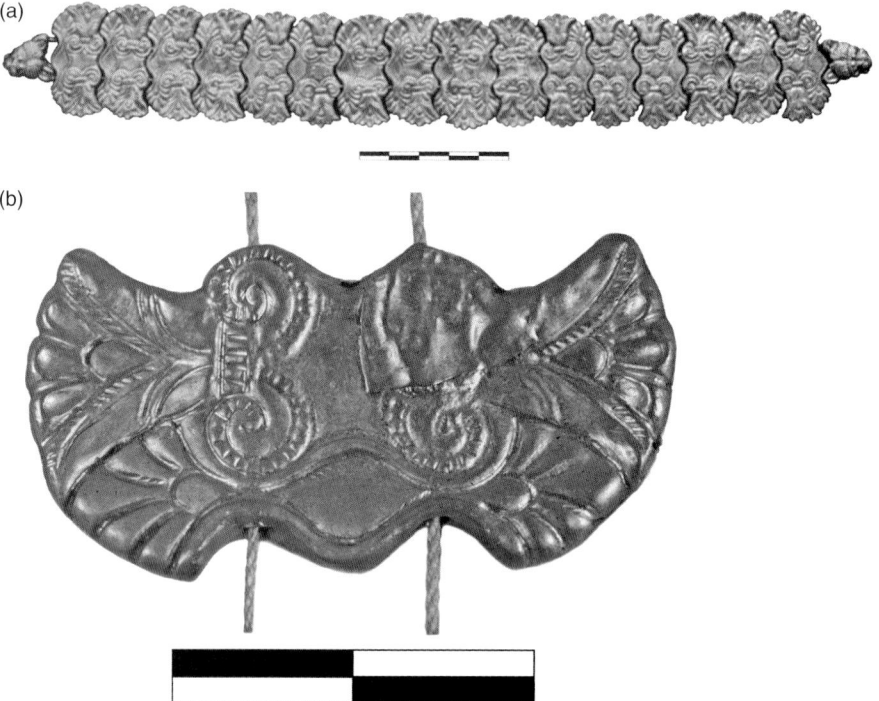

4.5. (A) Second gold necklace with links from the Child's Sarcophagus. Çanakkale Archaeological Museum. Troy Excavation Project photo. (B) Detail of second gold necklace with links from the Child's Sarcophagus. Gold leaf repair is visible at upper right. Çanakkale Archaeological Museum. Troy Excavation Project photo.

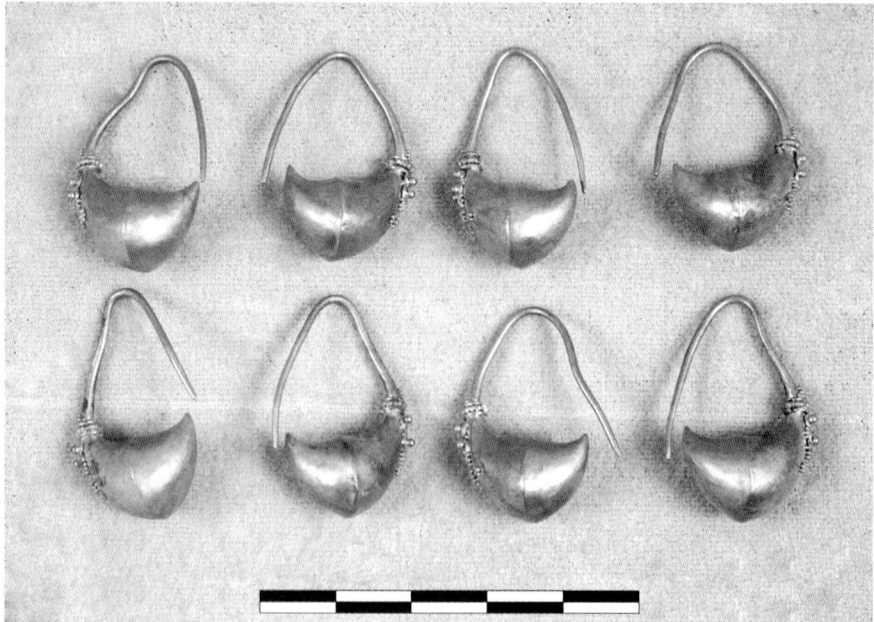

4.6. Gold earrings from the Child's Sarcophagus. Çanakkale Archaeological Museum. Troy Excavation Project photo.

4.7. Gold bracelets from the Child's Sarcophagus. Çanakkale Archaeological Museum. Troy Excavation Project photo.

4.8. Silver ladle and phiale from the Child's Sarcophagus. Çanakkale Archaeological Museum. Troy Excavation Project photo.

of the original liquid could be reconstructed, but the results, unfortunately, were limited. The organic contents consist of carbohydrates from plant sources, with no fats, oils, or natural resins in evidence.[16]

The wooden pyxis (Fig. 4.3) is of the same type as the one offered to the seated woman on the Polyxena Sarcophagus (Figs. 3.17 and 3.18). It consists of a shallow hemicycle divided into four compartments of equal size that were covered by a rotating lid.[17] The outer edge of the rim is decorated with a course of incised squares that echo the quadratic interior, while the underside featured a circular incised guilloche pattern ending in double spirals. Relief palmettes with four or five petals adorn sections of both the exterior and the interior. Four other small pyxides from western Turkey are nearly identical in shape: two from Ephesus, one from Lydia, and one from Tumulus D at Bayındır in Lycia.[18] The double spirals are paralleled in the Lydian piece, and the course of incised squares appears on one of the pyxides from Ephesus. The pyxis from the Child's Sarcophagus is the only one in this group to have been made of wood.

The only gift within the sarcophagus that would probably not have been found in the tomb of an adult is the wooden female protome carved from a single piece of wood, less than 8 cm in height (Fig. 4.2).[19] The protome terminates below the breast, and the face is long and narrow, with large eyes, a long straight nose, and slightly smiling, pursed lips. The strongly waved hair, crowned by a crescent-shaped crown, or stephane, is pulled behind ears adorned with large circular earrings, and the falling tresses completely cover her back. Judging by the remaining traces of paint, the face and the neck must have been white, the diadem red, and the hair yellow. The hairstyle can be paralleled on monumental stone sculpture at the end of the Archaic period, and the same earrings appear in the reliefs on the Polyxena Sarcophagus.[20]

The function of this piece is difficult to ascertain, although it must have been a toy. There appear to have been attachments at top and bottom: a small cylinder inserted into the hole on the top of the head, and a larger piece inserted into the hollow interior.[21] Greek dolls typically contained a small hole in the top of the head for the insertion of a tenon and string, and the protome from the Child's Sarcophagus may have had a similar function.[22] Dolls were not uncommon tomb gifts, and somewhat similar protomes have been discovered in fifth century B.C. tombs in southern Bulgaria.[23]

Although the range of gold jewelry is not unusual for western Asia Minor tombs of fifth century B.C. date, such an assemblage is rarely found in an unplundered context, and it reveals a considerable amount of information about funerary practices in this area. The child was deposited in the tomb with more jewelry than she would actually have worn during life, and it looks as if her entire jewelry box was deposited here. The only missing objects that one would have expected are rings and a mirror.[24]

The two necklaces placed around her neck were strikingly different. The larger one, which weighs more than 80 grams, consists of sixteen seed-like pendants alternating with five red glass beads and ending in teardrop-shaped terminals of red glass (Plate 14).[25] Each of the pendants hangs from an undecorated suspension bead approximately the same size as the glass beads. Five rows of feathered leaves appear on each bead, with small grains at the apices and a larger grain at the tip. The inlays on the gold necklace, which are held in place by beaded wires, are a dense, matte, opaque red glass with minute bubbles. Although no analysis was carried out, the glass is probably the copper red opaque glass prevalent in western Anatolian jewelry at this time.[26] The amount of wear on this necklace demonstrates that it had been in use for some time, like several of the other pieces of jewelry in the assemblage. Six of the pendants have lost the grains at their tips, and some of them have been dented or scraped.

The smaller necklace is composed of eighteen elements: two lion-head terminals with large forehead warts and sixteen hollow die-hammered pieces decorated with double lotus and palmettes (Fig. 4.5).[27] For the centerpiece, an additional double palmette component has been added to one side. One of the lotus spirals has been damaged and repaired with gold leaf, although it is barely perceptible. This necklace had clearly been in circulation for some time, as indicated by the repair, occasional traces of wear, and the unequal number of elements on either side of the center.

Still present on her arms were two gold bracelets, each of which weighs between 10 and 11 grams (Fig. 4.7).[28] The terminals are defined by Achaemenid-style antelope head terminals with incised beard, nose, and eyes. The oval depressions in the top of both antelope heads may once have contained inserts, although they were not discovered in the sarcophagus. Here too there are traces of sustained use: the heads are rather worn and the band is somewhat bent. Although the dimensions are the same, the heads are not identical in rendering or size, and the bracelets may not have been manufactured as a pair. Such Achaemenid-style antelope heads enjoyed great popularity in Asia Minor during the latter sixth and fifth centuries, as is well attested in the Granicus area.[29] The same style was used for the calf's head terminal of the ladle from this sarcophagus (Fig. 4.8) and for the ivory protome from the nearby Dedetepe tomb (Fig. 5.6).[30]

Eight boat-shaped gold earrings with vertical carination lay around her head, with four at each side (Fig. 4.6).[31] Each piece is made of two halves of sheet gold, with a weight of roughly 3 grams. The terminal has a band of beaded wire flanked by plain wire and a triangular cluster of grains above. Under the terminal on the short side of the body are two horizontal figure-of-eight spirals in filigree with grains in the scrolls; below are five granulated clusters composed of four or six grain lozenges. Such boat-shaped earrings with vertical carination were fairly common in western Asia Minor during the Late Archaic and Classical periods, and were possibly native to the areas of Lycia and Lydia.[32]

Judging by the find spot of the earrings, one might conclude that they were actually worn by the child at the time of interment, but there are no examples of multiple piercings for earrings in either the Greek or Persian worlds, and it seems likely that they were simply deposited on either side of the head.[33]

The deposition of a rather large group of earrings, both gold and silver, in the tombs of elite women and children appears to have been relatively common, with the numbers extending as high as twelve in the tombs of Thrace.[34]

It is worth noting that the attitudes toward jewelry as evinced by the two Kızöldün sarcophagi are not the same, even though we are presumably dealing with the same family during a relatively short period of time. No necklaces or bracelets are worn by the women in the Polyxena Sarcophagus reliefs, nor are the earrings of the same type. Mirrors are absent from the Child's Sarcophagus, as are fans, even though they are among the featured gifts in the Polyxena reliefs (Figs. 3.14–3.18). Missing from both are finger rings, fibulae, and gold appliqués, which one typically finds in contemporary tombs of elite females in Thrace and Asia Minor.[35]

The style of the jewelry fits well within the late sixth or early fifth century B.C., especially the use of spiral filigree in the earrings combined with granulated triangles.[36] Necklaces with seed-like pendants are attested by the Late Archaic period, as is the combination of gold and opaque glass.[37] The relatively large suspension beads, however, suggest a date somewhere in the fifth century, as do the decorative features on the gold link necklace. The motif of the lotus above two spirals appears on Cypriot coinage during the first half of the fifth century, and on other types of jewelry connected to Cyprus.[38] The Achaemenid-type lions are easily paralleled in sculpture and jewelry of the later sixth/first half of the fifth century, although they were used more often for bracelets than for necklaces.[39]

The precise date of burial cannot be fixed with certainty. The Child's Sarcophagus was certainly set into the tumulus after the Polyxena Sarcophagus had been interred, and the style of the doll and jewelry, viewed as a group, points to a date somewhere in the first quarter of the fifth century. The jewelry must have been in circulation for some time, considering the extent of wear and damage, which suggests a burial date sometime around the middle of the fifth century. This date would also fit well with the form of the alabastra in the sarcophagus.

Since the two sarcophagi occupied the same tumulus and date within forty to fifty years of each other, the occupants were undoubtedly members of the same family, and both featured implements associated with a celebratory after-life. The marked contrast between the surface finish of the two sarcophagi is therefore striking. Moreover, the size of the sarcophagus (2.25 m in length) seems somewhat large for an eight- to nine-year-old girl, although one cannot really speculate about standard conventions since no other children's sarcophagi of Archaic or Classical date have been discovered in this region. It is conceivable that regional marble workshops began to produce relatively simple marble sarcophagi in anticipation of unexpected or sudden deaths, so that purchase and delivery could occur relatively rapidly. In the case of this particular child, however, that seems unlikely: the cribra orbitalia from which the child suffered would probably have involved a rather lengthy illness, and there would have been enough time to order the sarcophagus well in advance of the burial.

This raises the issue of the manner in which the two sarcophagi were buried. Neither was placed on a foundation or within a stone chamber: the Polyxena Sarcophagus was surrounded by stacks of terracotta tiles that reached to the top of the reliefs; the Child's Sarcophagus was set directly into the earth (Fig. 3.3). When the Kızöldün excavations were published, the hypothesis was advanced that the Polyxena Sarcophagus had to have been used earlier than anticipated, thereby allowing an insufficient amount of time for the construction of the tomb chamber and necessitating the use of tiles to protect the reliefs of the sarcophagus.[40] This hypothesis should probably be modified. The construction of such chambers was most likely begun at approximately the same time as the sarcophagi, so that both would be ready prior to the death of the intended occupant. If the Child's Sarcophagus had been intended for a stone chamber, there would most likely have been enough time to complete it.[41]

We should therefore probably acknowledge that burial customs involving sarcophagi were different from what one would normally expect, at least in Asia Minor during the late sixth and early fifth centuries B.C. If a sarcophagus contained no exterior decoration, as in the case of the child at Kızöldün, no separate enclosure or protection was deemed necessary. If the sarcophagus did feature exterior decoration, then a layer of protection in the form of surrounding tiles was utilized in lieu of a special enclosure. It is noteworthy that no chambers were used for the simple Early Classical sarcophagi uncovered at Karaburun in Lycia – they were encased only in a pile of stones.[42]

One would like to be able to view the Gümüşçay Child's Sarcophagus in the context of other elite children's burials in both Greece and Anatolia, although this is difficult due to the limited number of comparanda: none of the excavated tombs of mainland Greece and Magna Graecia approaches the level of wealth evinced by the Polyxena Sarcophagus, nor is jewelry a regular feature of the assemblage.[43] The only consistently common components of children's graves across the Mediterranean are terracotta toys; vessels for eating and drinking also appear occasionally, although the "sympotic" format of the Kızöldün girl is duplicated in none of them, and such vessels appear more frequently in the graves of infants than in those of adolescents, at least in Athens.[44]

One of the few comparable Anatolian examples is Tumulus P at Phrygian Gordion, which contained the body of a four- to five-year-old boy.[45] Despite its date, nearly 300 years earlier than the Child's Sarcophagus at Kızöldün, the two are comparable in a surprising number of ways. The first involves the construction of the tumulus itself. The Gordion child was buried in one of the larger mounds at the site, with a lower diameter of 70 m, and in a wooden tomb chamber measuring 4.5 × 3.5 m. As the excavators noted, these are

4.9. The tumulus of Bozlartepe. Photo by the author.

unusually large tomb dimensions for a child of four- to five-years-old, and they proposed that the chamber had originally been intended for an adult but was reassigned when the child in question died unexpectedly.[46] The same situation may have existed at Kızöldün, and was probably a relatively frequent occurrence.

Like the girl at Kızöldün, the Gordion boy received toys as gifts, but on a much larger scale: a tiny bronze quadriga, painted vessels in the form of animals and birds, and a bronze caldron filled with miniature wooden animals. The funeral had been accompanied by a meal, the vessels of which (e.g., ladles, kraters, sipping bowls) were stacked under the bed and around the walls, with traces of food still present in some of them. Judging by the quantity of vessels, including ten dinoi (wine serving stands) and fourteen amphorae, the crowd assembled for the funeral must have been relatively large, although the vessels were not broken at the conclusion of the ceremony as in the Archaic and Classical tombs of western Asia Minor.[47]

During the period of Persian control in the Troad, the only other possible grave of a child lies at Bozlartepe, approximately 8 km north of Kızöldün and quite possibly part of the same estate (Fig. 4.9). The Bozlartepe tumulus has a diameter of only 27 m, which makes it the smallest of the tumuli in the area. Attempted looting in 2006 led to a rescue excavation undertaken under the auspices of the Çanakkale Archaeological Museum, which targeted an area where radar had detected an anomaly 2 m deep. We discovered no burial per se, although excavation yielded a large pile of Classical tiles at a depth of precisely 2 m. The decedent was most likely placed in a sarcophagus around which the tiles had been set, like the Polyxena Sarcophagus, and the tiles were then cast to the side when the sarcophagus was robbed.[48] Although tiles are notoriously difficult to date, these were of the same type as those found at Kızöldün and probably date to the fifth century B.C. The small size of the tumulus suggests that a child had been buried here, but the extent of the looting was so extensive that one can do no more than speculate.

Identifying other children's tombs in the Troad comparable to the one in Kızöldün has so far not been possible. A number of children's graves of Late Archaic/Classical date have been unearthed at Assos, but even though they occupied a privileged position directly outside the entrance to the city, the number and quality of the offerings are much more modest than those at Kızöldün and rarely include objects in precious metal.[49] This pattern again highlights the variation in wealth between the interior of the Troad and its coastal cities during the fifth century B.C., which would remain largely in place until the destruction of Daskyleion in 334. Since hyperostosis porosis appears to have been a chronic problem for children in this region during the later sixth/fifth centuries B.C., it seems likely that more tombs analogous to the one at Kızöldün await discovery on Persian-affiliated estates. In time, if the looters can be kept at bay, there should be enough evidence for a more systematic analysis of the roles played by age, class, and gender in western Asia Minor mortuary practices prior to the advent of Alexander.

FIVE

THE TOMBS OF THE GRANICUS RIVER VALLEY III: THE DEDETEPE TUMULUS

Our best evidence for the construction of tomb chambers in the Granicus region comes from Dedetepe, located approximately 7 km from the modern town of Gümüşçay (Plate 13).[1] The tumulus of Dedetepe, with a diameter of 65 m, is the largest of those identified in the Granicus River Valley, and at 60 m above sea level, it commands an excellent view of the surrounding area (Fig. 5.1).[2] The mound of Dedetepe is actually visible from the top of Kızöldün, and both were undoubtedly part of the same estate.[3]

Clandestine activity occurred here in 1994, although the robbers were unsuccessful in finding the tomb. Subsequent excavations under the direction of Nurten Sevinç unearthed a marble chamber measuring 3.60 × 4.20 m, with an interior height of 1.90 m, and it appears to have been built between 480 and 460 B.C. based on the associated pottery (Figs. 5.2–5.5, Plate 15). The tomb chamber had been robbed in antiquity, but two brightly painted marble klinai and some of the gifts deposited during the funeral service were still preserved (Fig. 5.5). The construction of the Dedetepe tumulus would have occurred after the burial of the Polyxena Sarcophagus but before that of the Child's Sarcophagus, which allows us to chart the funerary customs within a single estate throughout the first half of the fifth century B.C.

The evidence uncovered during excavation also clarifies the process of the tomb's construction. The door was doweled with lead to the threshold and flanking posts, and was sealed after the bodies had been interred in the completed chamber. As the mound rose, the chamber would have disappeared from

5.1. The Dedetepe tumulus. Photo by the author.

view, and the builders seem to have used shafts of wood situated at strategic points around the chamber to keep track of its location as the height of the mound increased.[4] When the fill reached the top of the poles, replacements would have been erected so that the center of the tumulus would always have been identifiable. None of the wooden shafts survives, but the chamber was surrounded by a series of holes, 0.20 m in diameter and more than 1 m in height, which suggests that the builders of the Dedetepe tumulus followed the same system that had been used earlier for the tumuli at Gordion (Fig. 5.3).[5]

The tomb per se is oriented on a northeast-southwest axis and constructed of white marble with gray veins from the nearby island of Proconnesus. The roof consists of four large marble blocks joined by iron clamps, while the walls were built with smaller rectangular marble blocks, laid in seven courses, that were joined by clamps smaller than those used in the ceiling.[6] The marble door on the southwest side was attached to the façade by dowels at right and left, and the long point-chiseled strip above the entrance was probably intended for an inscription naming the decedent, as in the Dardanus tomb near Ilion, although never incised (Fig. 5.4).[7]

The entrance was approached by an uncovered dromos with rubble walls that continue around the tomb chamber.[8] In front of the entrance, beneath some of these collapsed stones, was a burnt layer that included pottery and many pieces of charcoal. Under the burning was a layer of marble chips 10 cm

5.2. Excavation of the tomb chamber within the Dedetepe tumulus, looking north. Photo by the author.

thick that was concentrated in front of the threshold, around the walls, and under the tomb floor. This surely relates to the final trimming of the blocks once they had been set in place.

THE TOMB CHAMBER

Although the interior measurement of almost 29 m² strikes one as rather small, it is in fact one of the larger tomb chambers for which we have evidence

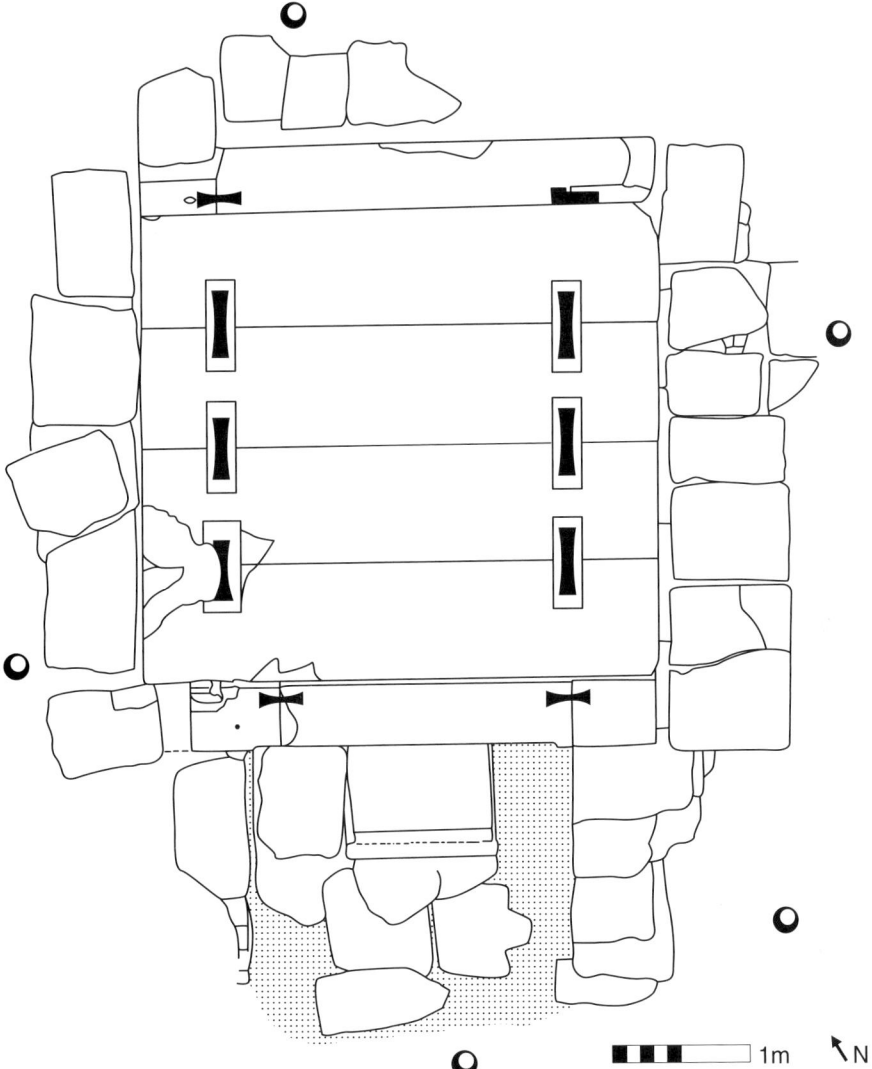

5.3. State plan of the Dedetepe tomb chamber, by Kate Clayton, based on an original by Nurten Sevinç. The five circles around the perimeter contained shafts of wood that enabled the builders to monitor the position of the chamber as the mound rose. Troy Excavation Project drawing.

(Fig. 5.5, Plate 15). The tomb chamber of the Lydian king Alyattes, which lay just north of Sardis, measures nearly 18 m², and the majority of the other chamber tombs of Lydia, as well as those in Lycia and Macedonia, are also smaller than Dedetepe.[9] Most of the above, however, were intended for single burials; those slated to receive two or more burials from the beginning were no doubt constructed with larger proportions.[10]

Both walls and ceiling have such well-polished surfaces that one can barely see the joins between the blocks (Plate 15). The absence of painting on the walls or the ceiling is somewhat surprising considering the elaborate paintings

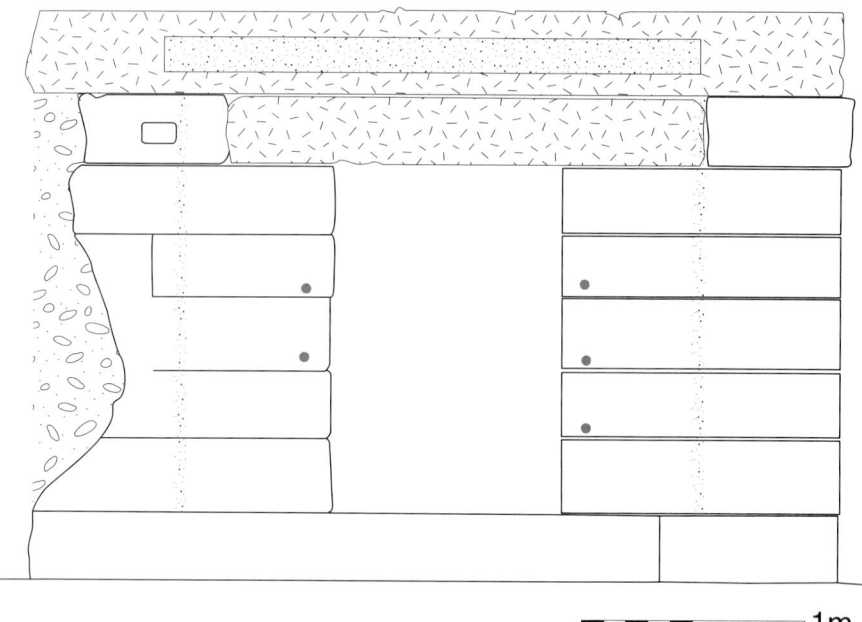

1m

5.4. Elevation of the front of the Dedetepe tomb, by Kate Clayton, based on an original by Nurten Sevinç. Troy Excavation Project drawing.

on the two klinai found inside the chamber, as well as on the Çan Sarcophagus (Plates 15–16; Fig. 6.2). What one does find throughout the tomb, however, are the handprints of the ancient robbers. It looks as if dirt adhered to their sweaty palms during the robbery, and they used the marble as a surface on which to clean them.

The floor is covered by five marble slabs, each 2 cm thick, and two marble klinai with separately carved legs were set against the north and west walls of the tumulus. On the upper section of each bed there is a slight concavity where the body was placed, although most of the bones had been pushed away in the course of the ancient robbery (Fig. 5.5, Plate 15). Both klinai were elaborately painted in an identical way, suggesting that they were probably made at the same time.[11] The head and base were decorated with rectangles outlined with a red band, and on either side of each was a hemispherical knob painted blue, no doubt in imitation of the rivet head that would have existed on wooden versions of the couch.[12] The curving outer side was decorated with nine parallel lines of more or less equal size, which suggests a mattress decorated with multicolored stripes.[13]

At the top of each leg is a meander of alternating blue and red, below which is a painted Ionic capital with blue for the volutes and red for the eyes (Plate 15). Between the volutes are a series of black and green rectangles in three horizontal rows. Underneath, at the juncture of bed and leg, are four very simple Ionic capitals in red, set back to back and oriented vertically. Above each capital

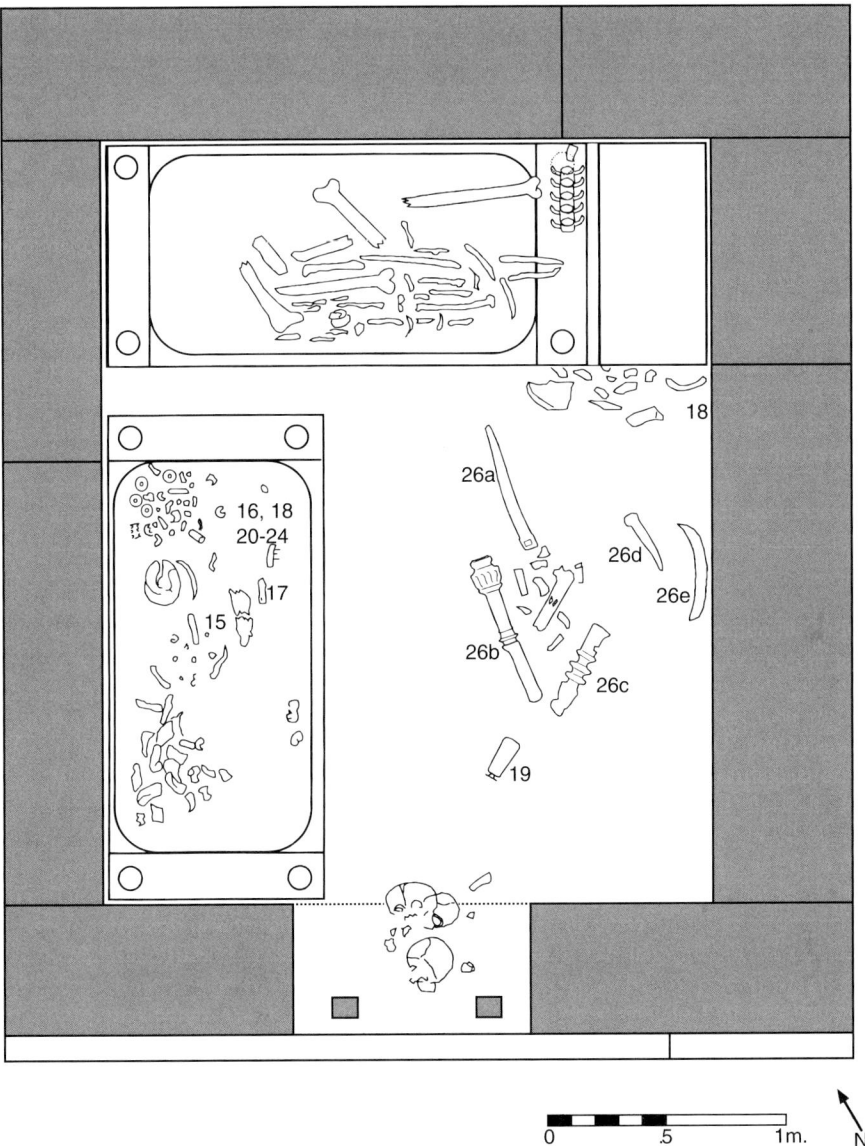

5.5. Interior plan of Dedetepe tomb chamber, by Kate Clayton, based on an original by Nurten Sevinç. Troy Excavation Project drawing.

is a small green rectangle with four vertical black lines, imitating the mortises on wooden prototypes.[14] The primary decoration on each leg is a kind of stylized plant, consisting of a base, three volute-like buds on either side, and a palmette at the top composed of alternating red and blue. The repetition of the volute shape ties together the horizontal and vertical elements of the bed, as does the consistent use of red and blue. The pigments included Egyptian blue and natural cinnabar, which were common in both Greek and Persian painting, and they were fixed to the marble with a pale yellow gesso.[15]

There is nothing especially unusual about the klinai: Ionic volutes and stylized palmettes were commonly used as kline decoration during the later sixth and fifth centuries B.C. throughout the Aegean, but the edges of the legs on either side of the volute buds were often carved away to create a more sculptural shape.[16] Perhaps the best comparanda are the stone klinai from the Late Archaic Aktepe tumulus in Lydia, although there the range of colors represented at Dedetepe is lacking.[17]

The kline at the north of the chamber held a skeleton but no skull. There were, however, three skulls at the tomb entrance as well as shattered pieces of skull and teeth in the center of the chamber (Fig. 5.5). Only the finger bone of the body on the west kline remained in place, and it was probably wearing an iron ring that was found on the kline.[18] Why the skulls would have been removed from the klinai is somewhat of a mystery: if the tombs were not plundered until the Hellenistic period, which seems logical, then the bodies would have completely decomposed, and any adornments would have fallen on the klinai. It seems likely that there were at least two looters, one of whom quickly examined the material on the west klinai and threw to the side anything without value, including the human remains, whereas the robber of the north kline threw only the skull to the side as he pulled objects of intrinsic value from the body.

A few objects, or fragments thereof, nevertheless still lay in place on the west kline. These consisted of seven knucklebones, one piece of wood, and a few fragments of ivory. The latter contained a splintered knife handle, originally 0.145 m long, that was decorated with a recumbent fallow deer facing left (Fig. 5.6).[19] The deer is depicted with antlers pressed against its back, while the front and rear legs are bent at the knee and virtually parallel to the antlers. A beard is outlined but not incised and leads to double-lobed ears that support the antlers. A nearly identical handle was found at Daskyleion, and the style has clearly been influenced by Persia rather than Greece.[20] Especially noteworthy are the double-lobed ears, which are common at Persepolis, the outlined beard leading to the ears, and the eye ridge with pronounced tear duct.[21]

Several fragments of hippo ivory were discovered on the west kline and appear to have belonged to musical instruments. Three are of cylindrical shape with cuttings for square and cone-shaped tuning pins that must have formed part of an instrument with strings, like the fragmentary instruments from the Dardanus tomb.[22] Four additional pieces, also of cylindrical shape, feature a central hole ca. 0.01 m in diameter and most likely belonged to an aulos. If so, then instruments of the same general type as those represented on side C of the Polyxena Sarcophagus must have been deposited in the Dedetepe tomb at the time of burial (Fig. 3.15).[23]

Thirty-five pieces of leather found under the north kline were completely dessicated and turned to powder when touched. The leather appeared to be

5.6. Ivory knife protome in the shape of a deer from the Dedetepe tomb. Çanakkale Archaeological Museum. Troia slide 31986.

tanned and of even thickness but contained no signs of stitching or holes, which would exclude the possibility that the pieces formed part of shoes.[24] A fragmentary alabastron was still in place on the kline, and another one, fortunately complete (H: 0.202 m), had been thrown toward the middle of the floor. Both were of the same type that one sees in the celebration relief on the Polyxena Sarcophagus (Figs. 3.15 and 3.16).

One especially exciting feature of these alabastra is that their exteriors are stained with patches of Tyrian purple, an indigo dye often used to color textiles.[25] The most likely conclusion is that ribbons freshly dyed in Tyrian purple were tied around the alabastra during the funeral service. Depictions on Attic white-ground lekythoi often feature similar ribbons wrapped around tombstones and tomb gifts, including alabastra, and the enthroned woman on the Polyxena Sarcophagus is approached by several attendants holding both alabastra and a ribbon.[26] Such beribboned alabastra were probably a common feature in ritual activity surrounding the burial, and the use of Tyrian purple, which was not inexpensive to acquire, would in itself have highlighted the wealth of the decedent's family during the service.[27]

The tomb robbing severely damaged some of the wooden objects in the tomb, but five wooden furniture legs with square mortises are relatively well preserved (Fig. 5.7). We cannot be certain of the kinds of furniture to which they belong nor the number of pieces of furniture that they represent. Three of the legs belong to different types, although they appear to have been more or less the same height (ca. 0.42 m). In the absence of bracing stretchers, it seems unlikely that one of the legs supported a bed for an additional corpse, and they probably belonged to two stools (*diphroi*) set in front of the two klinai, which is the standard scheme in scenes of funerary banquets.[28] Stools were usually slightly lower than klinai, and that is indeed the case here: the tops of the stools would have been 0.06 m lower than the bottom of the klinai. The existence of three distinct types does not necessarily create a problem – the front and rear

5.7. Wooden stool leg from the interior of the Dedetepe tomb. Çanakkale Archaeological Museum. Troia slide 19808.

legs of sympotic tables are often of two different types – however, no other examples exist of different leg types supporting a single stool.[29]

Two of the legs are nearly complete: one consists of a tapering shaft with no decoration, while the center of the other is turned with two grooves of equal height, below which is a bell-shaped element with down-turned leaves followed by a rounded foot. Only the upper section of the third leg is preserved, but there was clearly a turned section with three grooves of equal height followed by a relief rosette and lion's paw. The legs find their closest stylistic parallels in reliefs from Persepolis dating to the first quarter of the fifth century B.C., specifically those from the Apadana and the "Council Hall," and this corresponds to the date of the majority of the pottery.[30]

As I mentioned earlier, the Dedetepe and Kızöldün tumuli probably belonged to a single estate and contained burials of the same family. It is therefore not surprising that a number of objects depicted on the Polyxena Sarcophagus were also present in the Dedetepe tomb and on the Child's Sarcophagus. In the celebration reliefs on the Polyxena Sarcophagus, for example, women are shown carrying a pyxis and alabastra not unlike those in the latter tombs, while the fragmentary stringed instrument found at Dedetepe calls to mind the female musicians on the earlier sarcophagus (Fig. 3.15).[31] The legs of the kline represented on the sarcophagus, however, do not exhibit the same kind of Persianizing characteristics found on some of the stool legs from the Dedetepe tomb.

The Dedetepe chamber appears to have been designed for only two occupants, but three adult skulls were found inside, and there are fragments that may belong to a fourth one. Consequently, it looks as if several generations of the family were buried there, which means that the tomb would have been opened several times in the course of the fifth century.[32] The fact that the pottery spans several decades within the fifth century also supports such a reconstruction, and the same was true for the Late Classical/Hellenistic Dardanus Tomb near Troy. At least one of the klinai could have been shared by two bodies, which is a common depiction in painted and sculptural representations of symposia, although two skeletons have never been found together on a single funeral couch.[33]

Multiple burials would have required the door of the chamber to have been
sealed several times, and the system they used in antiquity is difficult for us to
reconstruct. The jambs show no signs of the door having been forced open and
subsequently resealed or that a succession of doors had been fixed in place as
new burials occurred. It looks as if the door had been sealed only once, which
suggests that the tomb was built with the expectation that it would be used for
several successive burials. The door must therefore not have been anchored in
place with lead dowels after the first burial. A series of stone slabs or fieldstones
set in front of the entrance, as at the Dardanus and Sardis tombs, could conceivably have been used, and since the tumulus was presumably in the middle
of the family's estate, with little immediate danger of robbery, it was not as
risky an option as it initially appears.[34]

THE FUNERAL CEREMONY

One of the most important results of the Dedetepe excavation is the evidence
it has provided for the reconstruction of Achaemenid-period funerary meals.
Determining the nature of drinking and dining at tumuli has always proved
difficult, since looting has frequently disrupted the ceramic assemblages and
the associated pottery is rarely published. In a few cases, judging by the assemblages, it looks as if the vessels could have been used by workers during the
construction of the tumulus: at Aktepe in Lydia, for example, the bowls were
clearly used as paint pots during the decoration of the tomb chamber.[35] At
Dedetepe, however, the deposit is more consistent, in terms of both assemblage
and find spot. All of the vessels were discovered in front of the entrance to the
tomb in a layer that included burned wood, and the entire deposit lay above a
stratum of marble chips clearly associated with the completion of the chamber.
The vessels included a chytra and lopas, used for cooking; several bowls for
serving what was cooked; and black glazed skyphoi remarkably similar in size,
style, and date.[36] Considering the circumstances of discovery, it seems likely
that the vessels relate to one event, that is, a cooked meal with wine that was
prepared and served at the time of burial, after which the vessels were broken
at the entrance to prevent reuse.[37] Similar skyphoi are held by symposiasts on
tomb stelae, and we should again assume that the iconography in gift presentation or symposium scenes reproduces elements of the funerary rites that
would have been conducted at the burial of the person represented in those
scenes.[38]

The burned wood with which the pottery was mixed could, of course,
relate to the preparation of the meal, but there is another possibility connected
to the burial. It seems virtually certain that the bodies of the deceased would
have been transported to the tumulus in wooden coffins set on the kind of
two-wheeled carts that are depicted in ekphora scenes on the Daskyleion

stelae. If the hearses were not reused, then it seems unlikely that the wooden coffins would have been, and excavations have shown that they were not placed within the tomb chamber. We should therefore probably imagine that they were ritually burned in the course of or at the conclusion of the funerary ceremony, with the charred wood deposited on or adjacent to the tomb, like the dismantled hearse. The burned wood found in front of the door of the Dedetepe tomb, which featured interior klinai, may derive from such a coffin, and the same may be true of the burned deposits occasionally found above Lydian tomb chambers.[39]

If one combines the discoveries from Dedetepe and Kızöldün, there is enough evidence to reconstruct the general outlines of the funeral ceremony in the Granicus River Valley. If the decedent had planned carefully during his or her life, then the sarcophagus or kline with the associated burial chamber would have been ordered far enough in advance that it would be ready for use when the need arose. If not, then the decedent's body might have been set on a kline next to that of another member of the family or placed in a sarcophagus that had originally been intended for someone else.

Regardless of whether a tomb chamber with klinai or a sarcophagus had been chosen as the manner of burial, the decedent would have been brought to the tumulus in a wooden sarcophagus, no doubt elaborately decorated, within the context of a formal ekphora with mourners and family members. The ekphora probably departed from the manor house of the estate where the tumulus was located, rather than from a city or town. The sarcophagus was moved in a two-wheeled chariot and concealed by fabric hanging from the cart's baldacchino-type roof.[40] If a stone sarcophagus had been chosen for burial, it would no doubt already have been positioned within the tumulus so that the body could be easily shifted from the wooden box to the stone one.[41]

No eulogies for an aristocrat in Achaemenid Anatolia have survived, but the decorations of the tombs at Çan, Kızılbel, and Karaburun emphasize the importance of physical prowess in the hunt and on the battlefield, and both themes would surely have been stressed in the funeral speech honoring the male decedents (Fig. 6.2 and Plates 18–24). A memorial meal also occurred, with the pottery used during the dining smashed in front of the tomb so that it could not be reused.

Considering the presence of musical instruments in some of the tombs, such as Dedetepe and Dardanus, it seems certain that music formed part of the funeral service, possibly with dancing, after which the instruments were deposited in the tomb along with the other gifts.[42] Those gifts would have included alabastra tied with fillets freshly dyed in Tyrian purple, pyxides, mirrors, knives, aryballoi, and fans, among others. Heirloom jewelry was also included, as were sympotic silver vessel sets and sympotic furniture, of both wood and marble, which evoked the setting of a dinner party within the tomb chamber.[43] Such an interior is beautifully illustrated by the Naip tomb on the northwest coast of the Marmara Sea, where the kline table was carved with relief reproductions of sympotic vessels, including plates, bowls, and salt cellars.[44]

Once the gifts had been set in place, the door of the tomb was sealed and/or the lid was lowered onto the sarcophagus. The funeral attendants dismantled the hearse and placed the wheels next to the tomb, then burned the wooden transport sarcophagi and left the charred wood *in situ*. The burial cavity was subsequently filled and the tumulus crowned by the terminal stone. Despite the high level of Achaemenid influence on the objects produced for the elite of Hellespontine Phrygia, there is no evidence for an adoption of Achaemenid burial customs, wherein the body was exposed and picked clean of flesh prior to burial.[45]

THE RESIDENCE OF THE TUMULI BUILDERS

The most pressing question still outstanding is where the aristocrats who commissioned these tumuli actually lived. Surveys of the area in 2004 and 2005, which utilized both surface collection and remote sensing, have finally suggested an answer. Between 1 and 2 km northwest of Dedetepe is a site known locally as Tepeağıl Tepe or Rüzgarlı Tepe, a long irregularly shaped mound encompassing nearly 15,400 m² (Plate 13).[46] The surface of the mound is covered with pottery and tiles, as were the adjacent fields, and magnetic prospection revealed the existence of walls beneath the central part of the mound.[47] The surface pottery consisted of a range of fine ware imports and suggests a short habitation from the Late Archaic period to the Early Hellenistic period, with no discernible pottery dating thereafter. All of the evidence points to this mound as the site of the elite residence in use at the time in which the tumuli at Kızöldün and Dedetepe were constructed.

Our best information regarding the appearance of these estates comes from Xenophon, who describes his attack on one such estate in the vicinity of Pergamon.[48] The fortifications were reportedly very high and extremely strong, with the walls of the towers eight bricks thick. Xenophon attacked the estate with three hundred soldiers, but nearly a thousand Persian-affiliated troops from regional fortresses came to offer protection, including many who were mercenaries in the service of the king. In the course of the raid the Greeks captured two hundred slaves, which was clearly only a part of the total. Although not all of the estates would have been this well defended, the Xenophon passage gives one a good sense of the number of personnel, both service and mercenary, who could be attached to the landowners.

An inscription from Didyma describes another such estate that was sold by Antiochus II to his divorced wife Laodice in 254/3 B.C.[49]

> We have sold to Laodice Pannukome and the manor-house and the land belonging to the village, bounded by the land of Zeleia and by that of Cyzicus and by the old road which used to run above Pannukome, but which has been plowed up by the neighboring farmers so that they might take the place for themselves…and any hamlets there may be in the land, and the folk who live there with their households and all their property…

The borders of the land are then described separately:

> from the east, from the land of Zeleia which adjoins the land of Cyzicus, the ancient royal road which runs to Pannukome above the village and the manor-house…; from this to the altar of Zeus which lies above the manor-house and which is, like the tomb, on the right of the road; from the tomb the royal road itself which leads through the Eupannese to the river Aesepus.

In this particular instance, the estate consists of a manor house and village to which a group of serfs were attached, as well as two major roads, one of which, "the old royal road," presumably extended to the satrapal capital at Daskyleion. N. Sekunda has estimated the size of the estate at ca. 100 km², although the area in question can be fixed only approximately somewhere between Zeleia and Cyzicus, in the general vicinity of the Aesepus, and no secure measurement of the original size can be determined.[50]

Along the royal road was an altar of Zeus – conspicuous enough to be mentioned and therefore probably of considerable size – and a *mneme*, or tumulus, which indicates the prominence that these mounds were accorded. Scattered throughout this area, according to Xenophon, were the *paradeisoi*, or aristocratic hunting grounds, although the only one that appears to have survived in the modern landscape is the Kuş Cenneti on Lake Manyas, near Daskyleion, which is now a wildlife preserve.[51]

The level of wealth attested by the tumuli along the Granicus River is not easily paralleled at the other coastal sites in the Troad during the same period. During the Persian Wars, and for half a century thereafter, the Aegean trade network that had been in place since the beginning of the Archaic period gradually disintegrated as control of the western Troad shifted *seriatim* from Persia to Mytilene to Athens.[52] Ilion was nearly uninhabited, as far as we can tell, although offerings continued to be made in the Sanctuary of Athena by visitors to the site.[53] No new urban projects are in evidence at Cyzicus, Lampsacus, or Assos, nor is it certain that any of these sites was striking coins during the first half of the fifth century B.C. The Athenian colony at Sigeion is probably the only site that grew more powerful, in tandem with the expansion of the Delian League into northwestern Turkey, although this has yet to be attested by excavation.

SIX

THE TOMBS OF THE GRANICUS RIVER VALLEY IV: THE ÇAN SARCOPHAGUS

During the period in which the Kızöldün and Dedetepe tombs were constructed, the Persians' control of most of the Troad was secure and the trade networks between the Aegean and inner Anatolia remained relatively intact.[1] During the second half of the fifth century, however, that stability became fragmented, at least in northwestern Asia Minor. The majority of the Troad and Hellespontine cities became members of the Delian League, including such Persian strongholds as Daskyleion and Zeleia, and power in the region shifted among Athens, Mytilene, and Persia during the remainder of the century. Defections from the Delian League steadily increased with the escalation of the Peloponnesian War, the final episode of which was played out at the Battle at Aegospotami, not far from Ilion, where the Spartans ultimately triumphed over Athens.[2]

The Spartans had succeeded in part due to their alliance with the Persians, who now regained most of the Troad, although the local satrap delegated control of the western half of his district to Zenis of Dardanus and his wife Mania, who stored their treasure in the mountain strongholds of Gergis, Cebren, and Scepsis (Plate 11).[3] Athenian control resumed for a brief period between 394 and 386, with Byzantium and the Hellespontine cities now forming part of their new naval league, but Persia continued to control most of the Troad until the Battle of Granicus in 334.

Considering the extent of the armed conflict and economic upheaval during the second half of the fifth century, it is not surprising that so few buildings

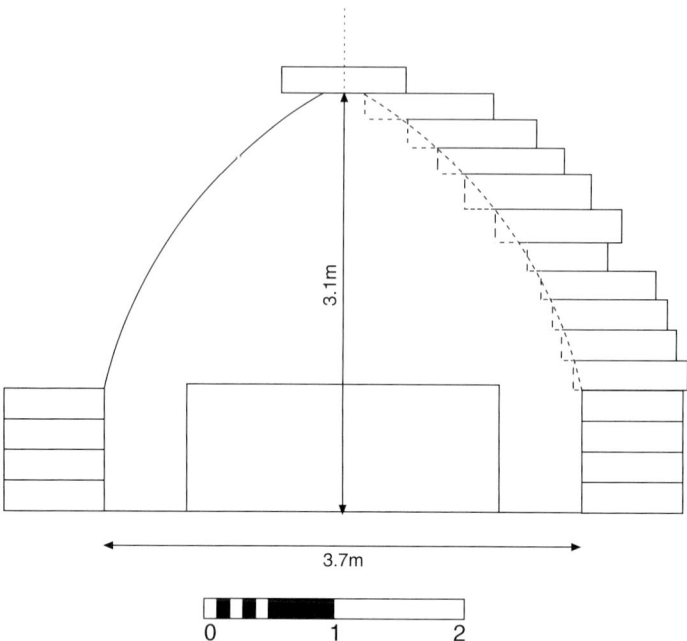

6.1. The reconstructed tomb chamber of the Çan tumulus, prepared by John Wallrodt for the Troy Excavation Project.

or monuments can be dated to that period, and artistic production would not resume in force until after the Peloponnesian War.[4] Within the Troad itself, the first work of sculpture from this period for which we have evidence is yet another sarcophagus, this time from the region of Çan, ca. 25 km to the south of the tumuli at Kızöldün and Dedetepe (Plate 17).[5] The reliefs that adorn this sarcophagus provide an unusually vivid evocation of the lifestyle of these Persian-affiliated landowners, and the tomb is surely one of many that still lie unexcavated.

Like the other tombs, the tumulus that held the Çan Sarcophagus was the target of plundering. In November 1998, looters used a backhoe to break into the tumulus, which is situated near the village of Altıkulaç 10 km to the northeast of Çan. The robbers were digging blindly, since there was no way to know what the tumulus contained, and their backhoe demolished the tomb chamber and damaged the left side of the marble sarcophagus within it (Figs. 6.1 and 6.2).

This sarcophagus, even in its damaged state, is an extraordinary find: the body is decorated with two relief scenes of hunting and battle, both of which had been brightly painted (Fig. 6.2 and Plates 18–24). Even though most of the relief surface was covered with a layer of mud at the time of the looting, it would have been clear that the sarcophagus was carved. Recognizing the potential value of the discovery, the looters dragged the sarcophagus out of the

6.2. The sarcophagus from the tomb chamber at Çan. The backhoe used by the looters smashed the left side of the sarcophagus, which was subsequently restored. Çanakkale Archaeological Museum. Photo by the author.

tumulus and transported it 5 km to the north, where they abandoned it in a forest. Why the sarcophagus was abandoned is unclear, but it was rediscovered and transported one week later to the Çanakkale Museum, where the painted reliefs were conserved with assistance from the Troy project under the general supervision of Donna Strahan. Amazingly, nearly all of the paint on the relief surface remained intact during this process. Most of the binding agent had dissipated over time, which meant that the pigment adhered more closely to the soil rather than to the stone surface; if the looters or the police had brushed the earth from the reliefs during discovery or transport, the paint would have quickly flaked off.

The 1998 looting was not the first assault on the tumulus. The sarcophagus had been robbed at some point in the Roman period, at which time the looters dislodged stones from the wall to create an opening into the chamber. This weakened the structure of the tomb and the vault eventually collapsed, although the general form of the tumulus remained intact. During the Late Byzantine period the top of the tumulus was used as a cemetery, and the graves fell into the tomb chamber when the looters began digging with their backhoe.

Only the foundations and the lowest course of the tomb chamber survive *in situ*, but its original form is clear (Fig. 6.1). The building consisted of a single circular corbel-vaulted chamber with a tamped earthen floor and an entrance at the east. The interior diameter of the tomb chamber is 3.70 m, which is only 1.30 m larger than the length of the sarcophagus, so there was a very limited amount of space within the tomb. Several of the Late Classical tombs in Thrace also have a beehive shape but they normally have a larger diameter, with a central column or relieving arches to support the vault.[6] The blocks used to construct the wall were of soft sandstone and featured drafted margins, while andesite-like stone was utilized for the roof.[7] Marble was employed only for the sarcophagus, which contained the body of an adult male of considerable strength whose left arm and leg had been broken, perhaps during a fall from his horse, as I will discuss below.

The style of the Çan Sarcophagus points to a date in the first quarter of the fourth century B.C., making it slightly more than a century later than the Polyxena Sarcophagus.[8] It has a length of 2.41 m, a width of 0.95 m, and a height of 0.85 m, which creates a ratio of 2.5:1 for length to width and 3:1 for length to height.[9] The lid is pitched, as was the case with the earlier sarcophagi from the Kızöldün tumulus, but the articulation consists only of three evenly spaced bars carved laterally across the lid (Plate 18).[10] It is somewhat surprising to find no architectural ornament on the body or lid, considering the elaborate decoration on the Polyxena Sarcophagus;[11] equally unusual is the inclusion of reliefs on only two sides, since the other examples from Lycia, Sidon, and Cyprus contained figural decoration on each face.

THE HUNTING SCENES

The front of the sarcophagus consists of two different scenes, a boar hunt at the right and a stag hunt at the left, with a tree in the center of the panel serving as a divider between the two (Plates 18–22).[12] The tree is leafless, as on the Polyxena Sarcophagus (Figs. 3.11 and 3.12), which was the favored scheme in figural arts of the fifth and fourth centuries B.C. The boar hunt is the better preserved of the two scenes, and features a single horseman galloping toward the right as two dogs attack the back and chest of a lone boar (Plates 19–21).[13] The boar rears up on its hind legs, as does the horse and one of the dogs, while the rider spears the boar between the eyes.[14]

The background of this hunt is painted green, which gives the impression that the scene is taking place in a wooded area. This conforms to the description of such hunts by Xenophon, who noted that boars usually lived in well-wooded areas because they were warm in winter and cool in summer.[15] Xenophon also commented on the number of *paradeisoi*, or hunting preserves, in the area of Daskyleion, and the hunt represented here may have occurred in one of them.[16]

The head and right hand of the hunter were damaged by both ancient and modern robbery attempts, but the lower part of the face is well preserved (Plate 20). Long red hair falls upon his shoulders, and his lips have been painted red. He wears a long-sleeved, ochre-colored tunic with *anaxyrides*, red shoes, and a purple-sleeved cloak or *kandys* around his neck, the ochre border of which indicates fur trim.[17] The back of the tiara hangs loose on his shoulder, and the side flaps have been drawn toward the chin but not tied beneath it, as in dynastic portraiture on Lycian coinage.[18] Tied to his belt is a Persian scabbard, or *akinakes*, held in place by two straps.[19]

The hunter holds a spear in his raised right arm, while his left hand clutches the reins at the base of the horse's neck.[20] The reconstruction of the spear is somewhat problematic. There is a distinct flat-chiseled line extending from the rider's hand to the boar's eye that clearly marks the spear's position, but the tip no longer survives. It looks as if the boar's head and the spear's tip were initially roughed out by the sculptor, who subsequently realized that the head was too large for the body. The boar's profile was then cut back slightly from the original line, which simultaneously erased the spear point. Carving a new spear point in the retooled area would have been impossible, because it would have involved a very deep cut into the marble. To resolve this, the sculptor lowered the relief of the shaft as it approaches the boar, which gives the impression that the spear is moving into the background and striking the boar's right eye.[21]

The hunter's horse is male, like the other animals on the sarcophagus, and has been presented with an ochre-colored body and red hooves. Its tail has been twisted, tied in a knot, and held in place by a red ribbon, the ends of which dangle below the knot.[22] The top of the mane appears to be gathered together and tied by another red ribbon; the remainder has been cut short and straight into what has been dubbed the "Lycian crewcut," which commonly adorns horses in so many Lycian monuments.[23] The horse is draped with a Persian ochre-colored saddle blanket that is trimmed with a thick red band and a side border of stepped half-merlons.[24]

The two dogs are painted in ochre as well and appear to be of the Laconian type. The one at the left claws and bites into the chest of the rearing boar from below, while the other has leaped onto his back and bites his shoulder just below the upper part of the mane (Plate 21).[25] The incisions on the dogs' ribs and the pronounced veins on their legs heighten our sense of their aggression and lend greater force to the narrative, as do the boar's wide-open mouth flanked by deep furrows, the large circular eyes, incisions on the forehead, and tensed muscles on shoulders and thigh.

The boar seems to look directly at the horse, and the two creatures' hooves nearly touch. The boar's body is painted purple with shading used to indicate the musculature, and one is immediately struck by its enormous size. Although the depictions of boars on works of art created in Asia Minor tend to be shown larger than those of Greece, no other monument features a boar of such massive proportions.[26] His long, drooping foreskin also contrasts sharply with the short and taut foreskins of all of the horses depicted, thereby making his gender more prominent than that of any of the other animals on the sarcophagus.[27]

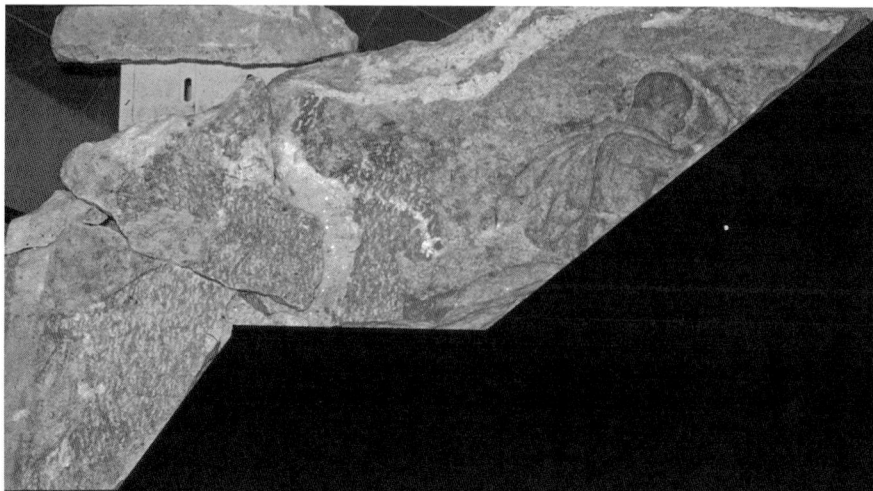

6.3. The broken section of the stag hunt showing two riders; the one at the left has been erased. Çanakkale Archaeological Museum. Troy Excavation Project photo.

Although the looters damaged the left half of the sarcophagus, there was clearly a second hunting scene on the opposite side of the tree featuring two riders on horseback and two diminutive stags moving toward the right (Fig. 6.3, Plates 18 and 22). The stag farthest to the right is positioned on the ground line and looks back toward the riders, while part of the second stag has been carved below the line and under the horse of the second rider. The two scenes have been distinguished by color: the background of the boar hunt was painted green, whereas that of the stag hunt is rendered in blue; the central tree therefore marks the border between two different locales as well as two different activities.[28]

The legs of the horseman at the right have been destroyed, but his torso and head are essentially intact. He holds a spear in front of him, with the top extending over his head and the point aimed toward the head of the stag by the tree. Billowing out behind him is a light ochre-colored cloak worn over a long-sleeved red tunic. Covering his chest is an ochre-colored breastplate that was probably fashioned of leather and secured by a belt.[29]

This rider's head is the better preserved of the two horsemen on this side of the sarcophagus, and features a bulbous nose, thick lips, a short unpainted goatee, and an incised line crossing the forehead (Plate 22). Unlike the goatee, the scalp hair is painted red, delineated by a series of vertical incisions, and cropped at the nape of the neck. The facial features are more highly individualized than those on any of the other heads on the sarcophagus, and it looks as if the sculptor intended to represent a specific person; in other words, to produce a portrait.

The early development of portraiture has consistently been associated with western Asia Minor during the Late Classical period, when the Çan

Sarcophagus was carved, primarily because this was the time when local mints began to produce coins with individualized portraits linked to the names of dynasts and satraps.[30] The die-cutters used a variety of techniques to add greater specificity to these images, including aquiline noses, thick lips, pointed beards, forehead creases, and receding hairlines. The rider on our sarcophagus appears to be yet another example of this trend toward greater individualization.[31]

Situated behind this horseman was a second equestrian figure, although much of it has been cut away from the relief surface, and all that remains is a point-chiseled shadow of the original image (Fig. 6.3, Plate 18). Nevertheless, the outline of the figure is still discernible, and the composition appears to have been the same as the rider just described, including targeted spear and billowing cloak. The back legs of the horse were pressed against the ground line and its tail was tied with red ribbons, like the other horses on this side.

The presence of a second rider in this scene is logical, since two stags are targeted for the hunt, but there is no easy explanation as to why this second horseman was removed. The only part of the figure that was not chiseled away is the beribboned tail of the horse, on which red paint is still preserved. This is a particularly important detail, in that the presence of paint indicates that the figure was carved and finished *before* it was removed. If there had been a structural flaw in the marble or if the sculptor had made an error during the carving, then work on the figure would surely have been halted prior to painting. By the same token, if the sculptor regarded the rider as an unsatisfactory element in the composition, it is likely that he would have realized this prior to completion. In fact, the removal of the rider unbalanced the composition since the two stags were now linked to only one equestrian.[32]

This second horseman appears to have been removed as an act of deliberate defacement, which would probably have involved the following scenario: the mutilated rider was originally intended to represent a specific person, presumably an associate of the decedent, whose identity was signaled by a portrait type as individualized as that of the first rider. After his portrait had been carved on the sarcophagus, the associate committed some egregious offense that prompted the erasure of his image. The sculptor could have made it appear as if no figure had been present by using the flat chisel to make the surface even with the background, but he instead left a rough, point-chiseled shadow of the erased figure, thereby deliberately highlighting the defacement. From what we can gather, these completed sarcophagi were carved well in advance of one's death and exhibited in the home of the man or woman who commissioned them. In this particular case, then, the reliefs would have functioned in an encomiastic and admonitory capacity simultaneously.[33]

This is an extraordinary discovery, since only a few examples of such sculptural defacement are known in Greece or Asia Minor prior to the Roman period.[34] In the Near East, however, there is evidence for such iconoclasm, especially in Assyria and Persia, and considering the extent of Persian influence on the iconographic program of the sarcophagus, it seems likely that the idea behind the defacement stems from the Near Eastern rather than the Greek tradition.[35] Iconoclasm is, of course, a by-product of the development of individualized portraiture, and its appearance in a biographical narrative such as this is not really surprising, although no contemporary parallels have been discovered.

THE BATTLE SCENE

As one turns to the short side of the sarcophagus, the iconography shifts from hunting to battle, with three characters moving against a painted blue background. The central figure is on horseback and spears a fallen opponent at the right, while the rider's henchman stands by at the left (Plates 18, 23, and 24).[36] This is the scene that one would have viewed when standing at the entrance of the tomb chamber, and its format recalls two other roughly contemporary funerary monuments: the Dexileos Relief in Athens and the Yalnızdam Stele in Lycia.[37]

The rider's costume is unprecedented in monumental art: a long-sleeved pink tunic is worn under a red cuirass with large shoulder pieces that extend as far as his elbow (Plate 24). The cuirass was probably made of leather, and the tall head-guard at the back may have had a frame of wickerwork to keep it in place, as in Persian shield design.[38] A red helmet, also probably representing leather, has a flat crown and completely covers the top, back, and sides of his head. An unpainted *akinakes* has been hung from the white belt of his cuirass, and he wears greaves and white shoes.

This type of armor is not featured on any of the Lycian tombs nor on any other monumental reliefs from Asia Minor, although it does appear in battle scenes on contemporary Graeco-Persian gems that date to approximately the same time as the Çan Sarcophagus.[39] Here too the design seems to have been partly influenced by Persian models. A cylinder seal from the Treasury at Persepolis, dated 470/69 B.C., depicts a warrior whose cuirass contains the same kind of head guard, although without the shoulder pieces, and the warrior lifts his spear in the same manner as the Çan rider.[40]

The rider grasps the reins in his left hand, while the right holds aloft a long spear that overlaps the upper border and runs into the fallen opponent's eye. The horse is shown in the same basic pose as those in the hunting scenes: rearing up on its hind legs and pushing with its front hooves the fallen opponent at the right. Its mane has been cut short and straight, while its tail has been twisted, tied into a knot at the end, and decorated with a red ribbon, as in the hunting scene. The horse's frontlet (*prometopidion*), shown as a single piece tied to the bridle, is larger than other known examples in that it encircles the eyes and covers both nose and forehead.[41] The ochre-colored saddle blanket has a border of stepped half-merlons at the left side, which is again reminiscent of the one depicted in the hunting scene.

The right half of the scene is occupied by a very pictorial landscape. A rocky outcropping painted in ochre features a series of curving lines that echo the form of the shields held by the other characters in this scene, and the rocks rise nearly to the top of the panel (Plate 23). Growing on the rocks at various heights are three trees with long curvilinear branches, the highest of which extend as far as the top and right edges of the sarcophagus. Perched on one of the highest branches, and carved almost totally on the upper border, is a falcon that watches the battle. Such an elaborate landscape setting is difficult to parallel in the sculpture of this period, and the Çan sculptors were probably influenced by pictorial models, some of which may have hung in the satrap's palace at Daskyleion.[42]

Sprawled on the rocks is the rider's opponent, wearing a long-sleeved white tunic but no greaves or shoes. He attempts to pull his sword from the scabbard and grasps the central handles of a rather small circular shield that he seems to be using to steady himself. Blood drips from his left knee and right foot as a result of the horse having pushed him onto the rocks.[43] His head is in three-quarter view and turned toward the rider, and the spear point grazes his right eye. His wavy hair, moustache, and bushy beard are all painted reddish-brown, and a white fillet is tied around the top of his forehead. The fillet probably marked the opponent as a Greek, and the dramatic contrast in costume and pose between rider and opponent seems to have been intended to emphasize the difference in ethnicity.[44]

The soldier standing at the left is partly concealed by the rider's horse, but his position, stance, and costume show him to be the rider's henchman. He is wearing a long-sleeved white tunic, red pants, and white shoes, and his curly hair, moustache, and full beard are painted red. In his raised left hand he holds a small round shield and two spears, while grasping a curving sword, or *macheira*.[45] The angle at which he holds the spears is parallel to the spear of the rider, thereby effectively creating a frame around the rider's head and torso.

The iconography of the henchman is unusual in several respects. Both he and his fallen Greek opponent are presented in three-quarter view, with similar hair and beards painted the same color. They also wear the same type of scabbard strap and carry identical shields. The long pants worn by the henchman clearly indicate that he fights on the Anatolian side, as does his display of replacement spears for the rider, yet the artist has gone out of his way to show that the soldier carries a sword different from that of the rider. The iconographic assemblage suggests that he is a Greek mercenary in the pay of the rider, who was almost certainly the local dynast who commissioned the sarcophagus.[46] Such mercenaries were, of course, commonplace at this time, and his inclusion here would have served as an additional manifestation of the dynast's wealth and power.[47]

Several unusual features in the battle scene point to its dependence on hunting iconography. Greek and Anatolian battle scenes always featured the hoplite shield, in which the arm passed through a *porpax*, or strap, in the center and grasped handles along the inner rim.[48] The small round shields with central handles used at Çan are rarely found in Archaic and Classical art, and when they do occur, it is in hunting scenes.

The pose and attributes of the henchman also derive from the hunt, and here we can turn to Xenophon for assistance. In describing the young men who accompany the Persian king on hunting expeditions, Xenophon reports that "they carry a light shield (*gerron*) and two spears, one to throw, the other to use in case of necessity in a hand-to-hand encounter."[49] This description conforms closely to the iconography of the Çan soldier, and a similar figure appears in a boar hunt on the grave stele found near Daskyleion, probably made at about the same time as the Çan Sarcophagus.[50] Such spear-bearing attendants are not featured in the surviving battle scenes from this period, and it looks as if the artist has simply modified a hunting figure for the battle.

The bird is also not a common element in either type of scene, although it appears occasionally in hunts near the speared animal.[51] The final link to the hunt is the manner in which the fallen Greek is being speared. In Classical and Hellenistic battle scenes, opponents were speared in a variety of places, but never in or between the eyes, whereas in boar hunts it was relatively common.[52] The artist's double use of the "speared-eye" motif effectively connects the two sides of the sarcophagus and establishes a link between the riders' two foes, human and animal.[53] In a sense, this linkage is reminiscent of the Polyxena Sarcophagus, which featured an iconographic conflation of human and animal sacrifice; here, however, the blurred line between hunt and battle was clearly intended to establish the prowess of the rider in both arenas.

BIOGRAPHICAL NARRATIVES

The Çan Sarcophagus can be assigned to a corpus of monuments that featured a biographical narrative of the decedent's life, most of which were created in western Asia Minor during the Late Classical period. All of the monuments are tombs, prepared while the dynast was still living, and the iconography ultimately derives from a long tradition of royal iconography in the Near East. The themes of hunt and battle consistently appeared together on these monuments, and the artists employed a variety of devices – costume, hairstyle, attributes – to indicate that the man who emerged victorious in battle was the same one who exhibited bravery in the hunt.[54]

Comparing the faces of the two principal figures on the Çan Sarcophagus is difficult since the upper section of the boar hunter's face was broken off during the robbery, while much of the warrior's face is covered by his armor. But in light of the popularity of biographical narratives in Anatolian funerary monuments of early fourth-century B.C. date, it seems virtually certain that the dynast who commissioned the Çan Sarcophagus appeared in both hunting and battle scenes. In other words, the cuirassed rider and boar hunter should represent the same man. To fortify the link between the two sides, the designers have maintained a similar rhythm in all three scenes: the horses and riders are posed in identical fashion, and the oblique angles of the spears in the hunt are picked up again by the spears in the battle (Plate 18).

If we combine the iconographic analysis with the proposed date of the sarcophagus, then we have evidence for an Anatolian dynast from the western part of Hellespontine Phrygia fighting a Greek in or around the first quarter of the fourth century B.C.[55] The unusual tree-laden, rocky landscape is very similar to the area around Çan, which is both wooded and mountainous, and the battle in question may have occurred in the vicinity.[56] During this period there were continual battles between Greek cities and Persian satraps, but the most devastating one within this area took place in 395 B.C., when the Spartan commander Agesilaos ravaged the region around the satrapal capital of Daskyleion and destroyed both villages and *paradeisoi*.[57] It is conceivable that the sarcophagus scene refers to that time, although Pharnabazos, the satrap of Daskyleion, also led his army into other areas of western Asia Minor, and the Çan dynast probably fought along with him.[58]

This is one of the few cases in which the bones of the decedent can be compared with the iconography on the exterior to see whether the two tell the same story. A large number of the decedent's bones were retrieved from the sarcophagus, and subsequent analysis by Henrieke Kiesewetter has revealed a wealth of information about his life and physical condition (Fig. 6.4). The bones belong to a young adult male of considerable strength, between 1.70 and 1.75 m in height, who died between the ages of twenty-five and twenty-eight. There are no signs of long-term malnutrition or hard physical work, although he apparently suffered from an infectious disease during his early childhood.[59] He experienced a devastating fall from a considerable height and sustained serious injuries: a broken arm and thigh, dislocated hip, fractured rib, and crushed vertebrae.

At the time of the accident, his recovery would have been in doubt: the blood vessels would have ruptured, and blood entering the fracture regions would have formed hematomas. The man remained alive for several years, although the thigh and arm healed in a misaligned position, and the arthritis that he subsequently contracted left him physically incapacitated for the rest of his life. Work on the sarcophagus undoubtedly began shortly after the injury and would probably have been completed well in advance of his death.

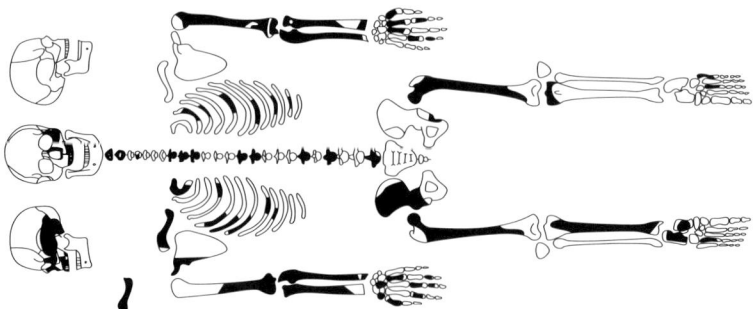

6.4. The skeleton within the Çan Sarcophagus. The surviving bones are in black. Drawing by Kate Clayton, based on an original by Henrieke Kiesewetter for the Troy Excavation Project.

The injury was probably caused by a fall from his horse, and the condition of the left arm suggests that it occurred during battle rather than hunting. Although the left humerus was broken, the left forearm shows no signs of injury, which would have been the case if a shield had been attached to the arm. The fracture of the humerus must have been caused by extreme torsion; in other words, the lower part of the arm was fixed while the upper part rotated in the course of the fall, and the shield or hand may have gotten caught in the reins.

Although there is no conclusive proof, it is tempting to posit that the injuries sustained by the man were caused during the combat depicted on the sarcophagus. As such, it would appear that victory over his opponent was not as triumphant as the iconography would lead us to believe. Indeed, he might well have lost the fight, although the reverse situation would have been presented on the sarcophagus since his family was paying the bills for its completion.

If this scenario is correct, then the sarcophagus would have been visually accessible during the course of several years, and it was probably viewed through a variety of lenses given the region's range of ethnicities and convergent iconographic traditions. Those familiar with illustrations of the *Odyssey* would have linked the speared-eye motif with the Blinding of Polyphemus, thereby applying a Homeric gloss to the scene and casting the cuirassed rider as a latter-day Odysseus.[60] Viewers who had traveled to Athens and Lycia and had examined the Dexileos and Yalnızdam monuments would have seen the sarcophagus as yet another example of an increasingly popular funerary format.[61] Perhaps most startling would have been the *damnatio* in the stag hunt, since the custom was so rare in northwestern Asia Minor, although Persians who had read the inscription of Darius I at Behistun would have known something of iconoclasm and mutilation of the enemy.[62]

The most striking aspect of the reliefs is the sharp intersection of hunting and battle iconography. Blurring the line between human and animal lends greater potency to the exposition of victory in that the prey is stripped of his humanity in order to heighten the viewer's assessment of the victor's achievement. The juxtaposition of hunting and battle scenes is particularly characteristic of Achaemenid Anatolia and the period immediately thereafter, with the Nereid monument at Xanthos and the Alexander Sarcophagus functioning as two of the most prominent examples, nor would it fall from favor in subsequent historical periods. Roman imperial sarcophagi, of course, are a case in point, and even on the eleventh-century A.D. Bayeux Tapestry one can find scenes of the hunt and preparation for battle linked within a single panel.[63]

THE SCULPTURAL WORKSHOP

Although the Çan Sarcophagus now strikes us as a unique product, it is probably only one of many that still lie buried in the hundreds of tumuli that encompass the Troad. Like the tombs at Kızöldün and Dedetepe, the marble for the sarcophagus came from Proconnesus, which had attained a high level of prosperity in the fifth and early fourth centuries B.C. (Plate 11). The island's contribution to the Delian League was assessed at three talents, and the statue of their principal goddess, the Dindymene Mother, was chryselephantine. Although Cyzicus would seize control of the island around 360 B.C., the marble quarries and their workshops were probably independent enterprises at the time in which the Çan Sarcophagus was carved.[64]

The accomplishments of the Proconnesian sculptors in antiquity are well known, but the Çan Sarcophagus demonstrates the skills of the painters tied to the workshops, as well as the range of colors at their disposal. Analysis of the pigments indicates the presence of malachite, occasionally mixed with lead white, vermilion, ochre, and Egyptian blue.[65] The painters alternated the color of the horses (ochre/pink) and the backgrounds (blue/green/blue) to suggest shifting locales and a heightened level of action. But what is truly remarkable is their use of shading, which appears on the trees, on the body of the boar, and on the boar hunter's cloak. The systematic development of shading is typically assigned to the late fifth century B.C., when it began to be employed in vase painting; until now, no evidence existed for its appearance in large-scale sculpture or painting prior to the second half of the fourth century B.C.[66] The Çan Sarcophagus validates the assumption that shadow contouring was already being utilized in monumental sculpture in the years around 400 B.C.

A number of sculptors must have worked on the sarcophagus, and, in general, the quality of carving on the front is better than that on the side: the figures are more carefully finished with the flat chisel and the edges are much crisper. This can be seen in particular when comparing such details as the tails of the horses, the branches of the trees, and the modeling of the animals' bodies. Nevertheless, the three-quarter views and anatomical foreshortening employed in the battle scene, combined with the highly pictorial landscape, indicate a high level of carving on this side as well.

The sculptural workshops on Proconnesus continued to operate until the Late Roman period, but the erection of monumental tumuli such as the one near Çan ceased after the Battle of Granicus in 334, even though they continued to be built in Thrace.[67] In the wake of that battle, which signaled the end of Persian domination in the Troad, the old estates began to break up and the surviving family members moved away. The description of one of these estates survives in a letter of Antiochus II from 254/3 B.C., and the disintegrating state of affairs is clear: the serfs who were tied to the estate had abandoned it, and one of the major avenues of approach had been plowed.[68]

That abandonment was probably accompanied by widespread looting, especially of the tumuli. While the estates were occupied, the tombs would have been well guarded, but they would have become easy and attractive targets once Persian control evaporated, and they were probably plundered continually throughout the Hellenistic and Roman periods.[69] Recent ceramic surveys of the region tell the same story: most of the areas were deserted in the last quarter of the fourth century B.C. in favor of the newly established coastal cities, and the population would not return in force until earthquakes and disease in the Late Roman period rendered the interior, once again, far more desirable than any of the cities on the coast.[70]

SEVEN

ILION, ATHENS, AND SIGEION DURING THE FIFTH AND FOURTH CENTURIES B.C.

One tends to regard the fifth century B.C. as a period of cultural and artistic excellence, and that was certainly true in Athens or the Persian satrapal capitals of Daskyleion, Sardis, and Kelainai, but one would have been hard-pressed to find anything even remotely analogous in the Greek cities of western Asia Minor, which are usually viewed as having been in the midst of a severe recession.[1] As control of the Troad shifted among Persia, Athens, and Mytilene, what had once been a stable system of supply and demand was shattered, leaving most of the coastal cities in such an impoverished state that we have little evidence for what life was like then.[2]

Ilion was certainly a case in point: habitation deposits dating to the fifth and early fourth centuries are extremely rare, which suggests that the site's population decreased dramatically during that period. A koinon or league of Troad cities was not yet in place, so the settlement was presumably supervised by the priests of the Athena Sanctuary, who probably numbered no more than a handful. Ironically, this sharp drop in the settlement's prosperity was accompanied by an increase in the recognition and exploitation of the site's Homeric foundations. The agents involved in that exploitation were drawn from a broad geographic area: Persia, Sparta, Athens, and Macedonia were all involved, and many of them made pilgrimages to the site even though there would have been few residents there to receive them. It is, in fact, this skeleton community that is so interesting in the context of Ilion's evolving identity, because it suggests that the promulgation of the site as the legendary Troy was now being driven by agents outside the settlement. As a consequence, the site's identity became unusually pliable due to the variety of political stages on which Ilion now found itself a player.

XERXES IN THE TROAD

The first of these stages involved the Persian king Xerxes, who visited the site with his army in 480 B.C. during his campaign against Greece. According to Herodotus, he "ascended to the citadel of Priam, having a desire to view it, and having viewed and inquired of all that was there, he sacrificed 1,000 oxen to Athena Ilias, while the Magi offered libations to the heroes."[3] This marked the inauguration of a long line of royal visits to Ilion that would extend throughout antiquity, and it demonstrates that the site could be just as captivating to the Persians as it had been to the Greeks.

We can reconstruct the basic features that Xerxes would have seen: the ruined Late Bronze Age fortifications, which had already been publicized as Priam's citadel during the Archaic period; the small temple of Athena with its relics of the Trojan War, including armor; and the surrounding Homeric tumuli to which the Magi paid homage. Given the fact that many of the stone buildings at the site had been damaged in a recent earthquake of considerable severity, the site must have looked as if it had just experienced a war; in other words, it would, in effect, have been costumed as the ruined city of Priam.[4]

The most interesting comment of Herodotus concerns Xerxes' sacrifice of 1,000 oxen to Athena Ilias in an ostensible acknowledgment of the legendary foundations of the site. The actual motive was surely to secure meat for his army, and such massive sacrifices of oxen and other animals must have been the norm in most of the cities through which Xerxes marched.[5] Calculating the number of men who would have been fed by 1,000 oxen is no easy feat, nor do we have any way of knowing whether the number mentioned by Herodotus is reliable, since the trash pits that would have held the bones have never been found. But if we assume that 1,000 cattle would have produced 100,000 kg of meat, with 0.3 kg (slightly more than 0.5 lb) per person, then more than 440,000 men could have been fed. The conditions must have been less than sanitary, and it is not surprising that some of the soldiers became ill with dysentery and ultimately died.[6] Others lost their lives during a storm at the base of Mt. Ida, and replacements were probably drawn from towns in the region, including Ilion.[7]

The loss of oxen would not have been the only impact on the area. The two pontoon bridges constructed by Xerxes across the Hellespont, probably between the towns of Abydos and Sestos, prompted one of the most extensive public works projects that the Troad had ever witnessed. According to Herodotus, 674 ships – both penteconters and triremes – were used to create

7.1. Stamp seal from Ilion with an intaglio of Ahuramazda, from sector F28, Lower City. Troy Excavation Project photo.

a two-lane bridge 1.5 km long, each of which was constructed of wooden planks that were probably more than 3.5 m wide. Twelve cables, each 1,500 m long, also formed part of the design, as did more than 1,300 anchors.[8]

Herodotus notes that Xerxes ordered his subject states in the area to provide the necessary ships and equipment, but a vast number of trees had to be felled, shipped, cut, and shaped into planks for the roadways, while large amounts of fiber had to be spun and twisted to make the cables, which meant that most of the spinning equipment in the region would have been pressed into service.[9] All of this would have occurred only one or two decades after a crippling earthquake, if we are interpreting the evidence from Assos correctly.[10]

These arrangements would also have required careful and systematic administration, especially in the areas where the pontoon bridge was erected, and two potential components of that system have been unearthed. One is a stone stamp seal from Ilion of oval conoid shape with an intaglio of Ahuramazda (Fig. 7.1).[11] It was found out of context in the Lower City but the style suggests a date in the early fifth century B.C., and it could easily be contemporary with Xerxes' march. The other discovery, a bronze lion weight with Aramaic inscription, was found near the eastern end of the pontoon bridge, at Abydos.[12] This too dates to the fifth century and may well be contemporary with the stamp seal from Ilion, although since both were found out of context and can be dated only generally by style, the attribution to Xerxes should be regarded merely as a possibility.[13]

The decimation of the region's livestock and agricultural surplus in 480 coupled with the drafting of its men for Xerxes' army would have been devastating, but more serious would have been the disruption of the region's delicate economy involving trade, tribute, and aristocratic support for local production, all of which were linked to Persian control of the Troad.[14] With the dissolution of this network and no subsequent compensatory replacement, there was no longer a viable foundation to sustain the local economy, and the powers that subsequently took control of the area were unable to restore the balance.

ATHENS IN THE TROAD/TROY IN ATHENS

It looks as if Ilion was controlled by Mytilene during the fifty-year period between the end of the Persian Wars and the island's takeover by Athens in 428, which is striking in itself.[15] This was the period in which Athens was emphasizing her pivotal role in the Trojan War and consequent claims to the Troad, so one might have expected Ilion to have been designated a protectorate of Sigeion, although there is no evidence for such a provision.[16] No changes in the region's administration appear to have occurred until 450 B.C., when Sigeion finally became a member of the Delian League. The Athenian decree that coincides with the year of Sigeion's entry highlights the town's desire for Athenian protection, presumably from Persia, as well as Athens' high regard for the town's residents, saluted as "*andres agathoi*" – a noteworthy adaptation of epic language.[17]

In 428, during the first phase of the Peloponnesian War, Athens took possession of all of its subject towns on the mainland, which included Ilion.[18] It is only at this point, in the 420s, that the archaeological record at Ilion demonstrates renewed activity. A small multiroom building was constructed at the southeast corner of the acropolis, on the site where the Bouleuterion would subsequently be erected.[19] Ceramics of late fifth-century date appear in the associated deposits, although on a very small scale, and two coins of late fifth/early fourth-century B.C. date have also been recovered: one from Tenedos, the other – of electrum – from the Ionian port of Phocaea.[20] Ilion's new membership in the Delian League would have required a building wherein administration could occur, and since the only real authority in Ilion at that time was the temple of Athena, the building should have been close to the temple precinct, which is the case for the multiroom structure. This building is, in fact, the only one of Classical date to have been uncovered thus far at Ilion, and it may be the "Prytaneion" to which several inscriptions at Ilion refer.[21]

By the second half of the fifth century, the majority of cities in the Troad were members of the Delian League, including such Persian strongholds as Daskyleion and Zeleia. In examining the list, Lampsacus and Cyzicus were assessed at the highest level – 12 and 9 talents, respectively; four cities (Abydos, Cebren, Proconnesus, and Tenedos) at 3 or 4 talents, three (Parium, Arisba, Ilion) at 2 talents, and two (Scepsis, Assos) at 1. This indicates the amount assessed, not what was actually paid, and the numbers should not necessarily be viewed as an index of economic power. Ilion, for example, may not have been able to manage any payment whatsoever.[22]

Not surprisingly, the allegedly pivotal role played by Athens in both the Ionian and Aeolian migrations became increasingly prominent as the fifth century B.C. progressed. The parentage of Ion, eponymous hero of Ionia, was continually reshaped until he emerged as a descendant of Apollo and Erechtheus, while Aeschylus has Athena essentially transfer her territories in the Troad to Athens in the *Eumenides*.[23] Another tradition maintained that as many as twelve cities in the Troad were actually founded by a son of Theseus named Acamas, although he reportedly allowed Ascanius and Scamandrius/Astyanax, the sons of Aeneas and Hector, respectively, to take the credit.[24]

Athens' increased promotion of its ties to the Homeric tradition coincided with a striking change in the iconographic configuration of the legendary Trojans. During the Archaic period, from Italy to the Aegean, the costume of the Trojans was virtually indistinguishable from that of the Greeks: both wore the same chitons, himations, and helmets, as well as the same basic hairstyle, and they worshipped the same gods.[25] After the conclusion of the Persian Wars, however, the Trojans began to be identified as people of the east in both word and image. The transformation had occurred in literature and civic spectacle at least by 456 B.C., when, in Athens, Aeschylus in the *Suppliants* described the Trojans as "Phrygians"; by the end of the fifth century B.C., Paris, Priam, and, on occasion, Troilus appeared in Athenian vase paintings in standard Persian costume with long trousers and tiaras (Fig. 7.2).[26] Blurring the distinction between Persians and Trojans simultaneously cast the allied Greek forces of the current wars in the role of their Homeric predecessors, with Athens as the leader. At the same time, the name "Troy" now acquired both Greek and Persian identities: those who had lived in the city during the Bronze Age were considered Asiatic, while the post–Bronze Age settlement belonged to an allied Hellenic society.[27]

All of this revisionism regarding Athenian involvement in the Trojan War was as prominent in the visual sphere as it had been in literature, especially on the Athenian Acropolis. As of the last quarter of the fifth century B.C., one of the most dazzling images adjacent to the Parthenon would have been a colossal bronze horse in the sanctuary of Artemis Brauronia.[28] Judging by the cuttings for the hooves, the horse must have been ca. 6 m tall – nearly two-thirds the height of the Parthenon's columns – and it was probably constructed ca. 420 B.C. around the conclusion of the first phase of the Peloponnesian War. Peering out of the horse, according to Pausanius, were four Greek soldiers, including Menestheus, Teucer, and two of the sons of Theseus, Damophon and Acamas.[29]

Although Pausanias provided no further description of the format, it seems likely that the four figures were positioned in trap doors in the sides, as they

7.2. Paris in Phrygian costume during the Judgment; Attic red-figure hydria, ca. 420–400 B.C. Karlsruhe, Badisches Landesmuseum. Photo courtesy Karlsruhe, Badisches Landesmuseum.

had appeared on Archaic and early Classical vases.[30] Only the foundations of the Brauronian precinct walls that would have framed the horse are preserved, but their width is slightly less than 0.60 m, which would suggest a wall hardly more than 3 m in height. If the horse had been situated near this wall, which seems likely, then the visitor passing the complex would have been able to see, above the wall, the horse's head and the men peering from the trap door, as in Polygnotos' painting of the same subject in the Knidian Lesche at Delphi (Plate 25).[31]

The precinct walls of the Brauronian sanctuary would therefore, at first glance, have suggested the walls of the Trojan citadel, a connection fortified by the Ilioupersis metopes on the north side of the Parthenon.[32] More significant, however, was the choice of men within the horse: other than the two sons of Theseus, the group included Menestheus, the king of Athens during the Trojan War, and Teucer, son of the king of Salamis, which had been an Athenian possession since the late sixth century B.C. Such a composition would have highlighted Athens' role in the Trojan conquest, thereby complementing the new literary accounts of the Aeolian Migration and lending greater credence to Athenian claims of primacy in the Troad.[33] The insertion of a Trojan horse in the shadow of the Parthenon would also have echoed

7.3. Athens, Propylaea, with remains of late Bronze Age fortification wall. Photo courtesy Jeffrey Hurwit.

the program of paintings in the Athenian Agora, where panels of Troy Taken and the Battle of Marathon were juxtaposed in the Stoa Poikile, and the entire scheme would have reinforced the news of Ilion's entry into the Delian League a few years earlier.[34]

There are two other noteworthy points of similarity between the acropolis of Athens and that of Ilion. Visitors to both sanctuaries would have been struck by the related design strategies employed for their monumental entrances: the ramp leading to the Athenaion at Ilion led the visitor past the monumental Late Bronze Age fortifications, and the same was true for the Propylaea on the Athenian acropolis, which was built against – and showcased – the remnants of a Bronze Age citadel wall (Fig. 7.3).[35] Both designs immediately engaged the viewer and advertised the illustrious ancestry of the city in question. In the case of Athens, though, such a proclamation also embellished the relatively insignificant role played by the city in the Homeric epics, as had their foundation of Sigeion within a distinctively Homeric landscape.

The second similarity involved ritual – specifically, the custom of the Locrian Maidens in Ilion and the office of the *arrhephoroi* on the Athenian acropolis, which is noteworthy in light of the increasingly stronger connections between Athens and Ilion.[36] In both precincts two young maidens would have lived on the acropolis for a year in the service of the goddess Athena, using subterranean passageways to exit the sanctuary by night.[37] There is, of course, no evidence that the two institutions were inaugurated at the same time or that one influenced the other, but visitors to the two sanctuaries, at least during the

Classical and Hellenistic periods, would undoubtedly have been struck by the correspondences between the two customs.

SPARTA, PERSIA, AND SIGEION IN LATE CLASSICAL ILION

The time at which Athenian control of Ilion ended is unclear, although it seems to have disintegrated by 411 B.C. when the Spartan admiral Mindarus sacrificed to Athena on the Ilion acropolis.[38] This was in the midst of the Peloponnesian War, which had enveloped the Hellespont by this point, and the two cities that had anchored Xerxes' pontoon bridge, Abydos and Sestos, were now controlled by Athens and Sparta, respectively.[39] Mindarus' speech at Ilion is not preserved, but one can imagine the inclusion of references to his kinsman, Menelaus, and the whole enterprise should probably be viewed as a Spartan attempt to co-opt the Homeric tradition, following the model set by Athens and Xerxes.

Defections from the Delian League steadily increased with the acceleration of the Peloponnesian War, the final phase of which was played out in northwestern Asia Minor. Attacks by both Spartan and Athenian commanders were waged on the Hellespontine and southern Marmara coasts, ending only in 405 with the battle at Aegospotami on the Gelibolu peninsula between Kallipolis and Sestos.[40] Several thousand Athenian sailors were executed at Abydos, and the coastal towns quickly fell to Sparta.

By the close of the fifth century B.C., Ilion and probably Sigeion as well formed part of a district controlled by a couple from Dardanos, Zenis and Mania, in the name of Pharnabazos, satrap at Daskyleion.[41] The focal points of that district were Gergis, Scepsis, and Cebren, but they also stationed a Greek mercenary garrison at Ilion, probably in or around the sanctuary of Athena. Political control would shift again in 399, when the Spartan commander Dercylidas freed Ilion and the surrounding towns from Persian control in the course of his war on the satrap Pharnabazos. The trade networks that crossed the region clearly suffered considerably during the subsequent Spartan invasion of 396/5, when a number of settlements and *paradeisoi* were burned along with Daskyleion itself.[42]

That invasion was led by Agesilaus II, who attempted to sacrifice at Aulis prior to sailing to Asia Minor, in direct imitation of Agamemnon before the Trojan War.[43] His stay in the Troad was short-lived, and a measure of stability returned during the reign of Ariobarzanes, who replaced Pharnabazos as satrap of Daskyleion in 387. War broke out again twenty years later, however, when Ariobarzanes joined the satraps of Cilicia and Cappadocia in revolt against King Artaxerxes II.[44] Sestos was subsequently besieged, and the forces of Ariobarzanes were saved only when Athens sent thirty ships and 8,000 mercenaries to assist him.[45] The satrap, in return, gave Sestos and Crithote to Athens, both of which were important components of the grain supply route, and Athenian citizenship was conferred on Ariobarzanes and his sons as a consequence.[46] At some point during this period, a statue of the satrap was erected in front of Ilion's temple of Athena – the first honorific statue at the site for which we have evidence.[47]

Following Ariobarzanes' execution in 362/1 B.C., the Athenian mercenary commander Charidemus seized Cebren, Scepsis, and Ilion. His deceit in capturing Ilion was described in detail by Aeneas Tacticus, and it bears repeating in full due to the unusual mix of narrative components.[48]

> His (Charidemus') instructions [to a slave of the governor of Ilion] were to take a horse with him when he went out that night… Once he was outside, Charidemus conferred with him and gave him about 30 of his mercenaries, wearing body armor and carrying daggers, shields, and pointed helmets. These the men led off in the dark, in shabby clothing – under which he concealed their weapons – and made to look like prisoners-of-war; the gates had been opened for him because of the horse, and of course the instant they were inside, the mercenaries go to work, killing the gatekeeper and generally behaving as mercenaries do. As soon as they were in control of the gates, some of Charidemus' troops who had been waiting nearby arrived and seized the inner city.[49]

Although Charidemus' seizure of Ilion certainly did occur and is attested by Demosthenes and Polyaenus as well, the version of Aeneas Tacticus reproduced above seems spurious in a number of details. The most significant error involves the description of strong walls with gates, since Troy was unwalled prior to 240/30 B.C.[50] Moreover, the principal features of the narrative – the horse, the element of disguise, the strong fortifications, and the arrival of troops that had been hiding at a distance, waiting for the gates to be breached – are clearly drawn from the *Odyssey*, thereby furnishing yet another example of the influence of the Homeric epics on later historical accounts of battles at Ilion.[51]

Charidemus' choice of sites for seizure is also worthy of comment. Cebren and Scepsis were large, well-fortified towns where the regional ruler Mania kept her treasure, and they were separated by only ca. 13 km.[52] Their attraction is clear, but the small, unwalled settlement of Ilion, approximately 42 km away from Scepsis and Cebren, is a more unusual selection from a military point of view. The city's value lay primarily in its symbolic status, but that status had grown exponentially during the prior 200 years and was well known on both sides of the Aegean. Ilion's inclusion in the miniature realm of Charidemus added an eye-catching temporal dimension to the conquests that would otherwise have been absent.[53]

The power base of Charidemus was of limited strength, and his control of the area evaporated within the year. Ilion's proxeny decree for the Athenian

7.4. Bronze coin of Sigeion, fourth century B.C., with reverse type of double-bodied owl. Photo courtesy of the American Numismatic Society.

commander Menelaus in 359 B.C. is usually interpreted as a testament to his liberation of the city at that time.[54] By 364/3 Sigeion and probably Ilion as well passed into the hands of the Athenian general Chares, who ruled it until the arrival of Alexander in 334.[55] Sigeion now began striking coins for the first time, and they appear to have been minted only during Chares' thirty-year reign. These were among the largest coins of the Troad, superseded only by those from Mytilene and Tenedos. Their eye-catching obverses featuring a three-quarter head of Athena, apparently adapted from late fifth century B.C. Syracusan types, with reverses of an owl with two bodies that symbolized the town's historical link to Athens (Fig. 7.4).[56]

Although the only reference to Ilion in the accounts of Chares' life is to his meeting with Alexander there in 334, recent discoveries around Ilion's Athenaion attest to the site's strong symbiotic relationship with Sigeion. The majority of the fourth-century B.C. coins unearthed at Ilion were struck at Sigeion, and most of the fineware and lamps from Ilion's late Classical deposits are either Attic or Atticizing, as at Sigeion.[57] Moreover, the size and design of Sigeion's new coins suggest the city's desire to be perceived as a player of prominence in the affairs of the Troad, which probably prompted the forging of every conceivable link with Ilion.

Those links were probably forged with other cities in the region as well, although the evidence is limited. A document relief from Sigeion, datable by style to the third quarter of the fourth century B.C., shows an armed Athena turning toward two men: one is bearded and clad in a himation; the other is a young soldier wearing a helmet and cuirass (Fig. 7.5). The name inscribed above the central figure does not survive, but "Athena" appears above the goddess, and "Protesilaus" above the soldier. The relief almost certainly signals an alliance among Hellespontine cities, each of which is represented by a god or hero, with Sigeion embodied by Athena and Elaious by Protesilaus.[58]

All of this attention to the Homeric tradition gradually prompted a rise in Ilion's fortunes. During the second and third quarters of the fourth century, when Ilion was controlled by Ariobarzanes and Chares, there are distinct signs of prosperity around the Athenaion and the West Sanctuary.[59] The fourth-century deposits in the former area feature a high number of fineware table vessels compared with other types of pottery, as well as a considerable increase in amphora types. In other words, there is a marked rise in evidence for ritual activities that featured eating and drinking, and the large number of Attic and Atticizing vessels suggests conscious imitation of Athenian sympotic activity.[60]

Associated with these vessels were large numbers of horse bones that show signs of both butchery and cooking, which, in turn, points to the sacrifice and

7.5. Document relief from Sigeion, fourth century B.C. Athena turns toward two men, one of whom has been labeled "Protesilaus." Fitzwilliam Museum, Cambridge. Photo courtesy Fitzwilliam Museum, Cambridge.

consumption of horses.[61] Equid sacrifice is attested in Achaemenid areas as well as in Greece and Cyprus during the Bronze Age, Archaic, and Classical periods, with both Poseidon and Anahita named as divine recipients of the offerings.[62] Given the unusual significance of the horse at Ilion, however, this particular assemblage probably supplies evidence for ritual activity in the Athenaion that was linked to the Homeric tradition. Achilles sacrificed horses over the funeral pyre of Patroclus in the *Iliad* (33.171f.), and a similar spirit may have been in force during the Athenaion sacrifices.

The same deposit also contained nineteen loom weights and spindle whorls, some of which were stamped with images of women weavers and, apparently, the cult statue of Athena Ilias. This suggests the manufacture of cloth as a feature of the Athenaion, and one is tempted to posit the weaving of a cloak for the statue of Athena in imitation of the Athenian Panathenaia.[63] Such weaving activities in honor of Athena must have occurred during the Hellenistic and Roman periods when Ilion's Panathenaic festival was in operation, and it is striking that the Late Classical weaving assemblage was found only 30 m to the west of the Pillar House, which had served as one of the principal weaving centers of the Late Bronze Age settlement.

As the sacrifices of Xerxes and Mindarus make clear, Ilion's Athenaion and the "Homeric" tumuli that surrounded it could be co-opted by either Greeks or Persians, and one would consequently expect offerings to Athena from both groups. There is now evidence for this phenomenon in the form of thick-walled "pale porous" mortaria, which imitate light colored stone vessels from Persepolis, Daskyleion, and other sites under Achaemenid control.[64] These too were used in ritual dining, presumably by dedicators associated with the satrapal court, and they span a period from ca. 525 to 325 B.C., with a notable gap in the fifth century B.C.[65] In other words, the site was accessible to and utilized by both Greeks and Achaemenids, who dined there in celebration of the same legendary battle.[66]

If viewed in this context, the Ariobarzanes statue erected in front of the Athenaion becomes all the more intriguing. As far as we know, this was the only honorific statue erected by Ilion during the entire fourth century B.C.[67] Even the wealthy Malousios, who sponsored the construction of the large theater at the close of the fourth century B.C., did not receive one, nor did Alexander.[68] There is no evidence that satraps set up statues of themselves in the cities of their realm, so it seems reasonable to conclude that the statue was dedicated by Ilion itself.

Although the statue disappeared long ago, its format can be reconstructed with a fair degree of certainty, and it probably reflected the dual identity of Ilion in the Late Classical period. By the time that Ariobarzanes' reign had begun, in 387 B.C., portraits had begun to exhibit individualized features, as demonstrated by the contemporary Çan Sarcophagus (Plate 24), and the same was no doubt true for the Ariobarzanes portrait.[69] The costume would have been Achaemenid, as in contemporary satrapal coinage, and would have featured a tiara, although the dedicatory inscription would have been written in Greek.[70] In other words, he would have resembled the Trojans in their post–Persian War iconographic configuration (Fig. 7.2).

There is still the question of when the statue of Ariobarzanes was erected, and why he seems to have been the only individual who received a statue at Ilion during the fourth century B.C. No evidence thus far uncovered offers a solution, but in light of the site's outreach to both East and West, the years between 367 and 361 emerge as the most likely period for its dedication. This was the time in which the satrap had given Sestos and Crithote to Athens, which had, in return, bestowed Athenian citizenship on him and his sons.[71] Ariobarzanes therefore embodied both of the worlds targeted by Ilion as potential benefactors, and the visual and verbal components of the statue's format would have evoked those worlds.

If the timing proposed here is correct, then the statue would have been erect for only a few years; it was lying on the ground in Athena's precinct by the time Alexander arrived in 334, and was probably toppled shortly after Ariobarzanes' assassination, possibly when the city had been seized by Charidemus. That it still lay on the ground twenty-five years later suggests a kind of *damnatio*, in fact even if not in intent, and again one is reminded of the figural mutilation on the Çan Sarcophagus (Fig. 6.3).

7.6. The fortification walls of Assos. Photo courtesy Bonna Wescoat.

I have concentrated on the fortunes of Ilion during the period between the King's Peace of 387 B.C. and the arrival of Alexander, but an increased level of prosperity and cultural enrichment would also have been visible in most of the towns of the Troad. Aristotle arrived in Assos around 347 and began lecturing in their gymnasium, where he was probably joined by Theophrastus, and Epicurus subsequently inaugurated a philosophical school at Lampsacus.[72]

It is Assos that has yielded our best evidence for new construction during this period. The city had been at least partially fortified during the sixth century B.C., the walls of which probably enabled Ariobarzanes to fend off attacks by Mausolus and Autophradates at the outset of his revolt from Artaxerxes II. During the tyrannies of Eubulus and his successor Hermias, around 350 B.C., the fortifications were completely rebuilt, with a circuit length of 3 km and a height of more than 19 m (Fig. 7.6).[73] This construction would have required reopening the regional andesite quarries that had been inactive for over a century; it would also have spurred the rapid development of concomitant industries, such as metalworking, timber, and carpentry, and must have pulled in laborers from the surrounding towns.

The same period almost certainly witnessed new construction in Sigeion and Lampsacus as well, and tombs from the region datable to the second half of the fourth century B.C. have yielded a wealth of elite gifts, including three gold wreaths, ten gold diadems with Dionysiac decoration, and costumes with sewn gold plaques.[74] Of the few surviving Troad grave monuments from this period, the most striking one comes from Sigeion and probably dates to the period in which Chares controlled the city. The unusual relief on the stele base, or *trapeza*, appears to depict a woman who had given birth to triplets, one of whom, judging by the iconography, died in childbirth.[75]

Also operating on a high level at this time were the quarries on Proconnesus, which shipped marble to Mausolus in Halicarnassus for the decoration of his palace and to the builders at Heraclea Pontica on the south shore of the Black Sea (Plate 11). At some point in the fourth century B.C. the island's prosperity increased to a point that it became an attractive target for takeover, and Cyzicus subsequently seized it and assumed control of the quarries, thereby gaining an important way station on the steadily increasing Black Sea grain trade.[76]

ALEXANDER AT ILION

All of these cities remained subject to the king until 334 B.C., when Alexander launched the first of his three major battles against the Persians. His forces traveled to Lampsacus, where the residents presented him with a dazzling stone intaglio, and then to Didymateiche (modern Gümüşçay), in the Granicus River Valley, as the Persians marched from Zeleia (modern Gönen).[77] The two forces assumed positions on either side of the Granicus River, not unlike the opposing Athenian and Spartan forces on either side of the Hellespont immediately prior to the Battle of Aegospotami. Alexander's infantry charged through the river diagonally, against the current, climbed the sloping banks, and engaged the Persian forces on the opposite side, some of whom were watching the conflict from the summits of the adjacent Graeco-Persian tombs (Plate 13).[78]

If the Persian troops were as organized as Arrian, Plutarch, and Diodorus indicate, with the cavalry on the river bank and the infantry on the hills, the visual effect would have been both overwhelming and intimidating, making it difficult for the Macedonians to determine whether there was a gap between Persian cavalry and infantry. Greatly in Alexander's favor, however, was the time of day in which the attack occurred – late afternoon, according to Arrian and Plutarch – which meant that the afternoon sun would have been shining directly in the eyes of the Persians.[79]

From the viewpoint of Ilion, Alexander's actions prior to that battle would have been as noteworthy as the victory itself. Before crossing the Dardanelles he sacrificed at the tomb of Protesilaus at Elaious, and then traveled directly to Ilion where he and his companion Hephaestion laid wreaths on the tumuli of Achilles and Patroclus, respectively.[80] Alexander reportedly anointed the gravestone of Achilles, after which he and his companions raced around the burial mound in apparent imitation of the funeral games for Patroclus.[81]

At Ilion itself, in addition to sacrificing to Athena, the Homeric heroes, and Priam on the altar of Zeus Herkeios, Alexander deposited his armor in the temple as a dedication to Athena, and took from it the finest armor remaining from the Trojan War, which he subsequently wore into battle.[82] According to Arrian, a shield taken from the temple was still being used during Alexander's battles in northwestern India. Throughout his campaigns, Alexander reportedly traveled with a copy of the *Iliad* – a practice that would be continually repeated by future warriors, including the allied forces in the Gallipoli campaign more than 2200 years later.[83]

Earlier commanders, notably Xerxes and Mindarus, had acknowledged Ilion's legendary heritage, but none had formulated such a wide-ranging, multifaceted program that targeted the citadel, the surrounding tumuli, and the relics of the war. Alexander, of course, differed from the earlier pilgrims in that he claimed descent from Achilles himself due to his mother Olympia's Molossian ancestry. Arrian alludes specifically to this link, noting that Alexander sacrificed to Zeus Herkeios, as patron of family ties, to "avert the anger against the family of Neoptolemus, whose blood still ran in his own veins."[84] Alexander's appropriation of military relics from the temple treasury was therefore particularly appropriate, and his own armor would subsequently have formed yet another component of the Homeric museum within the Athenaion. He also reportedly offered promises that his predecessors had failed to make, claiming that he would enlarge the Athena Sanctuary and make it the center of a religious assembly, although he died before those promises could be kept.[85]

At the time when Alexander departed for the Granicus River, Ilion still looked more or less as it had at the close of the Persian Wars, but the interim period had witnessed an acceleration in the town's metamorphosis into Homeric Troy. Implicit in that process was the presentation of the Trojan War as a metaphor for contemporary east-west conflict, although pejorative roles were assigned to neither side, thereby allowing Ilion to interface with a broader range of political powers. During the fifth and fourth centuries, this meant reaching out to Sigeion and Daskyleion, as surrogates of Athens and Persia, and to men as diverse as Ariobarzanes, Xerxes, Chares, and Alexander, among others. The votive assemblages of Ilion during the Late Classical period attest to the success of that outreach, and it was only the beginning of a period of economic prosperity tied to the Homeric framework into which the settlement had been situated.

EIGHT

ILION IN THE EARLY HELLENISTIC PERIOD

After his visit to Ilion in 334 B.C., Alexander raised the settlement to the status of polis, declared it free and exempt from taxation, and promised to fund a new sanctuary with sacred games (*agona hiera*).[1] The last provision, which was also the most expensive, remained unfulfilled at the time of his death, but Alexander's vision of the city's potential must have resonated strongly with the priests of the Athena Sanctuary, who probably constituted the primary authority there. Ilion had already grasped, several centuries earlier, the value of shaping and exploiting its identity as the site of the Trojan War, which included the Treasury with Homeric relics in the Sanctuary of Athena, the perennial penance of the Locrian Maidens, and the repackaging of the adjacent prehistoric settlement mounds as Homeric tumuli. Such programmatic initiatives had lured Xerxes and Alexander to the site, as well as lesser rulers such as Mindarus, Chares, and Charidemus. Not all of these visits, of course, had improved the city's fortunes: the activities surrounding Xerxes' visit, in fact, helped push the region into a decline that lasted more than 150 years, but by this point Ilion appears to have realized that a program focused on strengthening the site's Homeric credentials could lift its fortunes substantially if the necessary financial and political resources could be secured.

Those resources arrived during the reign of Antigonus I Monophthalmus, who had assumed control of all of Asia Minor in 315. He would be required to surrender some of that territory in 311, during a peace conference on the Hellespont with several of Alexander's successors, and would lose his life ten years later in a battle against Seleucus and Lysimachus, but during the course of Antigonus' reign the political structure of the Troad was significantly altered, with some of his innovations remaining in place through the late Roman period.[2] It also marked a period of prominence for Ilion, both financially and politically, as it did for most of the cities lying along the coast of the Troad.

Perhaps the most prominent innovation was the creation by synoecism, or consolidation, of an entirely new city in the center of the Troad's west coast, opposite Tenedos (Plate 26). The city was populated by the inhabitants of Cebren, Neandria, Scepsis, and Hamaxitus, among others, and named Antigoneia Troas after its founder, although it was subsequently changed to "Alexandria Troas" after Antigonus' death in 301. The town's large and well-protected harbor enabled it to emerge quickly as the Troad's most prosperous city and its financial capital.[3]

The political and religious center of the Troad, however, would now become Ilion. Around 310 Antigonus established a new league, or koinon, of Troad cities that was centered on the cult of Athena Ilias. There were eleven cities in the koinon during the first century of its existence, one fewer than the earlier Aeolian and Ionian Leagues, with membership extended to Abydos, Alexandria Troas, Assos, Dardanus, Gargara, Ilion, Lampsacus, Parium, Scepsis, Apamea Myrlea, and Chalcedon.[4] The vast majority of these were cities lining the south, west, and north coasts of the Troad; the only outliers were Scepsis, in the interior foothills of the Ida Mountains, and Chalcedon and Apamea Myrlea, which occupy the northeast and southeast corners of the Sea of Marmara. The last two cities had dropped out of the league after the third century B.C., but most of the others remained members as late as the third century A.D.

Such leagues greatly facilitated the administration of a kingdom as large as that of Antigonus, and at least two others were inaugurated at roughly the same time: a Cycladic League, centered on the Delian Sanctuary of Apollo, and a (revived) Ionian League, based at the League's old sanctuary to Poseidon, the Panionion, on the Mykale peninsula.[5] All three of these leagues – the Cycladic, Ionian, and Troad – were tied to a celebrated sanctuary that immediately conferred an aura of prestige on each of the member cities. This was particularly perceptible in the Troad koinon, in that each city was automatically linked to the Homeric tradition, as was Antigonus himself.

Shortly after the inauguration of the koinon, Ilion began to strike its first coins. The inception of coinage was a major advance for Ilion and needs to be viewed in the context of the other members of the koinon, nearly all of whom had begun striking their own coins much earlier.[6] Only Alexandria Troas, a new foundation, and Apamea Myrlea had not struck coins prior to 300 B.C. Ilion's coins were initially only bronze, with an obverse type of Athena in an Attic helmet, and a reverse of Athena Ilias wearing a polos and a long chiton, holding a distaff in her left hand and a raised spear decorated with an *infula* in

8.1. Silver coin struck by the mint of Ilion during the second century B.C., with reverse of Athena Ilias. Photo courtesy of the American Numismatic Society.

her right (Fig. 8.1).[7] This is generally regarded as an illustration of the cult statue within the Athenaion, and it essentially duplicates the description of the Palladion provided by Apollodorus in the first or second century A.D.:

And having prayed to Zeus that a sign might be shown to him, [Ilus] beheld by day the Palladion, fallen from heaven, lying before his tent. It was three cubits in height [ca. 1.5 m], its feet joined together; in its right hand it held a spear aloft, and in the other hand a distaff and a spindle.[8]

This image, slightly under life-size, therefore became yet another component of the settlement's Homeric foundations, and it effectively complemented the other features of the sanctuary that were tied to Trojan legends. The polos and columnar format that appear on the earliest coins associate it with the category of Anatolian cult statues that includes the Artemis of Ephesus, the Aphrodite of Aphrodisias, and apparently the Athena of Assos.[9] Although the use of spear and distaff was not especially common in the iconography of Athena, it was not unique, and one finds the same juxtaposition on Ionian and Lydian coins of the Hellenistic and Roman periods.[10]

Despite the residents' claims that their cult statue was the one worshipped by Priam, it was not modeled on the image of Athena described in the Homeric epics, which was seated, nor did it conform to the standard Palladion iconography in vase painting and the minor arts, which featured a helmeted Athena holding a spear and shield.[11] Since a number of other prominent cities, including Athens, Sparta, Argos, and, ultimately, Rome, claimed to possess the genuine Palladion, the priests of the Sanctuary may have favored an iconography distinct from all the others.[12]

The most prominent activity in each of the leagues was an annual festival, usually including athletic and musical events that provided cohesion for the member cities and prompted the development of a common identity for each league. At Delos the festivals bore the names of Antigonus and his son Demetrius (the "Antigoneia" and "Demetreia"), which were held in alternate years; at the Panionion, the festival was focused on Poseidon Helikonios, who had served as the patron deity of the league since its foundation in the early Archaic period.[13]

As the primary visual manifestation of its new public identity, the Troad koinon established a Panathenaea modeled on the festival in Athens. The inscriptions of the koinon refer to a parade with kanephoroi, a few of whom merited statues in the temenos; the crowning of Athena with a "stephanos aristeios"

8.2. Hellenistic relief from Ilion with equestrian contest. Photo by the author.

or "crown of valor"; and the sacrifice of cattle to the goddess.[14] The sacrificed cattle appear to have been hung from columns near the altar, as one can see on Ilion's coin reverses of the second century B.C.[15]

There were also musical competitions that probably included *rhapsodes* reciting the *Iliad* and the *Odyssey* as well as dramatic tragedies and athletic contests involving both gymnastic and hippic events.[16] The latter may in fact be represented on a damaged marble relief from Ilion showing a horseman approaching the finish line, marked by a herm, with a trumpeter placed between them (Fig. 8.2).[17] One unusual event was the *taurobolium*, in which a bull was chased by a horseman and tired out but not killed.[18] The culminating point of the festival was almost certainly a sacrifice in the Sanctuary of Athena.

A large market set up on this occasion probably featured specialty items produced by the member cities of the koinon. It is hard to believe that souvenirs were not sold on that occasion, as they were at the Athenian Panathenaea, but no miniature Panathenaic vessels, Homeric-themed figurines, or Trojan War memorabilia have yet come to light.[19] It is, of course, possible that the souvenirs were wooden, as they are today, and have not survived. Once the visitors arrived at Ilion, Hellenistic tour guides would have pointed to sites in the surrounding landscape, such as the place where Anchises and Aphrodite made love, the rock where Hesione, Priam's sister, was chained, or, if they were willing to travel further into the Troad, the point where Ganymede had been abducted by Zeus.[20]

As at Athens, the Panathenaic festivals occurred annually, in abbreviated form, and every four years as a full spectacle. The Athenian Panathenaea had been celebrated for slightly longer than a week during the month of Hekatombaion, which coincides roughly with our July–August. No such month is recorded in the Trojan calendar, but there was a month named Panathenaea in which the festival undoubtedly occurred, and it was probably close in time to but not overlapping with its Athenian counterpart.[21] The staggering of such festivals in the calendar would have allowed the residents to attend a series of festivals without fear of scheduling conflicts, as one sees in a long letter from Hadrian to the residents of Alexandria Troas.[22] Then, as now, such a position in the calendar would have decreased the chance of rain disturbing the festival.

What is particularly noteworthy here is that the koinon chose to define itself in Athenian terms, co-opting the spectacle of the Panathenaea as its primary festival. Ilion and its allies were not the only Asia Minor cities to select such a model for their local festivals – Sardis, Pergamon, and Priene made the same decision in the course of the Hellenistic period – but the Greek-speaking residents of Ilion and several of the neighboring cities had also presented themselves as descendants of the legendary Trojans, and it is striking that they chose Greek models to frame that presentation.[23]

In light of the league's emphasis on Athens and her signature festival, it seems surprising that Sigeion, an Athenian colony located less than 7 km away from Ilion, was never included among the league's members. Sigeion's fortunes had certainly decreased significantly by the end of the fourth century: the residents refused to submit to Lysimachus, who seized the city in 302 B.C. and installed a garrison there. The population may also have decreased substantially by this point judging by the limited amount of post-fourth-century pottery and coins discovered in the excavations, but the city was still in operation.[24]

All of the festivals were financed by dues that the member cities paid to the koinon, and each city was expected to supply cattle for sacrifice. An inscription set up in the Sanctuary of Athena in the late third century B.C. notes that the last two cities named above, Chalcedon and Myrlea, had not met their financial obligations to the festival.[25] Each was fined 2,000 drachms for forfeiting on their interest payments and for having provided no cattle for the festival. In other words, the delinquent status of these cities was published in stone in the Sanctuary in an attempt to coerce them into paying, although apparently they never did.[26] Such public censure was undoubtedly common in all sanctuaries related to the leagues.

BUILDING FOR THE PANATHENAEA

When Antigonus made the decision to organize the new league around the Sanctuary of Athena Ilias, he must have realized, as had Alexander, how much reconstruction would be necessary in order to provide the site with the buildings and facilities necessary for the administration and staging of such an elaborate festival. At this point, no construction had taken place at Ilion for at least

170 years; the Late Archaic buildings lay in ruins and there was no experienced work force in place to repair them. Nevertheless, by the end of the fourth century, the building industry at the site had not only rebounded, it had reached new heights of productivity with new sources of funding in place.

During this period Ilion undoubtedly relied on its fellow members of the League for assistance, especially Parium, Assos, and Lampsacus. All of those cities had enjoyed considerable prosperity in the fourth century B.C., as Ilion had not, and would have been in a position to provide both labor and technical expertise.[27] At the same time, the new port city of the region, Alexandria Troas, was being constructed from the ground up, which suggests that the logging, woodworking, stone quarrying, and metalworking industries in the Troad must have accelerated rapidly.

Ilion could rely on its own stone supplies for some sections of the new buildings. The soft limestone or marl that underlies the entire settlement is easily quarried and ideally suited for the foundations of monumental buildings as long as it is covered by earth or a harder limestone once it has been set in place. At the southern edge of the Lower City, nearly 400 m to the south of the citadel mound, large-scale quarrying had clearly begun by ca. 300 B.C., which suggests that a large local or regional work force had been established shortly after the foundation of the league. The remnants of their activities were still present in the deposits surrounding the quarry, including a random assortment of plates, bowls, and cups that each workman probably removed from his home for midday meals.[28]

Initial construction occurred in the three areas that were essential for the activities of the koinon: the agora, the Sanctuary of Athena, and the theater (Theater A). The first structure to be built was probably a new Bouleuterion, as was the case for the Panionion League that was revived at about the same time.[29] The new building, which provided an enclosed meeting space for the league's members, was constructed at the southeast corner of the mound directly above two earlier buildings that may have functioned as the town's prytaneion.[30] The complete ground plan cannot be reconstructed, but one of its rooms measured nearly 3 × 5 m, and a new retaining wall at the east supported the terrace on which it stood (Fig. 8.3, Plate 27).

In Athens, the Panathenaic procession moved through the agora and then to the acropolis, which was probably the formula followed at Ilion. This means that the *rhapsodes* who sang sections of the *Iliad* would have done so in the agora, which lay in front of the still-visible Late Bronze Age fortification wall (Fig. 8.4).[31] Here again, the ritual reinforced the Homeric associations of the surrounding architecture, which, in turn, lent historical validity to the Homeric epics. There are sections of the old fortification wall lining the north side of the agora that were certainly repaired or restored in the early Hellenistic period: one stretch was carefully repaired by several courses of headers and stretchers;

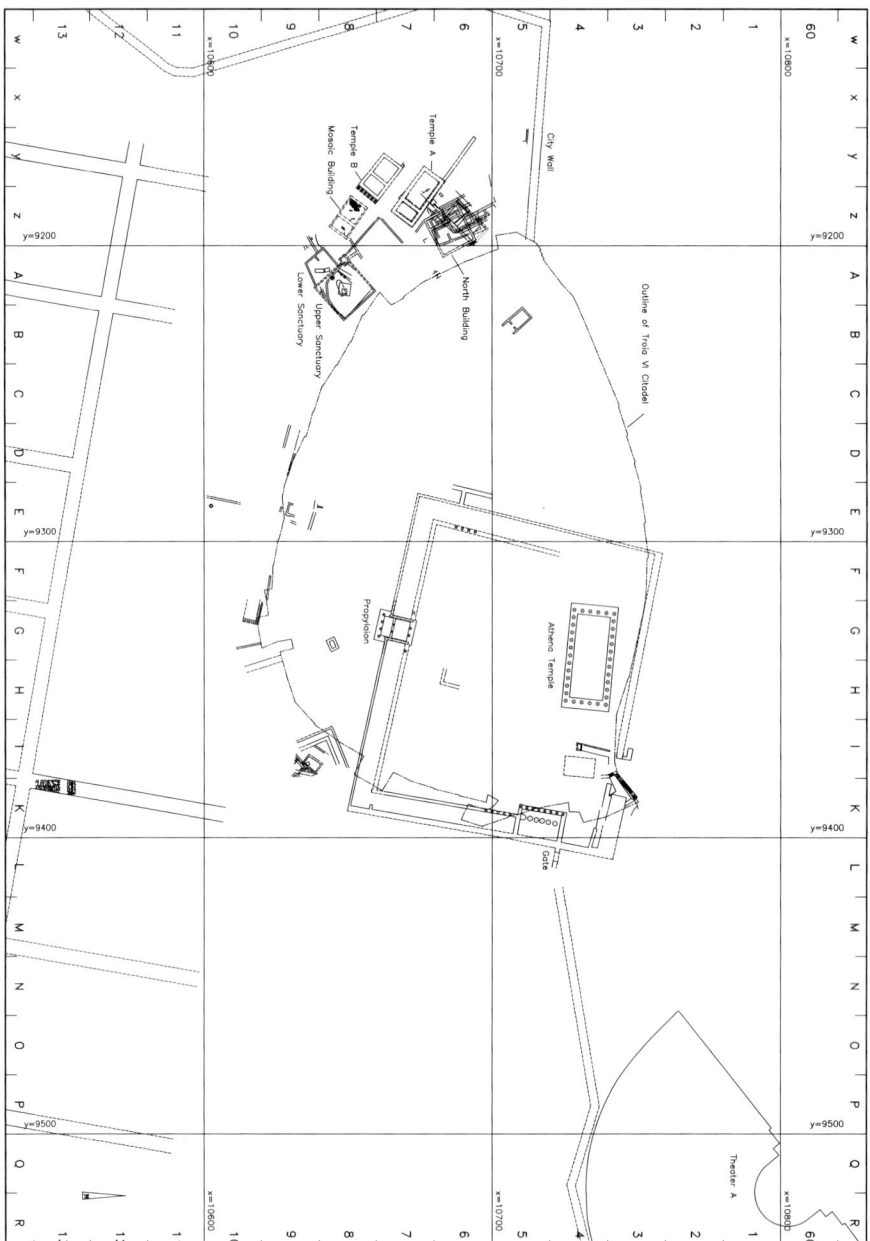

8.3. Plan of Troy VIII, during the Late Hellenistic period, prepared by Elizabeth Riorden for the Troy Excavation Project.

another badly damaged section was blocked from view completely by an entirely new wall. We cannot link these alterations to a specific decade, but they were probably planned shortly after the inauguration of the Panathenaic festival.

The largest and most elaborate component of the construction campaign was a new theater situated within a semicircular hollow near the northeast side

8.4. Aerial view of the agora of Ilion, looking west, with the reconstructed Late Bronze fortification wall running behind the Odeion. Troia slide 16258.

of the mound (Plate 8, Figs. 8.5 and 8.6).[32] The cavea was designed to hold nearly 10,000 spectators, which in itself suggests that the theater's construction was prompted by the creation of the league, with the festival's events drawing visitors from the entire Troad.[33] The orchestra was horseshoe-shaped, which is

8.5. The large theater (Theater A) on the northeast slope of the citadel mound. Troia slide 10576.

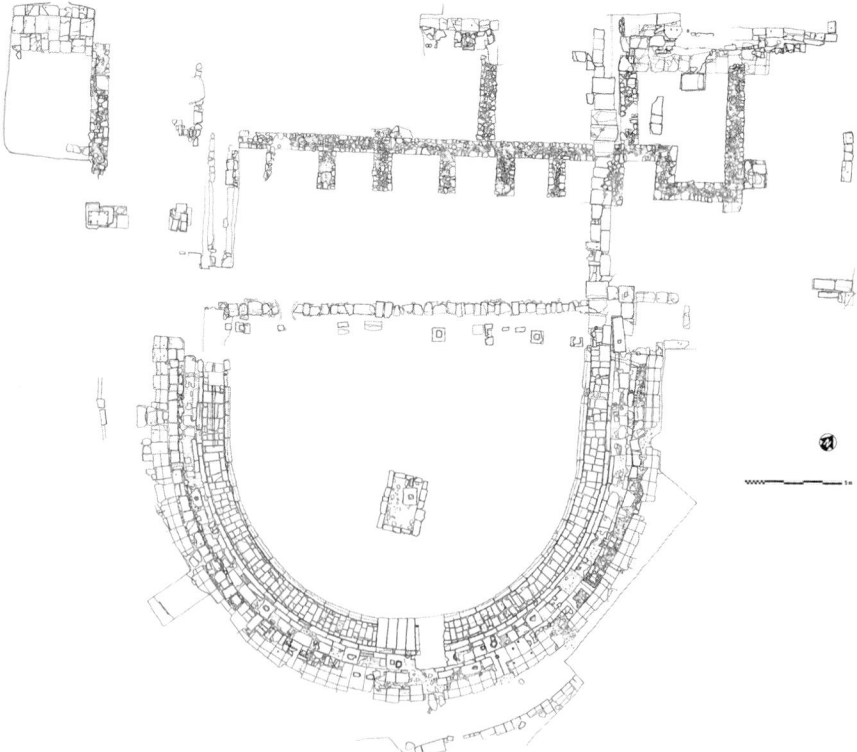

8.6. Plan of Theater A, drawn by Elizabeth Riorden for the Troy Excavation Project.

typical for Hellenistic theaters, and there was probably a wooden stage judging by the lack of stone architectural elements of Hellenistic date that have been found there.[34] The cavea was divided into thirteen sections, or cunei, but only three rows of limestone seats still remain in place, the others having been burned in lime kilns or spoliated for reuse.[35] One early Hellenistic inscription mentions dramatic contests in the Panathenaea, probably focused on Homeric subjects, which would undoubtedly have been staged there.[36]

Fortunately, there is secure epigraphic evidence in support of an Early Hellenistic date. An inscription set up in the Athena Sanctuary and datable to 306 B.C. contains six decrees in honor of Malousios, who represented his home city of Gargara on the league council.[37] Malousios provided the league with an interest-free loan of nearly 1,450 staters to build the theater and its skene, and contributed another 3,500 staters to cover expenses related to the theater, possibly the productions, as well as the erection of other unspecified buildings and the cost of embassies to Antigonus. Once the current bills were paid from the latter sum, the remainder was to be deposited in the Sanctuary of Athena, and whatever was not used would be returned to Malousios.[38]

It seems logical that plans for the rebuilding of the Sanctuary of Athena would have been prepared at this time since the temple was the culminating point of the festival's procession, but the Malousios inscription makes no reference to the provisions for a new temple – only to the construction of "other buildings" in addition to those in the theater. Consequently, the temple probably remained the "small and poor" affair that Alexander had seen, although one can imagine increased security installations to protect both the money from Malousios and the treasury of Homeric relics that were housed there.

We can put some of these costs for Ilion's theater into a broader fourth-century B.C. economic context. The gold:silver ratio at this time is likely to have been between 1:10 and 1:12, which would have yielded a rate of 20–24 drachms per stater. The 1,450 staters spent on Ilion's theater would therefore have amounted to a cost between 4.83 and 5.8 talents.[39] The price of the theater of Epidaurus was somewhere above 10 talents, or twice as much, and the temple of Asclepius at Epidaurus was 23 talents, or nearly four times as much.[40] It seems unlikely that any earlier building at Ilion had cost the equivalent of 5,000 staters, or any number close to that, and it indicates the heightened level of euergetism from which Ilion was now benefiting. In return for Malousios' beneficence, the city offered him a range of gifts: two gold crowns worth 300 and 1,000 drachms, respectively; places of honor for him and his descendants at the annual festival; and the erection of a stele attesting to his generosity in the Sanctuary of Athena.[41]

These were extraordinary honors, especially for Ilion, but they paled by comparison to the decrees for kings, one of which had been passed by Scepsis in recognition of their grant of autonomy from Antigonus. The king received an altar, temenos, sacrifice, games, a festival, and a statue that was to be crowned by a gold wreath valued at 100 staters.[42] Even more elaborate were the honors he received at Athens: gilded bronze statues of the king and his son Demetrius were set next to the Tyrannicides, and two of the city's tribes were named after them.

In 301, however, nine years after he had begun to launch such enormous changes in the Troad, Antigonus lay dead on the battlefield of Ipsos, near the modern city of Afyon in Phrygia. One of the victors in that battle, Lysimachus, now assumed control of Antigonus' holdings in Asia Minor, including the Troad, and would maintain that control until his defeat by Seleucus I at the Battle of Corupedium, near Sardis, twenty years later. The name of the new port city of Antigoneia was quickly changed to Alexandria (Troas) and construction activity appears to have increased significantly, as did the production of coinage. One new type that was struck at several Troad mints showed a seated Athena holding a Nike who crowns the name of Lysimachus with a wreath. This was, in a sense, a numismatic rendition of the kind of honors that had been voted to Antigonus at Scepsis several years earlier.[43]

Scholars have typically regarded Lysimachus as an even greater benefactor of the Troad than Antigonus, but the basis for that judgment is not as firm as one might think.[44] The evidence appears in a passage in Strabo (13.1.26 and 27) wherein the historian mentions, after a discussion of early Hellenistic Ilion, that Lysimachus built a temple and a city wall 40 stades in length.

> 13.1.26: It is said that the modern town of the Ilians was for a time a mere village containing the temple of Athena, a small and poor affair; but that when Alexander went there after the victory at Granicus he enriched the temple with votive offerings, gave the place the title of city, ordered the authorities to improve it by building, and proclaimed it free and exempt from taxation; and that later, after the downfall of the Persians, he sent a gracious letter promising to make of it a great city and eminent sanctuary, and to institute sacred games there. But after his death Lysimachus devoted his chief attention to the city where he built a temple and surrounded it with a city wall with a circuit of some forty stades, transferring to it the surrounding towns that were now old and decayed. Alexandria had already been founded by Antigonus and called Antigonia, but now changed its name, as piety seemed to require that the successors of Alexander should found their cities under his name in preference to their own. So it flourished and grew, and has now received a Roman colony and is one of the famous cities of the world.

> 13.1.27: So the modern Ilium was a sort of village-town when the Romans first set foot in Asia and expelled Antiochus the Great from the country within Taurus. At all events Demetrius of Scepsis says that when as a youth he visited the town about that time, he found the whole place so neglected that the houses had not even tiled roofs.

The section begins with a description of the impoverished state of Ilion when Alexander visited, as well as his plans to enlarge the city and move it toward greater prosperity. The problems begin once we arrive at the section dealing with Lysimachus. He is credited with building a fortification wall and a temple in the city that he had enlarged by synoecism. In the form in which this passage has come down to us, "the city where he built a temple" should technically refer to Ilion, since no other city is mentioned in the previous lines, and indicates that Lysimachus built the new temple of Athena promised by Alexander. But the larger context of this section speaks against such an interpretation, as does the recent archaeological evidence from Troy itself.

In 1872 George Grote proposed that this part of Strabo's manuscript must have been corrupted, and no other scenario seems possible.[45] It is clear that Lysimachus devoted the majority of his attention to something other than what Alexander had focused on ("but after his (Alexander's) death Lysimachus devoted his chief attention to the city where he built a temple") and the subsequent sentences indicate that this was Alexandria Troas. As we move forward to section 27, the phrase "καὶ τὸ Ἴλιον δ" conveys a sense of "meanwhile, back at Ilion." In other words, Strabo indicates Ilion's potential for grandeur, courtesy of Alexander, then says that this potential was realized instead by Alexandria Troas, and that is why Ilion remained a backwater town (the first sentences of 13.1.27).

As several scholars have noted, we have to assume the loss of at least a word and possibly a sentence that would have made it clear that the antecedent of "the city where he built a temple" was Alexandria and not Ilion.[46] Moreover, Strabo twice refers to the Sanctuary of Athena at Ilion as " *to ieron*," whereas in the next section he uses "*neos*" to describe the temple built by Lysimachus and omits the definite article, neither of which he would have done if the discussion referred to the same sacred place. In other words, Strabo varied his language to indicate that he was speaking of different structures.

This interpretation of the text is fortified by the material evidence from the sites of Troy and Alexandria Troas. There is now ceramic evidence regarding Ilion's temple of Athena, presented in detail below, which shows that construction could not have begun until at least thirty years after the death of Lysimachus. Moreover, the city wall of Alexandria is approximately 40 stades (7.4 km) in length, which is the number mentioned in Strabo's text, and it makes sense that Lysimachus would have focused on its construction since he was transforming Alexandria into one of the most important commercial centers of his kingdom. The city wall at Ilion, however, was 17 or 18 stades (ca. 3.2 km) in length, less than half of what Strabo indicates, and the pottery within the wall's foundation trench points to a construction date between 250 and 220 B.C. In terms of both size and date, then, the city wall of Ilion could not have been constructed by Lysimachus.[47]

We still need to consider Lysimachus' role in the development of Ilion, and how the residents viewed him. Scholarly assessments of the Troad during the early third century have alternately presented this period as one of prosperity or dictatorship based largely on two pieces of evidence: (1) the passage in Strabo, in which Lysimachus is named as donor of a temple and city walls, and (2) an anti-tyranny decree from Ilion dated to the early third century.[48] The latter is an extraordinarily powerful document written by a newly democratic Ilion, in which severe penalties are prescribed for anyone involved in tyranny or oligarchy. Their names were to be erased from all civic inscriptions, including those listing priests and benefactors, and their property divided evenly between the city and the children of those who died during the tyranny.[49]

Such a date would mean that the outrage expressed in the decree was directed toward the regime of Lysimachus, and scholars have understandably found this point difficult to reconcile with the Strabo passage that ostensibly presents Lysimachus as Ilion's most important Hellenistic benefactor. As I have argued above, the Strabo passage deals exclusively with Lysimachus' gifts to Alexandria Troas; there is no mention of any assistance to Ilion, and thus no reason to think that the residents enjoyed a special relationship with him.[50]

There are, however, good reasons for assuming an antagonistic relationship between Lysimachus and some of the cities of his kingdom. Strong anti-tyrannical movements followed his death, and at Heraclea Pontica the residents destroyed the citadel walls of the ruler who had been installed there by Lysimachus.[51] One can easily understand why resentment at Ilion ran high: the vast economic assistance promised by Alexander and no doubt expected from Lysimachus was instead given to Alexandria Troas. This was the city that Lysimachus designated as his communications center between Europe and Asia, and the buildup of the harbors there changed the commercial routes that traversed the area.[52] Synoecism enlarged the boundaries of the city and the new fortification wall made it easily defensible; Ilion, meanwhile, was still very vulnerable.

THE SELEUCIDS

In light of Ilion's chilly relationship with Lysimachus, it is no surprise that the city enthusiastically embraced the Seleucid dynasty, and especially the new ruler, Seleucus I, after Lysimachus' death. He received an inscribed altar in the most prominent site in the Agora, while one of Ilion's months was named "Seleukeios" in his honor, during which a festival with musical, gymnastic, and equestrian events was staged.[53] One day was devoted to a sacrifice to Apollo, with the city's twelve tribes marching in the procession, and the funds allotted to the tribes for the purchase of the sacrificial animals were to reach the same level as those intended for the festival of Athena. The inclusion of all twelve

8.7. Open-air, rectangular structure of early Hellenistic date next to the Troy VI South Gate.
Photo by Gebhard Bieg for the Troy Excavation Project.

tribes, several of which were named after Trojan heroes, would simultaneously
have called to mind the city's Homeric heritage.[54]

All we know about the original site of Seleucus I's altar is that it was erected
in the most prominent spot in the agora, and the only likely candidate lies
next to the Troy VI South Gate, which was now refashioned as the entrance to
the Sanctuary of Athena.[55] This was an open-air, rectangular structure of early
Hellenistic date with seats on three sides framing a pavement of stone (Figs. 8.3
and 8.7).[56] No altar was discovered there, but the architectural format would
be appropriate for a heroon, and its location next to the Athena Sanctuary's
entrance made it one of the most visible areas of the city. It was probably at this
time, in fact, that the flanking Troy VI walls were repaired with ashlar masonry.
The larger context here is also significant: the structure with seats was axially
aligned with the Propylaea of the Athena Sanctuary, the plans for which were
prepared during the reign of Antiochus Hierax, the great-grandson of Seleucus
I (Plate 8, Figs. 8.3 and 9.12). Both structures were excavated long ago and we
can no longer establish which one was constructed first, but their orientation
indicates a clear connection between them.[57]

Seleucus I died less than a year after the decree was formulated, and new
honors were quickly offered to his successor, Antiochus I, who received a
gilded bronze equestrian statue in the Athena Sanctuary. This was the first
such statue of its kind at Ilion and possibly the only image at that time in the

8.8. Silver tetradrachm from Ilion with portrait of Antiochus II on the obverse and a reverse of Apollo seated on an omphalos. Photo courtesy of the American Numismatic Society.

sanctuary, other than the cult statue of Athena.[58] Additional statues of Seleucus II or Antiochus Hierax, the sons of Antiochus II, appear to have been set up in the same area approximately thirty-five years later.[59] It is worth noting that the honorific month of Seleukios remained intact throughout the Hellenistic period, despite the frequent changes in political control of the region.[60]

All of this was new for Ilion, and one of the honors – the renaming of a month in the calendar – had occurred only once before, for Demetrius Poliorcetes at Athens.[61] It is not unlikely, in fact, that the idea for an honorific month actually derived from Athens, with which the Troad koinon enjoyed such close relations. The primary influence for the other honors, however, may have come from the Troad: in 311/10 B.C., Scepsis had offered an extensive series of honors to Antigonus I in recognition of his grant of autonomy, including an altar, statue, temenos, sacrifice, games, and a festival.[62] Many of these subsequently figured among the honors that Ilion offered to Seleucus I and Antiochus I, and it seems likely that Scepsis, now a member of the Troad koinon centered at Ilion, provided the impetus.

During the reign of Antiochus I's successor, Antiochus II, the mints of the Troad began to produce a new series of silver tetradrachms with the king's portrait on the obverse and a reverse type of Apollo seated on an omphalos (Fig. 8.8).[63] This was the first silver issue to be struck at Ilion, and the only one of Hellenistic date in which Athena Ilias was not the primary reverse type.[64] One would expect such an innovation to have led to die-sharing with the other cities of the Troad, and there is in fact evidence for one obverse die of Antiochus II that circulated among Ilion, Abydos, and Alexandria Troas.[65]

This series continued during the reigns of Seleucus II and his brother, Antiochus Hierax, and cast the entire area in a new light. The koinon of Antigonus had pulled many of the key cities of the Troad into a new political and religious configuration, but there was no fixed symbol in each of the cities that signaled their membership in a larger league. That symbol now existed in the form of the new Seleucid coinage, which marked the first time in which the cities were striking the same types and effectively presenting themselves as a unified region.

The dominance of Apollo on the reverse is to be expected since he was promoted as the divine patriarch of the Seleucid dynasty, but it must have seemed somewhat surprising in a region that was otherwise dominated by cults of Athena.[66] One sees a sign of this cultic imbalance in the provisions for Seleucus I's festival, which specified that the sacrificial victims for Apollo were to be of the same value as those intended for Athena.[67] The stipulation that the sacrifices should be equal suggests that there was a concern that otherwise they might not be.

There is one other Seleucid honor that merits discussion here, although the evidence is ambiguous. One of the honors given to Antigonus I by Scepsis was a temenos – an enclosed space that would have been intended for the king's cult.[68] There is no indication of such a temenos in the preserved Seleucid-era inscriptions from Ilion, but there are several mentions of a Basileion, or "peristyle of the kings," within the city, which was almost certainly connected to the ruler cult.[69] This must refer to either the Seleucids or the Attalids, since they were the only two dynasties that exercised control over Ilion for extended periods of time. The latter option seems unlikely, due to the fact that there is no evidence for civic honors offered to the Attalids other than naming one of Ilion's tribes "Attalis." A Seleucid attribution consequently seems more probable, although the Basileion's precise form and location are still unknown.[70]

The Basileion also played a role in the Ilieia, the third of Ilion's festivals, which is described in an inscription of the third century B.C. Each of the city's tribes, some of which were named after Trojan heroes, supplied an ox on which the name of the tribe was written.[71] The parade started at the Basileion and ran through the city, with the oxen ultimately sacrificed to Zeus Polieus. Two men were appointed as marshals and were authorized to hit with a stick anyone caught misbehaving.

The reference to a sacrifice to Zeus Polieus suggests the existence of an altar dedicated to him at Ilion, which was probably located within or near the Athena precinct, as at Pergamon and Athens. The Zeus Polieus altar on the Athenian acropolis was situated in an open-air walled precinct next to the Parthenon, and considering the influential role played by Athens in the configuration of Ilion's Athena cult, it is tempting to identify the open-air walled precinct next to the temple of Athena as the local Zeus Polieus cult site, which marked the termination of the Ilieia festival (Plate 8, Fig. 8.3).[72] This precinct occupied the entire southeast side of the Athena Sanctuary, approximately one-fifth of its total area, so the deity in question should have been

8.9. Colossal marble head of Zeus from the Athena Sanctuary. After Dörpfeld 1902, Beilage 54.

someone of high status who was closely connected to Athena, and Zeus Polieus is the most likely candidate.[73]

There is one additional discovery that supports this identification. The largest and most prominent discovery within the temenos was a colossal marble head of Zeus that belonged to a standing statue between 4.5 and 5 m high, probably carved in the later third or second century B.C. (Fig. 8.9). [74] The weathering at the top of the head indicates that the statue stood outside rather than in the cella, and the unfinished back points to a location against a wall rather than visible from all sides. Its original position in or near the walled precinct seems certain, and this is fortified by its discovery in the well to the north of the precinct.

When the Ilieia was first conceived is unclear, but it was certainly in operation during the Hellenistic period, and one inscription mentions its occurrence during the month of Panathenaios.[75] This suggests that the Ilieia and Panathenaia took place at roughly the same time, with the former complementing the latter and highlighting the allegedly Homeric configuration of the settlement within the context of the league's broader celebration.

Meanwhile, the members of the Troad League were benefiting from the same wave of prosperity that had embraced Ilion in the Early Hellenistic period, and the rise in material wealth can be charted most easily by examining the tomb assemblages. One-quarter of the burials in the Dardanus tumulus date to this period, as do a considerable number of gold diadems, headbands, medallions, and rings contained within it.[76] A similarly rich set of Early Hellenistic tombs was found at Lampsacus and Ilgardere on the Gallipoli peninsula, in which were preserved several gold wreaths and gold diadems with relief decoration of Dionysus and Ariadne.[77]

The gold diadems from the Hellespontine tombs are particularly important in that nearly all of them are identical in shape and were made from the same matrix, thereby again pointing to local production of gold jewelry.[78] The decoration of several of these diadems features women playing the aulos or lyre, and actual musical instruments of similar type have been found in tombs at both Dardanus and Lampsacus.[79] These are, of course, fragmentary, since several of them were made of wood, but their presence in tombs was no doubt far more common than the evidence now indicates, and they were probably played in the funeral service prior to burial.[80]

THE BUILDING PROGRAMS OF ANTIOCHUS HIERAX

In spite of the considerable attention that had been devoted to Ilion between ca. 310 and 240, the city was still unwalled and contained little more than a theater and a sanctuary with a small and apparently dilapidated temple. All of this would change in the 230s, when Antiochus Hierax, the son of Antiochus II, acquired control of most of Asia Minor. Although that control would endure for just over a decade, he would provide a level of financial support for the Troad that the region had never before witnessed, and the building industry flourished as a consequence.

This was a period marked by war throughout Asia Minor: the decision of Antiochus II to bequeath his kingdom to Seleucus II, the eldest son of his first marriage, provoked the Third Syrian War with Ptolemy III, which lasted from 246 to 242. The conclusion of that war was quickly followed by another one that involved Seleucus II and his brother, Antiochus Hierax, and is thus generally referred to as the War of the Brothers. To increase the strength of his armed forces Antiochus employed Gallic mercenaries, which subsequently pulled Attalus I and his kingdom of Pergamon into the conflict. By 226 both Seleucus II and Antiochus Hierax were dead, with Pergamon now emerging as the dominant power in the Troad.[81]

None of these conflicts affected the cities of the Troad in any significant way. On the contrary, this was an unusually prosperous period for the region due to the fact that Antiochus had chosen the Hellespont as the primary administrative and financial center of his kingdom. More than fifty obverse dies of Antiochus are attested at Hellespontine mints, including at least seventeen at Alexandria Troas, which appears to have served as Antiochus' capital; twelve at Lampsacus, two of which were also used at Abydos; and eight at Ilion.[82]

Antiochus devoted an unusual amount of attention to Ilion, which remained the capital of the koinon that bound all of these cities together. Other rulers, notably Alexander, had promised earlier to reshape the city so that its appearance would match the magnitude of its Homeric heritage, but Antiochus was the first to fulfill his promises. The new building program that he launched had an impact on every area of the settlement, but three components were more important than the others: a new precinct and temple of Athena, a new Bouleuterion, and a new city wall that would fortify the residential district in the Lower City. Based on the ceramics in the foundation trenches associated with the two projects, it looks as if all three projects were begun simultaneously in the 230s B.C.

This kind of program is somewhat reminiscent of Late Bronze Age Troy, when there had been another massive building campaign that added the citadel walls and the rock-cut ditch to the site's topography. The circuit of the new city wall would, in general, follow the line of the old ditch and would make use of some of the same materials. The Lower City quarries were still being mined for marl foundation stones, and by this point the limestone and granite quarries that surrounded Alexandria Troas were in full operation.[83]

Another source of building stone may have been the site of Sigeion itself, which was reportedly destroyed by Ilion sometime in the second half of the third century.[84] The mention of Ilion's involvement comes from Strabo, but it has always seemed surprising since the town had no standing army nor a very large population in the Hellenistic period. The episode would be more comprehensible, however, if it had taken place during Hierax's control of the Troad. He had secured an alliance with the Gallic mercenaries of Asia Minor and was therefore at war with Pergamon, which had strong political links to Athens. Given the importance of the Troad to Antiochus' kingdom, it is not unlikely that he would have looked with favor on and aided in the destruction of Sigeion, Athens' principal colony in the region.[85] It is also tempting to link that destruction to the inception of Ilion's building program during the third quarter of the third century.

This period also witnessed the establishment of the city's grid, at 11 degrees NE, which would remain in force until late antiquity.[86] The earliest structure so oriented was the portico surrounding the new Athena temple, with the streets of the Lower City and a massive new Bouleuterion following suit shortly thereafter (Fig. 8.3, Plate 29). The creation of such a grid appears to reflect a new conception of the settlement as a city that anticipated future growth on a large scale, not unlike the more powerful cities of the Troad such as Assos and Alexandria Troas. The koinon was the engine behind this change in outlook and presentation, but it was the patronage of the Seleucids and Attalids that would provide the means for implementation.

The koinon probably met in the new Bouleuterion, which was constructed above the small council house that had been built at the beginning of the Hellenistic period (Plate 27).[87] One of the most striking features of the new structure is that its back wall had actually been cut into the Troy VI citadel wall, which had to be partially dismantled as a consequence. Such an intervention was both costly and time-consuming, and it looks as if the builders were determined to have the new Bouleuterion draw its strength, both literally and figuratively, from the Bronze Age fortification walls.

Much of the third century Bouleuterion has been disturbed by later construction, but it clearly included an orchestral altar framed by a cavea that was, in turn, surrounded by an interior colonnade, and a broad staircase linked the back of the building to the Athena precinct. Its location near the road leading to the Temple of Athena was especially appropriate, since the Panathenaic festival was presumably planned in the Bouleuterion by the representatives of the koinon's cities.

The new fortification wall completely encircled the Lower City and joined to both sides of the Athena Sanctuary (Figs. 8.10, 8.11, Plate 29).[88] The north

8.10. The best-preserved stretch of the city wall north of the West Sanctuary, looking north. Troia slide 25047.

side of the Sanctuary, in effect, formed part of the northern trace of the wall, and it seems likely that the theater was also contained within the circuit.[89] The length of the wall has been estimated at 3.6 km, a measurement roughly analogous to those at Neandria (3.2 km) and Assos (more than 3 km), although the wall at Alexandria, with a length of 7.4 m, was nearly double the size of the others.[90]

In most parts of its trace, the wall was founded on bedrock and contained a rubble core between two ashlar faces, 2.50–3 m in width (Fig. 8.11). The limestone blocks generally featured pseudo-isodomic masonry, although the stones were sometimes interlocked at different levels, apparently to guard against any possible movement during earthquakes. The stones of the earlier Troy VI citadel wall were alternately used as foundations for the new wall or removed and reused in the new construction. Dörpfeld unearthed the remains of several round or half-round towers along the wall, and there are traces of a staircase on the southwest side of the citadel that led to the parados, or sentry walls.

The new fortification wall also featured a rock-cut ditch, U-shaped in section, as a primary line of defense.[91] In two areas near the city wall's southern trace, sectors f26 and s34, a rock cut ditch ca. 2 m deep and between 9 and 12 m wide was found 20–30 m in front of (to the south of) the wall.[92] Although the depth is comparable to that of the Late Bronze Age ditch, the width is nearly three times as large. The ditch's excavation would consequently have

8.11. The city wall north of the West Sanctuary, looking east. Troia slide 25053.

furnished a large quantity of marl for use in the wall's foundations, which surely increased the speed with which it was built.

The only gate in the wall that has been uncovered lies at the northeast corner of the citadel, on the road that would have led up from the main theater.[93]

8.12. The northeast gate of the Hellenistic and Roman city, looking south. Troy Excavation Project. Troia Neg. 96/205/8.

The gate featured two large limestone piers that probably supported an arch 3 m wide, next to which was an interior room or guardhouse (Figs. 8.3 and 8.12). A similar gate was almost certainly positioned at the northwest corner of the citadel, north of the West Sanctuary, although this corner of the site was heavily damaged by subsequent warfare and no trace of it now survives. A gate had occupied that spot during the second millennium B.C. (VI V), and the landscape probably favored an approach to the city there.

The wall makes two appearances in the historical sources of the third/early second century, both of which support a construction date in the later third century. Strabo mentions that when the Gauls first crossed the Hellespont in 278 B.C. Ilion had no walls, and they consequently chose not to occupy the settlement.[94] While describing the visit of the Scipios to Ilion in 190 B.C., Livy notes that the Roman army camped in the field below the walls, which were clearly standing by then.[95] One other passage, this one in Polybius, also refers to the walls, albeit in an indirect way. He relates the decision of Alexandria Troas to dispatch 4,000 men to Ilion to stop the Gallic siege of 217 B.C. Ilion could not have held off the Gauls, even for a short time, without a city wall already in place.[96]

The construction of the new city wall meant that the Lower City was now more secure than it had ever been, with approximately 72 hectares (178 acres) under protection. For a city that was still relatively small, this was an unusually large fortified area, roughly equivalent to that of Priene, and it suggests that Ilion's leaders were expecting considerable expansion to occur.[97] There had been traces of activity in this area already at the beginning of the Hellenistic period, but only at the southern edge of the Lower City, ca. 400 m to the south of the Bronze Age citadel, where workmen began quarrying stones for new buildings on and around the acropolis (sector w28).[98] A few houses of simple construction were later built in the vicinity of the quarries, ca. 260–240, but they may have been intended only as temporary shelter for agricultural workers and laborers.

More permanent housing was not constructed here until the third quarter of the third century B.C., when Ilion's population must have increased significantly as a result of the massive new building program. Less than 2 percent of the Lower City has been excavated, but magnetic prospection has produced a wealth of information concerning its plan during the Greek and Roman periods, some of which has been verified by trial trenches at strategic points.[99] The houses consisted of mud-brick walls on stone socles, which would continue to be the favored method of construction in the Lower City through late antiquity, and most were equipped with courtyards, wells, and drains.[100]

The contemporaneity of construction on the acropolis and in the Lower City created a perfect symbiotic relationship: a considerable number of trees must have been felled throughout the latter area to create more open space for the new housing and streets; meanwhile, an enormous amount of timber would have been necessary for the roofs of the new temple and its porticoes, as well as for scaffolding, and at least some of it must have come from the Lower City.[101]

The Spring Cave in sector t14, 180 m to the southwest of the citadel, now began to be mined again (Figs. 8.13 and 8.14).[102] Although the cave's potential

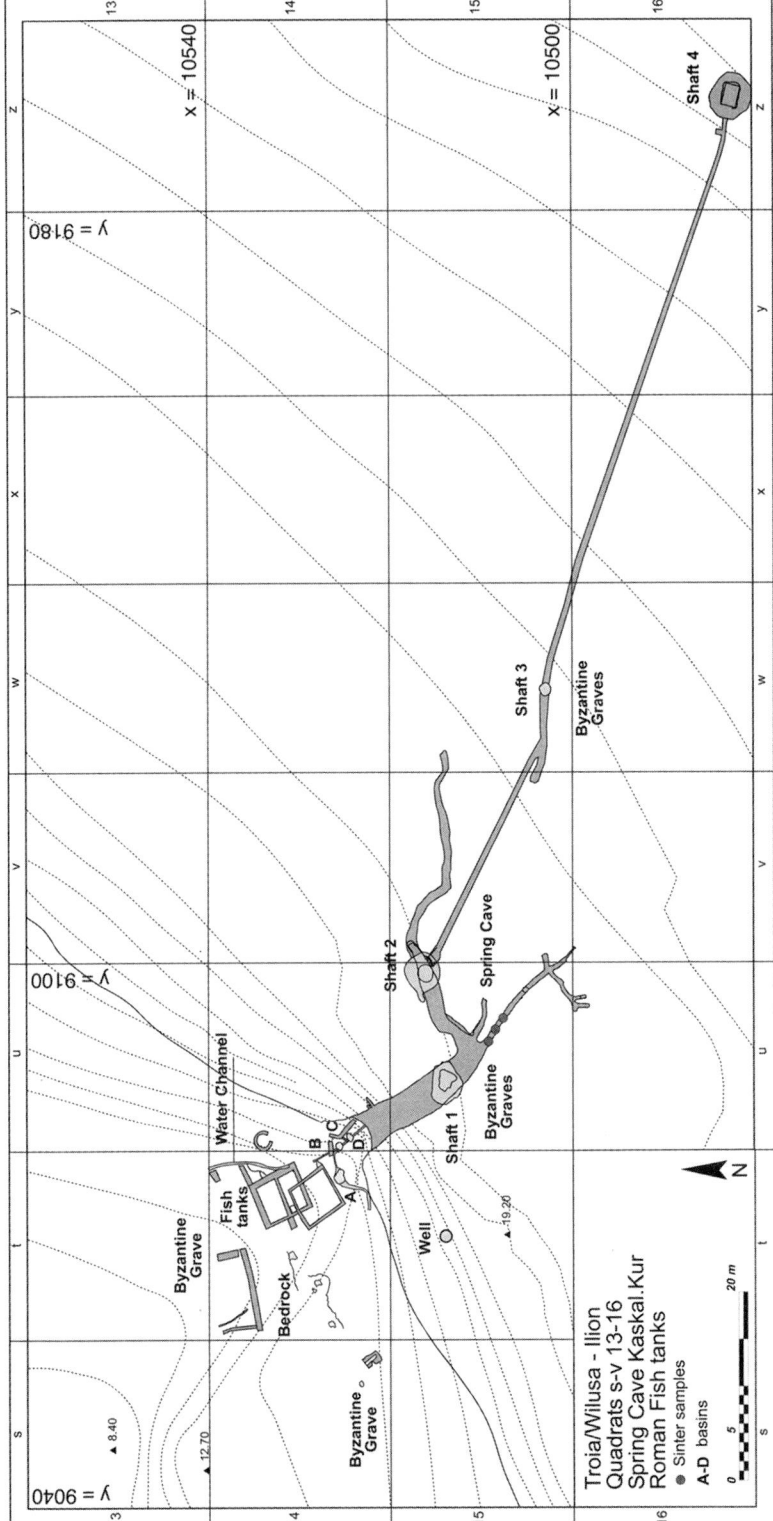

8.13. Plan of the Spring Cave in the Lower City. Drawing by Gebhard Bieg for the Troy Excavation Project.

8.14. View of the Spring Cave in the Lower City. Troia slide 34284.

as a water source was recognized already in the Early Bronze Age, exploitation of the cave's water during the post–Bronze Age period seems to coincide with the construction of the city wall. The importance of the cave to a growing community must have been recognized by this point, which was one of the reasons that the city wall was constructed 100 m to the west of the entrance, thereby protecting both the water and those who used it.[103]

The cave is one large aquifer, with water seeping from its walls and roof, and the tool marks throughout the interior reflect an attempt to expand the interior space of the cave and thus increase the amount of water it discharged. The entrance corridor branches off into three passages, each with smaller dependent corridors, and the central one extends for a length of more than 100 m. Cut into the roof of the central passage at staggered intervals are four funnel-shaped shafts intended to channel groundwater into the cave's main corridor, and at least two of the shafts end in basins in the floor of the cave.

This is a qanat system, first developed in Persia and widely used in the Near East, although such systems were rare in Asia Minor.[104] The only other example in this region lies in the vicinity of the Athenian colony of Sigeion; its date is uncertain, although the city's demolition in the third century B.C. provides a *terminus ante quem* for its construction, and it may have been begun as early as the time of Peisistratos.[105] It is not unlikely that Ilion's qanat was influenced by the one at Sigeion, since they are the only two such systems known from western Asia Minor.

THE TEMPLE OF ATHENA

The third component of this building program was a new temple of Athena, or Athenaion, which provided the cult of Athena Ilias with the kind of imposing shrine that Alexander had presumably envisioned a century earlier (Plate 8, Fig. 8.3). Upon completion, this building became the largest Doric temple in northwestern Asia Minor, slightly more substantial than the Assos temple and nearly twice as large as the temple of Athena at Pergamon.[106] It was constructed as a hexastyle peripteral Doric building, with pronaos and opisthodomos, featuring six by twelve columns and a two-stepped platform, or krepidoma (Fig. 8.15A, B).[107] The temple's footprint measured 16.40 m (north-south) by 35.70 m (east-west), which indicates a structure approximately 50 × 100 Doric feet, and so a hekatompedon.[108] This was, as far as we now, the first temple at Ilion to have been built of marble, and the last in the Mediterranean to have featured carved figural metopes.[109] Isotopic analysis of the marble shows that it derives from the Sea of Marmara, and therefore from the island of Proconnesus.[110] This was the best and most easily transportable marble in the region, and the most popular source for architectural elements at Ilion during the Hellenistic and Roman periods.

The dates assigned to the temple have vacillated between the Early Hellenistic and Augustan periods since its discovery in the 1870s, but excavations conducted around the Sanctuary during the 1990s have provided new evidence for its construction. The temple was part of a larger building program involving an expanded terrace and other structures, and the evidence for these is critical to establishing the date when construction began. To accommodate the new Athena temple and its altar, which were situated at the northern edge of the acropolis, an enormous terrace measuring 109 m east-west and 88 m north-south had to be constructed, thereby requiring the eastern side of the acropolis to be extended by about 20 m.[111] The platform was bordered by porticoes at the east, south, and west, but the northern side was left open so that the expansive view of the Dardanelles and the plains of Troy was not blocked.[112]

The new enlarged terrace would have required an enormous amount of fill as well as exceptionally strong walls to contain that fill. When work on the project began, the upper surface of the mound was no doubt marked by small mounds that contained the remains of Late Bronze Age buildings. All of these would have been sliced off by the leveling activities and used for terracing fill, but even more earth would have been necessary considering the enormous size of the new platform. Much of it must have come from the Athenaion's foundation trenches, which were nearly 9 m deep and would have produced an immense amount of fill. Those trenches must have been dug after the terrace walls had been set in place so that the earth they yielded could be used to fill the terrace.[113]

(A)

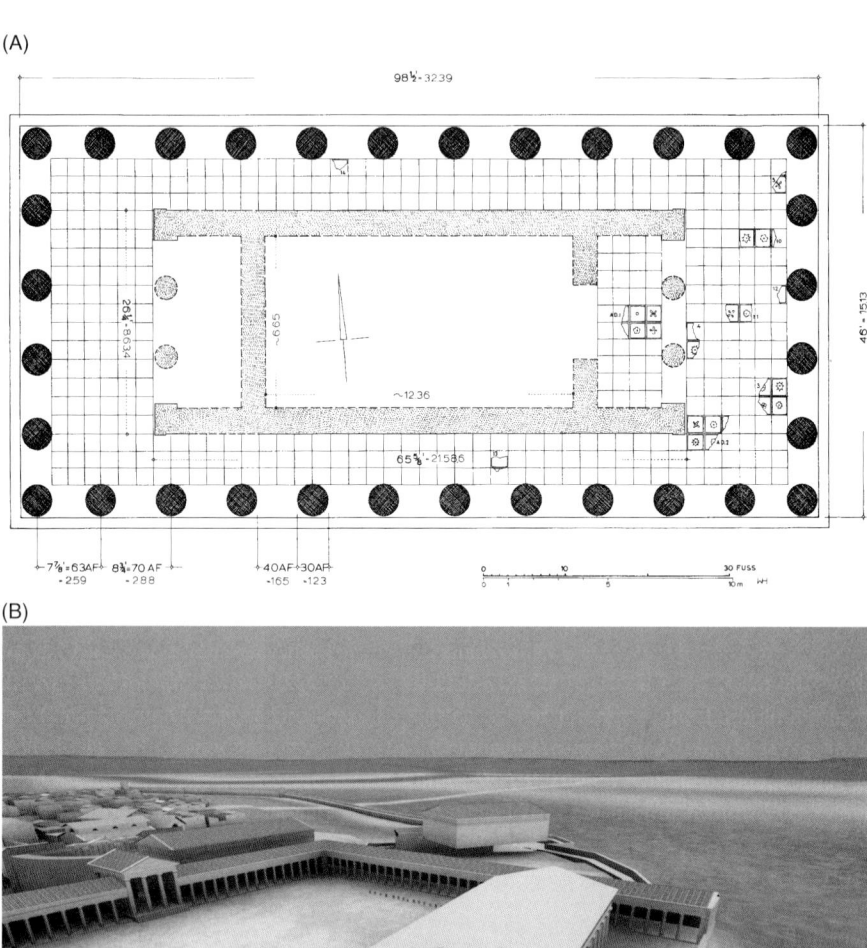

(B)

8.15. (A) The ground plan of the Athenaion, prepared by Elizabeth Riorden for the Troy Excavation Project. (B) Reconstruction of the Athena Sanctuary precinct, prepared by Elizabeth Riorden for the Troy Excavation Project.

The terrace fills should consequently provide a *terminus post quem* for the building of the temple. The latest pottery within those fills dates to the same period as that within the foundation trenches of the city wall, 250–220 B.C., which is what one would expect considering that the two structures were bonded. This means that construction work on the temple and the terrace on which it stood should date to the third quarter of the third century, which, in turn, strongly suggests that the temple and city wall were planned and begun simultaneously.[114] This proposed dating is reinforced by the style of the architectural decoration: the majority of the dated parallels, which come primarily from Pergamon, Samothrace, and Macedonia, fall either in the later third century or the first quarter of the second.[115]

There were undoubtedly several times within this period when economic or military problems forced construction to halt. It is hard to imagine work on the temple continuing without interruption in 223, when the renegade Seleucid prince Achaeus rampaged through the area, and this applies as well to the Gallic attack of 218 and the First and Second Macedonian Wars (214–205; 200–197 B.C.).[116] Such periods of hiatus were, of course, more the norm than the exception in Hellenistic temple construction, and it is conceivable that a few parts were not completed until the end of the second century, but at least part of the superstructure must have been finished during the period in which Ilion lay in the political orbit of the Attalids.

There are no inscriptions indicating a personal involvement or financing of the temple by Attalus I or Eumenes II, but there are several points that speak in favor of this, the most prominent of which are the strong technical and stylistic affinities between the Ilion Athenaion and the early Hellenistic architecture of Pergamon.[117] The Attalids certainly became benefactors of Ilion at a later point, as a gift of land by Attalus II to the Sanctuary of Athena Ilias indicates, and Attalid imagery would also have been a conspicuous part of the cityscape: a statue of Eumenes II stood prominently in the Sanctuary of Athena, and one of the tribes of Ilion was named "Attalis" in their honor.[118]

During the reign of Attalus I, in particular, Ilion constituted one of the principal links between Rome and Pergamon, as metropolis of the former and political ally/neighbor of the latter. When the treaty of Phoenice was concluded in 205 at the end of the First Macedonian War, Ilion and Pergamon – in that order – were the first two signatories on the Roman side.[119] At the same time, the cult of Cybele was formally brought to Rome, almost certainly because of the cult's Trojan origins, and it was Attalus whom the Romans approached to facilitate the transfer. The political and religious personae of all three cities were closely intertwined in the late third/early second centuries B.C., and Attalid economic assistance to Ilion would have been one way of forging an even stronger bond with Rome. Pergamon's ostentatious dedications in Athens in the late third/early second century were in large part intended to showcase the kingdom's role as successor to Athenian cultural excellence, and dedications at Ilion would have established a link with the Homeric foundations of that culture.[120]

THE METOPES OF THE TEMPLE

Since carved metopes in the Hellenistic period are so rare, the most frequently discussed component of the temple has always been the sculptural
decoration. Ilion's Athenaion is the last temple to feature metopic figural
sculpture, largely because Ionic and Corinthian were more popular orders.[121]
There would have been space for ten metopes on each of the short sides
and twenty-two on each of the long ones, adding up to a total of sixty-four
metopes if each of the sides were decorated. The earlier excavators identified
three different themes: a Gigantomachy, a battle between Greeks and Trojans
(Ilioupersis), and a Centauromachy. The one fragment associated with the
last theme has not been universally accepted, since it features only part of
a lined, bearded face that could belong to a giant as easily as a centaur.[122]
Nevertheless, to the first two themes we can add one more: recent excavations have produced a relief fragment of an Amazon that appears to be
carved from the same marble as the other elements of the temple.[123] Only
the upper torso survives, but the dimensions are in harmony with those of
the figures in the other temple metopes, and it is almost certainly a part of
the Athenaion decoration.

The Gigantomachy cycle was placed on the east side of the temple, as on the
Parthenon, and featured both biped and anguiped giants, as on the Pergamon
altar.[124] Since the Panathenaea commemorated Athena's victory in the
Gigantomachy, this cycle understandably had pride of place at the entrance.[125]
The best-preserved relief in this cycle features Athena striding vigorously to
the left and pulling the hair of a fallen giant with her left hand (Fig. 8.16).[126]
The same motif also appears on the Pergamon altar, but at Ilion her aegis has
been omitted and she grabs the giant with her (left) shield-bearing arm. The
latter configuration is extremely rare in ancient art: since the shield was always
attached to the left arm, the left hand generally grasped the rim straps and was
involved in no other action.[127] At Pergamon the configuration was reversed so
that the giant is at the left, and Athena pulls his hair with her right hand. In
other words, Ilion's version is in many respects a mirror image of what one
finds at Pergamon.

The metope with Helios, which is also the best preserved, began the
Ilioupersis cycle on the north side of the temple, as it did on the Parthenon
(Fig. 8.17).[128] The four-horsed chariot of Helios, which was shown rising and
traveling toward the west, featured an unusual combination of painting and
sculpture. The wheel of Helios' chariot was rendered by paint, the faint outlines of which could still be seen forty years ago, and painted wavy lines near
the base were probably intended to represent the sea.[129] The Macedonian star
that has been used for the nimbus of Helios can be found on a variety of media
in the Early Hellenistic period, in both Macedonia and western Asia Minor,

8.16. Metope of Athena and giant from the Athenaion, Pergamon Museum, Berlin. Photo courtesy of the Pergamon Museum, Berlin.

8.17. Metope of Helios from the Athenaion, Pergamon Museum, Berlin. Photo courtesy Pergamon Museum, Berlin.

8.18. Ilioupersis metope from the Athenaion. Achilles and Lykaon? Pergamon Museum, Berlin. Photo courtesy of the Pergamon Museum, Berlin.

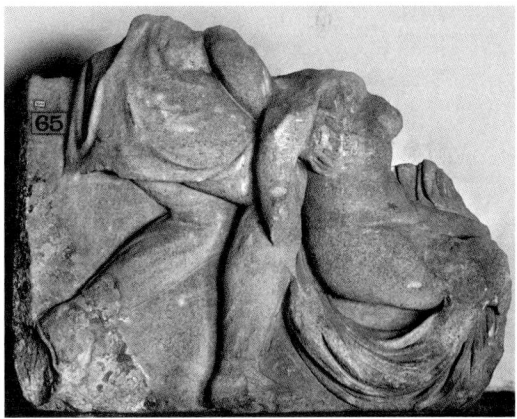

8.19. Ilioupersis metope from the Athenaion. The death of Sarpedon? Pergamon Museum, Berlin. Photo courtesy of the Pergamon Museum, Berlin.

and it complements the Macedonian influence on the Athenaion's architectural decoration.[130]

The other reliefs in this cycle cannot be identified with certainty. One features two warriors in combat: a soldier in chiton and cuirass striding toward the left grasps the hair of a kneeling foe wearing trousers (*anaxyrides*) and a chiton (Fig. 8.18).[131] The humbled easterner touches the knee of the Greek soldier with his left hand, and his right hand was probably raised to loosen the Greek's grasp of his hair, although it does not survive. The touching of the knee as an appeal for mercy is a common literary motif in the *Iliad*, and the iconography would fit several Greek-Trojan duels from the epic, although the most likely one is Achilles and Lykaon, the son of Priam, in Book XXI.[132]

Another metope depicts a man being carried from the battlefield: a standing Trojan in chiton and *anaxyrides* (trousers) grasps the upper torso of a nearly nude male whose legs would have been held by a now missing figure at the right (Fig. 8.19).[133] The man has a decidedly androgynous appearance, clearly intended to make him appear youthful, and there is no sign of life in his body. He must be Trojan, judging by the dress of the man carrying him, and the iconography would therefore fit Sarpedon, the young son of Zeus who was killed by Patroclus and carried from the battlefield by Hypnos and Thanatos. If so, then the two personifications assumed mortal guise here, as they sometimes do in vase painting.[134]

There are thirteen fragmentary reliefs that cannot be assigned with certainty to any of the aforementioned cycles, but most of them relate to fighting.[135] In any event, the presence of a Gigantomachy, Ilioupersis, and Amazonomachy suggests that a Centauromachy would originally have been included on the fourth side, and the only other temple in the eastern Mediterranean to have featured carved figural metopes on all four sides was the Parthenon.[136] It is difficult to believe that the koinon was not looking toward Athens, and the Parthenon in particular, when the temple was being designed and constructed. From the time of its formation in the Early Hellenistic period, the koinon had defined itself in Athenian terms, and Ilion's Athenaion was the geographic heart of the koinon.[137] All of this, of course, is somewhat ironic: the Greek-speaking residents of Ilion were emphasizing their links to the defeated Trojans of the Homeric epics, while simultaneously using Athenian models to frame those legendary connections.

It is worth noting that most of the rest of the Troad was also looking toward the west, at least in terms of architecture. There is evidence for twelve Troad temples prior to the Roman period, and at least eight of them were built in the Doric order.[138] This architectural signature served as one of the main components of the Troad's persona, as did the dominance of the cult of Athena, and visitors would have perceived the region as one that identified itself with mainland Greece, and especially Athens.[139]

OTHER STRUCTURES IN THE SANCTUARY

The Athenaion was only one component of a very large sanctuary, which encompassed over half of the area covered by the Bronze Age citadel, nearly 110 m east-west and nearly 90 north-south (Plate 8, Fig. 8.3). The exterior of the portico, facing the agora, was an unarticulated limestone wall; the interior was a single-story Doric façade of Proconnesian marble, behind which there were several rooms for storage and administration. The Propylaea was accessed via a road that led from the agora to the Athena Sanctuary, passing directly through the Troy VI South Gate that had served as the primary approach to the citadel during the Late Bronze Age. Although the road now occupied a higher level and was flanked by new ashlar balustrades, the ruined Troy VI fortification wall remained visible and would have activated the visitor's sense of the site's Homeric heritage.[140]

Whether marble paving extended throughout the temenos is uncertain, but it was certainly present between temple and altar.[141] No identifiable part of the altar's superstructure remains, but it would have been roughly two-thirds the length of the temple's east side, a ratio comparable to the altars of Athena Polias at Priene and Artemis at Magnesia (Figs. 8.3 and 8.15B). The placement of the well within the precinct (Ba) was especially unusual, and quite unlike that in any other sanctuary.[142] It was 14.50 m deep and axially aligned with the cult statue and the altar (Figs. 8.3, 8.15B, 8.20, and 8.21). The well-cut ashlar stones lining the well are bonded to those of the new temenos pavement, so the two are clearly contemporary.

Directly above Well Ba was a decorative marble enclosure that featured a three-stepped podium with a circular wall articulated by six pilasters, above which was marble lattice-work and possibly a conical roof (Fig. 8.21).[143] The well-head completely encircled the shaft and was at least 1.5 m in height, which was just high enough to prevent easy access to the water. In other words, the marble enclosure was intended both to monumentalize the well and to restrict the approach to it.[144] The only access lay in a new subterranean tunnel more than 2 m wide and 2.3 m high that extended at least 10 m toward the north.[145]

At first glance, this makes no sense: the designers created a new water source and situated it on the primary axis of the sanctuary, yet the water was available only to those who entered the tunnel. The most likely explanation for such an idiosyncratic topography is that it was designed to highlight the custom of the Locrian Maidens and thereby strengthen the site's Homeric associations. One of the requirements in this unusual cult was that the maidens were to stay out of the line of sight of the cult statue, which meant avoiding any activity on the central axis of the precinct. By placing the well on the temple's central axis, the maidens would have been compelled to use the subterranean passage to the well – on the same axis as the cult statue, but more than 2 m below it. The plans for this unorthodox architectural arrangement would have been drawn up at approximately the same time in which the Locrian tribute was revived, after a century's hiatus, and the new architectural organization is probably related to the revival.[146] The site's tour guides would now have been able to link the circuitous paths of the maidens to Ajax's rape of Cassandra in the

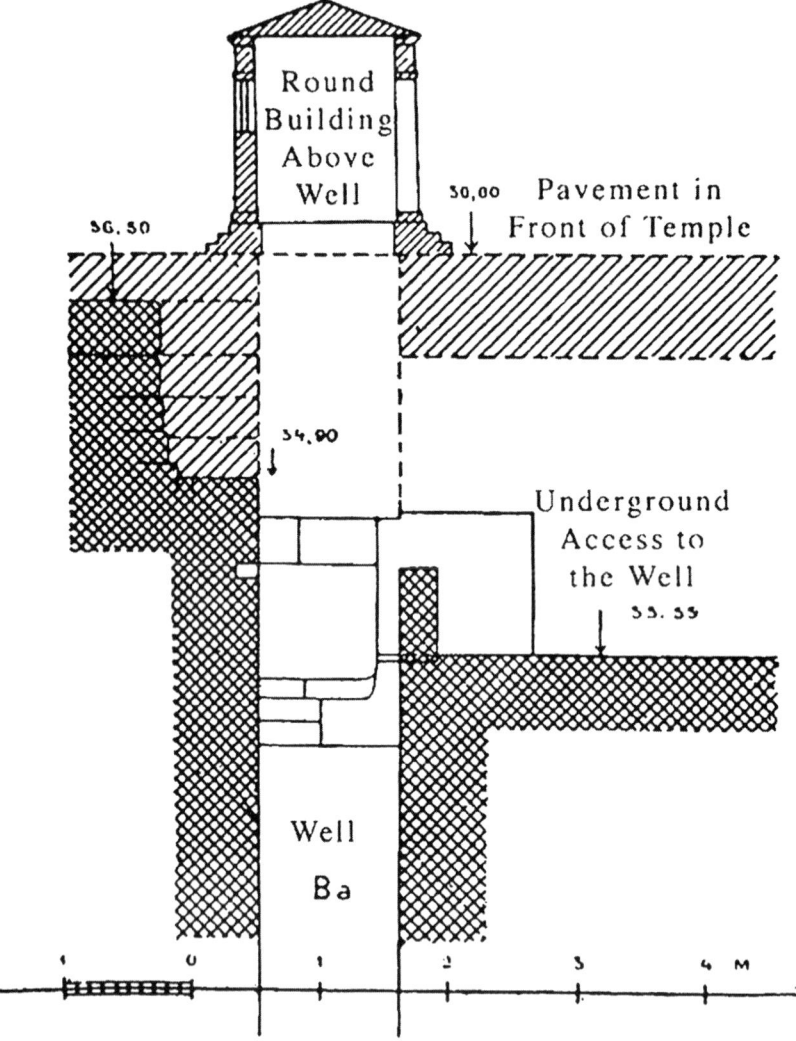

8.20. Section of Well Ba in the Athena Sanctuary, after Dörpfeld 1902, 178, fig. 68.

same locale. It was, in essence, a museum exhibit, with architecture and ritual closely linked.

That museum was not limited to Ilion's citadel: the surrounding landscape was punctuated with mounds that had probably been identified as the tombs of Greek and Trojan heroes as early as the Archaic period.[147] The most famous of these was the "tumulus of Achilles" at nearby Achilleion (now Sivritepe), which lay 4 km southwest of Troy (Fig. 8.22).[148] Excavation of the tumulus in 1998 and 1999 revealed that the original mound was a late Neolithic settlement, nearly 5 m high; it was monumentalized during the second quarter of the third century B.C., judging by the pottery, and raised to a height of 13 m above the surrounding area, an increase of approximately 8 m.[149] This would have been one of the largest public works projects that Ilion had attempted

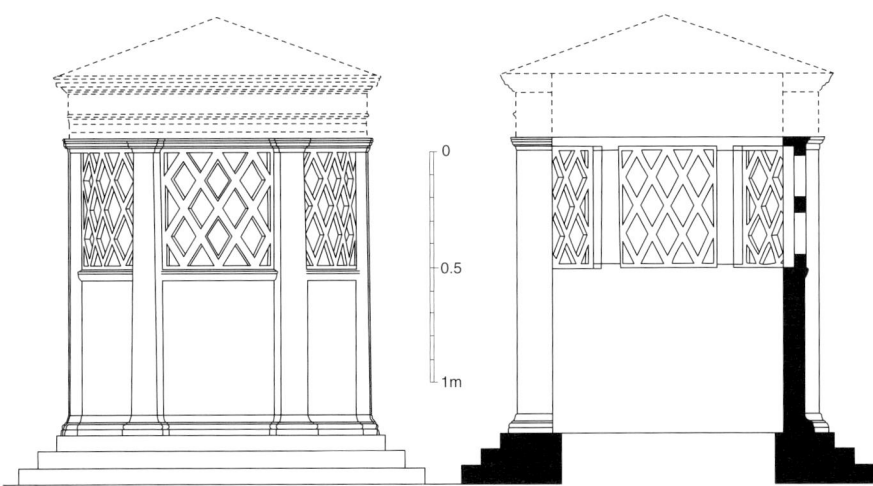

8.21. Reconstruction of the structure above Well Ba, drawing by Kate Clayton, after Dörpfeld 1902, 229, fig. 92.

8.22. Sivritepe, identified in antiquity as the Tumulus of Achilles. Troy Excavation Project photo.

up to this point, and it would have made the Tumulus of Achilles larger than any of the other mounds that had been linked to the graves of the Greek and Trojan heroes.

Such a monumental building project was surely a by-product of Ilion's burgeoning tourist industry and would have complemented both the temple treasury with Homeric relics and the recitations of the *Iliad* within the Panathenaic festival: the visitor could listen to the stories of the heroes' exploits, examine the remains of their armor and weapons, and pay homage to them at their burial sites. Meanwhile, the laborious movements of the Locrian Maidens throughout the sanctuary would have served as a continual reminder of the crime of Ajax, thereby blurring the line between past and present and effectively bridging the gap between Homeric Troy and Hellenistic Ilion.

A related development around this time was the growth of cults and cult sites of Homer, which, in turn, may have prompted increased tourism to the Troad.[150] A heroon of Homer was erected in the last quarter of the third century B.C. by Ptolemy IV in Alexandria, and Homeric cults are attested at Argos, Chios, Ios, and Smyrna during the Hellenistic period.[151] Images of Homer flanked by personifications of the *Iliad* and *Odyssey* now appeared on stelae commemorating victories in poetry contests, as demonstrated by the celebrated "Apotheosis of Homer" in the British Museum, and a broader embrace of the Homeric epics was readily apparent throughout the Aegean and eastern Mediterranean.[152]

Ilion's Homeric monuments were now being subjected to greater scholarly scrutiny by writers and scholars attempting to assess the historicity of the Trojan War and Ilion's actual relationship to it. Demetrius of Scepsis compared Homer's description of Trojan geography with the landscape around Ilion and concluded that Homeric Troy must lay elsewhere, while Hestiaea of Alexandria Troas examined the alluvial deposits to the north of Ilion ca. 200 B.C. and decided that the area must originally have been a bay and could not have supported a battle.[153] New literary assessments of Homeric geography also appeared in works by Apollodorus of Athens and Hegesianax, who, under the pen name of Cephalo of Gergis, wrote a novel that purported to be the true story of the Trojan War.[154]

The increased tourism was accompanied by looting. With the end of Persian domination in 334, the estates to which the imposing burial mounds were tied broke up and the families moved away. Tombs such as Kızöldün, Dedetepe, and Çan subsequently became easy and attractive targets for the new residents, who probably plundered them continually throughout the Hellenistic and Roman periods.[155] The objects looted from the tumuli, in general, appear to have been melted down for their intrinsic value rather than sold on the art market as rare antiques, unless they could somehow be linked to legendary characters, either Greek or Trojan, or presented as natural wonders in their own right.

Such Homeric relics were increasingly trumpeted as status symbols as the Hellenistic period progressed. The Temple of Athena at Lindos exhibited the quiver of Pandarus, the bracelets of Helen, and an electrum goblet, reportedly dedicated by Helen, which had the same measurement as her breast. The bronze spear of Achilles was housed in the Temple of Athena at Phaselis, and

the sword of Memnon lay in the Temple of Asclepius at Nicomedia. Any one
of these could conceivably have been plundered from an earlier tomb.[156]

OTHER MONUMENTS IN THE TROAD

Few of the other cities in western Asia Minor were in a position to showcase
antiquities that could be convincingly marketed as Trojan War memorabilia,
so they fashioned monuments and spectacles intended to attract just as much
attention and signal the extent of the power they wielded. Priene, Pergamon,
and Sardis inaugurated their own Panathenaic festivals, and Cyzicus put on
display a chryselephantine statue of Cybele – the only such statue of its kind in
Asia Minor.[157] All of these would have paled in comparison with the new construction at the site of Parium on the southern shore of the Sea of Marmara,
which built the largest altar that Asia Minor had ever seen. Usually referred
to as the Great Altar of Hermocreon, it was depicted on the city's coins and
measured one stade (186 m) in length, significantly larger than the Pergamon
altar (156 m in length), and nearly as sizable as that of Hieron in Syracuse (199
m long).[158]

At least one site in the Troad attempted to link its building programs to the
same Homeric heritage to which Ilion laid claim. This was the Sanctuary of
Apollo Smintheus, slightly less than 50 km south of Ilion, which lay within the
political orbit of Alexandria Troas (Plate 26). At some point around the middle
of the second century B.C. the Sanctuary constructed a new temple that was
slated to become the largest in the Troad, and nearly twice the size of Ilion's
temple to Athena Ilias (Fig. 8.23).[159] It was also, as far as we know, the only
Ionic temple in the Troad at the time in which it was built, and the only one,
other than the Artemision at Ephesus, to have featured sculpted column drums,
or *columnae caelatae*.[160]

The temple was located in the old city of Chrysa, where Apollo's priest
Chryses had allegedly lived at the time of the Trojan War, and the builders were
just as intent on repackaging and marketing that heritage as Ilion had been.
Unlike Ilion's Athenaion, however, the carved scenes on the column drums
and frieze focused solely on scenes from the *Iliad* and the *Ilioupersis*. Episodes
featuring the family of Chryses were included, as were several iconographically unique scenes, such as Achilles mourning at the deathbed of Patroclus
(Fig. 8.24) or Odysseus carrying one of the trees that would be used to construct the Trojan horse.[161] All of these subjects were no doubt amplified in the
annual Smintheia festival at the site, which probably echoed many of the same
themes that had been integrated into Ilion's Panathenaea.[162]

The visitor who traveled to these festivals during the third century B.C.
would have been struck by the extent to which cities of the region were

8.23. Temple of Apollo Smintheus. Troy Excavation Project photo.

8.24. Relief from the Temple of Apollo Smintheus: Achilles at the deathbed of Patroclus. Courtesy of Prof. Dr. Coşkun Özgünel.

unified, which was more remarkable than one might think. The kingdom of Wilusa had brought the Troad together under a single ruler, but from what we can tell, this involved only one major settlement and a collection of scattered villages. That unity splintered following the end of the Bronze Age due to a series of competing powers, coupled with the fact that the Ida Mountains effectively divided the region into northern and southern quadrants. All of this was largely reversed by the new koinon, which brought the coastal cities around the perimeter of the Troad into a single confederation, even though it excluded nearly all of the interior with the notable exception of Scepsis.

Athens as well as Athena provided the glue that held the confederation together, so it is not surprising that Doric developed into the region's architectural order of choice. Just as integral to the region's cohesion, however, was the increasingly prominent legendary heritage of the Troad that was now extended to all of the koinon's member cities. Ilion had thus far been the primary engine behind the promotion of the Troad's Homeric foundations, but other cities in the region would eventually pursue the same model as the Hellenistic period progressed, especially once Rome entered the political arena.

NINE

THE WEST SANCTUARY DURING THE HELLENISTIC PERIOD

The Homeric reconfiguration of the Athenaion, the agora, and the Troad tumuli during the third century B.C. is relatively easy to chart; less straight-forward is the evolving topography of the West Sanctuary on the southwest side of the citadel, which served as a locus of sanctity for more than 1500 years (Plate 8, Figs. 8.3, 9.1, and 9.2).[1] The earliest traces of activity there date to the period of Troy V (ca. 2000–1750 B.C.), but since the area occupies a strategic location between the Troy II stone ramp and the Spring Cave, it may have been occupied already in the Early Bronze Age. By the end of the eighth century, the complex was probably connected to the developing cult of the Homeric heroes at Ilion, with ritual dining occurring in the shadow of the damaged Late Bronze Age fortifications.

Identifying the cults that were enshrined in this complex during the Hellenistic and Roman periods has always been problematic. Unlike the Sanctuary of Athena, only a handful of inscriptions have been discovered dur-ing the fifteen years of the West Sanctuary's excavation, and from what we can gather, no ancient texts refer to the complex.[2] Consequently, any determina-tion regarding the identity of the gods worshipped there has to rest on the configuration of the architecture and associated small finds – an unenviable task given the long history of occupation and rebuilding in the area.

The evidence that does survive, however, leads one to the conclusion that this complex housed several cults that involved secret rites, at least during the Hellenistic period, which, in turn, appear to have been carefully cultivated to

9.1. State plan of the West Sanctuary, drawn by Elizabeth Riorden for the Troy Excavation Project.

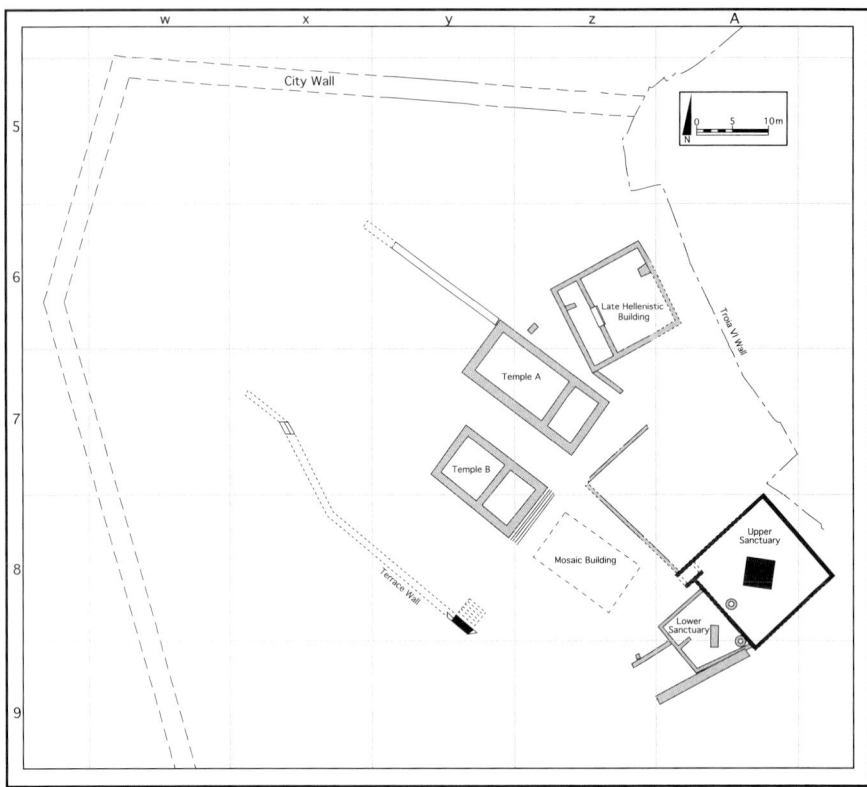

9.2. Phase plan of the West Sanctuary during the Hellenistic Period, prepared by Elizabeth Riorden for the Troy Excavation Project.

exploit the increasingly strong links between Ilion and Rome. In the discussion that follows, the evolving topography of the West Sanctuary is tied to a discussion of the ways in which those changes intersected with the gradual formulation of Rome's Trojan ancestry and the developing bonds of kinship between the two cities.

THE THIRD CENTURY B.C.

When construction at Ilion began again in the first quarter of the third century B.C., the West Sanctuary had been untended for more than 200 years, and a visitor's attention would have been drawn to the ruins of the walled Upper Sanctuary and the uneven sloping terrain that surrounded it. The foundations of the Late Archaic Temple were still in place, but the superstructure had collapsed, including the Aeolic capitals, and the entire area was covered with a dump that had probably been thrown down from the Sanctuary of Athena. Buildings began to be added again over the course of the next two centuries, however, and by the end of the second century B.C., the complex had become nearly as impressive as the Sanctuary of Athena, although the deities venerated there occupied a very different sphere of activity, as did the clientele to which it catered.

The first of the new structures (the "Early Hellenistic Building") was built in the northern part of the complex, directly above the ruined Archaic temples and roughly parallel to the still standing Late Bronze Age fortification wall (Figs. 9.1 and 9.2). The footprint of the building measured 16 × 10 m, which was even larger than the Late Archaic temple that had preceded it.[3] Two rooms of equal size opened onto a long vestibule 15 m in length, with the main entrance at the west. Although the threshold was fashioned from a rather roughly finished limestone block, the interior rooms were elaborately decorated with painted plaster imitation of drafted margin masonry, a technique that would subsequently be used to decorate the interior of the Mosaic Building further to the south.[4] The colors on the walls included red, pale pink, buff, mustard yellow, and white; one fragment featured panels of red and white with a drafted margin between them. Like the later Mosaic Building, the majority of the interior was probably white, with the colored imitation masonry confined to the lower part of the wall.

At the time in which it was constructed, the Early Hellenistic Building was the only standing structure in the West Sanctuary, and it probably served as the center of ritual activity during the first half of the third century. If Strabo was correct in categorizing the Archaic/Early Hellenistic temple of Athena as a "small and poor affair," then the Early Hellenistic Building would have been the most elaborate of the religious structures at Ilion at the time in which it was built.[5] The division of the building into two rooms may be significant given the dual altars in the Upper and Lower Sanctuaries and the two adjacent temples (A and B) subsequently constructed at the southwest – a subject to which I will return later in this chapter.[6]

The contents in the building were well protected: the threshold stone indicates that there were two doors occupying a length of 1.15m, with at least two locking mechanisms that actually constitute our earliest evidence for locked doors at the site. Excavation of the building yielded an iron double axe (Fig. 9.3), a gilded bronze sphinx statuette (Fig. 9.4), and the mold for a terracotta figurine of Athena.[7] The first two objects were the primary types on Hellenistic coins of Tenedos and Gergis, respectively, and they may have been symbols of or gifts from those cities.[8] The double axe has also been linked to the Cabiri/Dioscuri due to its discovery in the Samothrakeion at Delos and the Kabeireion at Thebes, and both cults may have been among those in operation here during the Hellenistic period.[9] The building also contained nearly two-thirds of the loom weights excavated in the West Sanctuary, as well as an equally high number of spindle whorls. It seems likely that this structure housed the principal weaving activities in the West Sanctuary and, indeed, perhaps served as one of the weaving centers within Ilion.[10]

9.3. Iron double axe from the Early Hellenistic Building in the West Sanctuary. Troia slide 15072.

9.4. Gilded bronze sphinx statuette from the Early Hellenistic Building in the West Sanctuary. Çanakkale Archaeological Museum. Troia slide 15132.

Throughout the complex we unearthed terracotta dedications, the majority of which were either Cybele figurines or votive plaques representing a horseman. Those of Cybele feature the same basic iconography: the goddess is seated on a high-backed throne, holding a tympanum in her left hand and a phiale in her right (Fig. 9.5).[11] Her head is covered by a high red polos, or a crenellated crown, usually placed over a veil, and a small yellow lion reclines on her lap. This calls to mind the lion skins that had decorated the altar precincts of the West Sanctuary during the Archaic period, and it seems likely that one of the deities worshipped there during the seventh and sixth centuries was a precursor to Cybele, if not Cybele herself.

The other frequent discoveries within the West Sanctuary's Hellenistic deposits were the so-called horseman plaques, all of which feature a youthful, unbearded man on a rearing horse, with a snake often situated beneath the horse (Fig. 9.6).[12] He wears a short tunic, riding boots, and a cloak that billows behind him, and is either bareheaded, wearing a

petasus, or (very rarely) a helmet. The plaques
were elaborately painted, although the colors
vary: the horse was red or white with a yellow
mane; the man, pinkish/red with blond hair
and a yellow or red cloak, and the snake, red
or yellow.[13] The iconography of the plaques
per se does not allow us to pin a particular
label on the figure represented, but within
the Hellenistic West Sanctuary he clearly
enjoyed a level of popularity equal to that of
Cybele.[14]

The third quarter of the third century B.C.
was one of the busiest periods of construction at Ilion, and the West Sanctuary was no
exception. The decision was made to erect a
new temple in the center of the complex as
well as a new terrace wall 13 m to the west
of it (Fig. 9.2).[15] Why the wall was built so far
to the west of the new buildings is unclear,
but there may have been activities associated
with the new complex that required a large

9.5. Terracotta figurine of Cybele from the West
Sanctuary. Çanakkale Archaeological Museum.
Troia slide 39912.

9.6. Horseman plaque from the West Sanctuary. Çanakkale Archaeological Museum. Troia slide
19531.

9.7. The staircase foundations of Temple B (at left) and the Mosaic Building with its robbed-out wall (at right), looking northeast. Troia slide 29316.

area of level ground. One possibility that comes to mind are tents for ritual dining, such as one finds in the Komyria festival of Zeus in his sanctuary at Stratonicea.[16] In any event, the new terrace would have dramatically increased the size of the West Sanctuary, and ritual activities would now have returned to the southern part of the complex for the first time in more than 350 years.

The new temple (the "Mosaic Building") measured ca. 8.5 × 13 m and contained a square cella and a deep pronaos that comprises one-third of the building (Figs. 9.2, 9.7, and 9.8).[17] Both rooms were paved with a dark green and white pebble mosaic that featured a floral and animal decoration around a circular emblema that is now completely missing. The wall decoration was equally elaborate: both cella and pronaos walls featured painted plaster imitation of drafted margin masonry with an Ionic molding of stucco above (Plate 28).[18] The wide range of colors included purple, red, white, blue, yellow, and blue with yellow or red veining, the latter clearly representing an imitation of marble revetment. At the rear of the cella was an aedicula with lateral wings that would have held the cult statue.[19] Such an installation would have entailed small columns at the front of the projections, and a canopy, probably gabled, that extended back over the statue. Torch bases, as in the Hieron on Samothrace, were positioned inside and outside the building.[20]

Although most of the Mosaic Building was stripped away in antiquity, several clues regarding its function still remained. The unusually large pronaos indicates that this was no ordinary temple, and the elaborate decoration within the cella suggests that some kind of activity occurred within the building, as

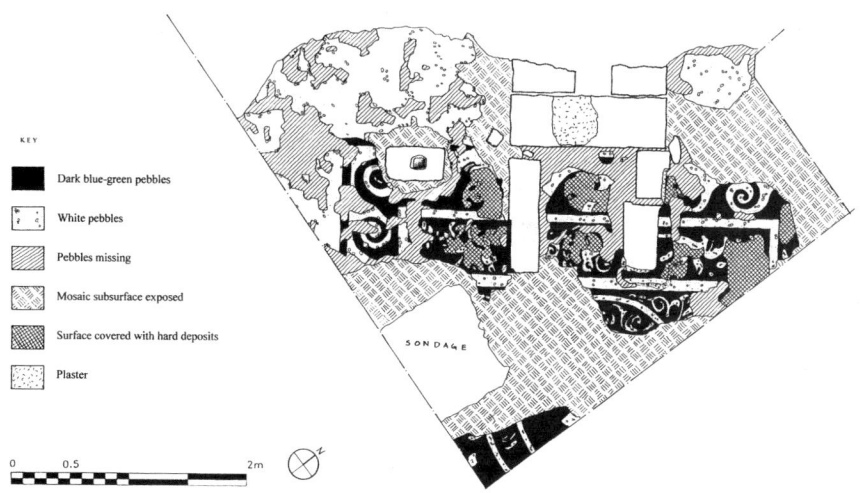

KEY

- Dark blue-green pebbles
- White pebbles
- Pebbles missing
- Mosaic subsurface exposed
- Surface covered with hard deposits
- Plaster

9.8. Drawing of the Mosaic Building, by Elizabeth Riorden for the Troy Excavation Project.

does the presence of the interior torch base and the substantial wear on the mosaic floor. Indeed, the mosaic was repaired at least four times, so traffic within the structure must have been especially heavy. All of these features lead in the same direction: at least by this point, the building must have become a locus for secret rites that would continue to be celebrated on an even larger scale during the second century B.C. But with which deity were the rites connected?

If we examine the associated small finds, there are some unusual patterns. Twenty percent of all terracotta figurines excavated within the West Sanctuary were found around the Mosaic Building – more than were yielded by any other structure within the complex. Sixty percent of these were horseman plaques, which suggests that his cult was more dominant in the Mosaic Building than anywhere else at the site.[21] I will return to the issue of the identity of the horseman and his role in Ilion's larger religious network after the other buildings in the complex have been discussed.

The decision to construct the Mosaic Building had a major impact on the much older Early Hellenistic Building, which lost its original function and became a workshop center that supported the new construction. Thirteen pits intended for bronze casting were dug in front of the old building, which effectively put the main part of it out of use (Fig. 9.9).[22] No fragments of the molds themselves survived, but the relatively large number of casting pits suggests a product with multiple components, which are best suited to a statue. Bronze statues were usually cast near the place where they were dedicated, so we should probably look for a site within the West Sanctuary itself.[23] The later casting pits were in operation at the time in which the Mosaic Building was

9.9. One of the mold bases within a pit in front of the Early Hellenistic Building, looking southeast. Troia slide 28976.

being constructed, which is the most logical candidate, and the discovery of a statue base within the building lends considerable plausibility to this proposal.

The Mosaic Building may have been tied to the new altar in the Upper Sanctuary, the orientation of which matched that of the recently planned altar in the Sanctuary of Athena (Plate 5, Figs. 2.7, 9.2, and 9.10).[24] The Upper Sanctuary altar was nearly 4 m square, and situated near the center of a new walled precinct, also square, that measured slightly more than 14 m on each side. This new altar was positioned directly over Archaic Altar A, with which it had a physical connection by virtue of a central stone-lined pit that reached the surface of the earlier altar. This suggests that the level of sanctity originally attached to the Upper Sanctuary had remained intact during the Classical period, even though there appears to have been no ritual activity in the complex at that time.

The original size of the precinct wall is unknown, but it is still preserved to a height of nearly 2.50 m, which meant that the activities inside the precinct would have been screened off from the surrounding area. As with the Mosaic Building, the layout suggests secret rites. The erection of such an enormous wall would have required a significant quantity of limestone and marl as well as a skilled construction crew. If the dating proposed above for the Upper Sanctuary is correct, then the construction activities would have coincided roughly with the building of Ilion's new city wall, one section of which was being erected along the northern border of the West Sanctuary.[25] It is conceivable that the West Sanctuary's late third-century building program was actually planned in concert with the city wall project in order to diminish the overall cost and facilitate the logistics of construction.

North of the Upper Sanctuary and east of the Mosaic Building was a large terraced area measuring 18 m north-south and possibly as much as 15 m east-west (Fig. 9.2). The north-south terrace wall appears to have extended as far as the Upper Sanctuary propylon, and the pottery within the makeup of the walls points to a construction date in the last quarter of the third century.[26] It is not unlikely that this zone was intended for ritual performances, as would be the case during the Early Roman period when a larger seating area or grand-stand was built immediately to the east.[27] If so, then some sort of Hellenistic seating may still remain to be found under the later grandstand.[28] We should probably view this terrace as a complement to the Mosaic Building and the Upper Sanctuary and assume that all of them were intended to form a cluster of adjacent ceremonial spaces.

The presence of such a ceremonial space surrounded by seating is paral-leled in other Hellenistic sanctuaries focused on mystery cults. The closest in form is that of the Demeter Sanctuary at Pergamon, with which Ilion had unusually strong political and religious links during the later third and second centuries B.C. Another relevant example can be found at Samothrace, where a circle of steps, presumably used as seats, surrounded a stone-paved space in the Sanctuary of the Megaloi Theoi, and theaters with a more traditional plan occupied the sanctuaries of the Cabiri at Boeotian Thebes and of Despoina at Lycosura.[29]

It is clear that the cults within the West Sanctuary experienced a discern-ible change from the early to the later third century. Although both the Early Hellenistic Building and the Mosaic Building featured polychromatic plas-ter wall decoration, the latter structure conformed more closely to what we would call a temple, with interior cult statue, and worship appears to have been focused primarily on the horseman cult. Whether the horseman was also venerated in the new adjacent altar precinct is impossible to judge, but the two new structures clearly attest to the inauguration of secret rites by the last quarter of the third century, at the latest.

THE SECOND CENTURY B.C.

After a likely mid-second-century B.C. earthquake, rebuilding in the West Sanctuary commenced immediately and would continue throughout much of the second half of the second century. This ambitious building program fea-tured an extensive agenda: two new temples (A and B) were placed adjacent to each other north of the Mosaic Building, with a new terrace wall to support them; a large square building with windows (the "Late Hellenistic Building") was constructed over part of the now ruined Early Hellenistic Building; a line of small adjacent rooms was appended to the northern side of the Late Hellenistic Building, also supported by a new terrace; a new temenos wall was built for the Upper Sanctuary; and a new precinct wall and altar were added in the Lower Sanctuary (Fig. 9.2).[30]

Never before had there been such a long and sustained period of building in the West Sanctuary. We can no longer judge whether all of these elements formed part of a master plan initially developed in the middle of the second century and gradually executed over the following fifty years, although this seems likely: Ilion needed at least seventy years to bring the plans for the new Athena sanctuary to fruition, and the West Sanctuary project was nearly as ambitious.[31] The identities of the agents driving this new program are difficult to pinpoint, but the Boule and the priests of the cult were undoubtedly among those who collaborated on the plans and the timing. It is worth noting that the West Sanctuary would have been the primary locus for construction at Ilion during the second half of the second century B.C., since the building projects in the agora and the Athena Sanctuary had already been completed.

The first of the new buildings was Temple B, which lay immediately north of the Mosaic Building and was clearly intended as its replacement (Figs. 9.2 and 9.7).[32] The temple was slightly larger than its predecessor but with the same distinctive size ratio of pronaos to cella (2:3), and its construction dates to the same time as the Mosaic Building's dismantlement. Whether the new temple had the same opulent interior as the Mosaic Building is unclear since only the foundations remain, but the fills surrounding the temple contained a relatively high percentage of horseman plaques, as had the Mosaic Building.

Tied to the construction of Temple B was a refashioning of the Upper Sanctuary, beginning with a rebuilding of the precinct wall and probably a new marble superstructure for the altar. The Lower Sanctuary also received a new altar (C) as well as its own temenos wall, which meant that there were two adjacent walled altar precincts with high precinct walls dominating the southern end of the complex.[33] The new altar faced east and abutted the earlier Altar B, although the new one was nearly twice the size of its predecessor and oriented at a slightly different angle, more in line with the Hellenistic altar in the Upper Sanctuary (Fig. 9.1).[34] The close juxtaposition of the Archaic and Hellenistic altars in the Lower Sanctuary is reminiscent of the physical link between the Late Archaic altar and Early Hellenistic Building in the Upper Sanctuary, and it surely represents an attempt to co-opt the sanctity associated with the earlier structure.[35]

Although there were no patches of burning that could be linked to animal sacrifice, a wealth of faunal remains was recovered in and around the Lower Sanctuary precinct. Domestic animals predominated over wild ones, and herd animals (cattle, sheep, goat, pig) appeared much more frequently than equids or dogs. The percentage of ovicaprids (sheep and goat) is higher than that of cattle and pig, and the ratio of sheep to goat is nearly 5:1. Whether this is somehow related to the weaving industry in the Sanctuary cannot be determined, but it remains a possibility.[36]

My guess would be that the Lower Sanctuary was accessible only from the upper one, with a portal located somewhere in the wall that divides them – probably between the propylon and well F, but the foundations in this area are so badly damaged that they provide no information about such a portal. There also appears to have been a kind of service corridor connected to the western side of the precinct, which provided a convenient mechanism for removing rubbish from the temenos without the necessity of carrying it through the ceremonial spaces (Figs. 9.1 and 9.12).[37]

During the last quarter of the second century two more major buildings were added to the complex. The earlier of the two (though not by many years) is Temple A, which was constructed next to Temple B and was clearly intended as its complement (Figs. 9.2, 9.11, and 9.12).[38] The two buildings are parallel to each other, with less than 6 m between them, and their facades are aligned. Both were also probably prostyle buildings, although whether hexastyle or tetrastyle in antis cannot be determined. The footprint of Temple A, however, was significantly larger, measuring 9 × 19 m, which made it the largest building in the West Sanctuary. The plans are also different: a comparison of the proportional relationship of pronaos to cella in the two temples yields a 2:3 ratio for Temple B, and 1:3 for Temple A. In other words, Temple A conforms more closely than its neighbor to the plan of a standard Greek temple of Hellenistic date.

Although Temple A had been stripped to its foundations, the associated fills yielded a relatively high number of small finds. The building accounted for slightly under 8 percent of the total terracotta figurines recovered in the West Sanctuary, and over 21 percent of this number are representations of Cybele. The marble head of a life-size lion was discovered near the entrance, so we should probably reconstruct the statue of a lion, or of Cybele with lions, in that spot.[39] The terraced area between Temple A and the Upper Sanctuary was still intact then, so there must have been performances that occurred directly in front of the temple.

Even though Temple A was significantly larger than Temple B, the alignment of their entrances, coupled with nearly identical widths, must have made them look like twins when one stood in front of them. The two temples were probably intended to operate in tandem with the twin altar precincts further to the south, which were also of unequal size. Such a link would have bound together the northern and southern sides of the complex for the first time since the Late Archaic period. Nevertheless, the high walls of the Upper and Lower Sanctuary precincts would have prevented the adherents of the cult from seeing those temples during the rituals that were conducted there.

9.10. Aerial view of the West Sanctuary from southwest. The Lower Sanctuary is at the left; the Upper Sanctuary at the right. Troia slide 16193.

Toward the end of the second century B.C. there was one additional ambitious building program focused on the northern sector of the complex, the most prominent component of which was a new, nearly square building (the "Late Hellenistic Building"), with a long vestibule leading into a single large room that was lit by windows on two sides (Plates 8 and 26; Figs. 8.1 and 9.11).[40] Considering the size of the threshold, nearly 2 m in length, the doors must have been enormous, and therefore more likely made of wood rather than metal. The roof featured tiles that were stamped "IΛI" for "Ilion," which are the only such examples uncovered at the site.[41]

Determining the function of the Late Hellenistic Building is problematic, since virtually all of its furnishings, including the doors and floor tiles, were stripped from the building prior to Fimbria's siege of the city in 85 B.C., discussed below. The only objects found inside were ten commercial amphorae and a matching pair of painted volute kraters, nearly 1 m high, that appear to be ceramic reproductions of fifth-century B.C. metalwork.[42] As John Hayes has noted, this was an unusual type probably intended for a specific function, either ritual or civic; beyond that, we are in the realm of speculation. The same ground plan was used for the principal building in the Samothracian Sanctuary on Delos, although we do not know the function of that structure, either.[43] One is tempted to associate the building with ritual dining on special occasions in the West Sanctuary, but since the building was emptied in antiquity, there is no ceramic evidence to prove or disprove the hypothesis.

9.11. The northern half of the West Sanctuary, looking southeast. The Late Hellenistic Building is at the left; the foundations of Temple A are at the right. Troia slide 16188.

DECIPHERING THE CULTS

I commented earlier on the prominence of Cybele here: terracotta figurines of the goddess outnumber those of any other deity at the site, and since nearly 40 percent of them have been discovered in the West Sanctuary, it seems clear that this was the center of her worship within the settlement.[44] Nevertheless, the range of finds and the complexity of the West Sanctuary plan indicate that she was not the only deity worshipped there. A significant clue to a secondary cult is provided by the horseman plaques that figured prominently in West Sanctuary assemblages during the third and second centuries B.C., but not in the Archaic or Roman periods. None of the plaques is inscribed, and the type is so generalized that pinning a label on the man and his significance is fraught with problems.[45] Nevertheless, if one considers the findspots of the plaques together with their historical context, one identity emerges as more likely than the others.

The horseman plaques' pattern of distribution at Ilion is quite distinctive. In addition to the West Sanctuary, they were dedicated in large numbers in the Sanctuary of Athena, in a walled precinct with its own propylon that occupied the entire southeast side of the temenos (Fig. 8.3).[46] As such, the horseman is the only deity at Ilion whose votive images were popular dedications in Ilion's two primary religious complexes. It was common practice in the Aegean to set up a heroon within a sanctuary, such as those of Neoptolemus at Delphi, Opheltes at Nemea, and Pelops at Olympia, and the Troad was, of course, filled with monumental tumuli that functioned as heroa themselves.[47] If one bears this pattern of homage in mind, coupled with the site's increasing emphasis on its Homeric affiliations, then it seems likely that the horseman represented a hero associated with the legendary heritage of Troy – one who was accorded cult status in Ilion and received offerings of a generic kind such as the horse and rider plaques.[48]

I have argued previously that the horseman should be considered as a representation of the Trojan hero Dardanus, whose great-grandson Ilus founded the city of Troy, and this remains the most plausible identification.[49] The iconography of the plaques is similar to that of the rider on coins from Dardanus, who surely represents the hero, and such an identification also fits well with his legendary history. Although not all of the ancient accounts of his life coincide in detail, Hellenistic and Roman authors generally agreed that the hero was a Samothracian by birth who subsequently founded the town of Dardanus, extended his rule over the surrounding area, and became the patriarch of the royal line of Troy.[50] He reportedly carried the images of both the Palladion and the Samothracian Gods to the Troad, and the local residents claimed that the cult image within Ilion's Athenaion was the actual statue that Dardanus had brought.[51] Placing a heroon of Dardanus in the same zone as the statue for whose existence he was responsible made perfect sense and would, in fact, have strengthened the Homeric credentials of the cult statue as well as Ilion's claim to Trojan ancestry.

The myths of Dardanus were frequently intertwined with those of Cybele during the Hellenistic and Roman periods: the Samothracian mysteries were reportedly introduced to him by Cybele or Attis; Dardanus brought the rites of Cybele to Asia; and his brother Iasion married her. Idaeus, the son of Dardanus, founded the sanctuary of Cybele on Mt. Ida and inaugurated her mysteries, while Electra, the mother of Dardanus, presented the sacred rites of Cybele on Samothrace when her daughter Harmonia married Cadmus.[52] In other words, the primary characters in the two cults consistently overlapped with one another, as well as with Troy and the Troad, and secret rites were common to both. Many of these accounts were formulated around the same time in which the precincts of the West Sanctuary were reconfigured, and a link between the new construction and the evolving nature of those cults seems highly likely.

To what extent did these religious and topographical changes tie into contemporary political developments? This was the period in which Rome began to promote its Trojan ancestry, and signs of the developing kinship between Troy and Rome became increasingly prominent as the Hellenistic period progressed. Roma herself periodically wore the Phrygian cap on Republican coinage as an indication of her origins in Troy, as did the Trojans in the *Aeneid*, and Trojan ancestry often figured prominently in interstate politics.[53] In responding to a diplomatic overture from Seleucus II, Rome asked him to relieve their kinsmen, the Trojans, from tribute, and when Flamininus dedicated his shields and gold wreath to Apollo at Delphi in 194, he referred to himself in the accompanying inscription as a descendant of Aeneas.[54] Shortly before the conclusion of the war with Antiochus III, both C. Livius Salinator and L. Scipio sacrificed to Athena at Ilion, as Xerxes and Alexander had done, and the latter's sacrifice was, according to Livy, in celebration of the common ancestry of Rome and Ilion.[55]

One of the critical elements in these new claims of kinship was Cybele, often referred to as the "Idaean Mother" since the Troad's Ida Mountains were regarded as her homeland. Cybele's cult had been brought from Asia Minor to Rome toward the end of the Second Punic War, almost certainly because of the goddess's link to the Troad and Rome's increasing emphasis on her legendary ancestry.[56] The official delegation from Rome charged with supervising the cult's transfer arrived in Asia Minor in 204, with Pergamon acting as the local agent of transfer since the majority of western Asia Minor was now controlled by the Attalids. There is no record of the delegation's visit to Ilion, although Varro notes that they traveled to Pergamon to acquire the black stone that symbolized the cult, and in light of Ilion's role as capital of the Troad koinon and ancestral city of the Romans, such a visit is not unlikely.[57] Once in Rome, the cult was housed in a new temple built on the southwest corner of the Palatine Hill, which had more legendary associations with Troy and its descendants than any other part of the city.[58]

All of these developments succeeded in conferring upon Ilion's West Sanctuary a status that it had never before possessed, in that their goddess had now been pulled into a larger political dimension that was tied to the primary power in the Mediterranean. Honors paid to Cybele in this complex could easily be packaged as reverence toward Rome, and funding for the West Sanctuary's new building program was therefore probably not difficult to secure, although we have no way of knowing who the donors were.

There may have been a third cult operating in the West Sanctuary. The stories of Cybele and Dardanus were consistently linked to the island of Samothrace, which is easily viewed from the Sanctuary on clear days.[59] An image of Cybele flanked by lions appeared on Samothracian coins, and she was regarded as one of the Megaloi Theoi worshipped in the island's sanctuary.[60] Both Dardanus and Cybele reportedly taught the Samothracian mysteries to the Trojans, while Dardanus' mother brought the sacred rites of Cybele to Samothrace.[61] The discovery of G2/3 ware at both Samothrace and Ilion suggests that the two areas had been in communication with each other since the seventh century B.C., and there are epigraphic attestations of their religious ties during the Hellenistic period: an inscription from Samothrace refers to initiates from Ilion, and two Hellenistic inscriptions to the Samothracian Gods have been discovered in or near Ilion.[62] More important, the Hellenistic fill to the south of the Lower Sanctuary yielded a West Slope kantharos, or drinking cup, inscribed with the words Μελίτηι τρία. "Melite," according to Strabo, was the ancient word for Samothrace, and the "tria" may refer to the dedication of three objects "to Samothrace."[63]

Several elements of the West Sanctuary's plan can be paralleled in other complexes that venerated the Samothracian Gods.[64] Open-air walled precincts were not common in Hellenistic sanctuaries, but another example (the "Altar Court") appears in the Megaloi Theoi Sanctuary on Samothrace, while the principal building in the Delian Samothracian Sanctuary evinces the same plan as Ilion's "Late Hellenistic Building."[65] There were also torch bases in front of and within the Hieron on Samothrace, which featured the same kind of painted plaster imitation of drafted margin masonry that one finds in Ilion's Mosaic Building.[66]

If one searches for an explanation as to why worship of the Samothracian Gods would have been included in a complex that also featured Cybele and Dardanus, one is led once again to the developing tradition of the Trojan origins of Rome. The Samothracian Gods came to be identified with the Trojan Penates, which were either brought from Samothrace to Troy by Dardanus, and then to Italy by Aeneas, or taken directly to Italy from Samothrace by Aeneas alone.[67] As Servius notes in his commentary on the *Aeneid*, the conflation of the Samothracian Gods and the Penates recast the Samothracians as kinsmen of the Romans by way of Aeneas.[68]

The connection among Samothrace, Aeneas, and the Penates began in the late third/early second century B.C., at more or less the same time in which Troy was being publicized as the mother city of the Romans, and the two developments should probably be viewed as complementary components within the evolving identity of Rome.[69] That identity was gradually being formulated by a wide variety of agents, including the Attalids, Ilion, Samothrace, and Rome herself. In essence, each was currying favor with the others while promoting its own self-interest, and religion provided the most expedient mechanism for satisfying everyone's objectives. By the second century, the cults of Cybele, Dardanus, the Samothracian Gods, and the Penates had been shaped so that each was linked to the other, and all were woven into the legendary traditions of Ilion, Rome, and Samothrace. Ilion's incorporation of all three cults into a single complex would have served as a particularly effective outreach tool to the latter two areas, as well as augmenting the site's political capital.

We may even be justified in speaking of a religious koiné within the north Aegean/northeast Asia Minor. The Samothracian Gods had been syncretized with the Cabiri at Delos and perhaps Samothrace, and the latter were also linked with the Penates and the Dioscuri as well as Demeter and the Corybantes.[70] Whether these deities were viewed as components of the West

Sanctuary's cultic network is difficult to say, but regional worship of the Cabiri is attested at Lemnos, Imbros, Pergamon, and Birytis, and another sanctuary of the Samothracian Gods existed at Scamandria.[71] All of these sanctuaries were in operation simultaneously, and one is tempted to view their associated cults as variations on a single theme, although the plans of the cult buildings differed markedly from each other.

Restoring the cults of Cybele, Dardanus, and the Samothracian Gods to the West Sanctuary still does not tell us whose names should be appended to Temples A and B. As I noted above, these two buildings were in use during the second century B.C. along with the two precincts, altars, and wells further to the south, and it therefore seems as if two gods were involved in the cult. The number two does figure prominently in the Samothracian mysteries and the cult of the Cabiri: by the second century B.C. both sets of gods had been identified with the Dioscuri, as had the Penates, and the Cabiri were frequently depicted in duos, such as on Hellenistic coins from the nearby mint of Birytis.[72] Nevertheless, there are no examples of the Dioscuri or the Cabiri receiving two distinct temples or altars, and it is noteworthy that there were no temples per se in the sanctuary on Samothrace. There were, however, two grades of initiation, the *myesis* and *epopteia*; if the same initiation process existed at Ilion, the two grades could conceivably have influenced the design of the Upper and Lower Sanctuaries.[73]

If we now step back and examine the broader development of the West Sanctuary during the first millennium B.C., it looks as if a female fertility deity was venerated in tandem with the Homeric heroes during the Archaic phase of the complex's operation. By the Hellenistic period, the heroic cults may have narrowed to that of Dardanus alone, while the fertility deity was syncretized to Cybele. The existence of those two cults then provided a convenient context for the inauguration of the Samothracian mysteries, which, in turn, brought the Penates of Aeneas back to the city from which they allegedly came. All of these developments strengthened significantly the evolving political connections between Ilion and Rome, which would gradually replace Pergamon as the site's new benefactor.

Those benefactions manifested themselves in a number of ways, some of which brought considerable economic benefits to Ilion. One of the provisions of the Peace of Apamea in 188 B.C. was that Ilion received immunity from taxation as well as the addition of the towns of Rhoeteum and Gergis, which provided Ilion with a view (from Gergis) of the entire Trojan plain. This meant that the tomb of Ajax was now under its control, as was the southern entrance to the Dardanelles.[74] The other members of the koinon benefited as well from Rome's acknowledgment of her Trojan ancestry. Dardanus, like Ilion, received freedom from taxation at the peace treaty of 188 in recognition of the consanguinity between the town's residents and Rome, and Lampsacus requested the same concessions from Rome after the Second Macedonian War in 197.[75]

TROJAN CULTS IN ITALY

Given the importance that Rome had attached to its Trojan ancestry during the Middle and Late Republic, one would expect symbols of Troy to permeate the landscape of the city and its surroundings during the same time. The date at which Rome's Trojan ancestry was first promoted is uncertain, but the literary evidence suggests that it was in place by the late fourth century B.C. The earliest sign of an awareness of Trojan ancestry is probably the restoration and enlargement of an Archaic tumulus at Lavinium, the city reportedly founded by Aeneas 28 km south of Rome. The tomb has usually been associated with the heroon of Aeneas described by Dionysius of Halicarnassus in his *Roman Antiquities*, and the renovation was probably a by-product of the emerging prominence of Troy in Roman society.[76]

This renovation is, in fact, comparable to the monumentalization of the Achilles tumulus at Ilion that occurred only a few decades later (Fig. 8.22). Both of these changes to the landscape were actually part of a much larger trend that is readily perceptible at the beginning of the Hellenistic period. Votive dedications began to be deposited at Bronze Age tumuli throughout Greece and the Aegean as civic and ethnic origins were explored with greater enthusiasm, and at roughly the same time, on Samothrace, a fictive Mycenaean tomb was constructed for one of the island's early heroes in the principal sanctuary.[77] None, however, pursued such legendary ancestral links as aggressively as Rome and Ilion, for whom Homeric foundations proved so mutually advantageous.

The first numismatic indication of this link occurred during the war with Pyrrhus of Epirus in the early third century B.C., when Roman bronzes featured the head of Roma wearing the Phrygian cap.[78] The cap had developed into a sign of Trojan status during the Classical period, and the Romans used it as such in their construction of a more complex symbol of civic identity.[79] That identity was also woven into an elaborate spectacle of Republican and Imperial date: the *lusus Troiae*, or Trojan Games.[80] The *lusus Troiae* was an equestrian parade and mock battle staged by Rome's patrician youths, generally between the ages of eight and fourteen, which probably involved between 200 and 300 boys during the early empire.[81] The date at which the ritual was introduced is unclear, but its Trojan links were fixed by the time Sulla revived it in the early first century B.C. Sulla's revival of the *lusus* as an elite Late Republican spectacle is not surprising given the emphasis on Venus as Roman matriarch in his political propaganda, but it developed into an even more popular custom under Augustus and his Julio-Claudian successors, since this was a dynasty that traced its origins directly to Aeneas.[82]

The most elaborate description of the *lusus Troiae* is provided in *Aeneid* V, in the account of the funeral games of Anchises, and Vergil's description of the

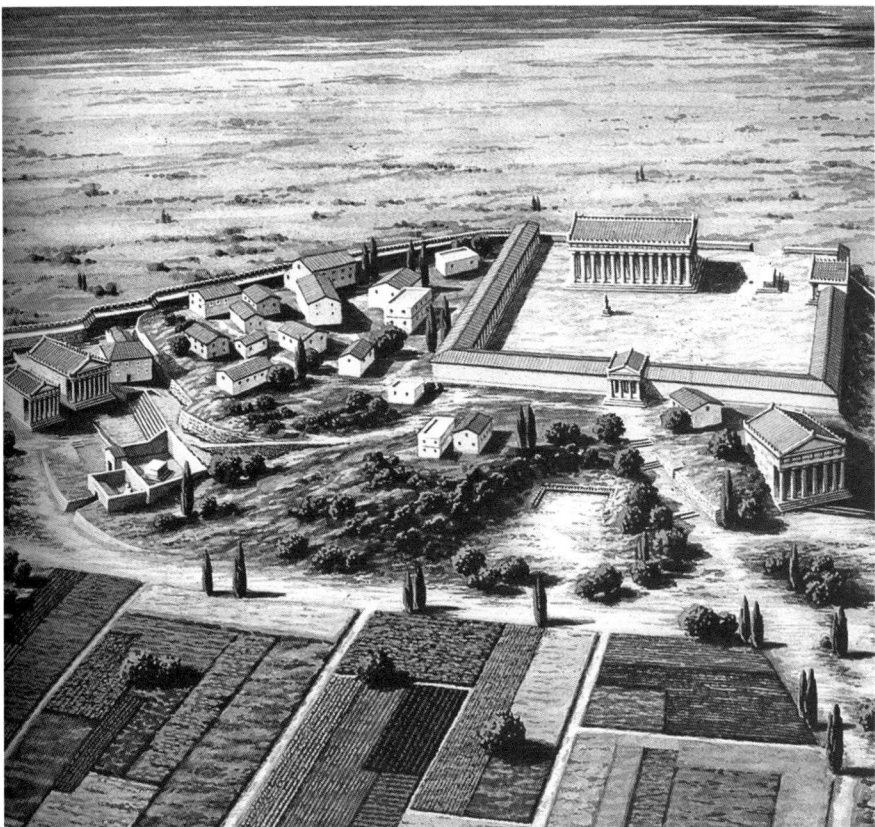

9.12. Conjectural reconstruction of Hellenistic Ilion, by Elizabeth Riorden. The West Sanctuary is at far left. Prepared by Elizabeth Riorden for the Troy Excavation Project.

pageant probably reflects the spectacle's format during the reign of Augustus.[83] The two most distinctive features of the boys' costume were a twisted metal torque, worn low, and a "tonsa corona," which is usually regarded as a garland of cut leaves.[84] The first attribute merits special attention. Torques often served as a sign of eastern status, such as those worn by the Persians, by Attis, the consort of Cybele (Fig. 9.13), and by Cybele's priests.[85] At first glance, then, a torque would seem a logical component of the boys' costume, since Troy was also located in the east. A survey of ancient Mediterranean imagery, however, reveals that the Trojans were never shown with torques, which means that its use in the *lusus Troiae* cannot have been stimulated by Trojan iconography per se.

Here one needs to examine the context of the ritual, for that holds the key to its visual configuration. The *lusus Troiae* always took place in the Circus Maximus, directly below the temple of Cybele on the Palatine Hill, where her priests also lived.[86] As noted above, torques formed part of the costume of both Attis and the priests, and a connection between the cult of Cybele and the

9.13. Silver plate with a bust of Attis from Hildesheim. Antikensammlung, Staatliche Museen zu Berlin-Preussischer Kulturbesitz, Inv. Misc. 3779, 4. Photo by Johannes Laurentius. Photo courtesy Staatliche Museen zu Berlin-Preussischer Kulturbesitz.

lusus Troiae would therefore have been readily apparent.[87] One would, in fact, expect exactly this kind of link in light of the legendary and historical interactions that had existed among Troy, Cybele, and Rome.[88]

It therefore looks as if the Trojan spectacle was structured so that a bond would be forged with the temple of Cybele that towered over the festivities, thereby creating yet another network of symbiotic relationships: the cult's Trojan origins were emphasized, as was Rome's Trojan ancestry, and Cybele's temple was pulled into the same legendary framework that had been so carefully constructed in the Troad. The rulers of Ilion had used a series of rituals to reconfigure the landscape that surrounded their citadel, and Rome was now following essentially the same model, with the cult of Cybele serving as the common denominator for the mutually beneficial relationship that both cities were constructing.

TEN

LATE HELLENISTIC AND EARLY IMPERIAL ILION

In his description of Hellenistic Ilion, Strabo mentions the site's poverty during the third century, its great revival in the second, and its destruction and return to poverty after Fimbria's attack in 85 B.C. Archaeology has demonstrated how inaccurate the third-century assessment was, but there is considerable evidence to support the economic revival of the second. This was a period when Ilion and several of the other cities in the Troad benefited from the political control of Pergamon, followed by Rome. It witnessed the completion of the Sanctuary of Athena – a complex that had been under construction for perhaps as long as eighty years, and an extensive building program in the West Sanctuary that encompassed most of the second half of the second century B.C.[1]

There was a substantial building program in Ilion's agora at the same time, although the scope is difficult to assess since so little of that area has been excavated. At some point in the second century, however, a new and enlarged Bouleuterion was constructed over its smaller third-century predecessor (Figs. 1.5, 8.3, and 10.1).[2] This was the first of the Bouleuteria to conform to the orientation of the Sanctuary of Athena, which meant that the link between the koinon's sanctuary and its place of assembly was stronger than ever before. Establishing that connection required the dismantling of a significant section of the Late Bronze Age citadel wall, but it also meant that the main door to the building was directly adjacent to the road leading to the Athenaion.

The new building was rectangular and measured 26 × 29 m, which was considerably larger than the Ekklesiasterion at Priene and slightly smaller than the

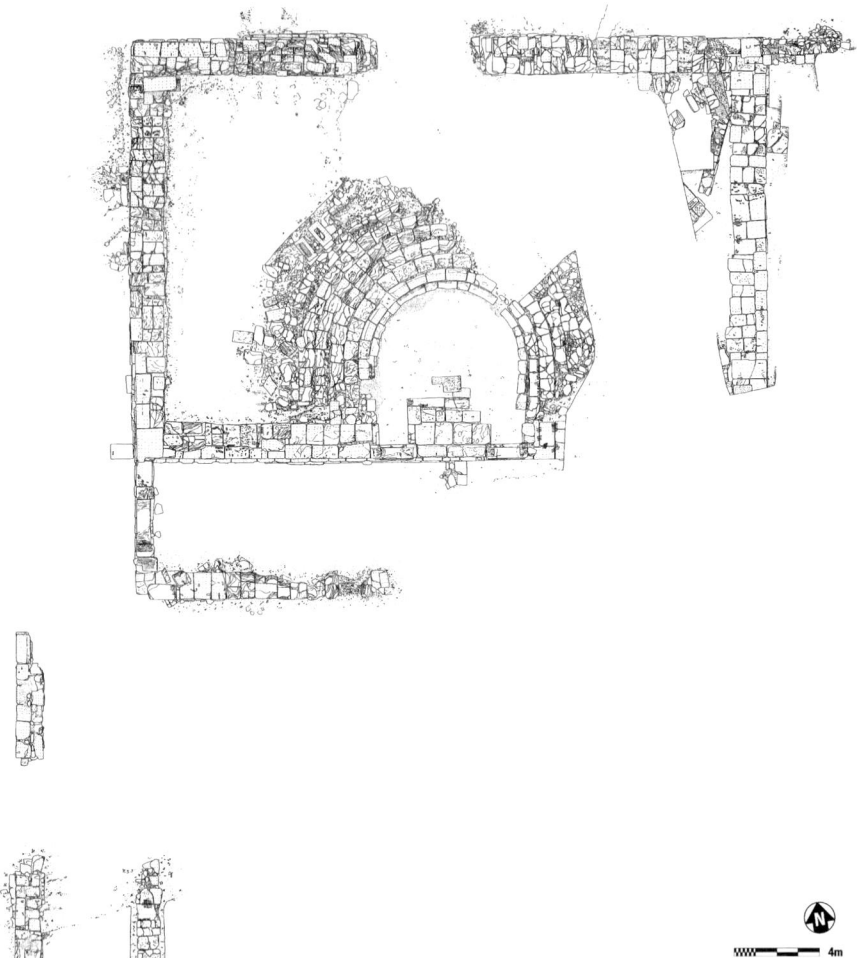

10.1. Plan of the Bouleuterion, drawn by Dieter Uhrig for the Troy Excavation Project.

Bouleuterion at Miletus.[3] The original appearance of the façade is uncertain; the order was certainly Doric, and it is usually restored as a decastyle building, although no associated columns appear to have been discovered during excavation.[4] The orchestra was decorated with colored marble – gray, white, and a brecciated purple laid around a centralized altar. Most of the seats in the horseshoe-shaped cavea were of limestone; only those on the lowest level were marble. At the back of the orchestra was a raised platform containing seats of honor that were separated from the rest of the cavea by a balustrade decorated with half columns. This is the only known ancient council chamber to have had such a platform in the orchestra, although it clearly functioned as reserved seating for leaders of the council and probably the koinon, not as a speaker's platform.

The road leading from the agora to the Sanctuary of Athena was now enlarged and must have been at least 10 m wide, although it narrowed gradually as it approached the old South Gate. Additional structures were built on the western side of the agora at the same time, but excavation has yielded only sections of walls, and their function cannot be determined.[5] Nevertheless, there must have been a gymnasium in this area judging by the surviving inscriptions, and one would expect stoas as well.[6]

The houses at the southern end of the Lower City continued to be occupied until ca. 130 B.C., when they were abandoned.[7] There appears to have been a desire around that time to live in an area closer to the acropolis, possibly because the district in the vicinity of the City Wall was perceived as too vulnerable, although greater proximity to the commercial activities in the agora may have played a role as well. There may also have been concern about a political danger: the Attalid prince Aristonicus, a brother of Eumenes II, had formed a sizable army after the bequest of Pergamon to Rome in 133, and had coerced several prominent cities in western Asia Minor into joining him, including Phocaea and Colophon. A residence closer to the citadel may have been deemed a safer choice in the wake of potential conflict.[8]

An increase in occupation in the central Lower City is, in fact, detectable at this time, and the buildings clearly housed prosperous families judging by the style of the architecture and associated pottery. Nevertheless, Ilion still seems to have been much more of a sanctuary than a city filled with houses during the Late Hellenistic period. There would certainly have been scattered homes for the administrators and employees of the sanctuaries and the Troad koinon, but no suburban district with planned houses such as one finds at this time at Priene and Pergamon.

THE ATTACK OF 85 B.C.

The literary accounts of Ilion's history in the early first century B.C. differ substantially from each other, although everyone agreed that the Roman commander G. Flavius Fimbria, legate of L. Valerius Flaccus, besieged the city in 85 B.C. because the residents refused to admit him.[9] That siege was one short chapter in the First Mithridatic War, in which Fimbria murdered Flaccus in Bithynia, took command of his forces, and battered both Mithridates and the towns of northwest Asia Minor.[10] Strabo, writing during the reign of Augustus, noted that Fimbria attacked Ilion for eleven days before subduing it, which indicates, by extension, the considerable strength of the city's fortification walls.[11]

Fimbria's army could have besieged the city from several sides, but the northwest, near the West Sanctuary, was certainly one of them, and it seems likely that there was a gate there, as in the Late Bronze Age. At least three buildings in the West Sanctuary caught fire: two temples (A and B) and the Late Hellenistic Building (Figs. 9.3 and 10.2). The fire may have started in the

10.2. The Late Hellenistic Building in the West Sanctuary, with destruction level, looking north. The City Wall can be seen further to the north. Troia slide 10947.

latter building, and the Hellespontine winds would have rapidly spread the flames to the adjacent temples.[12]

All of the West Sanctuary buildings had been emptied of their assemblages prior to Fimbria's arrival, so Ilion must have recognized the vulnerability of this area as well as the imminence of the attack. The fire in the Late Hellenistic Building was unusually intense: the interior walls are black and badly cracked by the fire. One man more than forty years old appears to have sought shelter in the Late Hellenistic Building at the point in which Fimbria's troops arrived, and his charred bones were found amid the destruction debris.[13] Everyone else seems to have vacated the Sanctuary before the attack occurred.

How desperate were the conditions elsewhere at Ilion? Substantial sections of every part of the city have been excavated, and there is no discernible evidence for damage anywhere else at this time, yet as the story of the Fimbrian attack began to be told, the scope of the destruction began to grow. Appian, summarizing the attack in the second century A.D., reported that Fimbria had demolished the city wall and burned the entire town, including the temple; not a house or statue remained standing.[14] Livy had earlier made the same point but claimed that the Palladion had miraculously survived. Augustine said only that Fimbria turned the town into a giant holocaust.[15]

When reading these historical accounts, we need to remember that the destruction of Homeric Troy was one of the most prominent tropes in ancient literature, and it substantially influenced subsequent accounts of attacks on Ilion. The actual damage was exaggerated in order to link more tightly the

Homeric and historic settlements.[16] We can see this in Augustine's description of Fimbria's attack on Troy, where the author continually juxtaposed the Homeric and Mithridatic Wars, as well as in Appian's account, where Fimbria was compared to Agamemnon.

Sulla visited Ilion shortly after Fimbria's attack, and one look at Ilion's new calendar demonstrates how desperately the city pinned its hopes of future benefactions on him. His visit literally triggered the beginning of a new era – in other words, Sulla's arrival marked year one of the new calendar, and subsequent events were intended to be measured by the number of years that had passed since the visit.[17] Strabo mentions that Sulla was responsible for substantial renovations at the site, but his main contribution may have involved only a confirmation of the city's freedom from taxes.

After Fimbria's attack, Ilion faced no further military conflicts during the first century B.C., but other cities in the region did, and Ilion was mindful of it. An inscription from Assos speaks of how difficult the conditions in the city were, and one of the stelae in Ilion's Athenaion records the miraculous appearance of Athena in Cyzicus when the city was besieged by Mithridates in 73 B.C.[18] Plutarch describes the situation in his *Life of Lucullus*: "It is related, too, that the goddess Athena appeared to many of the inhabitants of Ilion in their sleep, dripping with sweat, showing part of her peplos torn away, and saying that she had just come from assisting the Cyzicenes. And the people of Ilion used to show a stele which had on it certain decrees and inscriptions relating to this matter."

The other major problem that affected the Troad and, in fact, much of the eastern Mediterranean involved the pirates of Cilicia, whose power had been increasing since the second century B.C. In the years after 85 B.C. they attacked Samos and Samothrace and ravaged several of the cities on the west cost as far north as the Troad. An inscription from Ilion dated to 80/79 B.C. records the proconsul's dispatch of soldiers to Ilion, presumably to protect them from pirates, and Pompey's assistance against the pirates prompted Ilion to erect a statue of him in 62 B.C.[19]

The burgeoning economic depression in the Troad at this time is powerfully conveyed by a decree of the Troad koinon dating to 77 B.C.[20] The member cities of the league were having difficulty making their yearly payments to the koinon, and even a city as prominent as Lampsacus was forced to borrow money.[21] New low-interest loans had to be arranged, and several years later the interest rate had to be lowered even further, with the Athenaion's treasury now funding all of the cattle for sacrifice at the Panathenaea.[22] These conditions were by no means unique to the Troad: many of the traditional festivals in western Asia Minor were not held for several decades due to their great cost and the dearth of available funds.[23] Nevertheless, the decree mentioned above indicates that the Panathenaic festival should proceed as it had before, with no change in the usual procedures or provisions, and it must have gained renewed prominence merely by virtue of the fact that it continued to be held while so many other festivals did not.

The money for these and other loans would have been kept in the Ilion Athenaion, which belonged to the category of "temple banks" of which there is evidence for at least twenty-five, most of which also made loans.[24] Where exactly the money was kept is impossible to determine, since there was no standard practice in operation among the other eastern Mediterranean temple banks. Some cella floors contained a stone-lined vault that could require as many as four keys to open, whereas other sanctuaries preferred bronze strong boxes locked in the opisthodomos.[25] The latter would not have been an option at Ilion, if the plan is correctly restored, and the spoliation in the cella has removed any trace of a vault, if one ever existed. But there must have been temple guards (*hierophylakes*) who constantly patrolled the Sanctuary, as was done in other sanctuaries with treasures and/or banking operations.[26]

There appears to have been one additional misfortune experienced by Ilion during the first century B.C. At some point between the attack and the beginning of early Imperial building operations an earthquake brought down the upper courses of the northeast precinct wall in the West Sanctuary. The damage it inflicted on the other monuments can no longer be assessed, but the earthquake must have reached a level of 6.5 on the Richter scale to have dislodged so many heavy blocks, and it was yet another blow to a region that was already economically depressed.[27]

There is little activity datable to this interim period that is discernible in the archaeological record. Above the destruction debris in the West Sanctuary are several small areas of burning, probably the remains of campfires, which date to the mid-first century B.C.[28] The destruction debris pushed to either side of these fires may relate to temporary dwellings set up after one of the destructions, but there is otherwise no evidence for sustained habitation. Aside from a few coin issues of the koinon that continued to be struck at Ilion, the only other material culture surviving from this bleak period is the bronze burial urn of Herakleides of Dardanus, who had represented his town in the Panathenaea of 77 (Fig. 10.3).[29] The urn was discovered within the Dardanus tumulus, and the fact that this once handsome situla had been repaired and reused as a burial urn is a sober testament to the economic severity of the times.

Lucan supplied a fairly extensive discussion of Ilion's devastation when he recorded Julius Caesar's visit to the site in 48.[30] One of Lucan's goals was to juxtapose the impoverished condition of Ilion with the ruined state of Italy during the period of the Civil Wars, and the passage should not be regarded as an objective account of the city's appearance; nevertheless, the archaeological record attests to no new construction between Fimbria's attack and Caesar's visit, and a sizable part of the city must have resembled the ruinous condition that Lucan describes. Caesar, like Sulla, promised to restore the city to its former glory, although again, the only actual development appears to have involved a confirmation of Ilion's status as a city "*libera et immunis*."[31]

In Caesar's case, his concern for the city was spurred by more than Ilion's identification as the mother city of the Romans. As a member of the Julian family, he could trace his descent from Aeneas and Anchises, both of whom appeared on Caesarean coinage from the mint of Rome during the 40s B.C.[32] Ilion was, then, the ancestral city of his family, not unlike Aphrodisias, and promises of restoration allowed Caesar the opportunity to promote his own Trojan ancestry, as it would Augustus several decades later.

Julian ancestry had benefited the city once before: the censor in 89 B.C., L. Julius Caesar, had prevented the Roman *publicani* from taxing land belonging to the Sanctuary of Athena Ilias, in return for which both he and his daughter Julia received statues in the Sanctuary of Athena. These two statues would

10.3. Bronze burial urn of Herakleides of Dardanus, from the Dardanus tumulus, Çanakkale Archaeological Museum. Troy Excavation Project photo.

still have been visible in the Sanctuary of Athena at the time of Caesar's visit and would undoubtedly have been shown to him as an illustration of his family's benefactions, at which time their common ancestry would surely have been stressed.[33] It is hard to believe that the people of Ilion would not have voted a series of honors for Caesar as they had for the other benefactors of the city, although no such inscriptions survive.

THE AUGUSTAN AND JULIO-CLAUDIAN RENOVATION

Actual financial assistance would not arrive until the reign of Augustus, who visited Ilion ca. 20 B.C. during his tour of Asia.[34] Unlike the earlier visits of Alexander, Sulla, and Caesar, the visit of Augustus sparked a new campaign of building that would continue through the Julio-Claudian period, especially on the acropolis. Not surprisingly, it also marked a period of unbridled enthusiasm for the new dynasty in Rome. Nearly 80 percent of all Imperial images dedicated at Ilion were statues of the Julio-Claudian family, a few of which have survived, and Augustus in particular was hailed as *theos* and thanked for his unsurpassed benefactions.[35] Reconstructing the original location of these

10.4. Portrait of Augustus from the agora. Troy Excavation Project. Çanakkale Archaeological Museum. Neg. Troia 97/11–4.

statues is no longer possible in most cases, although a statuary group of Augustus and Tiberius was situated in the Bouleuterion, and at least one of the images of Augustus decorated the agora (Fig. 10.4).[36]

The largest of the new buildings was an enormous stoa-like structure (IXA) measuring 34 × 24 m; it was oriented toward the West Sanctuary, and its construction required the leveling of the mound's southwest side and the insertion of more supporting terrace walls at north and west (Figs. 1.5 and 10.5).[37] Much of the fill removed during the leveling was dumped directly into the West Sanctuary, thus raising the ground level between 1.5 and 2 m and burying much of the surface scarred by Fimbria's attack.[38] Probably constructed at the same time was another massive public building of similar plan and size (37 × 22 m) that was situated in front of and aligned with the south portico of the Athena precinct (IXB; Fig. 10.5).[39]

The function of neither of these buildings is known, but from what we can tell, everything on the old citadel mound was connected to the Sanctuary of Athena, and these are probably no exception. Whenever it was constructed, IXB would have provided a columnar façade for the southwest side of the Athenaion's precinct wall, which was otherwise unadorned, while the construction of IXA would, at least in part, have camouflaged the ruined West Sanctuary. It is worth noting that IXA was the largest building to have been constructed at Ilion up to this point, even if we include the monumental structures of Late Bronze Age date.[40]

Much of the stone for these buildings must have come from the West Sanctuary, which functioned as a kind of quarry during the early empire. An enormous number of limestone blocks were removed from most of the prominent Hellenistic structures, including the entire superstructure of Temple B, many of the wall blocks of the Late Hellenistic Building, and the precinct walls of the Upper and Lower Sanctuary. The only structure that was spared was the northeast wall of the Upper Sanctuary, which remained in place as a terrace wall.[41]

There is another indication of Augustus' assistance to the site, although its meaning has been continually debated. The evidence in question appears on one of the Athenaion's architrave blocks, now lost, which features an incised inscription of Augustus (Fig. 10.6): Αὐτοκράτ[ωρ Καίσαρ Θεοῦ] υἱὸς Σεβα[στὸς…].[42] Since the name of Augustus is in the nominative case, he

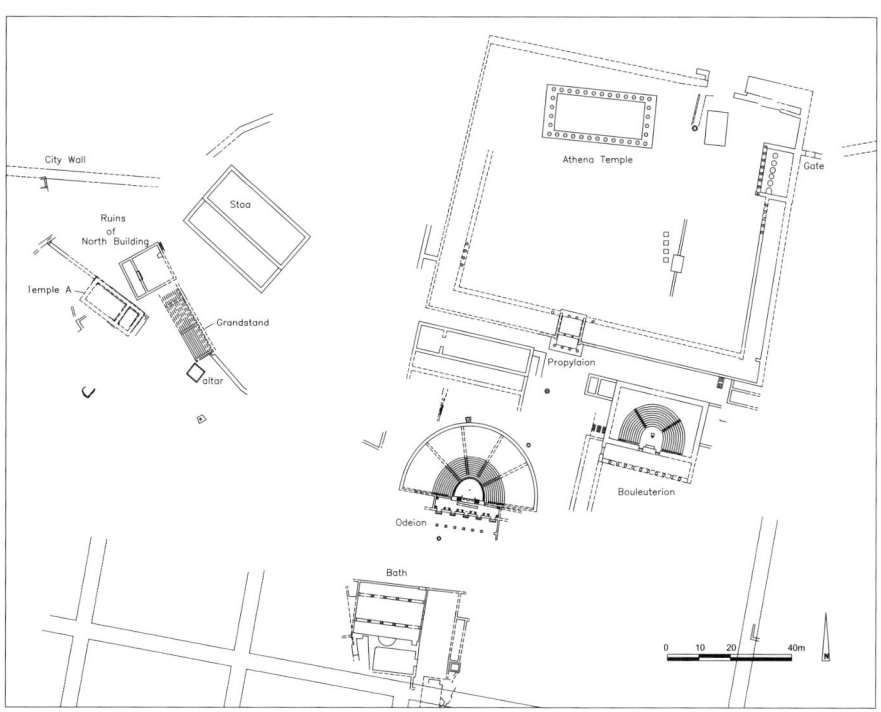

10.5. Plan of Troy IX, prepared by Elizabeth Riorden for the Troy Excavation Project.

10.6. Inscribed architrave block from the Athenaion. Drawing by Kate Clayton for the Troy Excavation Project based on an original by Goethert and Schleif 1962, Tafel 6a.

was clearly the donor, but the precise nature of his benefaction has always been unclear. Dörpfeld, following the accounts in Livy and Appian, proposed that the temple had been destroyed by Fimbria and subsequently rebuilt by Augustus; others have assumed that the inscription demonstrates the temple's initial construction in the Augustan period.[43] A renewed examination of the elements from the temple, portico, and propylaea, however, indicates no signs of repair or replacement, nor do the excavation reports mention the discovery of traces of fire in the vicinity of the temple. As a consequence, there is no reason to assume that the Athena Sanctuary was damaged in the late Hellenistic period and subsequently reconstructed.

Nevertheless, we need to reconcile all of this evidence with the fact that the name of Augustus appears in the nominative on the temple architrave, which means that he was responsible for some benefaction linked to the Sanctuary of Athena and, by extension, the koinon of Athena Ilias. There is still no satisfactory way to interpret the inscription. The only likely candidates are the two buildings mentioned above, IXA and IXB, which may be connected to the koinon. That connection, of course, cannot be proved, and one would still have to explain how the notice of the benefaction ended up on the temple.

It is also conceivable that other parts of the Ilion Sanctuary needed repair, having been damaged by earthquakes over the years, or that Antony seized part of the temple treasury, as he did the statue of Ajax from nearby Rhoeteum, and it was replenished by Augustus.[44] If the emperor had provided the koinon with additional land, as Attalus II had done, a record of the gift on the temple façade would also have been appropriate given the fact that the Athenaion was the heart of the koinon. But whatever the case, the benefactions of Augustus were probably focused on the koinon of Athena Ilias per se and did not involve the full-scale rebuilding of a temple destroyed by Fimbria.

The extent of the emperor's assistance might strike one as comparatively minor considering that Ilion was the mother city of both Rome and the ruling dynasty, but a survey of Early Imperial benefactions in Asia Minor shows that Augustus was far less generous than has been presumed. He either encouraged others in the city to come forward with money, freed up supplies in organizations that he controlled, or arranged for statues expropriated by Antony to be shipped back to their point of origin, as at Rhoeteum.[45]

Whatever the benefactions were, there is abundant evidence for Ilion's honors to Augustus and his dynasty in gratitude for them. A statue of Augustus was set up by a priest of the Imperial cult named Melanippides, which suggests either that the emperor received a new temple or altar precinct or that a pre-existing temple was reconfigured to include him.[46] No such temple dedication has come to light, but new temples to Augustus were being erected all around the Troad, at Cyzicus, Pergamon, Mytilene, among others, and Ilion may have followed the same model.[47]

Ilion's distinctive relationship with the Julio-Claudian dynasty was signaled through the addition of the epithet "συγγενῆς,"" or "kinsman," on Imperial statue bases, thereby highlighting the consanguineous connection of city and emperor by virtue of their common Trojan ancestors.[48] This practice, used only for men, began during the visits of Augustus, Agrippa, and Gaius Caesar during the last quarter of the first century B.C., and its final appearance was on the base of a statue of Nero, set up shortly after he argued before the Senate that Ilion's tax-exempt status should be continued.[49] This was a connection that no other city in Asia Minor could claim, and the fact that the current inhabitants of the city were Greeks was passed over in silence.

Throughout the Hellenistic period the Palladion had remained the dominant image on the city's coinage, and this was true during the Augustan period as well, but a new image now began to appear that was tied more specifically to the Troad's legendary heritage. The issue was contemporary with the new *syngenes* inscriptions and represented Aeneas carrying his father Anchises from Troy.[50] This was the only distinctively Trojan type struck during the first century A.D. at Ilion, which, in turn, was one of only two Mediterranean mints that employed the Aeneas type during the Augustan period – the other being Sicilian Segesta, which claimed to have been founded by Trojan refugees after the war.[51] The type is drawn almost exactly from Caesarian denarii struck in the East in 48 B.C., although the Palladion was omitted from the issue at Ilion. It is tempting to date the erection of Ilion's statue of Aeneas, hailed as "*patrios theos*," to the same period as the appearance of the Aeneas coins and the *syngenes* epithet, and it is noteworthy that Aeneas is the only one of the Homeric heroes to have merited such an appellation in the Troad's inscriptions.[52]

As the ancestral home of Aeneas, Ilion received visits from a variety of members of the Augustan and Julio-Claudian families, although not all were as rewarding as that of Augustus. When Agrippa and his wife Julia visited Ilion during his tour of Asia Minor between 16 and 13 B.C., she almost drowned while crossing the Scamander, and Agrippa levied the city with a fine of 100,000 drachms that was lifted only through the intercession of Herod the Great.[53] The statue offered to Agrippa was clearly a diplomatic overture on the part of Ilion, which seems to have appealed directly to Herod for intervention. If so, it seems likely that the request came from members of Ilion's Jewish community, even though there are no inscriptions that attest to that community's existence.[54]

In A.D. 18 there was another Imperial visit to Ilion: Germanicus, the eldest son of Tiberius, arrived with his wife Agrippina the Elder and their six-year-old son Caligula.[55] Shortly before their arrival, Agrippina had given birth on Lesbos to a daughter, Julia Livilla, and Germanicus, like Agrippa, would therefore have arrived at Ilion in the company of his family. He reportedly composed an epigram for the tomb of Hector, and Ilion probably voted a series of honors for the couple similar to those proposed by other cities in Asia Minor, although no such inscriptions at the site have survived.[56] Considering the disastrous situation that had prevailed during the visit of Agrippa nearly thirty-five years earlier, one can imagine that the Ilion's residents were solicitous to a fault.

There is a remarkable inscription to Germanicus' mother, Antonia the Younger, which probably dates to a few years after her son's visit.[57] The inscription appears on her statuary base and records her donation of funds to be used for the expenditures of local magistrates. The erection of a statue in gratitude for a benefaction was not unusual nor were the titles of Antonia herself. What is striking is the second part of the inscription, in which her daughter Livilla, wife of Drusus the Younger, was assimilated to the Aphrodite of Anchises. Livilla was therefore presented as a *genetrix* of the Julian dynasty, which, in turn, was simultaneously linked to Ilion's legendary heritage. The inscription is usually placed around the time of Germanicus' visit, but the emphasis on Livilla as "genetrix" strongly suggests a date shortly after 19, when she gave birth to twin sons.[58]

A similar model was embraced elsewhere in the region, with Julio-Claudian women freely associated with goddesses. Julia, daughter of Augustus, was linked to Aphrodite/Venus Genetrix at Assos, Lesbos, and Pergamon, while Livia was identified with older fertility goddesses, such as Demeter or Hera, at Assos, Lampsacus, and Pergamon.[59] Everyone recognized that the continuation of Imperial benefactions was tied to the maintenance of the Julian dynasty, and consequently followed an emphatically prospective approach in formulating their offers of honors.[60]

No coins from the local mint were issued during the Tiberian period, but upon the accession of Caligula in 37, a new issue was produced with facing busts of Augustus and Caligula coupled with a frontal Athena Ilias flanked by busts of Roma and the Senate.[61] This issue connected the new emperor with the dynasty's founder, conveniently editing Tiberius out of the sequence, while the reverse highlighted the links between Roman power and Ilion's patron deity.

Throughout the eastern Mediterranean there was a high level of enthusiasm surrounding Caligula's accession, in part because he had traveled in the company of Germanicus during their journey through Asia Minor in A.D. 18. Caligula was celebrated as "*neos Helios*" at Cyzicus, as Nero would later be at Aphrodisias, and his sister Drusilla was hailed as "*nea Aphrodite*."[62] Like many cities, Assos sent a delegation to Rome to pledge an oath of loyalty, a copy of which was discovered in the late nineteenth-century excavations at Assos.[63] In the midst of the congratulations was a statement mentioning that Caligula promised goodwill toward the city when he visited as a boy with his father Germanicus, and similar sentiments were surely expressed by Ilion. The enthusiasm was, of course, short-lived, since only four years later Caligula would be assassinated and his uncle Claudius hailed as emperor.

A high level of construction activity clearly continued during Claudius' reign, but there is very little that we can say about the original appearance of the buildings in question since only their dedicatory inscriptions survive.

10.7. Inscribed statuary base of the children of Claudius. Photo by the author.

The first involves a stoa dedicated by one Tiberius Claudius Philokles and his wife Claudia to Claudius, his fourth wife, Agrippina the Younger, and their children.[64] The inscription, which appeared on the *tabula ansata* of a fluted Doric column, indicates that Philokles dedicated the stoa and everything in it, thereby suggesting some substantial interior decoration. A similar Doric column with *tabula ansata* was found in the Sanctuary of Athena Ilias, and the two complexes were probably situated in close proximity to each other.[65]

One possible component of the stoa's decoration is a statuary group of Claudius' children, the inscriptions of which were found reused in the foundations of a late Roman portico southwest of the Bouleuterion (Fig. 10.7).[66] The group featured, from left to right, Antonia, daughter of Aelia Patina, Octavia and Britannicus, the children of Messalina, and Nero, son of Agrippina the Younger. The monument as we have it is incomplete, and Claudius and Agrippina were probably also included since children were usually shown with their parents in eastern Mediterranean dynastic imagery.

The statue of Nero shows a number of signs of being a later addition. The letters are smaller and more compressed, as if the letter cutter had to fit them onto a stone with little vacant space available. Moreover, he alone is called *syngenes* of the city, and only in his inscription are the Boule and Demos listed as dedicators. It therefore seems likely that the inscriptions were set up at two different times – the first three perhaps in the late 40s, and the statue of Nero

10.8. Inscribed Doric architrave with dedication to Claudius. Troia slide 14973.

added shortly after 53, at which time he argued before the Senate for a continuation of Ilion's status as a free city.[67] The *syngenes* title is almost certainly
related to that intercession.[68]

All that survives of the second Claudian building is part of a Doric architrave and frieze carved in one piece, but the identity of the dedicants is clear:
Claudius, Athena Ilias, and the Demos (Fig. 10.8).[69] Judging by its size, the
architrave probably belongs to a building approximately 70 percent the size of
the Athena portico, and so therefore quite a substantial structure.[70] On one of
the metopes is a circle of teardrop depressions that evoked the form of a phiale, probably accentuated with paint. Such a decorative treatment would have
called to mind another building of Hellenistic date in the Sanctuary of Athena
that was decorated with carved phialai, thereby highlighting the links between
the cults of Athena and the emperors.[71]

The identity of the dedicators of the building is problematic. There were
clearly two of them, although the first name was erased in antiquity along with
the conjunction between them, so that it would have looked as if the second
dedicator were solely responsible for the building. Most of the second name
has been damaged, but "Basilissa" can clearly be read, which suggests that the
erased section pertains to a king. The most attractive candidate is Mithridates
VIII, who was recognized as ruler of the Bosporan kingdom in 41.[72] Four years
later he attempted to break from Rome and, while preparing for war, sent his
brother Cotys as an envoy to Claudius with the intention of allaying any sus-
picions that might have existed. When Cotys revealed the plan to the emperor,

Mithridates was removed from power and his brother assumed the position of king. Undaunted, Mithridates proceeded to assemble a sizable army with the intent of laying siege to his former kingdom, but was ultimately defeated by the Roman army and sent as a hostage to Rome.

Mithridates VIII is mentioned in only one surviving inscription, discovered at Gorgippia in the Crimean peninsula and securely dated to 41.[73] In the inscription he is called "Philogermanikos" – an otherwise unattested title that was clearly intended to signal his close connection to Claudius, although his name was erased after his rebellion. Whether the lack of dedications to him is due to accident of survival or a comprehensive destruction is impossible to say, but the political situation in the Black Sea had not been this potentially dangerous since the reign of Mithridates VI, a lineal ancestor of Mithridates VIII. Ilion had nearly been destroyed during the Mithridatic Wars of the early first century B.C., and the events in the Bosporan kingdom during the Claudian period may have been uncomfortably reminiscent of the earlier situation. The name of his queen cannot be restored with certainty since only the first three letters survive ("Pai..."), but it may have been something like "Pairisades," "Pairisalos," or "Pairiphanes," all of which are attested in the Bosporan royal family.[74]

This is one of the few early Roman examples of an Imperial dedication by foreign royalty outside the formal boundaries of their kingdom. We should assume that the royal couple wrote a letter to Claudius requesting his permission to erect the building at Ilion and that the emperor consented to its construction. The dedication of the monument at Ilion meant that the new emperor was tacitly associated with the ancestral city of the Julian family, and the monument would have been guaranteed a higher level of visibility than a dedication in one of the cities of the monarch's own kingdom.[75]

The mint of Ilion issued four new types during the Claudian period that included Divus Augustus, Antonia, mother of Claudius, Britannicus alone, and facing busts of Nero and Britannicus.[76] Both Divus Augustus and Antonia had been honored on Claudian issues from the mint of Rome, as had Nero, but Britannicus was featured only on provincial coinage from the eastern Mediterranean, and his appearance here should be connected with the decidedly prospective approach of Greece and Asia Minor toward the Imperial family. With this series, Antonia becomes the first Imperial woman to appear on coins of Ilion. She had already been saluted as a benefactress of the city during the Tiberian period and had received a public statue in Ilion at that time, but both Julia, daughter of Augustus, and Livia had been honored earlier at Assos, Pergamon, and Mytilene, and it is surprising that Ilion had not followed suit.[77]

During the Neronian period there is little concrete evidence for new construction or monuments within the Troad. The mints of Ilion and Mytilene struck types of the new emperor and his mother Agrippina in direct response to similar issues from the Rome mint, and Alexandria Troas set up a statue to him, but otherwise there is no evidence for Imperial commemoration in the area.[78] The absence, of course, may be attributable to the senatorial *damnatio*.

In viewing the dynastic honors for the Imperial family within the Troad it is interesting to note the lack of references to the military exploits of the emperors, although this seems to have been the case throughout Asia Minor. The primary exceptions are Cyzicus, which erected an arch honoring Claudius' victory in Britain, and Aphrodisias, which built a Sebasteion featuring personifications of all subject peoples in the empire.[79] The latter city claimed the same bonds of kinship to Rome as did Ilion, so it is not surprising that their Sebasteion featured images of triumphant emperors juxtaposed with scenes of Aeneas' journey from Troy to Italy.

There are a few additional buildings that appear to have been added to Ilion during the Julio-Claudian period, although they cannot be placed in a particular reign. The most prominent of these was Ilion's first bath building, which lay near the west side of the agora and continued in operation throughout the third century (Figs. 10.5 and 10.9).[80] This site had probably been occupied by a Hellenistic gymnasium, of which only three sections of wall remain due to extensive later construction. All three walls were integrated into the new Julio-Claudian complex, which does not appear to have been large. There were at least two rooms, one of which measured approximately 11 × 7 m and was heated by a hypocaust system. The walls were faced with *opus reticulatum*, and although this technique could technically indicate a date in the first or second century A.D., *opus reticulatum* from the latter period generally incorporated brick into the construction, which is absent at Ilion, so a date in the early empire seems certain (Fig. 10.9).[81]

One of the rooms was paved with mosaics that featured images of athletes rendered in black silhouette on white ground (Fig. 11.12).[82] This is a technique that begins in Italy in the first century, although the majority of examples date to the second, and I suspect that the mosaics are tied to a second-century renovation.[83] The same date should probably be applied to Ilion's aqueduct (Fig. 11.13), which would mean that the Early Imperial baths relied on wells, cisterns, and the Spring Cave for their water, not unlike the baths at Alexandria Troas.[84]

The preserved inscriptions of Ilion unfortunately provide us with little information about the activities in the bath or about its genesis. The building certainly would have been used by the athletes preparing for the Panathenaea or Iliaea, some events of which occurred in the agora, and by those being coached for the *taurobolium*, a bullfight for the ephebes.[85] There was now also renewed occupation in the Lower City coupled with an increased population, and better bathing facilities would have been essential.[86]

10.9. Roman bath in the agora with wall of *opus reticulatum*, looking south. Photo by William Aylward for the Troy Excavation Project.

There is one other building that may have been erected at Ilion during the Julio-Claudian period, but it raises more questions than answers. The building is located in the agora and was originally free-standing, although it was subsequently incorporated into the Antonine bath/nymphaeum complex (Figs. 10.9, 10.10, and 11.12).[87] The most distinctive features are its small size (2.9 × 3.40 m) and its foundations, composed of a dark blue marble otherwise unattested at Ilion. The structure contained only one room, with a door that opened east into the agora.

From what we can gather, this was a peripatetic building, not unlike the Temple of Ares in the Athenian Agora; it was initially erected in another city during the Hellenistic period, then dismantled and re-erected at Ilion in the early empire. The molding profile points to a date in the later third or early second century B.C., but each of the blocks was subsequently labeled with twelve sequential letters of the Greek alphabet at the time in which it was moved and reassembled. Carl Blegen recorded no information about the pottery discovered in the building's foundations, but the latest ceramics under the neighboring limestone pavers date to the Claudian period, and the two building operations may have occurred at roughly the same time.[88]

The building's miniature format would be appropriate for a heroon, one of which was seen by the emperor Julian during his visit to Ilion in 354. Julian's shrine held a bronze statue of Hector and was very small (a "naiskos"), next to

10.10. Southeastern side of the Agora Bath, looking northwest. The Blue Marble Building is at upper right; the Antonine nympheum, in the center. Neg. Troia 99/68–33a.

which was a larger open-air shrine with a colossal statue of Achilles.[89] There is no evidence to link the Blue Marble Building with Hector's heroon, but it may easily have served a similar function. The structure's original home is a mystery, although the possibilities include the nearby cities of Sigeion, Rhoeteum, and Gergis, all of which had fallen under Ilion's control by the early second century B.C.

OTHER SITES AROUND THE TROAD

The reign of Augustus inaugurated a long period of peace in the Troad that would last for nearly 300 years, and new construction is attested throughout the region. Along the coast, slightly more than 20 km to the south, Alexandria Troas was in the process of becoming a large and prosperous Roman colony under the new name of Colonia Alexandria Augusta Troas. The colony's foundation date can be placed between 41 and 30 B.C., although it was supplemented by an additional contingent of veterans between 27 and 12 B.C. It was possibly then that the city received a grant of *Ius Italicum* that made it equal to other Augustan colonies on Roman soil; as a result, an image of Marsyas, symbolic of free cities, subsequently appeared as a type on their coinage.[90]

Alexandria continued to function as the principal port in the Troad, and construction must have been extensive judging by the results of the new excavations.[91] One of the newly discovered Early Imperial buildings is a Corinthian prostyle podium temple in the Agora, possibly connected to the Imperial cult, which was allegedly aligned with the point of sunrise on September 23, the birthday of Augustus.[92] Priests of both Julius Caesar and Augustus are attested epigraphically, and several other inscriptions reveal the scope of the city's homage to the Julio-Claudian dynasty.

One altar set up at the beginning of the Tiberian period is distinctive within the corpus of Julio-Claudian inscriptions from the Aegean. The dedication includes the names of Divus Augustus, Tiberius, Divus Julius Caesar, Julia Augusta, Gaius and Lucius Caesar, and Sextus Apuleius, consul in A.D. 29 and subsequently proconsul of Asia.[93] Dedications to Divus Augustus, Tiberius, and Julia Augusta were relatively common after A.D. 14, but the inclusion of the others is more unusual. In the eastern Mediterranean there was only one other dedication to Julius Caesar after A.D. 14 (in Elaea, near Pergamon); otherwise, the cult essentially disappeared.[94]

Given that the colony of Alexandria Troas may have been planned by Julius Caesar, his inclusion here is understandable, but it is worth noting that no other Roman colony followed suit.[95] Gaius and Lucius were members of the Julian family by blood, Tiberius by adoption; legally, the three men were brothers, and images of Gaius and Lucius were sometimes used in Tiberian dedications as a way of stressing Tiberius' connection to Augustus. The most striking addition is Sextus Apuleius, who was hailed as patron and benefactor in a number of Asia Minor cities: Assos dedicated a building to him, and a statuary group featuring him, his wife, and his daughter was set up at Cyme, but in none of these cities did the Julian family share an altar with him or any other proconsul.[96] Alexandria Troas was also one of the few Mediterranean cities to honor Claudius before his accession and to commemorate Drusus, son of Germanicus, during the Tiberian period.[97] In general, then, it looks as if the colony was much more active than the other cities of the Troad in honoring potential successors to the throne as well as their ancestors.

The nearby island of Lesbos also honored most of the Julio-Claudian emperors. At Eresus there were separate temples, in various parts of the city, to Augustus, Livia, Gaius, and Lucius, thereby imposing a Julio-Claudian dynastic stamp on the urban fabric of the city.[98] But the principal dynastic commemoration was reserved for the family of Germanicus, in part because Agrippina had given birth to her daughter, Julia Livilla, on the island. Statues of their children Nero and Drusus were set up during the later Tiberian period, and Agrippina was invoked as "*thea Aiolis karpophoros*" or the fruit-bearing goddess of Aeolis, which highlighted her role in the maintenance of the dynasty.[99]

An extraordinary series of small altars was produced in the city of Mytilene during the Caligulan period with dedications to Marcus Agrippa and Agrippa Postumus followed by the names of the siblings of Caligula. The altars may have been used in local Imperial festivals, and they demonstrate the loyalty that

10.11. Earthquake collapse at the Northeast Bastion, with two marble statues and architectural elements from the Athena Sanctuary. Troia digital image 31074.

an eastern city might continue to show its benefactors, even if they were dead or out of favor.[100]

Not all of the statues and honors dedicated at this time were focused on the Imperial family; wealthy benefactors who lived in the area were equally important, and the anticipated size of their potential contributions is amply demonstrated by Malousios of Gargara's overwhelming support during the Hellenistic period. Only a few statuary bases of Ilion's non-Imperial benefactors survive, but two slightly larger than life-size marble statues discovered in the earthquake collapse around the Northeast Bastion probably belong to this category (Fig. 10.11).[101]

The male is clad in a chiton and himation (Fig. 10.12A), while the woman has been presented in a Pudicitia type (Fig. 10.12B).[102] The woman's statue has been carved in one piece; the man's has a mortise for a separately made portrait, so they may not have been carved as a pair. Both of these types, however, were commonly used for images of civic benefactors during the empire, and given their findspots, they were probably set up by the koinon in gratitude for the benefactors' support of the Sanctuary of Athena.[103]

By the end of the Julio-Claudian period, Ilion's Sanctuary of Athena and the agora that faced it appear to have been functioning nearly as efficiently as they had in the late second century B.C., although the impact of the Mithridatic Wars would still have been firmly embedded within the memory of the inhabitants. The buildings of the West Sanctuary, destroyed in Fimbria's attack,

10.12. (A) Male statue from the Athena Sanctuary, Çanakkale Archaeological Museum. Troy Excavation Project photo. (B) Female statue from the Athena Sanctuary, Çanakkale Archaeological Museum. Troy Excavation Project photo.

continued to dominate the western side of the citadel as sober reminders of the chaotic political and economic situation during the first century B.C., as did a series of collapsed or collapsing houses in the Lower City.

Nevertheless, the tourism industry seems to have largely revived, even though one could no longer have seen the Locrian Maidens, who probably stopped coming around the beginning of the Mithridatic Wars. The recovery was due largely to the reigning dynasty's Trojan ancestry and to the Roman veterans living in the regional colonies of Alexandria Troas and Parium, all of whom were kinsmen of Ilion's inhabitants, at least in theory. This network of reconfigured kinships, now firmly anchored, would usher in a period of peace and prosperity that enabled Ilion to reach its maximum population, thereby becoming the kind of city that must have been envisioned by Alexander and Augustus.

ELEVEN

ILION FROM THE FLAVIANS TO THE BYZANTINES

The new Flavian dynasty founded by Vespasian in A.D. 69 had no connection to the Julian family that had been celebrated so enthusiastically at Ilion during the early first century, and the *syngenes*, or "kinsman," label now disappeared from local inscriptions. Nevertheless, the ties between Ilion and Rome had been so firmly established by this point that the emperors needed no familial connections to justify their continued acknowledgment of Ilion's privileged status. The period from the Flavians to Hadrian witnessed the largest number of construction projects in the city since the later third and second centuries B.C., when the region was under Seleucid and Attalid control. Repair, renovation, and rebuilding took place throughout the site, including the theater, agora, West Sanctuary, and Lower City. By the middle of the second century A.D., the public areas had assumed the appearance that they would maintain until late antiquity, and the entire region settled into a period of political stability and economic prosperity.[1]

Statues of the Flavian emperors were added to the city center and a new coin series celebrated the advent of the dynasty, with a reverse of Vespasian's sons, Titus and Domitian, facing the Palladion (Fig. 11.1).[2] The same reverse format had been used during the Caligulan period, albeit with Roma and the Senate flanking the Palladion, and in both cases the iconography signaled the close association between the new emperor and Ilion. The Palladion itself, however, had changed attributes: the polos disappeared in favor of a helmet, and she now carried a shield rather than the old distaff, thereby bringing her iconography closer to that of the Greek version of Athena and, by extension, Roma.[3]

There was a distinctive change also in the local mint's issue of Aeneas, which still constituted its only Homeric type. When these coins were first struck in the Augustan period, they included only Aeneas and his father Anchises, as on Caesarian denarii.[4] The Flavian issues now added the figure of a young Ascanius to the pair, thereby recreating the format of the Aeneas family statuary group that had been erected in 2 B.C. in one of the exedras of the Forum of Augustus (Fig. 11.2).[5]

11.1. Bronze coin from the mint of Ilion showing Titus and Domitian facing the Palladion. After Bellinger 1961, T127.

In both the sculptural and numismatic images of this group, Ascanius is dressed like an easterner with trousers and a Phrygian cap, whereas Aeneas is depicted as a Roman general in contemporary armor.[6] The figures therefore present a striking mix of East and West, with the father's costume representing the future, and his son's attributes signifying the past. This is the reverse of what one would expect, but it makes sense if one reconstructs the history of the group's creation. In the mid-Augustan period, the decision seems to have been reached to include both Roman and Asian iconography in *Aeneid* family groups – specifically, trousers and a Phrygian cap for Aeneas' son, and either a toga or contemporary armor for Aeneas. Such an addition succinctly conveyed the message that it was the destiny of Rome to dominate the East, from which it had originally come.

11.2. Bronze coin from the mint of Ilion showing the departure of Aeneas, Ascanius, and Anchises from Troy. After Bellinger 1961, T129.

Yet such a change in type involved a more complex set of issues than one might initially suspect: the status inherent in eastern costume could be either high or low, since it signified both the Trojan founders of the Roman people as well as their enemies in Parthia, who (from Rome's viewpoint) consistently sought to destroy what Rome had created. Both groups were fundamentally people of the East, and their costumes reflected that. The designers of the Forum of Augustus group dealt with the dual value of the iconography by adopting the Roman costume for Aeneas, to prevent him from looking like a Parthian, and assigning the eastern attributes to the child.[7]

One tends to assume that the new Aeneas iconography was immediately appropriated by cities throughout the Mediterranean, but it was embraced very slowly, perhaps because this unusual mix of east-west iconography coincided with a time of increased conflict between Romans and Parthians. Ilion was, in fact, the only city to utilize the new format during the entire first century A.D., and even there the mint waited at least seventy years before doing so.

THEATER A

It was probably during the Flavian period that Ilion's theater received its first stone skene, although the evidence is not as strong as one might wish. What is certain is that at some point in the last quarter of the first century A.D., the base of the cavea received a limestone water channel that emptied on either side into two new corbeled drains that evacuated the water toward the north (Figs. 8.5 and 8.6).[8] The drains passed directly below the new skene, and both were probably components of the new building campaign. In any event, the intersection of the two features demonstrates that the skene cannot be any earlier than the Flavian period, and the format of the lewis or lifting holes would be in harmony with such a date.[9]

The skene consisted of a series of rooms flanked by paraskenia and fronted by eight projections that probably constituted the foundations of four aediculae. The surviving elements formed part of a columnar façade with projecting and re-entrant cornices, although whether the aediculae were staggered among the floors, as in the Ephesian Library of Celsus, or aligned vertically, as in the Theater at Aspendos, cannot be determined. Such an architectural organization provides additional dating evidence for the skene's construction in that the aedicular format did not become popular in Asia Minor until the second half of the first century A.D. Since Ilion was not noted for its architectural innovation, it is rather surprising that they set up a façade of this type so quickly after its inauguration, although other cities of the koinon may again have provided assistance.

Most of the superstructure of the skene was burned in lime kilns or taken to the surrounding villages, but elements of the Doric, Ionic, and Corinthian orders survive, so we are probably dealing with a three-story building.[10] Two Corinthian capitals have been preserved nearly intact, as have several of the Corinthian cornices and one block from the raking sima of a pediment. None of these can be dated with precision, but the restrained carving points to a date not later than the first century A.D.[11] One has to admit, however, that the carving of the elements is not Asia Minor's best: the *caules* of the Corinthian capitals were left unfluted and the modilions on the cornices were rendered as simple rectangles.[12]

Schliemann found the traces of a wall parallel to and 1.5 m in front of the proskenion, along with a series of pierced blocks. These must relate to the *aulaeum*, or curtain, of the theater, and a series of cuttings along the base of the cavea must have been intended for large wooden poles that supported a

11.3. Balustrade block from Theater A inscribed with the name of Deiphobus. Troia slide 10573.

velum, or canopy, over the seats of honor.[13] Near one of the Schliemann dumps Blegen's team uncovered a fragmentary over-life-size draped female, a torso of Herakles, and the knee of an over-life-size male, some of which undoubtedly derive from statues that decorated the aediculae of the skene. Other sculptures discovered in this area are harder to place, such as two herms, one of which represented Herakles, and a reclining river god with cornucopia, perhaps the Scamander.[14]

It looks as if the sections of the theater were named after the local civic tribes.[15] One of the *balteus*, or parapet blocks, was incised with the name of "Deiphobus," the son of Priam who married Helen after the death of Paris (Fig. 11.3).[16] We have no way of knowing if one of Ilion's tribes actually bore his name, but another tribe was named "Panthous" after the Trojan elder who handed the Penates to Aeneas; a third was called "Alexandris," which probably refers to Paris rather than Alexander the Great; and a fourth bore the name of Assarakos, the son of Tros and grandfather of Anchises.[17] It is not unlikely that the Deiphobus inscription supplies yet another tribal name, and, if so, the theater would have evinced the same type of Homeric network that one finds in other sectors of the site.

THE WEST SANCTUARY AND THE LOWER CITY

The West Sanctuary had served primarily as a dumping ground and stone quarry during the Julio-Claudian period, but it too would be brought back to life during the last quarter of the first century A.D., although in a form significantly different from its Hellenistic manifestation. The new building program marked the first construction in the West Sanctuary in at least 160 years, and it was unusually ambitious: the Upper and Lower Sanctuaries were completely covered with earth, as was Temple B; a new altar aligned with a refurbished Temple A was built; and a new grandstand for performances was constructed on the eastern side of the complex (Plate 8, Figs. 2.7, 9.1, 9.11, and 10.5). The Late Hellenistic Building was left in its ruined state, with the back of the building now essentially functioning as a terrace wall (Fig. 10.2).[18]

An enormous quantity of earth would have been required to bury both the Upper and Lower Sanctuaries as well as the foundations of Temple B. Some of it would have become available during the leveling of the ground for the construction of Building IXA, directly above the West Sanctuary, but much more would have been necessary given the enormous spaces that had to be filled. Such massive quantities of earth would have completely removed many of the Hellenistic buildings in the complex from view, thereby camouflaging the fact that the earlier precinct walls of the Upper and Lower Sanctuaries had been spoliated. The new ground level extended throughout the complex, which meant that the northern and southern areas of the West Sanctuary now occupied the same level for the first time.

Once the ground level had been raised, the builders positioned a new altar to the north of the Upper Sanctuary's Hellenistic altar and shifted it slightly so that it was parallel to Temple A (Figs. 9.11, 10.5, and 11.4A).[19] This too constituted another innovation in planning: never before had an altar been aligned with its temple within the West Sanctuary, although the two structures were still separated by 22 m. The footprint of the new altar, at nearly 4.25 m square, was essentially the same as its Hellenistic predecessor; this made it easy to transfer the marble superstructure from the latter to the former, thereby producing the same kind of stepped altar facing the southeast.[20]

Temple A was also renovated at this time, although the extent of the renovation is unclear. In light of the intense fire in the neighboring Late Hellenistic Building, the temple must have sustained some damage, but since the building has been stripped to its foundations, there is not much evidence on which to draw in assessing that damage. A new foundation for the stairs at the front of the building was constructed with at least a few of the stones from the dismantled Upper Sanctuary precinct wall, and the area between the temple and the altar was now paved in marble.[21]

On the eastern side of the area between the renovated Temple A and the new altar rose a large grandstand, presumably intended for spectators watching ritual performances (Figs. 9.1, 10.4, and 11.4B).[22] The events were clearly expected to be relatively popular, and seating was planned accordingly: the grandstand's length was ca. 24.5 m, which provided seating for approximately

11.4. (A) The Roman altar in the West Sanctuary, looking northwest. The lower sections are modern restorations. Photo courtesy of the University of Cincinnati Classics Department, Troy Archives. (B) The Roman grandstand in the West Sanctuary during excavation. Photo courtesy of the University of Cincinnati Classics Department, Troy Archives.

360 people.[23] A colonnade was probably situated at the back of the grandstand, as in the Demeter sanctuary at Pergamon, and a new propylon, or stage entrance, occupied the narrow corridor that divided Temple A from the Late Hellenistic Building.[24] The latter construction would have lent an additional

note of drama to the festivities, which would have been lacking if the perform-
ers had simply entered with the spectators.

The cult activities in the newly rehabilitated complex must have deviated
significantly from their earlier manifestation. The high-walled precincts were
now completely covered, and there is no evidence for ritual activity within
Temple A or any other building. If the Sanctuary were linked to the cults of
Cybele and the Samothracian Gods during the Hellenistic period, the secret
rites associated with those cults would have had to change.[25]

An examination of the Early Roman small find assemblages in Ilion's sacred
and domestic contexts is particularly instructive in this regard. Terracotta figurines of Cybele began to appear in the houses of the Lower City only during the early first century A.D.;[26] at the same time, however, the horseman
plaques that had earlier been featured in the houses, as well as in the West
Sanctuary, suddenly disappeared. Whether the horseman cult remained active
in the Athenaion complex can no longer be determined, but the lack of such
plaques in sealed Roman strata near the Athenaion suggests that the cult there
had also been abandoned. It looks as if the Cybele cult shifted to the domestic
zone after the West Sanctuary was abandoned in 85 B.C., and once activity
resumed in the complex during the Flavian period, Cybele figurines began to
be featured in both areas, although her connection to the horseman cult was
terminated.

The majority of those votive terracottas were made in the Lower City,
where new houses and streets were being constructed with great rapidity. The
houses often encompassed residential, industrial, and commercial activities, so
one could have lived in the same building in which products were made and
sold. This appears to have been the case for one of the buildings in the center
of the Lower City, clearly a terracotta workshop, which contained two wells
and a basin next to an unusually large number of terracotta figurines and
bone implements, primarily tools or spoons (Fig. 11.5).[27] Excavation in the
surrounding area yielded a series of heavily used molds made of local clay
that were used to produce a variety of terracotta figurines, including Cybele,
Athena, incense burners, and herms, among others.[28]

One of the most distinctive features of this assemblage is the profusion of
large scale or life-size terracotta figures, all of which appear to have been made
within a relatively short period of time – the second half of the first century
A.D. If all of the specimens are gathered together, one ends up with an unusual
assemblage: the upper sections of several faces survive, as do three noses, fifteen fingers, and two toes (Fig. 11.6). With so many specimens preserved they
cannot have been a standard part of the decorative assemblage, and we should
probably interpret them as products kept within the workshop.

These Lower City buildings formed part of a network of insulae that can be
divided into three general groups based on size and shape: long rectangles at
the north, with a length:width ratio of nearly 1:3; slightly shorter rectangles at

11.5. View of the house in sectors I17 and I18, Lower City, looking south. The Early Roman phase, which contained the terracotta workshop, is represented by a well and basin. The colonnade foundation in the center dates to the late fourth century. Dia Troia 1484.

the south, with a length:width ratio of 1:2; and almost square rectangles in the center, coinciding with the south side of the agora (Plate 29).[29] Those in the north have a length of nearly 150 m; those at the south, 106 m; and those in the center, 80 m. The insulae were divided by a major north–south street that

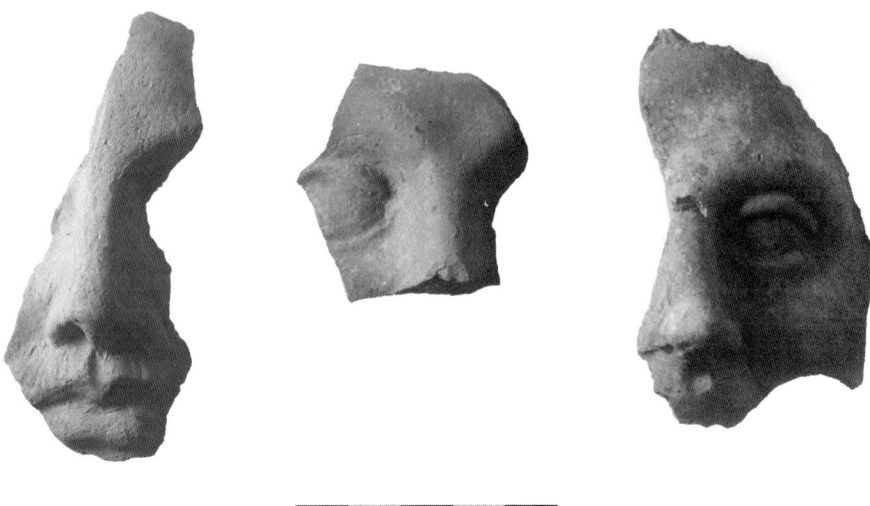

11.6. Lifesize terracotta figurine fragments from the center of the Lower City. Troia neg. 96–191–23.

was aligned with the main entrance at the Northeast Bastion (sectors K/L4) and continued along the east side of the agora. The grid to which these streets were aligned was laid out in the Early Hellenistic period, but the continuous blocks of housing that had been envisioned then began to appear only now, and would not reach their maximum size until the third century.

FROM HADRIAN TO THE ANTONINES

The Lower City and, indeed, the rest of Ilion appear to have flourished until ca. A.D. 100 when there was extensive destruction at Ilion: houses collapsed in the center and southern sections of the Lower City, and probably in the vicinity of the Spring Cave as well. There is evidence for an earthquake in A.D. 93 that would have registered 4.5 on the Richter scale (Mercalli intensity VI), which would not have been severe enough to destroy the buildings, as well as in A.D. 105 and 120 or 128.[30] Whatever the cause of the destruction was, it seems to have affected the entire city.[31] Shortly thereafter, one finds evidence for a massive cleanup, which involved filling in the wells in sectors u15 and u14/15 above the Spring Cave, as well as in C29, where more than 10 m of fill were dumped into the shaft.[32] The defensive ditch in front of the City Wall was also filled with dump at approximately the same time.[33]

Larger houses of much sturdier construction surrounded by new streets subsequently appeared in the center of the Lower City as well as along its southern edge, and the agora also became a locus for new building activity.[34] By the end of the Hadrianic period, the west side of the agora had been monumentalized with a new Odeion and an enlarged bath/gymnasium, which was

11.7. The tumulus of Ajax near Rhoeteum. Photo by the author.

now fed by water channeled from the foothills of Mt. Ida to the city via a new aqueduct (Figs. 10.5 and 11.11). Much of this beneficence is attributable to the emperor Hadrian himself, who visited the Troad in A.D. 124 during his tour of Greece and Anatolia.[35] This would have been the first imperial visit in over a century, since Germanicus passed through the area on his way to Syria, and the Troad's main coastal road appears to have been repaired in preparation for the emperor's arrival.[36]

Desperately in need of attention at this time was the Ajax mound, originally located in a vulnerable position on the shores of the Dardanelles. The tumulus had been consistently damaged by seawater over the years, and the bones of the occupant, allegedly nearly 5 m in height, had gradually become visible, according to Pausanias and Philostratus. This advanced deterioration reportedly prompted Hadrian to sponsor the construction of an entirely new tumulus well above sea level, nearly 2 km north of Ilion and roughly 1 km to the south of the Dardanelles (Fig. 11.7).[37] The unusual architectural framework that supported this new tumulus, still visible today, involved an outer circular vaulted passage, 3.5 m in width, which was connected to a central stone tower by a network of radiating walls. Such a format was never employed in pre-Roman tumulus construction, although it appears to have been popular in northwestern Asia Minor for tumuli of imperial date, and this is precisely the kind of architecture that one would expect for a tumulus built in the second century A.D.[38]

The mound now appears as battered as it did immediately prior to Hadrian's restoration, but in its original manifestation during the Hellenistic period, the tumulus of Ajax must have looked something like a park, with a seaside location, heroon, and a statue of Ajax so handsome that Antony carried it off to Alexandria, only to be later repatriated by Augustus.[39] Schliemann noted the existence of a statue by the tumulus in his day – "a mutilated marble statue of a warrior, draped and of colossal size" – but no trace of it remains today.[40] The tumulus has a diameter of at least 27 m and a height of 7 m, which would have required the transport of nearly 2,000 cubic meters of earth during the construction process.[41]

Hadrian's beneficence also appears to have extended to two buildings in Ilion's agora, although no inscriptions mentioning the emperor's name have been recovered from either building. One of these is the Odeion, built as a pendant to the bath-gymnasium, which was probably roofed even though no exterior supporting walls have been recovered (Plate 8, Figs. 10.5, 11.8, and 11.9).[42] The seating capacity was somewhere between 1700 and 2100 spectators, and therefore roughly the same capacity as the Bouleuteria at Aphrodisias and Ephesus.[43]

The cavea was divided into five cunei by four staircases, the highest section of which reached the same level as Building IXB behind it, and there may have been a link between the two.[44] The orchestra is fairly deep and surrounded by a limestone wall originally faced with marble and topped by a low marble cornice. When the theater was first built, the seats may have continued down to the level of the orchestra and were later removed to increase the distance between the spectators and the performance, although the area would have been too small for animal combats.[45]

The stage itself was wooden, as one can see from the joist pockets on the foundations, and was set within a stone frame connected to the cavea. The front of the stage included decorative semicircular and rectangular niches that were flanked by two staircases leading into the orchestra. Behind the stage was a polychromatic marble skene with four vertically aligned, two-storied aediculae – Ionic below and Corinthian above.[46] In a sense, this was a diminutive version of Theater A's skene in that both featured four stacked aediculae in a single line.

What was new here was the innovative use of colored marbles. Both stories featured gray marble columns, and additional columns of pinkish brecciated marble were later added in the wings. The range of marble revetment decorating the back wall of the skene was also extraordinary: opus sectile panels with geometric shapes were assembled from cipollino, pavonazzetto, Africano, Proconnesian white, and a pinkish brecciated marble. Most of these were quarried in Asia Minor, but it represented a new approach to architectural

11.8. The Odeion of Ilion, looking south. Troia slide 29795.

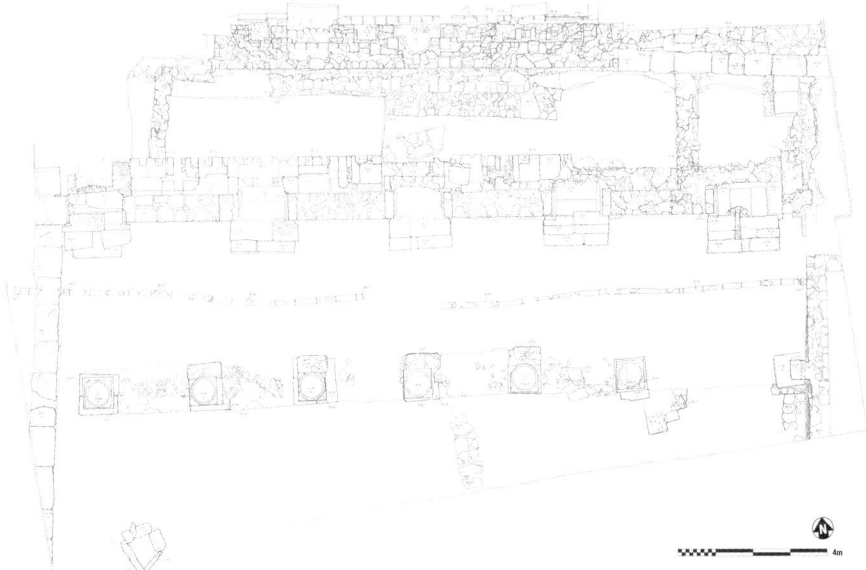

11.9. Plan of the Odeion, drawn by Elizabeth Riorden for the Troy Excavation Project.

decoration as well as a more magnanimous budget for construction costs than what one usually finds at Ilion.

Fortunately, part of the architrave dedicatory inscription was discovered during excavation, and the donor seems to have been a woman named Aristonoe, who reportedly paid for the skene and its sculptural decoration.[47] One of those

11.10. (A) Cuirassed statue of Hadrian from the Odeion, looking east. Troy Excavation Project photo. (B) The restored statue of Hadrian from the Odeion, Çanakkale Archaeological Museum. Troy Excavation Project photo.

sculptures, representing the emperor Hadrian, was found nearly intact during excavation and appears originally to have occupied one of the central aediculae on the upper level of the skene (Fig. 11.10).[48] This is the only imperial cuirassed statue to have been discovered at Ilion, although the cuirass type was also used for Hadrian on Ilion's coinage.[49] The statue is slightly over-life-size, with a paludamentum or military cloak draped over the left shoulder and arm. A scabbard occupies his left hand, and a separately attached element, probably a bronze spear, was originally positioned in the right hand.

The restrained carving of the portrait endows Hadrian with a decidedly youthful appearance: the beard and moustache have been lightly incised; the pupils are unincised; and there are no creases on the forehead or around the eyes, nor any use of the running drill in the hair.[50] The tight curls clustered in an arc above the forehead are a variant of Hadrian's "Imperatori 32" type, usually dated to the Early Hadrianic period, and a similar portrait appears on the cuirassed Hadrian from Thasos, which was probably made at more or less the same time as Ilion's Hadrian.[51] The simplicity of the cuirass is unusual: the decoration consists only of a gorgoneion on the breastplate and a thunderbolt

11.11. The Roman Bath in the Agora, looking south. Troy Excavation Project photo.

on the shoulder strap. In light of the fact that the statue was dedicated at Ilion, one would have expected the selection of a cuirass decorated with the Palladion situated above a Lupercal, which was one of Hadrian's most popular types in Greece and Asia Minor.[52] Without the accompanying inscription, in fact, it would have been difficult to determine whether the statue was private or imperial, and it highlights the disinclination at Ilion to spend money on elaborate sculptural compositions.

Little of the sculptural decoration that occupied the other aediculae can be reconstructed, although each of the aediculae was almost certainly occupied by a statue, so there should have been eight of them. Our discovery of the foot of a child perhaps indicates a statue of one of the Antonine children, as in the nymphaeum of Herodes Atticus at Olympia.[53] We should also probably reconstruct statues of Hadrian's wife, Sabina, his predecessors, Nerva and Trajan, and conceivably members of the donor's family.[54]

The Odeion appears to have been planned in tandem with the restoration and enlargement of the Augustan bath/gymnasium directly in front of it (Fig. 11.11).[55] The extent of the second-century A.D. renovation is difficult to determine, since the complex was excavated so long ago, but two likely components can be identified. One of them involved the insertion of *tubuli* in the walls of the hypocaust room to channel gasses from the furnace to the outside.[56] A new set of mosaic floors was probably also installed at this time, which included depictions of boxers; victor statues; bath attendants with strigils and oil pourers; cranes fighting pygmies (Fig. 11.12), some of whom were ithyphallic; and dolphins and hippocamps flanked by hydrias and kraters.[57]

11.12. Mosaic floor in the Roman Bath: pygmy fighting crane. Photo courtesy of the University of Cincinnati Classics Department, Troy Archives.

Most of these were rendered in black silhouette on white ground with the occasional flourish of color. The use of mosaic floors in such complexes does not seem to begin until the second century A.D., and although mosaic athletes in silhouette are attested in Italy in the later first century A.D., the majority of the examples date to the second century.[58]

Several inscriptions from Ilion and Alexandria Troas clarify the thoughts and activities of the athletes depicted in these mosaics. A marble grave stele found in Ilion's Lower City, dating to the second or third century A.D., contains an epigram in honor of a gladiator named Hilaros, who was honored as a friend of Ares and compared to Herakles:[59]

> You see me deceased, wayfarer, one daring in the stadiums, Hilaros, skilled (?) in arms and of the race of Ares (?). For just as they say that Herakles, having won 12 contests, has been joined to the immortal gods, I too, having fought 12, reached the end of my life.

The contests in which the athletes were engaged encompassed both sides of the Aegean, as is evident from a contemporary inscription honoring the athlete Pergamos, who won boxing competitions in the following games: the Pythia at Delphi, the Smintheia at Alexandria Troas, the Asklepieia in Epidaurus and Perinthus, the Kaisareia in Sparta, and the Smintheia and Hadrianeia in Coele.[60]

Some of the regulations relating to the contestants in these games have recently become clearer as a result of a newly discovered inscription from Alexandria Troas that contains three letters written by Hadrian to the international union of athletes. Among a series of proclamations, the emperor urged that the timing of civic or regional games be staggered so as to attract the greatest number of spectators, and detailed the punishment for athletes who misbehaved:

11.13. The Roman aqueduct in the village of Kemerdere. Troy Excavation Project. Troia slide 28091.

There must be some deterrent hanging over the contestants and those who err must be corrected, but not so that they are beaten by many persons at once, and only on their legs, and so that no one be crippled or incur any injury from which he will be worse at his profession itself.[61]

The aqueduct that would have supplied the water for Ilion's bath may have been set up during the same period (Fig. 11.13). The source of that water was somewhere in the foothills of the Ida Mountains, possibly in the vicinity of the villages of Salihler and Çamlıca, between 20 and 25 km to the east of the site.[62] The water was directed via clay pipes and underground channels, some of which have been discovered and mapped, as well as at least three bridges, the largest of which is located near the modern village of Kemerdere.[63] With a total length of 87 m and an arch span of 16 m, it represents the most impressive example of a Roman aqueduct still standing in the Troad. The construction technique, featuring dry laid ashlar masonry and mortared rubble, indicates a general date in the first or second century A.D., as does the relief head on the keystone that probably represents Apollo Thymbraios.[64] If, however, one links the new water system with the renovation of the bath complex, which seems logical, then the aqueduct should be placed in the Hadrianic period.

Such a date is also in harmony with the evidence from Alexandria Troas, a much larger and wealthier city that served as the primary port in the Troad. Philostratus notes that the city received its first aqueduct in A.D. 134/5, due to the beneficence of Hadrian and Herodes Atticus, having earlier used wells and cisterns.[65] It seems unlikely that Ilion would have received an aqueduct earlier than a colony as important to the regional economy as Alexandria Troas, although the two water systems may be more or less contemporaneous and could have been constructed by the same engineers.

Whether Alexandria Troas received the same level of support from Hadrian as Ilion is unclear, although one of the city's inscriptions refers to him as "restitutor" of the colony, which suggests significant benefactions.[66] The same may have been true for other cities in the Troad, and the region's projected enthusiasm for the emperor is clearly demonstrated by the inscriptions uncovered in the Olympieion at Athens. That complex had been intermittently under construction for more than 600 years and was finally dedicated by Hadrian in A.D. 131/2. Although it was ostensibly focused on Zeus, the complex reportedly contained 129 bronze statues of Hadrian dedicated by a variety of cities, and thus functioned as a center for the imperial cult.[67] Three of those statues were dedicated by cities in the Troad or on the Gallipoli peninsula: Alexandria Troas, Abydos, and Sestos.[68] Such a system of display would undoubtedly have become connected with issues of civic pride and prestige, and Ilion, as mother city of the Romans, probably dedicated a statue of Hadrian along with the others.

It was during the reign of Hadrian that Ilion expanded its range of legendary coin types to include Hector and Ganymede as well as Aeneas leaving Troy with Ascanius and Anchises.[69] Added to the latter type was a miniature Lupercal in exergue, which tied together the two key episodes in Roman legend.[70] Whether the expanded range was tied to Hadrian's visit to the city, to increased tourism, or to both cannot be determined, but it appears to have been prompted by local initiative – there was no corresponding set of legendary images that were struck by the mint of Rome or any other mint in the Troad.

That would change during the reign of Antoninus Pius, when a series of coins and medallions were struck in preparation for the festivities in 147 that celebrated the nine-hundredth-year anniversary of Rome's foundation.[71] The series included an abundance of legendary themes that encompassed Roman history from Troy to the Republic, including Aeneas (departure from Troy, arrival at Lavinium), Mars and Rhea Silvia, the Lupercal, and the Sabine women, among others.[72] These coins would have been in circulation at the time of the Secular Games and other celebrations in 147, at which time Antoninus also exempted the Arcadian village of Pallantium from taxation in recognition of the fact that it was the native city of Evander, who had colonized Rome's Palatine hill.[73]

Only two small issues were struck at Ilion during the reign of Antoninus, but when production resumed on a grander scale after the accession of Marcus Aurelius, large eye-catching sestertii and dupondii featured the most extensive array of Trojan subjects ever represented on Ilion's coins, including the Lupercal, Aeneas, Ganymede, and five types of Hector (Fig. 11.14), with Dardanus and

Priam added under Commodus.[74] This series also marked the return of the old Hellenistic type of Athena Ilias that had not been included on Ilion's coinage since the Augustan period. The size of the coins was similar to although not quite as large as the Antonine medallions with legendary scenes, which probably indicates that Ilion's series was prompted by the earlier anniversary issues.

One might have expected the other mints in and around the Troad to have followed the same model, since they had stressed their affiliations with the Homeric tradition in the past, but the response was limited: Alexandria Troas struck a Lupercal under Commodus, as did Parium, and Dardanus and Scepsis added Ganymede and Aeneas scenes during the Severan period, but no other such examples are attested.[75]

11.14. Coin from the mint of Ilion showing Hector throwing firebrands at the Greek ships. Troia slide 31119.

It is not unlikely that such coins were taken as souvenirs, which would explain why no Trojan War memorabilia have yet come to light in any of the excavations. This would also provide a rationale for the increase in the size of the coins, and in many cases, Ilion's tour guides could have pointed to the sites associated with the episodes depicted on those coins. There is, in fact, one piece of evidence in support of such a hypothesis, although it lacks a provenance: a bronze simpulum of Roman imperial date was decorated with coins from western Asia Minor mounted on the exterior, one of which features the Aeneas coin from the mint of Ilion.[76] It looks as if the decoration of the simpulum was intended to summarize the high points of a series of journeys, not unlike a stamp collection.

Did this renewed emphasis on the legendary history of Rome appear on contemporary monuments within Ilion? There is epigraphic evidence for the erection of statues of Aeneas, Ajax, Hector, and Priam at Ilion, and although none of them can be linked to a specific period, some of them are most likely Aurelian in date.[77] One other potential candidate, from Theater A, can be placed in this period with a fair degree of probability. In the course of his excavation of the theater, Schliemann found a marble block nearly 1.25 m square that was decorated with a relief shield whose center had been carved with a Lupercal on a rocky background (Fig. 11.15).[78] The relief has been organized like the reverse of a coin, with ground line and exergue decoration. The Lupercal format is the standard one, featuring a fig tree at the right and a wolf facing left with the twins beneath, although a few additional elements have been rendered in four niches or scalloped compartments: an eagle with outstretched wings to the left of the wolf's head, two facing stags at the top, and a seated Pan in the exergue.

11.15. Lupercal relief from Theater A, Pergamon Museum, Berlin. Photo by the author.

One can ascertain the date of the relief only by examining the history of the type. Lupercal images in the Hellenistic period were extremely rare: an image of Romulus and Remus was dedicated on Chios ca. 200 B.C. in recognition of Rome's intervention in the war with Antiochus III, but that seems to have been very much the exception.[79] This is true also for the Early Imperial period: cities tended to honor Rome with statues and cults to Roma herself rather than with images of the founders of the city. The type was featured on only two provincial coin issues during the first century A.D., and only twice in stone, as far as we know: on the Actium tropaeum in Nicopolis and the Sebasteion at Aphrodisias.[80]

The relative popularity of the Lupercal does not appear to have changed until the Antonine period, when it was featured on the coins and medallions commemorating the nine hundredth anniversary of Rome's foundation.[81] Only at this point did the Lupercal become relatively frequent as a reverse type on western Asia Minor coinage, including that of Ilion, and this is the most likely time for the relief to have been made.[82] Such a date would also be in harmony with the style and iconography of the relief: although the carving of the figures is rather crude, the relatively homogeneous size of the stones in the wolf's grotto conforms more closely to Lupercals dating to the Roman empire, and the grotto frame became a regular feature of the Lupercal only in the second century A.D.[83]

There is nothing in the history of Ilion ca. A.D. 150–250 that would point to a more specific date, but given Ilion's close diplomatic links to Rome, it seems likely that the city would not have waited long to respond to the anniversary celebrations, and the relief carving probably coincides roughly with Ilion's Lupercal coins. This would make the relief Aurelian and more or less contemporary with the Lupercal scene on the Parthian monument of Lucius Verus in Ephesus.[84]

The most unusual feature of the block is the fact that the relief has been carved within a shield. The inclusion of a figural motif on a shield was a frequent practice in the Hellenistic and Roman periods, although this was usually a portrait; when a multifigured scene appeared on a stone shield, it was generally carved in relief on the surface, not cut within its convex surface.[85] Such a technique would have been necessary, however, if the shield's surface had already been finished – in other words, if the insertion of the relief occurred during a secondary phase of carving.

The history of the relief's carving is related to the block's technical features. The form of the lifting hole is very close to those on the stones from the Athena temple, which suggests that the block was first fashioned as an architectural element in the Hellenistic period. Its dimensions are considerably larger than those of a metope, which would exclude its position on the skene frieze, and one would normally not expect to see such shields in the decoration of an ancient stage.[86] Shields of this type were, however, common features of Bouleuteria or heroa, and that may have been the original context of the block. It is noteworthy, in fact, that the diameter of the Ilion shield is nearly identical to that of the shields that decorated the Miletus Bouleuterion.[87] In other words, the Theater A shield block was probably created for another building altogether, which was most likely of Hellenistic date; at a later time, probably in the Antonine period, the block was brought to the theater where it was carved with the Lupercal. More such blocks may also have been brought to the theater from the same source and carved with other scenes of Rome's legendary history, although where and how they were set up remains a mystery.

In most cities of western Asia Minor, the Antonine period was one of enormous construction activity with increasingly complex aediculated columnar façades, many of which were incorporated into bath buildings. Ilion's volume of construction does not come close to matching that at Ephesus, Miletus, or the cities of Pamphylia, but there is enough evidence to indicate that a new marble nymphaeum was joined to the Hadrianic bath at some point in the second half of the second century (Figs. 10.5, 10.10, and 11.16).[88] This would have added a monumental flourish to the agora's southwest corner, and it was probably aligned with an equally monumental portico that was built along the western side of the agora at roughly the same time.[89]

The nymphaeum was built against the outer wall of the bath, facing the agora, and its total length would have been 15.5 m. The floor of the basin was constructed of waterproof plaster and bordered by a marble balustrade,

11.16. The nymphaeum next to the Agora Bath, looking southwest. Neg. Troia 99/99–27.

of which one piece was recovered and re-erected. Along the back wall of the basin was a large central pedestal flanked on each side by three smaller pedestals; these probably served as supports for columnar aediculae that would have framed statues in the six exedras. The varying sizes of the statuary supports suggest images of different types, one of which must have held a striding figure, judging by the orientation of the base, and therefore more likely an image of a god rather than an emperor.[90] A statue of a river personification found in the agora by Schliemann may also have occupied one of these niches, as at Miletus and Perge.[91]

The bath building may have been modified again around the same time. This included the transformation of the room with mosaics into a large apsed hall measuring nearly 21 × 16 m. Two lateral colonnades divided the room into three parts, with a new floor of alternating blue and white marble tiles now covering the earlier mosaics. The hypocaust room was also enlarged and vaulted, and a new series of rooms was added to the eastern side, one of which was probably the apodyterion, or changing room.[92]

These modifications probably coincided with the construction of yet another bath on the eastern side of the Lower City. The evidence for the building consists only of a line of large ashlar blocks lying in sector X/Y 11/12, about 350 m east of the Agora Baths, and a few notes in Carl Blegen's excavation report of 1932.[93] His exploration of the building yielded several rooms with marble floors, a hypocaust, large water channels and drains, and a marble bench, but no information on dating. Both baths were probably aligned with and fed by the new aqueduct, however, and the need for two baths would not

11.17. The water basins in front of the Spring Cave, looking northeast. From right to left are basins 1 (Flavian), 2 and 3 (Antonine). Troia slide 34246.

have arisen until the second century A.D., when the city's population increased significantly.

All of this activity involved significant changes in the city's water systems, several of which would have been visible in front of the Spring Cave on the northwestern side of the Lower City. At some point in the Flavian period an enormous stone-lined basin with *opus signinum* had been constructed in front of the cave; this basin, in turn, was replaced ca. A.D. 160/70 by two new adjacent basins with tiled floors, each measuring 5 × 3 m (Fig. 11.17).[94] The presence in the basin walls of terracotta tubes blocked at one end indicates their function as freshwater fish farms, wherein the tubes would have provided shade for the fish.[95] Such tank designs are described by Varro and Columella as especially appropriate for eels, a Roman delicacy, and an eel bone was actually unearthed in the Lower City.[96] Similar basins have been excavated in Crete, Egypt, and Italy, among others, but the Trojan examples are the only ones that have been found thus far in Asia Minor.

THE SEVERAN PERIOD

There appears to have been no diminution in the relationship between Ilion and Rome when the Severans came to the throne; the reign of the later Severan emperors, in fact, marked one of Ilion's most prosperous periods.[97] The local mint continued to produce large coins with innovative designs, such as Hector killing Patroclus, Herakles and Hesione, Apollo and Poseidon building the walls of Troy, and Anchises with Aphrodite in a *dextrarum iunctio*, although the coins of Aeneas now disappeared.[98] The revival of the old Athena Ilias images continued, with both Hector and Ilus sacrificing to or saluting the cult statue.[99] This device had been used during the Antonine period to show the emperor paying homage to Athena Ilias, and would later be modified at Alexandria Troas to depict Caracalla sacrificing to the image of Apollo Smintheus.[100]

The Athena Ilias type appears to have been issued in connection with Caracalla's visit to the Troad in A.D. 214, which was the first imperial visit to the area since that of Hadrian ninety years earlier.[101] Ilion commemorated the event with a type that featured a cuirassed Caracalla holding a small Nike in his hand, obviously intended as a prediction of victory in the Parthian Wars that were about to occur.[102] Both Dio and Herodian describe Caracalla's arrival at Ilion, which was programmed to echo that of Alexander the Great nearly 550 years earlier. The emperor reportedly wore Macedonian dress, complete with kausia, and was accompanied by a Macedonian phalanx to whose commanders Caracalla gave the names of Macedonian generals. As with the earlier visit of Hadrian, the coastal road of the Troad was again renovated.[103]

Like Alexander, Caracalla poured libations to Achilles, decorated his tumulus, and staged a race around it with his companions. He also dedicated a bronze statue of Achilles at Ilion, the location of which is not mentioned, but there may be a reference to it in a letter written 140 years later by Julian the Apostate in which he described his arrival at Ilion in A.D. 354.[104] Julian notes that Hector's image was still intact in a small temple at Ilion opposite a statue of Achilles that reportedly occupied the entire area of an unroofed court. From this description it appears that Hector's statue was more or less life-size and sequestered within a building, whereas that of Achilles was of colossal dimensions, on public view, and probably situated in such a way that it would have looked as if he were prepared to scale the walls. In this composition, the variation in scale was presumably intended to signal the outcome of the battle as well as the difference in ethnicity, since both would probably have been shown in Greek armor.[105] Whether this was the image dedicated by Caracalla is unclear, but it is the only Achilles statue at Ilion for which we have evidence.

Caracalla also constructed an enormous tumulus for his recently deceased freedman named Festus, now known as Üveciktepe, which lies approximately 7 km from Ilion (Fig. 11.18).[106] This is the largest of the Troad tumuli, with a diameter of 70 m and a height of 17 m, which makes it more than twice the size of the tumulus of Achilles. Herodian describes the enormous pyre on which the body of Festus was burned as well as the emperor's histrionic mourning, which was clearly intended as a re-enactment of the mourning of Achilles for Patroclus.[107]

This reverence for Ilion may have translated into an additional benefaction during the reign of Macrinus, the praetorian prefect who assassinated Caracalla

11.18. Caracalla's Tumulus of Festus at Üveciktepe. Photo by Ruestem Aslan for the Troy Excavation Project.

in A.D. 217. Since Macrinus occupied the throne for only fourteen months and suffered a senatorial *damnatio memoriae* after his assassination, not many inscriptions bearing his name have been found, but one of them appeared in the earthquake collapse of the Odeion.[108] The most interesting feature of the Ilion inscription is that Macrinus' name appears in the nominative case, which indicates a dedication on his part. The nature of the dedication would have been described in the now missing lower section of the inscription, but enough evidence exists to suggest that the benefaction in question relates to the Odeion. Beneath the marble paving at the west end of the stage there were enough coins and diagnostic pottery to indicate that the structure received its final form during the reign of Caracalla, or shortly thereafter, as did a new portico that separated the Odeion from the agora.[109] Given the findspot of Macrinus' inscription, it is possible that the city recognized him for a renovation that was funded by Caracalla but completed only during the reign of his successor.[110]

At some point in the later Severan period Ilion experienced a major destruction that brought down the houses in the central and southern parts of the Lower City. In light of the extensive damage that occurred throughout the site, an earthquake may well have been responsible, although there is no literary evidence for it.[111] Several enormous dumps were deposited in a large open area in the center of the Lower City, possibly deriving from the agora, and rebuilding commenced immediately.[112] A network of new stone-paved streets was laid at this time (Fig. 11.19), and there was a rise in the number of issues

11.19. View of the street along the south side of the house in sector K17, Lower City, looking northwest. Troia slide 1531.

struck by the local mint, wherein even inexperienced die-cutters were pressed into service to meet the increased demand.[113]

It was only now that occupation in the Lower City became dense, with the walls of one building abutting another. This period, in general, seems to have been an economic high point for Ilion as it was for other cities in western Asia Minor.[114] The density of Ilion's new housing suggests that during the second quarter of the third century there was a significant influx of new settlers there, who would, in turn, have played a role in stimulating the economy. If the early third-century disturbance affected the entire region, which seems likely, then there may have been a population shift from the smaller towns to Ilion, which still served as the capital of the Troad koinon.

Especially striking is the extent to which all of this parallels the history of the Hillside Houses at Ephesus, which comprise our best evidence for domestic occupation in western Asia Minor during the third century. Those houses had been severely damaged at the same time as the structures at Ilion, after which there was a similarly dramatic rise in reconstruction with new houses elaborately decorated with mosaics and wall paintings.[115] Other cities in western Asia Minor, especially in Ionia, benefited as well, and inscriptions refer to new construction, civic improvements, and elaborate spectacles.[116] There are no public buildings at Ilion whose construction can be placed in the second or third quarters of the third century, although a recently discovered milestone indicates additional road repairs during the reign of Gordian III.[117]

We also have a considerable amount of evidence for third-century industrial activity on the edge of the plateau above and to the east of Theater A. This is a 70 × 50 m area where magnetic prospection indicated the existence of nine kilns, one of which contained a rectangular firing chamber measuring 2 × 1.50 m, within which were ten fragmentary sausage-shaped distance pads for stacking pottery.[118] Such a nucleation of kilns was fairly common in the Roman world and allowed resources to be shared easily among workshops. This particular site was ideal for furnaces in that it was separate from the residential areas, and the strong winds from the Dardanelles would have pushed the smoke away from the city.[119] Not all of the kilns were necessarily intended for the production of clay objects: iron, bronze, and glass working are all possibilities.[120] In any case, the substantial clay beds throughout this area made it an ideal locale for the manufacture of pottery, tiles, and terracotta figurines.[121]

ILION DURING LATE ANTIQUITY

The Goths attacked Ilion in 262, as they had so many cities in the Aegean and Asia Minor.[122] According to Jordanes, a sixth-century A.D. author of the history of the Gothic invasions, the Goths crossed the Hellespont and sacked Ilion, which "had scarcely recovered from the famous war with Agamemnon, and was now destroyed anew."[123] There is, in fact, evidence for extensive destruction at Ilion ca. A.D. 260–70, although we cannot determine whether it was caused by an attack of the Goths, an earthquake, or a combination of the two.[124] Wells in the Lower City were filled with debris, as was at least one of the qanat shafts, while the fish farms in front of the Spring Cave were destroyed.[125] There was limited reconstruction following the disaster, but it seems to have been restricted to the center of the Lower City; nothing was rebuilt at its southern edge. It looks as if the residents once again abandoned that area and sought shelter closer to the acropolis, as they had done in the late second century B.C.

An unusual discovery within one of the newly filled wells may provide a glimpse of life at the time of the invasion. In the lowest fill of the well in sector w28 was a marble statuette of Cybele of the usual type, with a lion on her lap, a tympanum in her left hand, and a phiale in her right (Fig. 11.20).[126] The presence of such a complete and valuable artifact in this part of the Lower City, where the houses tended to be rather poor in all periods, is especially noteworthy, as is the statuette's deposition in the well.[127] Though slightly abraded in places, the image is whole and in good condition. Why the inhabitants would have thrown away such a valuable and attractive object is perplexing, and it is unlikely that an enemy would have dropped it there so carefully. A more likely hypothesis is that the inhabitants, fearing the impending devastation of the attackers, lowered the statuette into the well in an effort to hide it.[128]

In general, there appears to have been an economic downturn at Ilion after the Goths' attack, and that decline would continue until ca. A.D. 350.[129] A few

11.20. Marble statuette of Cybele from the well in sector w28, Lower City. Çanakkale Archaeological Museum. Troia slide 19152.

of the public buildings may also have been damaged during the decade following the attack, as suggested by a coin hoard of 218 antoniniani that was found in one of the rooms of the Agora Bath. The hoard consisted primarily of issues of the emperor Aurelian and had a closing date in the late 270s. Since there seems to have been no hiatus in habitation during this period, the most likely reason for the lack of retrieval would have been the destruction of the building.[130] By this point, the Panathenaea had almost certainly ended, and an epigraphic reference to a "new Panathenaea" suggests that its celebration during the third century A.D. may have been intermittent.[131]

Part of this decline can be associated with the economic crisis of the late third century, which ultimately led to price freezes and currency reform; another reason is probably the Diocletianic redistricting of Asia Minor, wherein Cyzicus was established as the new capital of the Troas and Lesser Phrygia.[132] This would have removed substantial commerce and income from Alexandria Troas, and Ilion's economy would have suffered indirectly as a consequence.

Nevertheless, Ilion was not forgotten by the emperors, nor the emperors by Ilion, even during the late third century. Inscriptions refer to a Tetrarchic gift of silver statues of Zeus and Asclepius to Athena Ilias, which, in turn, may have prompted Ilion to dedicate a monument to the Tetrarchs in the temenos of Athena, although the evidence requires some analysis.[133] During Dörpfeld's excavations of the precinct attributed here to Zeus Polieus, he found four bases, evenly spaced and identical in size, that were composed of spoliated elements.[134] They appear to have been set up at a time when some of the site's buildings had already fallen down, even though the Athenaion was still intact (Plate 8, Fig. 10.5). The fact that the four bases form part of a single series of Late Antique date, coupled with the epigraphic record of Diocletian's gifts to Athena, suggests that the bases originally supported statues of the Tetrarchs.[135] It is also worth noting that the position of the bases in front of the entrance to the precinct of Zeus Polieus meant that the Tetrarchic statues would have been juxtaposed with the colossal image of Zeus that had been set up there in the Hellenistic period. As such, it would have resembled the western side of the forum in Rome, which was decorated with images of the Tetrarchs and Jupiter on honorific columns.[136]

At least some imperial visits continued to occur. Constantine reportedly arrived in the early fourth century A.D. and considered moving the capital to either Ilion or Alexandria Troas, ultimately preferring the Bosphorus to the Dardanelles.[137] Two Late Antique historians, Sozomenus and Zosimus, asserted that Constantine had already begun building the walls of the new city near the tomb of Ajax before he changed his mind, and although historians have consistently attempted to affix a Constantinian label to various Late Roman walls in the vicinity of Ilion, there is no firm evidence that the construction of any new city was begun there by the emperor.

Ilion set up a statue of his son, Constantine II – one of the very few new statues in the city during the fourth century A.D. – but no evidence exists for any imperial benefactions either here or in Alexandria Troas at that time.[138] The future emperor Julian actually wrote a letter describing his arrival at Ilion in A.D. 354, wherein we learn that the heroon of Hector was still intact, as was a bronze statue of Achilles in an open-air precinct, possibly the one set up by Caracalla.[139] At some point in the Late Roman period a series of Greek epigrams was inscribed on statues of Homeric heroes (Priam, Hector, and Ajax) that probably stood in the Athenaion or the agora, perhaps around the time of Julian's visit.[140]

Julian was honored with a statue by the residents of Ilion, and his name may also have been featured on the temple, although here too the evidence is problematic.[141] One block of the temple's inscribed epistyle survives, with an incised inscription over which the bronze letters of a second inscription were subsequently placed (Fig. 11.21):[142]

Inscribed: Αὐτοκράτ[ωρ Καῖσαρ Θεοῦ] υἱός Σεβα[στὸς …]
Bronze:]οῦ Ἰουλ[

The bronze letters would have been at least 0.20 m in height, judging by the position of the holes. Other than Ilion, there are no examples in which a building inscription, once incised, was replaced by an identical inscription in bronze, and one can easily understand why. The surfaces that received these inscriptions were exposed to the elements year-round, and any plaster meant to cover an incised inscription would have quickly washed away, thereby leaving an ugly shadow under the gilded bronze letters.

The authors of the first monograph on the Athena temple assumed that both the incised and bronze inscriptions referred to Augustus, with one replacing the other within a very short period of time.[143] The bronze section was consequently restored as Θε]οῦ Ἰουλ[ίου υἱός].

Such a restoration is probably incorrect, since Caesar was never called "*theos Ioulios*" in the inscriptions of Ilion; Augustan inscriptions in the east generally refer to Caesar merely as "*theos*" or "*theos Kaisar*."[144] There is consequently no reason to associate the bronze letters with Augustus, and the fact that the bronze inscription obscures but does not completely erase the first one argues strongly against it. I suspect that the bronze inscription on Ilion's Athenaion

11.21. Inscribed architrave block from the Athenaion. After Goethert and Schleif 1962, Tafel 25b.

concerned a different emperor and was inset at a much later time. No words in the second inscription repeat those in the first, and only two fragmentary words survive from the bronze version: "]οῦ ᾽Ιουλ[."

The only certainties here are that (1) one of the words begins with "᾽Ιουλ"; (2) the name of an emperor was featured; and (3) the letters were set into the stone at a time when it would not have been considered anathema to deface or replace the name of Augustus. All of this evidence points toward a Late Antique date, and almost certainly to the emperor Julian. The preserved section of the inscription can easily be restored as "[Φλαβίου Κλαυδί]ου ᾽Ιουλ[ιανοῦ]," which is the usual formula for his name.[145] Julian's statue would probably have been erected at Ilion at the same time, and his name was probably added to the propylon architrave of the Aphrodisias Sebasteion as well, although it was later defaced.[146]

Shortly after this visit, and for the remainder of the fourth century, the Lower City of Ilion witnessed more building activity than any of the preceding centuries. Reconstruction in the middle of the Lower City included a monumental portico flanking one of the major streets as well as a large glass-working center with water channels in which we found abundant quantities of glass wasters, ingots, and slag (Fig. 11.22).[147] The manufacture of glass requires large quantities of silicate sand and an abundant supply of fuel, both of which were readily available due to the proximity of the Scamander River and the forests that encompass the foothills of Mt. Ida. Glass-working centers were probably a standard feature in many of the Troad cities, but Ilion is the only one in the region in which such a complex has been discovered.

11.22. Glass-working center in the Lower City, sector H17, looking west. Troia slide 10843.

11.23. Mosaic floor in the Late Roman house in sector D20, Lower City, looking south. Troia slide 12644.

The houses also became increasingly opulent in the late fourth century: two of them contained elaborate polychromatic mosaics with geometric schemes, including Solomon's knots and squares with chevrons (Fig. 11.23).[148] One also featured an elaborate painted plaster ceiling with floral designs, the edges of which were defined by a plaster bead and reel molding with a course of shells. The best comparanda for such decorated ceilings come from the Hillside Houses at Ephesus, although the example at Ilion is considerably later.[149] It is noteworthy that in none of Ilion's houses is there evidence for the private baths or opus sectile floors that one finds at Ephesus and Pergamon.[150]

11.24. The granite quarries at Koç Ali. Troy Excavation Project.

Some of the new construction gradually encroached upon the paved streets, thereby decreasing their width by several meters and spurring the spoliation of their stone pavers. This is part of a larger Late Antique trend in the eastern Mediterranean wherein commerce shifted from the agoras and forums to more residential areas along major roads, with the shops often set up behind new porticoes.[151] In spite of the fact that some of these structures were commercial as well as residential, there is no evidence of window grills to discourage theft, although the presence of keys indicates that the doors were locked.[152]

Very little granite was used in the new construction, but the granite quarries near Alexandria Troas were certainly still in operation during this period (Fig. 11.24). Newly quarried columns were shipped to Lepcis Magna in 313 for use in the restored Forum Vetus basilica, and both the *Theodosian Code* and the *Historia Ecclesiastica* indicate continued activity through the first quarter of the fifth century.[153] The granite quarries operating at that time were clearly engaged in the standardized production of monolithic column shafts, some of which were nearly 12 m in height, and when the quarries finally closed due to a drop in market demand, twenty-one of the shafts that had already been prepared for transport were simply abandoned at the quarry site.[154] All of this granite would have traveled to its final destination via the port of Alexandria Troas, where one of the ships tasked with transporting the columns was reportedly launched miraculously by the city's bishop, Silvanus, at the beginning of the fifth century.[155]

11.25. Mosaic floor of the Early Christian Church in the Lower City. Photo courtesy of the University of Cincinnati Classics Department, Troy Archives.

Ilion was also reportedly the seat of a bishopric until at least the ninth century A.D., but there is no indication that the temple of Athena was subsequently transformed into a church or that any churches were erected on the acropolis. The only church that has been identified at the site was excavated by Blegen on the eastern side of the Lower City. The total dimensions of the building were quite sizable, approximately 30 × 18 m, and it may have been Ilion's principal church during late antiquity. Some of the walls had clearly been spoliated, but the mosaic floor of the narthex was still intact and featured medallions filled with images of animals and birds (Fig. 11.25).[156] The church was probably constructed during the period of prosperity that occurred at Ilion on either side of A.D. 400, and it almost certainly lay near a pre-existing cemetery.

By the middle of the fourth century, the economic picture appears to have become considerably bleaker. The agora at Ilion gradually lost its commercial function due to the steady movement of shops to the Lower City, and it was being used as a cemetery by ca. A.D. 450.[157] A crippling blow occurred shortly after A.D. 500, when two sizable earthquakes struck the western Troad within a relatively short period of time.[158] Even before the earthquake struck, the city appears to have been largely abandoned: few small finds were discovered in the houses under the earthquake collapse, leading one to posit that most of the houses had been emptied of their contents by the beginning of the sixth century.

11.26. The early sixth century A.D. earthquake collapse at the Northeast Bastion, with blocked gate at left, looking southwest. Neg. Troia 96/205/10.

As in the Late Bronze Age, the remaining residents once again took shelter on the acropolis. The northeast gate of the city was completely blocked by a wall composed of fallen architectural elements (Fig. 11.26), and on the southern side of the acropolis, the survivors constructed another defensive wall composed of spoliated architectural elements set in a hard mortar. Both of these seem to have formed part of a new security system, and only one entrance to the acropolis may have remained open.[159]

How long habitation continued here is unclear, but on the southern side of the acropolis Blegen found three coins from the second half of the sixth century: Justin I and Sophia (565–8), Tiberius II (578–9), and Maurice Tiberius (587–8), while a coin of Heraclius (610–41) was unearthed on the west side of the Athena temenos. These are the latest Early Byzantine coins to have been found at the site, and it seems likely that the acropolis was the last locus of activity in post-earthquake Ilion.[160] The date of these coins is particularly important, because it indicates that at least a few of the residents survived the plague (probably bubonic) that swept through Asia Minor during the reign of Justinian.[161]

There was still a considerable amount of activity in this area of the Troad during the sixth century: Justinian built an enormous granary on the island of Tenedos so that grain ships from Egypt had a place to unload their cargo if the winds and currents of the Dardanelles hindered sailing, and an inscription from Abydos, probably dating to the reign of Anastasius I, records the tariffs imposed on ships crossing the Dardanelles.[162] All of this would have had little effect on Ilion or the coastal cities of the Troad, however, since their public buildings now lay in ruins.

THE GRANICUS RIVER VALLEY IN LATE ANTIQUITY

The last residents appear to have abandoned Ilion, including the acropolis, by the early seventh century A.D. That abandonment coincided with a complete restructuring of the Byzantine Empire, wherein new geographic units called themes were created. The Hellespont region was now joined to Bithynia with a new capital at Nicaea, which lay more than 300 km east of Ilion and Alexandria Troas.[163] A Heraclian hoard of silver ecclesiastical spoons found at Lampsacus in the mid-nineteenth century attests to the wealth of the local churches in the Troad, but the new administrative changes clearly had a negative effect on the area's commerce overall.[164]

Although the coastal cities lay in ruins, the interior of the Troad witnessed a significant increase in occupation: a recent survey of the area between the Granicus and Aesepus Rivers has revealed that nearly 30 percent of the pottery on the surface is Late Roman.[165] It looks as if the seismic activity along the coasts played a role in disrupting the regional waterways, which turned to swamps and ultimately prompted a rise in malaria, followed by plague. The coastal sites were therefore largely abandoned in favor of a return to the inland areas that had been sparsely inhabited since the end of Persian control. Indeed, many sites examined in the recent Granicus survey yielded virtually no pottery that dated between the Late Classical and Late Roman periods.

The Granicus River Valley did not experience the same diminution in construction activity that one finds in the coastal cities of the Troad during the late fifth and sixth centuries. The security of the roads that crossed through the Aesepus, Empelus, and Macestus River Valleys in the eastern Troad/Mysia were too important to leave unprotected, and new citadels were situated on high hills that, in some cases, provided views as far as the Sea of Marmara.[166] At least four such citadels were situated along the Aesepus river, which marked the main road from Cyzicus to Adramyttium and Pergamon, and the distance between them ranged from 6 to 33 km.[167]

Two of these, Alacaoluk and Asartepe, occupy very defensible terrain in the Aesepus River Valley and feature walls faced in ashlar masonry with neat headers and stretchers, especially on towers and around gates.[168] Alacaoluk is located on a high outcropping of bedrock that rises from the floor of a deep gorge about 15 km southwest of Gönen (Fig. 11.27).[169] The fortress has an oval shape, about 175 × 105 m in size, and the main citadel wall was fortified by an outer wall on the north and east sides. There are eleven towers overall, the largest of which is approximately 15 m in height.

11.27. Remains of the Late Roman citadel at Alacaoluk in the Granicus River Valley. Granicus Valley Survey Project.

The site of Asartepe is located 33 km southwest of Alacaoluk (Fig. 11.28).[170] The elevation of the citadel is extraordinarily high, with views of the Aesepus and Granicus River Valleys as well as the Sea of Marmara on clear days. The fortress is long and narrow, 325 m long and between 45 and 75 m wide. These walls are not as well preserved as those of Alacaoluk – the most intact tower is only about 7 m high – but aspects of the design and construction indicate that the two fortresses were contemporary. The fortress had ten towers (excluding bastions that flanked the gates) and three cisterns, while the large number of

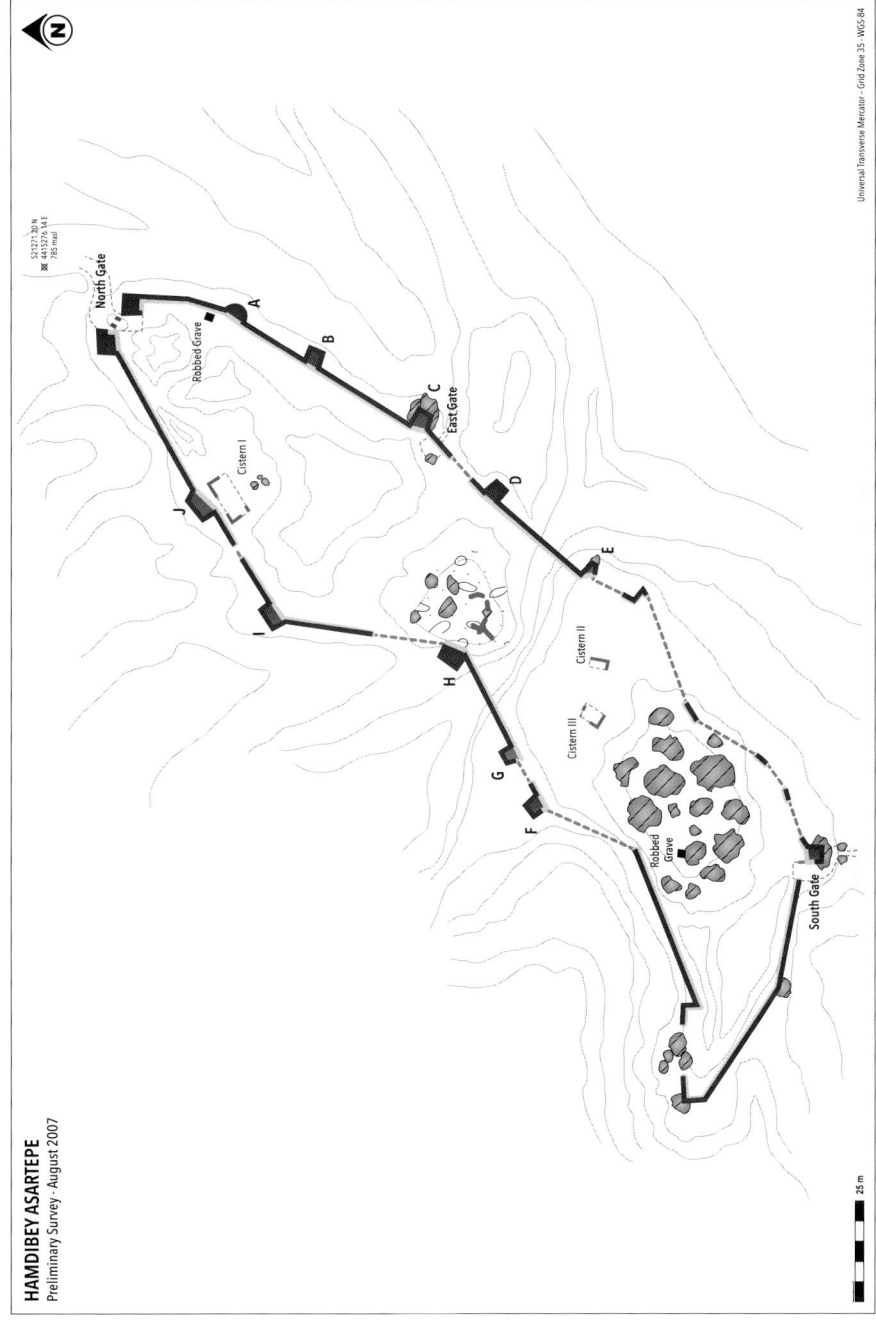

North Gate

Robbed Grave

A

B

C

East Gate

D

E

Cistern I

J

Cistern II

H

Cistern III

G

F

Robbed
Grave

South Gate

N

522271.20 N
445527634 E
785 masl

Universal Transverse Mercator - Grid Zone 35 - WGS-84

25 m

11.28. Plan of the Late Roman citadel at Asartepe in the Granicus River Valley, prepared by Gabriel Pizzorno for the Granicus Valley Survey Project.

273

millstones still present on the surface suggests grain storage and processing, which would have been vital for a garrison.

Both citadels were probably constructed during the reign of the emperor Anastasius I (A.D. 498–518). Anastasius built fortification walls across Thrace ca. A.D. 500, probably to counter military threats from the Bulgars, and similar walls were constructed across the Gallipoli peninsula around the same time.[171] These were enormous fortification projects, built as new lines of defense to supplement the existing walls in the face of increasing security problems, and the citadels at Asartepe and Alacaoluk may have been by-products of the building program. With the rise in population in the interior during the early sixth century A.D. coupled with a concomitant increase in commercial traffic, the construction of such citadels along major roads is to be expected.

Our attempts to chart the extent and size of Asia Minor settlements dating between the seventh and tenth centuries are usually foiled by the difficulty of recognizing and dating pottery produced at that time, along with the lack of documentary sources. Several inscriptions record Michael III's repairs of the city walls of Nicaea, Smyrna, and Ankara in the ninth century, and inhabitants of the countryside probably sought shelter in the largest fortified cities of their themes, such as Cyzicus and Assos, as they had done during the Late Bronze Age and the Mithridatic Wars.[172]

LATE BYZANTINE ILION

During the Middle Byzantine period a low level of activity continued, judging by the ninth-, tenth-, and eleventh-century coins that have been found on and around the mound, but this was probably related to the site's use as a lookout post on the Dardanelles, especially during the Byzantine–Selcuk wars of the late eleventh century.[173] New construction is not perceptible in the archaeological record until the Late Byzantine period, in the early thirteenth century, when the Nicaean empire would have controlled the area.[174] The revived settlement was clearly not a prosperous one: there was a considerable amount of stone robbing, and only a few new walls were built.

The center of habitation shifted to the Spring Cave at this point, probably because it was the most reliable water source still in operation at Ilion, and the West Sanctuary's proximity to the cave made it one of the main areas of activity.[175] A new building, perhaps a cellar or a storehouse, was set into the ground southwest of Temple B and built against earlier walls of Troy VI and VII.[176] The associated fills included an enormous amount of sgraffito pottery, the latest sherds of which date to the thirteenth century.[177] East of the terrace wall was another Late Byzantine structure containing numerous polychromatic glass bracelets, similar to those found in the area around the Spring Cave and in a series of thirteenth-century pits in the Lower City.[178] All of this construction

severely disturbed what remained of the
earlier temples in the West Sanctuary,
whose stones were clearly spoliated for
use in the new construction.

Even though the settlement was
probably not much larger than 500
people, cemeteries existed in at least
three different areas: the Spring Cave
(Fig. 11.29), Theater A, and the southwestern edge of the Lower City.[179] The
coffins were formed of limestone slabs,
some of which were reused architectural elements, and set in holes cut
directly out of the bedrock. This again
highlights the versatility of the Trojan
bedrock, which was alternately used as
a quarry, house foundations, rubbish
pits, bases for pithoi, and burial chambers throughout the Greek and Roman
periods.[180]

There was evidence for at least forty-
nine total burials above the Spring Cave,
of which sixteen were excavated, and at
least nineteen burials at the southwest-

11.29. The Late Byzantine necropolis above the Spring
Cave. Neg. Troia 97/124–1.

ern edge of the Lower City. As in the case of the cemetery adjacent to Theater
A, the bodies had been pulled out of their coffins and cast aside in order to
free up space for new burials, and several coffins contained more than one
skeleton.[181] Some of the heads were fixed in place with stone or tiles, with the
bodies oriented toward the east. Most of the tombs had been robbed in antiquity, but there were still a few finds, primarily of early thirteenth-century date:
two gilded earrings and a bronze reliquary, two silvered earrings, a multitude
of polychromatic glass bracelets, and a bronze coin in the mouth of one skeleton, which preserves an earlier Roman tradition.[182] The reliquary is our only
demonstrably Christian discovery in twenty-four years of digging.[183]

Of the forty-nine individuals from the Spring Cave cemetery, 39 percent
died before their eighteenth birthday and more than 30 percent died before
the age of five. The bodies of the adults, nearly all of whom died between the
ages of twenty and forty, clearly had a difficult life: the bones contain signs of
arthritis in the shoulders and sacrum, inflammation of the knee joints, and
degenerative curvature of the spine. The same is true of the children, who
suffered from osteomyelitis, meningitis, cribra orbitalia, anemia, hematomas,
and probably malaria.[184] In the contemporary cemetery next to Theater A,

however, there was virtually no sign of such sickness or of the ailments that plagued the adults buried above the Spring Cave. This variation in physical condition may be a sign of class differentiation, with the burials in the theater belonging to a more elite group.[185]

Several large Late Byzantine pits at the southwest corner of the Lower City indicate that a number of the residents had once again returned to the city's perimeter, probably because of the availability of large tracts of land for farming.[186] There is also secure evidence for continued use of the Lower City through the late fifteenth and early sixteenth century, probably for farming, although no Early Ottoman period structures have been unearthed. Habitation throughout the area seems to have increased at this point. One likely cause was the influx of Jewish refugees into Çanakkale at the end of the fifteenth century, after their expulsion from Spain by Ferdinand and Isabella; a rise in the number of Christian families during the second half of the sixteenth century can be documented as well, as can an additional influx of Greeks.[187] The linguistic culture of the area would again have become nearly as diverse as it had been during the period of Persian domination, but with a very different economic framework to support it.

TWELVE

THE CONCEPT OF TROY AFTER ANTIQUITY

The Late Roman earthquake that destroyed most of the standing buildings of Ilion had no effect on the Homeric heritage with which the site had been associated for over a millennium, and that heritage became even stronger as the Middle Ages progressed. Ilion's aura was based on something far more multifaceted than a city or a war, largely because Homer's epic had not really dealt with winners and losers, but rather with the shifting manifestations of humanity: war and peace, love and hate, and the emotional strength and fragility that accompany all of them. Consequently, Troy had the potential of serving as a legitimizing device for eastern nations as easily as those from the west, and therefore proved irresistible to the emerging nations of both medieval Europe and Asia.

Trojan ancestry had been carefully incorporated into the monuments and rituals of Rome during the early empire, and some of these customs were transferred to Constantinople after its foundation in the early fourth century A.D. The Palladion was enshrined in the new Forum of Constantine, which contained images representing the Judgment of Paris as well as a colossal bronze Apollo that had allegedly been taken from Ilion.[1] The Bath of Zeuxippus was decorated with twenty-nine statues linked to the Ilioupersis, or Sack of Troy, including a series of famous mythological couples such as Aeneas and Creusa, Menelaus and Helen, and Cassandra and Ajax.[2] As far as we can tell, the hippodrome contained no Trojan imagery, but the complex did feature images of the infants Romulus and Remus and served as the setting for the Lupercalia, one of Rome's oldest festivals.[3]

At the same time in which the center of power shifted from Rome to Constantinople, significant changes again occurred in the iconography of the Trojans, largely because eastern dress began to be treated very differently. Roman military costumes now began to include tightly sewn clothes, including long pants, and when figures clad in eastern garb were represented, they were generally holy men linked to the Judeo-Christian tradition such as Daniel, the Three Magi, or the Three Hebrews in the Fiery Furnace.[4] Parthian soldiers (now the Sassanians) who had worn the same costume were very infrequent additions to monumental displays in Constantinople; indeed, scenes of military triumph decreased significantly in number as the focus shifted toward an exposition of spiritual victory.[5] As a consequence, eastern dress now again acquired a generally positive connotation. It was only at this time that Trojan War cycles began to feature Aeneas in eastern clothing, including trousers and a Phrygian cap. The best examples come from the fourth/fifth century A.D. Vergilius Romanus manuscript and the Low Ham Mosaic in Britain, the iconography of which is based on the Vergilian story.[6] In a sense, this shifting Trojan iconography served as an index of the enormous changes in politics and religion that had just occurred.

Other than Vergil, the most widely read accounts of the Trojan War during the Medieval period were a pair of books written in Latin by alleged eyewitnesses to the war. Dares of Phrygia (Phrygius) reportedly fought on the side of Troy as a follower of Antenor; Dictys of Crete (Cretensis) was an associate of Idomeneus on the Greek side.[7] Since there were no Latin translations of Homer at that time and Greek was not widely read, the accounts of Dares and Dictys achieved enormous importance during the Medieval period, although they are actually literary forgeries of Late Antique date.[8] Both Dares and Dictys were especially popular in France and England and played significant roles in the construction of legendary genealogies and national identities, to which we now turn.

One tends to forget that between the sixth and twelfth centuries, most nation-states claimed Trojan ancestry in order to justify their occupation of parts of the old Roman Empire and place themselves in a position of equality with the emperors. By the beginning of the Renaissance, Troy had been claimed as a mother city by the Goths, Franks, Venetians, Normans, British, Turks, Scandinavians, and Byzantines, all of whom viewed themselves as the inheritors of the Roman Empire.[9] Such ancestry had the potential to unify virtually every region of Europe and the Near East, although it never functioned in that way, and claims of Trojan ancestry were frequently questioned as alliances shifted and wars were waged.

Even as early as the Augustan period, there were stories of Trojan exiles dispersing and traveling to different parts of Italy. In the *Aeneid*, Vergil included a reference to Antenor sailing to the northern Adriatic and founding Padua, while Livy added that he was accompanied by the Eneti (Paphlagonians), who gave their name to the "Veneti," and their arrival point was called "Troy."[10] Lucan, writing during the reign of Nero, noted that the Arverni tribe in central Gaul falsely claimed descent from Troy, but such stories nevertheless continued to circulate: Ammianus Marcellinus, writing in the last quarter of fourth century A.D., maintained that Trojan emigrants settled in Gaul, and by the fifth century Sidonius Apollinaris simply declared that the Arverni were of Trojan blood.[11]

Making the same claim were the Goths, who had actually sacked Ilion during the later third century A.D. The *Getica* of Jordanes, written in the sixth century, presented Telephus, mythical founder of Pergamon, as the ancestral king of the Goths, who had reportedly fought in the Trojan War along with the Amazons – recast here as ancestors of Gothic women. In formulating this sequence, Jordanes referred to Telephus as king of Moesia (modern Serbia) rather than Mysia, in northwestern Asia Minor, where Pergamon was actually located. This is an easy error to make since the same Greek word was used for Mysia and Moesia, and it had the effect of shifting the Troad and its environs much closer to the area where the Goths actually lived.[12]

Stories of the Trojan roots of the Gauls had been circulating continually since the first century A.D., so it is not surprising that the Franks ultimately embraced the same tradition.[13] Nevertheless, there appears to have been no standard version of the story until the seventh century, when the Frankish writer Fredegar constructed a new narrative that attempted to codify the ancestral links between the two groups. He believed that the Trojans left Troy following Priam's death and subsequently divided into two groups: one went to Macedonia and was considered to have included the ancestors of Alexander the Great; the other, under King Friga (a form of Phrygia), initially went to Phrygia, but subsequently traveled to Europe under the command of a new king named Francio (or Francus) and settled in the area between the Rhine, the Danube, and the North Sea.[14] The members of the second group were now called Franks, after Francio, and built a city on the model of Troy near the Rhine. Fredegar also mentions a third group of exiled Trojans under a King Torquatus, who initially settled on the banks of the Danube between the Ocean and Thrace, which coincides roughly with Scythia.

By the time of the Renaissance, Francio had been identified with Astyanax, the young son of Hector and Andromache who was killed during the sack of Troy in most ancient accounts, although not in the *Iliad* or in the tales of Dares and Dictys.[15] In the new tradition, Astyanax changed his name to Francus once he arrived in Gaul, just as the name of Ascanius had been altered to Iulus after the victory of the Trojans in Italy. It is unclear when this version of the story was formulated, although some have suggested that it was developed during the reign of the Frankish king Theudebert I (A.D. 534–48), the first of the barbarian kings to strike gold coins with his own name and image.[16]

Unlike the Franks, the Venetians could point to more specific references to their Trojan ancestry in Early Imperial literature, which crystallized around the figure of Antenor, Priam's advisor during the Trojan War.[17] Vergil mentions him as the founder of Padua, but in time he was also associated with the foundations of Aquileia and Venice, which meant that the construction of the earliest towns in northeastern Italy preceded the building of Rome itself.[18] With the late eleventh-century publication of the *Origo Civitatem Italie seu Venetiarum*, the Trojan foundation narrative had been firmly established, and Venice, rather than Constantinople, was presented as the legitimate successor to Rome.

The chronicle had acquired such weight that when a Late Roman sarcophagus containing a large skeleton was discovered in Padua in the late thirteenth century, the occupant was immediately identified as Antenor and provided with a heroon in the center of town, where it still survives intact.[19] Shortly thereafter, the central square of Treviso, 26 km to the north of Venice, was decorated with frescoes depicting the Trojan War, thereby following an increasingly popular model in European nation-states of commissioning visual programs of Troy as a complement to their ancestral claims.[20] Around the same time, one of the chroniclers argued that the Trojan emigrants had actually arrived in the lagoon of Venice, and Doge Enrico Dandolo maintained that Antenor had built the walls of Olivolo in Venice's Castello district.[21]

The Treviso paintings appear to derive from the *Roman de Troie*, written around A.D. 1175 by Benoit de St. Maure and largely based on the books of Dares and Dictys. The same author is generally regarded as having produced the *Chronique des Ducs de Normandie*, which followed the eleventh-century books *Gesta Normannorum* and *Historia Normannorum* in promoting a Trojan origin for the Normans. The founder in this case, once again, was Antenor, although the Norman account has him traveling to Dacia and Illyria.[22]

The British claimed Trojan origins as well by constructing a completely different kind of narrative. In Nennius' *Historia Brittonum* of the eighth century A.D., British ancestry was traced from Brutus, grandson of Aeneas, who was expelled from Italy and subsequently experienced the same type of wandering that Aeneas himself had faced, eventually arriving in Britain, which he named after himself.[23] The much later *History of the Kings of Britain* (ca. A.D. 1100–55) by Geoffrey of Monmouth was based extensively on the *Historia Brittonum*, although Brutus now became the great-grandson of Aeneas and founded London as Trinovantum or "New Troy."[24] The eleventh-century battles between the Normans and British were therefore, at least in theory, a conflict of kinsmen, although they were not presented as such at the time.

Meanwhile, the Scandinavians were making similar claims. The thirteenth century A.D. witnessed the composition of the *Prose Edda*, wherein Priam became Thor's grandfather, and Memnon, his father.[25] Once again one encounters the theme of Trojan emigrants separating into two groups after leaving the destroyed city: one traveling with Aeneas to Italy, the other with Thor's son Loridi to "Asialand" (Scythia), which was separated from "Tyrkland" by mountains. After twenty generations, in the period of Pompey the Great, Odin was crowned king and subsequently dispatched his sons to various regions of Scandinavia, including Denmark, Sweden, and Norway, where they established kingdoms.

The reference to "Tyrkland" in the Norse *Prose Edda* raises the issue of one additional claim to Trojan ancestry, this one involving the Turks, although the origins of that ancestral claim are somewhat cloudy. Already in the seventh century A.D. the Frankish writer Fredegar had mentioned that a group of exiled Trojans had settled on the banks of the Danube, having been led there by a King Torquatus, who gave his name to the nation of "Turquie."[26] Whether Fredegar intended this to refer to the Turks themselves is still unclear, but by the early twelfth century the name of Torquatus had been changed to Turcus, the eponymous founder of the Turks.[27] At roughly the same time, in the *Gesta Francorum*, there is reference to the Selcuk Turks' belief that they were related to the Franks, and a proposed relationship between the Franks and Turks was repeated a few years later in the *Historia Hierosolymitana*.[28]

By the early thirteenth century, Turcus had been identified as a son of Troilus and grandson of Priam, which made him a cousin of Francio, eponymous founder of the Franks.[29] This meant that Turks and Franks were kinsmen, at least in terms of legendary genealogies. The Turks were subsequently referred to by several distinctively Trojan names, including "Phryges" and "Troiani," and in time, the "Turki" were equated with "Teucri."[30] The same period witnessed yet another noteworthy change in the iconography of Trojan War scenes that were created by European artists: the Trojans now wore eastern costume intended to evoke the clothing of the Turks, thereby visually reinforcing the alleged ancestral connections between the two.[31] In principle, this was not so different from the changes in Trojan iconography shortly after the Persian Wars, when a shift in costume had effectively transformed Trojans into Persians.[32]

Examining these legendary genealogies as a group demonstrates the versatility of the Trojan tradition and its almost universal applicability, regardless of differences in ethnicities and national identities. In essence, nearly all of the nation-states in Europe and the Near East claimed to have been founded by Trojan refugees, which meant that virtually nothing remained of the Greeks. Although Greek was the official language of the Byzantine Empire as of the seventh century A.D., the Empire viewed itself as the continuation of Rome, and the Trojan decorative components in the public spaces of Constantinople reinforced that interpretation.[33] In other words, as strange as it may seem, not even Greece was Greek; it was Trojan.

Such was not the view of Constantinople's enemies, however, and their public speeches justifying battle against the Byzantines often referenced Trojan ancestry. Both Pierre of Bracheux, the French Crusader of the early thirteenth century, and Mehmet II, the Ottoman Sultan in the mid-fifteenth century, reportedly delivered similarly structured speeches after their respective conquests of Byzantine Constantinople, wherein they argued that they had avenged the attacks on their kinsmen, the Trojans, by sacking the capital city of the Greeks.[34]

Pierre of Bracheux is quoted as saying that "Troy belonged to our ancestors, and those who escaped from it came and settled in the country we come from; and because it belonged to our ancestors, we have come here to conquer land."[35] Mehmet's speech is more specific:

> God has reserved for me, through so long a period of years, the right to avenge this city and its inhabitants. For I have subdued their enemies and have plundered their cities and made them the spoils of the Mysians. It was the Greeks and Macedonians and Thessalians and Peloponnesians who ravaged this place in the past, and whose descendants have now through my efforts paid the just penalty, after a long period of years, for their injustice to us Asiatics at that time and so often in subsequent years.[36]

Other recorded vignettes underscore the same point: during the sack of Constantinople in A.D. 1204, the Venetians reportedly destroyed a statue of Helen in revenge for the Greek destruction of Troy, while Mehmet allegedly attacked a Greek woman in Hagia Sophia to avenge Ajax's rape of Cassandra.[37] The siege of Constantinople itself was often regarded as a latter-day Trojan War, and in some early Renaissance illuminated manuscripts of the attack on Troy, the ancient Greeks are shown wearing the Palaeologan hats of the Byzantine emperors.[38]

The claims to shared ancestry between Italians and Turks were exploited in a series of letters between popes and sultans that attracted considerable attention at the time, even though they were actually contemporary forgeries. A letter to Pope Clement VI from a Sultan Morbanus, written in the mid-fourteenth century A.D., inquired as to why the pope was helping the Venetians, since they were not of Trojan blood, unlike the Turks and Romans. The letter was updated over the course of the next century, with the names of new popes added as necessary, and was translated into French, Latin, and German.

Another letter, allegedly written by Mehmet II to Pius II in the mid-fifteenth century, made a more emotional appeal: "Father, we were Trojans, whatever you may think. We were the remnants of [the nation of] Priam whom the Greek generals could not destroy in their cruel war."[39] Not surprisingly, there were vehement denials of the Turks' Trojan ancestry, especially among the Venetians. One Genovese writer composed an epic poem following the loss of Euboea to the Turks in A.D. 1470 wherein the Venetian governor was compared to Priam, and Mehmet II was called "a new Achilles."[40]

Mehmet's speech about avenging the wrongs done to his Trojan kinsmen reportedly took place at the site of Troy itself, nine years after his sack of Constantinople.[41] This raises the issue of travel to Troy during the period in which these legendary genealogies were being formulated, and there were probably many more such journeys than the evidence now indicates. Once the *Iliad* had been translated into several languages in the fifteenth and sixteenth centuries and widely disseminated by virtue of the new printing press, travel to the Troad must have increased significantly.[42] Moreover, it seems likely that Early Modern ships entering the Dardanelles would have faced the same strong winds and currents that delayed maritime traffic in antiquity; consequently, passengers on the ships probably found themselves in the position of searching for something interesting to do while waiting for navigable conditions, and visits to the nearby site of Troy would undoubtedly have been a common occurrence.[43]

How many of these travelers were actually visiting the correct site? In a few instances there is enough anecdotal information for us to determine where they were going and what they were seeing. During the first half of the fourteenth century, for example, a German traveler named Ludolf von Suedheim describes the condition of the site: "no remains are to be seen except some foundations underwater in the sea, and in several places some stones and marble columns half-buried."[44] What he is actually describing is the coastal site of Alexandria Troas, which was often confused with Troy, even in antiquity, due to the similarity in names. The ruins of Alexandria at that time would probably have been the most impressive of those in the Troad, even though they dated no earlier than the Hellenistic period, and since the site lay west of Mt. Ida and directly opposite the island of Tenedos, it could be inserted into the Homeric narratives without much difficulty.

When Mehmet II visited Troy in 1462, however, his choice of site may have been more accurate. Michael Critoboulos, who described the Sultan's visit, notes that he inspected the heroic tombs and walked around the ruins of the city: "He spoke of the tombs of Achilles, of Ajax, and of the others, I mean, whom he called "blessed" because of their lasting fame and…because they were praised by the poet Homer."[45] Such tumuli are a distinctive feature of the environs of Troy and Sigeion, but less evident around Alexandria Troas, and Mehmet's speech was probably delivered at one of the former sites.[46]

By the end of the eighteenth century the Troad had been mapped, and a site labeled Hisarlık now appeared on the plans, although the ruins were linked to the "Novum Ilion" that had reportedly been established by Constantine.[47] In the 1870s, with the advent of Schliemann's excavations on the mound of Hisarlık, the Homeric narratives became closely intertwined with the stones of Ilion for the first time since late antiquity, and that connection has remained in force through the present. The residents of the site in antiquity had marketed those stones as Homeric relics, for which Strabo, among others, had criticized them. Schliemann found himself in a similar situation: his critics claimed that he was using the *Iliad* as a guidebook for where to dig and how to interpret what he found, and the current excavations have faced similar objections, which is the issue with which this book began.[48]

That the criticisms then and now should approach such a level of disquiet attests to the power of both the Trojan tradition and the site that has continually been linked to it, nor is there any reason to expect a diminution in that power in the face of shifting political and social conditions. This was abundantly illustrated in 1999, when Süleyman Demirel, the president of Turkey, used the occasion of his visit to Troy to stress the importance of the site for Turkey and for its relations to Europe. That was also the year in which Turkey was recognized as a candidate for full membership in the European Union (EU), and some argued that Turkey should be accepted into the EU because it was the home of Troy, arguably the most important component of the foundations of European culture.[49] In other words, the site itself had become a significant element in modern foreign policy as a consequence of its Homeric heritage, which was no different, really, from the political maneuvers that had continually reshaped it during the Greek and Roman periods.

As one travels through the Dardanelles today, approaching the narrowest point between Europe and Asia, there are two powerful reminders of the conflicts between East and West that have continually characterized this region, and here, too, the Homeric traditions are easily discernible. On the Asian side, in the city of Çanakkale, is the colossal wooden horse that had been used in the 2004 film *Troy*, standing as an obvious reminder of the area's connection to the wars of antiquity (Fig. 12.1).[50] Directly across the straits is one of the most prominent of the Gallipoli war memorials, with a striding soldier pointing toward a monumental inscription: "Stop Traveler! The soil you tread once witnessed the end of an era" (Fig. 12.2). Although the memorial in effect highlights the new political and military developments that gave rise to the Turkish Republic, the battle was just as tightly linked to the landscape's Homeric heritage. Several of the British soldiers who fought in the conflict viewed it as a second Trojan War, reading the *Iliad* on their way to Gallipoli and writing of Achilles in the poetry they composed.[51] Rupert Brooke, the British poet who died en route to the battle, anticipated the Homeric frame of the forthcoming conflict: "And Priam and his fifty sons wake up all amazed, and hear the guns, and shake for Troy again." Another poem of 1919 has the fallen fighters

12.1. The Trojan Horse from the Warner Brothers film *Troy* in Çanakkale. Photo by the author.

speaking of their legendary counterparts, as if the soldiers of Troy and Gallipoli were now bound by ties of kinship: "We are not lone, there are other graves by the Dardanelles. Men whom immortal Homer sang come to our ghostly campfires' glow. Greet us as brothers and tell us 'Lo, so to *our* deeds old Troy rang.'"[52]

Even in the war memorials, the link with the past is perceptible. One especially striking example is a bronze statuary group that shows a Turkish soldier carrying the wounded body of an Australian opponent (Fig. 12.3).[53] This is one of the few and perhaps the only known memorial in which the victor was represented carrying the body of his enemy from the battlefield, and it ultimately derives from an ancient statuary type frequently used in scenes of the Trojan War, such as Ajax carrying the deceased Achilles from the battlefield at Troy.[54]

In a sense, such an idiosyncratic iconography was in perfect harmony with the alleged Trojan ancestry of the two opponents, and although it hardly seems possible, that ancestry was embraced and promoted by virtually every nation that fought at Gallipoli. Mustafa Kemal Atatürk almost certainly did not have

12.2. Gallipoli War Memorial along the Dardanelles. Photo by the author.

the concept of shared Trojan ancestry in mind when he composed his letter to the British mothers whose sons died in the battle, but the words he wrote can be read that way:

> There is no difference between the Johnnies and the Mehmets to us where they lie side by side here in this country of ours. You, the mothers, who sent your sons from faraway countries, wipe away your tears; your sons are now lying in our bosom and are in peace. After having lost their lives on this land, they have become our sons as well.[55]

The two complementary images of the Trojan Horse and the Gallipoli soldier that now frame the Dardanelles effectively summarize so many of the themes that have characterized this region over the course of more than three millennia. The line between site and legend has continually been blurred, thereby endowing the landscape with a far more fluid identity than one finds in any other part of the ancient world. Since that landscape was shaped by tombs of both Greek and Trojan heroes, the site and its legendary heritage were easily co-opted by empires both east and west: Athens, Persia, and Rome between ca. 700 B.C. and A.D. 300, and by virtually all of Europe and the Near East thereafter.

The most distinctive feature of the landscape was the narrow width of the Dardanelles, a distance of only 1.2 km, which made it one of the easiest crossing points between continental Europe and Asia, and therefore a locus of continual

12.3. Gallipoli War Memorial of a Turkish soldier carrying the wounded body of an Australian opponent. Troy Excavation Project.

struggle between East and West. Throughout those battles that encompassed the Troad and its surroundings, the residents of Ilion rarely remained static in their identity; in fact, the persona they projected was usually just as versatile as the Homeric heritage they promoted. As a consequence, one finds them turning alternately toward Europe, Asia, or both directions simultaneously based on whatever seemed most politically advantageous or economically expedient. Therein lies the durability and attraction of the site and its monuments, as well as the rituals and traditions that have consistently embraced them.

NOTES

ACKNOWLEDGMENTS

1. The final publication volumes for the post–Bronze Age periods are focused on the three primary districts of the site, each of which represents a different sphere of activity. They include the Agora (William Aylward), the West Sanctuary (Carolyn Aslan, Mark Lawall, Kathleen Lynch, Billur Tekkök, and me), and the residential area of the Lower City (Sebastian Heath, Billur Tekkök, and me).

INTRODUCTION

1. Especially noteworthy is the relatively lengthy hiatus of forty to fifty years that followed the first two campaigns, during which Schliemann and Blegen launched new excavations in Greece in an attempt to acquire a more balanced perspective on the Bronze Age from both sides of the Aegean.
2. Earlier publications of post–Bronze Age material have evinced an inconsistent use of the names "Troy" and "Ilion." In this book I have used "Troy" in my discussions of the Bronze Age, Iron Age, and Archaic material, and "Ilion" for Classical, Hellenistic, Roman, and Byzantine periods, since this name for the site became common only in the fifth century B.C.
3. Rose 1999, 37.
4. Choiseul-Gouffier 1782–1822, chapters 13 and 14; Cook 1973, 160, 169; Easton 1991, 113–14.
5. Brunton 1939, 59–81; Cook 1973, 37; Easton 1991, 120–1; Bieg et al. 2006, 156, fig. 10 (AO554). The work took place "on the uppermost flat of the Hisarlık hill," according to William Eassie, Brunton's assistant: Eassie 1858, 153.
6. Robinson 1995; Allen 1999; Cook 1973, 35–6; Easton 1991, 119–25.
7. Schliemann 1881; 1884; Cook 1973, 38–40; Easton 2002; Aslan et al. 2008.
8. Dörpfeld 1894; 1902.

9. Friedmund Hueber and Elizabeth Riorden completed a revised version of the Dörpfeld color phase plan of Troy in 1994, which incorporated all of the remains discovered by Schliemann, Dörpfeld, and Blegen: Hueber and Riorden 1994.
10. Blegen et al. 1950; 1951; 1953; 1958; Blegen 1963.
11. Blegen et al. 1958, 259–307.
12. Blegen 1939, 228; Rose 1999, 37.
13. Blegen et al. 1950; 1951; 1953; 1958; Bellinger 1961; Thompson 1963. The *Archaeological Geology of Troy* was the last of the Blegen excavation monographs to be published (Rapp and Gifford 1982). The Greek inscriptions were published by Peter Frisch in 1975.
14. Korfmann 1991, 1. We also agreed to publish everything we found within a year of its discovery, and to that end, we founded an annual excavation journal (*Studia Troica*) that featured interdisciplinary studies dealing with all aspects of the Troad. The journal served as the initial scholarly venue for all articles dealing with newly excavated Trojan material, and nineteen volumes have appeared thus far.
15. Jansen 1992.
16. Jablonka 1995; 1996; Korfmann 1998b, 57–62; Korfmann 1999a, 23–5; Korfmann 2000, 32–7; Korfmann 2001c, 36–40; Korfmann 2002a, 20–3; Korfmann 2003, 6.
17. Strabo 13.1.27; Rose 1993, 98–105; Rose 1994, 76–86; Rose 1995, 82–97; Rose 1996, 97–101; Rose 1997c, 76–96; Rose 1998, 73–92; Rose 2000, 54–8.
18. Sevinç 1996; Sevinç et al. 1998; Sevinç et al. 1999; Sevinç et al. 2001.
19. Rose et al. 2007. Surveys of the western Troad have been conducted over the course of several years: Aslan et al. 2003; Bieg et al. 2006; 2008.
20. The magnetic readings in the area of the ditch were initially interpreted as a fortification wall: John Noble Wilford, "Outer 'Wall' of Troy

Now Appears to Be a Ditch," *New York Times*, September 28, 1993.

21. Mannsperger 1995; 1998.
22. Starke 1997; Latacz 2004.
23. Högemann 2000.
24. Korfmann 2000, 32. See also Korfmann 1999b.
25. Herodotus *Histories* 2.112–18; Thucydides *Histories* 1.3, 1.10, 2.41; Nagy 2010, 77–8.
26. Allen 1999, 219–21; Zavadil 2009.
27. Korfmann 1991, 1–2; Korfmann 1993, 35.
28. Korfmann 2001b, 17, 19.
29. Kolb 2003a, b; Kolb 2004; Kolb 2010; Korfmann 2002a, 27–30.
30. Zangger 1994; Hertel 2001; Hertel and Kolb 2003.
31. The debate dominated conversations at Troy between 2001 and 2005, culminating in a conference in Tübingen in February 2002 at which both groups presented their arguments for and against Troy's importance in the Late Bronze Age: Schweitzer 2001–2; Easton et al. 2002; Jablonka and Rose 2004.
32. Rose 2008.

ONE. TROY IN THE BRONZE AGE

1. Leaf 1923, xxxviii–xlvii; 41–2 (Strabo 13.1.1–2); *Iliad* 2.824; Herzhoff 2008.
2. Rapp and Gifford 1982, 43–58; Tenger 1999, 111–12.
3. Strabo 13.1.23; Leaf 1923, 133–5; Pernicka et al. 2003.
4. Purple dyers near Troy: Aristotle *Historia Animalium*, V. 15; on Lesbos: Singer 2008. For the evidence for purple dyers at Troy, see Jablonka and Rose 2004, 619; Çakırlar and Becks 2008, 87–103.
5. Özdoğan 2003.
6. Seventh millennium: Hoca Çeşme/Enez, near the current Greek/Turkish border. Sixth millennium: Uğurlu on Imbros, Karaağaçtepe on the European side of the Dardanelles, and Coşkuntepe in the southwest Troad, near the Smintheion. Other sites, possibly flooded by postglacial transgression or hidden under alluvium, probably await discovery: Özdoğan 1997, 26–8. See, in general, Erdoğu 2003; Harmankaya and Erdoğu 2003; Erdoğu 2011. I am grateful to Prof. Eva Rosenstock for considerable guidance here.
7. Sperling 1976; Korfmann 1995b; Gabriel 2000; 2006.
8. Gabriel et al. 2004; Niemeier 2005, 2; Gabriel 2006; Takaoğlu 2006; Aslan and Polat 2011.

Contemporary habitation is also attested on Thasos and Samothrace (Davis 2001, 42–3). For the northeast Aegean in general during the fifth and fourth millennia B.C., see Davis 2001, passim.

9. Özdoğan 1993b, 176, 183; Takaoğlu 2006, 291, 313.
10. Höckmann 2003. The maritime connections among the Black Sea, Bosphorus, Sea of Marmara, Dardanelles, and Aegean during the Late Chalcolithic and Bronze Age are still unresolved: Özdoğan 2003.
11. Özdoğan 1993b, 183; Jablonka 2010, 719. Kumtepe IA is dated to ca. 5000–4750, and Kumtepe IB to 3300–3000 B.C.
12. For a preliminary overview of Troy I settlements in the Troad, see Bieg et al. 2009.
13. Kayan 1991; 1995; 2000; Kraft et al. 2003.
14. Blegen et al. 1950; Blegen 1963, 39–58; Ünlüsöy 2006.
15. Hood 1981–2; Séfériadès 1985; Kouka 2002; Erkanal 2008; Ivanova 2008; Greaves 2010, 878.
16. Warner 1979. Troy I pottery has also been found on Imbros (Davis 2001, 86).
17. Blegen et al. 1950, figs. 190–2; Blegen 1963, 54–6; Thasos: Davis 2001, 42. Stelae of a similar type had appeared in the Crimean peninsula and the western Pontic steppes during the late fourth millennium: Anthony 2007, 336–9.
18. Korfmann 2001b; Sazcı 2005; Çalış-Sazcı 2006.
19. Blegen 1963, 59.
20. This extended also to Poliochni, where midthird millennium cylinder seals, possibly made in North Syria, have been found: Matsas 1995, 245; Aruz 2008, 274, Cat. 117.
21. Blegen 1963, 63.
22. City plans similar to that of Troy II have been found at Kanlıgecit, Turkish Thrace, and Küllüoba, near Eskişehir: Şahoğlu 2005, 345–6, 350; Efe 2006; Özdoğan 2010. The largest of the megarons at Kanlıgecit was 26 m long.
23. Korfmann 1999a, 11, fig. 11; Sazcı 2001; Çalış-Sazcı 2006, 206, 208.
24. Bachhuber 2009, 5.
25. Jablonka 2010, 719, 721.
26. Easton 2000, 81; Mansfeld 2001, 195–7; Ünlüsoy 2006, 142.
27. Schliemann 1881, 36, 211, 324–7.
28. Bachhuber 2009. There is no indication that wells were dug within the citadel at any point in Troy II, as they would be during the Late Bronze Age, but a large aquifer in the form of a cave in the Lower City began to be mined

at this time to increase the amount of water available for the inhabitants: Korfmann 1998b, 57–62; 1999a, 22–5; 2000, 32–7; 2001c, 36–40; 2002a, 20–3; Rose 1998, 102; 1999, 55–61; 2000, 61–5; Wolkersdorfer and Göbel 2004. The cave is located 180 m to the southwest of the citadel, in sector t14.

29. Şahoğlu 2005; Erkanal 2008; Wiencke 2010. Ramp at Thermi on Lesbos: Lamb 1936, 25; at Poliochni: Tiné and Traverso 2001, 26.

30. Jablonka 2001; 2006a.

31. They are in evidence, however, during the Late Bronze Age. One is attested at Samuha in the time of Hattusili III, in the mid-thirteenth century B.C.: KBo VI 29 ii 32–3; Otten 1976; Boysan-Dietrich 1987, 18.

32. Korfmann 1993, 25–8; 1997b, 62; 1999a, 20–2.

33. Koşay 1951; Özgüç and Temizer 1993; Bernabò Brea 1976, 284–98; Tolstikov and Treister 1996, 197; Nakou 1997; Sazcı and Treister 2006; Tiné and Traverso 2001, 44.

34. Tolstikov and Treister 1996; Easton 1997; Bryce 2006, 49–52; Sazcı 2007.

35. Easton 1997, 196; Korfmann 2001a; Sazcı and Treister 2006.

36. Ritual deposit: Bachhuber 2009.

37. Tolstikov and Treister 1996, 28–94. The bronze "frying pan" (no. 1) is probably a serving platter: Bachhuber 2009, 12.

38. All references are to Tolstikov and Treister 1996. Treasure B: 96–7; J: 134–42; L: 148–76; iron: 174, nos. 226, 232; carnelian and amber: 172, 175, 211.

39. Bass 1970. A roughly contemporary iron dagger was excavated at Alaca Höyük: Yalçın 1999.

40. Tolstikov and Treister 1996, 230; Sazcı and Treister 2006.

41. For the gilded axes, see Tolstikov and Treister 1996, 220. For the granulations, see Betancourt 2006; Tolstikov and Treister 1996, 231–2. For metalworking equipment, which includes stone molds, crucibles, ingots, and slag, see Easton 1997.

42. Apakidse 1999.

43. Blegen 1963, 70.

44. Manfred Korfmann grouped these three periods under the rubric "Anatolian-Troy Culture," because he believed their material culture evinced a greater interest in Anatolia than the Aegean.

45. Blegen 1963, 91–110; Blum 2006.

46. The fortification wall clearly extended across the northern side of the citadel, although the stones have now disappeared: Becks 2005. Blegen (1935a, 242) thought that the stones from the wall were used as building material in Sigeion during the Archaic period.

47. Klinkott 2004, 79–80.

48. Klinkott and Becks 2001; Klinkott 2004; Jablonka 2010, 721.

49. Wright 2005.

50. Dörpfeld 1902, 119–21; Blegen et al. 1953, 87. Naumann (1971, 247) linked the offsets to casement construction.

51. Jablonka et al. 1994; Jablonka 1995; Jablonka and Rose 2004, 617; Becks 2006, 157–9; Jablonka 2006a, 172–4; Jablonka and Pernicka 2009, 19–26.

52. Bennet 1997, 519.

53. Jablonka and Rose 2004, 616–20.

54. Jablonka 2006a; for Troy: Rose 2008, 409, n. 55; for Hattuşa: Seeher 2002; for Kanesh: Özgüç 1999; for Zincirli: Wartke 2005.

55. Gordion: Rose 2012; Bunimovitz 1992; Finkelstein 1992.

56. Korfmann 1986a; Kayan 1991, 89–90; Kraft et al. 2003, 373, fig. 9.

57. Korfmann 2001b, 17, fig. 23; Easton et al. 2002, 76–7; Hertel and Kolb 2003; Bryce 2006, 63–4.

58. Jablonka 1996, 86–92; Easton et al. 2002, 89–90.

59. Easton et al. 2002, 83; Jablonka and Rose 2004, 619.

60. Blegen et al. 1953, 219–29. The building measures 26 m in length and more than 12 m in width. The great hall is 15.5×8 m.

61. Blegen 1963, 138–9; Korfmann 1998a. Maureen Basedow has recently proposed that the Anta House should be dated to the Early Iron Age rather than the Late Bronze Age: Basedow 2009, 140. The most recent discussion of the Anta House appears in Pavúk forthcoming.

62. Becks et al. 2006a; Rigter and Thumm-Doğrayan 2004; Balfanz 1995; Mellink and Strahan 1998.

63. Pavúk 2007, 2010a, 2010b. The horse had already appeared during the Early Bronze Age at Kanlıgeçit in eastern Thrace, where horse bones comprised 15 percent of the faunal assemblages: Benecke 2002; Özdoğan 2010, 671. For the horse in western Asia in general, see Oates 2003, who notes that the domesticated horse had been introduced into North Syria and Mesopotamia by the late third millennium B.C.

64. Blegen et al. 1953, 15; Blegen 1963, 111–12; 145–6.

65. Macdonald et al. 2009; Niemeier 2005.

66. Davis 2001, 25; Girella and Pavúk forthcoming; Guzowska 2002; 2009; Matsas 1991; 1995; Mountjoy 1997c, 283–5; Mountjoy 1998, 34; Pavúk 2005. Excavations on Thasos have produced a lead weight consistent with Minoan metrology: Davis 2001, 83. Greaves (2010, 880) notes that there was probably no direct contact between Crete and the settlements in the north Aegean, but rather transfers through Minoanized centers, and Niemeier (2005, 4) has suggested that one of them would have been Miletus. For possible Minoan influence on a Troy VIIA pictorial krater, see Mountjoy 1997a, 2005.

67. Pavúk 2007, 299–301, 305; Pavúk 2010a; 2010b. The same situation prevailed on coastal Chalkidiki as well as at sites in the vicinity of Izmir, such as Liman Tepe and Panaztepe. I am grateful to Peter Pavúk and Penelope Mountjoy for guidance here.

68. Lamb 1936, 212–13; Mountjoy 1997b, 263; Mountjoy 2006.

69. Mountjoy and Mommsen 2006.

70. Blegen et al. (1953, 16) counted thirty-one pots as well as a mass of sherds deriving from 700–800 vessels.

71. Mountjoy 1998; Niemeier 2005, 10–16.

72. Pavúk 2010a.

73. Korfmann 1995a; Kolb 2004.

74. Beckman 1996; Hoffner 2009; Beckman et al. 2011.

75. Starke 1997; Hawkins 1998; Niemeier 2005, 17; Latacz 2004, 75–100; Easton et al. 2002, 98–100; Hajnal 2003, 29–32; Palaima 2007, 198.

76. Güterbock 1986, 35; Latacz 2004, 92–100; Hawkins 2005.

77. Aslan et al. 2003.

78. Watkins 1986; Blegen 1963, 116–17; Klinkott 2004, 79.

79. Bryce 1998, 135–7; Cline 1996.

80. Ünal et al. 1991; Cline 1996. There are two other potentially relevant finds. One is a terracotta bowl from Hattuša that is incised with the figure of a warrior who probably comes from the Aegean judging by his headgear: Niemeier 2005, 18–19; 2006, 51, fig. 4. The second is a silver bowl in Ankara that refers to a king Tudhaliyas who smote the land of Tarwiza. Although the dating is not secure, this may be another reference to the Taruisa in the Assuwa confederation against Tudhaliyas II: Hawkins 2005; Durnford 2010.

81. Güterbock 1986, 36.

82. The construction of the citadel walls of Hattuša was prompted by the invasion of the Kaska tribes, whose lands lay in the mountainous north of Anatolia along the south coast of the Black Sea. For the textual evidence for the construction, see Bryce 1998, 121. For the fortifications at Mycenae, see French 2010, 674.

83. This includes imports of local Milesian wares (pinkish with whitish wash) in both open and closed shapes, as well as Dodecanesian local wares, primarily matt-painted. The latter are almost exclusively jugs. I am grateful to Peter Pavúk for this information.

84. Sommer 1932; Güterbock 1983; Mountjoy 1998, 47–51; Niemeier 2002b; Easton et al. 2002, 101; Hope Simpson 2003; Latacz 2004, 121–8; Bryce 2006, 100–6; Beckman et al. 2011.

85. Bryce 2006, 57–60, 309–10; 2002, 259; Hope Simpson 2003; Vanschoonwinkel 1991, 399–404; Niemeier 1998; 1999; 2002a; 2002b; Mee 1998. See, however, Hajnal (2003, 35–41), who regards the association as not impossible, but yet to be proven.

86. Niemeier 2002a, 56–62; Benzi 2002, 377; Lemos 2007, 723. By contrast, the Mycenaean pottery from Troy never accounts for more than 5 percent of an assemblage (Peter Pavúk, pers. communication). See also Benzi 2002, 371; Mommsen et al. 2001, 181–94, 202–3; Mountjoy 1998, 34–45; 1997b, 262; 2006.

87. Cline 1994, 69; Bryce 2006, 58; Beckman et al. 2011, 3.

88. Both Mycenae and Thebes have been suggested as potential capitals, as has Rhodes, all of which have some points in their favor. The dominance of the Mycenaean royal family in the migration accounts is one of the reasons Mycenae has been regarded as the seat of the Great King of Ahhiyawa: Hope Simpson 2003, 233–5; Niemeier 1998, 44; 1999, 143–4; 2002b. The inclusion of Mycenae's name on the Mortuary Temple of Amenophis III at Thebes in Egypt has also been cited as an example of the city's elevated status in other Mediterranean regions, and thus a plausible seat for Ahhiyawa's king: Mellink 1983a, 139–40; Müller 2006, 220. Thebes in Greece has been considered a viable candidate since a cache of Linear B tablets discovered there refers to sites on Euboea, thereby suggesting (to some) that the latter was subject to the former: Latacz 2004, 238–47; Niemeier 2002b, 295;

Mountjoy 1998, 50. Some of these tablets include names that probably refer to Asia Minor: mi-ra-ti-jo (Milesios); to-ro-wo (possibly Troos); and si-mi-te-u (Smintheus, the epithet of Apollo in his sanctuary at Chryse, in the southern Troad): Benzi 2002, 365–6. For Rhodes, see Benzi 2002, 368–81; Mountjoy 1998, 50–1 (Rhodes together with Miletus); Càssola 1957, 334–37. For a more skeptical analysis, see Hall 2002, 50–2.

89. The importance of Ahhiyawa to the Hittites should not be exaggerated. As Alan Greaves (2010, 885) has noted, 25,000 tablets have been discovered at Hattuşa and only twenty-eight mention Ahhiyawa.

90. Beckman et al. 2011, 134–9, 270; Latacz 2004, 243–4; Wiener 2007, 17; Hoffner 2009, 290–2, no. 99.

91. For the geography of western Asia Minor during the Hittite period, see Starke 1997; Hawkins 1998; Melchert 2003, 5–7, 32, 35–40; Latacz and Starke 2006. The capital of Arzawa was Ephesus, or Apasa in Hittite.

92. Bryce 2006, 290–3; Hope Simpson 2003, 216–20.

93. Beckman et al. 2011, 69–100; Mountjoy 1998, 47; Bryce 2006, 58–9, 129–30; Benzi 2002, 360–1. See also Morris 1989, who has argued that visual references to these types of battles may be discernible in the Thera frescoes.

94. Niemeier 2005, 17.

95. Bryce 1998, 209–10; Niemeier 2005, 19–20. Miletus built new fortifications after Mursili's sack, which is reminiscent of Troy's construction of a fortification system around the time of the Assuwa revolt.

96. Beckman 1996, 87, no. 13; Bryce 1998, 247. Kukkunni was ruler of Troy during the reign of Suppiluliuma (1344–1322).

97. Beckman et al. 2011, 183–209. For the possible stroke, see Bryce 1998, 238–40.

98. Bryce 1998, 223–5.

99. Blegen 1963, 143–6.

100. Blegen 1963, 154.

101. Mountjoy 1997b; 1999b; Allen 1991; 1994; Mommsen and Pavúk 2007.

102. Blegen 1963, 147–50; Becks 2006.

103. Jablonka 1996; Jablonka and Rose 2004, 617.

104. Beckman et al. 2011, 101–22, 140–4, 251–2; Heinhold-Krahmer 1983; 1986; Singer 1983, 209–13; Hawkins 1998, 25–6; Latacz 2004, 122–5; Niemeier 2005, 17; Hoffner 2009, 293–313, nos. 100, 101.

105. Beckman et al. 2011, 140–4; Hoffner 2009, 293–6, no. 100.

106. Houwink Ten Cate 1983–4, 36; Bryce 2003, 77; Hoffner 2009, 300. The site of Thermi on Lesbos was destroyed in a vast conflagration in the Late Bronze Age, but this was probably not caused by the raids of Piyamaradu. Lamb (1936, 213) dated Thermi's destruction to the early twelfth century; subsequent analysis has revealed that the latest ceramics date to LHIIIA2, which would be late fourteenth century. If our chronologies are correct, then two or more generations would have separated Piyamaradu's attack on Lesbos from Thermi's conflagration, which probably occurred during the reign of Mursili II. I am grateful to Peter Pavúk for advice here.

107. Beckman et al. 2011, 47–8.

108. Beckman et al. 2011, 101–22; Hoffner 2009, 296–313, no. 101.

109. Beckman et al. 2011, 115; Hoffner 2009, 311.

110. Beckman 1996, no. 13; Latacz 2004, 76–8, 103–10. One of the Wilusan deities by whom the oath is sworn in the treaty is named "Kaskal. kur," which translates roughly as "underground water course." Korfmann believed that a cave on the northwest side of the Lower City, explored in part by Calvert and Schliemann, could conceivably relate to the underground waterway mentioned in the Alaksandu treaty, and thereby supply additional evidence for the Ilion–Wilusa link: Korfmann 1998b, 57–62; 1999a, 23–5; 2000, 32–7; 2001c, 36–40; 2002a, 20–3; 2003, 6.

111. For the dating of the treaty before the Battle of Kadesh, see Güterbock 1986, 35.

112. Niemeier (2005, 20) notes that the final fortification wall at Miletus, built after the Hittite sack, was of Anatolian type. As another indication of the change of rule, Niemeier (2006, 53) has frequently cited a Mycenaean krater from Miletus, dated ca. 1200 B.C., which features a Hittite horned crown.

113. Beckman et al. 2011, 50–68; Beckman 1996, no. 17; Cline 1991. Such a provision indicates that trade between Ahhiyawa and Assyria was in operation at that time, and there is one noteworthy example of it: a cache of lapis lazuli cylinder seals from Mesopotamia was discovered in Greek Thebes in a context datable to ca. 1220 B.C. or shortly before. The seals probably traveled to Greece via Cyprus, and Edith Porada has suggested that the seals were a gift

from the Assyrian king Tukulti-Ninurta I to the ruler of Thebes near the outset of the ban: Porada 1981–2; Cline 1994, 25–6.

114. Beckman et al. 2011, 61, 67.

115. Beckman et al. 2011, 123–33; Bryce 1998, 340; Van den Hout 1995, 91 with n. 112; Beckman 1996, no. 23A; Hoffner 2009, 313–21, no. 102.

116. S. Hiller 1975; Chadwick 1988, 90–3; Efkleidou 2002–3; Niemeier 2005, 16; Nikoloudis 2008, 47–8.

117. There were 70 women from Miletus, 26 from Halicarnassus, 20 or 21 from Cnidus, and 7 from Lemnos. For the analysis of To-ro-ja, see Palaima 2007. In the *Iliad*, Achilles sells war captives in Lemnos, Imbros, and Samothrace: *Iliad* 21.40–1, 23.740–7, 24.751–3; Donlan 1997, 652–3.

118. Bryce 2006, 115–17.

119. Bryce 1998, 340; Van den Hout 1995, 91 with n. 112.

120. Hawkins and Easton 1996. The seal was found in a VIIb1 or VIIb2 context, which would date approximately 100 years after the seal was made. Hieroglyphic Luwian has also been found at Dorylaion (modern Eskişehir): Darga and Starke 2003.

121. *Iliad* 6. 169; Bellamy 1989; Symington 1991; Pulak 1998, 216. The actual writing was done in wax set within the wooden frame.

122. Hoffner 2009, 7, and no. 75.

123. E.g., Kolb 2004; Hertel and Kolb 2003; Bryce 2006, 122–6.

124. Jablonka and Rose 2004, 625; Pavúk 2005.

125. Starke 1997; Darga and Starke 2003; Hawkins 2005; Bryce 2006, 74–7.

126. Mellink and Strahan 1998.

127. Blegen et al. (1953, 17, 18) thought that the ceramic anthropomorphic handles found at Troy shared some similarities with those from the Hittite levels of Alişar, about 80 km southeast of Hattuşa, but the Alişar examples are much older than those at Troy, and there is probably no direct connection between them.

128. Easton et al. 2002, 101–6.

129. Korfmann 1986c; 1995a.

130. Pulak 1998: 219; Kolb 2004, 591–5. The opposite opinion has been expressed by Jablonka 2003, 91–3; Jablonka and Rose 2004, 626, and Höckmann 2003. I thank Cemal Pulak and George Bass for their advice on this.

131. Özdoğan 2003. While investigating the connections between the Aegean and Black Seas during the Bronze Age, Manfred Korfmann

recognized that a broader geographical sphere of research was necessary, and he turned his attention toward the eastern Black Sea coast, launching excavations at two sites in Georgia, Didigora and Udabno: Korfmann et al. 1999; et al. 2002.

132. Bachhuber and Roberts 2009; Dickinson 2010.

133. Astour 1965, 255; Bryce 1998, 367–8.

134. RS 29.38.22–4; Linder 1981, 38–9; Singer 1987; Mountjoy 1998, 47. For the Hittite campaign conducted by Tudhaliyas IV against Lycia, see Hawkins 1995, 66–85.

135. Wiener 2007, 19.

136. Oren 2000.

137. Blegen 1963, 161.

138. Korfmann 1995b, 22–4; 1996, 34–9; 2001d, 401, fig. 449.

139. Korfmann 2002a, 18–19; Kiesewetter 2002. Within the burial were a bronze dagger and bronze pin. Two children were buried nearby: one, also probably dating to the seventeenth century B.C., was in a burial urn (Blegen et al. 1953, 165); the other, dated originally to the end of Troy V, was in a cist grave containing a Minoan or Minoanizing jug (Korfmann 1997b, 32–8). It has been re-dated to early Troy VI and is thus more or less contemporary with the other graves from the West Sanctuary (Pavúk 2007, appendix; Pavúk, forthcoming).

140. Blegen et al., 1953 370–91; Blegen 1963, 142–3; Becks 2002.

141. Angel 1951, 30.

142. Korfmann 1986a; Basedow 2000; 2002.

143. Lassen 1994; Pini 1992.

144. The end of habitation at Beşik Tepe will also have had an effect on external maritime trade with Troy during the Seventh Settlement in the twelfth century B.C.

145. Blegen et al. 1958, 141–3, 158–9; Becks et al. 2006b; Aslan 2009a.

146. Dörpfeld 1902, 195–6, fig. 75; Blegen et al. 1958, 141; Klinkott 2004, 68.

147. I thank Pavol Hnila for this information.

148. Aslan 2009a; Aslan and Hnila (forthcoming).

149. Blegen et al. 1958, 141–8; Koppenhöfer 1997, 316–47; Guzowska et al. 2003. For the Mycenaean pottery in these levels, see Mountjoy 1997a–c.

150. Sams 1992; Koppenhöfer 2002; Özdoğan 2010, 673. At least one of the VIIb1 houses was destroyed by fire (Mountjoy 1999b, 324), but there is no sign of a systematic destruction.

151. Guzowska et al. 2003, 239. Usage of the two categories was presumably determined by diet or ritual.

152. For this information I thank Pavol Hnila, who is publishing the Troy VII Handmade Coarse Ware. This represents a modification of Guzowska et al. 2003.

153. Blegen et al. 1958, 143; Koppenhöfer 1997, 305–6; Aslan 2002, 84; Guzowska et al. 2003, 236. Carolyn Aslan has informed me that the percentage of Handmade Burnished Wares in Protogeometric levels in the West Sanctuary is approximately 30 percent, whereas in trench D9, on the southern side of the citadel, the percentage is about 70 percent.

154. Lemos 2002, 84–97; Genz 1997; Hall 1997, 120; Bankoff et al. 1996; Sams 1992; Vanschoonwinkel 1991, 233–42; Rutter 1990; Small 1990; Bloedow 1985; Rutter 1975; Deger-Jalkotzy 1977, 40–8; Karageorghis and Kouka 2011. Rautman (1998) examines the issue from the perspective of Late Roman Cyprus. Handmade Burnished Ware has been discovered in levels that predate the collapse of the palaces: Small 1990, 8; Vanschoonwinkel 1991, 234–9.

155. Guzowska et al. (2003, 241–8) have argued that Handmade Coarse Ware was probably produced in Thrace and imported to Troy, but petrographic analysis by Farkas Pinter has demonstrated that it was all locally produced. See Pinter 2005, 177: "I was not able to identify any vessel fragment (of Knobbed Ware) in Troia which could certainly be of foreign origin."

156. Özdoğan 1993a, 160–2. For variants of Knobbed Ware at Daskyleion, see Bakır-Akbaşoğlu 1997, 231. Handmade ware begins to be found at Gordion in Phrygia around 1000 B.C., and at Kaman Kalehüyük (Kirsehir), although the shapes and decoration of the pottery at the latter sites are not duplicated at Troy: Sams 1994, 20–2; Omura 1991. For the ongoing excavations at Eceabat (Kilisetepe), see Sazcı 2012.

157. Pieniążek-Sikora 2003.

158. Dörpfeld 1902, 194; Blegen et al. 1958, 142.

159. Yakar 2003, 16; Sams 1992, 59.

160. Anthony 1990, 900–3; 1997, 24–5; Graham 1990.

161. MacGaffey 2000, 72–6.

162. Henrickson and Voigt 1998, 101. See also Voigt and Henrickson 2000, 46; Sams 1992; Vassileva 2005.

163. Strabo 12.8.3.

164. Blegen et al. 1958, 10–13.

165. Luce 1998; 2003.

166. Aslan et al. 2003; Easton et al. 2002, 100.

167. Cline 2008.

168. Beckman 1996, no. 27. Eteocles: Beckman et al. 2011, 120; Latacz 2004, 117; Niemeier 2005, 18; Wiener 2007, 15–16, n. 100. Atreus: West 2001a.

169. Blegen et al. 1958, 10–13.

170. S. Morris 1997, 539; Raaflaub 1997, 625.

171. Lorimer 1950; Bennet 1997, 532; Wiener 2007, 9. Donald Easton has recently argued that the Trojan Horse may be related to a wheeled battering ram of second millennium B.C. date: Easton 2010.

172. Hope Simpson and Lazenby 1970; Bryce 1998, 25–6.

173. *Iliad* 7: 339–42, 438–41; 12.50–4; Mannsperger 1998.

174. S. Morris 1997, 609; Bryce 2006, 130–5.

175. Burke 2007. The description of Priam's visit to Phrygia (*Iliad* 3.184–9) would be in harmony with the appearance of Gordion in the ninth or eighth century B.C., but not at an earlier time.

176. Sherratt 2010, 7, 10.

177. I have confined these remarks to the *Iliad*, but the description of Odysseus' palace in Ithaca could also be cited here, in that it has nothing in common with the complex administration of Late Bronze Age palaces as evinced by the Linear B tablets: I. Morris 1997; Raaflaub 1997, 625; Wiener 2007, 8.

178. Luke and Roosevelt 2009, 208–13.

179. Korfmann 1997b, 20.

TWO. TROY DURING THE ARCHAIC PERIOD

1. Dörpfeld 1902, 200–1; Blegen et al. 1958, 147–8; Basedow 2009, 132. Blegen proposed that during this interval the Trojans had retreated to the nearby hill of Ballı Dağ, although no such supporting evidence has been discovered: Aslan et al. 2003, 176–7.

2. Bérard 1959; Blegen et al. 1958, 147–8, 248–9; Cook 1962, 25–9; 1973, 360–3; Tenger 1999, 121–6; Vanschoonwinkel 1991, 405–21; Boardman 1999, 23–33; Fisher 2000, 17–20; Bayne 2000, 133–5, 265–8, 315–16.

3. Strabo 9.2.3, 5; 13.1.1–4, 58; 13.2.1; 13.3.2–3; 13.3.5; Leaf 1923, 43–5.

4. Rose 2008, 402–4.

5. Schliemann (1881, 127–8, 209–10, 587–8, 607; 1884, 237) was hard-pressed to find any actual evidence of an Aeolian colonization, but he assumed that it must have occurred at some point in the Iron Age, while Wilhelm Dörpfeld's historian, Alfred Brückner (Dörpfeld 1902, 573) linked the Aeolians' arrival to Lydian control of the Troad, during the Early Archaic period. Schliemann believed that there were similarities between Trojan handmade pottery and the bucchero pottery of Etruria. Noting Herodotus' statement about early Lydian migrations to Etruria, he assumed that the pottery dated prior to the migrations and therefore labeled the phase "Lydian."

6. Aslan 2002, 83–4; Mountjoy 1999b, 333–4; Lenz et al. 1998, 210, n. 46; Basedow 2009; Aslan 2009a.

7. VIIb3 as a chronological rubric was first coined by Korfmann (1995b, 22; 1997b, 27–8).

8. Catling 1998, 153–166; Aslan 2002, 83–4, 90–2. For Opountian Locris during the Protogeometric period, see Fossey 1990, 106–7. The NAA results will be published by Carolyn Aslan and Peter Graeve. John Papadopoulos had already questioned Catling's proposed links between Macedonia and Troy during the Protogeometric period, pointing out that the neck-handled amphoras at Torone differ in fabric, shape, and decoration from those at Troy: Papadopoulos 2005, 585.

9. Torone: Papadopoulos 2005, 576; Lemnos: Danile 2008, pl. II; 2011, 78–84; Clazomenae: Aytaçlar 2004, 22–4.

10. Catling 1998, 178; Catling and Lemos 1990, 1, 39, 55–6, 73–4, pl. 5j.

11. Papadopoulos 1997; Catling 1998; Mommsen et al. 2001, 194, 196, 203; Lemos 2002, 211–12. I am indebted to Carolyn Aslan for her observations on this issue.

12. Leaf 1923, 45; Hertel 1991; 1992.

13. For a similar approach with reference to Greeks in the Levant, see Waldbaum 1997.

14. Basedow 2006; Becks et al. 2006a; Basedow 2007; Basedow 2009; Aslan 2009a.

15. The finds include the bronze figurine of a worshipper, a bull figurine or rhyton, and one or two miniature stone axes. See Becks et al. 2006a, 27–46, 79–80; Aslan et al. *West Sanctuary* (forthcoming); Aslan and Hnila (forthcoming).

16. Rose 1997c, 80–3; 1998, 73–6; Basedow 2006; 2007; 2009; Aslan 2009a.

17. Amphora with incisions: Catling 1998, 164–6 (P459). Thymiaterion with animal frieze: Rose 1998, 74–7 (P584). In general, see Aslan 2009a, 149–50, and Aslan et al. *West Sanctuary* (forthcoming). Equally unusual are a series of horned handles with flared tops: Rose 1997c, 82–3 (P589, 597). The cross-hatched triangles appear to have been derived from Late Bronze Age ceramic traditions at Troy: Blegen et al. 1958, figs. 217, D45; 276(a); 279, 22a–c, as do the horned handles: 237, nos. 23–6. A Gray Ware thymiaterion may also conceivably have been used during this period, but it cannot be firmly dated: Rose 1997c, 83–4 (P534).

18. Blegen et al. 1958, 273–4; Aslan 2009a, 150.

19. Wallace 2003, 267–8 (Knossos); Klein 1997, 297 (Mycenae); Foley 1988, 145–7. See also Cook 1953a and b (Agamemnoneion at Mycenae). In general, see Antonaccio 1994, 86–90; Hall 1997, 138–40; and Coldstream 2000, 296. The Iron Age and Archaic architecture and stratigraphy in the West Sanctuary at Troy will be published by Carolyn Aslan.

20. Gorogianni 2011, 643–6.

21. Aslan 2002, 85–6; Basedow 2006, 18, 21, fig. 3; Rose 1995, 89–93; Rose 1997c, 76–86; 1998, 73–6; Basedow 2009, 135.

22. The height of the partition is unknown, but given the three large postholes set around it, the intention must have been to separate visually the cult object from the altar.

23. The base measured 0.23 m × 0.66 m, with a height of 0.50 m.

24. Becks et al. 2006a, 46–7, fig. 24; Aslan et al. *West Sanctuary* (forthcoming).

25. Aslan et al. *West Sanctuary* (forthcoming). For the development of the apsidal plan during the Protogeometric period, see Lemos 2002, 149–50. Compare the situation in the seventh century B.C. "Temple A" at Prinias, with internal hearth: Carter 1997, 87–9.

26. Rose 1995, 91–3; Koppenhöfer 1997, 310–13.

27. Basedow 2006; Aslan et al. *West Sanctuary* (forthcoming). On the interior, the evidence is primarily confined to the northwestern corner, although it is conceivable that they extended further than the evidence now suggests.

28. Aslan 2002, 85–6.

29. Carolyn Aslan has noted similarities between this structure and an Early Archaic (ca. 700 B.C.) temple in the Sanctuary of the Cabiri on Lemnos (Mazarakis Ainian 1997, 197). Both were approximately the same size, and

the Lemnian sanctuary featured mud-brick benches and a rectangular structure at the back of the building.

30. Blegen et al. 1958, 274–9; Rose 1997c, 89; Basedow 2006, 19–20; Aslan 2011, 412–17; Aslan et al. *West Sanctuary* (forthcoming). Hertel (2007, 118, nn. 94, 96) interprets the apsidal structure and stone circles as indicative of colonization, but supplies no mainland Greek examples as potential models.

31. Feasting also occurred in the vicinity of similar stone circles at Mycenae, Lefkandi, Asine, Nichoria, Naxos, Cyme, and Miletus. All comparanda are discussed in Aslan et al. *West Sanctuary* (forthcoming).

32. Blegen et al. 1953, 394–5.

33. The evidence has been collected in Aslan 2011. There was a 1 m wide entrance into the structure, but whether it was roofed is unclear. A similar oval structure of approximately the same date has been discovered on Lesbos, but its connection to cult activity is uncertain.

34. See *supra* n. 19.

35. *Vita* 1.15; *Vita* 2.11; *Greek Anthology* 7.153; Burke 2007; Nagy 2010, 36, 44. The epigram story is said to have come from Cyme, the native city of Midas' wife: *Vita* 2.11.

36. Arist. fr. 611; Pollux 9.83; Apollodorus 3.12.3; Bakır and Gusmani 1991; Bakır–Akbaşoğlu 1997; Neumann 1997; Gusmani and Polat 1999. The inscription published by Neumann is bilingual, in both Phrygian and Greek.

37. Sams 1994, 129.

38. For an overview of the evidence, see Wittke 2006.

39. Strabo 13.1.8, 22, 42, 65; Nicholas of Damascus *FGrH* 90 F 63; Leaf 1923, 61, 197, 317; Tenger 1999, 127–30.

40. Daskylus: Herodotus 1.8; Pausanias 4.21; royal hunts: Strabo 13.1.17; Xenophon, *Hell.* 4.1.15–16; Kaptan 2002, 94–9.

41. Strabo 13.1.22, 13, 1, 42; Leaf 1923, 126; Tenger 1999, 127–30.

42. Given the statement in Strabo and the naming of Daskyleion after Gyges' father, Lydian control had probably been established by the early seventh century B.C., during the reign of Gyges. It is conceivable that the Lydian losses to the Cimmerians in the middle of that century, coupled with an earthquake in the Troad, allowed other powers such as Lesbos to assume control over the Troad's cities with relative ease, at least until the arrival of Athens ca. 625

B.C. Even then, much of the Troad may have remained under Lydian control until the arrival of the Persians in the mid-sixth century B.C.

43. Aslan et al. *West Sanctuary* (forthcoming).

44. Lamb 1932; Spencer 1995, 277–87; Utili 2002; Lemos 2002, 148, 240; Bayne 2000, 200–17, 314. One of the apsidal buildings lay at the foot of the acropolis of Antissa; the other at Pyrrha.

45. Spencer 1995, 303–5.

46. Bayne 2000, 229–30; Fisher 1996; Aslan 2002, 92–3; Blegen et al. 1958, 253–5; Ilieva 2009. NAA: Mommsen et al. 2001, 196, 203. An early version of the ware already begins to appear in the eighth century B.C.: Aslan 2002, 86; 2009b.

47. Ilieva 2009; Aslan 2009b, 36a. For the production site of G2/3 ware, see Mommsen et al. 2001, 196, 203.

48. Aslan 2002, 86–7.

49. Spencer 1995, 294–5; Philipp 1981, 152; Kurtz and Boardman 1971, 176–7.

50. Spencer 1995, 293–6; Arslan and Sevinç 2003.

51. Spencer 1995, 293; Arslan and Sevinç 2003; Arslan 2003. This is especially apparent in the case of three semi-circular sheets of hammered gold of sixth century B.C. date whose style and iconography are easily paralleled in central and western Anatolia: Arslan 2003. A similar range of imports is evinced in the West Sanctuary of Troy, where the votive fibulae, of late eighth/early seventh century B.C. date, are paralleled in the Aegean islands and western coast of Asia Minor: Rose 1995, 91; Koppenhöfer 1997, 310–12; Sapouna-Sakellarakis 1978, 45–7, Type IIb; 57–9, Type IIIb; Caner 1983, 41–2, Type IVd; 44–5, Type Va.

52. Aslan 2009b.

53. Strabo 13.1.38. Blegen (1935a, 242) proposed that the northern fortification wall of Troy VI served as a source for Sigeion's stones.

54. Rose 1997c, 76–82; 1998, 73–4. The closest parallel is a late seventh-century B.C. temple at Klopedi on Lesbos: Aslan et al. *West Sanctuary* (forthcoming); Betancourt 1977, 82, fig 39; Spencer 1995, 299–301.

55. It is conceivable that the terrace walls were not added until the later sixth-century B.C. construction phase.

56. Rose 1997c, 80–1. The evidence consists of a cylindrical limestone base for a wooden column, several pebbled surfaces, and a hearth.

57. Rose 1997c, 80 (P544).

58. Blegen et al. 1958, 259–63; Rose 1995, 88–9; Rose 1997c, 76–86; Aslan et al. *West Sanctuary*

(forthcoming). Altar B measures 1.68 × 1.19 m with a height of 0.77 m; Altar A has a length of 5.50 and a width of 1.8 m.

59. Thompson 1963, 8–10.

60. I thank Carolyn Aslan for her perceptive analysis of this material.

61. Aslan 2002; Aslan et al. *West Sanctuary* (forthcoming).

62. Blegen et al. 1958, 256.

63. Fabiš 1996; 2003; Rose 2006, 141–2.

64. Lion scarab: SLS 5; bone fibula: BI 16; bronze fibula: BR 106; spindle whorl: SW 68.

65. Spindle whorls: SW 51, 52, 54, 67, 68, 106, 108; loom weights: LW 271; beads: GL 26, 33, 36, 37, 49, 61; ring: BR 106; arrows: BR 105, 115, 126, 127, 231. All of the Archaic small finds from the West Sanctuary will be published by Carolyn Aslan.

66. Blegen et al. 1958, 264, 268, fig. 290; swans/geese: TC 1015, 1025, 1070, 1487; painted heads: Blegen et al. 1958, fig. 290, no. 38–56; Rose 1997c, 88, fig. 15; standing women: Blegen et al. 1958, fig. 290, no. 38–68; Rose 1995, 88–9 (TC 999). All of these will be discussed in greater detail in Aslan et al. *West Sanctuary* (forthcoming).

67. Worth mentioning here is the Late Archaic lead medallion found at Scepsis that shows a fertility goddess with high *polos* standing on the back of a lion: Körpe and Körpe 2001.

68. The original top of Altar B does not survive, and it is conceivable that it featured a mortise similar to that above the base in the Terrace Building.

69. For the pottery from Cyme, see Frasca 1998; Bayne 2000, 310; Hertel 2007, 104; Lemos 2007, 717 ("no material earlier than Late Geometric").

70. Osborne 1996, 121–5; Ehrhardt 1983; Eder 1999, 646–6, s.v. Kolonisation (W. Eder). Elaia, near Pergamon, was reportedly founded by the Athenians at the time of the Trojan War, although there is no evidence that habitation at the site occurred before the seventh century B.C. (Pasinli 1976), and it was not one of the cities included in the Aeolian League by Herodotus (1.149). The earliest Gray Ware from Assos dates to the second half of the seventh century B.C.: Bayne 2000, 309–10; Utili 1999, 78–82; Gebauer 1992, 71. Gebauer's reference to a ninth-century B.C. sherd (1992, 87, no. 54) appears to be an error. Sites within the Ida mountains, such as Cebren and Neandria, also appear to have been settled for the first

time in the seventh century B.C.: Bayne 2000, 310–11; Leaf 1923, 223–40. For Sigeion, see infra, n. 72.

71. Our earliest sign of written Greek in Aeolis does not appear until the last quarter of the seventh century B.C., in the form of graffiti on sherds; stone inscriptions and coins were produced by the middle of the following century: Blegen et al. 1958, 266, 278, 280; Jeffery 1990, 72, 359–62, 366–7, 371, 416; Kraay 1976, 38–39; Blümel 1996, 10–11. In Ionia, the only site that has yielded Greek graffiti of seventh century B.C. date is Smyrna, and only two examples have been uncovered: Jeffery 1990, 345, no. 69 (end of seventh century B.C.?); 473, 68a (ca. 650 B.C.). The earliest coins with Greek legends were struck on Lesbos and Tenedos in the sixth century B.C.: *BMC Troas* xlv, lxiii.

72. Leaf 1923, 186–8; Cook 1973, 178–88; Graham 1983, 32–4, 192–4; Isaac 1986, 162–6; Nagy 2010, 143–6. The site of Sigeion has recently been surveyed along with some limited excavation: Bieg and Aslan 2006; Schäfer 2008; 2011; 2012, 258–9, figs. 13 and 14.

73. Page 1955, 152–61.

74. Page 1955, 131, 149–52, 170–1.

75. Herodotus 5.95.

76. Leaf 1923, 186–90.

77. It is much less likely that a temple to Athena at Sigeion would have been constructed by Lesbos prior to the Athenian colony's establishment. There were no temples to Athena on Lesbos, even though she occasionally appeared on coinage there, and judging by the pottery that has been discovered at Sigeion in rescue excavations, there was only a small settlement there prior to the Athenians' arrival (Reyhan Körpe, pers. communication).

78. Rose 2003, 46–7.

79. Rose 1999, 39; Aslan 2002, 87–8.

80. Berlin 2002; Wallrodt 2002. The terrace fills contain the same types of imported East Greek finewares that appear in contemporary deposits in the West Sanctuary, so they should probably be associated with ritual activity on the citadel, and therefore most likely with the temple of Athena.

81. Dörpfeld 1902, 177–81, 228–9; Rose 2003, 56–7.

82. Polybius 12.5.7; Lycophon *Alex.* 1141–73; Aeneas Tacticus 31.24; Strabo 13.1.40. The custom probably lasted for nearly 600 years, with a break only in the Late Classical/Early

Hellenistic period. For modern assessments of the custom, see Hughes 1991, 166–84; Graf 1978; Walbank 1967, 335–6; Leaf 1923, 191–3; Redfield 2003, 85–150.

83. Leaf 1923, 193.

84. Polybius 12.5.7.

85. Costamagna and Sabbione (1990, 32) place the foundation of the colony around 700 B.C., a quarter of a century earlier than the date supplied by Eusebius, but this is based on a few Corinthian imports in one of the tombs and does not necessarily signify the arrival of colonists.

86. The precise date for the custom's inauguration cannot be established. If we take literally Eusebius' proposed foundation date for the colony of Locri Epizephyri, then the custom must have begun by the first quarter of the seventh century B.C., at the latest, which means that the temple of Athena would have to have been in place by the late eighth century B.C. This is not impossible, since ritual activity had certainly occurred in the West Sanctuary by that date, but the removal of Archaic deposits by the Hellenistic builders of the new Athena temple means that we can probably never discern the time in which the first temple was built.

87. Taplin 1992; West 1995; 2001b.

88. Sivritepe: Schliemann 1881, 665–9; Dörpfeld 1902, 545–7; Cook 1973, 173–4; Korfmann 1985, 167; 1986b, 309–10; 1989, 474–81; Karaağaçtepe: Schliemann 1884, 254–62; Dörpfeld 1902, 547; Hanaytepe: Schliemann 1881, 706–20; Dörpfeld 1902, 548; Cook 1973, 122–3; Paşatepe: Schliemann 1881, 656–8; Cook 1973, 107–8; Bieg 2009.

89. Achilles built a mound for Patroclus, to which his own ashes were subsequently added, and the Trojans constructed a mound over Hector's ashes: *Iliad* 24.76ff; 23.245–8; *Odyssey* 24.80–4. Mounds were also built for Elpenor (*Odyssey* 12.9–15) and Eetion (*Iliad* 6.416–19).

90. Achilles and Patroclus: Strabo 13.1.32, 39; Arrian *Anab.* 1.11.12; Pliny *NH* 5.33, 124, 125; Lucian *Charon* 521; Quintus Smyrnaeus 7.402; Cassius Dio 77.16; Philostratus 51.12; Ajax: Pausanias 1.35.3; Philostratus 8.1; Strabo 13.1.30; Protesilaus: Herodotus 7.33, 9.116, 120; Pausanias 3.4, 5; Strabo 13.1.31; Pliny *NH* 16.88; *Anth. Pal.* 7.141, 385; Philostratus 1.1; Hector: Strabo 13.1.29; Lycophron *Alexandra* 1208ff.; Lucian *Deorum Conviv.* 12; Dio Chrysostum *Orat.* 11.179; Hecuba: Strabo 13.1.28; Priam:

Greek Anthology 55; Cook 1973, 133; Aisyetes: *Iliad* 2.792–794; Strabo 13.1.34, 37; Leaf 1923, 185–6; Luce 2003, 17–19; Bateia/Myrina: *Iliad* 2.811–15; Strabo 13.1.34; Luce 2003, 13–17; Ilus: *Iliad* 24.349–51; Strabo 13.1.25, 34; Luce 2003, 19–21; Antilochus: Strabo 13.1.32.

91. Caskey 1925, 25–6, no. 13.

92. The original tumulus of Ajax had been badly damaged by the Hadrianic period, which prompted the emperor to build a completely new tumulus in a more protected location. The first tumulus has never been identified, so its date of erection will always be unclear.

93. Arrian 1.11.7; Diodorus 17.18.1.

94. Plutarch *Alexander* 15.7.

95. Page 1955, 152–61.

96. Gorogianni 2011, 643–6.

97. Milesian colonization: Greaves 2007; Gorman 2001, 47–85; Ehrhardt 1983.

98. Coldstream 1976; Cook 1953a and b; Whitley 1988; Malkin 1994; Antonaccio 1995.

99. For modern assessments of the custom of the Locrian Maidens, see Hughes 1991, 166–84; Graf 1978; Walbank 1967, 335–6; Leaf 1923, 191–3; Wilhelm 1911; Redfield 2003, 85–150.

100. According to Philostratus (*Heroikos* 53.8–21), the Thessalians traveled annually to Troy to make sacrifices at the tomb of Achilles. This should probably be viewed as a status-building device in the same spirit as the custom of the Locrian Maidens.

101. For the temple of Athena Ilias at Physkeis in West Locris, see Lerat 1952, 156–8. For the tumulus of Achilles, now usually identified as Sivritepe, near Beşik Bay, see Cook 1973, 173–4; Rose 2000, 65–6; Korfmann 2000, 41–3; Hertel 2003, 161–75, 200–3. Excavation has shown it to have been a small Late Neolithic tumulus that was monumentalized in the third century B.C.

102. Tsetskhladze 2008. There are a number of tumuli near Sigeion, one of which was viewed as a likely candidate for Achilles' tomb and excavated by Choiseul-Gouffier and Schliemann in 1787 and 1882, respectively (Schliemann 1881, 654; 1884, 242–54; Leaf 1923, 165; Cook 1973, 161–2; Hertel 2003, 161–76; Bieg 2009, 242). Choiseul-Gouffier reportedly discovered a cremation burial together with Late Archaic/Early Classical pottery, including black-figured lekythoi (oil flasks). Another nearby tumulus, often linked to Patroclus, yielded pottery of similar date,

and both should probably be viewed as burials of wealthy Sigeion residents, not unlike those in the Granicus River Valley.

103. Boardman 1999, 264–5; Cook 1973, 178–88; Leaf 1923, 186–8; Graham 1983, 32–4, 192–4; Garnsey 1988, 118; Isaac 1986, 162–6; Viviers 1987; Stahl 1987, 221–3; Nagy 2010, 147–85. Aigner (1978) connects the Peisistratid retaking of Sigeion with the incorporation of the Homeric epics in the Athenian Panathenaia. For the tumulus of Achilles, see *supra*, n. 88.

104. Shapiro 1989, 154–6.

105. Hind 1998. A settlement was established ca. 570–560 B.C. at Achilleion, above Beşik Bay, when it was presumably controlled by Lesbos, but it lasted only until 530 B.C., ending for no particular reason that we can discern, since the final deposits do not coincide with the takeover by Peisistratus (Kossatz 1988).

106. Herodotus 5.94.1.

107. For the Homeric epics in the Panathenaea, see Hurwit 1985, 262–3; Nagy 1996, 65–106.

108. Leaf 1923, 163; Isaac 1986, 192–3. The elder Miltiades established a tyranny in the Chersonese (Herodotus 6.36–8), but this was not a colony per se.

109. Herodotus 9.116–20; Pausanias 1.34.2; 3.4.5. Cf. Philostratus *Heroicus* 2.1 and Pliny *NH* 16.8.8 commenting on the elaborate trees on the mounds of Protesilaus and Ilus. The treasure was ultimately stolen by Artyctes, one of Xerxes' governors, which suggests that it was in the process of formation during the sixth century B.C.

110. Elaious was probably founded only one or two decades after Sigeion, which meant that Athenian colonies would have occupied both sides of the entrance to the Dardanelles. For a different view of the location of Protesilaus' tomb, see Hertel 2003, 180–2.

111. I have qualified the language here because only the robbing trenches of the pronaos walls survive, and the position of the northeast wall is also based on robbing trenches.

112. Rose 1995, 82–93; 1997c, 76–86; 1998, 73–6; Lawall 2003. The measurements above relate only to the buildings per se, without including peristyles, since there is no firm evidence that the Late Archaic temple in the West Sanctuary had a peristyle. If peristyles are factored into the equation, both Assos and Neandria would have been significantly larger than the new temple at Troy.

113. The wall blocks are A664–70. These had been discovered in a ruined state during Hellenistic building construction and carefully reburied by the side of the new building. We discovered only one possible component of the superstructure's decoration: a terracotta disk acroterion with painted meander and a border of triangular teeth (AT 181).

114. Bases: A671, 672. For the Aeolic order, see Cook 1962, 84–6; Betancourt 1977, 58–112; Wiegartz 1994.

115. The height calculations are based on the elevations of the Aeolic temple at Klopedi, Lesbos, and the Old Palace at Larisa (Betancourt 1977, 86, fig. 42; pl. 45).

116. The mortise was an oval about 40 × 50 cm in size, which is approximately the same size as most of the mortises in the base of the Geneleos monument: Walter-Karydi 1985; Kienast 1992.

117. Within the eastern addition to the structure were ceramics of third century B.C. date: z6/7.342. For discussion of the platform, generally referred to as Structure 341, see Rose 1995, 86–8, and Aslan et al. *West Sanctuary* (forthcoming).

118. Cook and Nichols 1998, 93–196, 200–3 (Smyrna); Betancourt 1977, 73–88 (Larisa, Lesbos); Wiegartz 1994 (Neandria); Rose 1995, 86–88 (Troy); Basaran 2000 (Ainos).

119. Barletta 2001, 84–124.

120. Ragone 1990; Özkan 1994; Nagy 2010, 142–3.

121. Herodotus 1.149–51; Strabo 13.1.4; 13.1.39. The date at which the league was established is unclear. No excavations have occurred in the Sanctuary of Apollo at Gryneion, which served as the Aeolian League's headquarters, although Geometric pottery has been found on the surface: Ragone 1990; Özkan 1994. The headquarters of the Ionian league in the Panionion at Mykale have, however, been the subject of recent survey and excavation. A naiskos of late seventh century B.C. date was subsequently replaced (ca. 570–560 B.C.) by a much larger temple with assembly hall, 100 Attic feet in length, which was set within a fortified precinct of ca. 7 hectares: Lohmann 2007.

122. See *supra* n. 71.

123. Lydians: Pedley 1972, 18–25; Tenger 1999, 127–30.

124. The earliest Gray Ware from Assos dates to the second half of the seventh century B.C.: Bayne

2000, 309–10; Utili 1999, 78–82; Gebauer 1992, 71. Gebauer's reference to a ninth-century B.C. sherd (1992, 87, no. 54) appears to be an error.

125. Clarke 1898, 40–140; Wescoat 2012a.

126. Nothing remains of the Archaic temple of Athena at Sigeion, but this was an Athenian colony, and it is difficult to believe that the exterior order would not have been Doric. We can unfortunately say nothing about the order of the Archaic temple of Athena at Troy, since no elements have survived, but it appears to have been a simple building with no exterior ornamentation: Rose 2003, 74, n. 123.

127. Wescoat 2012a, 156–62.

128. At the same time, the polis of Mytilene, which had fought Athens over Sigeion, joined the Ionian and Dorian poleis situated along the western coast of Asia Minor in establishing the Hellenion precinct at Naucratis: Herodotus 2.178.2–3.

129. Wescoat 2012a, 100–24, 231–2, 239. The destruction of the temple of Athena at Assos is our best evidence for this earthquake in the Troad.

130. This section summarizes my arguments in Rose 2008.

131. Cf. Mountjoy and Hankey 1988, 30–2, with reference to the "Dorian Invasion."

132. See Herodotus 1.146.2–3.

133. Woolf 1998; Keay and Terrenato 2001. For Greek colonization on Sicily, see also Antonaccio 2001. The recently formulated models of Romanization could, in fact, be profitably applied to scholarly assessments of the early migrations.

134. The Ionians' annual contribution of oxen to Athens' Panathenaic festival also reinforced this connection: Barron 1964, 47.

135. Hall 2004, 41–2; Gosden 2001; Lyons and Papadopoulos 2002b.

136. Burkert 1992, 1–8; Boardman 1990a, 185–6. This attitude has been traced back to the Homeric period with reference to the Phoenicians: Winter 1995.

THREE. THE TOMBS OF THE GRANICUS RIVER VALLEY: THE POLYXENA SARCOPHAGUS

1. Balcer 1984, 95–325; Sekunda 1988; Tenger 1996; 1999, 131–3.

2. Rose et al. 2007, 104–5; Rose 2011b, 164.

3. Lawall 2002; Rose et al. 2007.

4. Attic: Tuna-Nörling 1999, 2001; Görkay 1999; Giudice et al. 2011. Lydian: Gürtekin-Demir 2002, 2003.

5. Wiegartz 1994, 125; Betancourt 1977, 73, 76, 79–80; 85.

6. Koenigs 1989; Jeffery 1990, 367, 372, no. 50. These two monolithic columns with base and capital would have reached a height of 2.65 m, and one of them contained a boustrophedon inscription. Jeffrey associated the column with Sidene, but the site was destroyed at least twenty-five years before the column was made (Strabo 13.1.42).

7. Sekunda 1988, 191, no. 10; 192, no. 13; Neumann 1997; Gusmani and Polat 1999; Lemaire 2001; Kaptan 2002, 194–210.

8. For an overview of settlements in the area, see Sekunda 1988; Kaptan 2003.

9. For Early Bronze Age habitation in the region, see Özdoğan 1989, 1993a, 2003; Sekunda 1988. For the evidence from Daskyleion, see Bakir 1995; Bakir-Akbasoğlu and Polat 1998; Kaptan-Bayburtluoğlu 1990; Nollé 1992; Briant 2002, 697–700.

10. Xenophon Hell. 4.1.15–16; Bakır 2003, 3.

11. Xenophon Cyr. 8.6.10; Balcer 1984, 195–210; Sekunda 1988; 1991.

12. Our best information regarding the appearance of the estates comes from Xenophon, who notes that one such estate in the vicinity of Pergamon had towers that were eight bricks thick within the fortification walls: Anabasis 7.8.7–9; Rostovtzeff 1923, 371–4; Balcer 1984, 211–14. Remote sensing at one potential settlement site near the tumuli at Dedetepe and Bozlartepe (Fig. 3.1) has revealed traces of walls as well as a dense accumulation of Classical sherds on the surface: Rose et al. 2007, 119–20. There are literary references to several important settlements in the region, the most prominent of which were Adrasteia, Sidene, Harpagion, and Didymateiche: Strabo 13.1.11; Leaf 1923, 68–72; Meritt et al. 1939, 481.

13. See, in general, Özgen and Öztürk 1996, 19–35; Roosevelt 2009, 99–100, 109, 115–16, 147–50.

14. Xenophon Anabasis 1.9.13; 4.6.11; 5.6.7; Herodotus 5.35; Hammond 1980.

15. Herodotus 1.93; Roosevelt 2009, 153; McLauchlin 1985, 126–39, 287–9.

16. The fieldwork was overseen primarily by Nurten Sevinç, former director of the Çanakkale Museum, and Reyhan Körpe, now a professor at Çanakkale University. The preliminary

publications are: Sevinç 1996; Sevinç et al. 1998; 1999; 2001. For sarcophagi in the tombs of Lydia, see Roosevelt 2009, 137–8.

17. The principal publications are Sevinç 1996; Sevinç et al. 1998, 314–16, 323; 2001, 402; Gilotta 1998; Steuernagel 1998; Schwarz 2001; Reinsberg 2001; 2004; Deppert 2006; Rose 2006, 143–6; 2007b; Neer 2012a.

18. Sevinç et al. 1999.

19. There is a photo in Gürsü 2001, 191.

20. Sevinç 1996, 252, 253, fig. 4.

21. For this information I thank Prof. Dr. Berna Alpagut of the Anthropology Department of Ankara University, who analyzed all of the human bones from this tumulus.

22. Littauer and Crouwel 1979, 146–7; Mellink 1973a, 299–301 (Karaburun); Fleischer 1983, 52–4 (Mourning Women Sarcophagus); Tappeiner 1986, esp. 90; Nollé 1992, 60–8 (Daskyleion); Crouwel 1992; Kökten-Ersoy 1998. The same kind of cart appears on the painted beams from the tomb at Tatarlı (Calmeyer 1992, 7–13; Summerer 2010, 151–68), and perhaps also within the tomb at Harta, Lydia (Özgen and Öztürk 1996, 38).

23. For the type, see Kökten-Ersoy 1998.

24. Xenophon *Cyropaedia* 7.3.4. This particular chariot was a "*harmamaxa*," a traveling vehicle for women: Tappeiner 1986; 86–7; Ateşlier 2002.

25. The Alexander Sarcophagus measures 3.02 m in length, 1.51 m in width, and 1.95 m in total height (Hitzl 1991, 181, no. 19). The Polyxena Sarcophagus is longer and wider, but slightly shorter. For the Sidamara sarcophagi, see Elderkin 1939, 102. For the comparative measurements, see Kleeman 1958, 45; Sevinç 1996, 252; Sevinç et al. 1999, 490; Hitzl 1991, Beilage I-III.

26. The measurements of the Mylasa sarcophagus were reported in the Turkish newspaper *Milliyet* on August 12, 2010, and the circumstances of its discovery appear in Brunwasser 2011. The length is 2.75 m (vs. 3.30 m for Polyxena); the width is 2.15 m (vs. 1.60 m for Polyxena); and the height is 1.85 m (vs. 1.78 m for Polyxena).

27. Hitzl 1991, nos. 17 (Lycian sarcophagus) and 18 (Mourning Women Sarcophagus).

28. The Çan Sarcophagus (Sevinç et al. 2001) has a length of 2.41 m, a width of. 95 m, and a height of. 85 m, which creates a ratio of 2.5:1 for length to width, and 3:1 for length to height. The Child's Sarcophagus (Sevinç et al. 1999)

measures 2.25 m in length and 0.88 m in width, with a total height of 1.07 m, which creates a length:width ratio of 2.5:1.

29. Relief palmettes on corner eggs are standard in Greek sarcophagus design: Kleeman 1958, pl. 1a; Von Graeve 1970, Taf. 1.1, 3,2; Langer-Karrenbrock 2000, Taf. 5. Weber (1999, 424) noted the similarities between the palmette decoration used for the Athena temple at Miletus and those on the corner eggs of the Polyxena Sarcophagus.

30. Ionic architraves of Late Archaic and Classical date usually have three fasciae: Ateşlier and Öncü 2004, 62–3. Two fasciae were also used in the monumental architecture of Daskyleion.

31. All three courses appear on the Alexander Sarcophagus, although not directly juxtaposed.

32. The next example seems to be the Mourning Women Sarcophagus, followed by the Alexander Sarcophagus.

33. The "Early Classical Building" and its connection to the lid of the Polyxena Sarcophagus have been discussed in depth by Suat Ateşlier (Ateşlier 2001; Ateşlier and Öncü 2004, 64–5).

34. On the early development of dentils, see Nylander 1970, 95–6, no. 236; Bingöl 1990, 103–8; Wesenberg 1996; Boardman 2000, 59, 79, 237 n. 167; Ateşlier 2001; Ateşlier and Öncü 2004, 64–6; Öncü 2004. The earliest in stone architecture appear to be from Labraunda, dated ca. 520–500 B.C. (Thieme 1993), although they appear in stone tower-house models earlier (Boardman 2000, 80, fig. 2.63).

35. The same proportional relationship was used for the dentils on the Nereid Monument at Xanthos, and the Limyra heroon of Perikles. See Roos 1976.

36. The removable dentils were not discovered during excavation.

37. Ateşlier 2001. The volutes of the capital, however, are upside-down. Suat Ateşlier has suggested that the architect responsible for constructing the "Early Classical Building" at Daskyleion was also involved in carving the sarcophagus, since the architectural ornamentation is so similar.

38. Kurtz and Boardman 1971, 267–72; Philipp 1981, 153–4 (Miletus, Ephesus, Chios); Gates 1983, 31–2 (Rhodes); Hitzl 1991, 8, 33, 43. Cyrus was interred in a gilded stone sarcophagus at Pasargadae: Strabo 15.3.7; Arrian *Anabasis* 6.29.4–11.

39. Isinda-Belenkli Pillar: Akurgal 1941, 52–97; Deltour-Levie 1982, 171–5; Lion Tomb: Akurgal

1941, 3–51; Demargne 1958, 29–36; Harpy Tomb: Demargne 1958, 37–76; Rudolph 2003.

40. For the literary and iconographic tradition, see Fontinoy 1950; Loraux 1987, 36–41; Hughes 1991, 61–2; Touchefeu-Meynier 1994; Bonnechere 1994, 251 n. 83; Van Straten 1995, 114; Steuernagel 1998; Gilotta 1998; Hedreen 2001, 134–6; Schwarz 2001; Ekroth 2005, 13–14.

41. Cook 1981, 129; Camporeale 1981, 205, no. 85 (tomb of Patroclus).

42. The hair-pulling motif was commonly used in scenes of battle (Gigantomachies and Centauromachies) as well as the Trojan War (Cassandra, Achilles with Trojan captives): Vian and Moore 1988, no. 332; Sengelin 1997, nos. 181, 191, 214, 406; Paoletti 1994, nos. 97, 104, 136, 176, 181; Holliday 1993, 179, fig. 63; Cook 1981, pl. 67, no. g29.

43. Beazley 1956, 97.27, 683; Touchefeu-Meynier 1994, 433, no. 26; Blome 2001, 138, fig. 144; Von Mehren 2002, 50; and Tuna-Nörling 1997, who demonstrates that Tyrrhenian amphorae were exported to Asia Minor. There is no obvious reason why Antiphates would have a hairstyle different from that of the other men.

44. The tumulus of Achilles appears in another scene of the sacrifice of Polyxena on a Clazomenaean sarcophagus: Cook 1981, 36, no. G8, pl. 48.3. It is difficult to judge whether the tumulus is crowned by a terminal stone or by a flaming altar. Cook (1981, 36, n. 80) noticed no flames. For an actual terminal stone in its socket, see Paton 1900, 68, fig. 4.

45. Euripides *Hecuba* ll. 342–78, 547–70; Gregory 1999, 87, 111–12.

46. The awkwardness is especially apparent in the drawing by Nurten Sevinç: Sevinç 1996, 256, fig. 9.

47. Similar walking sticks appear at Kızılbel (Mellink 1998, pl. Xb), Daskyleion (Nollé 1992, 178, Taf. 14a), and on the Harpy Tomb at Xanthos: Rudolph 2003, pls. 16, 19, 20, 25, 27, 30, 33. Hecuba uses a walking stick on an Attic red-figure cup, ca. 500 B.C. (Laurens 1988, 479, no. 56), and it is a regular feature of Nestor's iconography: Lygouri-Tolia 1994.

48. This figure was initially identified as Nestor, based primarily on his position on the Tyrrhenian amphora (Sevinç 1996, 258; Schwarz 2001, 36). Aged figures generally appear with a beard in both Greek and Graeco-Persian art: cf. the Late Archaic paintings from the Kızılbel

tomb in Lycia (Mellink 1998, pl. Xb), the Harpy Tomb reliefs from Xanthos (Rudolph 2003, pl. 16); the Daskyleion reliefs (Nollé 1992, 178, Taf. 14a); and the iconography of Priam (Neils 1994) and Nestor (Lygouri-Tolia 1994).

49. I owe the following Attic vase painting references to Prof. Timothy McNiven, who has written widely on the subject of Attic gesture. Athens, Agora P 18567: ABV 43.4 (near Sophilos); Bakır 1982, pl. 83, fig. 171; Moore 1986, pl. 121.1912; London E 254 (A): ARV 31.3 (Dikaios Painter); CVA British Museum 3, pl. 2.2a (Great Britain 167); New York 17.230.37 (B): ARV 498.1 (Deepdene Painter); Add 251; Richter 1923, 280, fig. 17; London E 363 (A): ARV 586.36; Boardman, *ARVA*, fig. 332; ARV 257.11 (Copenhagen Painter); Bloesch 1974, pl. 41 #245b; Louvre CA 1685 (A): ARV 1099.46 (Naples Painter); Zschietzschmann 1928, Beilage 18, fig. 116. A similar list, also provided by Prof. McNiven, appears in Weber-Lehmann 2005, 449, n. 29. See also Jannot 1984, 15, figs. 86, 113, 519 (Chiusi reliefs).

50. In some cases, the women's hair or hands cover their ears, and one cannot determine whether earrings exist. But the hair of figure 7 has been pulled back so that the viewer can see that she wears no earrings. This is true for none of the other women.

51. Euripides *Hecuba* l. 609, 658–709 (referred to as *archaia latris*); Gregory 1999, 48, 127.

52. Ferrari 1997, 31. For the iconography of mourning in general, see Mommsen 1997; Pedrina 2001; Huber 2001. Reinsberg (2001, 77) identifies the far left figure as a man, but the long hair falling down the back speaks in favor of a woman, as do her earrings.

53. Rudolph 2003, Taf. 16; Berger 1970, 130, fig. 146; Draycott 2008. For other examples, see Neumannn 1965, 139, fig. 69; Jannot 1984, figs. 86, 113 (Chiusi reliefs); Huber 2001, 262, nos. 199, 200 (white-ground lekythoi); Weber-Lehmann 2005, 447, fig. 2 (cippus in Florence).

54. Wiencke 1954; Shapiro 1991, 630–1, 643–4; Mommsen 1997; van Wees 1998, 19–41. The same gestures can be found in reliefs on Late Archaic cinerary urns from Chiusi: Jannot 1984, figs. 80, 86, 113, 120, 123, 133, 519.

55. There is a fragmentary Protoattic vase (ca. 650–630 B.C.) featuring men carrying a woman whose head must have faced upward judging by the position of her feet (Vermeule and Chapman 1971). The vase was initially

interpreted as a representation of Iphigenia on the grounds that if it were Polyxena, her head would have been directed toward the ground. The Kızöldün sarcophagus has shown that such a configuration is possible, and the scene is now generally identified as a representation of Polyxena's sacrifice (Hedreen 2001, 133, n. 40; Schwarz 2001, 39–47). If this is correct, then there were at least two depictions of the sacrifice in which Polyxena looked upward, one of which was made in Athens.

56. Prag 1985, 61–7. Aside from Polyxena, the only other woman to have been shown at such a moment is Penthesilea, on the name vase of the Penthesilea Painter (Berger 1994, 298, no. 34). Otherwise, she is shown either prior to or following her death by Achilles. Amazons are not infrequently depicted as wounded and bleeding, but not necessarily dying: Von Bothmer 1957, pls. 2.2, 3.1b, 37.1, 71.1, 3. The same does not apply to men, as demonstrated by, among others, the Trojans whose throats are being cut in the François Tomb paintings (Holliday 1993, 179, fig. 63), the Persians on the Alexander mosaic, and the paintings of the murder of Agamemnon and Aegisthus (Prag 1985, pls. 3, 15).

57. After the Archaic period, she was never again shown at the moment of death; cf. Pausanias 1.22.6 (Athenian Propylaia), where the moment just before the sacrifice was depicted.

58. Loraux 1987; Himmelmann 1997; Van Straten 1995, figs. 122–53; Gebauer 2002, Abb. 138; Ekroth 2005, 11–14, pl. 1.2.

59. Loraux 1987, 21, 32–3. If we examine similar scenes of sacrifice involving men, the examples are limited to Trojans killed by Achilles or Neoptolemus, which is not so surprising considering the number of instances in the *Iliad* in which warriors die with their throats cut, including Hector (Loraux 1987, 52). The best example is a Faliscan stamnos (ca. 400–350 B.C.) remarkably similar in a number of respects to the Polyxena Sarcophagus, wherein Achilles stands next to the tumulus of Patroclus, represented in half-oval form, and cuts the throat of a bound Trojan male whose hair he has grabbed with his other hand. There are seven depictions of this theme, including one in the François Tomb at Vulci, that appear to stem from a single prototype: Beazley 1947, 88–92; Messerschmidt 1930; Camporeale 1981, 205–6, nos. 85–95.

60. Burkert 1983; Van Straten 1995; 103–114. Himmelmann 1997; Gebauer 2002, 258; Ekroth 2005, pl. 1.2. For the throat as a locus of death in Greek tragedy, see Loraux 1987, 50–3.

61. Euripides *Hecuba* ll. 37–41, 93–7, 107–52, 205–10, 521–82; Gregory 1999, 109–14.

62. Messerschmidt 1930; Camporeale 1981, 205–6, nos. 85–7.

63. Euripides *Hecuba* 205–9; cf. also 147–52; 549; Loraux 1987, 35, 44–6, 56–60.

64. Van Straten 1995, figs. 115, 119–22, 157; Himmelmann 1997, 25, fig. 13; 27, fig. 15a; 28, fig. 16; 33, fig. 20a; Gebauer 2002, Abb. 134, 184; Ekroth 2005, pls. 1.1, 3.2.

65. Vermeule and Chapman 1971, 291; Prag 1985, 63; Van Straten 1995, 103–14. This in true also for Achilles' execution of Trojan captives on Faliscan vases: Camporeale 1981, 205, no. 85.

66. Aeschylus *Agamemnon* 232–5. See also Henrichs 1981, 198–208; Loraux 1987, 32, 34.

67. This is not true in every case, however: the paintings in the François Tomb in Vulci show Achilles slashing the throat of a Trojan captive, grabbing his hair, and pulling his head back so that he looks upward: Holliday 1993, 179, fig. 63.

68. Schwarz (2001, 46) has cited a red-figure column krater in Tekirdağ that may show Polyxena as the bride of Achilles, although the identification is not certain. For Achilles and Polyxena as lovers in the Hellenistic period, see Fontinoy 1950; Hughes 1991, 62.

69. For the literary tradition regarding the death of Achilles, see Kossatz-Deissmann 1981, 181–2.

70. *Iliad* 21, 275–8; 22.358–60. Apollo Thymbraios sanctuary: Hyg. *fab.* 110; Serv. ad Verg. *Aen.* 6, 57; Schol. Lykophron, *Alexandria* 269.

71. It is less likely that the tripod was intended to indicate that the tumulus of Achilles was situated in an area sacred to Apollo, such as the sanctuary of Apollo Thymbraios (Hedreen 2001, 135–6). There are no literary references to the placement of Achilles' tomb in a sanctuary of Apollo, nor would one expect this given their mutual antipathy.

72. Euripides *Hecuba* ll. 37–41, 93–7, 107–15.

73. See *infra* nn. 75–7.

74. Euripides *Hecuba* ll. 486–7.

75. It seems unlikely that the figure with the walking stick on the principal side of the sarcophagus is another representation of Hecuba at a different moment in the narrative. Both scenes appear to form parts of the same moment, and the two figures differ in dress and hairstyle.

76. Laurens 1988, no. 57; Badoni 1968, pl. 28.5.

77. Other examples would be the recumbent Cassandra clinging to the Palladion during the Ilioupersis (Paoletti 1994, 960–8), or Trojan male captives about to be sacrificed by Achilles (Holliday 1993, 179, fig. 63). An aged figure in squatting position also figures in mourning scenes of the Argive hero Amphiaraus: the hero's departure is lamented by a crouching seer who knows that the military campaign on which Amphiaraus embarks will lead to his death: Brownlee 1995, 366–7, fig. 21.5; Krauskopf 1981, 704, no. 75; Mellink 1998, 22–4, 59, pl. VIb (Kızılbel, Lycia).

78. For the Boston throne, see Simon 1959, 57–92; Baroni 1961, 28–30; Alscher 1963, 48–50; Young and Ashmole 1968; Guarducci 1987; Borelli 1993. For the Olympia pediment, see Ashmole and Yalouris 1967, 22 and fig. 67. An aged woman is also represented on one of the Locrian pinakes: Zancani Montuoro 1960, 46–7, pl. VIII, 1. Young and Ashmole have argued for the authenticity of the Boston Throne based on chemical analysis of the encrustation on the surface, but this has been forcefully challenged by Guarducci and Borelli, among others.

79. The same is true in vase painting; cf. Geropso, the old Thracian attendant of Herakles (Bundrick 2005, 72, fig. 43), and for aged men on Clazomenaean sarcophagi (Cook 1981, pl. 93.5–6). A more common way of indicating age for men in the Archaic period was the use of white hair: Shapiro 1991, 636, fig. 7, 638; Mellink 1998, 23–4, 30.

80. Hurwit 1982; Anderson 1997, 198–9; Hedreen 2001, 68–80. Palm trees and tripods are also occasionally used in scenes of the sacrifice of Troilus by Achilles (Hedreen 2001, 124–5, 171–2). Robertson (1990) has argued that there was considerable interaction between the iconography of Troilus and that of Polyxena. It is therefore conceivable that what we see on the Kızöldün sarcophagus is an example of the former influencing the latter.

81. Weber-Lehmann 2005, 446.

82. Hecuba and Cassandra were presented together on an Attic red-figure cup, ca. 500 B.C.: Laurens 1988, 479, no. 56.

83. The presence of the tree is interesting in itself in that no landscape elements appear in any other depictions of Polyxena's sacrifice. For bare trees, see Carroll-Spillecke 1985, 12, 14, 15–17, 29, 41–56, 153, 158, 163; Wegener 1985, 118–30, 157–62; Nollé 1992, pl. 9, Cat. S7; Pfrommer 1998, 87, 142–3, 165–6. Only a few trees were carved with leaves: pediment of the temple of Artemis at Corfu (Wegener 1985, 266, Cat. 1); Olive Tree Pediment (Ridgway 1999, 110); Golgoi sarcophagus (Hitzl 1991, 200–1, Cat. 37, Abb. 49); coin of Gortyna, 360–320 B.C. (Kraay 1976, pl. 7, 145). Both leafy and bare trees were represented on the frieze at Vergina: Carroll-Spillecke 1985, 153, and branches appear with leaves in one of the Late Archaic painted tombs of Lydia: Özgen and Öztürk 1996, 73, nos. 9, 10. Nearly all of the paint survives on the sarcophagus from Çan, and it is clear that the leaves were not painted: Sevinç et al. 2001, 400. Cassandra occasionally appears next to palm trees, symbolic of Apollo, in vase painting: Paoletti 1994, nos. 106, 202; Touchefeu 1981, no. 44 (Vivenzio hydria).

84. It has recently been argued that the enthroned figure on side C is a second representation of Polyxena, preparing for her marriage to Achilles in the underworld, which would thereby unify the two sides (Ateşlier and Öncü 2004, 59–61). But the romantic element of the story does not enter the literature until the Hellenistic period, and there is nothing in the iconography of the seated women or her attendants to suggest that we are dealing with Trojan women.

85. Compare the fan bearer in the tomb paintings of Karaburun: Mellink 1983b, 174. For the remains of Tyrian purple stains on alabastra, see the discussion of the Dedetepe tomb in Chapter 5.

86. Compare the mirrors from the tomb at Ikiztepe: Özgen and Öztürk 1996, 128, nos. 82–3.

87. Delavaud-Roux 1993; Ceccarelli 1998, 138–9, 246; Lesky 2000. For the helmets, see Pflug 1988.

88. For the kithara, see Byrne 1993; Lawergren 1993; Bundrick 2005, 26–9. For the aulos, see Bundrick 2005, 34–41. Kitharas also appear on a relief from the Lycian Isinda tomb (Akurgal 1941, fig. 12, pl. 12), and in the Late Archaic Painted House from Gordion (Lawergren 1985, 25–33, fig. 4). For women musicians in general, see Wegner 1963, 102–10.

89. For castanets in ancient Greece, see Wegner 1963, 212–14, pls. 8, 9, 28; Bundrick 2005, 46–7. Compare the male castanet players on Clazomenaean sarcophagus in London: Cook 1981, pl. 46, and on Late Archaic cinerary urns from Chiusi (Jannot 1984, fig. 174).

90. Wegner 1963, 212–14.

91. All of the following references are to Ceccarelli 1998. For Pyrrhic dancers with musicians: 165–85; for their appearance in funerary contexts: 53–7 (with Cook 1981, 116); for the foundation of the custom by Neoptolemus: 195–201. The Pyrrhic interpretation has been presented forcefully in Neer 2012a.

92. Harpy Tomb at Xanthos: Berger 1970, 148, 149, 153, and compare the corner winged figures of the footstool at Belevi (Richter 1966, fig. 325). Achaemenid Persian throne supports: Boardman 2000, figs. 2.27a, b, 3.39, 3.40, 4. The relevant mainland Greek examples include the throne of Zeus on a black-figure amphora showing the birth of Athena, where a youthful male stands between the two legs and supports the center with both arms (Richter 1966, fig. 57), and Zeus' throne on the Siphnian treasury frieze, where a maenad and satyr support the armrest (Kyrieleis 1969, pl. 24.1). It is not unlikely that the Kızöldün throne reflects the format of others that once existed in the satrap's palace at Daskyleion.

93. E.g., Kaptan 2002, figs. 7, 928, 32; Boardman 2000, fig. 3.27a. In the reliefs on the Harpy Tomb at Xanthos, a youthful winged figure carries the deceased to another world (Rudolph 2003, pls. 30–2), and a similar figure, carrying the lotus, appears above the departing warrior in the Kızılbel tomb (Mellink 1998, 59). See also Parrot 1961, 227, fig. 282; pl. XV (Til Barsib).

94. Özgen and Öztürk 1996, 43 (Aktepe), 72 no. 8; Rudolph 2003, pl. 1 (Harpy Tomb, Xanthos); Mellink 1998, 59 (Kızılbel); Parrot 1961, 101, fig. 110; pl. XV (Til Barsib).

95. Women traditionally sat on klinai rather than reclined, as one sees here and in the Daskyleion reliefs, but men were always represented in a reclining position.

96. Incorrectly identified as a plate of food in Sevinç 1996.

97. All of the figures in the two Trojan scenes (sides A and B) also have bare feet. A few of the women on side B wear shoes with a slightly curling tip, including the enthroned women (no. 20), several of her attendants (nos. 17, 19, 31, 32), and the aulos player (no. 23).

98. Polat 2007, figs. 1–2.

99. Brueckner 1907, 92–4, Abb. 5; Reinsberg 2001, 89. Sharing a kline in the context of wedding preparation was, however, very uncommon. This is the only example of such a sharing that I can find.

100. Stewart 1990, fig. 192; Ghirshman 1964, figs. 257, 259, 443, 444.

101. Similar disk-shaped earrings are worn in the tomb paintings at Aktepe: Özgen and Öztürk 1996, 45, fig. 83. The best discussion of the ear-cap earrings is Castor 1999, 68.

102. This is true for only two women in the gift presentation scenes: the enthroned woman on side C and the central seated woman on side D. It is conceivable that they represent the same person.

103. Mellink 1980, 97–8, figs. 3, 5, 6; Bingöl 1997, 38, figs. 24, 25. Castor (1999, 68) has suggested that these were made of a perishable material, such as leather or cloth. I thank Felix Pirson for calling my attention to these.

104. On Clazomenaean sarcophagi one also finds a notable absence of symposium scenes: Cook 1981, 131.

105. Ghirshman 1964, figs. 257–9, 443, 444; Tritsch 1942, 44–50; Mellink 1971, 254; Rudolph 2003, 31–3.

106. Rudolph 2003, pl. 1; Berger 1970, 129–42; Draycott 2008. Similar gift presentation iconography appears in the tomb paintings at Harta, Lydia: Özgen and Öztürk 1996, 46.

107. Polat 2007.

108. Pyrrhic dancers also appear in the ekphora represented on the painted wooden beams assigned to the Tartarlı tomb by Latife Summerer (cf. Özgen and Öztürk 1996, 45, fig. 84; Bingöl 1997, 39, fig. 27; Summerer 2010, fig. 2), and more such scenes will probably appear in time. The fact that so much of the iconography is unique is not really surprising: regional variation in Graeco-Persian art was strong, and the imagery in Lycian tombs was equally idiosyncratic, cf. Mellink 1971, 248.

109. Reinsberg 2001, 79–89; followed, in general, by Ateşlier and Öncü 2004; Weber-Lehmann 2005.

110. Oakley and Sinos 1993.

111. Kurtz and Boardman 1971, 77, 149, 215.

112. Lesky 2000, 85–123.

113. Bonfante 1989. Reinsberg (2001, 90) links the Pyrrhic dancers to a regional cult of Artemis, although that cult had no significance in this area until the Roman period: Hasluck 1910, 232–3.

114. Judging by the inscription on one of the Daskyleion reliefs, it looks as if they were made for non-elite patrons: Sekunda 1988; 192, no. 13; Nollé 1992, 19–22, no. S3, 119.

Differences in contemporary tomb types in Lycia have been viewed as an index of social position: Keen 1995.

115. The inclusion of myth and the focus on the moment of death are also included in Etruscan funerary monuments, as are musicians in tomb decoration, although very few are female: Messerschmidt 1930; Holliday 1993; Jannot 1984, figs. 116, 174.

116. Mellink 1998, 36, 38, 54–8.

117. Boardman 2007, 127; Neer 2012b, 211.

118. For contacts between Daskyleion and Lydia in the Late Archaic period, see Gürtekin-Demir 2003, 204–14.

119. Dentzer 1982; Borchhardt 1990 (e.g., the Nereid Monument at Xanthos, the Heroon at Trysa, and the Alexander Sarcophagus). The same is true for the painted sarcophagus from Çan, not far from Kızöldün, which was unquestionably the tomb of a male: Sevinç et al. 2001. For the epitaphs, see Bryce 1986, esp. 94–6 (early fourth century B.C.).

120. Fleischer 1983, 304. The dogs were greyhounds.

121. Laroche 1974, 134, no. 8; 135–6, no. 9. See also Schmidt-Dounas 1985, 144; Stewart 1993, 297.

122. Young 1981, 7.

123. Tomris Bakır has proposed that the sarcophagus was occupied by Hymaies, the son-in-law of Darius, who died somewhere in the Troad in 497 B.C: Ateşlier and Öncü 2004, 74; Herodotus 5.122; Balcer 1995, 183–4.

124. Judging by the elaborately painted tombs at Dedetepe and Çan (Plates 15, 16, 19–24), it seems clear that these sarcophagi were generally painted. Certainly, paint would have been planned for the rendering of ropes around the hands of Polyxena. One can exclude the possibility that the paint had gradually deteriorated, since the protective pan tiles placed around the reliefs at the time of burial were not removed until the Çanakkale Museum excavations in 1994.

125. Examples include the tombs of Kızılbel and Karaburun, the Daskyleion reliefs, and the tower-tombs of Limyra and Xanthos. The same tradition can be found in Lycian epitaphs of Late Classical date: Bryce 1986.

126. Rudolph 2003 (Harpy Tomb, Xanthos); Mellink 1973a, 299–301 (Karaburun).

127. Steuernagel 1998, 176) regards the seated woman on side C as a portrait of the deceased, as do Lesky (2000, 230), Reinsberg (2001, 89–92), and Weber-Lehmann (2005, 445).

128. Mellink 1973a, 299–301; 1998, 59–62.

129. The same type of object is well represented in the tombs of Lydia, and has been catalogued in Özgen and Öztürk 1996. Wine strainer: 109, no. 64; alabastra: 131, no. 86; pitchers: 78–81, nos. 16–22; pyxis: 132, no. 87.

130. Eggs: Kurtz and Boardman 1971, 77, 149, 215; Petrakos 1996, 22–4 (eggshells in the *soros* at Marathon). Eggs were also offered to the deceased on the Daskyleion reliefs (Nollé 1992, Taf. 3, 4) and on Archaic funerary reliefs from Sparta: Stibbe 1991, figs. 5, 7. Musical instruments: Sevinç et al. 1998, 314, 315, 320; Strauss 1994; Duyuran 1960 (Dardanos). Stringed instruments appear as well in scenes on white-ground lekythoi: Bundrick 2005, 66–71, 98–99.

131. Ceccarelli 1998, 53–7; Lesky 2000, 233; Bundrick 2005, 78–80, 89–90; Cook 1981, 33, Cat. G1, pl. 46 (Clazomenaean sarcophagus). Pyrrhic dancers also appear in the painted tomb from Tartarlı (Bingöl 1997, 39, fig. 27; Summerer 2010, 122–6.

132. Troilus at Kızılbel or on Clazomenaean sarcophagi: Mellink 1998, 58; Kaineus on Lycian sarcophagi: Schmidt-Dounas 1985, pls. 18–19.

133. Images of Lycian heroes were incorporated into the decoration of the tombs at Kızılbel, Trysa, Tlos, and Limyra: Mellink 1998, 53–4, 58; Borchhardt 1976, 82; 1993, 48; Childs 1978, 98–106.

134. Schmidt-Dounas 1985, 92–3.

135. Childs 1978, 13–14, 99–106; Ridgway 1997, 88–94.

136. Hitzl 1991, 62–5; Flourentzos 2007, 16–18.

137. Flourentzos 2007. For the Pasquino Group, see Ridgway 2002, 79–80.

138. Drapery: Stewart 1990, fig. 241 (Aegina pediment). Snail curls: Boardman 1978, fig. 145 (Aristodikos, ca. 510–500 B.C.), fig. 242 (kouros base from Athens, ca. 510 B.C.); Richter 1960, no. 134, fig. 377.

139. Boardman 1978, 242 (kouros base from Athens); Richter 1960, no. 134, fig. 377. See also Langlotz 1975, Taf. 52.10 (stele from Dikaia), and Steuernagel 1998, 166–7. On Archaic hairstyles in general, see Ridgway 1993, 77–9.

140. Mellink 1998, 47.

141. Langlotz 1975, Taf. 2.15, 3.7, 8 (Phocaean coinage); 108, 116–17, Taf. 33.4–6 (sphinx from Biga); Mellink 1980 (Painted House at Gordion).

142. H. Hiller 1975, Cat. No. O14, Taf. 9; Mellink 1980, 97, fig. 3 (Gordion); Özgen and Öztürk

1996, 43, fig. 79; 72, no. 8 (Aktepe, Lydia); Mellink 1998, pls. 11, 28 (Kızılbel, Lycia); Shapiro 1991, 630, fig. 1; 638, fig. 11; Huber 2001, 99, Abb. 7; 104, Abb. 8. They are not a feature of the funerary reliefs from Daskyleion: Nollé 1992.

143. This applies to the two sarcophagi in the Kızöldün tumulus (ca. 500 and 450 B.C.), the Dedetepe klinai and tomb chamber, and the Çan sarcophagus (400–375 B.C.). For its use, in general, see Zöldföldi and Satır 2003.

144. Özgen and Öztürk 1996, 23; Delemen 2006.

145. Asgari 1978; Asgari and Drew-Bear 2002; Vitruvius 2.8.10.

146. Vitruvius 10.2.15.

147. Walker 1985, 58–9. Both Vitruvius and Pliny comment on its use for the wall revetment of Mausolus' residence at Halicarnassus, and isotopic analysis indicates its extensive employment by the Hellenistic architects of Pergamon: Vitruvius 2.8.10; Pliny *NH* 36.6. For Pergamon, see Cramer et al. 2002.

148. Herodotus 4.137; Danoff 1974; Ateşlier 2001 (Daskyleion).

149. Ateşlier and Öncü 2004, 71–2.

150. Pausanias 8.46.4; Strabo 13.1.16. Some of the Late Archaic reliefs from Cyzicus would undoubtedly register as Proconnesian if they were tested.

151. For Late Archaic sculpture from the area of Cyzicus, see Langlotz 1975, 108, 116–17, Taf. 33.4–6 (sphinx); Akurgal 1961, 238, fig. 207 (charioteer relief); Akurgal 1965 (relief drum).

152. Istanbul Archaeological Museum Inv. no. 2813 T: Akurgal 1961, 238, fig. 207; Laviosa 1972–3, 413, fig. 17. There are two drill holes: one at the end of the mane knot; the other between the left and right arms of the charioteer.

153. Balcer 1984, 195–226.

154. Balcer 1972; Strabo 1.13.22.

155. Herodotus 6.31–2.

FOUR. THE TOMBS OF THE GRANICUS RIVER VALLEY II: THE CHILD'S SARCOPHAGUS

1. Sevinç 1996; Sevinç et al. 1998, 323; 1999; 2001, 402; Rose et al. 2007, 78–81, 120. For references to the second sarcophagus, see Sevinç 1996, 251, 253, fig. 3; Özgen and Öztürk 1996, 56–7, figs. 125, 126.

2. Even though the two sarcophagi lay at such different depths beneath the surface, in terms of absolute height, the Child's Sarcophagus was only 0.80 m above the Polyxena Sarcophagus, since the former was set into the sloping side of the tumulus.

3. For sarcophagi set in the floor of chamber tombs, see Özgen and Öztürk 1996, 53 (Basmacı); Kasper 1970 (Balıkesir). The tumuli that do cover sarcophagi tend to be quite low, e.g., Cook 1974 (Smyrna).

4. It measures 2.25 m in length and 0.88 m in width, with a total height of 1.07 m.

5. Similar examples occur at Halicarnassus (the "Carian Princess"): Özet 1994, Prag and Neave 1994; Chios: Kontoleon 1952, 525, fig. 7; Samos: Boehlau 1898, 14–15; Assos: Serdaroğlu 1995, 45; Sardis: Greenewalt et al. 1994, 35; Olynthos: Robinson 1942, 112–13 no. 577, 115 no. 595, and 158. The sarcophagi from Neandria (Koldewey 1891, 16), Topcatepe, Yuvarlankaya, and Basmacı (Özgen and Öztürk 1996, 29) also contain a simple surface finish. Only those from the first three sites are marble. On Archaic stone sarcophagi from the eastern Mediterranean, see, in general, Kurtz and Boardman 1971, 267–8; Philipp 1981, 150, 154; Schilardi 1984; Hitzl 1991, 24–41.

6. Stuart-Macadam 1992; Larsen 1997, 29–40. Cribra orbitalia was much rarer in the Archaic and Classical periods than it had been during the Bronze Age: Angel 1972, 100; 1978, 12. All of the bones were analyzed by Prof. Dr. Berna Alpagut of Ankara University.

7. Wolska and Wolski 1996; Wolska 2006.

8. Ladle: Mus. inv. no. 7672. H: 0.202; Dia. of bowl: 0.044; H of bowl: 0.015; L of calf's head: 0.012 m. Phiale: Mus. inv. no. 7673. D: 0.069; H: 0.009 m. A silver phiale of fifth century B.C. date was also discovered in the Dardanus tumulus: Sevinç and Treister 2003, 229.

9. For phiale comparanda, see Özgen and Öztürk 1996, 103–4, nos. 55–8; Waldbaum 1983, 145–6, nos. 968, 969; Von Bothmer 1984, 39, nos. 54, 56. For similar ladles, most of which have a height of ca. 0.20 m, see Pottier 1887; Strong 1966, 91–2; Waldbaum 1983, 24–32; Özgen and Öztürk 1996, 83–6, nos. 24–32; Oliver 1977, nos. 13, 15, 16; Von Bothmer 1984, 41, nos. 60, 61. Such ladles were occasionally found with strainers: Crosby 1943. Banquet iconography drawn from Greek sympotic imagery is standard in Asia Minor tomb decoration of the Archaic and Classical periods: Dentzer 1982; Mellink 1998; Delemen 2004.

10. A ladle and phiale were found together in the Dardanus tumulus (Duyuran 1960, 11), and a ladle and spouted dish were discovered in a tomb at Sardis (Waldbaum 1983, 146–7, nos. 965, 966; Özgen and Öztürk 1996, 105, no. 59). In a second tomb at Sardis, a phiale may have been positioned in the right hand of the skeleton: Greenewalt et al. 1994, 37. Tumulus D at Bayındır in Lycia yielded two ladles together with four omphalos bowls: Özgen and Özgen 1988, 188–9, nos. 34–9.

11. Below each of the lugs is a raised area of trapezoidal shape. The same trapezoidal projections below lugs appear on the alabastra from Dedetepe (Sevinç et al. 1998, 319, 320, no. 19) and from Kızılbel (Mellink 1998, 4 and pl. Vc, d), among others.

12. Sevinç et al. 1998, 318–20, nos. 14–19. For the examples from the Polyxena Sarcophagus: Sevinç 1996, 259, fig. 12, 13; Sevinç et al. 1998, 315, fig. 15. For the Dardanus tumulus examples: Duyuran 1960, 12; Kızılbel tomb: Mellink 1998, 4; Karaburun tomb: Dentzer 1982, 228; Sardis: Greenewalt et al. 1994, 35; Daskyleion relief: Dentzer 1982, 227, 284–5; Nollé 1992, 115; Thasos relief: Dentzer 1982, 256, 321; Ikiztepe tomb: Özgen and Öztürk 1996, 51, 121–4 nos. 75–8, 131 no. 86. In the Ikiztepe tomb there were at least fourteen intact alabastra, four of silver and ten of alabaster.

13. Two ovoid flasks with a height of 0.21 m were also found within the sarcophagus. These are often discovered in graves dating to the later sixth and fifth centuries B.C.: Cook and Dupont 1998, 134; Boehlau 1898, 147–8, pl. VII.5; Sparkes and Talcott 1970, pl. 39 no. 1161.

14. H: 0.069 m. For other tomb gifts on which traces of textiles are preserved, see Özgen and Öztürk 1996, nos. 38 (silver phiale), 223 (bronze jug), 225 (bronze bowl), and p. 53. The dress of the deceased was decorated with sewn gold appliqués at Lampsacus (Körpe and Treister 2002, 442–3, no. 7) and Dardanus (Sevinç and Treister 2003, 229, 239).

15. Grose 1989, 111–13, 151–2, nos. 119, 120; Harden 1981, 91 nos. 226, 227; Bischop 1993, 212–13 no. 2.

16. The samples were subjected to Fourier transform infrared microspectroscopy (FT-IR) and gas chromatography–mass spectrometry (GC-MS) analysis at the Williamstown Conservation Laboratory in Massachusetts.

17. Mus. inv. no. 8739. D of box: 0.085; W (with projections): 0.093; H: 0.024; L of lid: 0.094; pres. W. of lid: 0.035 m.

18. Ephesus: Hogarth 1908, pl. XLI nos. 18–20, and p. 193; Erdemgil et al. 1989, 121. Lydia: Özgen and Öztürk 1996, no. 87. Bayındır, Lycia: Özgen and Özgen 1988, 33, 48 fig. 58, 194 no. 58.

19. Museum inv. no.: 8738. H: 0.077; W of body: 0.032; Th: 0.03 m.

20. See, e.g., Boardman 1978, figs. 118 and 159; Richter 1968, figs. 578–82. For earrings on the Polyxena sarcophagus, see Sevinç 1996, 260, and Sevinç et al. 1998, 315 figs. 15, 16, 18. The stephane is fairly common for both dolls and protomes: see, e.g., Higgins 1954, nos. 856, 857, 913; Goldman and Jones 1942, 384, nos. 8–11 (terracottas from Halai).

21. For the hole on the head of dolls, see Higgins 1954, 248, pls. 132, 133, nos. 856, 909, 930.

22. For doll typology, see Elderkin 1930; Higgins 1954, 248ff., nos. 701, 721, 734; Schmidt 1977, 114–28; Rühfel 1984, figs. 72, 73, 100a. The terracotta protome of a peplophoros (late fifth century B.C.) was discovered in a tomb in the Kerameikos (Vierneisel-Schlörb 1964, 98, no. 4, pl. 55.2), but it is much larger than the one from Kızöldün.

23. Dolls as tomb gifts for children: Schmidt 1977, 124, no. 327 (Athens); Serdaroğlu 1995, 50; Stupperich 1992, 15; 1993, 21, 25; Mrogenda 1990, 42, 47–8, nos. 24, 25; 135 (Assos); Kurtz and Boardman 1971, 204 (Olynthos), 209. For dolls in southern Bulgarian tombs of children: Filow 1934, 90–1; for dolls on grave stelai, see Schmidt 1977, 121, 124–7. Children's tombs on Samos sometimes contained whistles and miniature terracotta wagons: Boehlau 1898, 21.

24. But mirrors were included in elite tombs in the region, at least during the late Classical and Early Hellenistic periods: Körpe and Treister 2002, 443–4, cat. no. 12 (sarcophagus at Lampsacus), Sevinç and Treister 2003, 232 (Dardanus tumulus); Bieg 2002, 456–63 (Kumkale).

25. Mus. inv. no. 7677; total L: 0.285; H of pendant with suspension bead: 0.030 m.

26. Brill-Cahill 1988.

27. Mus. inv. no. 7676. Full L: 0.29; Weight: 69 grams. Each link, except the center piece, has a length of 0.037, width of 0.018, and thickness of 0.002 m.

28. Mus. inv. nos. 7674 and 7675. D: 0.051; Th: 0.002; W of deer head: 0.004. Each of these weighs between 9.7 and 10.9 grams.

29. For the type, see Maxwell-Hyslop 1971, 246–51; Rehm 1992, 25–30, nos. A.63-A.84; Deppert-Lippitz 1998, 92–3. See also Öztürk 1998, 41.

30. A similar type was found in the fourth-century B.C. tomb of a noblewoman at Halicarnassus: Özet 1994, 91, fig. 5.

31. Mus. inv. nos. 7678, 7679, 7680, 7681. H: 0.029; W: 0.018; Th: 0.0115 m.

32. Özgen and Öztürk 1996, 164, nos. 113, 144; 214–17 (Lydian punches for boat-shaped earrings); Öztürk 1998, 43–5. For similar examples, see Muscarella 1974, no. 69; Naumann 1980, nos. 35, 36. For the type in general, with reference to the tombs at Assos, see Reiblich 1993, 1996.

33. For girls wearing earrings in Greek art, see, e.g., Rühfel 1984, figs. 51, 88, 100a.

34. Filow 1934, 39–58 (Kukuva Mogila), 82–97 (Mushavitza), 127–42 (Arabadzijskata Mogila). See also Boehlau 1898, 45–6, no. 45 (ten silver earrings in a tomb on Samos).

35. Filow 1934 (Thrace); Kohler 1980 (Gordion); Hanfmann 1983, 63 (Sardis); Özet 1994 (Halicarnassus); Özgen and Öztürk 1996, 128, nos. 82, 83; 207–10, nos. 178–82 (Lydia).

36. Maxwell-Hyslop 1971, 230, pls. 213–14 (7th–6th c.); Naumann 1980, no. 38 (late 6th–early 5th); Deppert-Lippitz 1985, 148–9, fig. 96 (500–450); Pierides 1971, 31, pl. XX, 5–6 (ca. 475–400); Silantyeva 1976, figs. 3–7; Williams and Ogden 1994, 152, no. 93 (ca. 400). In general, see Higgins 1980, 122.

37. Özgen and Öztürk 1996, nos. 108, 212; Öztürk 1998, 42–4. For the use of glass in jewelry, see Higgins 1980, 41–4.

38. Williams and Ogden 1994, nos. 71, 164, 179; Deppert-Lippitz 1985, 139, fig. 88, pl. 8; Kraay 1976, 303–4, pl. 64, nos. 1097–8; Treister 1996, 174; Griefenhagen 1975, 109, pl. 75, 1. A gold necklace, reportedly found on Cyprus and dating ca. 475–450, is decorated with double palmettes, spirals, and rosettes: Deppert-Lippitz 1985, 142 fig. 91, color plate IXb. For Achaemenid-style lions, see Ghirshman 1964, figs. 240, 265, 286, 303, 306; Amandry 1958, pl. 8.4.

39. For Archaic/Classical bracelets or armrings with lion head terminals, see Özgen and Öztürk 1996, p. 59, nos. 111, 130; Williams and Ogden 1994, 189; Deppert-Lippitz 1985, fig. 82; Rehm 1992, A.37, 40, 44, 46; Higgins 1980, pl. 30A.

40. Sevinç et al. 2001, 402.

41. For sarcophagi set in the floor of chamber tombs, see Özgen and Öztürk 1996, 53 (Basmacı); Kasper 1970 (Balıkesir). The tumuli that do cover sarcophagi tend to be quite low, e.g. Cook 1974 (Smyrna).

42. Mellink 1971, 250; 1975, 352–353 (460 B.C.).

43. Most museum objects associated with children's tombs lack an archaeological context, e.g., Neils and Oakley 2003, 303–4, nos. 118–20.

44. Houby-Nielsen 2000; Neils and Oakley 2003, 174–9; Wescoat 1989, 113–18, nos. 37–48; Vierneisel-Schlörb- 1964; Stroszeck 2002.

45. The skeletal remains do not allow identification of sex, but the tumulus included three bronze belts and a parasol fragment that would presumably have been included only in the tomb of a male: Young 1981, 17–20, 74–5.

46. Young 1981, 7.

47. All of the contents of the child's tomb (Tumulus P) are described in Young 1981, 1–77.

48. We can date that robbery to the early second century A.D., since a pitcher, cup, and lamp of Hadrianic date were found in the midst of the tiles.

49. Stupperich 1990, 1992, 1993, 1996, 2006; Wolska 1992, 2006; Wolska and Wolski 1996. For an overview of children's burials in mainland Greece, see Neils and Oakley 2003, 174–9.

FIVE. THE TOMBS OF THE GRANICUS RIVER VALLEY III: THE DEDETEPE TUMULUS

1. Sevinç et al. 1998; Rose et al. 2007, 78. For tomb chambers in Lydian tumuli, see Roosevelt 2009, 139–40.

2. By comparison, the diameter of the Kızöldün tumulus is 33 m, that of the Çan tumulus is 30 m, and that of Karaburun in Lycia is 35 m.

3. Sevinç et al. 1998.

4. Sevinç et al. 1998, 308.

5. Young 1981, 2, 196.

6. Each of the blocks measures 3.54 m in length and 0.83 m in width, with a thickness of 0.37 m. On the north and south sides, swallow-tail clamps, 0.28 m long, join the walls to the ceiling blocks. For the type, see Orlandos 1966, 102–4.

7. The threshold measures 0.22 m thick, 1.45 m long, and 1.10 m wide. There are three dowel holes at the right and two at the left, some of which still contained lead. The inset strip above the entrance measures 2.35 m in length and 0.35 m in height. For the Dardanus inscription, see Sevinç and Treister 2003, 216, 245 n. 8 (late sixth century B.C.).

8. Compare the construction of the Aktepe tumulus in Lydia: Özgen and Öztürk 1996, 40, fig. 71.

9. The following measurements are in square meters. In Lydia, Harta: 11.92; Ikiztepe: 11.36; Aktepe: 35.52; Alyattes: 17.95. In Lycia, Kızılbel: 6.86; Karaburun: 15.27. In Macedonia, most of the tombs measure ca. 3 × 3 m.: Delemen 2006, 254.

10. This does not apply to Ikiztepe 2, in Lydia, which has an interior measurement of 11.36 m² (Özgen and Öztürk 1996, 48–52). But one of the klinai was placed in the middle of the chamber, and it may not have been intended originally for two burials.

11. For the application of painting to marble in antiquity, see Brinkmann 1994, 31–3.

12. The same knobs appear in the Naip tomb at Tekirdağ, and at Aktepe in Lydia, among others: Delemen 2006, 256; Özgen and Öztürk 1996, 42, fig. 78.

13. The progression of colors from top to bottom is as follows: green, yellow, blue, yellow, red, blue, yellow, green, and red.

14. The same painted mortises occur on the kline from the Aktepe tomb: Özgen and Öztürk 1996, 42, fig. 78; 70, no. 6.

15. Wallert 1995; Stodulski et al. 1984.

16. Boardman 1990b, 126; Dentzer 1982, R64; Berger 1970, figs. 149, 154; Kyrieleis 1969, 168–77 and Tafel 19.2, 3; 20.2; 21.3; Richter 1966, figs. 109, 110, 312, 313, 316, 319–21, 441. See also Andronikos 1984, 34, fig. 13; Knigge 1976, 62, fig. 22 (Kerameikos); Delemen 2006, 258, fig. 6.

17. Özgen and Öztürk 1996, 42, 70 no. 6.

18. The outer diameter is 0.029 m.

19. For the same kind of construction, although without the iron projections, see Stucky 1985, pl. 9, fig. 23.

20. Amandry 1958, figs. 12, 28, 29; Stucky 1985, 30, pl. 10, figs. 33a and b, 34; pl. 12, fig. 7; Koch 1992, figs. 26, 182b; cf. Özgen and Öztürk 1996, 83 no. 24. Another ivory shaft found on the west kline was also attached to a piece of iron (Sevinç et al. 1998, 318–20, no. 16), and was probably a second knife handle.

21. Sevinç et al. 1998, 312, 320, no. 17. For double-lobed ears at Persepolis, see Terrence 1965, 24.

22. Duyuran 1960, pl. 14a. The pieces are catalogued from largest to smallest. A, H: 0.025, preserved diameter: 0.025; B, H: 0.025, preserved diameter 0.02; C, H: 0.027, preserved diameter: 0.015 m. For stringed instruments in Archaic and Classical Greek areas, see Paquette 1984, 86–203; Roberts 1981; Wegner 1963.

23. Similar bone pieces, almost certainly from an aulos, were found in a fourth-century B.C. sarcophagus at Lampsacus: Körpe and Treister 2002, 444–5, no. 15.

24. Sevinç et al. 1998, 322 (D. Strahan). The largest piece was 0.06 m long. The soles of leather shoes were recovered from the Dardanus tomb, although the lack of signs of stitching at Dedetepe would argue against such an identification: Duyuran 1960, 12; Sevinç and Treister 2003, 220.

25. Sevinç et al. 1998, 322. The conservation of the alabastra was carried out by Donna Strahan, who also directed the analysis.

26. Sevinç 1996, 259, fig. 13.

27. Kurtz 1975, pl. 64.3; Kurtz and Boardman 1971, 104–6, 123–4, 148; Oakley 1990, 42–3, pl. 110, no. 139, pl. 113, no. 141. Tyrian purple was also used in the elite tombs of Phrygia, especially during the eighth century B.C.: Young 1956; 1981, 9.

28. See Richter 1966, figs. 201–35; Dentzer 1982, figs. 318, 332, 638; Delemen 2006, 256–9; and, in general, Boardman 1990b, 127–9.

29. Dentzer 1982, R62, R64, R296, R342b, R486; Nollé 1992, Cat. S7, Taf. 10b; Richter 1966, figs. 50, 52, 63, 290, 316, 332, 616.

30. Baker 1966, fig. 209; Kyrieleis 1969, 35–41, and Tafel 9; Calmeyer 1996, pls. 72–5. The same kinds of legs appear in the reliefs from the Harpy Tomb in Xanthos: Berger 1970, fig. 148. For the dates of the Apadana and "Council Hall," see Root 1979, 90–5, 98–100. For increased Persian influence on the development of Greek furniture in the fourth century B.C., see Kyrieleis 1969, 141, 146–51; Bernard 1970. A few Persian-related finds have recently been unearthed in the Troad. An Achaemenid seal of the early fifth century B.C. was discovered in 1988 in Troy's Lower City (Miller-Collett and Root 1997), and an imitation Persian lead medallion of sixth-century B.C. date appeared in the excavations at Scepsis, in the southern part of the Troad (Körpe and Körpe 2001). It depicts a god on the back of a lion, in front of which stands a worshipper.

31. Compare also the alabastra from the Ikiztepe tomb: Özgen and Öztürk 1996, 131, no. 86.

32. For analysis of the bones, we thank Prof. Dr. Berna Alpagut of Ankara University. Compare the tomb at Dardanus, in operation

from the sixth century B.C. through the first or second century A.D., which contained forty-two skulls: Sevinç and Treister 2003, 220. Six skulls appeared in a recently excavated fourth-century B.C. sarcophagus at Lampsacus: Körpe and Treister 2002, 430–4.

33. E.g., Richter 1966, 363, 451, 454, 458, 603, 616.

34. Dardanus: Sevinç and Treister 2003, 219; Sardis: Ramage 1972, 11–15; Hanfmann 1983, 58.

35. Dinç 1993, 89; Roosevelt 2003, 186–7. For Lydian funerary ceremonies, see Roosevelt 2009, 176–82.

36. Billur Tekkök initially dated these skyphoi to different periods within the late sixth and early fifth century B.C. but is now inclined to date them to a single period: Sevinç et al. 1998, 317–18.

37. Petrakos 1996, 22–4. In the *soros* at Marathon, the vessels used during the funerary banquet had also been smashed intentionally at the end of the ceremony.

38. E.g., Nollé 1992, Taf. 3a; Dentzer 1982, fig. 620.

39. Roosevelt 2003, 173–4; McLauchlin 1985, 157–8.

40. Fleischer 1983, Tafel 36–9, 45, 46; Summerer 2010, 153.

41. This means that the elaborately decorated sarcophagi, such as that of Polyxena, would not have formed part of the ekphora, although they were probably ordered in advance and exhibited in the home until the time of death. The sleds that brought the stone sarcophagi to the tumulus were presumably reused, since they had not formed part of the ekphora.

42. Sevinç et al. 1998, 314–15, 320, nos. 20–1; Strauss 1994; Duyuran 1960.

43. Sevinç et al. 1998; Delemen 2006, 256–64.

44. Delemen 2006, 257–8.

45. Boyce 1975, 113–14, 325.

46. Measurement: 230 × 90 m; footprint: 15393.80 m; elevation: 6.5 m. For manor houses in Lydia, see Roosevelt 2009, 112–15.

47. Rose et al. 2007, 81–5, 119–20.

48. *Anabasis* 7.8.9ff.; 7.8.7f.; Rostovtzeff 1923, 371–4; Balcer 1984, 211–14.

49. Welles 1934, 89–104, nos. 18–20.

50. Sekunda 1988, 186–7; Wiegand, 1904, 274–85; Hasluck 1910, 106–7. See also, in general, Maffre 2006; 2007.

51. Xenophon *Hell.* 4.1.15–16; Bakır 2003, 3.

52. Cook 1961.

53. Berlin 2002, 141; Lawall 2002, 212–14.

SIX. THE TOMBS OF THE GRANICUS RIVER VALLEY IV: THE ÇAN SARCOPHAGUS

1. Lawall 2002, 212; Kaptan 2002, 2003.

2. Strauss 1987; Yavuz and Körpe 2006.

3. Xenophon *Hell.* 3.1.18–20; Leaf 1923, 104, 173.

4. Cook 1961, 9; Borchhardt 1976, 20; Demargne 1979, 295; Borchhardt 1980, 7; Childs 1981, 61 and n. 31; Bryce 1986, 99–114; Bruns-Özgan 1987, 34; Childs and Demargne 1989, 373, 380, 385, 394; Zahle 1991, 149, 152; Ridgway 1997, 78.

5. Sevinç et al. 2001; Rose 2006, 145–6; Bieg 2006; Ma 2008.

6. Kitov 1997, 36–43. Note that the tomb interior on page 37 is printed upside-down.

7. A similar juxtaposition of sandstone and andesite was used in the Late Archaic tomb at Ikiztepe in Lydia: Özgen and Öztürk 1996, 49.

8. For a detailed analysis of the dating, see Sevinç et al. 2001, 399–400.

9. The measurements were taken at the base. The height of the lid alone is 0.25 m. There is a similar ratio of length to width on the Satrap's Sarcophagus from Sidon (ca. 420 B.C.) and on the Child's Sarcophagus from Kızöldün (ca. 450 B.C.; here, Fig. 4.1). The Polyxena Sarcophagus (ca. 500–490 B.C.) and the fourth-century B.C. Sidonian sarcophagi have a length to width ratio of approximately 2:1. For the comparative measurements, see Kleeman 1958, 45; Sevinç 1996, 252; Sevinç et al. 1999, 490; Hitzl 1991, Beilage I-III.

10. There is nothing similar in Hitzl (1991) or Winter (1993). A comparable roof design appears on a Late Classical marble sarcophagus from Lampsacus, now in the courtyard of the Çanakkale Museum (Inv. no. 7497).

11. Sevinç 1996, 255.

12. For other examples in which boar and stag hunts have been combined, see Demargne 1974, pl. 32 (Payava Sarcophagus); Fleischer 1983, pls. 12, 13 (Mourning Women Sarcophagus); Nollé 1992, pl. 9, Cat. 57 (Çavusköy Stele); Tiverios 1997a, 272, fig. 4 (relief lekythos from Kertch); Mellink 1998, 32–4, 53 (Kızılbel). See also the comments of Mellink in Özgüç 1971, 92–3.

13. On boar hunts in general, see Kleeman 1958, 125–39; Hull 1964, 103–5. For other examples on fourth-century B.C. tombs, see Demargne 1974, pls. 34.3, 56; Zahle 1979, 328, no. 19; Fleischer 1983, pl. 12.2.

14. Xenophon (*On Hunting* 10.16) advises spearing a boar in the throat, but in the visual tradition they were usually speared between the eyes or on the forehead: Furtwängler 1900, pls. XI, 2, 3, XII, 10; Zwierlein-Diehl 1969, pl. 41 no. 187; Boardman 1970, nos. 885, 905, 924–6; Anderson 1985, 28.

15. Xenophon, *On Hunting* 10.6.

16. Xenophon, *Hellenica* 4.1.15, 33–6; Borchhardt 1968b, 166; Miller 1997, 124; Bakır 2003, 3.

17. For the fur-trimmed *kandys*, see Pollux 7.58; Mellink 1973a, pl. 46.9. Red shoes also appear at Karaburun (Mellink 1972, 267) and on a painted amphora from Kültepe (Özgüç 1971, 30–1, 92–3).

18. Zahle 1982, pl. 16.5, 7, 8, 11.

19. The same arrangement appears in the Persepolis reliefs: Schmidt 1953, pls. 37, 65c, 98, 100.

20. For similar examples in which the arm throwing the spear was held in front of the hunter, rather than behind him, see Furtwängler 1900, IX. 2, 3; Brandt 1968, pl. 30 no. 251; Zwierlein-Diehl 1969, pl. 41 no. 187; Boardman 1970, nos. 843, 886, 905, 925, 975.

21. The insertion of a separate metal spear would have been the easiest solution to the problem, but metal attachments were generally avoided in Graeco-Persian and Lycian sculpture: Ridgway 1997, 88, 130; 1990, 44–5.

22. For the topknot and tail decoration in Graeco-Persian art, see Schmidt 1953, pls. 37, 52; Metzger 1963, pl. 38.2; Borchhardt 1968b, 164–165 and pl. 43; Mellink 1972, 267; von Graeve 1970, pls. 31–3; Knauer 1990, 302–3; Nollé 1992, 58 and pl. 13a; Özgen and Öztürk 1996, 69 no. 4; Cohen 1997, pl. IVb; Bittner 1985, 226–37; Pfrommer 1998, 78–93. Decorated tails frequently appear on Graeco-Persian gems: Furtwängler 1900, pl. XI.2–3; Zwierlein-Diehl 1969, pl. 41, no. 187; Boardman 1970, nos. 831, 881, 924, 927.

23. See, e.g., Benndorf 1884, fig. 6 (Trysa); Demargne 1974, pl. 32 (Payava Sarcophagus); Fleischer 1983, pl. 13.2 (Mourning Women Sarcophagus); Nollé 1992, 55–7 (Daskyleion reliefs).

24. For saddle decoration, see Bittner 1985, 238–41; Knauer 1990, 282–3, 303–5; Nollé 1992, 59–60; Pfrommer 1998, 48–56.

25. For the Laconian breed of dogs, see Hull 1964, 31–3. A similar boar/dog format occurs in the painted frieze at Vergina (Andronikos 1984, 102–3), on the Mourning Women Sarcophagus (Fleischer 1983, pl. 14.2), and on Graeco-Persian gems (Boardman 1970, no. 897).

26. See Boardman 1970, 312. Boars in Late Archaic vase painting and gems could also be enormous: Schauenburg 1969, pls. 5, 7–9; Boardman 1968, 152, pls. 36, 37. Compare the much smaller boar on the roughly contemporary Lycian sarcophagus from Sidon (Schmidt-Dounas 1985, Tafel 11.1), although the boar on the small frieze of the Mourning Women Sarcophagus, painted red, is also quite large (Fleischer 1983, pl. 12.2).

27. Compare the long foreskin of the boar on the Lycian sarcophagus from Sidon: Schmidt-Dounas 1985, pl. 11.1.

28. A change in color to indicate a change in locale was probably also used on Hellenistic narrative friezes, such as the Telephos frieze at Pergamon: Ridgway 1999, 124.

29. This kind of hunting chest guard is difficult to parallel, but it seems to be represented on Graeco-Persian gems: Anderson 1985, 69, fig. 25a.

30. The earliest attempts at portraiture date to the Late Archaic period (Akurgal 1986, 9–14 [life-size marble portrait of local dynast or satrap]), and they occur sporadically during the fifth century B.C.: Cahn and Gerin 1988; Cahn and Mannsperger 1991; Metzler 1971, 143–4. See also Bruns-Özgan 1987, 86–7, 136 Cat. F22, pl. 26.1; Demargne 1974, pl. 44 (Payava Sarcophagus); and in general, Ridgway 1990, 110–11; 1997, 126–7. Most scholars would identify the individualized portraits on coins as local dynasts: Schwabacher 1968; Morkholm and Zahle 1976; Kraay 1976, 271–83; Robertson 1975, 506–7; Bodenstedt 1982; Zahle 1982; 1991.

31. An individualized portrait in Persian garb also appears in one of the reliefs of the Lycian Sarcophagus, which is roughly contemporary with Çan: Schmidt-Dounas 1985, 20, pl. 51.

32. Throughout Graeco-Persian art there is typically one animal per hunter: Akurgal 1941, 55 Abb. 7 (Isinda-Belenkli tomb); Demargne 1974, pl. 32 (Payava Sarcophagus); Boardman 1970, fig. 965.

33. Lycian inscriptions indicate that the construction of the tombs dates to the lifetime of the dynasts who paid for them: Laroche 1974, 134, no. 8; 135–6, no. 9; Stewart 1993, 297, 298.

34. Hipparchus, son of Charmos (480 B.C.): Lycurgus, *Contra Leocratem* 117–19; Philip V of Macedon (200 B.C.): Livy 31.44.4; Briscoe 1972, 151; Habicht 1970, 189–90 and n. 6; associates of Mithridates VI on Delos: Erciyas 2006, 140. For pre-Roman *damnationes* in general,

see Vittinghoff 1936, 18–19; Metzler 1971, 357; 1973, 14–20.

35. See, in particular, Nylander 1980 and Bahrani 1995 on the Near Eastern tradition. For Egyptian examples: Schulman 1969–70, 36–48; Dorman 1988, 141–64; Tyldesley 1996, 216–26 (Hatshepsut and Senenmut). Several figures in the Apadana reliefs at Persepolis were also defaced (Schmidt 1953, pls. 105, 136, 137, 140–1).

36. For the motif of rider and fallen foe in battle, see Borchhardt 1968a, 226 Abb. 39, 238 (Kadyanda); Mellink 1972, pl. 60, fig. 23 (Karaburun); Bruns-Özgan 1987, 182, 279–80, Cat. S12; Cohen 1997, 28–35.

37. Discussed together in Ridgway 1997, 3–9.

38. For leather as a material for corselets, see Miller 1993, 52–3. For wickerwork in shields, see von Graeve 1970, 100; Bittner 1985, 158; Eustathius *Comm.* 1924 (*Od.* c 184). Compare the arm pieces in Scythian armor of the fifth/fourth century B.C.: Reeder 1999, 112–13, no. 10.

39. Furtwängler 1900, pl. XI.9; Maximova 1928, 650 Abb. 2, 658 Abb. 15; Boardman 1970, 314, 326, and nos. 881–3. Flat-topped hats are worn by men in the Persepolis reliefs (Schmidt 1953, pl. 22, 27–30, 32), but in battle the headgear was usually a soft tiara made of cloth (Bittner 1985, 193–8, and pls. 20–32).

40. Schmidt 1957, 11, 16–17, 29–30, and plate 9 (Seal no. 30 [PT4 655]), dated to the sixteenth year of Xerxes' reign. The equestrian type per se does not appear in the monumental or minor arts of Persia; it developed in the western satrapies under influence from Greece: Farkas 1969.

41. Bittner 1985, 234, n. 1; Littauer and Karageorghis 1969; Kunze 1967, 184–95.

42. Rocky outcroppings appear frequently in votive reliefs, especially those dedicated to Pan (Carroll-Spillecke 1985, 56–63; Ridgway 1981, 134, no. 14; 1997, 108, n. 32). Rough terrain also appears in the battle scene on the Payava sarcophagus (Demargne 1974, 77–8, pl. 40), the Nereid monument at Xanthos (Childs and Demargne 1989, pl. 65.2; Ridgway 1997, 81), Trysa (Ridgway 1997, 92), and Boeotian stelai (Ridgway 1997, 170–1, 195). There are far better parallels in Macedonian tomb paintings, such as the landscape at Vergina: Andronikos 1984, 102–19; Ginouvès 1993, 161–4.

43. Compare the bleeding opponents in the paintings at Karaburun (Mellink 1972, 267), and on the Alexander Sarcophagus (Ridgway 1999, 122).

44. Krug 1968, 131–5. There was no attempt to make the Anatolian's skin darker than that of the Greek, although on the Alexander Sarcophagus the Persians were shown with darker skin: Ridgway 1999, 122.

45. For the *macheira*, see Snodgrass 1967, 97–8 and fig. 50; Best 1969, 7–8, fig. 5; Bittner 1985, 171–4 and pl. 12; Ensoli 1987, tav. XI.c.1; Litvinskij and Picikian 1995, 111–17, and fig. 10.

46. The mercenaries who fought with Cyrus carried the Greek *macheira* (Xenophon, *Anabasis* 1.8.6).

47. For mercenaries on the Alexander mosaic, see Hölscher 1973, 139–40; Stewart 1993, 137; Cohen 1997, 8; Pfrommer 1998, 105–6; on the tomb of Perikles at Limyra: Borchhardt 1976, 122; Ridgway 1997, 96.

48. Connolly 1981, 51–4; Ducrey 1986, 47–52.

49. Xenophon, *Cyropaedia* 1.2.9.

50. Borchhardt 1968b, 206–8; Pfuhl and Möbius 1977, 30–1, no. 73, and pl. 19; Nollé 1992, 27–30, 114–17, Cat. S7. Compare also the assistant with spear in the stag hunt from the Daskyleion area: Nollé 1992, 21–2, Cat. S3.

51. Cremer 1984, 91 and pl. 6C; Nollé 1992, 30–1, Cat. 58 and Taf. 11 (stele from Bursa); Boardman 1970, no. 844 (Graeco-Persian gem).

52. See *supra* n. 14 (boar speared in eye). There are two Graeco-Persian gems in which the spear is aimed toward the face of the opponent: Boardman 1970, nos. 881, 883. See also Xenophon, *Anabasis* 1.8.27, where a javelin was thrown under the eye of Cyrus.

53. The iconographic conjunction of the two scenes is reminiscent of Xenophon's statement (*Cyropaedia* 8.1.34ff.) that the hunt was viewed as training for war.

54. For the biographical tradition in Graeco-Persian monuments, see Kleeman 1958, 107–51, 156; Mellink 1972, 268; 1973a, 299, 301; 1973b, 158; Demargne 1974, 57–58, 69–71, 121; Childs 1978, 91–7, 102; Jacobs 1987, 59–64; Childs and Demargne 1989, 253–7; Nollé 1992, 128; Ridgway 1997, 81–4, 101–102; Mellink 1998, 51–3. For monuments in which battle and hunt are combined, see Akurgal 1941, 55 Abb 7; Deltour-Levie 1982, 171–4 (tomb of Isinda-Belenkli); Demargne 1974, pl. 32 (Payava Sarcophagus); Zahle 1979, 344 no. 69; Childs and Demargne 1989, 280 (Nereid monument, Xanthos); Mellink 1998, 22–6, 30–8 (Kızılbel). In general, see also Borchhardt 1976, 75; Bruns-Özgan 1987, 149–56; Messerschmidt 1989,

87–92; Nollé 1992, 1–2, 70–4, 76–9, 92–3; Ferron 1993, 185–97, 208–20; Jacobs 1987, 57–8. For epigraphic attestations of the decedent's skills in hunting and battle, see Bryce 1986, 94–6 (early fourth century B.C.).

55. For other such battles in Graeco-Persian art, see Mellink 1972, 268; 1973b, 158 (Karaburun); Bruns-Özgan 1987, 114–15; Ridgway 1997, 7–9 (Yalnızdam); Childs and Demargne 1989, 259–70 (Nereid monument, Xanthos). It is difficult to assign the names of dynasts to these tombs. The Payava Sarcophagus is inscribed, but the name of Perikles does not appear on his tomb at Limyra, nor that of Erbbina on the Nereid monument at Xanthos.

56. Aside from the Çan Sarcophagus, only one other battle relief has been found in the Daskyleion area, and no good photos of it have ever been published: Macridy 1913, 354, figs. 5, 6; Borchhardt 1968b, 169 n. 48, 205–6, no. 1; Sekunda 1988, 190 no. 5; Nollé 1992, 37–8 Cat. FV, pl. 15a and b. The relief seems to have disappeared.

57. For the location and history of Daskyleion, see Munro 1912; Cook 1983, 208–18; Sekunda 1988; Kaptan-Bayburtluoğlu 1990; Petit 1990, 181–6; Sekunda 1991; Zahle 1991; Briant 1996, 357–8, 518–19; Ruzicka 1997, 110–18. For recent excavations at the site, see Bakır 1995; Bakır-Akbaşoğlu and Polat 1998.

58. For a discussion of nobles and landholders in Persian satrapies, see Sekunda 1988; 1991; and Osborne 1975. Sekunda (1988, 183) estimates that there were 600 Persian noblemen in the satrapy of Hellespontine Phrygia. Bieg (2006) has argued that the cuirassed rider represents Spithridates, the hyparch of the satrap Pharnabazos, fighting a Mysian, while the hunting scene shows Pharnabazos himself with Spithridates and a member of the latter's family. Ma (2008) also identifies Mysians here.

59. Kiesewetter in Sevinç et al. 2001, 405–8.

60. Attic black- and red-figure vases with mythological scenes were popular at Daskyleion and the other estates in Hellespontine Phrygia: Görkay 1999; Tuna-Nörling 1997, 1999, 2001.

61. Ridgway 1999, 309. The format had already been used during the early fifth century in the tomb paintings of Lycian Karaburun: Mellink 1972, pl. 60, fig. 24; 1973a, pl. 45, fig. 8.

62. Malbran-Labat 1994.

63. Grape 1994, 104; Maguire 1994, 191–3, 197. An excellent Middle Byzantine comparandum for

the Çan Sarcophagus is provided by an ivory casket from Troyes, dated to the tenth/eleventh century A.D., where two armed, equestrian emperors flanking a city are paired with two hunters spearing a lion (Evans and Wixom 1997, 205, fig. 141). Although the poses of hunters and warriors are not identical, the link between the two subjects within the context of ruler exaltation is clear. I owe this reference to Henry Maguire.

64. Pausanias 8.46; Hasluck 1910, 169, 214–16; Meritt et al. 1950, 26.

65. Strahan in Sevinç et al. 2001, 404–5.

66. For the development of shading and its use in vase painting, see Brommer 1969; Robertson 1975, 411–12, 423–7; Bruno 1977, 23–30; Yalouris 1982, 263–4; Koch-Brinkmann 1999, 76–9, 96–8; Koch 2000, 137–53. For its appearance ca. 350–300 B.C., see Ginouvès 1993, 158–9, pl. 137 (Tomb of Eurydice, Vergina); Andronikos 1984, 97–119 ("Philip's Tomb," Vergina); Ridgway 1999, 116 (Lefkadia metopes); von Graeve 1970, Farbtafel II; Ridgway 1999, 122 (Alexander Sarcophagus); Cohen 1997, pl. I (Alexander mosaic); Vassiliev 1959, pls. 33–44 (Kazanlak); Sprenger and Bartoloni 1977, pl. 213 (Amazon Sarcophagus from Tarquinia).

67. Archibald 1998, 282–303.

68. Welles 1934, 89–104, nos. 18–20. See also the confiscation of land at Zeleia after the battle of Granicus: Corsaro 1984.

69. A lamp was also left behind by the looters of the Bozlartepe tumulus, near Dedetepe (Rose and Körpe 2007, 110) and by those who robbed the painted tomb at Karaburun in Lycia (Mellink 1971, 251). The foundation of a new colony could also spur looting: Carpenter and Bon 1936, 298; Strabo 8.6.23 (Corinth).

70. Rose et al. 2007, 104.

SEVEN. ILION, ATHENS, AND SIGEION DURING THE FIFTH AND FOURTH CENTURIES B.C.

1. Cook 1961; Berlin 2002, 141; Lawall 2002, 212–13.

2. Lawall 2002, 211–15; Cook 1961. A silver omphalos bowl and spoon were dedicated in the Dardanos tumulus during the mid-fifth century B.C., but such elite dedications were very much the exception in coastal cities of the Troad during the Classical period, even though they were common in the monumental tumuli

along the Granicus and Aesepus Rivers: Sevinç and Treister 2003, 239, 240, 243; Sevinç et al. 1999.

3. Herodotus 7.43; Georges 1994, 59–63; Erskine 2001, 84–5.

4. For the earthquake, see Wescoat 2012a, 100–24, 231–2, 239.

5. Herodotus 7.43; 8.115. These numbers rely on similar experiments that appear in a discussion of late Mycenaean feasting: Stocker and Davis 2002, 192, n. 60; Isaakidou et al. 2002, 91.

6. Herodotus 8.115.

7. Herodotus 7.42.

8. Herodotus 7.25.1, 33, 34, 36; 8.117; 9.114–15, 121; Arrian *Anabasis* 5.7.2; Hammond and Roseman 1996.

9. Herodotus 7.21.2.

10. Wescoat 2012a, 100–24, 231–2, 239.

11. Miller-Collett and Root 1997. A small figure in sketchy style has been cut on the side of the seal. This was initially identified as a bird but is more like a fish (Boardman 2000, 243, n. 19). It seems likely that the fish was added to the seal shortly after it was made, which may have occurred at Daskyleion judging by the seal's style.

12. Miller-Collett and Root 1997, 358–9.

13. Another object with Persian iconography, slightly later in date, has been found at Scepsis, at the base of the Ida Mountains in the center of the Troad. This is a lead medallion, ca. 530 B.C., featuring a goddess standing on a lion and facing a worshipper: Körpe and Körpe 2001.

14. Lawall 2002, 211–15.

15. Lawall 2002, 212.

16. Rose 2008, 418–19.

17. Meiggs 1972, 117; Whitehead 1993, 44; Berlin 2002, 140; Meritt 1936, 360–363. For Sigeion in general, see Schäfer 2008, 2011, 2012.

18. Thucydides 3.50.3; Strabo 13.1.39. The town's inclusion in the Athenian Tribute Lists of 425 and 422 under the "Aktaian" rubric indicates that it had once been a Mytilinean possession: Meritt et al. 1939, I, 157, col. 3, l. 132; III, 223–4.

19. Berlin 2002, 141.

20. Lawall 2002, 210; Berlin 2002, 141 (C519; C668). No coins of fifth- and early fourth-century B.C. date appear to have been found in earlier campaigns of excavation. The same pattern is visible in the Classical assemblages from the West Sanctuary, which will be published by Kathleen Lynch.

21. Rose 1999, 47; Frisch 1975, no. 24, l. 20; no. 25, l. 25; no. 51, l. 28; Miller 1978, 194, nos. 328–30. The Prytaneion is not mentioned in Ilion's inscriptions after the third century B.C., when the Bouleuterion was constructed. Frisch (1975, no. 53) restores "Prytaneion" in a second-century B.C. inscription, but the restoration is not certain, and I suspect that the new Bouleuterion may have put the Prytaneion out of use.

22. Hasluck 1910, 165–6; West and Meritt 1925; Bellinger 1961, 1–2; Ruschenbusch 1983; Tenger 1995. The "Didymateiche" in the Athenian Tribute Lists (Meritt et al. 1939, 481) is not the town of the same name on the Granicus River.

23. Aeschylus *Eum.* 397–402; Hall 1997, 55–6.

24. For Akamas: Vanschoonwinkel 1991, 306–8. The reports are based on the writings of Dionysus of Chalkis, a scholiast of Euripides' *Andromache*, who was active sometime in the fourth or second century B.C.: Erskine 2001, 107–8. The foundations included Scepsis, Chryse (Smintheion), and Daskyleion.

25. Castriota 1992, 102–9; Woodford 1993; Miller 1995, 450; Hall 1997, 46; Erskine 2001, 61–92; Rose 2002a.

26. Aeschylus *Suppliants* 548; Strabo 14.3.3; Schol. A Homer *Il.* 2.862 (=1.348.61 Erbse); *TGF* 3.364 and frg. 446 (Radt) = frg. 242 (Mette); Römer 1924, 93. Homer uses "Phrygian" only for the allies of the Trojans, e.g., *Iliad* 2.862, 3.184. See also Hall 1988; 1989, 132–3, 212–17; Miller 1995, 458–61, 464 n.e 48; Kossatz-Deissmann 1997, 94 (Troilus); Neils 1994 (Priam); Hampe 1981, 521–2 (Paris/Alexandros).

27. Pelops also sometimes wore the Phrygian cap, since he came from Western Asia (Triantis 1994, 287). Astyanax does not wear the Phrygian cap until the Roman period: Touchefeu 1984. The only appearance of Aeneas with a Phrygian cap during the Classical/Hellenistic period occurred on coins of Ainos: Calciani 1981a, 382, no. 5 (ca. 400–350 B.C.). See also Chapter 11, n. 7.

28. Pausanias 1.23.7–8; *IG* I.3, 895; Raubitschek 1949, 208–9, no. 176, 524; Hamdorf 1980; Higbie 1997, 291; Hurwit 1999, 198, 229. Two of the inscribed foundations of the horse were found in the Brauronian sanctuary, thereby pinpointing its original location. The dedicator of the horse was Charidemos, son of Euangelos, and the sculptor was Strongylion.

29. Pausanias refers to the men in two groups, which may mean that there were two windows,

one on each side, with two heroes in each window: Hamdorf 1980.

30. Walter 1962, Beilage 54.2; Froehner 1892, Taf. 2; Woodford 1993, 108, fig. 100; Stevens 1936, 460, fig. 14 (reconstruction). Walter (1962, 194) has proposed that the Acropolis bronze was the prototype for the horse depicted on the red-figure fragment of an Ilioupersis, now in Würzburg.

31. Pausanias 10.26.2; Hamdorf 1980, 234.

32. The adjacent statuary group of Phrixus on the ram (Pausanias 1.24.1) served as another visual reference to Asia Minor. It is worth noting that Poseidon's horse in the Parthenon's west pediment would have been within the same angle of vision as the upper section of the Brauronian horse.

33. The horse was set up at the end of the Archidamian War, when a treaty favorable to Athens had been concluded with Sparta. The construction would have been temporally flanked by the completion of the temple of Athena Nike and the carving of the Victories in the associated parapet reliefs (Hurwit 1999, 213–14). Although the superficial intent of the new horse was to highlight the alleged Athenian role in the victory at Troy, it may have been read by some as an expression of Athenian authority in Greece immediately following the first phase of the Peloponnesian War. The same significance applies to the colossal bronze horse at Delphi, dedicated ca. 414 B.C. by Argos after their battle with Sparta (Pausanias 10.9.12; Pouilloux and Roux 1963, 53–4, 60–6). Judging by the cuttings for the hoofs, the two horses were approximately the same size.

34. Pausanias 1.15.1; Castriota 1992, 96–133; Erskine 2001, 70–72.

35. Hurwit 1999, 75–6, 158–9, 194.

36. For the *arrhephoroi*, see also Pausanias 1.27.3; Deubner 1932, 9–17; Burkert 2001, 37–63; Hurwit 1999, 42–3, 199–200; Boulé 1987, 83–123; Simon 1983, 38–46. Pausanias mentions that there were two, while Harpocration indicates four: 1991, 45, A239.

37. For the subterranean passage, see Broneer 1933; Travlos 1971, 72–5, 228–32.

38. Xenophon *Hellenica* 1.1.4.

39. For their history, see Strabo 13.1.22; Leaf 1923, 116–33; Isaac 1986, 195–9.

40. Strauss 1987; Yavuz and Körpe 2006.

41. Xenophon *Hell.* 3.1.18–20.

42. Xenophon *Hell.* 3.4.12–14; 4.1.33. The battle scene on the Çan sarcophagus may relate to the

Spartan invasion of 396/5 B.C.: Sevinç et al. 2001, 401–2; Behrwald 2005.

43. Xenophon *Hell.* 3.4.3–4.

44. Weiskopf 1989, 26–58; Leaf 1923, 128–9; 295–6; Tenger 1999, 141.

45. Diodorus 15.90.3, 91; Xenophon, *Agesilaos* 2.26; Isocrates *Antidosis* 108, 111–12.

46. Demosthenes, *Against Aristocrates* 141, 202; Weiskopf 1989, 34–35; Buckler 1980, 256–257; Kallet 1983, 246. The name of Philiscus of Abydos, hyparch of Ariobarzanes, was inscribed on the base of the statue of Chabrias in the Athenian Agora: Burnett and Edmonson 1961.

47. Diodorus 17.17.6.

48. Demosthenes, *Against Aristocrates* 154.

49. Aeneas Tacticus: 24.5–8; Hunter and Handford 1927, 183–5.

50. Aylward and Wallrodt 2003.

51. Polyaenus 3.14. "Troy was captured a second time, again outgeneraled by a horse."

52. For the walls of both cities and their dating, see Schulz 2000.

53. Here I am indebted to the analysis of Andrea Berlin (2002).

54. Frisch 1975, 57–8, no. 23; *SIG*³ no. 188.

55. Leaf 1923, 129, 190; Tenger 1999, 141; Arrian 1.11; Moysey 1984.

56. Mannsperger 2006, 269; *BMC Troas* xxxiii–iv, 86–8; Berlin 2002, 142–3. The contemporary coins of Abydos, Assos, and Dardanus appear to have been the same size as those at Sigeion. For the Syracusan types, see Erhart 1978, 220–6. The three-quarter Athena type appears also on fourth-century B.C. Lycian coinage.

57. Berlin 2002, 137; Berlin and Lynch 2002.

58. Meyer 1989, A81; Canciani 1994, 555, no. 7; Lawton 1995, 18–19. The relief is in the Fitzwilliam Museum at Cambridge, Inv. GR 13.1865.

59. The sectors in question are D9, southwest of the Athenaion, and z-A, 6–8 (West Sanctuary).

60. Most, and possibly all of the lamps are Attic imports; approximately one-third of the fine tableware was imported from Athens, and the remainder is Atticizing: Berlin 2002; Berlin and Lynch 2002.

61. Fabiš 2002.

62. Kosmetatou 1993; Nobis 1976–7; Kadletz 1976, 170.

63. Wallrodt 2002.

64. Berlin 2002, 139, 140, 146. In the West Sanctuary, pale porous ware accounts for nearly half of the coarse ware that was uncovered in the Late

Archaic deposits, which is nearly 10 percent of the overall assemblage. I owe this analysis to Carolyn Aslan. Many fragments of these pale porous mortaria have been found in Rhoeteum, Tavolia (Aianteion?), Sigeion, Achilleion, and Ballı Dağ, to name only the sites around Troy: Bieg 2006, 35, Abb. 9.

65. Andrea Berlin (2002) has suggested that these were offerings rather than components of a table service, but Kathleen Lynch, who is publishing the Classical pottery from the West Sanctuary, noted that the ratio of drinking vessels to food receptacles to pale porous basins was 2:2:1, which suggests that the basins were used in dining.

66. One cannot exclude the possibility that the stamp seal with image of Ahuramazda (SLS 4; Miller-Collett and Root 1997) was initially an Achaemenid dedication to Athena Ilias.

67. The erection of honorific statues appears to be, in general, a post–Peloponnesian War phenomenon: Rhodes and Osborne 2003, 46.

68. For the Malousios inscription, see Frisch 1975, no.1; Robert 1966a, 19–23; Verkinderen 1987.

69. Sevinç et al. 2001, 394.

70. For a late Archaic predecessor of the Ariobarzanes statue, see Akurgal 1986, 9–14; for portraiture on coinage in the late fifth/early fourth century B.C., see Cahn and Gerin 1988; Cahn and Mannsperger 1991; Metzler 1971, 143–4; and in general, Ridgway 1990, 110–11; 1997, 126–7.

71. Crithote lay on the northern end of the Thracian Chersonese, near the juncture of the Hellespont and the Sea of Marmara. For its location, see Külzer 2008, 476.

72. Strabo 13.1.19, 13.1.57; Leaf 1923, 107, 296–7; Pavese 1961; Gaiser 1985.

73. McNicoll 1997, 182–190. Schulz (2000, 15–16) has identified six different phases.

74. Körpe 2004; Körpe and Treister 2002; Sevinç and Treister 2003, 229, 239, 244.

75. Budde and Nicholls 1964, 11–12, no. 27; Pfuhl and Möbius 1977, 34, no. 86; Dasen 2001, 77. For other fourth-century B.C. grave stelae from the Troad, see Pfuhl and Möbius 1977, no. 87 (Sigeion), no. 71 (Lampsacus); Schäfer 2008, 12, fig. 13a; 2012, 259, fig. 15.3 (Sigeion).

76. Herodotus 4.137, 6.33; Strabo 13.1.16; Pausanias 8.46.4; Leaf 1923, 89–91; Danoff 1974.

77. For the intaglio gift to Alexander, probably a quarzite stone from the nearby gold mines at Astyra, see Pliny NH 37.12; Theophrastus, De lapidis 32. For the mines, see Strabo 13.1.23; Leaf 1923, 133–5. The fullest account of the fourth-century B.C. road system in the Troad is Foss 1977. See also Bosworth 1980, 107–9.

78. Arrian 1.13–16; Plutarch *Alexander* 16; Diodorus 17.18–19; Hammond 1980, 76, 86. See also Polyaenus 4.3.16; Justin 11.6.2; Hammond 1980; Foss 1977; Badian 1977; Nikolitsis 1974; Rose et al. 2007, 73, 115–17.

79. Badian 1977, 290–1.

80. Arrian 1.11.5–8, 12.1; Strabo 13.1.26; Diodorus 17.18, 21; Plutarch *Alexander* 15; Erskine 2001, 105–6, 228–31; Hertel 2003, 238 44.

81. The word used by Plutarch is "stele," so the reference is not to a "phallos" or terminal stone situated at the summit. Strabo notes that the tumulus of Ajax featured a temple and statue of the hero (13.1.30), which suggests that the heroic tumuli around Ilion may have been more elaborately decorated than other tumuli in western Anatolia.

82. Arrian 1.11.7–8; Diodorus 17.17.6–7; 17.18.1; Plutarch *Alexander* 15.7. For an analysis of Alexander's actions at Ilion, see Cohen 1995, 484–6, 487–98.

83. Strabo 13.1.27; Plutarch *Alexander* 8.2, 26.1–2; Arrian 6.9.3. For the role of Homer in the Gallipoli campaign, see Vandiver 2010.

84. Arrian 1.11.8.

85. Strabo 13.1.26; Diodorus 18.4.5. Bellinger (1961, 3) notes that the institution or *revival* of the religious synedrion of Athena should date to 310 B.C., but Strabo's passage makes it clear that no synedrion had existed before the early Hellenistic period.

EIGHT. ILION IN THE EARLY HELLENISTIC PERIOD

1. Strabo 13.1.26; Leaf 1923, 141–4.

2. For the Hellespontine conference, see Welles 1934, 1–12, no. 1.

3. Leaf 1923, 233–40; Bellinger 1961, 78–151; Cook 1973, 198–204; Ricl 1997; Schwertheim and Wiegartz 1994; 1996; Schwertheim 1999; 2011.

4. Bellinger 1957; Frisch 1975, xi–xiv, nos. 1–18; Verkinderen 1987; Billows 1990, 218–20; Knoepfler 2010.

5. Cycladic League: Laidlaw 1933, 95–102, 134; Buraselis 1982, 41–3, 60–7; Billows 1990, 118, 220–25. Ionian League: Billows 1990, 217–20. In general, Tarn 1948, 231–2.

6. Bellinger 1957; 1961.

7. For a discussion of the statue, see Dörpfeld 1902, 510–14 (H. von Fritze); Lacroix 1949, 103–12; Bellinger 1961, 15; Frazer 1979, 38–40, n. 2; Demargne 1984, 963 no. 58 a; Barchiesi 1998; Erskine 2001, 117; Mannsperger and Mannsperger 2002, 1089–101. After the Augustan period an image of a helmeted Athena flanked by shield and spear began to appear on reverse types from the local mint, although the traditional version reappeared in the Antonine period. Von Fritze (Dörpfeld 1902, 511–13; Mannsperger and Mannsperger 2002, 1095) assumed that the changes were tied to the creation of a new cult statue, but divine images on coins changed frequently in antiquity as new styles and trends became dominant, and there is no reason to posit a corresponding change in the form of the cult statue. See Lacroix 1949, 108–9, citing the changes in the representation of the cult statue of Apollo Smintheus.

8. Apollodorus *Bibliotheca* 3.12.3; translated by Frazer 1979, 38–9. The only difference between this description and the numismatic image is the omission of the spindle in the left hand. This type of Athena Ilias also appeared on late Classical loom weights that appear to have been associated with weaving activities in the Sanctuary of Athena: Wallrodt 2002. The *infula* was a common decoration on cult statues throughout the Mediterranean: Vergil *Aeneid* 2.168 (Palladion in Rome); Lacroix 1949, 122–4 (cult statue of Athena at Assos), 130; Fleischer 1973, 108.

9. Fleischer 1973, 108, 388, and *passim*; Lacroix 1949, 107–11, 122–4; Lazzarini 1984; Mannsperger and Mannsperger 2002. One of the cult statues of Artemis in the Archaic Artemision at Ephesus had the same measurements as the Athenaion Palladion (ca. 1.5 m): Radner 2001, 236 fig. 3.

10. Head 1892, 155, no. 15, pl. XVII, 12 (Lebedos); 1901, 322, no. 153, pl. XLI, 9 (Thyatira); Lacroix 1949, 111–12. The cult statue of Athena at Erythrai held distaffs in both hands: Pausanias 7.5.9.

11. Strabo 13.1.41; Leaf 1923, 194–6; *Iliad* 6.92, 273; 9.455; *Odyssey* 6.305. For the standard iconography, see Demargne 1984, 965–9, 1019, nos. 67–117; Moret 1997.

12. Lippold 1949, 176–9; Lacroix 1949, 102–3; Krumme 1993 (Athens); Plutarch *Quaest. Gr.* 48 (Sparta); Pausanias 2.23.5 (Argos); Dionysius of Halicarnassus, *AntRom* 1.68–9;

2.66.5 (Rome); and in general, Lippold 1949. Nevertheless, the Roman coins of the nearby town of Dardanus featured the standard Palladion type (Rose 1993, 104–5), and on one Antonine issue from the mint of Ilion, the cult statue of Athena Ilias was shown holding a miniature version of the standard type (Bellinger 1961, 60, T198, 199).

13. Billows 1990, 217–20; Lohmann 2005. For the Demetrieia and Antigoneia, see *IG* 11.2.154A, l. 42; *IG* 11.4.1036; Tarn 1948, 395.

14. Kanephoroi: Frisch 1975, nos. 15–17; crowning of Athena: Frisch 1975, no. 32. See Shear 2001, 45–6, 130, 195. There is evidence for seventy-three inscriptions from Ilion's Sanctuary of Athena, most of which are either stelae or statue bases. They deal primarily with benefactors to the Sanctuary or the administration of the koinon: Rose 2003, 66–9.

15. Dörpfeld 1902, 514–16 (von Fritze); Bellinger 1961, 31 T80. On local coins of Imperial date a cow was shown hanging from a tree that faced the image of Athena, which probably suggests that there was some landscaping within the Sanctuary, at least during the second and third centuries A.D.: Bellinger 1961, 54 T166, 167; 60 T198, 199; 64–5 T219, 221; Wroth 1894, xxviii–xxix (there associated with Ilus).

16. See Shapiro 1992, 72–5, and Shear 2001, 365, for a description of *rhapsodes* in the Athenian Panathenaea. Aside from the vague reference to musical events in Frisch no. 10, we have no specific mention of the *rhapsodes*, but the basic elements of the Panathenaea in Athens seem to have been copied here, and since the site's identification with Homeric Troy was the main component of its identity, the recitation of the *Iliad* must have been a part of the festival. For the tragedies in the theater, see Frisch 1975, no. 2; for the athletic events: Frisch 1975, no. 10.

17. SS 79; Rose 2003, 61. For trumpeter comparanda, see Fless 1995, 89, 90, 106 Kat. 18, 111 Kat. 46 II.

18. Frisch 1975, no. 12; Robert 1940, 318. This event is mentioned on eastern gladiator stelae, but apparently it did not form part of the Athenian Panathenaea (Shear 2001).

19. For the market see Frisch 1975, no. 3; for souvenirs sold at the Athenian Panathenaea see Shear 2001, 432.

20. Lucan *Pharsalia* 9. 970–3; Strabo 13.1.11 (Ganymede/Memnon); 13.1.33 (Paris, Oenone).

21. For the month of Panathenaea, see Frisch 1975, no. 52, ll. 16–18. For an exhaustive treatment of the subject, see Shear 2001, especially 7–8.

22. Petzl and Schwertheim 2006; Jones 2007, 155, letter 2.1. I am grateful to Julia Shear for advice on the timing of the festivals.

23. For the Panathenaic festivals of Pergamon, Priene, and Sardis, see Hansen 1971, 7, 124, 448, 458; Carter 1983, 90–91; Welles 1934, no. 23 (Eumenes II).

24. For Lysimachus' attack on the city in 302, see Diodorus Siculus 20.107.2. The boats of Perseus of Macedon docked there in 168 B.C. (Livy 44.28.6), but there is no reference to the city. Strabo (13.1.39) says that Sigeon was destroyed by Ilion for insubordination at some point in the Hellenistic period. The recent excavations of Thomas Schäfer have been very limited in scope, but the latest pottery and coins are of fouth century B.C. date (Schäfer 2011; 2012). Reyhan Körpe, however, found Early Hellenistic pottery there during the Çanakkale Museum rescue excavations in 2001 (personal communication), and an inscription of Sigeion dating to ca. 300–250 B.C. shows that the city was still functioning then: Daux 1956; Robert 1966b, 177–8; Migeotte 1984, 261–2, no. 78.

25. Frisch 1975, no. 5.

26. As a comparison, those citizens of Ilion fined by the College of the Prytaneis had their names inscribed on a marble stele, together with the amount of their fines, and the stelae were probably set up in the agora: Frisch 1975, no. 65.

27. Leaf 1923, 80–5 (Parium), 92–7 (Lampsacus), 289–300 (Assos).

28. Berlin 1999, 146.

29. Carter 1983, 28. For the Panionion excavations, see Lohmann 2004; 2005; 2007.

30. Rose 1999, 46–7.

31. Kanephoroi: Frisch 1975, nos. 15–17; crowning of Athena: Frisch 1975, no. 32. See now Shear 2001, 45–6, 130, 195.

32. Rose 1991; 1992, 46–9; 1993, 105; Hertel 2003, 143–4; Sear 2006, 356–7.

33. The capacity was estimated at 9650 by Sear (2006, 356), and at 6,000 by Schliemann (1884, 211).

34. Bieber 1961, 127, 253.

35. The only stone from the theater that appears to be of Hellenistic date is a nearly square block with shield motif, into which a Lupercal has been carved (Rose 1991), but this was almost certainly brought into the theater from another

site during the second century A.D., as I argue in Chapter 11.

36. Frisch 1975, no. 2.

37. Robert 1966a, 19–23, 69; Frisch 1975, no. 1; Verkinderen 1987; Migeotte 1984, no. 79; Moretti 2010, 154, 160, 180–1.

38. What exactly the staters funded is unclear: the vast majority of the seats have been robbed, and bedrock is almost immediately below them. The water channel appears to be early Imperial, as does the stage building. The first skene was almost certainly wooden.

39. For valuable advice on this subject, I thank Andrew Meadows, Deputy Director of the American Numismatic Society.

40. Burford 1966, 296–300; 1969, 76, 82–3. The text is fragmentary, but Burford estimates the cost of the Epidaurus theater at more than 10 talents. If we use the following conversions (1 talent = 6,000 drachms; 1 stater = 20–24 drachms), then Ilion's theater would have cost between 29,000 and 34,800 drachms (20 × 1450/24 × 1450), which would indicate a number between 4.83 and 5.8 talents. The cost of the Delos theater, built in the mid-third century B.C., cannot be estimated: Fraisse and Moretti 2007, 235.

41. Frisch 1975, no. 1, ll. 14, 21, 30–4, 49–53. For honors to other benefactors of Ilion during the third century B.C., see Rigsby 1999 and 2004. The former inscription honored Agonippus of Dyme in Achaia, who was crowned annually in the theater. The second honored a woman of Cyzicus who appears to have donated money to the city.

42. Diodorus 20.46.2; *OGIS* I, nos. 5, 6; Scott 1928, 144; Simpson 1959, 402.

43. Morkholm 1991, 81.

44. Lund 1992, 121, 127; Landucci Gattimoni 1992, 238; Franco 1993, 127–30.

45. Grote 1872, 300 n. 2.

46. Leaf 1923, 142–3. The wording used by Strabo at the beginning of section 26 is: τὴν δὲ τῶν Ἰλιέων πόλιν. If the same formula had been employed by Strabo to describe Alexandria Troas, the line could have read "τῆς τῶν Ἀλεξανδρείων πόλεως" but not "τῆς πόλεως Ἀλεξανδρείας," which was Leaf's restoration. See also Rose 1997c, 98.

47. For a full presentation of the ceramic evidence, see Rose 1997c, 93–8; Tekkök 2000. The third major activity of Lysimachus mentioned by Strabo – the synoecism of towns – must also refer to Alexandria. Strabo identifies the towns that were synoecised in section 13.1.47, and they

are linked to Alexandria. Livy (38.39.10) notes that the cities around Ilion were not incorporated into her territory until the early second century B.C.

48. Brückner in Dörpfeld 1902, 581–2; Frisch 1975, 62–80, no. 25; Buraselis 1982, 95; Funck 1994; Koch 1996; Landucci Gattinoni 1997; Tenger 1999, 144–5.

49. For *damnatio memoriae* in the Greek and western Persian spheres, see Sevinç et al. 2001, 394–5; Lund 1992, 239 n. 72.

50. Alfred Bellinger (1961, 22, T32–5) proposed that there was additional evidence for this relationship in Ilion's coinage. He identified four issues featuring the deified Alexander/seated Athena as posthumous Lysimachus types struck by the Ilion mint between 228 and 190, and argued that a numismatic salute to Lysimachus over fifty years after his death does not conform to his image as a tyrant. On the latter score he is right, but there is no reason to attribute these coins to Ilion. All of the Hellenistic types of Athena struck at the site showed the Palladion cult statue, and the coins in question contain a seated type with no mention of Ilion in the legend. Moreover, none of these coins has ever been found at Ilion, and they should consequently be assigned to a different mint.

51. For Heraclea, see Burstein 1976, p. 87; Lund 1992, 75–7, 119–20, 188–9; Bittner 1998, 44–54; Memnon XIII, 9; *FgrHist* 434 F 5. The destruction deposit at Heraclea has been found: Hoepfner 1966, 10, 25. There were also revolts at Erythrai (Lund 1992, 84–5, 126–7; Welles 1934, 82–3). The anti-tyranny decree from Nisyros has wording very similar to the one from Ilion: *Syll.* 3, 1220 = *IG* 12.3, 387. In general, see Leaf 1923, 143–4.

52. Ricl 1997, 15–20.

53. For the honors, see Frisch 1975, no. 10, l. 3, and no. 31; Robert 1937, 172–84; Bellinger 1961, 4; Piejko 1991b. Despite Piejko's attempts to assign the inscription to Seleucus II, the arguments of Robert and Frisch remain the most convincing. In 281 cultic honors were also offered to Seleucus I on Lemnos immediately after the island recovered its freedom: Habicht 1970, 89–90. For the months, see Scott 1931, 202.

54. Rose 1993, 105.

55. Part of the late Bronze Age tower next to the South Gate remained visible during the

Hellenistic period, as did the stone stelae that flanked it: Korfmann 2003, 17.

56. Rose 1993, 108. The complex measures 12 × 7 m. The foundations of the seats consist of three courses, all limestone, each of which is 0.24 m high.

57. Dörpfeld 1894, 41; 1902, 132, fig. 43.

58. Frisch 1975, no. 32; Piejko (1991a, 41) regards this as a statue of Antiochus III.

59. Frisch 1975, nos. 38 and 62; Piejko 1991b, 122–6, no. 3; 127, no. 4.

60. Frisch 1975, no. 10, l. 3 (77 B.C.).

61. Plutarch *Demetrius* 12.2; Scott 1931, 201–2.

62. Diodorus 20.46.2; *OGIS* I, nos. 5, 6; Scott 1928, 144.

63. Newell 1941, 319–58; Seyrig 1958; Houghton 1978; 1983, 58–9, 65, no. 3; Morkholm 1991, 123–7.

64. Bellinger 1961, 17–20, T9–30. The first issue (Antiochus II) featured a small image of Athena Ilias next to Apollo on the reverse (Bellinger 1961, T9).

65. Newell 1941, 328–31; Morkholm 1991, 123.

66. Piejko 1991b, 133–6.

67. Robert 1937, 179.

68. Scott 1928, 153, 156. The Athenians of Lemnos dedicated temples to both Seleucus I and his son Antiochus I.

69. Frisch 1975, no. 52, l. 29; no. 104, l. 7.

70. For the Ilion tribe named "Attalis": *CIG* 3616; Frisch 1975, no. 121.

71. For the tribes of Ilion, see Frisch 1975, nos. 121–4; Rose 1993, 105; Cohen 1995, 153.

72. For the Athenian sanctuary of Zeus Polieus, see Hurwit 1999, 190–2. For a discussion of the archaeological evidence for the walled precinct at Ilion, see Rose 2003, 57–58; Hertel 2003, 111–12. Dörpfeld's (1902, 229–30) discovery of a large cache of terracotta horseman plaques in the vicinity of the precinct would also be in harmony with such an identification: it is likely that the plaques represent the Trojan hero Dardanus, who was a son of Zeus, as I argue in Chapter 9.

73. Compare the open-air precinct to the Pelopeion at Olympia, which had its own propylon: Scott 2010, 149, 154, 157, 187.

74. Dörpfeld 1902, 438; Bieber 1961, 180, figs. 776–8; Landwehr 1990, 107 no. G4, 112, 117, pl. 72; Tiverios 1997, 348 no. 264; Rose 2003, 58–9.

75. Frisch 1975, nos. 51, 52 (third/second century B.C.); Preuner 1926, 128–31. The Ilieia also featured gymnastic contests. A number of Asia

Minor sanctuaries had eponymous festivals that occurred every four years. The Great Didymeia, for example, involved music, oratory, dance, and athletic games: Magie 1950, 884–885, n. 83; 941, n. 37; Haussoullier 1902, 46–7.

76. Sevinç and Treister 2003, 243. The weight of most of the diadems is slightly more than one gram.

77. Körpe and Treister 2002; Körpe 2004. The Lampsacus tombs also yielded a gold ring with stamped bee decoration, a gold appliqué of Nike, and a bronze mirror.

78. Sevinç and Treister 2003, 244; Körpe and Treister 2002, 437, 445–6.

79. Strauss 1994; Körpe and Treister 2002, 444–5; Körpe 2004. The fragmentary musical instruments from Dedetepe are also relevant here: Sevinç et al. 1998, 314–15.

80. Also worthy of mention is a tomb in Kumkale that yielded a bronze mirror with relief decoration of Eros holding a cornucopia, dating to ca. 300 B.C.: Bieg 2002, 456–63. Further to the north, across the Sea of Marmara, was the monumental Naip tumulus with marble furniture and a silver sympotic set, ca. 320–300 B.C.: Delemen 2006.

81. Rizzo 1974, 83–8; Hansen 1971, 33–9; Capdetrey 2007, 295–7.

82. Houghton 1978; Boehringer 1993.

83. Ponti 1995; Williams-Thorpe 2008.

84. Strabo 13.1.39; Leaf 1923, 190.

85. The latest evidence from Sigeion appears to be a proxeny inscription dating to the first half of the third century B.C.: Daux 1956; Robert 1966b, 177–8; Gatti 1967; Migeotte 1984, 261–2, no. 78.

86. Aylward and Wallrodt 2003, 106; Jablonka 1995, 49. The earliest preserved walls in the Lower City, which lie in sector y28/29, date to ca. 260–240 B.C. (Berlin 1999, 77–9; Aylward 1999, 161–4). Several of the walls are parallel to the Bronze Age ditch; the others are oriented north-south. The grid appears to have been inaugurated only with the houses built after 225 B.C. (H2 occupation).

87. Rose 1999, 46–7; Aylward 2000, 122–3. The new building measured 16 m east-west and probably slightly more north-south.

88. Rose 2008, 409, n. 55.

89. Aylward and Wallrodt 2003, 97.

90. Aylward and Wallrodt 2003, 103–4.

91. For comparable examples, see McNicoll 1986, 309–13.

92. Jablonka 1996, 87; Korfmann 2001c, 32–6.

93. Rose 1997c, 96–7.

94. Strabo 13.1.26.

95. Livy 37.37.2.

96. Polybius 5.111.2f; Grote 1872, 300, n. 2; Walbank 1967, 633.

97. For the fortifications of Priene, see McNicoll 1997, 50.

98. Berlin 1999, 75–7; Aylward 1999, 166–9.

99. Jansen 1992; Becker et al. 1993; Becker and Jansen 1994; Jansen et al. 1998; Blindow et al. 2000; Korfmann 2004, 23, fig. 14.

100. Jablonka 1995, 49–61; 1996, 73–8; Rose forthcoming.

101. New terrace walls were also installed along the south side of the acropolis at this time: Rose 1999, 41–2.

102. Korfmann 1998b, 57–62; 1999a, 22–5; 2000, 32–7; 2001c, 36–40; 2002a, 20–3; Rose 1998, 102; 1999, 55–61; 2000, 61–5; Wolkersdorfer and Göbel 2004; Rose 1999, 60; Aylward and Wallrodt 2003, 94, fig. 5. This refers to the first post–Bronze Age use of the cave for water. The sinter from within the cave, when analyzed using the uranium/thorium method, yielded a mid-third-millennium date, which indicated that it had been in use already in the early Bronze Age: Frank et al. 2002.

103. Relation of the cave and City Wall: Rose 1999, 60; Korfmann 2001c, 32–3; Aylward and Wallrodt 2003, 100–1.

104. Forbes 1964, 156–63; Tölle-Kastenbein 1990, 39–42; Crouch 1993, 117; Briant 2001.

105. Bieg and Aslan 2006, 137–42.

106. The Athenaion would, however, have been dwarfed by the Ionic Temple of Apollo Smintheus, built ca. 150 B.C., which was nearly twice its size: Özgünel 2001; 2003; Hoepfner 1990. For the basic bibliography on the Athenaion, see Schliemann 1881, 608–9, 622–5; 1884, 198–210; Dörpfeld 1894, 67–81; 1902, 207–30, 429–36, 438–9, 442–3, 558–66, 576–82, 588–91; Leaf 1912, 115–44; 1923, 141–9; Blegen 1937b, 557–8; Goethert and Schleif 1962 (reviews: Scichilone 1962; Delvoye 1963; Tomlinson 1963; Scranton 1963; Gerkan 1963; Kähler 1964; Picard 1964); Holden 1964; Hoepfner 1969; Jucker 1969; Sussenbach 1971, 38–47; Knell 1973; Ridgway 1990, 150–4; Schmidt-Dounas 1991; Rose 1992, 45–6; Rumscheid 1994, 145–50; Webb 1996, 47–51; Rose 1997c, 93–8; Hoepfner 1997, 32, 48; Ridgway 2000, 117–18; Pohl 2002, 14–15, 17, 58, 204.

107. Hoepfner 1997, 48, 173 n. 88. The width of the temple, assuming a two-stepped stylobate, would have been 15.97 m. The two-stepped krepidoma is not per se a distinctly third-century feature, since it appears on the Late Archaic Temple of Athena at Assos (Clarke 1898, 58–68), but it does appear in third-century architecture at Pergamon, such as the Temple of Athena Polias and Temple R in the Gymnasium (Hoepfner 1997, 34, 47–8, 173 n. 88).

108. There is no reason to restore any half columns in the temple, as Goethert and Schleif (1962) have done (fig. 4D).

109. At least some of the roof tiles were also made of marble: Goethert and Schleif 1962, 18; Aylward 2005a, 155–6, 171, n. 141.

110. The conclusions regarding marble provenance are based on the studies of Dr. Judit Zöldföldi (Zöldföldi and Satır 2003).

111. The eastern boundaries of the Archaic/Classical terrace probably followed the line of the Troy VI fortification walls fairly closely, which would explain why the Troy VI wall in I/K6/7 was strengthened during the Archaic period: Dörpfeld 1902, 116; Rose 2003, 35–6.

112. The architects of the Sanctuary of Athena Polias at Pergamon adopted the same approach, leaving the west side of the Sanctuary open so that the panoramic view of the Caicus River valley was unobstructed. For this type of approach to sanctuary construction during the Hellenistic period, see Lehmann 1954.

113. Dörpfeld 1902, 218.

114. A bronze coin of Alexandria Troas found within the temple construction deposits dates to 281–261 B.C., which supports the dating proposed here: Bellinger 1961, 83, no. A28; Troy Excavation Notebooks/Inventory of Coins for 1937, no. 28.31. The discovery of the coin is described in the excavation notebook of J. Sperling, 1937, pp. 29 and 92 (dated April 21).

115. Rose 2003, 37–42. For an opposing view, attributing the temple to Lysimachus, see Hertel 2004, although he does not incorporate into his analysis the latest fieldwork and research on the temple.

116. Walbank et al. 1984, 430–2; Polybius 5.87.1–5; 111.1–7. There is no evidence that Achaeus seized Ilion or the cities of the Troad in 223: Ma 1999, 56, n. 13.

117. Hoepfner 1997, 32, 47–8. See also Tomlinson 1963.

118. For the gift of Attalus II, see Welles 1934, 253–5, no. 62. For the statue of Eumenes II, dedicated by his brother Attalus II, see Frisch 1975, no. 41; for the Ilion tribe named "Attalis," which marched in the Ilieia festival, see CIG 3616; Frisch 1975, no. 121 (still in existence in 69 A.D.); Kosmetatou 2001. See also Polybius 5.78.6, which deals with the bonds between Attalus I and the Hellespontine cities. For Attalid involvement in the Troad in general, see Tenger 1999, 149–159.

119. Gruen 1990, 31–2; McShane 1964, 111, 113; Magie 1950, 744–6, n. 35.

120. On the foreign policy of the Attalids, see in general McShane 1964, 60–1; Allen 1983, 34–5; Stewart 2005, 220–6.

121. Lehmann and Spittle 1982, 261; Ridgway 1990, 152–154; 2000, 104, 129–30 n. 4; Rumscheid 1994, 146; Webb 1996, 6, 21–2, 42, 48.

122. Schmidt-Dounas (1991, 391–2) identified it as a giant, and Goethert and Schleif (1962, 29) thought the same.

123. SS51; Rose 1997, 101; Rose 2003, 49, fig. 15; Ridgway 2000, 136–7 n. 48.

124. Schliemann 1884, 199–201; Dörpfeld 1902, 430–8; Goethert and Schleif 1962, 23, 26–31; Holden 1964, 19–23; Vian and Moore 1988, 206, no. 22; Ridgway 1990, 152–4; Webb 1996, 48–9.

125. Goethert and Schleif 1962, 26 no. 4, pl. 43 (Athena with biped giant); 27 no. 7, pl. 44; 27–8 no. 8, pl. 45a (anguiped giant); 27 no. 6, pl. 46 a, b; 29 no. 16, pl. 48c.

126. Schliemann 1884, 199, no. 108; Dörpfeld 1902, 433; Goethert and Schleif 1962, 26 no. 4; Schmidt-Dounas 1991, 379–82, 389.

127. But this is somewhat reminiscent of the battle scene on the Çan Sarcophagus, where the henchman of the rider grasps two spears in his left hand, and the shield is also attached to this arm: Sevinç et al. 2001, figs. 11, 16.

128. Schliemann 1884, 199, 202; Dörpfeld 1902, 430–1; Goethert and Schleif 1962, 24–5, no. 1; Holden 1964, 6–18; Jucker 1969; Ridgway 1990, 152–3; Yalouris 1990, 1031 no. 380; Schmidt-Dounas 1991, 372–9, 390–1; Webb 1996, 48–9; Knittlmayer and Heilmeyer 1998, 200–1, no. 119; Andreae 2001, 72–3, 18/19. For the Parthenon Helios, see Brommer 1967, 39–41 (Nord I).

129. Jucker 1969, 249–51.

130. Vergina larnax/gold disks: Andronikos 1984, figs. 136, 143, 144, 155; tetradrachms of

Demetrius Poliorcetes: Ginouvès 1993, 65, fig. 56; Lampsacus staters: Wroth 1894, 84, pl. XIX.14; Pergamene phialai: Bohn 1885, Taf. XXIX.3. The long and short rays of the Helios crown also appear in South Italian vase painting (Trendall and Cambitoglou 1982, 923, 924 Nr. 88 Taf. 359), on Achaean hemidrachms from the second half of the fourth century, and on a gold brooch of Hellenistic date in the Louvre (Yalouris 1990, 1021, no. 167; 1024, no. 247). There is an excellent discussion of the Helios metope in Schmidt-Dounas 1991, 372–8; Jucker 1969; and Ridgway 1990, 153.

131. Schmidt-Dounas 1991, 387–8.

132. *Iliad* XXI, 34–118; Rose 2003, 53.

133. Schmidt-Dounas 1991, 383–7; Holden 1964, 24–5.

134. Von Bothmer 1994, 698–700.

135. Goethert and Schleif 1962, 27–8 no. 8 (pl. 45a); 28 no. 9 (pl. 45b); 28 no. 10 (pl. 46 c, d); 29 no. 13 (pl. 47a); 29 no. 14 (pl. 47b); 30 no. 21 (pl. 47c); 29 no. 15 (pl. 47d); 30 no. 18 (pl. 48a); 29 no. 17 (pl. 48b); 30 no. 19 (pl. 48d); 30 no. 22 (pl. 49 c, d).

136. If the metopes on the fourth side had been uncarved, one would expect that a few smooth metopes with these dimensions would have been found at or near the site, and none has ever appeared.

137. The overwhelming influence of Attica is especially apparent in a fourth-century B.C. votive deposit in sector D9, southwest of the Athena Sanctuary: Berlin 2002; Berlin and Lynch 2002.

138. For Assos, see Serdaroğlu 1995, 82–90; Wescoat 1987; Wescoat 2012a. For the Doric temple of Athena at Scepsis: Xenophon *Hellenica* 3.1.21; Cook 1973, 345; *Antiquities of Ionia* V (1915) 32; for Gergis: Xenophon *Hellenica* 3.1.22–3; Cook 1973, 350. Since Sigeion was a colony of Athens, it is usually assumed that the temple was built in the Doric order, although there are no remains of it. Temples A and B in the West Sanctuary at Ilion were also Doric, although only a few fragments from the superstructure survive. For the early Hellenistic Doric temple at Alexandria Troas, see Pohl 1999.

139. See Berlin 2002 for an extensive commentary on the mutually advantageous links between Athens and Ilion. The Ilians were certainly not the only ones attempting to appropriate the glory of Classical Athens by repeating elements of the Acropolis building program: the

Erechtheion caryatids appeared on the heroon of Pericles at Limyra (Borchhardt 1970); the Athena Parthenos was copied for the library at Pergamon (Weber 1993); and Priene and Sardis established Panathenaic festivals (Hansen 1971, 7, 124, 448, 458; Welles 1934, no. 23 [Eumenes II]). But only at Ilion can the influence of the Parthenon be detected in the design of the primary temple.

140. Aylward 2005a, 162. The road appears to have been composed of flat and sloping sections, and was enlarged in the second century B.C.

141. Dörpfeld 1894, 76.

142. There are examples of wells situated within sanctuaries, but the only other potential example of a well placed between temple and altar occurs at Aphrodisisas (Theodorescu 1990, fig. 1), although the well in question is preserved within a Byzantine church. For wells in sanctuaries, see Koenigs 1991, 222 (Didyma); Crouch 1993, 146 (Corinth, Asklepieion), 179 (Pompeii, south of the Doric Temple); Hurwit 1999, 330 n. 79 (Athens, wells sunk into bedrock on north flank of acropolis). Dörpfeld (1902, 177, 228) assigned Well Ba to Troy VI but could offer no solid evidence for the dating, and he admitted that it could also belong to a later period. It is conceivable that the well was dug in the Late Bronze Age and monumentalized only in the third century B.C., but that would mean that the well was in operation for over 1000 years. The fact that the residents dug Well Bh to the north of the temenos suggests that Ba was not yet in operation at that time. All of the evidence points to a third-century origin for well Ba.

143. Dörpfeld 1902, 228. Most of the pieces of the well-head were found in the shaft, and although no sections of a roof were unearthed, there must have been a covering of some sort to keep the water clean.

144. Dörpfeld originally assumed that one part of the well was left open to facilitate access to the water, but there is evidence for vertical slabs on each of the base stones (Leaf 1912, 126–7), which means that the well-head completely blocked direct access to the water.

145. The ceiling would have been 1 m below the level of the temenos pavement. The only subterranean corridors in sanctuaries that I have been able to find are linked to divine epiphanies, e.g., the Asklepieion and the Sanctuary of the Egyptian Gods at Pergamon: Radt 1988, 228–39, 250–71, esp. 268–70.

146. The custom had ceased at the time of the Third Sacred War (356–346 B.C.) and was revived roughly a century later through the arbitration of a King Antigonus – almost certainly Antigonus Gonatus: Momigliano 1945, 53, no. 1; Huxley 1966b, 162, n. 41.7 (Aelian fr. 47).

147. Schliemann 1881, 665–9; Dörpfeld 1902, 545–7; Cook 1973, 173–4; Korfmann 1985, 167; 1986b, 309–10; 1989, 474–81; Hertel 2003, 161–3.

148. Sivritepe: Schliemann 1881, 665–9; Dörpfeld 1902, 545–7; Cook 1973, 173–4; Korfmann 1985, 167; 1986b, 309–10; 1989, 474–81; Bieg 2009, 242; Karaağaçtepe: Schliemann 1884, 254–62; Dörpfeld 1902, 547; Bieg 2009, 227–8; Hanaytepe: Schliemann 1881, 706–20; Dörpfeld 1902, 548; Cook 1973, 122–3; Bieg 2009, 215–16; Paşatepe: Schliemann 1881, 656–658; Cook 1973, 107–8; Bieg 2009, 244.

149. Rose 1999, 61–3; 2000, 65–6.

150. Erskine 2001, 49–50.

151. Fraser 1972, 447–9; Brink 1972; Erskine 2001, 50.

152. Pinkwart 1965.

153. Hestiaea: Strabo 13.1.36; Leaf 1923, 181–4; Cook 1973, 186–8; Ricl 1997, 19, T168. Demetrius of Scepsis: Strabo 13.1.33–4; Leaf 1923, xxvii–xxviii, 139, 141, 169–71; Erskine 2001, 106–7; Dueck et al. 2005, 140–1.

154. Apollodorus: Leaf 1923, 167. Hegesianax: Strabo 1.13.27; Leaf 1923, 103–4, 147; Ricl 1997, 19, T 167–8.

155. Xenophon *Anabasis* 7.8.9ff; 7.8.7f.; Rostovtzeff 1923, 371–374; Welles 1934, 89–104, nos. 18–20.

156. Lindos: Blinkenberg 1912, 73, 118, B70; 74–5, B83; Higbie 2001, 119–21; Pliny *NH* 33.81; Phaselis: Pausanias 3.3.8. Nicomedia: Pausanias 3.3.8. In general, see Scheer 1996; Erskine 2001, 112–26.

157. Pausanias 8.46.4; Hasluck 1910, 214–22; Lapatin 2001, 12. The statue had been seized from Proconnesus in the fourth century B.C.

158. Altar of Hermocreon: Strabo 10.5.7, 13.1.13; Leaf 1923, 84–5; Wroth 1892, 97–8, nos. 40–50.

159. Özgünel 2001; 2003; Hoepfner 1990; Webb 1996, 52–4.

160. For the type, see Rügler 1988.

161. Özgünel 2001, 378–9, figs. 114, 115 (Odysseus with tree); 2003, 274, figs. 22, 23 (Achilles and Patroclus).

162. Ricl 1997, nos. 52, 4–5; 53, 7; 54, 3–4; Frisch 1975, no. 125. The cult statue was allegedly by Scopas of Paros (Strabo 13.1.48), but the statue shown on the coins (Bellinger 1961, 81) is an Archaistic statue that in no way resembles Scopas' style. At the time in which Scopas lived, the cult of Apollo Smintheus appears to have been centered in the small Troad town of Hamaxitus, and it seems unlikely that they would have commissioned him to produce a cult statue. In general, see Lacroix 1949, 76–87.

NINE. THE WEST SANCTUARY DURING THE HELLENISTIC PERIOD

1. Excavations in the West Sanctuary began during the Blegen campaign, and constituted one of the primary areas of excavation between 1992 and 2002: Blegen et al. 1951, 295–8; 1958, 259–307; Rose 1993, 98–105; Korfmann 1994, 24–7; Rose 1994, 76–86; Korfmann 1995b, 19–24; Rose 1995, 82–97; Korfmann 1996, 33–9; Rose 1996, 97–101; Fabiš 1996, 217–27; Korfmann 1997b, 32–47; Rose 1997c, 76–92; Korfmann 1998b, 31–41; Rose 1998, 73–90; Korfmann 1999a, 15–16; Rose 1999, 49–52; Korfmann 2000, 21–8; Rose 2000, 54–8; Korfmann 2001c, 14–22; Korfmann 2002a, 13–19; Kiesewetter 2002; Korfmann 2003, 11–14; Becks et al. 2006a; Aslan 2011.

2. Rose 2003, 60–3.

3. Rose 1994, 83; 1995, 96–7; 1997c, 87–8; 1998, 77–9; Lawall 2003, 84–5. For the measurements of the Late Archaic temple, see Rose 1997c, 104, n. 4. The Early Hellenistic Building was probably the largest building that had been constructed at Ilion up to this point. The Early Hellenistic Bouleuterion measured 6.00 × 7.80 m.

4. Lawall 2003, 84. The wall painting was inventoried as WD71–4, 76.

5. Strabo 13.1.26; Rose 2003, 31–5.

6. It is conceivable that the altars in the Upper and Lower Sanctuaries were still in operation during this period, but there is insufficient evidence to support their continued use: Lawall 2003, 85–6.

7. Rose 1994, 78–9.

8. Double axe: IL31; sphinx: BR61. For the double axe on coins from Tenedos: Wroth 1894 pp. xlvi–xlvii, 91–4; for the sphinx: pp. xxix–xxx, 55.

9. Chapouthier 1935b, 81, fig. 104; 1935a, 111, 238; Hemberg 1950, 152 n. 6; 186, 204.

10. For weaving equipment in Asia Minor sanctuaries, see Simon 1986, 263–70.

11. Thompson 1963, 57–8, 77–84; Miller 1991, 45–6; Tekkök et al. 2001, 371–2. For enthroned statuettes of Cybele, see Simon 1997, nos. 26–54.

12. Dörpfeld 1902, 442–3; Thompson 1963, 56–7, 108–16; Miller 1991, 48–9; Barr 1996; Rose 1998, 88–9. The earliest plaques are nearly square, roughly 0.13 m on each side, although they subsequently become more rectangular, with a height usually ranging between 0.09 and 0.11, and a width between 0.11 and 0.13 m.

13. For a color illustration, see Barr 1996, 157, figs. 37 and 38. The colors of the rider at Corinth were similar: Davidson 1952, 110–13.

14. Thompson (1963, 116) suggested Hector. Tin foil had regularly been applied to the small votive plaques that were often discovered with those of the horseman (Aylward et al. 2011, 68–9), which featured quivers, thunderbolts, and Herakles knots, among other subjects. As such, the plaques would have acquired a silver appearance very different from the polychromatic terracottas that surrounded them.

15. Rose 1997c, 91–2; 1998, 91; 2000, 54–7. The new terrace wall was over 1 m thick.

16. Şahin 1981, 92–3, no. 203 (under Marcus Aurelius).

17. Rose 1995, 94–5; Rose 1998, 85–6; Lawall 2003, 86–7.

18. WD 77–81, 91, 95–9.

19. I owe this suggestion to William Aylward.

20. Samothrace: Lehmann 1969, II, 73, fig. 384; Corinth: Bookidis and Stroud 1997, 201.

21. For earlier discussions of the horseman plaques, see *supra*, n. 12.

22. Rose 1998, 79–85. For a description of the installation, see Mattusch 1988, 229; Bol 1985, 118–35; Zimmer 1990, 83, 121, 123, 136–7, 211–13; Haynes 1992, 75–76.

23. Zimmer 1990, 74, 156–8; Haynes 1992, 75.

24. Blegen et al. 1958, 303–4.

25. Aylward and Wallrodt 2003.

26. The terrace was initially published as a second-century B.C. construction (Rose 1995, 95), but a re-examination of the pottery in and under the walls has shifted the date to the last quarter of the third century B.C.

27. Rose 1997c, 92; Lawall 2003, 89–90.

28. Such a Hellenistic grandstand is shown in Elizabeth Riorden's reconstruction of the second century B.C. West Sanctuary in Korfmann 2001e, 65, fig. 66.

29. Pergamon: Bohtz 1981, 36–8; Radt 1988, 207–8. Samothrace and Thebes: Lehmann and Spittle 1964, 138–9; Sear 2006, 408; Lykosoura: Sear 2006, 400. For ancient references to music and dance in the Samothracian sanctuary, see Lewis 1959, nos. 214–20; Cole 1989, 1576.

30. Lawall 2003, 87–9.

31. Rose 2003, 42–3.

32. Rose 1998, 86–7; 2000, 55–7. Marl was used above a course of very small limestone blocks in the foundations of Temple B, which is rather unusual at Ilion, although the small limestones were completely different from the large well-cut blocks that one finds in the terrace wall: Rose 1997c, 91, 106 n. 61.

33. Rose 1995, 93–4; 1997c, 89–91. The Lower Sanctuary's precinct wall, measuring 8.5 × 9.5 m, framed a space about half the size of the Upper Sanctuary. Only the marl foundations remain in place, but they have the same width as those of the Upper Sanctuary, which suggests that the two precincts were enclosed by walls of similar height. Blegen proposed an Early Hellenistic date for the Lower Sanctuary temenos wall, thereby making it contemporary with that of the Upper Sanctuary, but the latest pottery in the foundation trenches dates to the middle of the second century B.C.

34. Blegen et al. 1958, 306. The length of the Archaic altar (B) was 1.77 m; the length of the second-century altar (C) was 3.13 m. Both had the same width (1.25 m).

35. The same situation prevailed in sector z6/7 in the northern part of the Sanctuary, wherein the corner of the Early Hellenistic Building was planned so that it abutted the Late Archaic altar.

36. This summary has been derived from Fabiš 1996.

37. *Contra* Rose 1997c, 91.

38. Rose 1993, 100; 1994, 80–2; 1995, 95; 1997c, 88–91; 1998, 90–2.

39. SS31. The small finds of Hellenistic and Roman date will be published in Rose forthcoming.

40. Rose 1993, 100–4; 1994, 76–80; 1995, 85–8; 1997c, 92; 1998, 89; 1999, 51; Lawall 2003, 89. The structure measured 11.5 × 9.5 m, with a long vestibule leading into a single large room. The foundations are nearly 1.50 m deep.

41. Rose 1993, 100–4. For comparanda from other sites, see the stamped tiles from Pella (Petsas 1978, 20–1 and 79–80), and Lysimachia in Aetolia (Klaffenbach 1936, 364 = *IG* IX 1 no. 130). For other examples of stamped tiles from sanctuaries, see Orlandos 1966, 93–5.

42. Hayes 1995b. The vessels are P379, 410. A few fragmentary glass vessels were found around the exterior of the building.

43. Chapouthier 1935b, 62, fig. 82.

44. Between 1988 and 2002, seventy-one figurines of Cybele were found in the West Sanctuary, out of 186 discovered throughout the site during the same period.

45. For the type in general, which has a great deal in common with that of the Thracian rider, see Hampartumian 1979; Goceva and Oppermann 1979; Tudor 1976, 26–34, 137–42; Oppermann 1981; Dimitrova 2002. For the type on coins, see Bellinger 1961, nos. 1, 131–6; Wroth 1894, 48–50.

46. Rose 1998, 88–9; 2003, 57–8. This precinct is linked to the cult of Zeus Polieus in Chapter 8.

47. These are attested by archaeological and literary sources. A few examples include Neoptolemus/Pyrrhus at Delphi, Opheltes at Nemea, and Pelops at Olympia. For the Homeric tumuli, see Rose 1999, 61–3.

48. Salapata 1997.

49. Rose 1998, 88–9; Lawall 2003, 97–9.

50. Thraemer 1901; Lewis 1959, nos. 32, 36, 53a–75; 142, 150, 182–4, 189, 192; Cole 1984, 304; Burkert 1985, 284; Kahil 1986.

51. Dionysius of Halicarnassus I 68.3–4 and I 69, 104; Strabo 7, frg. 49. For the coins of Dardanus, see Wroth 1894, 48–50. The description of the Palladion in Apollodorus (*Bibliotheca* 3.12.3) matches the image of Athena's cult statue on Hellenistic coins of Ilion: Rose 2003, 59–60. In Amy Barr's survey of the horseman plaques (Barr 1996, 135), she questioned whether Dardanus would have been shown without the Palladion since it figured so prominently in his exploits. The Palladion, however, was never a standard feature of Dardanus iconography. A small image of the Palladion appears on the reverse of coins from the Dardanus mint (Wroth 1894, 48–9, nos. 4–7 [there called Athena Promachos]), and Dardanus carries the Palladion on an early Severan issue from that mint (Rose 1993, 104), but it is otherwise absent from his images. For the iconography of Dardanus in general, see Kahil 1986; for the Palladion: Demargne 1984, 965–9.

52. Lewis 1959, nos. 31, 59, 142, 144–5.

53. Roma with Phrygian cap: Di Filippo Balestrazzi 1997, 1050, no. 11; Crawford 1974, nos. 19.2, 21.1, 22.1, 24.1, 27.5.

54. Suetonius *Claudius* 25.3; Plutarch *Flamininus* 12.6–7; Gruen 1992, 46–8.

55. Livy 37.9.7; 37.37. 1–3. Livy's description of the visit of Livius Salinator makes it sound as if he received embassies from Elaious, Dardanus, and Rhoeteum at Ilion itself, which would probably have occurred in the Bouleuterion.

56. Gruen 1990, 11–33; 1992, 31–51; Lawall 2003, 101–3. For Cybele's connection with Troy, see Rose 1998, 87–90; Roller 1999, 263–86.

57. Varro, *De Lingua Latina* 6.15; Gruen 1990, 15–19.

58. Ovid *Fasti* 4.183; *Aeneid* 4.215; 12.97–100; Beard 1994, 173–7; Roller 1998, 129–130; 1999, 301–9; Galinsky 1969, 9. For the sacred associations of the Palatine, see Wiseman 1984, 126; Coarelli 1993a, b; 1996; Pensabene 1999; Tagliamonte 1999. For the role of Pergamon in the transfer of the cult, see Gruen 1990, 11–33; 1992, 31–51; and Kuttner 1995.

59. Ilion's visibility from Samothrace was a point stressed by several ancient authors: Lewis 1959, nos. 80, 81, 83.

60. Cybele on coins: BMC Thrace 1877, 215; Lehmann 1975, 27, fig. 9; Cole 1984, 3; Burkert 1985, 282; Simon 1997, 761, no. 107.

61. Lewis 1959, nos. 31, 59, 60, 142, 144–5.

62. G2/3 Ware: Fisher 1996; Aslan 2011; Aslan et al. forthcoming. Ilion inscriptions: Cohen 1996 (inventoried as I29); Robert and Robert 1964, 188–90, no. 272; Frisch 1975, no. 44 (= Cole 1984, no. 46). The Sestos inscription is dated 209–205 B.C. Samothrace inscription: *IG* XII 8, 206, ll. 4–5.

63. Rose 1998, 89; 1999, 50; Lawall 2003, 95. The graffito is P411. For Strabo's use of Melite for Samothrace, see 10.3.19 (= Lewis 1959, no. 163).

64. In my initial discussion of the Samothracian Gods (Rose 1998, 87–90), I cited a sympoliteia inscription between Ilion and Scamandria (ca. 100 B.C.), which included mention of a Sanctuary of the Samothracian Gods, as evidence for the existence of such a sanctuary at Ilion. The inscription was subsequently interpreted in the same way by Mark Lawall (2003, 93–5). It is now clear that the sanctuary in question lay at Scamandria (Rose 2003, 62), and the inscription per se provides no evidence for a Samothracian sanctuary at Ilion.

65. For the "Altar Court," see Lehmann and Spittle 1964; Lehmann 1967, 429–32. Delos: Chapouthier 1935b, 62, fig. 82 (premiere état).

66. Torches: Lehmann 1969 I: 135–8; II: 17–18, 31–2, 55, 73–4. Masonry style painting: Lehmann and Spittle 1964; Lehmann 1969, 138–42, 204–12 (the Hieron); Bruno 1969, 314–16; McCredie 1965, 108–10; 1968, 221–2; 1979, 13, 33–4; 1988, 120.

67. Hemberg 1950, 294, 305; Lewis 1959, nos. 179–85, 189, 190; Cole 1984, 100–103; 1989, 1588–96; Mambella 1994.

68. Servius in Aeneidem 3.12 = Lewis 1959, no. 179; Burkert 1993, 187.

69. Cole 1989, 1589; Wescoat 2012b.

70. Delos: Chapouthier 1935b; Samothrace: Strabo 10.3.19–21; Daumas 1997; Burkert 1993, 191; Graf 1999, 126–127; Cole 1984, 1–2. In general, see Schachter 2003.

71. Lemnos and Imbros: Strabo 10.3.21; Levi 1966; Accame 1941–3; Birytis: Wroth 1894, 40–41; Pergamon: Wroth 1892, 117 (there identified as Dioscuri [?]); Scamandria: Rose 2003, 62.

72. For the connection between the Samothracian Gods and the Dioscuri, see Chapouthier 1935b, 71–77; 1935a, 153–84; Hemberg 1950, passim and Karte IV; Lewis 1959, nos. 168, 174a, 175, 179, K. Lehmann 1975, 26; Cole 1984, 3, 77, 78, 82; Hermary 1986, 592; Vollkommer-Glökler 1997, 821–2, 827. For links between the Cabiri/Dioscuri and Cybele, see Chapouthier 1935a, 153–84; Hemberg 1950, 82–3. For the coins of Birytis, see Wroth 1894, 40–1; Mannsperger 1989, nos. 2571–75; Vollkommer-Glökler 1997, 822, no. 305. See also *supra*, n. 8, for the connection between the double axe and the Cabiri/Dioscuri.

73. For the two grades of initiation, see Lehmann 1969 II, 3–50; Lehmann 1975, 32; Cole 1984, 26–37; Burkert 1985, 283; Cole 1989, 1571–79; Burkert 1993; Clinton 2003.

74. Livy 38.39.10; Strabo 13.1.30. Leaf (1923, 105–6) argued that Gergis should be identified with Ballı Dağ; whether Ilion's control also extended to Elaious, on the north side of the Dardanelles, is uncertain (Leaf 1923, 163). The Troad town of Kokkylion may also have come under Ilion's control at this time: Rigsby 2007.

75. Livy 38.39; *Syll*. 3. 591, lines 18–19, 21–2, 24–5, 30–1, 54–6, 60–1; Gruen 1992, 49.

76. Dionysius of Halicarnassus Ant. Rom. 1.64.4–5; Giuliani 1981, 169–77; Torelli 1984, 11–15; Gruen 1992, 23–5, 28; Holloway 1994, 135–8.

77. McCredie 1974; Alcock 1991.

78. Roma with Phrygian cap: Di Filippo Balestrazzi 1997, 1050, no. 11; Crawford 1974, nos. 19.2,

21.1, 22.1, 24.1, 27.5. For the iconography of the Phrygian cap, see Schneider 1986, 123–4 with note 866; Seiterle 1985.

79. Pyrrhus himself reportedly commented on the Trojan ancestry of the Romans: Pausanias 1.12.1; Gruen 1990, 12.

80. For the *lusus Troiae*, see Schneider 1927; Mehl 1956; Williams 1960, 145–57; Weinstock 1971, 88; Fuchs 1990.

81. Boys of nobility in *lusus Troiae*: Dio 49.43.3; 48.20.2.

82. Suetonius *Caesar* 39.2; *Augustus* 43.2; *Tiberius* 6.4; *Claudius* 21.3; Dio 54.26.1, 55 10.6–7, 59.11.2; Pliny 8.65. The *lusus Troiae* was held in conjunction with Caesar's triumph in 46 B.C., the dedications of the Theater of Marcellus, the temples of Mars Ultor, Divus Julius Caesar, and Divus Augustus, the funeral of Drusilla, and the Saecular Games of A.D. 47.

83. *Aeneid* 5.545–603.

84. Williams 1960, 148. Augustus awarded a gold torque to one of the boys who was injured in the lusus Troiae: Suetonius *Augustus* 43.

85. Herodotus 8.113.3 (as Persian marks of distinction); King Darius: Pfrommer 1998, pls. 6 and 8; generic Persians: Boardman 2000, 215, figs. 5.93c,d; Xenophon *Anabasis* 1.5.8 (gifts to foreign princes by Persians). For Attis: Vermaseren and De Boer 1986, nos. 345, 361; priests of Cybele: Vermaseren 1977a, no. 250; Roller 1998; 1999, 290–1, 297–303. In general, see Schuppe 1937.

86. Wiseman 1982.

87. In the *Aeneid*, Aeneas and the Trojans were actually compared with the priests of Cybele: *Aeneid* 4.215, 9.617–20, 12.97–100; Roller 1999, 302–4.

88. Pensabene 1996; Roller 1999, 263–85; Tagliamonte 1999; Vermaseren 1977b, 41–3; Wiseman 1984, 126.

TEN. LATE HELLENISTIC AND EARLY IMPERIAL ILION

1. For the duration of the construction of the Athenaion, see Rose 2003, 42–3.

2. Strabo 13.1.27; Dörpfeld 1902, 230–4. ; Rose 1992, 49–54; 1999, 46–7; Aylward 2000, 109–26.

3. McDonald 1943, 273; Gneisz 1990, 197.

4. Dörpfeld was the excavator and did not cite his evidence for such a reconstruction. Hellenistic Bouleuteria in Asia Minor tended not to have façades with free-standing columns; they may

have been engaged, although no engaged columns were discovered during excavation. The Doric entablature elements from the east side of the building were found in a Late Roman earthquake collapse: Rose 1992, 49–54.

5. One wall of ashlar blocks runs underneath the Odeion for a length of at least 9 m and may have been connected to a stoa: Rose 1998, 96; Aylward 2000, 98–101.

6. Frisch 1975, nos. 2, 31.

7. Aylward 1999, 174–6; Berlin 1999, 147–51.

8. Carrata Thomes 1968. There is no evidence for foreign attack on the city in the second half of the second century B.C., as proposed in Aylward 1999, 176.

9. The attack would have occurred sometime in the spring of 85: Münzer 1909.

10. Magie 1950, 226–30; Erskine 2001, 237–45.

11. Strabo 13.1.27; Leaf 1923, 148.

12. See Thompson 1981 for a discussion of the deliberate destruction of sacred buildings by an invading army, with special reference to Athens.

13. Rose 1993, 103 (z6.33.1); Wittwer-Backofen and Kiesewetter 1997, 521–2.

14. Appian 12.53; Livy Periochae 83; Obsequens 56b.

15. Augustine, De Civ. Dei III.7. Schliemann (1881, 176–8) discussed the variation in accounts between Strabo and Appian, and also argued that Strabo was the more trustworthy source.

16. The same bias underlies Lucan's description of Julius Caesar's visit to a post-Fimbrian Ilion: Pharsalia 9.964–79, 999. Even during the Gallipoli campaign, British soldiers read the Iliad while traveling to the Dardanelles: Wood 1998, 34–35.

17. Frisch 1975, no. 10, lines 2–3.

18. Plutarch Lucullus 10.3); I. Assos 11a.

19. Inscription of 80/79 B.C.: Frisch 1975, no. 73. Statue of Pompey: Winter 1996b, 175–94. The dedication on the statue base also noted his piety toward Athena Ilias, and it may have been set up in the Sanctuary of Athena.

20. Frisch 1975, no. 10.

21. Cicero II. Verr. I.74; Magie 1950, 1120 n. 24.

22. Frisch 1975, 34–47, nos. 10 and 11; Broughton 1938, 558–60; Santangelo 2007, 58–60. For a comparable law at Ephesus dating to 85 B.C., see SIG³ 792, ll. 28ff.

23. Magie 1950, 239, 1119, n. 22, citing Pergamon and Miletus.

24. Bogaert 1968, 239–40; Broughton 1938, 888–900. The priests of the Athenaion would also have supervised the production of the silver drachms and tetradrachms (from bullion stored in the Sanctuary) that formed the primary precious metal coinage of the koinon: Robert 1966a, 36–41.

25. Bogaert 1968, 285–7. The vault in the cella of the Asklepieion at Kos, constructed in the early third century B.C., was 2.15 m long, 1.53 m wide, and nearly 1 m deep: Herzog 1928, 37–9; Schatzmann 1932, 36. The keys to the vault's four locks were kept by the priests of Asclepius, the hierophylax, and the Sanctuary treasurers: Herzog 1928, no. 14, 37–9. There were similar stone-lined pits at Gortyna, Lebena, Epidaurus, and Miletus: Bogaert 1968, 285.

26. For references to such guards, see Sokolowski 1969, no. 60 (Epidaurus); Aristotle, Ath. Const. 24.3 (Athens); IG 14.291 (Segesta); Herzog 1928, 6, no. 1, l. 3; 37, no. 14, ll. 5, 12 (Kos); Rehm 1958, 129, no. 142, l. 4 (Didyma); and, in general, Hasaki 1995, 71–6. For security arrangements on the Athenian acropolis, see Harris 1995, 8, 266–7.

27. Blegen 1937a, 43; 1939, 218; Blegen et al. 1958, 304. This would be a level of VIII on the Mercalli scale, and 5.5 on the Richter scale. Blegen offered conflicting interpretations of the event, initially attributing the damage to a violent earthquake, and later (1958) associating it with Fimbria's attack. The former interpretation is surely the correct one; the Late Roman earthquake brought down the limestone blocks from the Athena temenos wall in the same way: Rose 1996, 98; Korfmann 2001c, 30–1; Rose 2003, 64–5.

28. For a general account of the history of the city between the periods of Fimbria and Julius Caesar, see Winter 1996b, 175–94.

29. Frisch 1975, no. 10, ll. 7–8; Sevinç and Treister 2003, 230–1, no. 62; 241–2. Bellinger (1961, 35–7) placed several issues in the period from 85 to 65 B.C. One of the moneyers, however, is named in an Augustan inscription of the koinon, so the coin chronology is not certain. The moneyer in question, Agathes, son of Menophilos (Frisch 1975, no. 12), was agonothetes and agoranomos of the Panathenaea and funded the taurobolium, a bullfighting event for ephebes. For the Augustan dating, see Robert, Op. Min. Sel. 1027; for the taurobolium: Robert 1940, 315–16.

30. Lucan Pharsalia 9.964–79; Erskine 2001, 19–22, 247–50.

31. Strabo 13.1.27; Leaf 1923, 148–9.

32. Weinstock 1971, 5, 129–30, 183, 292.

33. L. Julius Caesar: Frisch no. 71; Tuchelt 1979, Ilion 01. Julia: Frisch no. 72; Tuchelt 1979, Ilion 02.

34. Halfmann 1986, 158; *IGR* 4.203.

35. Unsurpassed benefactions: Frisch 1975, no. 81, where he is also hailed as "theos." Those portraits that survive represent Augustus (Actium type), Gaius Caesar, Tiberius ("adoption" type), and Agrippina the Younger. None of these is of especially high quality, and the portrait of Agrippina the Younger looks as if it has been recut. Augustus: Rose 1998, 93–4; Gaius Caesar: Inan and Rosenbaum 1966, 57, no. 2; Pollini 1987, 97–8, no. 9; Boschung 1993, 203, no. 283; Tiberius: Inan and Rosenbaum 1966, 62, no. 13; Agrippina the Younger: Inan and Alföldi-Rosenbaum 1979, 150–2, no. 98; Romano 2006, 206–9, no. 103. There is epigraphic evidence for three statues of Augustus at Ilion: Frisch 1975, nos. 81–3.

36. Statues in the Bouleuterion: Dörpfeld 1902, 230–4; Frisch 1975, nos. 83, 89. Portrait in the agora: Rose 1998, 93.

37. Dörpfeld 1902, 114 fig. 36, 204 (sectors A4 and A6/7). For the pottery in the foundations, see A5/6 107, 113, 365, 368; Rose 2003, 63, 79 n. 278. One of the stones contained an incised delta.

38. Blegen et al. 1958, 304. The limestone water channel in Theater A was also built at this time: R60.117, 120 (ceramic Behälter from the foundation trench); Rose 1992, 47–8.

39. Dörpfeld (1902, 234) excavated both buildings. In the case of IXA, an Augustan date is secure, since part of the foundation trench was excavated in 2000. Nothing remains of IXB, although the well immediately to the west of it (Bv) was filled with Augustan ceramics (Hayes 1995b), which suggests construction activity in the area during that period. Dörpfeld (1902, 210, fig. 78) found part of a limestone entablature below the building, which appears to be Hellenistic in date and supplies a *terminus post quem* for IXB.

40. Building IXA occupies 782 m². By way of comparison, the Temple of Athena occupied 577 m², and the Bouleuterion, 765 m². Only the Agora Bath would surpass it in size.

41. We did uncover one piece of evidence for this transfer of stones during the excavation of IXA's limited remains. In the foundations of this building was a stone with an incised delta, other examples of which were used in the Hellenistic temenos wall of the Upper Sanctuary. For the excavation, see Korfmann 2002a, 7–9, although Building IXA is not mentioned.

42. Goethert and Schleif 1962, 37; Frisch 1975, no. 84.

43. See Rumscheid 1994, 145–50; Rose 2003, 28–31.

44. For Antony's theft of the Ajax statue, see Strabo 13.1.30. An earthquake at Troy during the first half of the second century B.C. may have shaken the painted plaster from the walls of the Mosaic Building, but there is no evidence that any structures in the Sanctuary were affected. If the propylon had been damaged in that earthquake, it would probably have been repaired immediately, since the town was extremely prosperous at that time. Guidoboni (1989) found no ancient literary references to this quake.

45. There were repairs in the Sanctuary of Artemis at Ephesus (Winter 1996a, 307–9, nos. 3–7), and the Hekateion at Lagina (Winter 1996a, 310, no. 11; Webb 1996, 108, 120 n. 113; Şahin 1982, 14–15, nos. 511, 512), but there is no certain evidence for new buildings funded by Augustus. The two examples most often cited, Iconium in Galatia (Mitchell 1987, 22; *IGR* 3.262) and the Hekateion at Lagina (Winter 1996a, 340 no. 17), are not secure. The patron of the Iconium theater skene was actually Nero: Ramsay 1918, 169–70; Winter 1996a, 345 no. 52. The Hekateion at Lagina had been occupied and pillaged by the Parthians under Labienus, but there is no sign of any restoration on the temple itself (Schober 1933, 16). The new construction there during the early empire, consisting of four porticoes and a propylon, was sponsored by a wealthy citizen of Lagina, M. Ulpius Heraclitus (Şahin 1982, 67, no. 668 Laumonier 1937, 274; 1938, 269 n. 3). There is no indication of a significant involvement by Augustus. On occasion the benefactions consisted solely of repatriating statues that had been taken by Antony, and the Emperor's name would be added to the original base: *Res Gestae* c. 24; Strabo 13.1.30; Pliny *NH.*34.58; Fränkel 1890–5, I 125–6, no. 216B; II 229–30 no. 301, 509; Magie 1950, 470; Gruen 1992, 117 n. 165 (for Scipio Aemilianus as model). Stephen Mitchell (1987, 24) sums up well the situation involving Imperial benefactions in the provinces: "[the emperor's] ownership of important sources of raw materials enabled him to support building projects in the most basic way;

his control of revenue made it possible for him to subsidize construction simply by offering tax exemption." For a list of examples of Augustan assistance in Asia Minor, see Winter 1996a, 306–11, 338–42.

46. Frisch 1975, nos. 83, 85; 1984, 15.

47. Price 1984, 249, no. 5; 250, no. 7; 251, no. 16; 252, no. 19.

48. Frisch 1975, nos. 82, 86, 87, 89, 91.

49. Halfmann 1986, 158 (Augustus); 163–4 (Agrippa); 166–8 (Gaius Caesar); 168–70 (Germanicus); 188–210 (Hadrian); 223–30 (Caracalla and Macrinus).

50. Bellinger 1961, T115, T134, T140, T148, T154, T208, T210 (Aeneas). None of the coins is preserved well enough to illustrate, but the type is very similar to Fig. 11.2 here, although without Ascanius.

51. *RPC* I, no. 652 (Segesta). The type would be added to the repertoire of several other eastern mints during the late second and early third centuries A.D., including the Troad mints of Scepsis and Dardanus: *BMC Troas* 51 (Dardanus), 85 (Scepsis).

52. Frisch 1975, 236–7, no. 143.

53. Nicolaus of Damascus frg. 3 Müller (*FHG* III p. 350) = frg. 134 Jac. (*FGH* II p. 421f.). For dedications to the Agrippan family in the eastern Mediterranean, see Rose 1997a, 13–14.

54. Josephus *AJ* 16.26; Magie 1950, 479; Shürer 1973, 292 n. 15; Braund 1984, 82.

55. Tacitus *Annals* 2.43, 54; Josephus *Ant. Jud.* 18.2.5; Suetonius *Caligula* 1; Magie 1950, 497–8; Halfmann 1986, 168–70. Gaius Caesar, the eldest adoptive son of Augustus, may also have stopped at Ilion in or around A.D. 1 when he was proconsul of Asia and traveled via Samos or Chios on his voyage east: Rose 1997a, 17–18; 2005, 45–50.

56. Epigram of Germanicus: *Anthologia Latina* II, 798; Tacitus *Annals* 2.54.2; Halfmann 1986, 30–1, 168–9;

57. Frisch 1975, no. 88; Rose 1997a, 28; Trillmich 1978, 3.

58. Rose 1997a, 28.

59. Assos: Merkelbach 1976, nos. 16, 17, 19; Mytilene: *IG* 12.2, no. 537; *IGR* 4.9; 4.114; Lampsacus: Frisch 1978, no. 11; Pergamon: *RPC* 2359; Rose 1997c, 13.

60. One would expect celebrations of the Imperial family to have been incorporated into the local festivals of the Troad, but the closest we come is a redefined festival at the Sanctuary of Apollo Smintheus, which began to bear the name "Smintheia Pauleia" as a tribute to Paullus Fabius Maximus, proconsul of Asia in 11 B.C.: Robert *Op. Min. Sel.* I 1969, 629–32; Ricl 1997, 83. At other sanctuaries in the eastern Mediterranean one sees a fusion of emperor and god in the titulature of the local festival, such as the Sebasta Heraea on Samos or the Dionysia Caesarea at Teos: Price 1984, 103–4. Worship of Livia was incorporated in the cult of Athena Polias at Cyzicus, and the local Panathenaea was celebrated in Livia's honor: Hasluck 1910, 184.

61. Bellinger (1961, 43) argued that this should not be construed as a representation of Athena Ilias, but the iconography is very similar to what had been used in the past, and the legend IΛI actually touches the image of Athena. She was surely intended to stand as a symbol for Ilion. The only Tiberian issues within this general area come from the island of Lesbos: *BMC Troas* no. 38 and 193 (Germanicus and Agrippina at Methymna and Mytilene, respectively), no. 186 (Tiberius and Divus Augustus), nos. 187–92 (Tiberius and Livia).

62. *IGR* 4.145; Hasluck 1910, 185. Nero as *"neos Helios"*: Reynolds 1981, 324, no. 9; *IGR* 3.345; *SEG* 18, 566; *SIG*³ 814.

63. Merkelbach 1976, no. 26.

64. Frisch 1975, 192–3, no. 90.

65. For a description on the column with *tabula ansata*, see Dörpfeld 1894, 139, where it is compared with the similar example from the sanctuary of Athena Ilias, for which see Aylward 2005a, 147, figs. 37, 38, and 148.

66. Frisch 1975, no. 91; Pontes 1996; Rose 1997a, 178–9, no. 120.

67. Tacitus *Annals* 12.58.1; Suetonius *Claudius* 25.3; *Nero* 7.2.

68. If the statues were set up at the times suggested above, then the statue of Britannicus would have been erected when he was eight or nine years old, and that of Nero at the age of sixteen; consequently, Nero's image would have been larger than that of his stepbrother and rival for the throne, and the inequality in status would have been readily apparent.

69. Rose 1994, 95–7; *SEG* 14 (1994) 983.

70. It seems unlikely that Building IXB should be associated with this Claudian dedication or with the Stoa of Philokles due to the unusual form of the dedicatory inscriptions on the latter two structures. Given its size, IXB should have featured a dedication in large letters evenly spread

across the architrave. The Philokles dedication appears on a column's *tabula ansata*, while
the second Claudian dedication is written in
small letters within a compressed space on the
architrave.

71. Rose 1994, 96, fig. 23. The Athena Ilias architrave was found in the late Roman earthquake
collapse near the Northeast Bastion; Rose
1997c, 98–101; Jablonka 2006b, 12–15. It probably belongs to a building of late Hellenistic
date.

72. Dio 60.8, 60.28.7; Tacitus *Annals* 12.15–21;
Anderson 1963, 752–3; Gajdukevic 1971, 340–
343; Levick 1990, 157–8.

73. *IosPE* II 400; Minns 1913, 597, n. 2, 653, no. 43;
Boltunova 1954; Robert and Robert 1956,
146, no. 194; *SEG* 16 (1959) 439; *CIRB* 656–7,
no. 1123; Gajdukevic 1971, 341 n. 22; Safrai and
Stern 1974, 156.

74. Detschew 1957, 353.

75. The dedication of a monument to a benefactor in a city with high visibility was one of the
components of Hellenistic euergetism: Rose
1997b.

76. Bellinger (1961, T124) dates the issue of Nero
and Britannicus to the first year of Nero's
reign, but it has plausibly been assigned to the
late Claudian period by the editors of *RPC* I,
390, 392.

77. Livia: Assos (Merkelbach 1976, no. 19);
Methymna (*RPC* 1.1563); Pergamon (*RPC*
1.2359). Julia: Sestos (*IGR* 1.821); Mytilene
(*IGR* 4.114); Assos (Merkelbach 1976, no. 16;
IGR 4.257 [there incorrectly identified as
Livia]); Pergamon (*RPC* I.2359); Lesbos (*IGR*
4.9).

78. Bellinger 1961, no. T125; *BMC Troas* no. 194
(Mytilene); Ricl 1997, 57, no. 18 (Alexandria
Troas).

79. Smith 1990; Rose 1997a, 171–2, cat. 110; 164–9,
Cat. no. 105.

80. Blegen 1934, 245–6; Aylward 2000, 154–62. A
bath at Assos was dedicated at the same time:
Merkelbach 1976, nos. 16, 17.

81. Blake 1947, 253; Adam 1994, 129–34. All of the
examples of *opus reticulatum* in Asia Minor have
been collected in Spanu 1996. See also Schneider
2008, 70–2, and Torelli 1980, 154–5 (Tulul Abu
El Alayig, in Palestine, near Jericho).

82. These were reported in Blegen 1934, 245–6,
and Blegen et al. 1950, 10, pls. 118–19. They will
be published by William Aylward in his monograph on the Agora.

83. Silhouetted athletes: Blake 1936, 162–7. For the
popularity of black and white figural mosaics
in general, see Clarke 1979. For early mosaics
in bath buildings in Asia Minor, see Steskal and
la Torre 2008, 260, pls. 231, 269, 270, 372, 373
(Vedius Gymnasium, Ephesus); Von Gerkan
and Krischen 1928, 131–5, 141. The second
century A.D. marked the period of greatest
popularity for bath-gymnasium complexes
in Roman Greece and Turkey: Yegül 1992;
Farrington 1999.

84. Philostratus *Lives of the Sophists II* 1 (548); Ricl
1997, T125; Boatwright 2000, 116–18.

85. One of the benefactors of the *taurobolium*,
Agathes, son of Menophilos, was also *ago-
nothetes* and *agoranomos* of the Panathenaea:
Frisch 1975, no. 12; Robert, *Op. Min. Sel.* 1027;
Robert 1940, 315–16. He donated forty bulls
for the *taurobolium*.

86. Rose 2000, 64; Kozal 2001 (R1 construction
and occupation); Rose 1999, 53–4.

87. Blegen 1934, 246; Aylward 2000, 143–53.

88. Rose 2000, 60.

89. For the visit, see Julian *Epistles* 19.

90. Ricl 1997, 20–1, 66–7, no. 34; Römhild 2011.

91. Ricl 1997, 66, no. 34; Görkay 2002. A man
named Gaius Fabricius Tuscus was honored at
Alexandria for overseeing building operations
there during the Tiberian period.

92. Görkay 2002, 228. The same alignment was
allegedly used for the temple in the Aphrodisias
Sebasteion.

93. Halfmann 1987. The altar was found in the village of Mahmudiye, but Halfmann has argued
convincingly that it must have been brought
from Alexandria Troas, some 14 km away.

94. Rose 1997a, 217, n. 24.

95. Ricl (1997, 20) proposed that the colony may
have been planned by Caesar and carried out
by the triumvirs.

96. Merkelbach 1976, no. 24a (Assos); Engelmann
1976, no. 18 (Cyme).

97. Ricl 1997, 54–5, nos. 14, 15.

98. *IG* 12, Suppl. 124, ll. 11–18; Rose 1997c, 151–2,
Cat. no. 84.

99. Rose 1997a, 24–5. The fact that Germanicus is
called "neos theos" in the dedication to Nero
and Drusus strongly suggests a date not long
after his death in 19.

100. *IGR* 4.78. For example, the name of Pompey,
Mytilene's great benefactor, continued to
appear on small altars produced during the
Augustan period: *IGR* 4.79, 80.

101. Jablonka 2006b, 14–15.

102. For the types, see Smith 2006, 158–60, no. 41; 164–6, no. 45; 179–80, no. 51; Bieber 1977, 133 and fig. 612 (Baebia from Magnesia).

103. For other statue bases from the area, see Rose 2003, 68–9. The statue base of A. Claudius Caecina, which was discovered by Schliemann in this area, held a colossal bronze statue: Schliemann 1881, 637–8; Frisch 1975, no. 106.

ELEVEN. ILION FROM THE FLAVIANS TO THE BYZANTINES

1. A Flavian inscription from the Sanctuary of Athena records the receipt of *argyra aristeia,* which indicates that the Athenaion's treasury continued to receive precious metals: Frisch 1975, nos. 96, 97, 103.

2. For the statues, see Frisch 1975, no. 92. The group featured images of the deified Titus and Vespasian, and Domitian was no doubt also included. For the coins, see Bellinger 1961, T127. As Frisch has shown (1975, 211), there is no evidence for a Gens Flavia temple at Ilion, as Vermeule (1968, 458) proposes.

3. Mannsperger and Mannsperger 2002.

4. Bellinger 1961, T115 (Augustan); 129 (Flavian); Calciani 1981a, s.v. "Aeneas," no. 131.

5. Bellinger 1961, T115 (Augustan); 129 (Flavian); Calciani 1981a, s.v. "Aeneas,"no. 131. For the iconography of the flight of Aeneas, see Fuchs 1973. The group would eventually be copied throughout the empire in a variety of media, such as the painting on the façade of a Pompeian house (Spinazzola 1953, fig. 183) and a relief from the Aphrodisias Sebasteion (Erim 1989, 56, fig. 80).

6. Paribeni 1984, 862–3, s.v. "Ascanius."

7. Rose 2002a, 337–9; 2005, 34–44. In general, eastern attributes were applied to the young (Ascanius, Ganymede, Astyanax), the old (Priam), and the cowardly (Paris), but not adult Trojan males such as Aeneas and Hector. This is nicely illustrated by a bronze issue from the mint of Otus in Phrygia, which depicts the departure of Aeneas (*BMC Phrygia* 345, no. 14). Aeneas wears contemporary Roman armor, but Ascanius and Anchises are shown with Phrygian caps. See also Chapter 7, n. 27.

8. Schliemann 1881, 109–10, 610–11; 1884, 210–13, 230–1, nos. 12–13; Dörpfeld 1902, 239; Blegen 1932, 447–8; 1935a, 246–7; Rose 1991; 1992, 46–9; 1993, 105; Sear 2006, 356–7. I thank

Billur Tekkök for advice on the dating of pottery from the foundation trench of the water channel. This supersedes my comments on the date in Rose 1991.

9. Bernardi Ferrero (1970, 138) proposed a date in the third century A.D. for the skene, but one of the two architectural elements that she cites in support of this date (140, fig. 207) is a coffered ceiling block of Hellenistic date from the Athenaion (Rose 2003). For advice on the lewis holes, I thank William Aylward.

10. One of the skene roof tiles had been stamped with the word "theatron": Rose 1992, 48.

11. One of the capitals is from an anta, the other from a column. There are two tiers of acanthus leaves and thin unfluted caules from which rise diagonal volutes and central helices that extend into the abacus. The closest parallels come from the lower story of the Theater at Ephesus, dated to around A.D. 66 (Vandeput 1997, 171 and pl. 83.3), and the Delphinion at Miletus (Heilmeyer 1970, 85, fig. 23.4), although there are strong regional variations. For the development of the Corinthian capital in Asia Minor during the empire, see Vandeput 1997, 170–174; Heilmeyer 1970, 78–105. I thank Lut Vandeput for her advice on the dating of these elements.

12. Bernardi Ferrero 1970, 140, fig. 206.

13. Sear 2006, 90.

14. Schliemann 1884, 214–15; Blegen 1933, 495; Rose 1991.

15. The naming of theater sections after local tribes was not uncommon in antiquity: Wiseman 1973, 71 (Stobi); Jones 1987, 365–7; Ritti 1985, 118–22; Robert and Robert 1976, 554–5, no. 668; Kolb 1974, 255–70 (Hierapolis in Phrygia); Erskine 2001, 104.

16. Rose 1993, 105, 114, n. 40.

17. Frisch 1975, 223–6, nos. 121–3; Jones 1987, 298–300. For Panthous, see *Aeneid,* 2. 429–30. The inscription referring to the phyle of Assarakos was found by Gebhard Bieg in one of the cemeteries of Akçapinar and will be published by him in the Troy Final Publication series. Lucan refers to the houses of Assarakos when he describes Caesar's visit to Ilion: Lucan 9.966–968; Hertel 2003, 159.

18. Lawall 2003, 89–91. The only marble inscription to have been found in the West Sanctuary, I56, features a dedication to Titus or Domitian.

19. Blegen et al. 1958, 304. The altar was set on a foundation of small stones at least 2.30 m deep.

20. The transfer was accomplished with no apparent damage to the associated blocks; the only signs of change are the two sets of clamp cuttings.

21. Rose 1993, 98.

22. Blegen et al. 1958, 304, 306; Rose 1993, 100.

23. Blegen et al. 1958, 304, 306; Rose 1999, 51. Blegen assumed that the northern wall of the Late Hellenistic Building was the northern terminus of the grandstand and estimated the original length as 39 m. For the southern side of the grandstand, see Rose 1993, 102 fig. 4; 1996, 98; 1998, 74, fig. 2. One stone from the northern edge of the grandstand can be seen in the scarp in Rose 1994, 83, fig. 9 (upper right corner).

24. Blegen 1937b, 586; Blegen et al. 1958, 306. The stone foundations, which were constructed directly in front of the Troy VI fortification wall, appear as no. 18 in Blegen et al. 1958, fig. 375, and in fig. 156. For the Demeter sanctuary at Pergamon, see Bohtz 1981, 36–8; Radt 1988, 207–8.

25. For the Samothracian cult during the Roman period, see Cole 1984, 87–103; 1989, 1569–96. The Lehmanns believed there was a change in the cult on Samothrace ca. A.D. 200: Lehmann 1969, vol. 2, 42–50.

26. E.g., TC400, 422, 423, 477, 1550. The chronological distribution of small finds is discussed in more detail in Rose *West Sanctuary* forthcoming.

27. The final analysis of this complex will be published in Rose forthcoming. For a preliminary analysis, see Korfmann 1991, 21; Miller 1991.

28. Thompson 1963, 84, no. 51; Miller 1991, 56. Compare the situation in the "terra-cotta factory" at Olynthus: Robinson 1930, 108–11.

29. Jablonka 1995, 49; Hübner and Giese 2006. Compare the insulae at Abdera, Piraeus, and Priene: Hoepfner and Schwandner 1994, 307.

30. Tekkök et al. 2001, 344–6; Rapp and Gifford 1982, 50; Guidoboni 1989, 229, no. 107 (Aeolis, A.D. 105); 233, no. 112 (Cyzicus, A.D. 120 or 128).

31. Defensive ditch: Korfmann 2001c, 34–36.

32. Tekkök et al. 2001; Rose 2000, 64.

33. f26.94; g28.13.

34. Kozal 2001. For a contemporary rise in house construction at Pergamon, see Wulf 1999, 206–8.

35. Philostratus *Heroicus* 8.1; Magie 1950, 613 and 1470 n. 6; Halfmann 1986, 43, 191.

36. Ricl 1997, 85, no. 55; Vermeule 1995, 473; Frisch 1975, 198, no. 94. Three inscriptions involving Hadrian have been uncovered at Ilion, but all are extremely fragmentary: Frisch 1975, nos. 93, 94, and 94a. One inscription, possibly an altar, dates between A.D. 129 and 138; another may date to the time of his visit, and involves one of the sanctuaries; the third may be a letter from Hadrian to Ilion.

37. Pausanias 1.35.3; Philostratus *Heroicus* 8.1; Schliemann 1881, 652–3; Winnefeld in Dörpfeld 1902, 543; Leaf 1923, 157–8; Cook 1973, 88–89; Hertel 2003, 176–8. Schliemann (1881, 652) connected the original burial with a tumulus on the Hellespont nearly 550 m to the north of the Hadrianic tumulus, but this was doubted by Winnefeld (Dörpfeld 1902, 543).

38. Lechevalier 1802, 303; Schliemann 1881, 103, 652–3; 1884, 343–344; Dörpfeld 1902, 543; Leaf 1923, 157–8; Hertel 2003, 176–8. Three tumuli in the vicinity of Ilion feature this technique, and it occurs also in tumuli at Pergamon: see Pirson forthcoming. A lamp of Hadrianic date was found in the fill above the vaulted entrance: Bieg 2009, 242–3.

39. Strabo 1.31.30.

40. Schliemann 1881, 103.

41. The volume of the tumulus was calculated using a model of its present-day slope. Erosion over millennia has naturally reduced the mass of the mound's mantle, and this figure is therefore assumed to represent the lower limit for the amount of earth originally required for the structure. I owe this calculation to Gabriel Pizzorno.

42. Dörpfeld 1902, 234; Blegen 1939, 216–18; Rose 1992, 54–5; 1994, 89–90; 1997c, 101–2; 1998, 92–7; Aylward 2000, 138–43; Sear 2006, 357; Riorden 2007. Whether there was a predecessor to the Odeion prior to the second century A.D. can no longer be determined. I mentioned in 1994 that an earlier Odeion of Augustan date must have existed (Rose 1994, 88–91), but the evidence is insufficient to support such a conclusion. For an overview of the building, see Aylward 2000, 138–43.

43. Bier 2008; 2011. The seating estimate comes from Sear 2006, 357.

44. Up to seventeen rows of seats still remained in place at the time of initial excavation in the 1930s: Blegen 1939, 216–18.

45. Rose 1994, 99 n. 47.

46. The earlier reconstructions of the Odeion have shown broken pediments crowning the two central aediculae (Riorden 2007, 50, fig. 1), although William Aylward, who is publishing the Odeion, has noted that the one surviving broken pediment block could fit only on the lower story, which seems unlikely. He has restored the broken pediments in the paradoi.

47. Frisch 1975, no. 158.

48. Rose 1994, 91–3; Evers 1994, 353, no. 141 bis; Rose 2011a, 287.

49. SS 39. Pres. H: 1.41; W: 0.96; D: 0.52. For other statues of Hadrian from Asia Minor, see Inan and Rosenbaum 1966, nos. 29–35; Inan and Rosenbaum 1979, nos. 43–8. For statues of Hadrian in theaters, see Fuchs 1987, 176–7. The pose conforms to Group V in Stemmer 1978, 56–72.

50. The running drill has, however, been used to render the locks of the Gorgoneion and the leather straps of the cuirass. We may be dealing with two artists here: one who carved the body and another who finished the head.

51. For the type, see Evers 1994, 352, 141 bis; Wegner 1956, 20–4; Fittschen and Zanker 1985, 54–7. For the Thasos statue, see Rolley and Salviat 1963; Stemmer 1978, 86–7; Fittschen and Zanker 1985, 46, n.e 5e, and 51, n. 8c.

52. Wegner 1956, 68; Stemmer 1978, 160–1.

53. Foot: SS62. The width of the foot is 0.08m. For the Olympia statue, see Bol 1984, 31–45.

54. The mixing of private and imperial statues on aediculated facades became increasingly common in second-century A.D. Greece and Asia Minor: Rose 1997b, 113–17.

55. Blegen 1935a, 245–6; Rose 2000, 58–61; Aylward 2000, 154–62.

56. Tubuli: Rook 1979, 305–6 (Central Baths, Pompeii; Suburban Baths, Herculaneum). Most of the tubuli systems in Asia Minor baths (Yegül 1992, 363–6) are second-century A.D. in date.

57. These were reported in Blegen 1935a, 245–6, and Blegen et al. 1950, 10, pls. 118–19. They will be published by William Aylward in his monograph on the agora. For ithyphallic pygmies in Roman bath mosaics, see Clarke 1998, 119–42; Clarke 2007, 74–81.

58. Yegül 1992, 304 (Ephesus). For early mosaics in bath buildings in Asia Minor, see Steskal and la Torre 2008, 260, pls. 231, 269, 270, 372, 373 (Vedius Gymnasium, Ephesus); Von Gerkan and Krischen 1928, 131–5, 141. Silhouetted athletes: Blake 1936, 162–7. For the popularity of black and white figural mosaics in general, see Clarke 1979. I thank John Clarke for advice on the dating of the mosaics.

59. Rose 1999, 54–5. The inscription was discovered in quadrant ss18. We cannot connect any of the funerary stelae honoring athletes with specific graves, but bronze or iron strigils have been found within several burials of Roman date: IL 97, 103; Korfmann 2005, 16. Strigils of iron were also found by Blegen in Late Roman tombs on the western and southern sides of the citadel: Blegen 1932, 441; 1935b, 582.

60. Frisch 1975, no. 125.

61. Petzl and Schwertheim 2006, 10, ll. 28–32; Jones 2007, 154 (letter 1.3).

62. Aylward et al. 2002; Aylward 2006.

63. For the water channel discovered near Ilion, see Rose 1999, 61; Aylward 2006, 111.

64. Aylward 2006, 110.

65. Philostratus VS 2.1 (548); Ricl 1997, T125; Boatwright 2000, 116–18. Part of the aqueduct of Alexandria Troas has been located near Pinardere, ca. 19 km southeast of Alexandria Troas: Jewett and Stupperich 2008, 349–57.

66. Ricl 1997, nos. 20, 21.

67. Pausanias 1.18.6; Benjamin 1963, 58–9; Spawforth and Walker 1985, 93–4; Willers 1990, 48–51.

68. Abydos: IG 3.472; Alexandria Troas: CIL 3.7282; Sestos: IG 3.484. Statues were also erected by Cyzicus (IG 3.477) and Thasos (IG 3.476). See also Graindor 1934, 50–1, n. 2; 66–8.

69. Bellinger 1961, T134–6, T140.

70. Bellinger 1961, 48, T134.

71. BMCRE IV, nos. 1300–1 and 1319–21; Dulière 1979, 166–9; Dabrowa 2004.

72. Toynbee 1944, 143–4, 193–4; Hill 1970, 91–2.

73. Pausanias 8.43; Aur. Victor De Caes. 15.

74. Bellinger 1961, 50–61; Vermeule 1995.

75. Bellinger 1961, A206, A227; Wroth 1894, 51 (Dardanus), 85 (Scepsis); 1892, 105–8 (Parion).

76. Vermeule 1995, 474–6. For the market, see Frisch 1975, no. 3; for souvenirs sold at the Athenian Panathenaia, see Shear 2001, 432.

77. Frisch 1975, nos. 141–5.

78. Schliemann 1884, 212, no. 122; Dörpfeld 1902, 437–8. Rose 1991, 71; Dulière 1979, 122, 229; Rose 2011a, 288–9. The height of the relief is 1.26 m; the width is 1.17 m.

79. For the Chios Lupercal, which cost 1000 Attic drachms, see Moretti 1980; Derow and Forrest 1982; Wiseman 1995, 161. Images of Romulus and Remus also figured in the decoration of

the Attalid temple of Apollonis at Cyzicus (early second century B.C.), but they were shown as adults with their mother, Servilia (Merkelbach and Stauber 2001, 38–9).

80. The Lupercal appeared on coins struck by the colony of Apamea (Augustan) and Laodicea (Domitianic): *RPC* I, no. 2009; *RPC* II, no. 1295. For Nicopolis, see Zachos 2001, fig. 28; for Aphrodisias, see Smith 1990, 100.

81. *BMCRE* IV, nos. 1300–1, 1319–21; Dulière 1979, 166–9.

82. T151, T157, T171, T182 (Lupercal). The Lupercal first appeared on coins of Ilion during the Hadrianic period (T134), as an exergue filler below the type of Aeneas leaving Troy, but it would not be used as a primary reverse type until the reign of Marcus Aurelius. Lupercal types were struck by a number of colonies during the Antonine period, probably in response to the anniversary celebrations in Rome: *BMC Lycia, Pamphylia, Pisidia* 177 (Antioch in Pisidia); *BMC Peloponnesus* 27 (Patras); Wroth 1892, 105–8 (Parion). Other provincial mints followed suit during the Severan period: *BMC Phrygia* 237, 252 (Hierapolis); Head 1901, 194, 200 (Philadelphia); 316 (Thyatira); *BMC Galatia, Cappadocia, Syria* 15, 16 (Antioch); 259–61 (Laodiceia ad Mare); 286 (Damascus).

83. Weigel 1992, 296.

84. Landskron 2006, 111, Abb. 16.

85. The Lupercal decorating Roma's shield on the column base of Antoninus Pius and Faustina is a case in point: Vogel 1973, 33, figs. 3–5.

86. An exception is the Hellenistic theater in Lycian Termessos, which had decorative shields along the front of the stage: Bernardi Ferrero 1970, Tav. III; p. 23, fig. 23.

87. It is noteworthy that the diameter of the Ilion shield is nearly identical to that of the shields that decorated the Miletus Bouleuterion: Knackfuß 1908, 52. The diameter of the Miletus shield is 1.28 m; the Ilion shield is 1.15 m. It is conceivable that the shield block was brought to Ilion from another city, not unlike the Blue Marble Building during the early empire.

88. Rose 2000, 59–60; Aylward 2000, 163–73. The ceramics in the construction fill of the nymphaeum's water pipes (E12/13.39, 41, 44) date between A.D. 150 and 180, which supplies a *terminus post quem* for the nymphaeum's construction.

89. For the portico, see Aylward 2000, 173–5. The columns were granite and the capitals Corinthian. The remains were excavated by Blegen (Aylward 2000, 62–3), but he supplied no evidence for dating.

90. One measured 1.10 × 0.80 m, with the short end facing front, and the other was 0.50 × 0.60 m. The imperial family was rarely represented in action poses (e.g., Niemeyer 1968; Bol 1984), but gods were (Lambrinoudakis 1984, pl. 301, fig. 44 [Apollo]; Kahil and Icard 1984, pl. 592, fig. 27 [Artemis]).

91. Two column capitals (one Ionic [A776], one Corinthian [A777]) had been set against the front of the nymphaeum, probably after the Late Roman earthquake. The Ionic capital is small enough to have been used in the aediculae of the nymphaeum, but the Corinthian capital most likely belonged to another building in the agora. For the river personification statue, see Schliemann 1884, 214, no. 126; Aylward 2000, 167.

92. Aylward 2000, 159.

93. Blegen 1932, 446.

94. Rose 1999, 55–61; 2000, 61–5; Korfmann 2001c, 36–40.

95. See, in general, Higginbotham 1997, 23–4, figs. 1–3, 70, 90–3.

96. Columella, *De Re Rustica* viii.16–19; Varro, *De Re Rustica*, iii.17, Rose 1999, 55–9. For the eel bone, see Uerpmann and Van Neer 2000, 176.

97. There is also evidence for benefactions in the Sanctuary of Athena Ilias during the second and third centuries A.D. in the form of inscriptions added to the architraves of the temenos porticoes, but they are so fragmentary that one cannot determine what precisely is being commemorated: Aylward 2005a, 149–54, 163–66.

98. Bellinger 1961, T175 (Marcus Aurelius and Athena); T214 (Hector and Patroclus); T217 (Herakles and Hesione); T219 (Anchises and Aphrodite);

99. Bellinger 1961, T220 (Ilus and Athena); T237 (Hector and Athena).

100. Bellinger 1961, T175 (Marcus Aurelius and Athena); A271 (Caracalla and Apollo).

101. Halfmann 1986, 104, 224, 230.

102. Bellinger 1961, T261; Dio 77.16.7; Herodian 4.8.3.

103. Ricl 1997, 87–8, no. 57.

104. Julian *Ep.* 19; Sage 2000, 215.

105. Hector, like Aeneas, was never shown in Phrygian garb during the empire.

106. Schliemann 1881, 658–65; Dörpfeld 1902, 539–42; Cook 1973, 172–3; Bieg 2009, 243–4.
107. Herodian 4.8.4–5.
108. Dio 79.2.5–6; Cavuoto 1983, 42–8, 61; Rose 1998, 96–7; *SEG* 48 (1998), no. 1478.
109. Rose 1997c, 101–2; 1998, 93.
110. Aylward 2000, 140.
111. Tekkök et al. 2001, 344; Rose (forthcoming. There are two candidates for the earthquake: the first took place in A.D. 235 in Nicomedia, which is not very far from Ilion: Robert 1978, 398. The second occurred during the reign of Gordian III and severely affected Aphrodisias (Guidoboni 1989, 241, no. 124 [A.D. 241]; AE 1984, 875), but this is too far away.
112. Kozal 2001, 314, 318. In y28/29, a massive cleanup was followed by new construction, and in the makeup of one of the walls was a sherd of ARS 50a. A single sherd of the same type appeared in the enormous dumps in K17. In both cases, a date within the second quarter of the third century A.D. is indicated. It is noteworthy that a few sherds of ARS 50a also appeared in the dump/reconstruction levels in the Hillside Houses at Ephesus: Ladstätter 2002, 21. For contemporary dumps at Pergamon, see Wulf 1999, 209–11. For all of this information I have relied on the advice of Sebastian Heath and Billur Tekkök, who will be publishing this material.
113. The width of the streets is 7 m: Rose 1999, 53–4. By way of comparison, I supply street widths for other Roman cities in Anatolia: Antioch, 6.80 m; Perge, 13 m; Side, 9 m; Sardis, 12.50 m; Cremna, 3–4 m: Crawford 1990, 124; Mitchell 2000. For the coins, see Bellinger 1961, 75–6 (Gordian III).
114. Magie 1950, 692–3, 1559, n. 9.
115. Ladstätter 2002, 11, 19, 38; Tür 2002, 57. Zimmermann 2002, 111: "*Im Hanghaus 2 kommt es im 2. Viertel des 3. Jhs., wohl als Folge eines Erdbebens, zu einer umfassenden Bauphase mit teilweiser Neuorganisation der Nutzung und fast durchgängiger Neuausstattung der Räume.*" The majority of the mosaics and wall paintings from the Ephesian houses, formerly dated to the fourth and fifth centuries, have now been redated to the second quarter of the third century: Zimmermann 2002; Parrish 1999, 511–13.
116. Magie 1950, 692–3, 1559, n. 9. This rise in the economy, however, is not visible in the material record of Pergamon: Wulf 1999, 209–11.

117. The Roman road in question probably crossed the Granicus near the modern village of Çınarköprü and led through Didymateiche toward Zeleia. For other western Asia Minor milestones with the names of Gordian III and Valerian/Gallienus, see the lists in French 1988, 451–2, 457, and Rose et al. 2007, 110–13.
118. Jansen 1992, 66–7. One of the kilns, in sector Y59, appears to be of late second-century B.C. date, and the sondage around it yielded the support for the oven floor, two pottery supports, and large quantities of mud-brick and vitrified tiles: Korfmann 1992, 33; Rose 1992, 56; Korfmann 2005, 13–16. The walls seem to have been covered during the Early Roman period. For the firing chamber type, see Swan 1984, 40.
119. For the siting of kilns, see Peacock 1982, 38–43; Scheibler 1983, 107–8, Swan 1984, 49; Arubus and Goldfus 1995.
120. Swan 1984, 49.
121. Compare the situation in Corinth, where the clay beds were next to the potters' quarter: Stillwell 1948, 3.
122. Tybout 1992; Tenger 1999, 171.
123. Jordanes *Getica* XX 108; Mierow, 1915, 82.
124. For the Gallienic earthquake of A.D. 262, which severely damaged Ephesus, see Guidoboni 1989, 242–3, no. 126 (A.D. 262); Ladstätter 2002, 26–9. No damage from that earthquake is apparent in the houses of Pergamon: Wulf 1999, 212.
125. Lower City well: Tekkök et al. 2001, 363–72; qanat shaft: Korfmann 2002a, 20–3; fish farms: Rose 1999, 59. Extensive dumping at this time also occurred at Pergamon: Wulf 1999, 99, 134. The description of the dumps at Pergamon is very close to those in the center of Ilion's Lower City.
126. Rose 1995, 99–100; Tekkök et al. 2001, 371–2 (S. Wallrodt). For enthroned statuettes of Cybele, see Simon 1997, nos. 26–54.
127. Berlin 1999, 146–51; Kozal 2001.
128. Due to the excellent preservation of the statuette, it is unlikely that it was already being reused as building material during the third century A.D. There are no traces of mortar or recarving.
129. New construction in western Asia Minor following the attack of the Goths was primarily focused on the construction or repair of city walls (Magie 1950, 712, 1567; Foss 1976, 3; Abbasoğlu 2001, 187), although there was some

new construction in city centers (Broughton 1938, 756; Abbasoğlu 2001, 183).

130. Blegen 1932, 446; Bellinger 1961, 201–11; Aylward 2000, 60. The same situation prevailed in the baths at Metropolis, where a coin hoard had a closing date of A.D. 272: Harl 2006. A hoard discovered in Çanakkale had a closing date of A.D. 283–4, although nearly all of the coins had been amassed between 266 and 274: Pflaum and Bastien 1969.

131. *CIG* 3620; Magie 1950, 870 n. 53; Frisch 1974; Ricl 1997, 81–2, no. 50.

132. Erim and Reynolds 1970; Erim and Reynolds 1971; Hasluck 1910, 192; Tenger 1999, 171–3.

133. Frisch 1975, nos. 96, 97, 103.

134. Three had been discovered at the time of the publication of *Troja 1893*: Dörpfeld 1894, 82.

135. Rose 2003, 63.

136. L'Orange 1984, 10–11.

137. Zosimus 2.23.1; Sozomen 2.3.2; Cook 1973, 158–9; Sage 2000, 217–18.

138. Statue of Constantine II: Frisch 1975, no. 99.

139. Julian *Ep.* 19; Sage 2000, 215; Hertel 2003, 155–6. He also visited Alexandria Troas : Ricl 1997, 182, T19.

140. Frisch 1975, nos. 141, 142, 145.

141. For the statue, see Frisch 1975, no. 100.

142. Dörpfeld 1902, 223–5; Goethert and Schleif 1962, 37; Frisch 1975, no. 84; Rose 2003, 65–6; Hertel 2004. The incised letters are certainly Augustan in date and can be paralleled on other Augustan inscriptions from Ilion: Frisch 1975, nos. 81–3, 85. They feature barely perceptible seriphs, and the crossbars of the "A"s are formed by intersecting diagonal strokes rather than a single horizontal line. The inscribed block has now disappeared.

143. Goethert and Schleif 1962, 37

144. During the Augustan period, Caesar was referred to as "*theos Ioulios*" only in Greek versions of the *Res Gestae*, and there it was a direct translation of "Divus Iulius": Damon 1995, 60 no. 2. The only use of the term during the Tiberian period that I have found in Asia Minor appears on a statue of the emperor at Cyme: Engelmann 1976, no. 20 = *IGR* 4.1739.

145. For the Aphrodisias propylon dedication, see Erim 1986, 112 (the two lower fasciae of the architrave, later erased). Two other inscriptions to Julian at Aphrodisias were also erased: Rouché 1989, 35–42, nos. 19 and 20. For the dedication to Julian at Ilion, see Frisch 1975,

no. 100. For the inscriptions of Julian in general, see Arce 1984, 93–176, esp. 109–12, 154–66. To his list add *SEG* 37 (1987), no. 863 [Iasos]; 41 (1991) no. 1544 [Askalon], 1614 [Prokynema, Egypt]; 45 (1995) no. 1682 [Yirce, Mysia]; 47 (1997) no. 2066 [Jerash]; 48 (1998) nos. 1912, 1913 [Jerash].

146. For the Aphrodisias propylon dedication, see Erim 1986, 112 (the two lower fasciae of the architrave, later erased). Two other inscriptions to Julian at Aphrodisias were also erased: Rouché 1989, 35–42, nos. 19 and 20. The dedication to Julian at Ilion is in Latin, which is interesting in itself. Altogether, five Latin inscriptions can be confidently attributed to Ilion, four of which concern Late Roman emperors (Alexander Severus, Diocletian, Constantine II, and Julian: Frisch 1975, nos. 95, 98–100). None of the inscriptions associated with Athena or the koinon was in Latin. On the use of Greek vs. Latin in Asia Minor during the fourth century A.D., see Van Dam 2007, 184–216.

147. Rose 1992, 55–6; 1997c, 102–3; 1998, 101–2; 1999, 52–4.

148. Rose 1994, 93–4; Rose forthcoming.

149. Strocka 1977, 58, fig. 91; 91, fig. 349. Another preserved ceiling (36, fig. 27) contains interlocking squares with floral elements. For the new chronology, see Scherrer 2001, 77–9.

150. Wulf-Rheidt 1998; Wulf 1999; Ladstätter 2002.

151. Foss 1976, 16, 42–3; 1979, 54–67; Rautman 1995, 52; Lang-Auinger 2003, 333.

152. Four keys were found (IL15, IL16, IL55, BR175) and one locking device (IL137).

153. Ponti 1995; Williams-Thorpe 2008; Reynolds and Ward-Perkins 1952, 132, no. 467; Ricl 1997, 236, T139 (Codex Theodosianus), 234–5, T134 (Historia Ecclesiastica 7.37). There is no evidence that the quarries continued operations after ca. 420 A.D.

154. Ponti 1995, 313–17.

155. *Historia Ecclesiastica* 7.37; Ponti 1995, 319, n. 36.

156. Blegen 1935b, 582–83; Blegen et al. 1950, 13; Frisch 1975, 242–3, no. 156 (inscription); Sage 2000, 219; Rose 2001, 280.

157. Rose 1993, 110; Wittwer-Backofen and Kiesewetter 1997, 522.

158. Rose 1997c, 96–101. The coins and pottery associated with the earthquake collapse include extensive amounts of LRC Hayes Form 3,

which allows us to date the catastrophe to the first quarter of the sixth century.

159. Blegen et al. 1953, 101–2; Rose 1997c, 99; 2003, 64.

160. Two coins of Justinian (A.D. 518–65) were found in H17, in the center of the Lower City (C55, 58), and a nummus, apparently of Justinian (C143), was found under one of the blocks of the Bouleuterion (Rose 1992, 53). The coins of Maurice Tiberius, Tiberius II, Justin, and Heraclius were not catalogued by Bellinger in his monograph on the coins of Troy, but they appear in Blegen's unpublished inventory of coins: p. 12 no. 144 (Justin); no. 146 (Maurice Tiberius); no. 152 (Tiberius II); p. 18 no. 224 (Heraclius). The inventory is preserved in the archives of the University of Cincinnati Classics Department. See also Rose 2003, 65.

161. For the plague, see Allen 1979.

162. Granaries: Procopius *De Aedif.* 5.1 (ca. A.D. 560); tariffs: Durliat and Guillou 1984.

163. Hasluck 1910, 193–4.

164. Hauser 1992, 31–42.

165. Rose et al. 2007, 71, 105.

166. Wiegand 1904, 335–9.

167. See the plan at the back of Hasluck 1910. A few of these can be dated by literary sources, such as Achyraus, near Hadrianoutherai (Balıkesir), which was built by John Comnenus to guard the southern roads (Niketas Choniates *Annals* 44B). At the site of Babayaka, about 5 km southeast of Gönen, a large ecclesiastical complex with mausoleum was constructed in the fifth or sixth century: Rose 2011b, 165–6.

168. Rose 2011b, 167–9. The existence of both had been noted by nineteenth-century topographers who dated them generally to the Byzantine period, but a sketch existed only for Alacaoluk, which was done quickly: Wiegand 1904, 274, 337–8.

169. Wiegand 1904, 335–9, with fig. 47; Hasluck 1910, 104, fig. 11.

170. Mordtmann 1855; Wiegand 1904, 274; Hasluck 1910, 110–11 (identified as Palaeoscepsis); Rose 2011b, 167–9.

171. Crow 1995; Greatrex 1995; Crow and Ricci 1997; Crow 2007.

172. Foss and Winfield 1986, 111–14, 142–5; Çaylak Türker 2010.

173. Bellinger 1961, 181, nos. 354–8. These include one of Leo V and Constantine (A.D. 813–20), three of Basil II and Constantine VIII (976–1025), and

one each of Romanus III (1028–34), Romanus IV (1067–71), and Michael VII (1071–78). For the Troad during the Byzantine-Selcuk wars, see Hasluck 1910, 195–7.

174. Angold 1975, 103, 241. The Latins were driven out of the area by John Vatatzes in A.D. 1224. Nine thirteenth-century coins have been found, of which seven can be attributed to the Nicaean empire (Theodore Lascaris and John Vatatzes): Bellinger 1961, 182.

175. Rose 1998, 102–3; 1999, 51–2, 60–1; Kiesewetter 1999; Rose 2000, 57–8; 2001, 280–1; Korfmann 2001c, 31–2.

176. The building was approximately 4 × 3 m in size with only a tamped floor, and it featured slightly curved rubble walls composed of very small stones.

177. For Ilion's Byzantine pottery, see Böhlendorf 1997; 1998. Hayes 1995a presents the pottery from the Late Byzantine pits in the Lower City. The associated coins are C8–6, 831, 832, all of which date to the first half of the thirteenth century A.D.

178. For the jewelry, which consists mostly of multicolored bracelets, see GJ86, 88, 90, 93, 94. The Late Byzantine phases of the Ilion will be published by Kathleen Quinn.

179. The population estimate comes from Christian Wolkersdorfer, based on the water discharge from the Spring Cave at this time: Wolkersdorfer and Göbel 2004. For the Spring Cave, see Rose 1999, 55–61; 2000, 65; Korfmann 2000, 37–8; 2001c, 31–4. By comparison, in A.D. 1218–19 Lampsacus had a recorded population of only 173 households: Angold 1975, 110. For the cemeteries, see Blegen et al. 1953, 391–4 (B trenches); Rose 1992, 48–9; Jablonka 1995, 60 (p. 28); Wittwer-Backofen and Kiesewetter 1997; Kiesewetter 1999.

180. For the quarry, pithos bases, and rubbish pits in w28 and p28, see Jablonka 1995, 52–60; for the house foundations in y28/29, see Jablonka 1996, 73–8.

181. Kiesewetter 1999; Jablonka 2006b, 17–21.

182. Rose 1998, 102. For the reliquary, see Pitarakis 2006; coin in skeleton's mouth: notebook of Marion Rawson 1935, B trenches, book IV, p. 19; silvered earrings: Jablonka 2006b, 17–21. The glass bracelets from the current excavations will be published by Kathleen Quinn. For those from the Blegen excavations, see the 1932 notebook of Marion Rawson, M Trenches, pp. 21, 32, 47, 109.

183. Blegen found only one Christian inscription: Blegen 1935b, 583; Frisch 1975, no. 156.
184. Kiesewetter 1999, 421–3.
185. Wittwer-Backofen and Kiesewetter 1997, 524.
186. Jablonka 1995, 58–61 (p. 28); Hayes 1995a; Korfmann 2001c, 31–4 (f26).
187. Cook 1973, 376–7; Quataert 1994. See also Inalcık 1994, 179–409, for the increase in trade in the sixteenth century.

TWELVE. THE CONCEPT OF TROY AFTER ANTIQUITY

1. Bassett 2004, 201–4 cat. 109B; 205, cat. nos. 107, 113, 114. Alexandria Troas is a more likely provenance for the Apollo statue.
2. Bassett 2004, 51–5.
3. Bassett 2004, 64, 231, cat. no. 147.
4. For the change in costume, see Wright 1993, 97. In the cities of Greece and Asia Minor, belt buckles or ornaments, which indicate the existence of trousers, are usually found in levels dating to the fourth century A.D. or later: Weinberg 1952, 265–6 (Corinth); Waldbaum 1983, 117 (Sardis); at Troy, BR226. For the iconography of Daniel, see Koch 2000, 151–4; Wessel 1966; for the Three Magi, see Koch 2000, 157–60; Vikan 1990; Cumont 1932–3; for the Three Hebrews, see Weitzmann 1979, 399, 425–6 no. 383, 430–1 no. 388.
5. If we survey the evidence for triumphal monuments in early Christian Constantinople, only one featuring enemy warfare – the column of Arcadius – focused on the campaign against the Goths, whose costume was very different from that of the Trojans: Becatti 1960, 151–264; Weitzmann 1979, 79–80 no. 68. Both eastern and western figures appeared on the base of the Column of Arcadius as representations of the two parts of the empire (Becatti 1960, 258–60, pl. 74b). Such is also the case for the base of the Obelisk of Theodosius (Ploumis 1997, 128–30). See also Weitzmann 1979, 33–5 no. 28; Delbrueck 1929, 188–96 no. 48 (Barberini diptych); 196–200 no. 49 (Milan diptych).
6. Rosenthal 1972; Weitzmann 1979, 227–8 no. 204; Calciani 1981a, nos. 199–202; Wright 1992, 81–124. See also the fourth-century A.D. mosaic from Low Ham with scenes from the *Aeneid*: Calciani 1981a, no. 159; Weitzmann 1979, 201 fig. 25.
7. Gudeman 1894; Griffin 1907; Frazer 1966; Buchthal 1971, 65; Diop 2009; Goldwyn 2010, 79–111.

8. There are fragments of a Greek version of Dictys, probably dating to the first or second century A.D., although the Latin version can be placed in the fourth century. The manuscript of Dares dates to the fifth or sixth century.
9. Hay 1957, 48–50; Yates 1975, 130–3; Graus 1989; Federico 2003; Goldwyn 2010, 112–38.
10. Livy 1.1; *Aeneid* 1.242–9.
11. Lucan *BC* 1.427; Ammianus Marcellinus 15.9.5; Sidonius Apollinaris *Epistulae* 7.7.2.
12. Jordanes *Getica* 8.57, 9.60; Soby 2002, 242–3. The same mistake was made by the Augustan author Hyginus, who locates the court of King Teuthras in Moesia rather than Mysia: Hyginus 99 Auge, cf. Fantham 2003.
13. Ewig 1997; Cohen 2004; Goldwyn 2010, 114.
14. Fredegar, *Chronicles* 2.4–6; 3.2; Barlow 1995; Wallace-Hadrill 1960, xi–xii.
15. Meserve 2008, 60–2.
16. Barlow 1995, 87, 93. The Habsburgs traced their descent from both the Franks and the Julian family, so they, too, were able to claim Trojan ancestry: Wandruszka 1964, 14–23.
17. Brown 1996, 13, 25, 31, 41–2, 70–4; Das 2004; Goldwyn 2010, 136–8.
18. Cessi, *Origo civitatem italie seu venetiarum*, 7. 32–3; Brown 1996, 13, 41. Beginning in the eleventh century there were lists of towns with Trojan origins, although Venice was not included until the thirteenth century: Martin da Canal, *Cronique des Veniciens* 60 (ca. A.D. 1250–75); Buchthal 1971, 59.
19. Buchthal 1971, 59; Braccesi 1984; Brown 1996, 32.
20. Coletti 1935, 47–8; Buchthal 1971, 60. Compare the contemporary monumental paintings of the destruction of Troy in the palace of the archbishop of Patras, a likely reference to the Franks' Trojan descent: Jacoby 1986, 170.
21. Buchthal 1971, 60; Brown 1996, 25.
22. Buchthal 1971, 3; Loud 1981, 113–14; Albu 2001, 13–16, 237–8.
23. *Historia Brittonum* I.10–11. An alternate version in I.18 presents Brutus as the great-grandson of Rhea Silvia, which still provided him with Trojan ancestry. See also Federico 2003; Dalton 2005.
24. Geoffrey of Monmouth Book 1, Chapters 3–17; Yates 1975, 50; Ingledew 1994; Dalton 2005. Paris had also been founded as "New Troy": Yates 1975, 138, 222.
25. The account is contained in the prologue of the *Prose Edda*, composed by Snorri Sturluson. See Byock 2005 for the edited edition, as well

as Frank 1909; Lincoln 2001; Goldwyn 2010, 132–5.

26. Fredegar, *Chronicarum quae dicuntur Fredegarii Scholastici libri IV*, 45–6; Meserve 2008, 47–8.

27. Meserve 2008, 52–3.

28. *Gesta Francorum et aliorum Hierosolymitanorum*, ed. B. A. Less (Oxford 1924), 20; Meserve 2008, 56; Hankins 2003, 334–41.

29. Rigord, De gestis Philippi Augusti Francorum Regis, in *Recueil des historiens des Gaules et de la France*, 17:17; Meserve 2008, 52: early thirteenth century A.D. The story was later adopted by Vincent of Beauvais and Martin of Troppau, but it was not followed by everyone: Rigord, a French monastic historian writing ca. A.D. 1200, maintained that the descendants of Turcus served as ancestors of the northern Europeans who would later fight the Franks: Meserve 2008, 54. Venetian Doge Andrea Dandolo, writing in A.D. 1354, made a similar claim: Meserve 2008, 62.

30. Phryges and Troiani: Florence chancellor Colucci Salutati (A.D. 1389) and Augustinian friar Andrea Biglia (A.D. 1420s). The evidence for these equations and the Teucri is carefully presented by Meserve 2008, 25–34. Meserve (2008, 37) also cites the writing of Filippo da Rimini, Venetian chancellor of Corfu, who referred to the Turks as Teucri and to Mehmet II as Tros, the eponymous founder of Troy. See also Hankins 2003, 330–1.

31. Harper 2005.

32. Rose 2002a.

33. Bassett 2004, 51–5, 201–4.

34. Pierre of Bracheux: Jacoby 1986, 171; Noble 2005, 138–40; Mehmet II: Babinger 1978, 112, 210; Reinsch 1983, 60, 90–1; Sage 2000, 211–13.

35. McNeal 1969, 122.

36. Critoboulos, *History of Mehmed the Conqueror*, trans. C. T. Riggers (Princeton, 1954), 181–2.

37. Venetians: Niketas Choniates, *Annals* 360 (chapter 652); Brown 1996, 17. Mehmet: Pertusi and Carile 1983, 138–41; Hankins 2003, 334; Meserve 2008, 37.

38. Brown 1996, 70–3.

39. Both letters are carefully analyzed in Meserve 2008, 35–9, with Meserve's translation of this letter on p. 39.

40. Among the most vocal critics were the Venetian Doge Andrea Dandolo (Meserve 2008, 62) and Pope Pius II (Hay 1957, 85). For the reference to Mehmet as Achilles: Giorgio Freschi, *Eubois* (Naples: Sixtus Riessinger, A.D. 1470–1); Meserve 2008, 32.

41. Sage 2000, 211–13.

42. Cook 1973, 14–44; Easton 1991.

43. Spencer 1952, 333; Easton 1991, 111, citing Nicephorus Gregoras (A.D. 1295–1360), who waited four days to enter the Hellespont.

44. Patton 1951, 28–9; van der Vin 1980, 580–1.

45. Critoboulos 4.11.5; Philippides and Hanak 2011, 211.

46. Easton 1991, 112. Yenişehir/Sigeion was also frequently mistaken for Troy at that time.

47. Cook 1973, 23–35; Easton 1991, 113–19.

48. Schliemann 1884, xiii–xxviii; Allen 1999, 219–21; Mannsperger 1995; 1998; Kolb 2004; 2010.

49. Korfmann 2000, 47–8.

50. The horse had accompanied the premieres of the *Troy* film in Germany and Japan. It was leased to the city of Çanakkale for nineteen years, and cost $66,000 to move and install in its current location. It was dedicated on March 18, 2004, the eighty-ninth anniversary of the Turkish victory at Gallipoli.

51. Vandiver 2010, 228–80; Hart 2011, 72. One of the young French fighters, Jean Giraudoux, used the setting of the Trojan War for a slightly veiled discussion of World War I diplomacy in his play *The Trojan War Will Not Take Place*.

52. Brooke: Marsh 1918, 177; anonymous poem of 1919: Jaquet 1919, 76.

53. Aydoğan 1995; Rose 2007a; Rose 2011a, 291.

54. Ridgway 2002, 79–80.

55. Hickey 1995, 339.

BIBLIOGRAPHY

Abbasoğlu, H. 2001. "The Founding of Perge and Its Development in the Hellenistic and Roman Periods." In *Urbanism in Western Asia Minor: New Studies on Aphrodisias, Ephesos, Hierapolis, Pergamon, Perge and Xanthos*, edited by D. Parrish, 173–88. JRA Supplement 45. Portsmouth, R.I.

Accame, S. 1941–3. "Iscrizioni del Cabirio di Lemno." *ASAtene* 19–21 (n.s. 3–5): 75–105.

Adam, J.-P. 1994. *Roman Building: Materials and Techniques*. London.

Aigner, H. 1978. "Sigeion und die Peisistradische Homerförderung." *RhM* 121: 204–9.

Akurgal, E. 1941. *Griechische Reliefs des VI. Jahrhunderts aus Lykien*. Berlin.

Akurgal, E. 1961. *Die Kunst Anatoliens von Homer bis Alexander*. Berlin.

Akurgal, E. 1965. "Neue Archaische Bildwerke aus Kyzikos." *AntK* 8: 99–103.

Akurgal, E. 1986. "Neue archaische Skulpturen aus Anatolien." In *Archaische und klassische griechische Plastik: Akten des internationalen Kolloquiums vom 22.-25. April 1985 in Athen*, edited by H. Kyrieleis, 1–14. Mainz am Rhein.

Albu, E. 2001. *The Normans in Their Histories: Propaganda, Myth and Subversion*. Woodbridge, UK.

Alcock, S.E. 1991. "Tomb Cult and the Post-Classical Polis." *AJA* 95: 447–67.

Alcock, S.E. 1994. "The Heroic Past in a Hellenistic Present." *EchCl* 13: 221–34.

Allen, P. 1979. "The "Justinianic" Plague." *Byzantion* 49: 5–20.

Allen, R.E. 1983. *The Attalid Kingdom*. Oxford.

Allen, S.H. 1991. "Late Bronze Age Grey Wares in Cyprus." In *Cypriot Ceramics: Reading the Prehistoric Record*, edited by J.A. Barlow, D.L. Bolger, and B. Kling, 151–67. Philadelphia.

Allen, S.H. 1994. "Trojan Grey Ware at Tel Miqne-Ekron." *BASOR* 293: 39–51.

Allen, S.H. 1999. *Finding the Walls of Troy: Frank Calvert and Heinrich Schliemann at Hisarlik*. Berkeley, Calif.

Alscher, L. 1963. *Götter vor Gericht. Das Fälschungsproblem des Bostoner Throns. Die klassisch-griechische Kunst und die Archäologen. Ergänzungsband zu Griechische Plastik II, 2*. Berlin.

Amandry, P. 1958. "Orfèvrerie achéménide." *AntK* 1: 9–23.

Anderson, J.G.C. 1963. "The Eastern Frontier from Tiberius to Nero." In *The Cambridge Ancient History X. The Augustan Empire (44 B.C.–A.D. 70)*, edited by S.A. Cook, F.E. Adcock, and M.P. Charlesworth, 743–80. Cambridge.

Anderson, J.K. 1985. *Hunting in the Ancient World*. Berkeley, Calif.

Anderson, M.J. 1997. *The Fall of Troy in Early Greek Poetry and Art*. Oxford.

Andreae, B. 2001. *Skulptur des Hellenismus*. Munich.

Andronikos, M. 1984. *Vergina*. Athens.

Angel, J.L. 1951. *Troy: The Human Remains*. Supplementary Monograph 1. Princeton, N.J.

Angel, J.L. 1972. "Ecology and Population in the Eastern Mediterranean." *WorldArch* 4: 88–105.

Angel, J.L. 1978. "Porotic Hyperostosis in the Eastern Mediterranean." *Medical College of Virginia Quarterly* 14: 10–16.

Angold, M. 1975. *A Byzantine Government in Exile: Government and Society under the Lascarids of Nicaea (1204–1261)*. Oxford.

Anthony, D.W. 1990. "Migration in Archaeology: The Baby and the Bathwater." *American Anthropologist* 92: 895–914.

Anthony, D.W. 1997. "Prehistoric Migration as Social Process." In *Migrations and Invasions in Archaeological Explanation*, edited by J. Chapman and H. Hamerow, 21–32. BAR-IS 664. Oxford.

Anthony, D.W. 2007. *The Horse, The Wheel, and Language: How Bronze-Age Riders from the Eurasian Steppes Shaped the Modern World*. Princeton, N.J.

Antonaccio, C.M. 1994. "Placing the Past: The Bronze Age in the Cultic Topography of Early Greece." In *Placing the Gods: Sanctuaries and Sacred Space in Ancient Greece*, edited by S.E. Alcock and R. Osborne, 79–104. Oxford.

Antonaccio, C.M. 1995. *An Archaeology of Ancestors: Tomb Cult and Hero Cult in Early Greece* Lanham, Md.

Antonaccio, C.M. 2001. "Ethnicity and Colonization." In *Ancient Perceptions of Greek Ethnicity*, edited by I. Malkin, 113–57. Washington, D.C.

Apakidze, J. 1999. Lapislazuli-Funde des 3. und 2. Jahrtausends v.Chr. in der Kaukasusregion: Ein Beitrag zur Herkunft des Lapislazuli in Troia." *Studia Troica* 9: 511–25.

Arce, J. 1984. *Estudios sobre el Emperador Fl. Cl. Juliano: fuentes literarias, epigrafía, numismatics*. Madrid.

Archibald, Z. 1998. *The Odrysian Kingdom of Thrace: Orpheus Unmasked*. Oxford.

Arslan, N. 2003. "Goldbleche aus Tenedos." *IstMitt* 53: 251–63.

Arslan, N., and N. Sevinç. 2003. "Die eisenzeitlichen Gräber von Tenedos." *IstMitt* 53: 223–50.

Arubas, B., and H. Goldfus. 1995. "The Kilnworks of the Tenth Legion Fretensis." In *The Roman and Byzantine Near East: Some Recent Archaeological Research*, 95–107. JRA Supplement 14. Ann Arbor, Mich.

Aruz, J. 2008. *Marks of Distinction: Seals and Cultural Exchange between the Aegean and the Orient (ca. 2600–1360 B.C.)*. CMS Beiheft 7. Mainz am Rhein.

Asgari, N. 1978. "Roman and Early Byzantine Marble Quarries of Proconnesus." In *The Proceedings of the Xth International Congress of Classical Archaeology, Ankara – Izmir, 1973*, edited by E. Akurgal, 467–80. Ankara.

Asgari, N., and T. Drew-Bear. 2002. "The Quarry Inscriptions of Prokonnesos." In *ASMOSIA V, Interdisciplinary Studies on Ancient Stone: Proceedings of the Fifth International Conference of the Association for the Study of Marble and Other Stones in Antiquity, Museum of Fine Arts, Boston, June 1998*, edited by J. Herrmann, N. Herz, and R. Newman, 1–19. London.

Ashmole, B., and N. Yalouris. 1967. *Olympia: The Sculptures of the Temple of Zeus*. London.

Aslan, C.C. 2002. "Ilion before Alexander: Protogeometric, Geometric, and Archaic Pottery from D9." *Studia Troica* 12: 81–129.

Aslan, C.C. 2009a. "End or Beginning? The Late Bronze Age to Iron Age Transformation at Troia." In *Forces of Transformation. The End of the Bronze Age in the Mediterranean*, edited by C. Bachhuber and R.G. Roberts, 144–51. Oxford.

Aslan, C.C. 2009b. "New Evidence for a Destruction at Troia in the Mid 7th Century B.C." *Studia Troica* 18: 33–58.

Aslan, C.C. 2011. "A Place of Burning: Hero or Ancestor Cult at Troy." *Hesperia* 80: 381–429.

Aslan, C.C., and P. Hnila. Forthcoming. "Migration and Integration at Troy from the End of the Late Bronze Age to the Iron Age." In *Nostoi: Indigenous Culture, Migration and Integration in the Aegean Islands and Western Anatolia during the Late Bronze and Early Iron Age*, edited by N. Stampolidis, Ç. Maner, and K. Kopanias. Istanbul.

Aslan, C.C., K. Lynch, and M. Lawall. Forthcoming. *The West Sanctuary of Troy during the Iron Age and Archaic Period*. Mainz am Rhein.

Aslan, R. 2003. "The Relationship between Man and Landscape in the Troad during the Ottoman Period." In *Troia and the Troad: Scientific Approaches*, edited by G.A. Wagner, E. Pernicka, and H.-P. Uerpmann, 31–42. Berlin.

Aslan, R., and F. Polat. 2011. "Çanakkale Boğazı'nın Suları Altındaki Kalkolitik Yerleşim." *Aktüel Arkeoloji Dergisi* 24: 38–9.

Aslan, R., G. Bieg, P. Jablonka, and P. Krönneck. 2003. "Die mittel- bis spätbronzezeitliche Besiedlung (Troia VI und Troia VIIA) der Troas und der Gelibolu-Halbinsel: Ein Überblick." *Studia Troica* 13: 165–213.

Aslan, R., A. Sönmez, and R. Körpe. 2008. "Heinrich Schliemanns Ausgrabungen in Troia nach osmanischen Quellen." *Studia Troica* 18: 237–48.

Astour, M.C. 1965. "New Evidence on the Last Days of Ugarit." *AJA* 69: 253–8.

Ateşlier, S. 2001. "Observations on an Early Classical Building of the Satrapal Period at Daskyleion." In *Achaemenid Anatolia. Proceedings of the First International Symposium on Anatolia in the Achaemenid Period*, edited by T. Bakır, H. Sancisi-Weerdenburg, G. Gürtekin, P. Briant, and W. Henkelman, 147–68. Leiden.

Ateşlier, S. 2002. "Pers Ölü Gömme Geleneğinde 'Cenaze-Harmamaksa'lari.'" *Olba* 5: 77–95.

Ateşlier, S., and E. Öncü. 2004. "Güçüşçay Polyksena Lahiti Üzerine Yeni Gözlemler: Mimari ve Ikonografik Açidan Bakış." *Olba* 10: 45–87.

Aydoğan, Nasit Bora. 1995. *Çanakkale: 80th Anniversary of the Gallipoli Campaign*. Çanakkale.

Aylward, W. 1999. "Studies in Hellenistic Ilion: The Houses in the Lower City." *Studia Troica* 9: 159–86.

Aylward, W. 2000. "The Roman Agora at Ilion and Its Predecessors." Ph.D. diss., University of Cincinnati.

Aylward, W. 2005a. "The Portico and Propylaia of the Sanctuary of Athena Ilias at Ilion." *Studia Troica* 15: 127–75.

Aylward, W. 2005b. "Security, Synoikismos, and Koinon as Determinants for Troad Housing in Classical and Hellenistic Times." In *Ancient Greek Houses and Households: Chronological, Regional, and Social Diversity*, edited by B. Ault and L. Nevett, 36–53. Philadelphia.

Aylward, W. 2006. "The Aqueduct of Ilion (Troy) and the Supply of the City's Nymphaeum and Bath." In *Cura Aquarum in Ephesus: Proceedings of the Twelfth International Congress on the History of Water Management and Hydraulic Engineering in the Mediterranean Region, Ephesus/Selçuk, Turkey, October 2–10, 2004*, edited by G. Wiplinger, 107–15. BABesch Supplement 12. Dudley, Mass.

Aylward, W., and J. Wallrodt. 2003. "The Other Walls of Troia: A Revised Trace for Ilion's Hellenistic Fortifications." *Studia Troica* 13: 89–112.

Aylward, W., G. Bieg, and R. Aslan. 2002. "The Aqueduct of Roman Ilion and the Bridge across the Kemerdere Valley in the Troad." *Studia Troica* 12: 397–427.

Aylward, W., W. Marx, and D. Strahan. 2011. "Elemental Identification of Artifacts and Pigments from Ancient Ilion with X-ray Fluorescence." *Studia Troica* 11: 57–117.

Aytaçlar, N. 2004. "The Early Iron Age at Klazomenai." In *Klazomenai, Teos and Abdera: Metropoleis and Colony. Proceedings of the International Symposium held at the Archaeological Museum of Abdera, 20–21 October 2001*, edited by A. Moustaka, 17–41. Thessaloniki.

Babinger, F. 1978. *Mehmed the Conqueror and His Time*. Princeton, N.J.

Bachhuber, C. 2009. "The Treasure Deposits of Troy: Rethinking Crisis and Agency on the Early Bronze Age Citadel." *AnatSt* 59: 1–18.

Bachhuber, C., and R.G. Roberts, eds. 2009. *Forces of Transformation: The End of the Bronze Age in the Mediterranean*. Oxford.

Badian, E. 1977. "The Battle of the Granicus: A New Look." In *Archaia Makedonia II: Papers Read at the Second International Symposium Held in Thessaloniki, 19–24 August 1973*, 271–93. Thessalonike.

Badoni, F.P. 1968. *Ceramica campana a figure nere*. Florence.

Bahrani, Z. 1995. "Assault and Abduction: The Fate of the Royal Image in the Ancient Near East." *Art History* 18.3: 363–82.

Baker, H. 1966. *Furniture in the Ancient World*. London.

Bakır, G. 1982. *Sophilos*. Mainz am Rhein.

Bakır, T. 1991. "Eine neue phrygische Inschrift aus Daskyleion." *EpigAnat* 18: 157–64.

Bakır, T. 1995. "Archäologische Beobachtungen über die Residenz in Daskyleion." *Pallas* 43: 269–85.

Bakır, T. 2003. "Daskyleion (Tayaiy Drayahya) Hellespontine Phrygia Bölgesi Akhaemenid Satraplığı." *Anadolu* 25: 1–26.

Bakır, T., and R. Gusmani. 1991. "Eine neue phrygische Inschrift aus Daskyleion." *EpigAnat* 18: 157–64.

Bakır–Akbaşoğlu, T. 1997. "Phryger in Daskyleion." In *Frigi e frigio. Atti del 1° Simposio Internazionale, Roma, 16–17 Ottobre 1995*, edited by R. Gusmani, M. Salvini, and P. Vannicelli, 229–38. Rome.

Bakır–Akbaşoğlu, T., and G. Polat. 1998. "Daskyleion 1997." *Kazı Sonuçları Toplantısı* 20: 577–82.

Balcer, J.M. 1972. "The Date of Herodotus IV, 1. Darius' Scythian Expedition." *HSCP* 76: 99–132.

Balcer, J.M. 1984. *Sparda by the Bitter Sea: Imperial Interaction in Western Anatolia*. Chico, Calif.

Balcer, J.M. 1995. *The Persian Conquest of the Greeks, 545–450 B.C.* Konstanz.

Balfanz, K. 1995. "Eine spätbronzezeitliche Elfenbeinspindel aus Troia VIIa." *Studia Troica* 5: 107–16.

Bankoff, H.A., N. Meyer, and M. Stefanovich. 1996. "Handmade Burnished Ware and the Late Bronze Age of the Balkans." *JMA* 9: 193–209.

Barbanera, M. 2003. *Ranuccio Bianchi Bandinelli: Biografia ed epistolario di un grande archeologo.* Biblioteca d'arte Skira 8. Milan.

Barchiesi, A. 1998. "The Statue of Athena at Troy and Carthage." In *Style and Tradition: Studies in Honor of Wendell Clausen*, edited by P.E. Knox and C. Foss, 130–40. Stuttgart.

Bardill, J. 2012. *Constantine, Divine Emperor of the Christian Golden Age*. Cambridge.

Barford, P.M. 2001. *The Early Slavs: Culture and Society in Early Medieval Eastern Europe*. Ithaca, NY.

Barker, G., and T. Rasmussen. 1998. *The Etruscans*. Oxford.

Barletta, B. 2001. *The Origins of the Greek Architectural Orders*. Cambridge.

Barlow, J. 1995. "Gregory of Tours and the Myth of the Trojan Origins of the Franks." *Fruehmittelalterliche Studien* 29: 86–95.

Baroni, F. 1961. *Osservazioni sul "Trono di Boston."* Rome.

Barr, A.E. 1996. "Horse and Rider Plaques at Ilion: A Preliminary Study of the Hellenistic Hero Cult in Asia Minor." *Studia Troica* 6: 133–57.

Barron, J.P. 1964. "Religious Propaganda of the Delian League." *JHS* 84: 35–48.

Basaran, S. 2000. "Aeolische Kapitelle aus Ainos (Enez)." *IstMitt* 50: 157–70.

Basedow, M. 2000. *Beşik Tepe: Das spätbronzezeitliche Gräberfeld*. Studia Troica Monograph 1. Mainz am Rhein.

Basedow, M. 2002. "Cemetery and Ideology in the West Anatolian Coastal Region." In *Mauerschau: Festschrift für Manfred Korfmann*, edited by R. Aslan, S. Blum, G. Kastl, F. Schweizer, and D. Thumm, 469–74. Remshalden-Grünbach.

Basedow, M. 2006. "What the Blind Man Saw: New Information from the Iron Age at Troy." In *Common Ground: Archaeology, Art, Science, and Humanities. Acta of the XVIth International Congress of Classical Archaeology, August 2003*, edited by C. Mattusch, A. Brauer, and A.A. Donohue, 18–22. Oxford.

Basedow, M. 2007. Troy without Homer: the Bronze Age-Iron Age Transition in the Troad." In *Epos: Reconsidering Greek Epic and Aegean Bronze Age Archaeology. Proceedings of the 11th International Aegean Conference, Los Angeles, UCLA, The J. Paul Getty Villa, 20–23 April 2006*, edited by S.P. Morris and R. Laffineur, 49–58. Aegaeum 28. Liège.

Basedow, M. 2009. "The Iron Age Transition at Troy." In *Forces of Transformation: The End of the Bronze Age in the Mediterranean*, edited by C. Bachhuber and R.G. Roberts, 131–42. Oxford.

Bass, G.F. 1970. "A Hoard of Trojan and Sumerian Jewelry." *AJA* 74: 335–41.

Bassett, S. 2004. *The Urban Image of Late Antique Constantinople*. Cambridge.

Baughan, E. 2004. "Anatolian Funerary Klinai: Tradition and Identity." Ph.D. diss., University of California, Berkeley.

Bayne, N. 2000. *The Grey Wares of North-West Anatolia in the Middle and Late Bronze Age and the Early Iron Age and Their Relation to the Early Greek Settlements*, Bonn.

Beard, M. 1994. "The Roman and the Foreign: The Cult of the 'Great Mother' in Imperial Rome." In *Shamanism, History, and the State*, edited by T. Nicholas and C. Humphrey, 164–90. Ann Arbor, Mich.

Beazley, J.D. 1947. *Etruscan Vase Painting*. Oxford.

Beazley, J.D. 1956. *Attic Black-Figure Vase-Painters*. Oxford.

Becatti, G. 1960. *La colonna coclide istoriata: problemi storici, iconografici, stilistici.* Rome.

Becker, H. J., and H.G. Jansen. 1994. "Magnetic Prospektion 1993 der Unterstadt von Troia und Ilion." *Studia Troica* 4: 105–14.

Becker, H., J. Faßbinder, and H.G. Jansen. 1993. "Magnetische Prospektion in der Untersiedlung von Troia 1992." *Studia Troica* 3: 117–34.

Beckman, G. 1996. *Hittite Diplomatic Texts.* Atlanta, Ga.

Beckman, G., T.R. Bryce, and E.H. Cline. 2011. *The Ahhiyawa Texts.* Atlanta, Ga.

Becks, R. 2002. "Bemerkungen zu den Bestattungsplätzen von Troia VI." In *Mauerschau: Festschrift für Manfred Korfmann,* edited by R. Aslan, S. Blum, G. Kastl, F. Schweizer, and D. Thumm, 295–306. Remshalden-Grünbach.

Becks, R. 2003. "Troia VII: The Transition from the Late Bronze Age to the Early Iron Age." In *Identifying Changes: The Transition from Bronze to Iron Ages in Anatolia and Its Neighboring Regions,* edited by B. Fischer, H. Genz, E. Jean, and K. Köroglu, 41–53. Istanbul.

Becks, R. 2005. "Die nördliche Burgmauer von Troia VI." *Studia Troica* 15: 99–120.

Becks, R. 2006. "Troia in der späten Bronzezeit: Troia VI und Troia VIIa." In *Troia: Archäologie eines Siedlungshügels und seiner Landschaft,* edited by M. Korfmann, 155–67. Mainz am Rhein.

Becks, R., W. Rigter, and P. Hnila. 2006a. "Das Terrassenhaus im westlichen Unterstadtsviertel von Troia." *Studia Troica* 16: 27–88.

Becks, R., P. Hnila, and M. Pieniazek-Sikora. 2006b. "Troia in der frühen Eisenzeit: Troia VIIb1–VIIb3." In *Troia: Archäologie eines Siedlungshügels und seiner Landschaft,* edited by M. Korfmann, 181–8. Mainz am Rhein.

Behrwald, R. 2005. *Hellenika von Oxyrhynchos.* Texte zur Forschung 86. Darmstadt.

Bellamy, R. 1989. "Bellerophon's Tablet." *CJ* 84: 289–307.

Bellinger, A.R. 1957. "The Earliest Coins of Ilium." *ANSMN* 7: 43–9.

Bellinger, A.R. 1961. *Troy: The Coins.* Troy Excavations Supplementary Monograph 1. Princeton, N.J.

Benecke, N. 2002. "Die frühbronzezeitlichen Pferde von Kırklareli-Kanlıgeçit, Thrakien, Türkei." *Eurasia Antiqua* 8: 39–59.

Benjamin, A. 1963. "The Altars of Hadrian in Athens and Hadrian's Panhellenic Program." *Hesperia* 32: 57–86.

Benndorf, O. 1884. *Reisen in südwestlichen Kleinasien.* Vienna.

Bennet, J. 1997. "Homer and the Bronze Age." In *A New Companion to Homer,* edited by I. Morris and B. Powell, 511–34. Leiden.

Benzi, M. 2002. "Anatolia and the Eastern Aegean at the Time of the Trojan War." In *Omero Tremila anni dopo,* edited by F. Montanari, 343–406. Rome.

Bérard, J. 1959. "La migration éolienne." *RA:* 1–28.

Berger, E. 1970. *Das Basler Arztrelief: Studien zum griechischen Grabund Votivrelief um 500 v. Chr. und zur vorhippokratischen Medizin.* Basel.

Berger, E. 1994. "Penthesileia." *LIMC* VII: 296–305.

Berlin, A.M. 1999. "Studies in Hellenistic Ilion: The Lower City. Stratified Assemblages and Chronology." *Studia Troica* 9: 73–157.

Berlin, A.M. 2002. "Ilion before Alexander: A Fourth Century B.C. Ritual Deposit." *Studia Troica* 12: 131–65.

Berlin, A.M., and K. Lynch. 2002. "Going Greek: Atticizing Pottery in the Achaemenid World." *Studia Troica* 12: 167–78.

Bernabò Brea, L. 1976. *Poliochni: città preistorica nell'isola di Lemnos.* Rome.

Bernard, P. 1970. "Sièges et lits en ivoire d'époque hellénistique en Asia central." *Syria* 47: 327–43.

Bernardi Ferrero, D. 1970. *Teatri classici in Asia Minore III.* Rome.

Best, J.G.P. 1969. *Thracian Peltasts and Their Influence on Greek Warfare.* Groningen.

Betancourt, P.P. 1977. *Aeolic Style in Architecture: A Survey of its Development in Palestine, the Halikarnassos Peninsula, and Greece, 1000–500 B.C.* Princeton, N.J.

Betancourt, P.P. 2006. "Joining Techniques of Early Bronze Age Trojan Jewelry." *Studia Troica* 16: 89–95.

Bieber, M. 1961. *The History of the Greek and Roman Theater.* Princeton, N.J.

Bieber, M. 1977. *Ancient Copies*. New York.

Bieg, G. 2002. "Neue Funde aus der Troas: Eine archaische Bronzepunze aus Ophryneion und ein hellenistischer Klappspiegel mit Erosrelief aus der Umgebung von Kumkale, Provinz Çanakkale." *Studia Troica* 12: 451–66.

Bieg, G. 2006. "Die Perser in der Troas." In *Tekmeria: Archäologische Zeugnisse in ihrer kulturhistorischen und politischen Dimension. Beiträge für Werner Gauer*, edited by N. Kreutz and B. Schweizer, 25–39. Münster.

Bieg, G. 2009. "Bollwerke der Herrschaft: Burgen und Festungen; Antike Stätten: Spuren vergangener Macht und Größe; Antike Steinbrüche und Tumuli." In *Stadt und Landschaft Homers. Ein historisch geografischer Führer für Troia und Umgebung*, edited by V. Höhfeld, 177–224. Mainz am Rhein.

Bieg, G., and R. Aslan. 2006. "Eine Quellhöhle in Spratt's Plateau (Subaşi Tepe): Wo lag Sigeion?" *Studia Troica* 16: 133–45.

Bieg, G., B. Tekkök, and R. Aslan. 2006. "Die spätrömische Besiedlung der Troas: ein Überblick." *Studia Troica* 16: 147–70.

Bieg, G., K. Belke, and B. Tekkök. 2008. "Die mittel- bis spätbyzantinische Besiedlung innerhalb des Nationalparks 'Troia und die Troas.'" *Studia Troica* 18: 163–97.

Bieg, G., S. Blum, R. Körpe, N. Sevinç, and R. Aslan. 2009. "Yeşiltepe: Eine Siedlung der Frühen Bronzezeit am Oberlauf des Skamanders." *Studia Troica* 18: 199–227.

Bier, L. 2008. "The Bouleuterion at Aphrodisias." In *Aphrodisias Papers 4: New Research on the City and its Monuments*, edited by C. Ratté and R.R.R. Smith, 144–68. Portsmouth, R.I.

Bier, L. 2011. *The Bouleuterion at Ephesos*. Vienna.

Billows, R.A. 1990. *Antigonos the One-Eyed and the Creation of the Hellenistic State*. Berkeley, Calif.

Bingöl, O. 1990. "Überlegungen zum ionischen Gebälk." *IstMitt* 40: 101–8.

Bingöl, O. 1997. *Malerei und Mosaik der Antike in der Türkei*. Mainz am Rhein.

Bischop, D. 1993. "Gläser griechischer und römischer Zeit." In *Ausgrabungen in Assos 1991*, edited by Ü. Serdaroğlu and R. Stupperich, 211–57. Asia Minor Studien Band 10. Bonn.

Bittner, A. 1998. *Gesellschaft und Wirtschaft in Herakleia Pontike: Eine Polis zwischen Tyrannis und Selbstverwaltung*. Bonn.

Bittner, S. 1985. *Tracht und Bewaffnung des persischen Heeres zur Zeit der Achaimeniden*. Munich.

Blackman, D.J. 1973. "Comment." In *Bronze Age Migrations in the Aegean: Archaeological and Linguistic Problems in Greek Prehistory*, edited by R.A. Crossland and A. Birchall, 315. London.

Blake, M. 1936. "Roman Mosaics of the Second Century in Italy." *MAAR* 13: 67–214.

Blake, M. 1947. *Ancient Roman Construction in Italy from the Prehistoric Period to Augustus*. Washington, D.C.

Blegen, C.W. 1932. "Excavations at Troy, 1932." *AJA* 36: 431–51.

Blegen, C.W. 1934. "Excavations at Troy, 1933." *AJA* 39: 6–34.

Blegen, C.W. 1935a. "Excavations at Troy, 1934." *AJA* 38: 223–48.

Blegen, C.W. 1935b. "Excavations at Troy, 1935." *AJA* 39: 550–87.

Blegen, C.W. 1937a. "Excavations at Troy, 1936." *AJA* 41: 17–51.

Blegen, C.W. 1937b. "Excavations at Troy, 1937." *AJA* 41: 553–97.

Blegen, C.W. 1939. "Excavations at Troy, 1938." *AJA* 43: 204–28.

Blegen, C.W. 1963. *Troy and the Trojans*. New York.

Blegen, C.W., J.L. Caskey, M. Rawson, and J. Sperling. 1950. *Troy I: The First and Second Settlements*. Princeton, N.J.

Blegen, C.W., J.L. Caskey, and M. Rawson. 1951. *Troy II: The Third, Fourth, and Fifth Settlements*. Princeton, N.J.

Blegen, C.W., J.L. Caskey, and M. Rawson. 1953. *Troy III: The Sixth Settlement*. Princeton, N.J.

Blegen, C.W., C.G. Boulter, J.L. Caskey, and M. Rawson. 1958. *Troy IV: Settlements VIIa, VIIb and VIII*. Princeton, N.J.

Blegen, E.P. 1933. "News Items from Athens." *AJA* 37: 491–5.

Blegen, E.P. 1936. "News Items from Athens." *AJA* 40: 371–7.

Blindow, N., H.G. Jansen, and K. Schröer. 2000. "Geophysikalische Prospektion 1998/99 in der Unterstadt von Troia." *Studia Troica* 10: 123–34.

Blinkenberg, C. 1912. *La chronique du temple lindien*. Copenhagen.

Bloedow, E.F. 1985. "Handmade Burnished Ware or Barbarian Pottery and Troy VIIB." *PP* 40: 161–99.

Bloesch, H. 1974. *Tier in der Antike*. Zurich.

Blome, P. 2001. "Der Mythos in der griechischen Kunst. Der Troianische Krieg findet statt." In *Troia: Traum und Wirklichkeit*, edited by B. Theune-Großkopf, U. Seidel, G. Kastl, M. Kempa, R. Redies, and A. Wais, 118–53. Stuttgart.

Blum, S. 2006. "Troia an der Wende von der frühen zur mittleren Bronzezeit: Troia IV und Troia V." In *Troia: Archäologie eines Siedlungshügels und seiner Landschaft*, edited by M. Korfmann, 145–54. Mainz am Rhein.

Blümel, W. 1996. "Zum Verhältnis zwischen Gemeinsprache und Dialekt am Beispiel des Aiolischen der Troas." In *Die Troas: neue Forschungen zu Neandria und Alexandria Troas II*, edited by E. Schwertheim and H. Wiegartz, 9–14. Bonn.

Boardman, J. 1968. *Archaic Greek Gems*. Evanston, Ill.

Boardman, J. 1970. *Greek Gems and Finger Rings*. London.

Boardman, J. 1978. *Greek Sculpture: The Archaic Period*. London.

Boardman, J. 1990a. "Al Mina and History." *OJA* 9: 169–90.

Boardman, J. 1990b. "Symposium Furniture." In *Sympotica: A Symposium on the Symposium*, edited by O. Murray, 122–31. Oxford.

Boardman, J. 1999. *The Greeks Overseas: Their Early Colonies and Trade*. New York.

Boardman, J. 2000. *Persia and the West*. London.

Boardman, J. 2007. Review of *In Sepulkral-und Votivdenkmäler östliches Mittelmeergebiete (7 Jh. v. Chr.- 1 Jh. n. Chr.): Kulturbegegnungen im Spannungsfeld von Akzeptanz und Resistenz. Akten des Internationalen Symposiums Mainz am Rhein, 1–3 November 2001*, edited by R. Bol and D. Kreikenbom. *JHS* 127: 229.

Boatwright, M.T. 2000. *Hadrian and the Cities of the Roman Empire*. Princeton, N.J.

Bodenstedt, F. 1982. "Vorstufen der Porträtkunst in der ostgriechischen Münzprägung des 5. und 4. Jh. v. Chr." In *Proceedings of the 9th International Congress of Numismatics*. edited by T. Hackens and R. Weiller, 95–9. Louvain-la-Neuve.

Boehlau, J. 1898. *Aus ionischen und italischen Nekropolen. Ausgrabungen und Untersuchungen zur Geschichte der nachmykenischen griechischen Kunst*. Leipzig.

Boehringer, C. 1993. "Antiochos Hierax am Hellespont." In *Essays in Honor of Robert Carson and Kenneth Jenkins*, edited by M. Price, A. Burnett, and R. Bland, 37–47. London.

Bogaert, R. 1968. *Banques et banquiers dans les cités grecques*. Leiden.

Böhlendorf, B. 1997. "Byzantinische Keramik des Beşik-Tepe." *Studia Troica* 7: 363–444.

Böhlendorf, B. 1998. "Ein byzantinisches Gräberfeld in Troia/Ilion." *Studia Troica* 8: 263–73.

Bohn, R. 1885. *Das Heiligtum der Athena Polias Nikephoros*. Altertümer von Pergamon 2. Berlin.

Bohn, R. 1889. *Altertümer von Aegae*. Berlin.

Bohtz, C. 1981. *Das Demeter-Heiligtum*. Altertümer von Pergamon 13. Berlin.

Bol, P. 1985. *Antike Bronzetechnik*. Munich.

Bol, R. 1984. *Das Statuenprogramm des Herodes-Atticus-Nymphäums*. Berlin.

Boltunova, A.I. 1954. "On the Inscription IosPE 400." *VDI* 1: 168–76.

Bonfante, L. 1978. "History Art: Etruscan and Early Roman." *AJAH* 3: 136–62.

Bonfante, L. 1989. "Nudity as a Costume in Classical Art." *AJA* 93: 543–70.

Bonnechere, P. 1994. *Le sacrifice humain en Grèce ancienne*. Athens.

Bookidis, N., and R. Stroud. 1997. *The Sanctuary of Demeter and Kore: Topography and Architecture*. Corinth 18.3. Princeton, N.J.

Borchhardt, J. 1968a. "Dynastische Grabanlagen von Kadyanda." *JdI* 83: 174–238.

Borchhardt, J. 1968b. "Epichorische, gräko-persisch beeinflußte Reliefs in Kilikien." *IstMitt* 18: 161–211.

Borchhardt, J. 1970. "Das Heroon von Limyra: Grabmal des Lykischen Königs Perikles." *AA*: 353–90.

Borchhardt, J. 1976. *Die Bauskulptur des Heroons von Limyra: Das Grabmal des lykischen Königs Perikles*. Berlin.

Borchhardt, J. 1980. "Zur Deutung lykischer Audienzszenen." In *Actes du colloque sur la Lycie antique*, edited by H. Metzger, 7–14. Paris.

Borchhardt, J., ed. 1990. *Götter, Heroen, Herrscher in Lykien.* Munich.

Borchhardt, J. 1993. *Die Steine von Zemuri.* Vienna.

Borelli, L.V. 1993. "Postilla alla questione del "Trono" di Boston." *BdA* 77: 55–62.

Borgolte, M. 2001. "Europas Geschichten und Troia: Der Mythos im Mittelalter." In *Troia: Traum und Wirklichkeit*, edited by B. Theune-Großkopf, U. Seidel, G. Kastl, M. Kempa, R. Redies, and A. Wais, 190–203. Stuttgart.

Boschung, D. 1993. *Die Bildnisse des Augustus.* Berlin.

Bosworth, A.B. 1980. *A Historical Commentary on Arrian's History of Alexander. Volume I: Commentary on Books I–III.* Oxford.

Boulé, P. 1987. *La fille d'Athenes. La religion des filles à Athenes à l'epoque classique. Mythes, cultes, et societé.* Paris.

Boyce, M. 1975. *A History of Zoroastrianism I.* Leiden.

Boysan-Dietrich, N. 1987. *Das hethitische Lehmhaus aus der Sicht der Keilschriftquellen.* Heidelberg.

Braccesi, L. 1984. *La leggenda di Antenore da Troia a Padova.* Venice.

Brandt, E. 1968. *Antike Gemmen in deutschen Sammlungen. Munich.* Munich.

Braund, D. 1984. *Rome and the Friendly King: The Character of the Client Kingship.* London.

Bravo, B. 1980. "Sulan: Représailles et justice privée contre des étrangers dans les cités grecques." *AnnPisa* 10: 675–987.

Briant, P. 1996. *Histoire de l'empire perse de Cyrus à Alexandre.* Paris.

Briant, P. 2001. *Irrigation et drainage dans l'antiquité, qanats et canalisations souterraines en Iran, en Égypte, et en Grèce.* Paris.

Briant, P. 2002. *From Cyrus to Alexander: A History of the Persian Empire.* Winona Lake, Ind.

Brill, R.H., and N. Cahill. 1988. "A Red Opaque Glass from Sardis and Some Thoughts on Red Opaque in General." *JGS* 30: 16–27.

Bringmann, K., and H. von Steuben, eds. 1995. *Schenkungen hellenistischer Herrscher an griechische Städte und Heiligtümer I: Zeugnisse und Kommentare.* Berlin.

Brink, C.O. 1972. "Ennius and the Hellenistic Worship of Homer." *AJP* 93: 547–67.

Brinkmann, V. 1994. *Beobachtungen zum formalen Aufbau und zum Sinngehalt der Friese des Siphnierschatzhauses.* Enneptal.

Briscoe, J. 1972. *A Commentary on Livy. Books XXXI–XXXIII.* Oxford.

Brommer, F. 1967. *Die Metopen des Parthenon.* Mainz am Rhein.

Brommer, F. 1969. "Eine Lekythos in Madrid." *MM* 10: 155–71.

Broneer, O. 1933. "Excavations on the North Slope of the Acropolis in Athens." *Hesperia* 2: 329–417.

Broughton, T.R.S. 1938. "Roman Asia." In *An Economic Survey of Ancient Rome*, edited by F. Tenney, 499–916. Paterson, N.J.

Brown, P.F. 1996. *Venice and Antiquity: The Venetian Sense of the Past.* New Haven, Conn.

Brownlee, A.B. 1995. "Story Lines: Observations on Sophilan Narrative." In *The Ages of Homer: A Tribute to Emily Townsend Vermeule*, edited by J.B Carter and S.P. Morris, 363–72. Austin, Tex.

Brueckner, A. 1907. "Athenische Hochzeitgeschenke." *AM* 32: 79–122.

Bruneau, P. 1970. *Recherches sur les cultes de Délos à l'époque hellénistique et à l'époque impériale.* Paris.

Bruneau, P. 1983. *Guide de Delos.* Paris.

Bruno, V.J. 1969. "Antecedents of the Pompeian First Style." *AJA* 73: 305–17.

Bruno, V.J. 1977. *Form and Colour in Greek Painting.* London.

Bruns-Özgan, C. 1987. *Lykische Grabreliefs des 5. und 4. Jahrhunderts v. Chr.* Tübingen.

Brunton, J. 1939. *John Brunton's Book.* Cambridge.

Brunwasser, Matthew. 2011. "The Tomb of Hecatomnus – Milas, Turkey." *Archaeology* 64.1: 25.

Bryce, T.R. 1985. "A Reinterpretation of the Milawata Letter in the Light of the New Join Piece." *AnatSt* 35: 13–23.

Bryce, T.R. 1986. *The Lycians in Literary and Epigraphic Sources.* Copenhagen.

Bryce, T.R. 1998. *The Kingdom of the Hittites.* Oxford.

Bryce, T.R. 2002. *Life and Society in the Hittite World.* Oxford.

Bryce, T.R. 2003. "History." In *The Luwians,* edited by H.C. Melchert, 27–127. Leiden.

Bryce, T.R. 2006. *The Trojans and Their Neighbors.* London.

Buchthal, H. 1971. *Historia Troiana: Studies in the History of Mediaeval Secular Illustration.* London.

Buckler, J. 1980. *The Theban Hegemony, 371–362 B.C.* Cambridge.

Budde, L., and R.V. Nicholls. 1964. *A Catalogue of the Greek and Roman Sculpture in the Fitzwilliam Museum.* Cambridge.

Bundrick, S. 2005. *Music and Image in Classical Athens.* Cambridge.

Bunimovitz, S. 1992. "The Middle Bronze Age Fortifications in Palestine as a Social Phenomenon." *Tel Aviv* 19: 221–34.

Buraselis, K. 1982. *Das hellenistische Makedonien und die Ägäis: Forschungen zur Politik des Kassandros und der drei ersten Antigoniden (Antigonos Monopthalmos, Demetrios Poliorketes und Antigonos Gonatas) im ägäischen Meer und in Westkleinasien.* Munich.

Burford, A. 1966. "Notes on the Epidaurian Building Inscriptions." *BSA* 61: 254–333.

Burford, A. 1969. *The Greek Temple Builders at Epidauros.* Liverpool.

Burgess, J.S. 2005. "Tumuli of Achilles." *The Homerizon: Conceptual Interrogations in Homeric Studies.* http://chs.harvard.edu/publications. sec/classics.ssp.

Burke, B. 2007. "Gordion of Midas and the Homeric Age." In *Epos: Reconsidering Greek Epic and Aegean Bronze Age Archaeology. Proceedings of the 11th International Aegean Conference, Los Angeles, UCLA, the J. Paul Getty Villa, 20–23 April 2006,* edited by S.P. Morris and R. Laffineur, 151–6. Aegaeum 28. Liège.

Burkert, W. 1983. *Homo Necans: The Anthropology of Ancient Greek Sacrificial Ritual and Myth.* Berkeley, Calif.

Burkert, W. 1985. *Greek Religion.* Cambridge, Mass.

Burkert, W. 1992. *The Orientalizing Revolution: Near Eastern Influence on Greek Culture in the Early Archaic Age.* Cambridge, Mass.

Burkert, W. 1993. "Concordia Discors: The Literary and the Archaeological Evidence on the Sanctuary of Samothrace." In *Greek Sanctuaries: New Approaches,* edited by N. Marinatos and R. Hägg, 178–91. London.

Burkert, W. 2001. *Savage Energies: Lessons of Myth and Ritual in Ancient Greece.* Chicago, Ill.

Burnett, A.P., and C.N. Edmonson. 1961. "The Chabrias Monument in the Athenian Agora." *Hesperia* 30: 74–91.

Burstein, S. 1976. *Outpost of Hellenism: The Emergence of Heraclea on the Black Sea.* Berkeley, Calif.

Byock, J.L. 1988. *Medieval Iceland: Society, Sagas, and Power.* Berkeley, Calif.

Byock, J.L., ed. 2005. *The Prose Edda: Norse Mythology.* London.

Byrne, M. 1993. "The Dardanos Fragments and the 40° Angular Lyre." *The Galpin Society Journal* 46: 3–25.

Cahn, H.A. 1975. "Dynast oder Satrap." *SchwMbll* 25: 84–91.

Cahn, H.A. 1989. "Le monnayage des satrapes: iconographie et signification." *RÉA* 91: 97–106.

Cahn, H.A., and D. Gerin. 1988. "Themistocles at Magnesia." *NC* 148: 13–20.

Cahn, H.A., and D. Mannsperger. 1991. "Themistocles Again." *NC* 151: 199–202.

Çakırlar, C., and R. Becks. 2008. "'Murex' Dye Production at Troia: An Assessment of Archaeomalacological Data from Old and New Excavations." *Studia Troica* 18: 87–103.

Calciani, F. 1981a. "Aeneas." *LIMC* I: 381–96.

Calciani, F. 1981b. "Anchises." *LIMC* I: 761–4.

Çalış-Sazcı, D.. 2006. "Die Troianer und das Meer: Keramik und Handelsbeziehungen der sog. 'Maritimen Troia-Kulter.'" In *Troia: Archäologie eines Siedlungshügels und seiner Landschaft,* edited by M. Korfmann, 201–8. Mainz am Rhein.

Calmeyer, P. 1992. "Zwei mit historischen Szenen Bemalte Balken der Achaimenidenzeit." *MüJb* 43: 7–18.

Calmeyer, P. 1996. "Achaimenidische Möbel und Kussu Sa Sarrute." In *The Furniture of Western Asia, Ancient and Traditional,* edited by G. Herrmann, 223–31. Mainz am Rhein.

Cameron, A. 2011. *The Last Pagans of Rome.* Oxford.

Camp, J. 2001. *The Archaeology of Athens.* New Haven, Conn.

Camporeale, G. 1981. "Achle." *LIMC* I: 200–14.

Canciani, F. 1994. "Protesilaos." *LIMC* VII: 554–60.

Caner, E. 1983. *Fibeln in Anatolien.* Munich.

Capdetrey, L. 2007. *Le pouvoir séleucide: territoire, administration, finances d'un royaume hellénistique (312–129 avant J.-C.).* Rennes.

Carpenter, R., and A. Bon. 1936. *The Defenses of Acrocorinth and the Lower Town.* Corinth 3.2. Cambridge, Mass.

Carrata Thomes, F. 1968. *La rivolta di Aristonico e le origini della provincia romana d'Asia.* Torino.

Carroll-Spillecke, Maureen. 1985. *Landscape Depictions in Greek Relief Sculpture: Development and Conventionalization.* New York.

Carter, J.B. 1997. "*Thiasos* and *Marzeah*: Ancestor Cult in the Age of Homer." In *New Light on a Dark Age: Exploring the Culture of Geometric Greece*, edited by S. Langdon, 72–112, Columbia, Mo.

Carter, J.C. 1983. *The Sculpture of the Sanctuary of Athena Polias at Priene.* London.

Caskey, J.L. 1935. "New Inscriptions from Troy." *AJA* 39: 588–92.

Caskey, L.D. 1925. *Catalogue of Greek and Roman Sculpture.* Cambridge, Mass.

Càssola, F. 1957. *La Ionia nel mondo miceneo.* Naples.

Castor, A. 1999. "Enotia: The Contexts of Greek Earrings, Tenth to Third Century B.C." Ph.D. diss., Bryn Mawr College.

Castriota, D. 1992. *Myth, Ethos, and Actuality: Official Art in Fifth-Century B.C. Athens.* Madision, Wis.

Catling, R.W.V. 1998. "The Typology of the Protogeometric and Subprotogeometric Pottery from Troia and Its Aegean Context." *Studia Troica* 8: 151–87.

Catling, R.W.V., and I.S. Lemos. 1990. *Lefkandi II: The Protogeometric Building at Toumba, Part 1: The Pottery.* London.

Cavuoto, P. 1983. *Macrino.* Naples.

Çaylak Türker, A. 2010. "Bizans Döneminde Çanakkale Boğazı ve Yerleşim Modelleri: Skamander Vadisi." *Anadolu ve Çevresinde Ortaçağ* 4: 53–94.

Ceccarelli, P. 1998. *La pirrica nell'antichità greco romana: studi sulla danza armata.* Pisa.

Chadwick, J. 1956. "The Greek Dialects and Greek Pre-history." *GaR* 3: 38–50.

Chadwick, J. 1988. "The Women of Pylos." In *Texts, Tablets, and Scribes: Studies in Mycenaean Epigraphy and Economy*, edited by J.-P. Olivier and T.G. Palaima, 42–95. *Minos* Supplement 10. Salamanca.

Chapouthier, F. 1935a. *Les dioscures au service d'une déese: étude d'iconographie religieuse.* Bibliothèque des Écoles Francaises d'Athènes et de Rome 137 (ser. 1). Paris.

Chapouthier, F., 1935b. *Le sanctuaire des dieux de Samothrace.* Exploration Archéologique de Délos 16. Paris.

Chapouthier, F., A. Salac, and F. Salviat. 1956. "Le Theater de Samothrace." *BCH* 80: 118–46.

Childs, W.A.P. 1978. *The City-Reliefs of Lycia.* Princeton, N.J.

Childs, W.A.P. 1981. "Lycian Relations with Persians and Greeks in the Fifth and Fourth Centuries Re-examined." *AnatSt* 31: 55–80.

Childs, W.A.P., and P. Demargne. 1989. *Fouilles de Xanthos VIII: Le monument des néréides et le décor sculpté.* Paris.

Choiseul-Gouffier, M.-G.-F.-A de. 1782–1822. *Voyage pittoresque de la Grèce.* Paris.

CIRB. 1965. *Corpus Inscriptionum Regni Bosporani.* Leningrad.

Clairmont, C. 1993. *Classical Attic Tombstones.* Kilchberg.

Clarke, J. 1979. *Roman Black and White Figural Mosaics.* New York.

Clarke, J. 1998. *Looking at Lovemaking: Constructions of Sexuality in Roman Art, 100 B.C.–A.D. 250.* Berkeley, Calif.

Clarke, J. 2007. *Looking at Laughter: Humor, Power, and Transgression in Roman Visual Culture, 100 B.C.–A.D. 250.* Berkeley, Calif.

Clarke, J.T. 1898. *Report on the Investigations at Assos, 1882, 1883, Part 1.* New York.

Cline, E.H. 1991. "A Possible Hittite Embargo against the Mycenaeans." *Historia* 40: 1–9.

Cline, E.H. 1994. *Sailing the Wine-Dark Sea: International Trade and the Late Bronze Age Aegean.* BAR-IS 591. Oxford.

Cline, E.H. 1996. "Assuwa and the Achaeans: The 'Mycenaean' Sword at Hattusas and Its Possible Implications." *BSA* 91: 137–51.

Cline, E.H. 2008. "Troy as a 'Contested Periphery': Archaeological Perspectives on Cross-Cultural and Cross-Disciplinary Interactions Concerning Bronze Age Anatolia." In *Anatolian Interfaces: Hittites, Greeks and Their Neighbours: Proceedings of an International Conference on Cross-Cultural Interaction, September 17–19, 2004, Emory University, Atlanta, GA*, edited by B.J. Collins, M. Bachvarova and I. Rutherford, 11–19. Oxford.

Clinton, K. 2003. "Stages of Initiation in the Eleusinian and Samothracian Mysteries." In *Greek Mysteries: The Archaeology and Ritual of Ancient Greek Secret Cults*, edited by M. Cosmopoulos, 50–78. London.

Coarelli, F. 1993a. "Auguratorium." *LTUR* I: 143.

Coarelli, F. 1993b. "Casa Romuli (Cermalus)." *LTUR* I: 241–2.

Coarelli, F. 1996. "Lupercal." *LTUR* III: 198–9.

Cohen, A. 1997. *The Alexander Mosaic*. Cambridge.

Cohen, G.M. 1995. *The Hellenistic Settlements in Europe, the Islands, and Asia Minor*. Berkeley, Calif.

Cohen, G.M. 1996." A Dedication to the Samothracian Gods." *Studia Troica* 6: 201–7.

Cohen, P. 2004. "In Search of the Trojan Origins of the French: The Uses of History in the Elevation of the Vernacular in Early Modern France." In *Fantasies of Troy: Classical Tales and the Social Imaginary in Medieval and Early Modern Europe*, edited by A. Shepard and S.D. Powell, 63–80. Toronto.

Coldstream, J.N. 1976. "Hero Cults in the Age of Homer." *JHS* 96: 8–17.

Coldstream, J.N. 2000. "Evans's Greek Finds: The Early Greek Town of Knossos, and Its Encroachment on the Borders of the Minoan Palace." *BSA* 95: 259–99.

Cole, S.G. 1984. *Theoi Megaloi: The Cult of the Great Gods at Samothrace*. Leiden.

Cole, S.G. 1989. "The Mysteries of Samothrace during the Roman Period." *ANRW* II.18.2: 1564–98.

Coletti, L. 1935. *Treviso*. Bergamo.

Connolly, P. 1981. *Greece and Rome at War*. Englewood Cliffs, N.J.

Connor, R. 1993. "The Ionian Era of Athenian Civic Identity." *PAPS* 137: 194–206.

Cook, J.M. 1953a. "The Agamemnoneion." *BSA* 48: 30–68.

Cook, J.M. 1953b. "The Cult of Agamemnon at Mycenae." In *Geras Antoniou Keramopoullou*, 112–18. Athens.

Cook, J.M. 1961. "The Problem of Classical Ionia." *PCPS* 187: 9–18.

Cook, J.M. 1962. *The Greeks in Ionia and the East*. London.

Cook, J.M. 1973. *The Troad: An Archaeological and Topographical Study*. Oxford.

Cook, J.M. 1975. "Greek Settlement in the Eastern Aegean and Asia Minor." In *Cambridge Ancient History*, 3rd edition, vol. 2, pt. 2, edited by I.E.J. Edwards, C.J. Gadd, N.G.L. Hammond, and E. Sollberger, 773–804. Cambridge.

Cook, J.M. 1983. *The Persian Empire*. New York.

Cook, J.M., and R.V. Nichols. 1998. *Old Smyrna Excavations: The Temples of Athena*. London.

Cook, R.M. 1974. "Old Smyrna: The Clazomenian Sarcophagi." *Papers of the British School at Athens* 69: 555–60.

Cook, R.M. 1981. *Clazomenian Sarcophagi*. Mainz am Rhein.

Cook, R.M., and P. Dupont. 1998. *East Greek Pottery*. London.

Corsaro, M. 1984. "Un decreto di Zelea sul recupero dei terreni pubblici (Syll.³, 279)." *AnnPisa* 3.14: 441–93.

Costamagna, L., and C. Sabbione. 1990. *Una città in Magna Grecia, Locri Epizefiri: guida archeologica*. Reggio Calabria.

Cramer, T., K. Germann, and W.D. Heilmeyer. 2002. "Petrographic and Geochemical Characterization of the Pergamon Altar (Telephos Frieze) Marble in the Pergamon Museum, Berlin." In *ASMOSIA VI, Interdisciplinary Studies on Ancient Stone: Proceedings of the Sixth International Conference of the Association for the Study of Marble and other Stones in Antiquity, Museum of Fine Arts, Boston, June 1998*, edited by L. Lazzarini, 285–91. Padua.

Crawford, J. S. 1990. *The Byzantine Shops at Sardis*. Archaeological Exploration of Sardis, Monograph 9. Cambridge.

Crawford, M. 1974. *Roman Republican Coinage*. London.

Cremer, M. 1984. "Zwei neue graeco-persische Stelen." *EpigAnat* 3: 87–99.

Crosby, M. 1943. "A Silver Ladle and Strainer." *AJA* 47: 209–16.

Crouch, D. 1993. *Water Management in Ancient Greek Cities.* New York.

Crouwel, J.H. 1992. *Chariots and Other Wheeled Vehicles in Iron Age Greece.* Amsterdam.

Crow, J. 1995. "The Long Walls of Thrace." In *Constantinople and Its Hinterland: Papers from the Twenty-seventh Spring Symposium of Byzantine Studies, Oxford, April 1993,* edited by C. Mango and G. Dagron, 109–24. Brookfield, Vt.

Crow, J. 2007. "The Infrastructure of a Great City: Earth, Walls and Water in Late Antique Constantinople." In *Technology in Transition: A.D. 300–650,* edited by L. Lavan, E. Zanini, and A Sarantis, 251–85. Leiden.

Crow, J., and A. Ricci, 1997. "Investigating the Hinterland of Constantinople: Interim Report on the Anastasian Long Walls." *JRA* 10: 235–62.

Cultraro, M. 1999. "'Non è tutt' oro quel che luce': per una rilettura del riposiglio di oreficerie di Poliochni." In *Epi ponton plazomenoi: simposio italiano di studi egei,* edited by V. la Rosa and L. Vagnetti, 41–52. Rome.

Cumont, F. 1932–3. "L'adoration des Mages et l'art triumphal de Rome." *AttiPontAcc* 3: 81–105.

Curtius, E. 1855. *Die Ionier vor der ionischen Wanderung.* Berlin.

Curtius, E. 1892. *The History of Greece I.* New York.

Curty, O. 1995. *Les parentés legendaires entre cités grecques: catalogue raisonné des inscriptions contenant le terme syngeneia et analyse critique.* Geneva.

Dabrowa, E. 2004. "Lupa Romana sur les revers des monnaies des villes d'Asie Mineure." In *Ad Fontes! Festschrift für Gerhard Dobeschzum 65. Geburtstag am 15. September 2004 dargebracht von Kollegen, Schülern und Freunden,* edited by H. Heftner and K. Tomaschitz, 479–83. Vienna.

Dalton, P. 2005. "The Topical Concerns of Geoffrey of Monmouth's Historia Regum Britanniae: History, Prophecy, Peacemaking, and English Identity in the Twelfth Century." *Journal of British Studies* 44: 688–712.

Damon, C. 1995. *Res Gestae divi Augusti.* Bryn Mawr, Pa.

Danile, L. 2008. "La cultura materiale tra la fine dell'età del Bronzo e gli inizi dell'età dell Ferro." In *Hephaestia 2000–2006: ricerche e scavi della Scuola archeologica italiana di Atene in collaborazione con il Dipartimento di archeologia e storia delle arti dell'Università di Siena: atti del seminario, Siena, Certosa di Pontignano, 28–29 maggio 2007,* 39–53. Paestum.

Danile, L. 2011. *Lemno, 2: Scavi ad Efestia, 1. La ceramic grigia di Efestia. Dagli inizi dell'Età del ferro all'Alto-arcaismo.* Athens.

Danoff, C.M. 1974. "Prokonnesos." *RE* 14: 560–1.

Darbyshire, G., S. Mitchell, and L. Vardar. 2000. "The Galatian Settlement in Asia Minor." *AnatSt* 50: 75–97.

Darga, M., and F. Starke. 2003. "Eine Tonbulle mit hieroglyphen-luwischem Siegelabdruck aus Šarhöyük-Dorylaion." *Studia Troica* 13: 161–4.

Das, S. 2004. "The Disappearance of the Trojan Legend in the Historiography of Venice." In *Fantasies of Troy: Classical Tales and the Social Imaginary in Medieval and Early Modern Europe,* edited by A. Shepard, and S.D. Powell, 97–114. Toronto.

Dasen, V. 2001. "Les jumeaux dans l'imaginaire funeraire grec." In *Les Pierres de l'offrande: autour de l'oeuvre de Christoph W. Clairmont,* edited by G. Hoffmann, 72–89. Kilchberg, Switzerland.

Daumas, M. 1997. "Des Cabires thébains aux Grands Dieux de Samothrace: Aspects d'une recherche sur un culte a mystères." *RA* 1: 201–9.

Daumas, M. 1998. *Cabiriaca: recherches sur l'iconographie du culte des Cabires.* Paris.

Daux, G. 1956. "Décret de Sigée trouvé en Corse." *BCH* 80: 53–6.

Davidson, G.R. 1952. *Corinth XII: The Minor Objects.* Princeton, N.J.

Davis, J.L. 2001. "The Islands of the Aegean." In *Aegean Prehistory: A Review,* edited by T. Cullen, 19–94. Boston.

Deger-Jalkotzy, S. 1977. *Fremde Zuwanderer im spätmykenischen Griechenland: zu einer Gruppe handgemachter Keramik aus den Myk. III C Siedlungsschichten von Aigeira.* Vienna.

Delavaud-Roux, M.-H. 1993. *Les danses armées en Grèce antique.* Aix-en-Provence.

Delbrueck, R. 1929. *Die Consular-Diptychen und verwandte Denkmäler*. Berlin.

Delemen, İ. 2004. *Tekirdağ Naip tümülüsü*. Istanbul.

Delemen, İ. 2006. "An Unplundered Chamber Tomb on Ganos Mountain in Southeastern Thrace." *AJA* 110: 251–73

Deltour-Levie, C. 1982. *Les piliers funéraires de Lycie*. Louvain-la-Neuve.

Delvoye, C. 1963. Review of *Der Athenatempel von Ilion*, by F.W. Goethert and H. Schleif. *AntCl* 32: 358–9.

Demargne, P. 1958. *Fouillles de Xanthos I: les piliers funéraires*. Paris.

Demargne, P. 1974. *Fouillles de Xanthos V: tombes-maisons, tombes rupestres et sarcophages*. Paris.

Demargne, P. 1979. "Recherches en Lycie d'après des publications nouvelles." *RA* 291–5.

Demargne, P. 1984. "Athena." *LIMC* II: 955–1044.

Dentzer, J.-M. 1982. *Le motif du banquet couché dans le Proche-Orient et le monde grec du VIIe au IVe siecle avant J.-C.* Bibliothèque des Écoles Francaises d'Athènes et de Rome 246. Paris.

Deppert, K. 2006. "Überlegungen zum Polyxena-Sarkophag von Çanakkale." In *Tekmeria: Archäologische Zeugnisse in ihrer kulturhistorischen und politischen Dimension. Beiträge für Werner Gauer*, edited by N. Kreutz and B. Schweizer, 89–102. Münster.

Deppert-Lippitz, B. 1985. *Griechischer Goldschmuck*. Mainz am Rhein.

Deppert-Lippitz, B. 1998. "Greek Bracelets of the Classical Period." In *The Art of the Greek Goldsmith*, edited by D. Williams, 91–104. London.

Derow, P., and W. Forrest. 1982. "An Inscription from Chios." *BSA* 77: 79–82.

Detschew, D. 1957. *Die thrakischen Sprachreste*. Vienna.

Deubner, L. 1932. *Attische Feste*. Berlin.

DeVries, K. 1990. "The Gordion Excavation Seasons of 1969–1973 and Subsequent Research." *AJA* 94: 371–406.

DeVries, K. 2000. "The Nearly Other: The Attic Vision of Phrygians and Lydians." In *Not the Classical Ideal: Athens and the Construction of the Other in Greek Art*, edited by B. Cohen, 338–63. Leiden.

Di Filippo Balestrazzi, E. 1997. "Roma." *LIMC* Supplement: 1048–68.

Dickens, G. 1905–6. "Damophon of Mesene." *BSA* 12: 109–36.

Dickinson, O. 2010. "The Collapse at the End of the Bronze Age." In *The Oxford Handbook of the Bronze Age Aegean*, edited by E.H. Cline, 483–90. Oxford.

Dimitrova, N. 2002. "Inscriptions and Iconography in the Monuments of the Thracian Rider." *Hesperia* 71: 209–29.

Dinç, R. 1993. "Lydia Tümülüsleri." Ph.D. diss., Ege University.

Dinsmoor, W. 1940. "The Temple of Ares at Athens." *Hesperia* 9: 1–52.

Dinsmoor, W. 1973. *The Architecture of Ancient Greece*. New York.

Diop, S. 2009. "L'image troyenne et sa fonction narrative chez Darès de Phrygie et Dictys de Crète." In *Reconstruire Troie: permanence et renaissances d'une cité emblématique*, edited by M. Fartzoff, M. Faudot, E. Geny, and M.-R. Guelfucci, 121–43. Besançon.

Dommelen, P. van. 1998. "Punic Persistence: Colonialism and Cultural Identities in Roman Sardinia." In *Cultural Identity in the Roman Empire*, edited by R. Laurence and J. Berry, 25–48. London.

Dommelen, P. van. 2001. "Cultural Imaginings: Punic Tradition and Local Identity in Roman Republican Sardinia." In *Italy and the West: Comparative Issues in Romanization*, edited by S. Keay and N. Tarrenato, 68–84. Oxford.

Donlan, W. 1997. "The Homeric Economy." In *A New Companion to Homer*, edited by I. Morris and B. Powell, 649–67. Leiden.

Dorman, P.F. 1988. *The Monuments of Senenmut: Problems in Historical Methodology*. London.

Dörpfeld, W. 1894. *Troja 1893: Bericht über die im Jahre 1893 in Troja veranstalteten Ausgrabungen*. Leipzig.

Dörpfeld, W. 1902. *Troja und Ilion: Ergebnisse der Ausgrabungen in den vorhistorischen und historischen Schichten von Ilion 1870–1894*. Athens.

Draycott, C. 2008. "Bird-Women on the Harpy Monument from Xanthos, Lycia: Sirens or Harpies?" In *Essays in Classical Archaeology for Eleni Hatzivassiliou 1977–2007*, edited by D. Kurtz, 145–53. Oxford.

Ducrey, P. 1986. *Warfare in Ancient Greece*. New York.

Dueck, D., H. Lindsay, and S. Pothecary, eds. 2005. *Strabo's Cultural Geography: The Making of a Kolossourgia*. Cambridge.

Dulière, C. 1979. *Lupa Romana: recherche d'iconographie et essai d'interpretation*. Brussels and Rome.

Durliat, J., and A. Guillou. 1984. "Le tarif d'Abydos (vers 492)." *BCH* 108: 581–598.

Durnford, S. 2010. "How Old Was the Ankara Silver Bowl When Its Inscriptions Were Added?" *AnatSt* 60: 51–70.

Duyuran, R. 1960. "Decouverte d'un tumulus près de l'ancienne Dardanos." *Anatolia* 5: 9–12.

Eassie, W. 1858. *Romaic Beauties and Trojan Humbugs*. London.

Easton, D.F. 1991. "Troy before Schliemann." *Studia Troica* 1: 111–29.

Easton, D.F. 1997. "The Excavation of the Trojan Treasures, and Their History up to the Death of Schliemann in 1890." In *The Spoils of War: World War II and Its Aftermath: The Loss, Reappearance, and Recovery of Cultural Property*, edited by E. Simpson, 194–9. New York.

Easton, D.F. 2000. "Schliemann's 'Burnt City.'" *Studia Troica* 10: 73–83.

Easton, D.F. 2002. *Schliemann's Excavations at Troia, 1870–1873*. Studia Troica Monographien 2. Mainz am Rhein.

Easton, D.F. 2010. "The Wooden Horse: Some Possible Bronze Age Origins." In *Ipamati kistamati pari tumatimis: Luwian and Hittite Studies Presented to J. David Hawkins on the Occasion of His 70th Birthday*, edited by I. Singer, 50–63. Tel Aviv.

Easton, D.F., J.D. Hawkins, A.G. Sherratt, and E.S. Sherratt. 2002. "Troy in Recent Perspective." *AnatSt* 52: 75–109.

Eder, B. 2004. "Antike und moderne Mythenbildung: Der Troianische Krieg und die historische Überlieferung." In *Griechische Archaik: Interne Entwicklungen, externe Impulse*, edited by R. Rollinger and C. Ulf, 105–24. Berlin.

Eder, W. 1999. "'Grosse' griechische Kolonisation." *Der Neue Pauly* 6: 653–64.

Efe, T. 2006. "Anatolische Wurzeln: Troia und die frühe Bronzezeit im Westen Kleinasiens." In *Troia: Archäologie eines Siedlunghügels und seiner Landschaft*, edited by M. Korfmann, 15–28. Mainz am Rhein.

Efkleidou, K. 2002–03. "The Status of Outsiders within Mycenaean Pylos: Issues of Ethnic Identity, Incorporation and Marginality." *Minos* 37–8: 269–92.

Ehrhardt, N. 1983. *Milet und seine Kolonien: Vergleichende Untersuchung der kultischen und politischen Einrichtungen*. New York.

Ekroth, G. 2005. "Blood on the Altars? On the Treatment of Blood at Greek Sacrifices and the Iconographical Evidence." *AntK* 48: 9–29.

Elderkin, K. 1930. "Jointed Dolls in Antiquity." *AJA* 34: 455–79.

Elderkin, G.W. 1939. "The Sarcophagus of Sidamara." *Hesperia* 8: 101–15.

Emlyn-Jones, C.J. 1980. *The Ionians and Hellenism: A Study of the Cultural Achievement of the Early Greek Inhabitants of Asia Minor*. London.

Engelmann, H. 1976. *Die Inschriften von Kyme*. Bonn.

Ensoli, S. 1987. *L'heróon di Dexileos nel ceramico di Atene*. Rome.

Erciyas, D.B. 2006. *Wealth, Aristocracy and Royal Propaganda under the Hellenistic Kingdom of the Mithradatids in the Central Black Sea Region of Turkey*. Leiden.

Erdemgil, S., et al. 1989. *Ephesus Museum Catalogue*. Istanbul.

Erdoğu, B. 2003. "Visualizing Neolithic Landscape: The Early Settled Communities in Western Anatolia and Eastern Aegean Island." *EJA* 6: 7–23.

Erdoğu, B. 2011. "A Preliminary Report from the 2009 and 2010 Field Seasons at Uğurlu on the Island of Gökçeada." *Anatolica* 37: 45–65.

Erhart, K.P. 1978. *The Development of the Facing Head Motif on Greek Coins and Its Relation to Classical Art*. New York.

Erim, K. 1986. *Aphrodisias: City of Venus Aphrodite*. New York.

Erim, K. 1989. *Aphrodisias: A Guide to the Site and Its Museum*. Istanbul.

Erim, K., and J. Reynolds. 1970. "The Copy of Diocletian's Edict on Maximum Prices from Aphrodisias in Caria." *JRS* 60: 120–41.

Erim, K., and J. Reynolds. 1971. "Diocletian's Currency Reform: A New Inscription." *JRS* 61: 171–7.

Erkanal, H. 2008. "Liman Tepe: New Light on Prehistoric Aegean Cultures." In *The Aegean in the Neolithic, Chalcolithic and the Early Bronze Age. Proceedings of the International Symposium Urla–İzmir (Turkey) 1997*, edited by H. Erkanal, H. Haptmann, V. Şahoğlu, and R. Tuncel, 179–90. Ankara.

Erskine, A. 2001. *Troy between Greece and Rome: Local Tradition and Imperial Power*. Oxford.

Evans, H., and W. Wixom, eds. 1997. *The Glory of Byzantium: Art and Culture of the Middle Byzantine Era, A.D. 843–1261*. New York.

Evers, C. 1994. *Les portraits d'Hadrian: typologie et ateliers*. Brussels.

Ewig, E. 1997. "Le mythe troyen et l'histoire des Francs." In *Clovis: histoire et memoire. Le baptême de Clovis, l'evenement*, edited by M. Rouche, 817–47. Paris.

Fabiš, M. 1996. "Archaeofaunal Remains from the Lower Sanctuary: A Preliminary Report on the 1994 Excavations." *Studia Troica* 6: 217–27.

Fabiš, M. 2002. "Ilion before Alexander: The Archaeofaunal Remains from D9." *Studia Troica* 12: 245–74.

Fabiš, M. 2003. "Troia and Fallow Deer." In *Troia and the Troad: Scientific Approaches*, edited by G.A. Wagner, E. Pernicka, and H.-P. Uerpmann, 263–76. Berlin.

Fantham, E. 2003. "Pacuvius: Melodrama, Reversals and Recognitions." In *Myth, History and Culture in Republican Rome. Studies in Honour of T.P. Wiseman*, edited by D. Braund and C. Gill, 98–118. Exeter.

Farkas, A. 1969. "The Horse and Rider in Achaemenid Art." *Persica* 4: 57–76.

Farrington, A. 1999. "The Introduction and Spread of Roman Bathing in Greece." In *Roman Baths and Bathing: Proceedings of the First International Conference on Roman Baths held at Bath, England, 30 March–4 April 1992*, edited by J. De Laine and D.E. Johnston, 57–66. JRA Supplement 37. Portsmouth, R.I.

Federico, S. 2003. *New Troy: Fantasies of Empire in the Late Middle Ages*. Minneapolis, Minn.

Ferrari, G. 1997. "Figures in the Text: Metaphors and Riddles in the Agamemnon." *CP* 92: 1–45.

Ferron, J. 1993. *Sarcophages de Phénicie*. Paris.

Filow, B.D. 1934. *Die Grabhügelnekropole bei Duvanlij in Südbulgarien*. Sofia.

Finkelstein, I. 1992. "Middle Bronze Age '"Fortifications": A Reflection of Social Organization and Political Formations." *Tel Aviv* 19: 201–21.

Fisher, S.M. 1996. "Troian 'G 2/3 Ware' Revisited." *Studia Troica* 6: 119–32.

Fisher, S.M. 2000. "Ceramics and Culture: The Archaic Finewares of Ilion." Ph.D. diss., University of Cincinnati.

Fittschen, K., and P. Zanker. 1985. *Katalog der römischen Porträts in den Capitolinischen Museen und den anderen kommunalen Sammlungen der Stadt Rom*. Mainz am Rhein.

Fleischer, R. 1973. *Artemis von Ephesus und verwandte Kultstatuen aus Anatolien und Syrien*. Leiden.

Fleischer, R. 1983. *Der Klagefrauensarkophag aus Sidon*. Tübingen.

Fless, F. 1995. *Opferdiener und Kultmusiker auf stadtrömischen historischen Reliefs: Untersuchungen zur Ikonographie, Funktion und Bennennung*. Mainz am Rhein.

Flourentzos, P. 2007. *The Sarcophagus of Palaipafos*. Lefkosia.

Foley, A. 1988. *The Argolid 800–600 B.C.: An Archaeological Survey, Together with an Index of Sites from the Neolithic to the Roman Period*. Göteborg.

Fontenrose, J. 1978. *The Delphic Oracle: Its Responses and Operations*. Berkeley, Calif.

Fontinoy, C. 1950. "Le sacrifice nuptial de Polyxene." *AntCl* 19: 383–96.

Forbes, R.J. 1956. *Studies in Ancient Technology IV*. Leiden.

Forbes, R.J. 1964. *Studies in Ancient Technology I*, 2nd ed. Leiden.

Foss, C. 1976. *Byzantine and Turkish Sardis*. Cambridge.

Foss, C. 1977. "The Battle of the Granicus: A New Look." In *Archaia Makedonia II: Papers Read at the Second International Symposium Held in Thessaloniki, 19–24 August 1973*, 495–502. Thessaloniki.

Foss, C. 1979. *Ephesus after Antiquity: A Late Antique, Byzantine, and Turkish City*. Cambridge.

Foss, C., and D. Winfield. 1986. *Byzantine Fortifications: An Introduction*. Pretoria.

Fossey, J.M. 1990. *The Ancient Topography of Opountian Lokris*. Amsterdam.

Fraisse, P., and J.-C. Moretti. 2007. *Le théatre: exploration archéologique de Délos*. Paris.

Franco, C. 1993. *Il regno di Lisimaco: strutture amministrative e rapporti con le citta*. Pisa.

Frank, N., A. Mangini, and M. Korfmann. 2002. "230Th/U Dating of the Trojan 'Water Quarries.'" *Archaeometry* 44: 305–14.

Frank, T. 1909. "Classical Scholarship in Medieval Iceland." *AJP* 30: 139–52.

Fränkel, M. 1890–5. *Die Inschriften von Pergamon*. Altertümer von Pergamon 8. Berlin.

Frasca, M. 1998. "Osservazioni preliminari sulla ceramica arcaica di Kyme in Turchia." In *Studi su Kyme eolica: Atti della giornata di studio della Scuola di specializzazione in archeologia dell'università di Catania, Catania, 16 maggio 1990*, 49–70. Catania.

Fraser, P. 1972. *Hellenistic Alexandria*. Oxford.

Frazer, J.G., ed. and trans. 1979. *Apollodorus: The Library, Volume I: Books 1–3.9*. Loeb Classical Library 121. New York.

Frazer, R.M. 1966. *Dares and Dictys: An Introduction to the Study of Medieval Versions of the Story of Troy*. Bloomington, Ind.

French, D.H. 1988. *Roman Roads and Milestones of Asia Minor*. Oxford.

French, E. 2010. "Mycenae." In *The Oxford Handbook of the Bronze Age Aegean*, edited by E.H. Cline, 671–9. Oxford.

Frisch, P. 1974. "Zwei Athleteninschriften aus der Troas." *ZPE* 13: 38–9.

Frisch, P. 1975. *Die Inschriften von Ilion*. Inschriften griechischer Städte aus Kleinasien 3. Bonn.

Frisch, P. 1978. *Die Inschriften von Lampsakos*. Bonn.

Frisch, P. 1984. "Gaius und Lucius Caesar in Ilion (I.K. 3, Ilion, Nr. 85 a)." *EpigAnat* 4: 15.

Froehner, W. 1892. "Troianische Vasenbilder." *JdI* 7: 25–31.

Fuchs, H. 1990. *Lusus Troiae*. Cologne.

Fuchs, M. 1987. *Untersuchungen zur Ausstattung römischer Theater in Italien und den Westprovinzen des Imperium Romanum*. Mainz am Rhein.

Fuchs, W. 1973. "Die Bildgeschichte der Flucht des Aeneas." *ANRW* I.4: 615–32.

Funck, B. 1994. "Seleukos Nikator und Ilion: Einige Beobachtungen zum Verhältnis von König und Staat im frühen Hellenismus." *HZ* 258: 317–37.

Furtwängler, A. 1900. *Die antiken Gemmen*. Berlin.

Gabriel, U. 2000. "Mitteilung zum Stand der Neolithikumsforschung in der Umgebung von Troia." *Studia Troica* 10: 233–8.

Gabriel, U. 2006. "Ein Blick zürück: das fünfte Jahrtausend vor Christus in der Troas." In *Troia: Archäologie eines Siedlunghügels und seiner Landschaft*, edited by M. Korfmann, 355–60. Mainz am Rhein.

Gabriel, U., R. Aslan, and S. Blum. 2004. "Alacalıgöl: eine neuentdeckte Siedlung des 5. Jahrtausends v. Chr. in der Troas." *Studia Troica* 14: 121–33.

Gajdukevic, V.F. 1971. *Das Bosporanische Reich*. Berlin.

Gaiser, K. 1985. *Theophrast in Assos: zur Entwicklung der Naturwissenschaft zwischen Akademie und Peripatos*. Heidelberg.

Galinsky, K. 1969. *Aeneas, Sicily, and Rome*. Princeton, N.J.

García-Ramón, J.L. 1975. *Les origines postmycéniennes du groupe dialectal éolien: étude linguistique*. Salamanca.

Gardner, P. 1887. *Catalogue of the Greek Coins of Peloponnesus in the British Museum*. London.

Garnsey, P. 1988. *Famine and Food Supply in the Graeco-Roman World: Responses to Risk and Crisis*. Cambridge.

Gates, C. 1983. *From Cremation to Inhumation: Burial Practices at Ialysos and Kameiros during the Mid-Archaic Period, ca. 625–525 BC*. UCLA Occasional Paper 11. Los Angeles, Calif.

Gatti, C. 1967. "Aspetti della εὐεργεσία nel mondo ellenistico." *PP* 94: 192–213.

Gebauer, J. 1992. "Die archaische geglättete graue Keramik." In *Ausgrabungen in Assos 1990*, edited by Ü. Serdaroğlu and R. Stupperich, 65–101. Bonn.

Gebauer, J. 2002. *Pompe und Thysia: Attische Tieropferdarstellungen auf Schwartz- und rotfigurigen Vasen*. Munster.

Genz, H. 1997. "Northern Slaves and the Origin of Handmade Burnished Ware: A Comment on Bankhoff et al. (JMA 9 [1996] 193–209)." *JMA* 10: 109–11.

Georges, P. 1994. *Barbarian Asia and the Greek Experience: From the Archaic Period to the Age of Xenophon*. Baltimore, Md.

Geppert, K. 2006. "Überlegungen zum Polyxena-Sarkophag von Çanakkale." In *Tekmeria: Archäologische Zeugnisse in ihrer kulturhistorischen und politischen Dimension. Beiträge für Werner Gauer*, edited by N. Kreutz and B. Schweizer, 89–102. Münster.

Gerkan, A. von, 1963. Review of *Der Athenatempel von Ilion*, by F.W. Goethert and H. Schleif. *DLZ* 84: 239–41.

Ghirshman, R. 1964. *The Arts of Ancient Iran from Its Origins to the Time of Alexander the Great*. New York.

Gilotta, F. 1998. "Gümüşçay e l'etruria: due ambienti a confronto." *RdA* 22: 11–18.

Ginouvès, R. 1993. *La Macedoine: de Philippe II à la conquête romaine*. Paris.

Girella, L., and P. Pavúk. Forthcoming. "Minoanisation, Acculturation, Hybridisation: The Evidence of the Minoan Presence in Northeastern Aegean between Middle and Late Bronze Age." In *Nostoi: Indigenous Culture, Migration and Integration in the Aegean Islands and Western Anatolia during the Late Bronze and Early Iron Age*, edited by N. Stampolidis, Ç. Maner, and K. Kopanias. Istanbul.

Giudice, F., E. Giudice, G. Giudice, F. Muscolino, and G. Sanfilippo Chiarello. 2011. "Attic Imports to Anatolia: The Construction of a Reference Framework." In *SOMA 2009: Proceedings of the XIII Symposium on Mediterranean Archaeology, Selcuk University of Konya, Turkey, 23–24 April 2009*, edited by H. Oniz and E. Aslan, 81–91. Oxford.

Giuliani, C.F. 1981. "Santuario delle tredici are, hcroon di Enea." In *Enea nel Lazio: Archeologia e mito, bimillenario virgiliano, Roma, 22 settembre–31 dicembre 1981, Campidoglio, Palazzo dei Conservatori*, 169–77. Roma.

Gneisz, D. 1990. *Das antike Rathaus: das griechische Bouleuterion und die frührömische Curia*. Vienna.

Goceva, Z., and M. Oppermann. 1979. *Monumenta Orae Ponti Euxeni Bulgaricae*. Corpus Cultus Equitis Thracii 1. Leiden.

Goethert, F.W., and H. Schleif. 1962. *Der Athenatempel von Ilion*. Berlin.

Goldwyn, A.J. 2010. "A Literary History of the Trojan War from Antiquity to the Middle Ages." Ph.D. diss., City University of New York.

Görkay, K. 1999. "Attic Black-Figure Pottery from Daskyleion." In *Studien zum antiken Kleinasien IV*, edited by K. Fuhrmeister, 1–100. Asia Minor Studien 34. Bonn.

Görkay, K. 2002. "An Early Imperial Podium Temple in Alexandria Troas." In *Patris und imperium: kulturelle und politische Identität in den Städten der römischen Provinzen Kleinasiens in der frühen Kaiserzeit: Kolloquium Köln, November 1998*, edited by C. Berns, 217–32. Leuven.

Goldman, H., and F. Jones. 1942. "Terracottas from the Necropolis of Halai." *Hesperia* 11: 365–421.

Gorman, V.B. 2001. *Miletos, The Ornament of Ionia: A History of the City to 400 B.C.E.*, Ann Arbor, Mich.

Gorogianni, E. 2011. "Goddess, Lost Ancestors, and Dolls: A Cultural Biography of the Ayia Irini Statues." *Hesperia* 80: 635–55.

Gosden, C. 2001. "Postcolonial Archaeology: Issues of Culture, Identity, and Knowledge." In *Archaeological Theory Today*, edited by I. Hodder, 241–61. Malden, Mass.

Graf, F. 1978. "Die lokrischen Mädchen." *Studi Storico Religiosi* 2: 61–79.

Graf, F. 1999. "Kabeiroi." *Der neue Pauly, Enzyklopädie der Antike* 6: 123–7.

Graham, A.J. 1978. "The Foundation of Thasos." *BSA* 73: 61–98.

Graham, A.J. 1983. *Colony and Mother City in Ancient Greece*, 2nd ed. Chicago.

Graham, A.J. 1990. "Pre-Colonial Contacts: Questions and Problems." In *Greek Colonists and Native Populations*, edited by J.-P. Descoeudres, 45–60. Oxford.

Graindor, P. 1934. *Athènes sous Hadrien*. New York.

Grainger, J.D. 1996. "Antiochus III in Thrace." *Historia* 45: 329–43.

Grant, M. 1950. *Roman Anniversary Issues: An Exploratory Study of the Numismatic and Medallic Commemoration of Anniversary Years 49 B.C.–A.D. 375*. Cambridge.

Grape, W. 1994. *The Bayeux Tapestry: Monument to a Norman Triumph.* New York.

Graus, F. 1989. "Troja und Trojanische Herkunftssage im Mittelalter." In *Kontinuität und Transformation der Antike im Mittelalter*, edited by W. Erzgräber, 25–45. Sigmaringen.

Greatrex, G. 1995. "Procopius and Agathias on the Defenses of the Thracian Chersonese." In *Constantinople and Its Hinterland: Papers from the Twenty-seventh Spring Symposium of Byzantine Studies, Oxford, April 1993*, edited by C. Mango and G. Dagron, 125–30. Brookfield, Vt.

Greaves, A.M. 2007. "Milesians in the Black Sea: Trade, Settlement and Religion." In *The Black Sea in Antiquity: Regional and Interregional Economic Exchanges*, edited by V. Gabrielsen and J. Lund, 9–22. Aarhus.

Greaves, A.M. 2010. "Western Anatolia." In *The Oxford Handbook of the Bronze Age Aegean*, edited by E.H. Cline, 877–89. Oxford.

Greenewalt, C.H., Jr. 1972. "Two Lydian Graves at Sardis." *CSCA* 5: 113–45.

Greenewalt, C.H., Jr., M. Rautman, and C. Ratté. 1994. "The Sardis Campaigns of 1988 and 1989." In *Preliminary Excavation Reports: Sardis, Paphos, Caesarea Maritima, Shiqmim, Ain Ghazal*, edited by W.G. Dever, 1–43. Annual of the American Schools of Oriental Research 51. Ann Arbor, Mich.

Gregory, J. 1999. *Euripides, Hecuba: Introduction, Text, and Commentary.* Atlanta, Ga.

Greifenhagen, A. 1975. *Schmuckarbeiten in Edelmetall, Band II. Eizelstücke.* Berlin.

Griffin, N. 1907. *Dares and Dictys: An Introduction to the Study of Medieval Versions of the Story of Troy.* Baltimore, Md.

Grose, D.F. 1989. *Early Ancient Glass: The Toledo Museum of Art. Core-Formed, Rod-Formed, and Cast Vessels and Objects from the Late Bronze Age to the Early Roman Empire, 1600 B.C. to A.D. 50.* New York.

Grote, G. 1872. *A History of Greece I.* London.

Gruen, E. 1990. *Studies in Greek Culture and Roman Policy.* Leiden.

Gruen, E. 1992. *Culture and National Identity in Republican Rome.* Ithaca, N.Y.

Guarducci, M. 1987. "Il cosidetto Trono di Boston." *BdA* 43: 49–62.

Gudeman, A. 1894. "Literary Fraud among the Romans." *TAPA* 25: 140–64.

Guidoboni, E., ed. 1989. *I terremoti prima del Mille in Italia e nell' area mediterranea.* Bologna.

Gürsü, E. 2001. *Biga/Pegai.* Biga.

Gürtekin-Demir, R.G. 2002. "Lydian Painted Pottery at Daskyleion." *AnatSt* 52: 111–43.

Gürtekin-Demir, R.G. 2003. "Imported Painted Pottery from Asia Minor to Daskyleion in the Achaemenid Period." In *Achaemenid History XIII. A Persian Perspective: Essays in Memory of Helene Sancisi-Weerdenburg*, edited by W.F.M. Henkelman and A. Kuhrt, 203–26. Leiden.

Gusmani, R., and Y. Polat. 1999. "Ein phrygisches Graffito aus Daskyleion." *Kadmos* 38: 50–64.

Güterbock, H.G. 1983. "The Hittites and the Aegean World: Part 1. The Ahhiyawa Problem Reconsidered." *AJA* 87: 133–8.

Güterbock, H.G. 1986. "Troy in Hittite Texts? Wilusa, Ahhiyawa, and Hittite History." In *Troy and the Trojan War*, edited by M.J. Mellink, 33–44. Bryn Mawr, Pa.

Guzowska, M. 2002. "Traces of Minoan Behavioural Patterns in the North-East Aegean." In *Mauerschau: Festschrift für Manfred Korfmann*, edited by R. Aslan, S. Blum, G. Kastl, F. Schweizer, and D. Thumm, 585–94. Remshalden-Grünbach.

Guzowska, M. 2009. "En vogue Minoenne…On the Social Use of Minoan and Minoanising Objects in Troia." In *The Minoans in the Central, Eastern and Northern Aegean: New Evidence*, edited by C.F. Macdonald, E. Hallager, and W.-D. Niemeier, 243–9. Athens.

Guzowska, M., I. Kuleff, E. Pernicka, and M. Satir. 2003. "On the Origin of Coarse Wares of Troia VII." In *Troia and the Troad: Scientific Approaches*, edited by G.A. Wagner, E. Pernicka, and H.-P. Uerpmann, 233–49. Berlin.

Habicht, C. 1970. *Gottmenschentum und griechische Stadte.* Munich.

Hajnal, I. 2003. *Troia aus sprachwissenschaftlicher Sicht: die Struktur einer Argumentation.* Innsbruck.

Halfmann, H. 1986. *Itinera Principum: Geschichte und Typologie der Kaiserreisen im Römischen Reich.* Stuttgart.

Halfmann, H. 1987. "Ein neuer Statthalterkult in der Provinz Asia." *EpigAnat* 10: 83–90.

Hall, E. 1988. "When Did the Trojans Turn into Phrygians? Alcaeus 42.15." *ZPE* 73: 15–18.

Hall, E. 1989. *Inventing the Barbarian: Greek Self-Definition through Tragedy.* New York.

Hall, J.M. 1997. *Ethnic Identity in Greek Antiquity.* New York.

Hall, J.M. 2002. *Hellenicity: Between Ethnicity and Culture.* Chicago, Ill.

Hall, J.M. 2004. "Culture, Cultures and Acculturation." In *Griechische Archaik: Interne Entwicklungen, externe Impulse,* edited by R. Rollinger and C. Ulf, 35–50. Berlin.

Hamdorf, F.W. 1980. "Zur Weihung des Chairodemos auf der Akropolis von Athens." In *Stele: Tomos eis Mnemon N. Kontoleon,* 231–5. Athens.

Hammond, N.G.L. 1980. "The Battle of the Granicus River." *JHS* 100: 73–88.

Hammond, N.G.L., and L.J. Roseman. 1996. "The Construction of Xerxes' Bridge over the Hellespont." *JHS* 116: 88–107.

Hampartumian, N. 1979. *Moesia Inferior (Romanian Section) and Dacia.* Corpus Cultus Equitis Thracii 4. Leiden.

Hampe, R. 1981. "Alexandros." *LIMC* I: 494–529.

Hanfmann, G.M.A. 1983. *Sardis from Prehistoric to Roman Times: Results of the Archaeological Exploration of Sardis 1958–1975.* Cambridge, Mass.

Hankins, J. 2003. "Renaissance Crusaders: Humanist Crusade Literature in the Age of Mehmed II." In *Humanism and Platonism in the Italian Renaissance I: Humanism,* edited by J. Hankins, 293–424. Rome.

Hansen, E.V. 1971. *The Attalids of Pergamon.* Ithaca, N.Y.

Harden, D.B. 1981. *Catalogue of Greek and Roman Glass in the British Museum.* London.

Harl, K. 2006. "A Hoard of Roman Antoniniani from the Bath at Metropolis, Ionia." *AJN* 18: 75–111.

Harmankaya, S., and B. Erdoğu. 2003. "The Prehistoric Sites of Gökçeada, Turkey." In *From Villages to Towns: Studies Presented to Ufuk Esin,* edited by M. Özdoğan, H. Hauptmann, and N. Başgelen, 459–79. Istanbul.

Harper, J. 2005. "Turks as Trojans, Trojans as Turks: Visual Imagery of the Trojan War and the Politics of Cultural Identity in Fifteenth-Century Europe." In *Translating Cultures: Postcolonial Approaches to the Middle Ages,* edited by A.J. Kabir and D. Williams, 151–79. Cambridge.

Harris, D. 1995. *The Treasures of the Parthenon and Erechtheion.* Oxford.

Hart, P. 2011. *Gallipoli.* London.

Hasaki, E. 1995. "Temenos: Delimiting Sacred Space." M.A. thesis, University of Cincinnati.

Hasluck, F.W. 1910. *Cyzicus.* Cambridge.

Haubold, J. 2002. "Wars of Wissenschaft: The New Quest for Troy." *IJCT* 8: 564–79.

Hauser, S. 1992. *Spätantike und frühbyzantinische Silberlöffel.* Münster.

Haussoullier, B. 1902. *Études sur l'histoire de Milet et du Didymeion.* Paris.

Hawkins, J.D. 1995. *The Hieroglyphic Inscription of the Sacred Pool Complex at Hattusa.* Wiesbaden.

Hawkins, J.D. 1998. "Tarkasnawa King of Mira: 'Tarkondemos,' Boğazköy Sealings and Karabel." *AnatSt* 48: 1–31.

Hawkins, J.D. 2005. "A Hieroglyphic Luwian Inscription on a Silver Bowl in the Museum of Anatolian Civilizations, Ankara." *Studia Troica* 15: 193–204.

Hawkins, J.D., and D.F. Easton. 1996. "A Hieroglyphic Seal from Troia." *Studia Troica* 6: 111–18.

Hay, D. 1957. *Europe: The Emergence of an Idea.* Edinburgh.

Hayes, J. 1995a. "A Late Byzantine and Early Ottoman Assemblage from the Lower City in Troia." *Studia Troica* 5: 197–210.

Hayes, J. 1995b. "Early Roman Well Group from the Troia Excavations, 1992." *Studia Troica* 5: 185–96.

Hayes, J. 1995c. "Two Kraters 'After the Antique' from the Fimbrian Destruction in Troia." *Studia Troica* 5: 177–83.

Haynes, D. 1992. *The Technique of Greek Bronze Statuary.* Mainz am Rhein.

Head, B. 1892. *Catalogue of the Greek Coins of Ionia in the British Museum.* London.

Head, B. 1901. *Catalogue of the Greek Coins of Lydia in the British Museum.* London.

Head, B. 1906. *Catalogue of the Greek Coins of Phrygia in the British Museum.* London.

Hedreen, G. 2001. *Capturing Troy: The Narrative Functions of Landscape in Archaic and Early Classical Greek Art.* Ann Arbor, Mich.

Heilmeyer, W.-D. 1970. *Korinthische Normalkapitelle: Studien zur Geschichte der römischen Architekturdekoration.* Heidelberg.

Heinhold-Krahmer, S. 1983. "Untersuchungen zu Piyamaradu (Teil I)." *Orientalia* 52: 81–97.

Heinhold-Krahmer, S. 1986. "Untersuchungen zu Piyamaradu (Teil II)." *Orientalia* 55: 47–62.

Hemberg, B. 1950. *Die Kabiren.* Uppsala.

Henrichs, A. 1981. "Human Sacrifice in Greek Religion: Three Case Studies." In *Le sacrifice dans l'antiquité,* edited by J.-P. Vernant, 195–242. Geneva.

Henrickson, R., and M. Voigt. 1998. "The Early Iron Age at Gordion: The Evidence from the Yassıhöyük Stratigraphic Sequence." In *Thracians and Phrygians: Problems of Parallelism. Proceedings of an International Symposium on the Archaeology, History and Ancient Languages of Thrace and Phrygia, Ankara, 3–4 June 1995,* edited by N. Tuna, Z. Aktüre, and M. Lynch, 79–106. Ankara.

Hermary, A. 1986. "Dioskouroi." *LIMC* III: 567–93.

Hertel, D. 1991. "Schliemanns These vom Fortleben Troias in den "Dark Ages" im Lichte neuer Forschungsergebnisse." *Studia Troica* 1: 131–44.

Hertel, D. 1992. "Zum Problem der Historizität der Sage vom Trojanischen Krieg: Kämpfe in der Frühphase der äolischen Kolonisation Nordwestkleinasiens als historisches Substrat der Tradition." In *Heinrich Schliemann: Grundlagen und Ergebnisse moderner Archäologie 100 Jahre nach Schliemanns Tod,* edited by J. Herrmann, 177–81. Berlin.

Hertel, D. 2001. *Troia: Archäologie, Geschichte, Mythos.* Munich.

Hertel, D. 2003. *Die Mauern von Troia.* Munich.

Hertel, D. 2004. "Zum Heiligtum der Athena Ilias von Troia IX und zur frühhellenistischen Stadtanlage von Ilion." *AA* 177–205.

Hertel, D. 2007. "Die aiolische Siedlungsraum (Aiolis) am Übergang von der Bronze- zur Eisenzeit." In *Frühes Ionien: Eine Bestandsaufnahme. Panionien Symposium,* edited by J. Cobet, 97–122. Mainz am Rhein.

Hertel, D., and F. Kolb. 2003. "Troy in Clearer Perspective." *AnatSt* 53: 71–88.

Herzhoff, B. 2008. "Der Flusskatalog der Ilias (M 20–23) – ältestes literarisches Beispiel geometrischer Raumerfassung?" In *Antike Naturwissenschaft und ihre Rezeption, Vol. 18,* edited by J. Althoff, S. Föllinger, and G. Wöhrle, 101–38. Trier.

Herzog, R. 1928. *Heilige Gesetze von Kos.* Berlin.

Heyder, W., and A. Mallwitz. 1978. *Die Bauten im Kabirenheiligtum bei Theben II.* Berlin.

Hickey, M. 1995. *Gallipoli.* London.

Higbie, C. 1997. "The Bones of a Hero, the Ashes of a Politician: Athens, Salamis, and the Usable Past." *ClAnt* 16: 278–307.

Higbie, C. 2001. "Homeric Athena in the Chronicle of Lindos." In *Athena in the Classical World,* edited by S. Deacy and A. Villing, 105–25. Leiden.

Higbie, C. 2003. *The Lindian Chronicle and the Greek Creation of their Past.* Oxford.

Higginbotham, J. 1997. *Piscinae.* Chapel Hill, N.C.

Higgins, R. A. 1954. *Catalogue of the Terracottas in the Department of Greek and Roman Antiquities, British Museum. Vol. 1: Greek: 730–330 B.C.* London.

Higgins, R. A. 1980. *Greek and Roman Jewellery,* 2nd ed. London.

Hill, G. F. 1897. *Catalogue of the Greek Coins of Lycia, Pamphylia and Pisidia in the British Museum.* London.

Hill, P. V. 1970. *The Dating and Arrangement of the Undated Coins of Rome, A.D. 98–148.* London.

Hiller, H. 1975. *Ionische Grabreliefs der ersten Hälfte des 5. Jahrhunderts v. Chr.* Istanbuler Mitteilungen Beiheft 12. Tuebingen.

Hiller, S. 1975. "Ra-mi-ni-ja: mykenisch-kleinasiatische Beziehungen und die Linear B-Texte." *ZivaAnt* 25: 388–412.

Himmelmann, N. 1997. *Tieropfer in der griechischen Kunst.* Oplanden.

Hind, J. 1998. "Megarian Colonisation in the Western Half of the Black Sea." In *The Greek Colonisation of the Black Sea,* edited by G. R. Tsetskhladze, 131–52. Stuttgart.

Hitzl, I. 1991. *Die griechischen Sarkophage der archaischen und klassichen Zeit.* Jonsered.

Höckmann, O. 2003. "Zu früher Seefahrt in den Meerengen." *Studia Troica* 13: 133–60.

Hodder, I., ed. 1978. *The Spatial Organization of Culture.* Pittsburgh, Pa.

Hodot, R. 1990. *Le dialecte éolien d'Asie: la langue des inscriptions, VIIe s. a.C.-IVe s. p.C.* Paris.

Hoepfner, W. 1966. *Herakleia Pontike-Ereğli: eine baugeschichtliche Untersuchung.* Graz.

Hoepfner, W. 1969. "Zum Entwurf des Athena-Tempels in Ilion." *AM* 84: 165–81.

Hoepfner, W. 1990. "Bauten und Bedeutung des Hermogenes." In *Hermogenes und die hochhellenistische Architektur: Internationales Kolloquium in Berlin vom 28. bis 29. Juli 1988 im Rahmen des 13. Internationalen Kongresses für Klassische Archäologie veranstalten vom Architekturreferat des DAI*, edited by W. Hoepfner and E.-L. Schwandner, 1–34. Mainz am Rhein.

Hoepfner, W. 1997. "The Architecture of Pergamon." In *Pergamon: The Telephos Frieze from the Great Altar*, edited by R. Dreyfus and E. Schraudolph, 23–57. San Francisco, Calif.

Hoepfner, W., and E.-L. Schwandner. 1994. *Haus und Stadt im klassischen Griechenland.* Berlin.

Hoffner, H.A. 2009. *Letters from the Hittite Kingdom.* Atlanta, Ga.

Hogarth, D.G. 1908. *Excavations at Ephesus: The Archaic Artemisia.* London.

Högemann, P. 2000. "Zum Iliasdichter: Ein anatolischer Standpunkt." *Studia Troica* 10: 183–98.

Holden, B. 1964. *The Metopes of the Temple of Athena at Ilion.* Northampton, Mass.

Holliday, P. 1993. "Narrative Structures in the François Tomb." In *Narrative and Event in Ancient Art*, edited by P. Holliday, 175–97. Cambridge.

Holloway, R.R. 1994. *The Archaeology of Early Rome and Latium.* London.

Hölscher, T. 1973. *Griechische Historienbilder des 5. und 4. Jahrhunderts vor Chr.* Munich.

Hood, S. 1981–2. *Excavations in Chios, 1938–1955: Prehistoric Emporio and Ayio Gala.* BSA Supplements 15/16. London.

Hood, S. 1995. "The Bronze Age Context of Homer." In *The Ages of Homer: A Tribute to Emily Townsend Vermeule*, edited by J.B Carter and S.P Morris, 25–32. Austin, Tex.

Hope Simpson, R. 2003. "The Dodecanese and the Ahhiyawa Question." *BSA* 98: 203–37.

Hope Simpson, R., and J.F. Lazenby. 1970. *The Catalogue of Ships in Homer's Iliad.* Oxford.

Hopkins, K., and M. Beard. 2005. *The Colosseum.* London.

Houby-Nielsen, S. 2000. "Child Burials in Ancient Athens." In *Children and Material Culture*, edited by J. Sofaer Derevenski, 51–166. London.

Houghton, A. 1978. "The Seleucid Mint at Lampsacus." *ANSMN* 23: 59–68.

Houghton, A. 1983. *Coins of the Seleucid Empire from the Collection of Arthur Houghton.* New York.

Houwink Ten Cate, P.H.J. 1983–4. "Sidelights on the Ahhiyawa Question from Hittite Vassal and Royal Corrrespondance." *JEOL* 28: 33–79.

Huber, I. 2001. *Die Ikonographie der Trauer in der Griechischen Kunst.* Mannheim.

Hübner, C., and S. Giese. 2006. "Geomagnetische Prospektion 2002 bis 2005 in der Unterstadt von Troia." *Studia Troica* 16: 125–9.

Hueber, F., and E. Riorden. 1994. "Plan von Troia 1994 and Troia. Freiliegende Ruinen und Besucherwege 1994." *Studia Troica* 4: 115–20.

Hughes, D. 1991. *Human Sacrifice in Ancient Greece.* London and New York.

Hull, D.B. 1964. *Hounds and Hunting in Ancient Greece.* Chicago.

Hunter, L.W., and S.A. Handford. 1927. *Aeneas on Siegecraft.* Oxford.

Huppert, G. 1965. "The Trojan Franks and Their Critics." *Studies in the Renaissance* 12: 227–41.

Hurwit, J. 1982. "Palm Trees and the Pathetic Fallacy in Archaic Greek Poetry and Art." *CJ* 77: 193–9.

Hurwit, J. 1985. *The Art and Culture of Early Greece, 1100–480 B.C.* Ithaca, N.Y.

Hurwit, J. 1999. *The Athenian Acropolis: History, Mythology, and Archaeology from the Neolithic Era to the Present.* New York.

Huxley, G.L. 1966a. *The Early Ionians.* London.

Huxley, G.L. 1966b. "Troy VIII and the Lokrian Maidens." In *Ancient Society and Institutions: Studies Presented to Victor Ehrenberg on His 75th Birthday*, edited by E. Badian, 147–64. Oxford.

Ilieva, P. 2009. "G 2–3 Ware" and the Non-Greek Populations on the North Aegean Coast (Some Preliminary Notes on Its Distribution Pattern and Its Contextual Characteristics)." In *Greeks and Thracians in Coastal and Inland Thrace during the Years before and after the Great Colonization: Proceedings of the International Symposium,*

Thasos, 26–27 September 2008, edited by Z.I. Bonias and J.Y. Perreault, 109–21. Thasos.

İnalcık, H. 1994. "The Ottoman State: Economy and Society, 1300–1600." In *An Economic and Social History of the Ottoman Empire, 1300–1916*, edited by H. İnalcık and D. Quataert, 9–410. Cambridge.

Inan, J., and E. Rosenbaum. 1966. *Roman and Early Byzantine Portrait Sculpture in Asia Minor*. London.

Inan, J., and E. Alföldi-Rosenbaum. 1979. *Römische und frühbyzantinische Porträtplastik aus der Türkei: Neue Funde*. Mainz am Rhein.

Ingledew, F. 1994. "The Book of Troy and the Genealogical Construction of History: The Case of Geoffrey of Monmouth's Historia regum Britanniae." *Speculum* 69: 665–704.

IosPE. 1890. *Inscriptiones Antiquae Orae Septentrionalis Ponti Euxini, Vol. II: Inscriptiones Regni Bosporani Continens*, edited by B. Latyschev. St. Petersberg.

Isaac, B. 1986. *The Greek Settlements in Thrace until the Macedonian Conquest*. Leiden.

Isaakidou, V., P. Halstead, J.L. Davis, and S.R. Stocker. 2002. "Burnt Animal Sacrifice in Late Bronze Age Greece: New Evidence from the Mycenaean 'Palace of Nestor,' Pylos." *Antiquity* 76: 86–92.

Ivanova, M. 2008. *Befestigte Siedlungen auf dem Balkan, in der Ägäis und in Westanatolien, ca. 5000–2000 v. Chr.* Münster.

Jablonka, P. 1995. "Ausgrabungen südlich der Unterstadt von Troia im Bereich des Troia VI-Verteidigungsgrabens: Grabungsbericht 1994." *Studia Troica* 5: 39–79.

Jablonka, P. 1996. "Ausgrabungen im Süden der Unterstadt von Troia im Bereich des Troia VI-Verteidigungsgrabens: Grabungsbericht 1995." *Studia Troica* 6: 65–96.

Jablonka, P. 2001. "Ein Stadtmauer aus Holz: Das Bollwerk der Unterstadt von Troia II." In *Troia: Traum und Wirklichkeit*, edited by B. Theune-Großkopf, U. Seidel, G. Kastl, M. Kempa, R. Redies, and A. Wais, 391–4. Stuttgart.

Jablonka, P. 2003. "The Link between the Black Sea and the Mediterranean since the End of the Last Ice Age: Archaeology and Geology." In *Troia and the Troad: Scientific Approaches*,

edited by G.A. Wagner, E. Pernicka, and H.-P. Uerpmann, 77–94. Berlin.

Jablonka, P. 2006a. "Leben ausserhalb der Burg: Die Unterstadt von Troia." In *Troia: Archäologie eines Siedlunghügels und seiner Landschaft*, edited by M. Korfmann, 167–80. Mainz am Rhein.

Jablonka, P. 2006b. Vorbericht zu den Arbeiten in Troia 2005." *Studia Troica* 16: 3–26.

Jablonka, P. 2010. "Troy in Regional and International Context." In *The Oxford Handbook of Ancient Anatolia*, edited by S. Steadman and G. McMahon, 717–33. Oxford.

Jablonka P., and E. Pernicka. 2009. "Vorbericht zu den Arbeiten in Troia 2007 und 2008." *Studia Troica* 18: 3–32.

Jablonka, P., and C.B. Rose. 2004. "Late Bronze Age Troy: A Response to Frank Kolb." *AJA* 108: 615–30.

Jablonka, P., H. König, and S. Riehl. 1994. "Ein Verteidigungsgraben in der Unterstadt von Troia VI. Grabungsbericht 1993." *Studia Troica* 4: 51–73.

Jacobs, B. 1987. *Griechische und persische Elemente in der Grabkunst Lykiens zur Zeit der Achämenidenherrschaft*. Jonsered.

Jacoby, D. 1986. "Knightly Values and Class Consciousness in the Crusader States of the Eastern Mediterranean." *Mediterranean Historical Review* 1: 170–3.

Janik, L., and H. Zawadzka. 1996. "One Europe, One Past?" In *Cultural Identity and Archaeology*, edited by P. Graves-Brown, S. Jones, and C. Gamble, 116–24. London.

Janko, R. 1982. *Homer, Hesiod and the Hymns: Diachronic Development in Epic Diction*. Cambridge.

Janko, R. 1992. *The Iliad, A Commentary: Books 13–16*. Cambridge.

Jannot, J.-R. 1984. *Les reliefs archaïques de Chiusi*. Rome.

Jansen, H.G. 1992. "Geomagnetische Prospektion in der Untersiedlung von Troia." *Studia Troica* 2: 61–70.

Jansen, H.G. 2006. "Das unsichtbare Troia sichtbar gemacht: Chancen und Ergebnisse der Anwendung neuer Prospektionsmethoden." In *Troia: Archäologie eines Siedlunghügels und seiner Landschaft*, edited by M. Korfmann, 309–16. Mainz am Rhein.

Jansen, H.G., and N. Blindow. 2003. "The Geophysical Mapping of the Lower City of Troia/Ilion." In *Troia and the Troad: Scientific Approaches*, edited by G.A. Wagner, E. Pernicka, and H.-P. Uerpmann, 325–40. Berlin.

Jansen, H.G., T.L. Kienlin, A.E. Patzelt, M. Waldhör, and J. Wilhelm. 1998. "Geophysikalische Prospektion 1996/97 in der Unterstadt von Troia." *Studia Troica* 8: 275–84.

Jaquet, E.R., ed. 1919. *These Were the Men: Poems of the War 1914–1918*. London.

Jeffery, L.H. 1990. *The Local Scripts of Archaic Greece: A Study of the Origin of the Greek Alphabet and Its Development from the Eighth to the Fifth Centuries B.C.*, 2nd ed. Oxford.

Jewett, R. and R. Stupperich. 2008. "Wanderungen in der Troas." In *Vom Euphrat bis zum Bosporus: Kleinasien in der Antike. Festschrift für Elmar Schwertheim zum 65. Geburtstag*, edited by E. Winter, 349–57. Asia Minor Studien 26. Bonn.

Jones, A.H.M. 1971. *The Cities of the Eastern Roman Provinces*. Oxford.

Jones, C.P. 1993. "The Decree of Ilion in Honor of a King Antiochus." *GRBS* 34: 73–92.

Jones, C.P. 1999. *Kinship Diplomacy in the Ancient World*. Cambridge, Mass.

Jones, C.P. 2007. "Three New Letters of the Emperor Hadrian." *ZPE* 161: 145–56.

Jones, N. 1987. *Public Organization in Ancient Greece: A Documentary Study*. Philadelphia.

Jorro, F.A., ed. 1985. *Diccionario micénico*. Madrid.

Jucker, H. 1969. "Zur Helios-Metope aus Ilion." *AA*: 248–56.

Kadletz, E. 1976. "Animal Sacrifice in Greek and Roman Religion." Ph.D. diss., University of Washington.

Kahil, L. 1986. "Dardanos." *LIMC* III: 352–3.

Kahil, L., and N. Icard. 1984. "Artemis." *LIMC* II: 618–753.

Kähler, H. 1964. Review of *Der Athenatempel von Ilion*, by F.W. Goethert and H. Schleif. *Gnomon* 36: 79–87.

Kallet, L. 1983. "Iphicrates, Timotheus, and Athens, 371–360 B.C." *GRBS* 24: 239–52.

Kaptan, D. 2002. *The Daskyleion Bullae: Seal Images from the Western Achaemenid Empire*. Leiden.

Kaptan, D. 2003. "A Glance at Northwestern Asia Minor during the Achaemenid Period." In *Achaemenid History XIII. A Persian Perspective: Essays in Memory of Heleen Sancisi-Weerdenburg*, edited by W.F.M. Henkelman and A. Kuhrt, 189–202. Leiden.

Kaptan-Bayburtluoğlu, D. 1990. "A Group of Seal Impressions on the Bullae from Ergili/Daskyleion." *EpigAnat* 16: 15–25.

Karageorghis, V., and O. Kouka, eds. 2011. *On Cooking Pots, Drinking Cups, Loomweights and Ethnicity in Bronze Age Cyprus and Neighbouring Regions: An International Archaeological Symposium Held in Nicosia, November 6th–7th 2010*. Nicosia.

Kasper, S. 1970. "Eine Nekropole nordwestlich von Soma." *AA*: 71–83.

Katz, J. 2005. Review of *Troy and Homer: Towards a Solution of an Old Mystery*, by J. Latacz. *JAOS* 125: 422–5.

Kayan. İ. 1991. "Holocene Geomorphic Evolution of the Beşik Plain and Changing Environment of Ancient Man." *Studia Troica* 1: 79–92.

Kayan. İ. 1995. "The Troia Bay and Supposed Harbour Sites in the Bronze Age." *Studia Troica* 5: 211–35.

Kayan. İ. 2000. "The Water Supply of Troia." *Studia Troica* 10: 135–44.

Keaney, J.J. 1991. *Harpocration: Lexeis of the Ten Orators*. Amsterdam.

Keay, S., and N. Terrenato, eds. 2001. *Italy and the West: Comparative Issues in Romanization*. Oxford.

Keen, A. 1995. "The Tombs of Lycia: Evidence for Social Stratification?" In *The Archaeology of Death in the Ancient Near East*, edited by S. Campbell and A. Green, 221–5. Oxford.

Kienast, H. 1992. "Die Basis der Geneleos-Gruppe." *AM* 107: 29–42.

Kiesewetter, H. 1999. "Spätbyzantinische Gräber bei der Quellhöhle in der Unterstadt von Troia/Ilion." *Studia Troica* 9: 411–35.

Kiesewetter, H. 2002. "Ein trepanierter Schädel aus Troia VI." *Studia Troica* 12: 73–80.

Kitov, G. 1997. "The Thracian Valley of the Kings in the Kazanlak Region." In *Glorie di tracia: l'oro più antico, i tesori, i miti*, edited by R. Berti and E. La Porta. Florence.

Klaffenbach, G. 1936. "Neue Inschriften aus Ätolien." *Sitzungsberichte der Preussischen Akademie der Wissenschaften zu Berlin, philologisch-historische Klasse*: 358–88.

Kleeman, I. 1958. *Satrapen-Sarkophag aus Sidon*. Berlin.

Klein, N.L. 1997. "Excavation of the Greek Temples at Mycenae by the British School at Athens." *BSA* 92: 247–322.

Kleiner, G., P. Hommel, and M. Müller-Wiener. 1967. *Panionion und Melie*. Berlin.

Klinkott, M. 2004. "Die Wehrmauern von Troia VI: Bauaufnahme und Auswertung." *Studia Troica* 14: 33–85.

Klinkott, M., and R. Becks. 2001. "Wehrmauern, Türme und Tore: Bauform und Konstruktion der troianischen Burgbefestigung in der VI. und VII. Siedlungsperiode." In *Troia: Traum und Wirklichkeit*, edited by B. Theune-Großkopf, U. Seidel, G. Kastl, M. Kempa, R. Redies, and A. Wais, 407–14. Stuttgart.

Knackfuß, H. 1908. *Das Rathaus von Milet*. Milet I.2. Berlin.

Knauer, E.R. 1990. "Multa egit cum regibus et pacem confirmavit. The Date of the Equestrian Statue of Marcus Aurelius." *Römische Mitteilungen* 97: 277–306.

Knell, H. 1973. "Der Athenatempel in Ilion. Eine Korrektur zur Grundrissrekonstruktion." *AA*: 131–3.

Knigge, U. 1976. *Der Südhügel*. Kerameikos Band 9. Berlin.

Knittlmayer, B., and W.-D. Heilmeyer. 1998. *Die Antikensammlung: Altes Museum Pergamonmuseum*. Berlin.

Knoepfler, D. 2010. "Les agonothètes de la confédération d'Athéna Ilias." *Studi Ellenistici* 24: 33–62.

Koch, C. 1996. "Die Wiederherstellung der Demokratie in Ilion." *ZSav* 113: 32–63.

Koch, H. 1992. *Es kündet Dareios dder König... Vom Leben im persischen Grossreich*. Mainz.

Koch, G. 2000. *Frühchristliche Sarkophage*. Munich.

Koch-Brinkmann, U. 1999. *Polychrome Bilder auf weissgrundigen Lekythen: Zeugen der klassischen griechischen Malerei*. Munich.

Koenigs, W. 1989. "Zwei Säulen aus Biga." *IstMitt* 39: 289–95.

Koenigs, W. 1991. *Westtürkei: von Troia bis Knidos*. Munich.

Kohler, E. 1980. "Cremations of the Middle Phrygian Period at Gordion." In *From Athens to Gordion: Papers of a Memorial Symposium for Rodney S. Young*, edited by K. DeVries, 65–89. Philadelphia.

Kökten, H. 1998. "Conservation and Reconstruction of Phyrgian Chariot Wheels from Mysia." In *Thracians and Phrygians: Problems of Parallelism. Proceedings of an International Symposium on the Archaeology, History and Ancient Languages of Thrace and Phrygia, Ankara, 3–4 June 1995*, edited by N. Tuna, Z. Aktüre, and M. Lynch, 131–46. Ankara.

Kökten-Ersoy, H. 1998. "Two Wheeled Vehicles from Lydia and Mysia." *IstMitt* 48: 107–33.

Kolb, F. 1974. "Zur Geschichte der Stadt Hierapolis in Phrygien: Die Phyleninschriften." *ZPE* 15: 255–70.

Kolb, F. 2003a. "Ein neuer Troia-Mythos? Traum und Wirklichkeit auf dem Grabhügel von Hisarlik." In *Troia: Traum und Wirklichkeit. Ein Mythos in Geschichte und Rezeption*, edited by H.-J. Behr, G. Biegel and H. Castritius, 8–40. Braunschweig.

Kolb, F. 2003b. "War Troia eine Stadt?" In *Der neue Streit um Troia. Eine Bilanz*, edited by C. Ulf, 120–45. Munich.

Kolb, F. 2004. "Troy VI: A Trading Center and Commercial City?" *AJA* 108: 577–614.

Kolb, F. 2010. *Tatort "Troia": Geschichte, Mythen, Politik*. Paderborn.

Koldewey, R. 1891. *Neandria*. Programm zum Winckelmannsfeste der Archäologische Gesellschaft zu Berlin, no. 51. Berlin.

Kontoleon, N. 1952. "Anaskaphai en Chio." *Prakt* 520–30.

Koppenhöfer, D. 1997. "Troia VII: Versuch einer Zusammenschau einschließlich der Ergebnisse des Jahres 1995." *Studia Troica* 7: 295–353.

Koppenhöfer, D. 2002. "Buckelkeramik und Barbarische Ware in Troia: Anmerkungen zur Herkunft." In *Mauerschau: Festschrift für Manfred Korfmann*, edited by R. Aslan, S. Blum, G. Kastl, F. Schweizer, and D. Thumm, 679–704. Remshalden-Grünbach.

Korfmann, M. 1983. "Red Cross Bowl: Angeblicher Leittyp für Troja V." In *Beiträge zur Altertumskunde. Festschrift für Kurt Bittel*, edited by R. M. Böhmer and H. Hauptmann, 291–27. Mainz am Rhein.

Korfmann, M. 1985. "Beşik-tepe: Vorbericht über die Ergebnisse der Grabung von 1983." *AA*: 157–94.

Korfmann, M. 1986a. "Beşik Tepe: New Evidence for the Period of the Trojan Sixth and Seventh Settlements." In *Troy and the Trojan War*, edited by M.J. Mellink, 17–28. Bryn Mawr, Pa.

Korfmann, M. 1986b. "Beşik-tepe: Vorbericht über die Ergebnisse der Grabung von 1984." *AA*: 303–63.

Korfmann, M. 1986c. "Troy: Topography and Navigation." In *Troy and the Trojan War*, edited by M.J. Mellink, 1–16. Bryn Mawr, Pa.

Korfmann, M. 1988. "Beşik-tepe: Vorbericht über die Ergebnisse der Grabung von 1985 und 1986." *AA*: 391–404.

Korfmann, M. 1989. "Beşik-tepe: Vorbericht über die Ergebnisse der Arbeiten von 1987 und 1988." *AA*: 473–81.

Korfmann, M. 1991. "Troia: Reinigungs- und Dokumentations-arbeiten 1987, Ausgrabungen 1988 und 1989." *Studia Troica* 1: 1–34.

Korfmann, M. 1992. "Troia: Ausgrabungen 1990 und 1991." *Studia Troica* 2: 1–41.

Korfmann, M. 1993. "Troia: Ausgrabungen 1992." *Studia Troica* 3: 1–37.

Korfmann, M. 1994. "Troia: Ausgrabungen 1993." *Studia Troica* 4: 1–50.

Korfmann, M. 1995a. "Troia: A Residential and Trading City on the Dardanelles." In *Politeia: Society and State in the Aegean Bronze Age. Proceedings of the 5th International Aegean Conference, University of Heidelberg, Archaologisches Institut, 10–13 April 1994*, edited by R. Laffineur and W.-D. Niemeier, 173–83. Aegaeum 12. Liège.

Korfmann, M. 1995b. "Troia: Ausgrabungen 1994." *Studia Troica* 5: 1–38.

Korfmann, M. 1996. "Troia: Ausgrabungen 1995." *Studia Troica* 6: 1–63.

Korfmann, M. 1997a. "Hisarlık und das Troia Homers: Ein Beispiel zur kontroversen Einschätzung der Möglichkeiten der Archäologie." In *Ana šadî Labnāni lū allik. Beiträge zu altorientalischen und mittelmeerischen Kulturen: Festschrift Wolfgang Röllig*, edited by

B. Pongratz-Leisten, H. Kühne, and P. Xella, 171–84. Neukirchen-Vluyn.

Korfmann, M. 1997b. "Troia: Ausgrabungen 1996." *Studia Troica* 7: 1–71.

Korfmann, M. 1998a. "Stelen vor den Toren Troias: Apaliunas-Apollon in Truisa/Wilusa?" In *Light on Top of the Black Hill: Studies Presented to Halet Çambel*, edited by G. Arsebük, M.J. Mellink and W. Schirmer, 471–8. Istanbul.

Korfmann, M. 1998b. "Troia: Ausgrabungen 1997." *Studia Troica* 8: 1–70.

Korfmann, M. 1999a. "Troia: Ausgrabungen 1998." *Studia Troica* 9: 1–34.

Korfmann, M. 1999b. "Zusammenfassung des Kolloquiumsbeitrages und des Vortrages 'Homer als Zeitzeuge für die Ruinen von Troia im 8. Jahrhundert v.u.Z.'" *WürzJbb* 23: 35–41.

Korfmann, M. 2000. "Troia: Ausgrabungen 1999." *Studia Troica* 10: 1–52.

Korfmann, M. 2001a. "Der 'Schatz A' und seine Fundsituation." In *Beiträge zur Vorderasiatischen Archäologie Winfried Orthmann Gewidmet*, edited by J.-W. Meyer, M. Novak, and A. Pruss, 212–35. Frankfurt.

Korfmann, M. 2001b. "Troia: Traum und Wirklichkeit. Eine Einführung in das Thema." In *Troia: Traum und Wirklichkeit*, edited by B. Theune-Großkopf, U. Seidel, G. Kastl, M. Kempa, R. Redies, and A. Wais, 4–23. Stuttgart.

Korfmann, M. 2001c. "Troia/Wilusa: Ausgrabungen 2000." *Studia Troica* 11: 1–50.

Korfmann, M. 2001d. "Die Troianische Hochkultur (Troia VI und VIIa): Eine Kultur Anatoliens." In *Troia: Traum und Wirklichkeit*, edited by B. Theune-Großkopf, U. Seidel, G. Kastl, M. Kempa, R. Redies, and A. Wais, 395–406. Stuttgart.

Korfmann, M. 2001e. "Wilusa/(W)ilios ca. 1200 v. Chr. – Ilion ca. 700 v. Chr.: Befundberichte aus der Archäologie." In *Troia: Traum und Wirklichkeit*, edited by B. Theune-Großkopf, U. Seidel, G. Kastl, M. Kempa, R. Redies, and A. Wais, 64–76. Stuttgart.

Korfmann, M. 2002a. "Die Arbeiten in Troia/Wilusa 2001: Work in Troia/Wilusa." *Studia Troica* 12: 1–33.

Korfmann, M. 2002b. "Ilios, ca. 1200 BC – Ilion, ca. 700 B.C." In *Omero Tremila anni dopo*, edited by F. Montanari, 209–26. Rome.

Korfmann, M. 2003. "Die Arbeiten in Troia/ Wilusa 2002: Work in Troia/Wilusa." *Studia Troica* 13: 3–25.

Korfmann, M. 2004. "Die Arbeiten in Troia/ Wilusa 2003: Work in Troia/Wilusa." *Studia Troica* 14: 3–31.

Korfmann, M. 2005. "Die Arbeiten in Troia/ Wilusa 2004: Work in Troia/Wilusa 2004." *Studia Troica* 15: 3–26.

Korfmann, M., K. Pizchelauri, and P. Jablonka. 1999. "Vorbericht zu den Ausgrabungen in der Siedlung Didi Gora, Ostgeorgien, 1997 und 1998." *Studia Troica* 9: 527–49.

Korfmann, M., K. Pizchelauri, J.-K. Bertram, and G. Kastl. 2002. "Vorbericht zur 3. Grabungskampagne am Didi Gora im Jahre 1999 mit einem Anhang zu den Auswertungsarbeiten im Jahre 2000 (Kachetien/Ostgeorgien)." *Studia Troia* 12: 467–500.

Korfmann, M., N. Frank, and A. Mangini. 2006. "Eingang in die Unterwelt: Die Höhle von Troia und ihre Datierung." In *Troia: Archäologie eines Siedlunghügels und seiner Landschaft*, edited by M. Korfmann, 337–42. Mainz am Rhein.

Körpe, R. 2004. "A New Gold Diadem from Ilgardere." *Studia Troica* 14: 141–5.

Körpe, R., and F. Körpe. 2001. "A Lead Medallion from Skepsis in the Troad." *Studia Troica* 11: 421–6.

Körpe, R., and M. Treister. 2002. "Rescue Excavations in the Necropolis of Lampsacus, 1996." *Studia Troica* 12: 429–50.

Körpe, R., and M.F. Yavuz. 2009. "Sigeion and Its Foundation." In *SOMA 2007 Proceedings of the XI Symposium on Mediterranean Archaeology, Istanbul Technical University, 24–29 April 2007*, edited by C.O. Aygün, 230–2. BAR-IS 1900. Oxford.

Koşay, H. 1951. *Les Fouilles d'Alaca Höyük: Enterprises par la Societe d'histoire Turque: Rapport Preliminaire sur les Traveux en 1937–39*. Ankara.

Kosmetatou, E. 1993. "Horse Sacrifices in Greece and Cyprus." *JPR* 7: 31–41.

Kosmetatou, E. 2001. "Ilion, the Troad, and the Attalids." *Ancient Society* 31: 107–32.

Kossatz, A.-U. 1988. "Zur archaischen Keramik vom Beşik-Yassitepe." *AA*: 398–404.

Kossatz-Deissmann, A. 1981. "Achilleus." *LIMC* I: 37–200.

Kossatz-Deissmann, A. 1997. "Troilos." *LIMC* VIII: 91–4.

Kouka, O. 2002. *Siedlungsorganisation in der Nord- und Ostägäis während der Frühbronzezeit*. Rahden.

Kozal, E. 2001. "Studies in Roman Ilion: The Lower City. Stratified Domestic Assemblages." *Studia Troica* 11: 309–42.

Kraay, C.M. 1976. *Archaic and Classical Greek Coins*. Berkeley, Calif.

Kraft, J.C., I. Kayan, H. Brückner, and G. Rapp. 2003. "Sedimentary Facies Patterns and the Interpretation of Paleogeographies of Ancient Troia." In *Troia and the Troad: Scientific Approaches*, edited by G.A. Wagner, E. Pernicka, and H.-P. Uerpmann, 361–78. Berlin.

Krauskopf, I. 1981. "Amphiaraos." *LIMC* I: 691–713.

Kreikenbom, D. 1992. *Griechische und römische Kolossalportrats bis zum späten ersten Jahrhundert nach Christus*. Berlin.

Krenz, P., and E. Wheeler. 1994. *Polyaenus: Strategems of War*. Chicago, Ill.

Krug, A. 1968. *Binden in der griechischen Kunst: Untersuchungen zur Typologie, 6.-1. Jahrh. v. Chr.* Hosel.

Krumme, M. 1993. "Das Heiligtum der "Athena beim Palladion" in Athen." *AA*: 213–27.

Külzer, A. 2008. *Ostthrakien (Europe). Tabula Imperii Byzantini* 12. Vienna.

Kunze, E. 1967. *VIII Bericht über die Ausgrabungen in Olympia*. Berlin.

Kurtz, D. 1975. *Athenian White-Ground Lekythoi: Patterns and Painters*. Oxford.

Kurtz, D., and J. Boardman. 1971. *Greek Burial Customs*. London.

Kuttner, A. 1995. "Republican Rome Looks at Pergamon." *HSCP* 97: 157–78.

Kyrieleis, H. 1969. *Throne und Klinen: Studien zur Formgeschichte altorientalischer und griechischer Sitz- und Liegemobel vorhellenistischer Zeit*. Berlin.

Lacroix, L. 1949. *Les reproductions de statues sur les monnaies grecques*. Paris.

Ladstätter, S. 2002. "Die Chronologie des Hanghauses 2." In *Das Hanghaus 2 von Ephesos: Studien zu Baugeschichte und Chronologie*, edited by F. Krinzinger, 9–40. Vienna.

Laidlaw, W.A. 1933. *History of Delos*. Oxford.

Lamb, W. 1931–2. "Antissa." *BSA* 32: 41–67.

Lamb, W. 1932. "Grey Wares from Lesbos." *JHS* 52: 1–12.

Lamb, W. 1936. *Excavations at Thermi on Lesbos*. Cambridge.

Lambrinoudakis, W. 1984. "Apollo." *LIMC* II: 183–327.

Landskron, A. 2006. "Repräsentantinnen des Orbis Romanus auf dem sog. Partherdenkmal von Ephesos. Personifikationen und Bildpropaganda." In *Das Partherdenkmal von Ephesos. Akten des Kolloquiums, Wien, 27.–28. April 2003*, edited by W. Seipel, 103–27. Milan.

Landucci Gattinoni, F. 1992. *Lisimaco di Tracia*. Milan.

Landucci Gattinoni, F. 1997. "La legittimazione della vendetta nell' uccisione del tiranno: Il caso della leggge di Ilio." In *Amnistia, perdono e vendetta nel mondo antico*, edited by M. Sordi, 201–16. Contributi dell' Istituto di Storia Antica 23. Milan.

Landwehr, C. 1990. "Die Sitzstatue eines bärtigen Gottes in Cherchel: Zur Originalität römischer Vatergottdarstellungen." In *Phyromachos-Probleme*, edited by B. Andreae, N. Himmelmann, and G. De Luca, 101–22. Mainz am Rhein.

Lang-Auinger, C., ed. 2003. *Hanghaus 1 in Ephesos: Funde und Ausstattung*. Forschungen in Ephesos VIII.4. Vienna.

Langer-Karrenbrock, M.-T. 2000. *Der lykische Sarkophag aus der Königsnekropole von Sidon*. Münster and Hamburg.

Langlotz, E. 1975. *Studien zur nordostgriechischen Kunst*. Mainz am Rhein.

Langmann, G. 1967. "Eine spätarchaische Nekropole unter dem Staatsmarkt zu Ephesos." In *Festschrift für Fritz Eichler zum achtzigsten Geburtstag*, 103–23. Vienna.

Lapatin, D.S. 2001. *Chryselephantine Statuary in the Ancient Mediterranean World*. Oxford.

Laroche, E. 1974. "Les épitaphes lyciennes." In *Fouilles de Xanthos V: tombes-maisons, tombes rupestres et sarcophages*, edited by P. Demargne, 123–48. Paris.

Larsen, C.S. 1997. *Bioarchaeology*. Cambridge.

Lassen, H. 1994. "Zu den beiden Bronzebeinringen aus dem Gräberfeld an der Beşik-Bucht in der Troas." *Studia Troica* 4: 127–42.

Latacz, J. 2002a. "Troia, Wilios, Wilusa: Drei Namen für ein Territorium." In *Mauerschau: Festschrift für Manfred Korfmann*, edited by R. Aslan, S. Blum, G. Kastl, F. Schweizer, and D. Thumm, 1103–21. Remshalden-Grünbach.

Latacz, J. 2002b. "Wilusa (Wilios/Troia): Zentrum eines hethitischen Gliedstaates in Nordwest-Kleinasien." In *Die Hethiter und ihr Reich: das Volk der 1000 Götter*, edited by H. Willinghöfer, 196–201. Stuttgart.

Latacz, J. 2004. *Troy and Homer: Towards a Solution of an Old Mystery*. Oxford.

Latacz, J., and F. Starke. 2006. "Wilusa und die Grossen Vier: Troia in der politischen Landschaft." In *Troia: Archäologie eines Siedlungshügels und seiner Landschaft*, edited by M. Korfmann, 57–70. Mainz am Rhein.

Laumonier, A. 1937. "Recherches sur la chronologie des pretres de Panamara." *BCH* 61: 236–98.

Laumonier, A. 1938. "Recherches sur la chronologie des pretres de Lagina." *BCH* 62: 251–84.

Laurens, A.-F. 1988. "Hekabe." *LIMC* IV: 473–81.

Laviosa, C. 1972–3. "Un rilievo arcaico di Iasos e il problema del fregio nei templi ionici." *ASAtene* n.s. 34–5: 397–418.

Lawall, M. 2002. "Ilion before Alexander: Amphoras and Economic Archaeology." *Studia Troica* 12: 197–243.

Lawall, M. 2003. "'In the Sanctuary of the Samothracian Gods': Archaeology of Cult at Ilion." In *Greek Mysteries: The Archaeology and Ritual of Ancient Greek Secret Cults*, edited by M. Cosmopoulos, 79–111. London.

Lawergren, B. 1985. "A Lyre Common to Etruria, Greece, and Anatolia." *Acta Musicologia* 57: 25–33.

Lawergren, B. 1993. "Lyres in the West (Italy, Greece) and East (Egypt, The Near East), ca. 2000–400 B.C." *OpRom* 19: 55–76.

Lawton, C. 1995. *Attic Document Reliefs*. Oxford.

Lazzarini, L. 1984. "La prima monetazione della panegiria a Ilio." *RIN* 86: 3–8.

Leaf, W. 1912. *Troy: A Study in Homeric Geography*. London.

Leaf, W. 1923. *Strabo on the Troad, Book XIII, Cap. 1*. Cambridge.

Lebrun, R. 1976. *Samuha: foyer religieux de l'Empire Hittite*. Louvain-le-Neuve.

Lechevalier, J.B. 1802. *Voyage de la Troade*. Paris.

Lehmann, K. 1975. *Samothrace: A Guide to the Excavations and the Museum*. 4th ed. Locust Valley, N.Y.

Lehmann, K., and D. Spittle. 1964. *Samothrace 4.2: The Altar Court*. New York.

Lehmann, P. 1954. "The Setting of Hellenistic Temples." *JSAH* 13: 15–19.

Lehmann, P. 1967. "Letter to the Editor of AJA." *AJA* 71: 429–32.

Lehmann, P. 1969. *Samothrace 3.1: The Hieron*. Princeton, N.J.

Lehmann, P., and D. Spittle. 1982. *Samothrace 5: The Temenos*. Princeton, N.J.

Lemaire, A. 2001. "Remarques sur source épigraphiques et domination achémenide en Asie Mineure." In *Achaemenid Anatolia. Proceedings of the First International Symposium on Anatolia in the Achaemenid Period*, edited by T. Bakır, H. Sancisi-Weerdenburg, G. Gürtekin, P. Briant, and W. Henkelman, 21–35. Leiden.

Lemos, I.S. 2002. *The Protogeometric Aegean: The Archaeology of the Late Eleventh and Tenth Centuries BC*. Oxford.

Lemos, I.S. 2007. "The Migrations to the West Coast of Asia Minor: Tradition and Archaeology." In *Frühes Ionien: Eine Bestandsaufnahme. Panionien Symposium*, edited by J. Cobet, 713–27. Mainz am Rhein.

Lenz, D., F. Ruppenstein, M. Baumann, and R. Catling. 1998. "Protogeometric Pottery at Troia." *Studia Troica* 8: 189–222.

Lerat, L. 1952. *Les Locriens de l'ouest*. Paris.

Lesky, M. 2000. *Untersuchungen zur Ikonographie und Bedeutung antiker Waffentänze in Griechenland und Etrurien*. Munich.

Levi, D. 1966. "Il Cabirio di Lemno." In *Charisterion eis Anastasion K. Orlandon* III, 110–32. Athens.

Levick, B. 1990. *Claudius*. London.

Lewis, N. 1959. *Samothrace 1: The Ancient Literary Sources*. London.

Lincoln, B. 2001. "The Center of the World and the Origins of Life." *History of Religions* 40: 311–26.

Linder, E. 1981. "Ugarit: A Canaanite Thalassocracy." In *Ugarit in Retrospect: Fifty Years of Ugarit and Ugaritic*, edited by G.D. Young, 31–42. Winona Lake, Ind.

Lippold, G. 1949. "Palladion." *RE* 18.2: 171–201.

Littauer, M.A., and J.H. Crouwel. 1979. *Wheeled Vehicles and Ridden Animals in the Ancient Near East*. Leiden.

Littauer, M.A., and V. Karageorghis. 1969. "Note on Prometopidia." *AA* 84: 152–60.

Litvinskij, B.A., and I.R. Picikian. 1995. "An Achacmenian Griffin-Handle from the Temple of the Oxus: The Makhaira in Northern Bactria." In *In the Land of the Gryphons: Papers on Central Asian Archaeology in Antiquity*, edited by A. Invernizzi, 107–29. Florence.

Lohmann, H. 2004. "Mélia, le Panionion et le culte de Poséidon Héliconios," In *Les cultes locaux dans les mondes grecs et romain: actes du colloque de Lyon, 7–8 juin, 2001*, edited by G. Labarre, 31–49. Lyon.

Lohmann, H. 2005. "Melia, das Panionion und der Kult des Poseidon Helikonios." In *Neue Forschungen zu Ionien: Fahri Işık zum 60. Geburtstag gewidmet*, edited by E. Schwertheim and E. Winter, 57–91. Bonn.

Lohmann, H. 2007. "The Discovery and Excavation of the Archaic Panionion in the Mycale (Dilek Daglari)." *Kazı Sonuçları Toplantısı* 28: 575–90.

L'Orange, H.P. 1984. *Das spätantike Herrscherbild von Diokletian bis zu den Konstantin-Söhnen 284–361 n. Chr*. Berlin.

Loraux, N. 1987. *Tragic Ways of Killing a Woman*. Cambridge, Mass.

Lorimer, H.L. 1950. *Homer and the Monuments*. London.

Loud, G.A. 1981. "The 'Gens Normannorum': Myth or Reality?" In *Anglo-Norman Studies IV: Proceedings of the Battle Conference, 1981*, edited by R.A. Brown, 104–16. Woodbridge, U.K.

Luce, J.V. 1998. *Celebrating Homer's Landscapes: Troy and Ithaca Revisited*. New Haven, Conn.

Luce, J.V. 2003. "The Case for Historical Significance in Homer's Landmarks at Troia." In *Troia and the Troad: Scientific Approaches*, edited by G.A. Wagner, E. Pernicka, and H.-P. Uerpmann, 9–30. Berlin.

Luke, C., and C. Roosevelt. 2009. "Central Lydia Archaeological Survey: Documenting the Prehistoric through Iron Age Periods." In *Tree-Rings, Kings, and Old World Archaeology and Environment: Papers Presented in Honor of Peter Ian Kuniholm*, edited by S. Manning and M.J Bruce, 199–217. Oxford.

Lund, H. 1992. *Lysimachus: A Study in Early Hellenistic Kingship*. London.

Lygouri-Tolia, E. 1994. "Nestor." *LIMC* VII: 1060–5.

Lyons, C.L., and J.K. Papadopoulos. 2002a. "Archaeology and Colonialism." In *The Archaeology of Colonialism*, edited by C.L. Lyons and J.K. Papadopoulos, 1–26. Los Angeles, Calif.

Lyons, C.L., and J.K. Papadopoulos, eds. 2002b. *The Archaeology of Colonialism*. Los Angeles, Calif.

Ma, J. 1999. *Antiochus III and the Cities of Western Asia Minor*. London.

Ma, J. 2008. "Mysians on the Çan Sarcophagus? Ethnicity and Domination in Achaimenid Military Art." *Historia* 57: 243–54.

Macdonald, C.F., E. Hallager, and W.-D Niemeier, eds. 2009. *The Minoans in the Central, Eastern and Northern Aegean: New Evidence*. Athens.

MacGaffey, W. 2000. *Kongo Political Culture: The Conceptual Challenge of the Particular*. Bloomington, Ind.

Macridy, T. 1913. "Reliefs gréco-perses de la region de Dascylion." *BCH* 37: 340–58.

Maffre, F. 2006. "Phrygie maritime, Phrygie hellespontique, satrapie de Phrygie helles-pontique face au Pseudo-Skylax §93–96." *Colloquium Anatolicum* 5: 127–98.

Maffre, F. 2007. "Indigenous Aristocracies in Hellespontine Phrygia." In *Persian Responses: Political and Cultural Interaction within the Achaemenid Empire*, edited by C. Tuplin, 117–41. Swansea.

Magie, D. 1950. *Roman Rule in Asia Minor*. Princeton, N.J.

Maguire, H. 1994. "Imperial Gardens and the Rhetoric of Renewal." In *New Constantines: The Rhythm of Imperial Renewal in Byzantium, 4th–13th Centuries: Papers from the Twenty-sixth Spring Symposium of Byzantine Studies, St Andrews, March 1992*, edited by P. Magdalino, 181–98. Aldershot.

Malbran-Labat, F. 1994. *La version akkadienne de l'inscription trilingue de Darius à Behistun*. Rome.

Malkin, I. 1994. *Myth and Territory in the Spartan Mediterranean*. Cambridge.

Malkin, I. 1998. *The Returns of Odysseus: Colonization and Ethnicity*. Berkeley, Calif.

Malkin, I., ed. 2001. *Ancient Perceptions of Greek Ethnicity*. Washington, D.C.

Mambella, R. 1994. "Penates." *LIMC* VII: 288–91.

Mannsperger, B. 1995. "Die Funktion des Grabens am Schiffslager der Achäer." *Studia Troica* 5: 343–56.

Mannsperger, B. 1998. "Die Mauer am Schiffslager der Achaier." *Studia Troica* 8: 287–304.

Mannsperger, B., and D. Mannsperger. 2002. "Die Ilias ist ein Heldenepos: Ilosgrab und Athena Ilias." In *Mauerschau: Festschrift für Manfred Korfmann*, edited by R. Aslan, S. Blum, G. Kastl, F. Schweizer, and D. Thumm, 1075–87. Remshalden-Grünbach.

Mannsperger, D. 1989. *Sylloge Nummorum Graecorum: Deutschland. Münzsammlung der Universität Tübingen*. Mysien-Ionien 4. Munich.

Mannsperger, D. 2006. "Von Zahlungsmittel zum Leitartefakt: Münzen und Münzfunde in Ilion." In *Troia: Archäologie eines Siedlungshügels und seiner Landschaft*, edited by M. Korfmann, 265–74. Mainz am Rhein.

Mansfeld, G. 2001. "Die Kontroll-Ausgrabungen des 'Pinnacle E4/5' im Zentrum der Burg Troia." *Studia Troica* 11: 51–308.

Marsh, E. 1918. *Rupert Brooke: A Memoir*. New York.

Marvin, M. 1989. "Copying in Roman Sculpture: The Replica Series." In *Retaining the Original: Multiple Originals, Copies, and Reproductions*, 29–45. Washington, D.C.

Matsas, D. 1991. "Samothrace and the Northeastern Aegean: The Minoan Connection." *Studia Troica* 1: 159–79.

Matsas, D. 1995. "Minoan Long Distance Trade: A View from the Northern Aegean." In *Politeia: Society and State in the Aegean*

Bronze Age. Proceedings of the 5th International Aegean Conference, University of Heidelberg, Archaologisches Institut, 10–13 April 1994, edited by R. Laffineur and W.-D. Niemeier, 235–47. Aegaeum 12. Liège.

Mattusch, C. 1988. *Greek Bronze Statuary from the Beginnings through the Fifth Century B.C.* Ithaca, N.Y.

Maximova, M.E. 1928. "Griechisch-persische Kleinkunst in Kleinasien nach den Perserkriegen." *JdI* 43: 647–78.

Maxwell-Hyslop, K.R. 1971. *Western Asiatic Jewellery c. 3000–612 B.C.* London.

Mazarakis Ainian, A. 1997. *From Rulers' Dwellings to Temples: Architecture, Religion and Society in Early Iron Age Greece (1100–700 B.C.).* Jonsered.

McCredie, J.R. 1965. "Samothrace: Preliminary Report on the Campaigns of 1962–64." *Hesperia* 34: 100–24.

McCredie, J.R. 1968. "Samothrace: Preliminary Report on the Campaigns of 1965–67." *Hesperia* 37: 200–34.

McCredie, J.R. 1974. "A Samothracian Enigma." *Hesperia* 43: 454–9.

McCredie, J.R. 1979. "Samothrace: Supplementary Investigations, 1968–1977." *Hesperia* 48: 1–44.

McCredie, J.R. 1988. "Samothrace in the Classical Period." In Πρακτικά του XII Διεθνούς Συνεδρίου Κλασικής Αρχαιολογίας, Αθήνα 4–10 Σεπτεμβρίου 1983, 4, 119–23. Athens.

McDonald, W. 1943. *Political Meeting Places of the Greeks*. Baltimore.

McInerney, J. 2001. "Ethnos and Ethnicity in Early Greece." In *Ancient Perceptions of Greek Ethnicity*, edited by I. Malkin, 51–74. Washington, D.C.

McLauchlin, B. 1985. "Lydian Graves and Burial Customs (Asia Minor)." Ph.D. diss., University of California, Berkeley.

McNeal, E.H., ed. 1969. *The Conquest of Constantinople by Robert de Clari*. New York.

McNicoll, A.W. 1986. "Developments in Techniques of Siegecraft and Fortification in the Greek World, ca. 400–100 B.C." In *La fortification dans l'histoire du monde grec: actes du colloque international: la fortification et sa place dans l'histoire politique, culturelle et sociale du monde grec*, edited by P. Leriche and H. Tréziny, 305–13. Paris.

McNicoll, A.W. 1997. *Hellenistic Fortifications from the Aegean to the Euphrates*. Oxford.

McNiven, T.J. 1982. "Gestures in Attic Vase Painting: Use and Meaning, 550–450 B.C." Ph.D. diss., University of Michigan.

McShane, R.B. 1964. *The Foreign Policy of the Attalids of Pergamon*. Urbana, Ill.

Mee, C.B. 1998. "Anatolia and the Aegean in the Late Bronze Age." In *The Aegean and the Orient in the Second Millennium B.C.: Proceedings of the 50th Anniversary Symposium, Cincinnati, 18–20 April 1997*, edited by E.H. Cline and D. Harris-Cline, 137–47. Aegaeum 18. Liège.

Mehl, E. 1956. " Troiaspiel." *RE* Suppl. 8: 888–905.

Meiggs, R. 1972. *The Athenian Empire*. Oxford.

Melchert, H.C., ed. 2003. *The Luwians*. Boston.

Mellink, M.J. 1971. "Excavations at Karataş-Semayük and Elmalı, Lycia, 1970." *AJA* 75: 245–55.

Mellink, M.J. 1972. "Excavations at Karataş-Semayük and Elmalı, Lycia, 1971." *AJA* 76: 257–69.

Mellink, M.J. 1973a. "Excavations at Karataş-Semayük and Elmalı, Lycia, 1972." *AJA* 77: 293–303.

Mellink, M.J. 1973b. "Karatas-Semayük and Elmalı, 1971." *TürkArkDerg* 20: 155–66.

Mellink, M.J. 1975. "Excavations at Karataş-Semayük and Elmalı, Lycia, 1974." *AJA* 79: 349–55.

Mellink, M.J. 1980. "Archaic Wall Paintings from Gordion." In *From Athens to Gordion. Papers of a Memorial Symposium for Rodney S. Young*, edited by K. DeVries, 91–8. Philadelphia.

Mellink, M.J. 1983a. "The Hittites and the Aegean World: Part 2. Archaeological Comments on Ahhiyawa-Achaians in Western Anatolia." *AJA* 87: 138–41.

Mellink, M.J. 1983b. "Wall Paintings of West Anatolian Tombs: Elements of a Tradition." *Kazı Sonuçları Toplantısı* 5: 171–4.

Mellink, M.J. 1995. "Homer, Lycia, and Lukka." In *The Ages of Homer: A Tribute to Emily Townsend Vermeule*, edited by J.B Carter and S.P Morris, 33–44. Austin, Tex.

Mellink, M.J. 1998. *Kızılbel: An Archaic Painted Tomb Chamber in Northern Lycia*. Philadelphia.

Mellink, M.J., and D. Strahan. 1998. "The Bronze Figurine from Troia VIIa." *Studia Troica* 8: 141–9.

Meritt, B.D. 1936. "Greek Inscriptions." *Hesperia* 5.3: 355–430.

Meritt, B.D., H.T. Wade-Gery, and M.F. McGregor. 1939. *The Athenian Tribute Lists*. Cambridge.

Meritt, B.D., H.T. Wade-Gery, and M.F. McGregor. 1950. *The Athenian Tribute Lists III*. Cambridge.

Merkelbach, R. 1976. "Strabo XIII 1, 26 (Ilion und Alexandreia Troas)." *ZPE* 23: 241–2.

Merkelbach, R., and J. Stauber. 2001. *Steinepigramme aus dem griechischen Osten*. Stuttgart.

Merker, I.L. 1970. "The Ptolemaic Officials and the League of the Islanders." *Historia* 19: 141–60.

Meserve, M. 2008. *Empires of Islam in Renaissance Historical Thought*. Cambridge.

Messerschmidt, F. 1930. "Probleme der Etruskischen Malerei des Hellenismus." *JdI* 45: 62–90.

Messerschmidt, W. 1989. "Historische und ikonographische Untersuchungen zum Alexandersarkophag." *Boreas* 12: 64–92.

Metzger, H. 1963. *Fouilles de Xanthos II: L'acropole lycienne*. Paris.

Metzler, D. 1971. *Porträt und Gesellschaft: Über die Entstehung des griechischen Porträts in der Klassik*. Münster.

Metzler, D. 1973. "Bilderstürme und Bilderfeindlichkeit in der Antike." In *Bildersturm: Die Zerstörung des Kunstwerkes*, edited by M. Warnke, 14–29. Munich.

Meyer, M. 1989. *Die Griechischen Urkundenreliefs*. *AM* Beiheft 13. Berlin.

Mierow, C.C. 1915. *The Gothic History of Jordanes*. Princeton, N.J.

Migeotte, L. 1984. *L'emprunt public dans les cités grecques: recueil des documents et analyse critique*. Québec and Paris.

Miller, M.C. 1995. "Priam, King of Troy." In *The Ages of Homer: A Tribute to Emily Townsend Vermeule*, edited by J.B Carter and S.P Morris, 449–65. Austin, Tex.

Miller, M.C. 1997. *Athens and Persia in the Fifth Century B.C.: A Study in Cultural Receptivity*. Cambridge.

Miller, Stella G. 1991. "Terracotta Figurines: New Finds at Ilion, 1988–89." *Studia Troica* 1: 39–68.

Miller, Stella G. 1993. *The Tomb of Lyson and Kallikles: A Painted Macedonian Tomb*. Mainz am Rhein.

Miller, Stephen G. 1978. *The Prytaneion: Its Function and Architectural Form*. Berkeley, Calif.

Miller-Collett, Stella. 2010. "Two Painted Chamber Tombs of Northern Lycia at Kızılbel and Karaburun." In *Tatarlı: The Return of Colours*, edited by L. Summerer and A. von Kienlin, 318–29. Istanbul.

Miller-Collett, Stella G., and M.C. Root. 1997. "An Achaemenid Seal from the Lower City." *Studia Troica* 7: 355–62.

Minns, E.H. 1913. *Scythians and Greeks*. Cambridge.

Mitchell, S. 1987. "Imperial Building in the Eastern Roman Provinces." In *Roman Architecture in the Greek World*, edited by S. Macready and F.H. Thompson, 18–25. London.

Mitchell, S. 1999. "Archaeology in Asia Minor 1990–1998." *AR* 45: 125–91.

Mitchell, S. 2000. "The Settlement of Pisidia in Late Antiquity and the Byzantine Period: Methodological Problems." In *Byzanz als Raum. Zu Methoden und Inhalten der historischen Geographie des östlichen Mittelmeerraumes*, edited by K. Belke, F. Hild, J. Koder, and P. Soustal, 139–52. Vienna.

Mitchell, S. 2004. "Troas." In *An Inventory of Archaic and Classical Poleis*, edited by M.E. Hansen and T.H. Nielsen, 1000–17. Oxford.

Momigliano, A. 1945. "The Locrian Maidens and the date of Lycophron's Alexandra." *CQ* 39: 49–53.

Mommsen, H., D. Hertel, and P.A. Mountjoy. 2001. "Neutron Activation Analysis of the Pottery from Troy in the Berlin Schliemann Collection." *AA*: 169–211.

Mommsen, H., and P. Pavúk 2007. "Provenance of the Grey and Tan Wares from Troia, Cyprus, and the Levant." *Studia Troica* 17: 25–41.

Mommsen, Heidi. 1997. *Exekias I: Die Grabtafeln*. Mainz am Rhein.

Moore, M.B. 1986. *Attic Black-Figured Pottery*. Athenian Agora 23. Princeton, N.J.

Mordtmann, A.D. 1855. "Ruines de Scepsis en Troade." *RA* 11: 767–70.

Moret, J.-M. 1997. *Les pierres gravees antiques representant le rapt du Palladion.* Mainz am Rhein.

Moretti, J.-C. 2010. "Le cout et le financement des théâtres grecs." In *L'argent dans les concours du monde grec,* edited by B. Le Guren, 147–88. St. Denis.

Moretti, L. 1980. "Chio e la lupa capitolina." *RivFil* 108: 33–54.

Morgan, C. 1999. *Isthmia VIII: The Late Bronze Age Settlement and Early Iron Age Sanctuary.* Princeton, N.J.

Morkholm, O. 1991. *Early Hellenistic Coinage from the Accession of Alexander to the Peace of Apamea.* Cambridge.

Morkholm, O., and J. Zahle. 1976. "The Coinages of the Lycian Dynasts Keriga, Kherêi and Erbbina." *ActaArch* 47: 47–90.

Morris, I. 1997. "Homer and the Iron Age." In *A New Companion to Homer,* edited by I. Morris and B. Powell, 535–59. Leiden.

Morris, S.P. 1989. "A Tale of Two Cities: The Miniature Frescoes from Thera and the Origins of Greek Poetry." *AJA* 93: 511–35.

Morris, S.P. 1997. "Homer and the Near East Morris." In *A New Companion to Homer,* edited by I. Morris and B. Powell, 599–623. Leiden.

Morris, S.P. 2007. "Troy between Bronze and Iron Ages: Myth, Cult, and Memory in a Sacred Landscape." In *Epos: Reconsidering Greek Epic and Aegean Bronze Age Archaeology. Proceedings of the 11th International Aegean Conference, Los Angeles, UCLA, The J. Paul Getty Villa, 20–23 April 2006,* edited by S.P. Morris and R. Laffineur, 59–68. Aegaeum 28. Liège.

Most, G., ed. 2006. *Hesiod.* Cambridge, Mass.

Mountjoy, P.A. 1997a. "A Trojan Mycenaean Pictorial Krater." *Studia Troica* 7: 269–74.

Mountjoy, P.A. 1997b. "Local Mycenaean Pottery at Troia." *Studia Troica* 7: 259–67.

Mountjoy, P.A. 1997c. "Troia Phase VIf and Phase VIg: The Mycenaean Pottery." *Studia Troica* 7: 275–94.

Mountjoy, P.A. 1998. "The East Aegean–West Anatolian Interface in the Late Bronze Age: Mycenaeans and the Kingdom of Ahhiyawa." *AnatSt* 48: 33–67.

Mountjoy, P.A. 1999a. *Regional Mycenaean Decorated Pottery.* Rahden.

Mountjoy, P.A. 1999b. "Troy VII Reconsidered." *Studia Troica* 9: 295–346.

Mountjoy, P.A. 2005. "A Trojan Mycenaean Pictorial Krater Revisited." *Studia Troica* 15: 121–6.

Mountjoy, P.A. 2006. "Mykenische Keramik in Troia: ein Überblick." In *Troia: Archäologie eines Siedlungshügels und seiner Landschaft,* edited by M. Korfmann, 241–52. Mainz am Rhein.

Mountjoy, P.A., and V. Hankey. 1988. "LH IIIC Late versus Submycenaean: The Kerameikos Pompeion Cemetery Reviewed." *JdI* 103: 1–37.

Mountjoy, P.A., and H. Mommsen. 2006. "Neutron Activation Analysis of Mycenaean Pottery from Troia (1988–2003 Excavations)." *Studia Troica* 16: 97–123.

Moysey, R.A. 1984. "Chares and Athenian Foreign Policy." *CJ* 80: 221–7.

Mrogenda, U. 1990. "Figürliche Terrakotten." In *Ausgrabungen in Assos 1990,* edited by Ü. Serdaroğlu and R. Stupperich, 35–53. Bonn.

Müller, M. 2006. "Ex oriente lux? Troia und Ägypten im Geflecht der internationalen Beziehungen." In *Troia: Archäologie eines Siedlungshügels und seiner Landschaft,* edited by M. Korfmann, 219–26. Mainz am Rhein.

Munro, J.A.R. 1912. "Dascylium." *JHS* 32: 56–67.

Münzer, F. 1909. "C. Flavius Fimbria (no. 88)." *RE* 4.2: 2599–601.

Murray, A.C. 1998. "Post vocantur Merohingii: Fredegar, Merovech and 'Sacral Kingship.'" In *After Rome's Fall: Narrators and Sources of Early Medieval History, Essays Presented to Walter Goffart,* edited by A.C. Murray, 121–52. Toronto.

Muscarella, O. 1974. *Ancient Art: The Nobert Schimmel Collection.* Mainz am Rhein.

Nagy, G. 1996. *Homeric Questions.* Austin, Tex.

Nagy, G. 2010. *Homer the Classic.* Washington, D.C.

Nagy, G. 2012. *Homer the Preclassic.* Berkeley, Calif.

Nakou, G. 1997. "The Role of Poliochni and the North Aegean in the Development of Aegean Metallurgy." In *Hē Poliochnē kai hē proïmē epochē tou Chalkou sto Voreio Aigaio: diethnes synedrio Athēna, 22–25 Apriliou 1.* 634–48. Athens.

Naumann, F. 1980. *Antike Schmuck. Vollständiger Katalog der Sammlung und der Sonderausstellung. Staatliche Kunstsammlungen Kassel.* Kassel.

Naumann, R. 1971. *Architektur Kleinasiens*, 2nd ed. Tübingen.

Neer, R. 2012a. "'A Tomb both Great and Blameless': The Polyxena Sarcophagus in Canakkale." *Res: Anthropology and Aesthetics.* 61/2: 98–115.

Neer, R. 2012b. *Greek Art and Archaeology: A New History, c. 2500–c. 150 BCE.* New York.

Neils, J. 1994. "Priam." *LIMC* VII: 507–22.

Neils, J., and J.H. Oakley. 2003. *Coming of Age in Ancient Greece: Images of Childhood from the Classical Past.* New Haven, Conn.

Neumannn, G. 1965. *Gesten und Gebärden in der griechischen Kunst.* Berlin.

Neumannn, G. 1997. "Die zwei Inschriften auf der Stele von Vezirhan." In *Frigi e frigio. Atti del 1° simposio internazionale, Roma 16–17 ottobre*, edited by R. Gusmani, M. Salvini, and P. Vannicelli, 13–31. Rome.

Newell, E.T. 1941. *The Coinage of the Western Seleucid Mints from Seleucus I to Antiochus III.* Numismatic Studies 4. New York.

Niemeier, W.-D. 1998. "The Mycenaeans in Western Anatolia and the Problem of the Origins of the Sea Peoples." In *Mediterranean Peoples in Transition: Thirteenth to Early Tenth Centuries B.C.E., in Honor of Professor Trude Dothan*, edited by S. Gitin, A. Mazar, and E. Stern, 17–65. Jerusalem.

Niemeier, W.-D. 1999. "Mycenaeans and Hittites in War in Western Asia Minor." In *Polemos: le contexte guerrier en Égée à l'âge du Bronze. Actes de la 7e Rencontre égéenne internationale, Université de Liège, 14–17 avril 1998*, edited by. R. Laffineur, 141–55. Aegaeum 19. Liège.

Niemeier, W.-D. 2001. "Archaic Greeks in the Orient: Textual and Archaeological Evidence." *BASOR* 322: 11–32.

Niemeier, W.-D. 2002a. "Die analysierten mykenischen Keramikfunde aus Milet und Ephesus." In *Töpferzentren der Ostägäis: archäometrische und archäologische Untersuchungen zur mykenischen, geometrischen und archaischen Keramik aus Fundorten in Westkleinasien*, edited by M. Akurgal, M. Kerschner, H. Mommsen, and W.-D. Niemeier, 56–62. Vienna.

Niemeier, W.-D. 2002b. "Hattusa und Ahhiyawa im Konflikt um Millawanda/Milet." In *Die Hethiter und ihr Reich: das Volk der 1000 Götter*, edited by H. Willinghöfer, 294–9. Stuttgart.

Niemeier, W.-D. 2005. "Minoans, Mycenaeans, Hittites and Ionians in Western Asia Minor: New Excavations in Bronze Age Miletus-Millawanda." In *The Greeks in the East*, edited by A. Villing, 1–36. London.

Niemeier, W.-D. 2006. "Zwischen Mykene und Hattusa: Westkleinasien und die Ägais in der mittleren und späten Bronzezeit." In *Troia: Archäologie eines Siedlungshügels und seiner Landschaft*, edited by M. Korfmann, 47–56. Mainz am Rhein.

Niemeyer, H.G. 1968. *Studien zur statuarischen Darstellung der römischen Kaiser.* Berlin.

Nikolitsis, N. 1974. *The Battle of the Granicus.* Stockholm.

Nikoloudis, S. 2008. "Multiculturalism in the Mycenaean World." In *Anatolian Interfaces: Hittites, Greeks and Their Neighbours: Proceedings of an International Conference on Cross-cultural Interaction, September 17–19, 2004, Emory University, Atlanta, GA*, edited by B.J. Collins, M. Bachvarova and I. Rutherford, 45–56. Oxford.

Nobis, G. 1976–7. "Tierreste aus Tamassos auf Zypern." *Acta Praehistorica at Archaeologica* 7–8: 271–300.

Noble, P. 2005. "Epic Heroes in Thirteenth Century French Chroniclers." In *The Medieval Chronicle III: Proceedings of the 3rd International Conference on the Medieval Chronicle Doorn/Utrecht 12–17 July 2002*, edited by E. Kooper, 135–46. Amsterdam.

Nollé, M. 1992. *Denkmäler vom Satrapensitz Daskyleion.* Berlin.

Nylander, C. 1970. *Ionians in Pasargadae: Studies in Old Persian Architecture.* Uppsala.

Nylander, C. 1980. "Earless in Nineveh: Who Mutilated 'Sargon's' Head?" *AJA* 84: 329–37.

Oakley, J.H. 1990. *The Phiale Painter.* Mainz am Rhein.

Oakley, J.H., and R. Sinos. 1993. *The Wedding in Ancient Athens.* Madison, Wis.

Oates, J. 2003. "A Note on the Early Evidence for Horse and the Riding of Equids in Western

Asia." In *Prehistoric Steppe Adaptation and the Horse*, edited by M. Levine, C. Renfrew, and K. Boyle, 115–27. Cambridge.

Oliver, A., Jr. 1977. *Silver for the Gods: 800 Years of Greek and Roman Silver*. Toledo, Ohio.

Omura, S. 1991. "1990 yılı Kaman-Kalehöyük kazıları." *Kazı Sonuçları Toplantısı* 13: 319–36.

Öncü, E. 2004. "Erken İon Yapılarında Architrav ve Geisipodes." *Olba* 10: 151–67.

Opper, T. 2006. "Ein Fundkomplex von Terrakotten aus der Nekropole von Assos." In *Ausgrabungen in Assos 1993*, edited by R. Stupperich, 131–80. Bonn.

Oppermann, M. 1981. "Thrakische und danubische Reitergötter und ihre Beziehungen zu orientalischen Kulten." In *Die orientalischen Religionen in Römerreich*, edited by M.J. Vermaseren, 520–30. Leiden.

Oren, E., ed. 2000. *The Sea Peoples and Their World: A Reassessment*. Philadelphia.

Orlandos, A. 1966. *Les materiaux de construction et la technique architecturale des anciens Grec*. Paris.

Osborne, M.J. 1975. "The Satrapy of Mysia." *Graz Beitr* 3: 291–334.

Osborne, R. 1996. *Greece in the Making: 1200–479 BC*. London.

Otten, H. 1976. Review of *Samuha: foyer religieux de l'Empire Hittite*, by R. Lebrun. *ZA* 66: 301–5.

Özdoğan, M. 1989. "1988 Yılı Trakya ve Marmara Bölgesi Araştırmaları." *Araştırma Sonuçları Toplantılan* 7: 443–57.

Özdoğan, M. 1993a. "The Second Millennium of the Marmara Region: The Perspective of a Prehistorian on a Controversial Historical Issue." *IstMitt* 43: 151–63.

Özdoğan, M. 1993b. "Vinča and Anatolia: A New Look at a Very Old Problem, Or Redefining Vinča Culture from the Perspective of Near Eastern Tradition." *Anatolica* 19: 173–93.

Özdoğan, M. 1997. "Anatolia from the Last Glacial Maximum to the Holocene Climatic Optimum: Cultural Formations and the Impact of the Environmental Setting." *Paléorient* 23: 25–38.

Özdoğan, M. 2003. "The Black Sea, the Sea of Marmara and Bronze Age Archaeology: An Archaeological Predicament," In *Troia and the Troad: Scientific Approaches*, edited by G.A. Wagner, E. Pernicka, and H.-P. Uerpmann, 105–20. Berlin.

Özdoğan, M. 2006. "Neolithic Cultures at the Contact Zone between Anatolia and the Balkans: Diversity and Homogeneity at the Neolithic Frontier." In *Aegean-Marmara-Black Sea: The Present State of Research on the Early Neolithic*, edited by I. Gatsov and H. Schwarzberg, 21–8. Langenweissbach.

Özdoğan, M. 2010. "Eastern Thrace: The Contact Zonc between Anatolia and the Balkans." In *The Oxford Handbook of Ancient Anatolia*, edited by S. Steadman and G. McMahon, 657–82. Oxford.

Özet, M.A. 1994. "The Tomb of a Noble Woman from the Hekatomnid Period." In *Hekatomnid Caria and the Ionian Renaissance*, edited by J. Isager, 88–96. Halicarnassian Studies I. Odense.

Özgen, E., and I. Özgen. 1988. *Antalya Museum*. Istanbul.

Özgen, I., and J. Öztürk. 1996. *Heritage Recovered: The Lydian Treasure*. Istanbul.

Özgüç, T. 1971. *Kültepe and Its Vicinity in the Iron Age*. Ankara.

Özgüç, T. 1999. *Kültepe-Kaniš/Neša sarayları ve mabetleri*. Ankara.

Özgüç, T., and R. Temizer. 1993. "The Eskiyapar Treasure." In *Aspects of Art and Iconography: Anatolia and Its Neighbors: Studies in Honour of Nimet Özgüç*, edited by M.J. Mellink, E. Porada, and T. Özgüç, 613–68. Ankara.

Özgünel, C. 1978. "Spätgeometrische Keramik in Bayrakli (Alt-Smyrna)." In *Les céramiques de la Grèce de l'est et leur diffusion en occident*, 17–26. Paris.

Özgünel, C. 2001. *Smintheion: Troas'ta Kutsal Bir Alan*. Ankara.

Özgünel, C. 2003. "Das Heiligtum des Apollo Smintheus und die Ilias." *Studia Troica* 13: 261–91.

Özgünel, C. 2008. "Eine neugefundene Columna Caeleta des Apollon Smintheus Tempels in der Troas." In *Vom Euphrat bis zum Bosporus: Kleinasien in der Antike: Festschrift für Elmar Schwertheim zum 65. Geburtstag*, edited by E. Winter, 513–16. Bonn.

Özkan, T. 1994. "1992 Yili Gryneion kazisi çalismalari." *Müze Kurtarma Kazılari Semineri* 4: 1–15.

Öztürk, J. 1998. "Lydian Jewellery." In *The Art of the Greek Goldsmith*, edited by D. Williams, 41–7. London.

Page, D.L. 1955. *Sappho and Alkaios: An Introduction to the Study of Ancient Lesbian Poetry*. Oxford.

Palaima, T. 2007. "Ilios, Tros and Tlos: Continuing Problems with to-ro, to-ro-o, to-ro-wo, to-ro-ja, wi-ro and a-si-wi-ja/a-si-wi-jo." In *Stefanos Aristeios Festschrift fur Stefan Hille zum 65. Geburtstager*, edited by F. Lang, C. Reiholdt, and J. Weilhartner, 197–204. Vienna.

Paoletti, O. 1994. "Kassandra." *LIMC* VII: 956–70.

Papadopoulos, J.K. 1997. "Innovations, Imitations and Ceramic Style: Modes of Production and Modes of Dissemination." In *TEXNH: Craftsmen, Craftswomen and Craftsmanship in the Aegean Bronze Age: Proceedings of the 6th International Aegean Conference, Philadelphia, Temple University, 18–21 April 1996*, edited by R. Laffineur and P. Betancourt, 449–61. Aegaeum 16. Liège.

Papadopoulos, J.K. 2005. *The Early Iron Age Cemetery at Torone*. Los Angeles, Calif.

Paquette, D. 1984. *L'instrument de musique dans la céramique de la Grèce antique*. Paris.

Paribeni, E. 1984. "Ascanius." *LIMC* II: 860–3.

Parrish, D. 1999. "House (or Wohneinheit) 2 in Hanghaus 2 at Ephesos: A Few Issues of Interpretation." In *100 Jahre Österrreichische Forschungen in Ephesos: Akten des Symposions Wien 1995*, edited by H. Friesinger and F. Krinzinger, 507–13. Vienna.

Parrot, A. 1961. *The Arts of Assyria*. New York.

Pasinli, A. 1976. "Elaea'dan gelen kabartmalı bir pithos." *TürkArkDerg* 23: 57–66.

Paton, W.R. 1900. "Sites in East Caria and South Lydia." *JHS* 20: 57–80.

Patton, J.M. 1951. *Chapters on Medieval and Renaissance Visitors Greek Lands*. Princeton, N.J.

Pavese, C. 1961. "Aristotele e i filosofi ad Asso." *PP* 16: 113–9.

Pavúk, P. 2005. "Aegeans and Anatolians. A Trojan Perspective." In *Emporia: Aegeans in Central and Eastern Mediterranean. Proceedings of the 10th International Aegean Conference: Italian School of Archaeology, Athens, 14–18 April 2004*, edited by R. Laffineur and E. Greco, 269–79. *Aegaeum* 25. Liège.

Pavúk, P. 2007. "What Can Troia Tell Us about the Middle Helladic Period in the Southern Aegean?" In *Middle Helladic Pottery and Synchronisms*, edited by F. Felten, W. Gauss, and R. Smetana, 295–308. Vienna.

Pavúk, P. 2010a. "Between the Aegean and Anatolia: The Shifting Character of Troy in the Middle and Late Bronze Age." *BICS* 53: 128–9.

Pavúk, P. 2010b. "Minyan or Not: The Second Millennium Grey Ware in Western Anatolia and its Relation to Mainland Greece." In *Mesohelladika: La Grèce continentale au Bronze Moyen*, edited by A. Philippa-Touchais, G. Touchais, S. Voutsaki, and J.C. Wright, 931–43. BCH Supplement 52. Athens.

Pavúk, P. Forthcoming. *Troia VI-Früh und Mitte. Keramik, Stratigraphie, Chronologie*. Studia Troica Monographs 3. Mainz am Rhein.

Peacock, D.P.S. 1982. *Pottery in the Roman World: An Ethno-archaeological Approach*. London.

Pedley, J.G. 1972. *Ancient Literary Sources on Sardis*. Archaeological Exploration of Sardis 2. Cambridge, Mass.

Pedrina, M. 2001. *I gesti del dolore nella ceramics attica (VI–V secolo a.C.): per un'analisi della comunicazione non verbale nel mondo gredo*. Venice.

Pensabene, P. 1996. "Magna Mater Aedes." *LTUR* III: 206–8.

Pensabene, P. 1999. "Scalae Caci." *LTUR* IV: 239–40.

Pernicka, E., C. Eibner, Ö. Öztunalı, and G.A. Wagner. 2003. "Early Bronze Age Metallurgy in the Northeast Aegean." In *Troia and the Troad: Scientific Approaches*, edited by G.A. Wagner, E. Pernicka, and H.-P. Uerpmann, 143–72. Berlin.

Pertusi, A., and A. Carile, eds. 1983. *Testi inediti e poco noti sulla caduta di Constantinopoli*. Bologna.

Petit, T. 1990 *Satrapes et satrapies dans l'empire achéménide de Cyrus le Grand à Xerxès Ier*. Paris.

Petrakos, B. 1996. *Marathon*. Athens.

Petsas, P. 1978. *Pella: Alexander the Great's Capital*. Thessaloniki.

Petzl, G., and E. Schwertheim. 2006. *Hadrian und die dionysischen Künstler: drei in Alexandria Troas neugefundene Briefe des Kaisers an die Künstler-Vereinigung*. Bonn.

Pflaum, H.-P., and P. Bastien. 1969. *La trouvaille de Canakkale (Turquie)*. Wetteren.

Pflug, H. 1988. "Chalkidische Helme." In *Antike Helme: Sammlung Lipperheide und andere Bestande des Antikenmuseums Berlin*, 137–50. Mainz am Rhein.

Pfrommer, M. 1998. *Untersuchungen zur Chronologie und Komposition des Alexandermosaiks auf antiquarischer Grundlage*. Mainz am Rhein.

Pfuhl, E., and H. Möbius. 1977. *Die ostgriechischen Grabreliefs*. Mainz am Rhein.

Philipp, H. 1981. "Archaische Gräber in Ostionien." *IstMitt* 31: 149–66.

Philippides, M., and W.K. Hanak. 2011. *The Siege and the Fall of Constantinople in 1453*. Burlington, Vt.

Picard, C. 1964. Review of *Der Athenatempel von Ilion*, by F.W. Goethert and H. Schleif. *RA*: 89–91.

Piejko, F. 1988. "The Treaty between Antiochus III and Lysimacheia." *Historia* 37: 151–65.

Piejko, F. 1991a. "Antiochus and Ilion." *ArchPF* 37: 9–50.

Piejko, F. 1991b. "Seleucus II and Ilium." *ClMed* 42: 111–38.

Pieniążek-Sikora, M. 2003. "Some Comments on Northwest Pontic and North Aegean Settlement Architecture in the Last Quarter of the Second Millennium B.C." In *Identifying Changes: The Transition from Bronze to Iron Ages in Anatolia and Its Neighboring Regions*, edited by B. Fischer, H. Genz, E. Jean, and K. Köroglu, 29–39. Istanbul.

Pierides, A. 1971. *Jewelery in the Cyprus Museum*. Nicosia.

Pini, I. 1992. "Zu den Siegeln aus der Beşik-Nekropole." *Studia Troica* 2: 157–63.

Pinkwart, D. 1965. *Das Relief des Archelaos von Priene und die "Museum des Philiskos*. Lassleben.

Pinter, F. 2005. "Provenance Study of the Early Iron Age Knobbed Ware in Troia, NW Turkey and the Balkans: Petrographic and Gochemical Evidence." Ph.D. diss., University of Tübingen.

Pipili, M. 1997." Ilioupersis." *LIMC* VIII: 650–7.

Pirson, F. Forthcoming. "Die Tumuli von Pergamon." In *Tumulus as Sema: Space, Politics, Culture and Religion in the First Millennium BC*, edited by O. Henry and U. Kelb. Istanbul.

Pitarakis, B. 2006. *Les croix-reliquaires pectorales byzantine en bronze*. Paris.

Ploumis, I.M. 1997. "Gifts in the Late Roman Iconography." In *Patron and Pavements in Late Antiquity*, edited by S. Isager and B. Poulsen, 125–41. Odense.

Pohl, D. 1999. "Der dorische Tempel von Alexandria Troas." In *Die Troas: neue Forschungen III*, edited by E. Schwertheim, 85–93. Bonn.

Pohl, D. 2002. *Kaiserzeitliche Tempel in Kleinasien unter besonderer Berucksichtigung der hellenistischen Vorläufer*. Asia Minor Studien 43. Bonn.

Polat, G. 2007. "Daskyleion'dan Yeni bir Anadolu-Pers Stele." In *The Achaemenid Impact on Local Populations and Cultures in Anatolia (Sixth–Fourth Centuries B.C.)* edited by İ. Delemen, 215–24. Istanbul.

Pollini, J. 1987. *The Portraiture of Gaius and Lucius Caesar*. New York

Pollitt, J.J. 1978. "The Impact of Greek Art on Rome." *TAPS* 108: 155–74.

Pontes, H. 1996. "Inscriptiones Iliacae: Two Epigraphical Notes from Ilion." *Studia Troica* 6: 209–16.

Ponti, G. 1995. "Marmor Troadense: Granite Quarries in the Troad. A Preliminary Survey." *Studia Troica* 5: 291–320.

Porada, E. 1981–2. "Cylinder Seals Found at Thebes in Boeotia." *AfO* 28: 1–70.

Pottier, E. 1887. "Cyathus." In *Dictionnaire des antiquités grecques et romaines d'après les textes et les monuments, ouvrage redigé par une societé d'ecrivains speciaux, d'archeologues et de professeurs sous la direction de Ch. Daremberg et Edm. Saglio*, I.2, 1675–7. Paris.

Pouilloux, J., and G. Roux. 1963. *Enigmes á Delphes*. Paris.

Prag, A.J.N.W. 1985. *The Oresteia: Iconographic and Narrative Tradition*. Warminster.

Prag, J., and R. Neave. 1994. "The Tomb of a Noble Woman from the Hekatomnid

Period." In *Hecatomnid Caria and the Ionian Renaissance: Acts of the International Symposium at the Department of Greek and Roman Studies, Odense University, 28–29 November, 1991*, edited by J. Isager, 97–109. Odense.

Preuner, E. 1926. "Panegyris des Athena Ilias." *Hermes* 61: 113–33.

Price, S.R.F. 1984. *Rituals and Power: The Roman Imperial Cult in Asia Minor*. Cambridge.

Pulak, C. 1998. "The Uluburun Shipwreck: An Overview." *IJNA* 27: 188–224.

Quataert, D. 1994. "The Age of Reforms, 1812–1914." In *An Economic and Social History of the Ottoman Empire, 1300–1916*, edited by H. İnalcık and D. Quataert, 759–946. Cambridge.

Raaflaub, K. 1997. "Homeric Society." In *A New Companion to Homer*, edited by I. Morris and B. Powell, 624–48. Leiden.

Radner, K. 2001. "Kompositstatuen vom Typus der Ephesia aus dem vorkroisoszeitlichen Heiligtum: Zur Herstellung und Pflege von Götterstatuen im östlichen Mittlemeerraum und im Vorderen Orient im frühen ersten Jahrtausend." In *Der Kosmos der Artemis von Ephesos*, edited by U. Muss, 233–63. Vienna.

Radt, W. 1985. "Ein hölzerner hellenistischer Sarkophag aus Elaia bei Pergamon." *IstMitt* 35: 139–72.

Radt, W. 1988. *Pergamon: Geschichte und Bauten, Funde und Erforschung einer antiken Metropole*. Cologne.

Ragone, G. 1990. "Il tempio di Apollo Gryneios in Eolide: Testimonianze antiquarie, fonti antiche, elementi per la ricerca topografica." *Studi ellenistici* 3: 9–112.

Ramage, A. 1972. "The Fourteenth Campaign at Sardis (1971)." *BASOR* 206: 9–39.

Ramsay, W.R. 1918. "The Utilization of Old Epigraphic Copies." *JRS* 38: 124–92.

Rapp, G., and J. Gifford. 1982. *The Archaeological Geology*. Troia Supplementary Monograph 4. Princeton, N.J.

Rathje, A. 1990. "The Adoption of the Homeric Banquet in Central Italy in the Orientalizing Period." In *Sympotica: A Symposium on the Symposium*, edited by O. Murray, 279–88. Oxford.

Rathje, A. 1994. "Banquet and Ideology." In *Murlo and the Etruscans*, edited by R. De Puma and J.P. Small, 95–9. Madison, Wis.

Ratté, C. 1993. "Lydian Contributions to Archaic East Greek Architecture." In *Les grands ateliers d'architecture dans le monde égéen du VIe siecle av. J.-C.* edited by J. Courtils and J.-C. Moretti, 1–12. Paris.

Raubitschek, A.E. 1949. *Dedications from the Athenian Akropolis: A Catalogue of the Inscriptions of the Sixth and Fifth Centuries B.C.* Cambridge, Mass.

Rautman, M. 1995. "A Late Roman Townhouse in Sardis." In *Forschungen in Lydien*, edited by E. Schwertheim, 49–66. Bonn.

Rautman, M. 1998. "Handmade Pottery and Social Change: The View from Late Roman Cyprus." *JMA* 11: 81–104.

Redfield, J.M. 2003. *The Locrian Maidens: Love and Death in Greek Italy*. Princeton, N.J.

Reeder, E. (ed.). 1999. *Scythian Gold: Treasures from the Ancient Ukraine*. New York.

Rehm, A. 1958. *Die Inschriften*. Didyma II. Berlin.

Rehm, E. 1992. *Der Schmuck der Achämeniden*. Münster.

Reiblich, E. 1993. "Ringe und Ohrringe aus der Westtor-Nekropole von Assos." In *Ausgrabungen in Assos 1991*, edited by Ü. Serdaroğlu and R. Stupperich, 163–78. Bonn.

Reiblich, E. 1996. "Ringe und Ohrringe aus der Westtor-Nekropole von Assos." In *Ausgrabungen in Assos 1992*, edited by Ü. Serdaroğlu and R. Stupperich, 127–37. Bonn.

Reinsberg, C. 2001. "Der Polyxena-Sarkophag in Çanakkale." *Olba* 4: 71–99.

Reinsberg, C. 2004. "Der Polyxena-Sarkophag in Çanakkale." In *Sepulkral-und Votivdenkmäler östliches Mittelmeergebiete (7 Jh. v. Chr.–1 Jh. n. Chr.): Kulturbegegnungen im Spannungsfeld von Akzeptanz und Resistenz. Akten des Internationalen Symposiums Mainz, 1–3 November 2001*, edited by R. Bol and D. Kreikenbom, 199–217. Möhnesee.

Reinsch, D. 1983. *Critobuli Imbriotae historiae*. Berlin.

Reynolds, J. 1981. "New Evidence for the Imperial Cult in Julio-Claudian Aphrodisias." *ZPE* 43: 317–27.

Reynolds, J., and J. Ward-Perkins. 1952. *The Inscriptions of Roman Tripolitania*. Rome.

Rhodes, P.J., and R. Osborne. 2003. *Greek Historical Inscriptions: 404–323 BC*. Oxford.

Richter, G.M.A. 1923. "Red-Figured Athenian Vases Recently Acquired by the Metropolitan Museum of Art." *AJA* 27: 265–85.

Richter, G. 1960. *Kouroi: Archaic Greek Youths*. London.

Richter, G. 1966. *The Furniture of the Greeks, Etruscans and Romans*. London.

Richter, G. 1968. *Korai*. London.

Ricl, M. 1997. *The Inscriptions of Alexandria Troas*. Bonn.

Ridgway, B.S. 1981. *Fifth Century Styles in Greek Sculpture*. Princeton, N.J.

Ridgway, B.S. 1990. *Hellenistic Sculpture I: The Styles of ca. 331–200 B.C.* Madison, Wis.

Ridgway, B.S. 1993. *The Archaic Style in Greek Sculpture*. Rev. ed. Chicago, Ill.

Ridgway, B.S. 1997. *Fourth Century Styles in Greek Sculpture*. Madison, Wis.

Ridgway, B.S. 1999. *Prayers in Stone: Greek Architectural Sculpture (ca. 600–100 B.C.E.)*. Berkeley, Calif.

Ridgway, B.S. 2000. *Hellenistic Sculpture II*. Madison, Wis.

Ridgway, B.S. 2002. *Hellenistic Sculpture III: The Styles of ca. 100–31 B.C.* Madison, Wis.

Rigsby, K. 1999. "Greek Inscriptions from Ilion, 1997." *Studia Troica* 9: 347–52.

Rigsby, K. 2004. "A Greek Inscription from Troia, 2003." *Studia Troica* 14: 117–20.

Rigsby, K. 2007. "A New Greek Inscription from Troia." *Studia Troica* 17: 43–6.

Rigter, W., and D. Thumm-Doğrayan. 2004. "Ein hohlgeformter Stier aus Troia." *Studia Troica* 14: 87–99.

Riorden, E. 2007. "The Odeion of Ilion: A Proposed Reconstruction and Some Implications." *Studia Troica* 17: 47–55.

Ritti, T. 1985. *Hierapolis I: Fonti letterarie ed epigrafiche*. Rome.

Rizzo, F.P. 1974. *Studi ellenistico-romano*. Palermo.

Robert, J., and L. Robert. 1956. "Bulletin épigraphique." *REG* 69: 104–91.

Robert, J., and L. Robert. 1964. "Bulletin épigraphique." *REG* 77: 127–259.

Robert, J., and L. Robert. 1976. "Bulletin épigraphique." *REG* 89: 415–595.

Robert, J., and L. Robert. 1983. *Fouilles d'Amyzon en Carie. Tome 1: Exploration, histoire, monnaies, et inscriptions*. Paris.

Robert, L. 1937. *Études anatoliennes: Recherches sur les inscriptions grecques de l'Asie Mineure*. Paris.

Robert, L. 1940. *Les gladiateurs dans l'Orient grec*. Paris.

Robert, L. 1951. *Études de numismatique grecque*. Paris.

Robert, L. 1966a. *Les monnaies antiques en Troade*. Geneva.

Robert, L. 1966b. "Sur un décret d'Ilion et sur un papyrus concernant des cultes royaux." In *Essays in Honor of C. Bradford Welles*. 175–212. New Haven, Conn.

Robert, L. 1978. "Stèle funéraire de Nicomédie et séismes dans les inscriptions." In Documents d'Asia Mineure." *BCH* 102: 395–408.

Roberts, H. 1981. Reconstructing the Greek Tortoise-Shell Lyre." *WorldArch* 12: 303–12.

Robertson, M. 1975. *A History of Greek Art*. Cambridge.

Robertson, M. 1990. "Troilos and Polyxena: Notes on a Changing Legend." In *Eumousia: Ceramic and Iconographic Studies in Honour of Alexander Cambitoglou*, edited by P. Descoeudres, 63–70. Sydney.

Robertson, N. 1983. "The Riddle of the Arrhephoroi at Athens." *HSCP* 87: 241–88.

Robinson, D.M. 1930. *Excavations at Olynthos II. Architecture and Sculpture: Houses and Other Buildings*. Baltimore, Md.

Robinson, D.M. 1942. *Necrolynthia: A Study in Greek Burial Customs and Anthropology. Excavations at Olynthos XI*. Baltimore, Md.

Robinson, M. 1995. "Frank Calvert and the Discovery of Troia." *Studia Troica* 5: 323–41.

Roebuck, C. 1959. *Ionian Trade and Colonization*. New York.

Roller, L.E. 1998. "The Ideology of the Eunuch Priest." In *Gender and the Body in the Ancient Mediterranean*, edited by M. Wyck, 118–35. Oxford.

Roller, L.E. 1999. *In Search of God the Mother: The Cult of Anatolian Cybele*. Berkeley, Calif.

Rolley, C., and F. Salviat. 1963. "Une statue d'Hadrien sur l'agora de Thasos." *BCH* 87: 548–78.

Rollinger, R., and C. Ulf, eds. 2004. *Griechische Archaik: Interne Entwicklungen, externe Impulse.* Berlin.

Romano, I.B. 2006. *Classical Sculpture: Catalogue of the Cypriot, Greek, and Roman Stone Sculpture in the University of Pennsylvania Museum of Archaeology and Anthropology.* Philadelphia.

Römer, A. 1924. *Die Homerexegese Aristarchs.* Paderborn.

Römhild, J.-H. 2011. "Römische Bürger in der Troas." In *Studien zum antiken Kleinasien VII*, edited by E. Schwertheim, 159–80. Bonn.

Rook, T. 1979. "The Effect of the Evolution of Flues upon the Development of Architecture." In *Roman Brick and Tiles: Studies in Manufacture, Distribution, and Use in the Western Empire*, edited by A. McWhirr, 303–8. Oxford.

Roos, P. 1976. "Observations on the Internal Proportions of the Ionic Dentil in the Aegean." *RA*: 103–12.

Roosevelt, C. 2003. "Lydian and Persian Period Settlement in Lydia." Ph.D. diss., Cornell University.

Roosevelt, C. 2009. *The Archaeology of Lydia: From Gyges to Alexander.* Cambridge.

Root, M.C. 1979. *The King and Kingship in Achaemenid Art: Essays on the Creation of an Iconography of Empire.* Acta Iranica 19. Leiden.

Rose, C.B. 1991. "The Theater of Ilion." *Studia Troica* 1: 69–77.

Rose, C.B. 1992. "The 1991 Post-Bronze Age Excavations at Troia." *Studia Troica* 2: 43–60.

Rose, C.B. 1993. The 1992 Post-Bronze Age Excavations at Troia." *Studia Troica* 3: 97–116.

Rose, C.B. 1994. "The 1993 Post-Bronze Age Excavations at Troia." *Studia Troica* 4: 75–104.

Rose, C.B. 1995. "The 1994 Post-Bronze Age Excavations at Troia." *Studia Troica* 5: 81–105.

Rose, C.B. 1996. "The 1995 Post-Bronze Age Research and Excavations at Troia." *Studia Troica* 6: 97–101.

Rose, C.B. 1997a. *Dynastic Commemoration and Imperial Portraiture in the Julio-Claudian Period.* Cambridge.

Rose, C.B. 1997b. "Imperial Image in the Eastern Mediterranean." In *The Early Roman Empire in the East*, edited by S.E. Alcock, 108–20. Oxford.

Rose, C.B. 1997c. "The 1996 Post-Bronze Age Excavations at Troia." *Studia Troica* 7: 73–110.

Rose, C.B. 1998. "The 1997 Post-Bronze Age Excavations at Troia." *Studia Troica* 8: 71–113.

Rose, C.B. 1999. "The 1998 Post-Bronze Age Excavations at Troia." *Studia Troica* 9: 35–71.

Rose, C.B. 2000. "Post-Bronze Age Research at Troia, 1999." *Studia Troica* 10: 53–71.

Rose, C.B. 2001. "Von Konstantin bis Mehmet II: Ilion in byzantinischer Zeit." In *Troia: Traum und Wirklichkeit*, edited by B. Theune-Großkopf, U. Seidel, G. Kastl, M. Kempa, R. Redies, and A. Wais, 280–2. Stuttgart.

Rose, C.B. 2002a. "Bilingual Trojan Iconography." In *Mauerschau: Festschrift für Manfred Korfmann*, edited by R. Aslan, S. Blum, G. Kastl, F. Schweizer, and D. Thumm, 329–50. Remshalden-Grünbach.

Rose, C.B. 2002b. "Ilion in the Early Empire." In *Patris und Imperium: Kulturelle und politische Identität in den Städten in den römischen Provinzen Kleinasiens in der frühen Kaiserzeit. Kolloquium Köln, November, 1998*, edited by C. Berns, H. von Hesber, L. Vandeput, and M. Waelkens, 33–47. BaBesch Supplement 8. Leuven.

Rose, C.B. 2003. "The Temple of Athena at Ilion." *Studia Troica* 13: 27–88.

Rose, C.B. 2005. "The Parthians in Augustan Rome." *AJA* 109: 21–75.

Rose, C.B. 2006. "Ilion." In *Stadtgrabungen und Stadtforschung im westlichen Kleinasien*, edited by W. Radt, 135–58. Istanbul.

Rose, C.B. 2007a. "Designing Monuments to War and Tragedy." In *Festschrift für Coşkun Özgünel zum 65. Geburtstag*, edited by E. Öztepe and M. Kadıoğlu, 305–14. Ankara.

Rose, C.B. 2007b. "The Tombs of the Granicus River Valley." In *The Achaemenid Impact on Local Populations and Cultures in Anatolia (Sixth–Fourth Centuries B.C.)*, edited by İ. Delemen, 247–64. Istanbul.

Rose, C.B. 2008. "Separating Fact from Fiction in the Aeolian Migration." *Hesperia* 77: 399–430.

Rose, C.B. 2011a. "Greek and Roman Sculpture and Coinage in Ilion." In *Roman Sculpture in Asia Minor*, edited by F. D'Andri and I. Romeo, 279–93. Portsmouth, R.I.

Rose, C.B. 2011b. "Troy and the Granicus River Valley in Late Antiquity." In *Archaeology and the Cities of Asia Minor in Late Antiquity*, edited by O. Dally and C. Ratté, 151–71. Ann Arbor, Mich.

Rose, C.B. 2012. "Introduction." In *The Archaeology of Phrygian Gordion, Royal City of Midas*, edited by C.B. Rose, 1–19. Philadelphia.

Rose, C.B., ed. Forthcoming. *The Hellenistic and Roman Houses of the Lower City of Ilion*. Mainz am Rhein.

Rose, C.B., ed. Forthcoming. *The West Sanctuary of Ilion: Hellenistic and Roman Phases*. Mainz am Rhein.

Rose, C.B., and R. Körpe. 2007. "The Granicus River Valley Survey Project, 2006." *Araştırma Sonuçları Toplantısı* 25: 103–16.

Rose, C.B., B. Tekkök, and R. Körpe, et al. 2007. "Granicus River Valley Survey Project, 2004–2005." *Studia Troica* 17: 65–150.

Rosenthal, E. 1972. *The Illuminations of the Vergilius Romanus (Cod. Vat. Lat. 3867): A Stylistic and Iconographical Analysis*. Zurich.

Rostovtzeff, M. 1923. "Notes on the Economic Policy of the Pergamene Kings." In *Anatolian Studies Presented to Sir William Mitchell Ramsay*, edited by W. Buckler, 359–90. Manchester.

Roueché, C. 1989. *Aphrodisias in Late Antiquity*. London.

Rudolph, C. 2003. *Das "Harpyien-Monument" von Xanthos: Seine Bedeutung innerhalb der spätarchaischen Plastik*. London.

Rügler, A. 1988. *Die columnae caelatae des jungeren Artemisions von Ephesos*. Tübingen.

Rühfel, H. 1984. *Das Kind in der Griechischen Kunst*. Mainz am Rhein.

Rumscheid, F. 1994. *Untersuchungen zur kleinasiatischen Bauornamentik des Hellenismus*. Beiträge zur Erschliessung hellenistischer und kaiserzeitlicher Skulptur und Architektur 14. Mainz am Rhein.

Ruschenbusch, E. 1982. "Ein Bürgerliste von Koresia und Iulis auf Keos." *ZPE* 48: 175–88.

Ruschenbusch, E. 1983. "Tribut und Bürgerzahl im ersten athenischen Seebund." *ZPE* 53: 125–43.

Rutter, J.B. 1975. "Ceramic Evidence for Northern Intruders in Southern Greece at the Beginning of the Late Helladic IIIC Period." *AJA* 79: 17–32.

Rutter, J.B. 1990. "Some Comments on Interpreting the Dark-Surfaced Handmade Burnished Pottery of the 13th and 12th Century BC Aegean." *JMA* 3: 29–48.

Ruzicka, S. 1997. "The Eastern Greek World." In *The Greek World in the Fourth Century*, edited by L.A. Tritle, 107–36. London.

Safrai, S., and M. Stern. 1974. *The Jewish People in the First Century*. Philadelphia.

Sage, M. 2000. "Roman Visitors to Ilium in the Roman Imperial and Late Antique Period: The Symbolic Functions of a Landscape." *Studia Troica* 10: 211–31.

Şahin, M.Ç. 1981. *Die Inschriften von Stratonikeia. Teil I: Panamara*. Bonn.

Şahin, M.Ç. 1982. *Die Inschriften von Stratonikeia. Teil II.I: Panamara*. Bonn.

Şahoğlu, V. 2005. "The Anatolian Trade Network and the Izmir Region during the Early Bronze Age." *OJA* 24: 339–61.

Sakellariou, M.V. 1958. *La migration grecque en Ionie*. Athens.

Sakellariou, M.V. 1990. *Between Memory and Oblivion: The Transmission of Early Greek Historical Traditions*. Paris.

Salapata, G. 1997. "Hero Warriors from Corinth and Lakonia." *Hesperia* 66: 245–60.

Salzmann, D. 1982. *Untersuchungen zu den antiken Kieselmosaiken: von den Anfangen bis zum Beginn der Tesseratechnik*. Archäologische Forschungen 10. Berlin.

Sams, G.K. 1992. "Observations on Western Anatolia." In *The Crisis Years: The 12th Century B.C., from Beyond the Danube to the Tigris*, edited by W.A. Ward and M.S. Joukowsky, 56–60. Dubuque, Iowa.

Sams, G.K. 1994. *The Gordion Excavations, 1950–1973, Final Reports IV: The Early Phrygian Pottery*. Philadelphia.

Santangelo, F. 2007. *Sulla, the Elites and the Empire: A Study of Roman Politics in Italy and the Greek East*. Leiden.

Sapouna-Sakellarakis, E. 1978. *Die Fibeln der griechischen Inseln*. Munich.

Sazcı, G. 2001. "Gebäude mit vermutlich kultischer Funktion: Das Megaron in Quadrat G6." In *Troia: Traum und Wirklichkeit*, edited by B. Theune-Großkopf, U. Seidel, G. Kastl, M. Kempa, R. Redies, and A. Wais, 384–90. Stuttgart.

Sazcı, G. 2005. "Troia I–III, die maritime Troia-Kultur und Troia IV–V, die anatolische Troia-Kultur: eine Untersuchung der Funde und Befunde im mittleren Schliemanngraben (D07, DO8)." *Studia Troica* 15: 35–98.

Sazcı, G. 2007. *The Treasures of Troia*. Istanbul.

Sazcı, G. 2012. "Maydos Kilisetepe Höyüğü. 2010 Yılı Kazıları." *Kazı Sonuçları Toplantısı* 33.2: 389–408.

Sazcı, G., and M. Treister. 2006. Troias Gold – Die Schätze des dritten Jahrtausends vor Christus." In *Troia: Archäologie eines Siedlungshügels und seiner Landschaft*, edited by M. Korfmann, 208–18. Mainz am Rhein.

Schachter, A. 2003. "Evolution of a Mystery Cult: The Theban Kabiroi." In *Greek Mysteries: The Archaeology and Ritual of Ancient Greek Secret Cults*, edited by M. Cosmopoulos, 112–42. London.

Schäfer, T. 2008. "Sigeion Yüzey Araştırmaları 2005–2007." *Araştırma Sonuçları Toplantısı* 26.2: 1–12.

Schäfer, T. 2011. "Sigeion, Troas Bericht über die 1. Grabungskampagne 2009." *Kazı Sonuçları Toplantısı* 33: 407–20.

Schäfer, T. 2012. "Sigeion, Troas Bericht über die 2. Grabungskampagne 2010." *Kazı Sonuçları Toplantısı* 33.2: 239–59.

Schalles, H.-J. 1985. *Untersuchungen zur Kulturpolitik der pergamenischen Herrscher im dritten Jahrhundert vor Christus*. Istanbuler Forschungen 36. Tübingen.

Schatzmann, P. 1932. "Asklepieion, Baubeschreibung und Baugeschichte." In *Kos: Ergebnisse der deutschen Ausgrabungen und Forschungen I*, edited by R. Herzog. Berlin.

Schauenburg, K. 1969. *Jagddarstellungen auf griechischen Vasen*. Berlin.

Scheer, T.S. 1996. "Ein Museum griechischer 'Frühgeschichte' im Apollon-tempel von Sikyon." *Klio* 78: 353–73.

Scheibler, I. 1983. *Griechische Topferkunst: Herstellung, Handel, und Gebrauch der antiken Tongefässe*. Munich.

Scherrer, P. 2001. "The Historical Topography of Ephesus." In *Urbanism in Western Asia Minor: New Studies on Aphrodisias, Ephesos, Hierapolis, Pergamon, Perge and Xanthos*, edited by D. Parrish, 57–96. JRA Supplement 45. Portsmouth, R.I.

Schilardi, D. 1984. "Representations of Free-Standing Sarcophagi on Attic, White-Ground Lekythoi." In *Ancient Greek and Related Pottery: Proceedings of the International Vase Symposium in Amsterdam, 12–15 April, 1984*, edited by H.A.G. Brijder, 264–70. Amsterdam.

Schliemann, H. 1881. *Ilios: The City and Country of the Trojans*. New York.

Schliemann, H. 1884. *Troja: Results of the Latest Researches and Discoveries on the Site of Homer's Troy and in the Heroic Tumuli and Other Sites, Made in the Year 1882*. New York.

Schmidt, E.F. 1953. *Persepolis I: Structures, Reliefs, Inscriptions*. Chicago, Ill.

Schmidt, E.F. 1957. *Persepolis II: Contents of the Treasury and Other Discoveries*. Chicago, Ill.

Schmidt, R. 1977. *Die Darstellung von Kinderspielzeug und Kinderspiel in der griechischen Kunst*. Vienna.

Schmidt-Dounas, B. 1985. *Der lykische Sarkophag aus Sidon*. Tübingen.

Schmidt-Dounas, B. 1991. "Zur Datierung der Metopen des Athena-Tempels von Ilion." *IstMitt* 41: 363–415.

Schneider, E.E. 2008. *Elaiussa Sebaste*. Istanbul.

Schneider, K. 1927. "Lusus Troiae." *RE* 13: 2059–67.

Schneider, R. 1986. *Bunte Barbaren: Orientalenstatuen aus farbigem Marmor in der römischen Repräsentationskunst*. Worms.

Schober, A. 1933. *Der Fries des Hekateions von Lagina*. Baden bei Wien.

Schulman, A.R. 1969–70. "Some Remarks on the Alleged 'Fall' of Senenmut." *JARCE* 8: 29–48.

Schulz, A. 2000. *Die Stadtmauern von Neandreia in der Troas*. Asia Minor Studien 38. Bonn.

Schuppe, E. 1937. "Torques." *RE²* 6: 1800–5.

Schürer, E. 1973. *The History of the Jewish People in the Age of Jesus Christ (175 B.C.–A.D. 135)*. Edinburgh.

Schwabacher, W. 1968. "Lycian Coin-Portaits." In *Essays in Greek Coinage Presented to Stanley Robinson*, edited by C.M. Kraay and G.K. Jenkins, 111–24. Oxford.

Schwarz, G. 2001. "Der Tod und das Mädchen: Frühe Polyxena Bilder." *AM* 116: 35–50.

Schweitzer, B. 2001–2. "Das Troia-Symposium in Tübingen: Eine Diskussion um Geschichte und Archäologie." *Hephaistos* 19: 7–38.

Schwertheim, E., ed. 1999. *Die Troas: neue Forschungen III*. Bonn.

Schwertheim, E., ed. 2011. *Studien zum antiken Kleinasien VII*. Bonn.

Schwertheim, E., and H. Wiegartz, eds. 1994. *Neue Forschungen zu Neandria und Alexandria Troas*. Bonn.

Schwertheim, E., and H. Wiegartz, eds. 1996. *Die Troas: neue Forschungen zu Neandria und Alexandria Troas II*. Bonn.

Scichilone, G. 1962. Review of *Der Athenatempel von Ilion*, by F.W. Goethert and H. Schleif. *ArchCl* 14: 119–27.

Scott, K. 1928. "The Deification of Demetrius Poliorcetes." *AJP* 49: 137–66.

Scott, K. 1931. "Greek and Roman Honorific Months." *YCS* 2: 201–78.

Scott, M. 2010. *Delphi and Olympia: The Spatial Politics of Panhellenism in the Archaic and Classical Periods*. Cambridge.

Scranton, R. 1963. Review of *Der Athenatempel von Ilion*, by F.W. Goethert and H. Schleif. *AJA* 67: 228–9.

Sear, F. 2006. *Roman Theatres: An Architectural Study*. Oxford.

Seeher, J. 2002 *Hattusha Guide: A Day in the Hittite Capital*. Istanbul.

Séfériadès, M. 1985. *Troie I: Matériaux pour l'étude des sociétés du nord-est égéen au début du bronze ancien*. Paris.

Seiterle, G. 1985. "Die Urform der Phrygischen Mütze." *AntW* 16: 2–13.

Sekunda, N. 1988. "Persian Settlement in Hellespontine Phrygia." In *Achaemenid History III. Method and Theory: Proceedings of the London 1985 Achaemenid History Workshop*, edited by A. Kuhrt and H. Sancisi-Weerdenburg, 175–96. Leiden.

Sekunda, N. 1991. "Achaemenid Settlement in Caria, Lycia, and Greater Phrygia." In

Achaemenid History VI. Asia Minor and Egypt: Old Cultures in a New Empire: Proceedings of the Groningen 1988 Achaemenic History Workshop, edited by H. Sancisi-Weerdenburg and A. Kuhrt, 83–143. Leiden.

Sengelin, T. 1997. "Kentauroi et Kentaurides." *LIMC* VIII: 671–721.

Serdaroğlu, Ü. 1995. *Assos: Behramkale*. Istanbul.

Sevinç, N. 1996. "A New Sarcophagus of Polyxena from the Salvage Excavations at Gümüşçay." *Studia Troica* 6: 251–64.

Sevinç, N., and T. Takaoğlu. 2004. "The Early Bronze Age on Tenedos/Bozcaada." *Studia Troica* 14: 135–40.

Sevinç, N., and M. Treister. 2003. "Metalwork from the Dardanos Tumulus." *Studia Troica* 13: 215–60.

Sevinç, N., C.B. Rose, D. Strahan, and B. Tekkök-Biçken. 1998. "The Dedetepe Tumulus." *Studia Troica* 8: 305–27.

Sevinç, N., C.B. Rose, and D. Strahan. 1999. A Child's Sarcophagus from the Salvage Excavations at Gümüşçay." *Studia Troica* 9: 489–509.

Sevinç, N., R. Körpe, M. Tombul, C.B. Rose, D. Strahan, H. Kiesewetter, and J. Wallrodt. 2001. "A New Painted Graeco-Persian Sarcophagus from Çan." *Studia Troica* 11: 383–420.

Seyrig, H. 1958. "Parion au 3e siècle avant notre ère." In *Centennial Publication of the American Numismatic Society*, edited by H. Ingholt, 603–26. New York.

Shapiro, A. 1991. "The Iconography of Mourning in Athenian Art." *AJA* 95: 629–56.

Shapiro, H.A. 1989. *Art and Cult under the Tyrants in Athens*. Mainz am Rhein.

Shapiro, H.A. 1992. "Mousikoi Agones: Music and Poetry at the Panathenaia." In *Goddess and Polis: The Panathenaic Festival in Ancient Athens*, edited by J. Neils, 53–75. Princeton, N.J.

Shear, J. 2001. "Polis and Panathenaia: The History and Development of Athena's Festival." Ph.D. diss., University of Pennsylvania.

Sherratt, A.G., and E.S. Sherratt. 1993. "The Growth of the Mediterranean Economy in the Early First Millennium BC." *WorldArch* 24: 361–78.

Sherratt, E.S. 2010. "The Trojan War: History or Bricolage?" *BICS* 53: 1–18.

Shürer, E. 1973. "A History of the Jewish People in the Age of Jesus Christ." Edinburgh.

Silantyeva, P. 1976. "Spiral Pendants from Bosporan Necropoles." *Trudy Gosudarstvennogo Ermitaza* 17: 123–37.

Simon, C.G. 1986. "The Archaic Votive Offerings and Cults of Ionia." Ph.D. diss., University of California, Berkeley.

Simon, E. 1959. *Die Geburt der Aphrodite*. Berlin.

Simon, E. 1983. *Festivals of Attica: an Archaeological Commentary*. Madison, Wis.

Simon, E. 1997. "Kybele." *LIMC* VIII: 744–66.

Simpson, R.H. 1959. "Antigonus the One-Eyed and the Greeks." *Historia* 8: 385–409.

Singer, I. 1983. "Western Anatolia in the Thirteenth Century B.C. According to the Hittite Sources." *AnatSt* 33: 205–17.

Singer, I. 1987. "Dating the End of the Hittite Empire." In *Hethitica VIII: Acta Anatolica*, edited by R. Lebrun, 413–21. Louvain.

Singer, I. 2008. "Purple-Dyers in Lazpa." In *Anatolian Interfaces: Hittites, Greeks and Their Neighbours: Proceedings of an International Conference on Cross-Cultural Interaction, September 17–19, 2004, Emory University, Atlanta, GA*, edited by B.J. Collins, M. Bachvarova and I. Rutherford, 21–43. Oxford.

Small, D.B. 1990. "Handmade Burnished Ware and Prehistoric Aegean Economics: An Argument for Indigenous Appearance." *JMA* 3: 3–25.

Smith, P. 1886. *The Ancient History of the East, from the Earliest Times to the Conquest by Alexander the Great*. New York.

Smith, R.R.R. 1990. "Myth and Allegory in the Sebasteion." In *Aphrodisias Papers: Recent Work on Architecture and Sculpture*, edited by C. Rouechel and K.T. Erim, 89–100. Journal of Roman Archaeology Supplementary Series 1. Ann Arbor, Mich.

Smith, R.R.R. 2006. *Roman Portrait Statuary from Aphrodisias*. Aphrodisias 2. Mainz am Rhein.

Snodgrass, A.M. 1967. *Arms and Armour of the Greeks*. London.

Snodgrass, A.M. 1987. *An Archaeology of Greece: The Present State and Future Scope of a Discipline*. Berkeley, Calif.

Snodgrass, A.M. 1994. "The Euboeans in Macedonia: A New Precedent for Westward Expansion." In *Apoikia: i più antichi insediamenti Greci in Occidente: funzioni e modi dell'organizzazione politica e sociale: scritti in onore di Giorgio Buchner*, edited by B. D'Agostino and D. Ridgway, 87–93. Naples.

Soby, A. 2002. *Cassiodorus, Jordanes, and the History of the Goths: Studies in a Migration Myth*. Copenhagen.

Sokolowski, F. 1969. *Lois sacrées des cités grecques*. Paris.

Soleti, V.M. 2003. "Gli studi sul Trono Ludovisi e sul Trono di Boston dalla scoperta al 2000." *AnnBari* 46: 5–116.

Sommer, F. 1932. *Die Ahhijava Urkunden*. Munich.

Spanu, M. 1996. "L'opus reticulatum e mixtum nelle province asiatiche." In *L'Africa romana 11.2. Atti dell'XI Convegno di studio, Cartagine 15–18 dicembre 1994*, edited by M. Khanoussi, P. Ruggeri and C. Vismara, 923–39. Ozieri.

Sparkes, B.A., and L. Talcott. 1970. *Black and Plain Pottery of the 6th, 5th and 4th Centuries B.C. The Athenian Agora* 12. Princeton, N.J.

Spawforth, A., and S. Walker. 1985. "The World of the Panhellenion, 1. Athens and Eleusis." *JRS* 75: 78–104.

Spencer, N. 1995. "Early Lesbos between East and West: A Grey Area of Aegean Archaeology." *BSA* 90: 269–306.

Spencer, T. 1952. "Turks and Trojans in the Renaissance." *Modern Language Review* 47: 330–3.

Sperling, J.W. 1976. "Kum Tepe in the Troad: Trial Excavation, 1934." *Hesperia* 45: 305–64.

Spinazzola, V. 1953. *Pompei alla luce degli scavi nuovi di Via dell'Abbondanza*. Rome.

Sprenger, M., and G. Bartoloni. 1977. *The Etruscans: Their History, Art, and Architecture*. New York.

Stahl, M. 1987. *Aristokraten und Tyrannen im archaischen Athen: Untersuchungen zur Überlieferung, zur Sozialstruktur und zur Entstehung des Staates*. Stuttgart.

Starke, F. 1997. "Troia im Kontext des historisch-politischen Umfeldes Kleinasiens im 2. Jahrtausend." *Studia Troica* 7: 447–87.

Stemmer, K. 1978. *Untersuchungen zur Typologie, Chronologie und Ikonographie der Panzerstatuen.* Berlin.

Steskal, M., and M. la Torre. 2008. *Das Vediusgymnasium in Ephesus: Archaeologie und Baubefund.* Forschungen in Ephesus XIV.1. Vienna.

Steuernagel, D. 1998. "Ein spätarchaischer Sarkophag aus Gümüşçay im Museum von Çanakkale. Ikonographische Beobachtungen." In *Archäologische Studien in Kontaktzonen der antiken Welt,* edited by R. Rolle and K. Schmidt, 165–77. Göttingen.

Stevens, G.P. 1936. "The Periclean Entrance Court of the Acropolis of Athens." *Hesperia* 5: 443–520.

Stewart, A.F. 1977. *Skopas of Paros.* Park Ridge, N.J.

Stewart, A.F. 1990. *Greek Sculpture: An Exploration.* New Haven, Conn.

Stewart, A.F. 1993. *Faces of Power: Alexander's Image and Hellenistic Politics.* Berkeley, Calif.

Stewart, A.F. 1997. "Telephos/Telepinu and Dionysos: New Light on an Ancient Myth." In *Pergamon: The Telephos Frieze from the Great Altar,* R. Dreyfus and E. Schraudolph, 109–19. San Francisco, Calif.

Stewart, A.F. 2005. *Attalos, Athens, and the Akropolis: The Pergamene "Little Barbarians" and Their Roman and Renaissance Legacy.* Cambridge.

Stibbe, C.M. 1991. "Dionysus in Sparta." *BABesch* 66: 1–44.

Stillwell, A. 1948. *The Potters' Quarter.* Corinth 15.1. Princeton, N.J.

Stocker, S.R., and J.L. Davis. 2002. "Animal Sacrifice, Archives, and Feasting at the Palace of Nestor." *Hesperia* 73: 179–95.

Stodulski, L., E. Farrell, and R. Newman. 1984. "Identification of Ancient Persian Pigments from Persepolis and Pasargadae." *Studies in Conservation* 29: 143–54.

Strauss, B.S. 1987. *Athens after the Peloponnesian War: Class, Faction, and Policy, 403–386 B.C.* Ithaca, N.Y.

Strauss, M. 1994. "Instruments à cordes dans un tumulus et la musique des morts." In *La pluridisciplinarité en archéologie musicale: IVe rencontres internationales d'archéologie musicale de l'ICTM, Saint-Germain-en-Laye, 8–12 octobre 1990,* edited by C. Homo-Lechner and A. Bélis, 102–10. Paris.

Strocka, V.M. 1977. *Die Wandmalerei der Hanghäuser in Ephesos. Forschungen in Ephesos 8.1.* Vienna.

Strong, D.E. 1966. *Greek and Roman Gold and Silver Plate.* London.

Stroszeck, J. 2002. "Das Grab des Euphoros." In *Die griechische Klassik: Idee oder Wirklichkeit,* 468–72. Mainz am Rhein and Berlin.

Stuart-Macadam, P. 1992. "Anemia in Past Human Populations." In *Diet, Demography, and Disease: Changing Perspectives on Anemia,* edited by P. Stuart-Macadam and S. Kent, 151–70. New York.

Stucky, R. 1985. "Achämenidische Hölzer und Elfenbeine aus Ägypten und Vorderasien im Louvre." *AntK* 28: 7–32.

Stupperich, R. 1990. "Vorbericht über die Grabung in der Westtor-Nekropole von Assos in Sommer 1989." In *Ausgrabungen in Assos 1990,* edited by Ü. Serdaroğlu and R. Stupperich, 7–22. Bonn.

Stupperich, R. 1992. "Zweiter Vorbericht über die Grabung in der Westtor-Nekropole von Assos in Sommer 1991." In *Ausgrabungen in Assos 1990,* edited by Ü. Serdaroğlu and R. Stupperich, 1–31. Bonn.

Stupperich, R. 1993. "Dritter Vorbericht über die Grabung in der Westtor-Nekropole von Assos in Sommer 1991." In *Ausgrabungen in Assos 1991,* edited by Ü. Serdaroğlu and R. Stupperich, 1–35. Bonn.

Stupperich, R. 1996. "Vierter Vorbericht über die Grabung in der Westtor-Nekropole von Assos in Sommer 1992." In *Ausgrabungen in Assos 1992,* edited by Ü. Serdaroğlu and R. Stupperich, 1–31. Bonn.

Stupperich, R. 2006. "Fünfter Vorbericht über die Grabung in der Westtor-Nekropole von Assos in Sommer 1993." In *Ausgrabungen in Assos 1993,* edited by Ü. Serdaroğlu and R. Stupperich, 1–26. Bonn.

Summerer, L. 2010. "Wall Paintings." In *The Return of Colours,* edited by L. Summerer and A. von Kienlin, 120–85. Istanbul.

Sussenbach, U. 1971. *Frühhellenismus im griechischen Kampf-Relief; Versuch einer Rekonstruktion der Stilentwicklung vom Mausoleum von*

Halikarnassos bis zum Grossen Altarfries von Pergamon. Bonn.

Swan, V. 1984. *The Pottery Kilns of Roman Britain.* London.

Symington, D. 1991. "Late Bronze Age Writing-Boards and Their Uses: Textual Evidence from Anatolia and Syria." *AnatSt* 41: 111–23.

Tagliamonte, G. 1999. "Palatium, Palatinus Mons (fino alla prima età repubblicana)." *LTUR* IV: 14–22.

Takaoğlu, T. 2006. "The Late Neolithic in the Eastern Aegean: Excavations at Gülpinar in the Troad." *Hesperia* 75: 289–315.

Taplin, O. 1992. *Homeric Soundings: The Shaping of the Iliad.* Oxford.

Tappeiner, M. 1986. "Ein Beitrag zu den Wagenzügen auf den Stelen aus Daskyleion." *EpigAnat* 7: 81–96.

Tarn, W.W. 1948. *Alexander the Great.* Cambridge.

Taşlıklıoğlu, Z., and P. Frisch. 1975. "New Inscriptions from the Troad." *ZPE* 17: 101–14.

Tekkök, B. 2000. "The City Wall of Ilion." *Studia Troica* 10: 85–96.

Tekkök, B., S. Wallrodt, C.Y. Gündem, and C.B. Rose. 2001. "Two Roman Wells in the Lower City of Ilion Quadrats C29 and w28." *Studia Troica* 11: 343–382.

Tenger, B. 1995. "Phoroshöhe und Bevölkerungszahl. Die Athener Tributlisten als Indikator für die Größe der Einwohnerschaft einer Polis?" In *Studien zum antiken Kleinasien III*, edited by D. Pohl, 139–60. Asia Minor Studien 16. Bonn.

Tenger, B. 1996. "Troas zwischen Königsfrieden und Ankunft Alexanders." In *Die Troas: neue Forschungen zu Neandria und Alexandria Troas II*, edited by E. Schwertheim and H. Wiegartz, 125–47. Bonn.

Tenger, B. 1999. "Zur Geographie und Geschichte der Troas." In *Die Troas: neue Forschungen III*, edited by E. Schwertheim, 103–80. Bonn.

Terrence, E. 1965. "Sumptuary Arts of Ancient Persia." *BMFA* 63: 3–33.

Themelis, P.G. 1998. "The Sanctuary of Demeter and the Dioscouri at Messene." In *Ancient Greek Cult Practice from the Archaeological Evidence: Proceedings of the Fourth International Seminar on Ancient Greek Cult, organized by the*

Swedish Institute at Athens, 22–24 October 1993, edited by R. Hägg, 157–86. Stockholm.

Theodorescu, D. 1990. "La restitution de l'Aphrodision." In *Aphrodisias Papers: Recent Work on Architecture and Sculpture*, edited by C. Rouechel and K.T. Erim, 49–65. *Journal of Roman Archaeology* Supplementary Series 1. Ann Arbor, Mich.

Thieme, T. 1993. "The Architectural Remains of Archaic Labraunda." In *Les grand ateliers d'architecture dans le monde egéen du VIe siecle av. J.-C.*, edited by J. Des Courtils and J.-C. Moretti, 47–55. Paris.

Thomas, R. 2001. "Ethnicity, Genealogy, and Hellenism in Herodotos." In *Ancient Perceptions of Greek Ethnicity*, edited by I. Malkin, 213–33. Washington, D.C.

Thompson, D.B. 1963. *Troia: The Terracotta Figurines of the Hellenistic Period.* Princeton, N.J.

Thompson, H. 1981. "Athens Faces Adversity." *Hesperia* 50: 343–55.

Thraemer, E. 1901. "Dardanos (3)." *RE* 4.2: 2164–78.

Tiné, S., and A. Traverso. 2001. *Poliochni: The Earliest Town in Europe.* Athens.

Tiverios, M. 1997a. "Die von Xenophantos Athenaios signierte grosse Lekythos aus Pantikapaion: Alte Funde neu betrachtet." In *Athenian Potters and Painters: The Conference Proceedings*, edited by J.H. Oakley, W.D.E. Coulson, and O. Palagia, 269–84. Oxford.

Tiverios, M. 1997b. "Zeus." *LIMC* VIII: 310–74.

Tölle-Kastenbein, R. 1990. *Antike Wasserkultur.* Munich.

Tolstikov, V., and M. Treister. 1996. *The Gold of Troy: Searching for Homer's Fabled City.* New York.

Tomlinson, R. 1963. Review of *Der Athenatempel von Ilion*, by F.W. Goethert and H. Schleif. *JHS* 83: 219–20.

Torelli, M. 1980. "Innovazioni nelle tecniche edilizie romane tra il I sec. a.C. e il I sec. d.c." In *Tecnologia, economia e società nel mondo romano*, 139–62. Como.

Torelli, M. 1984. *Lavinio e Roma: riti iniziatici e matrimonio tra archeologia e storia.* Roma.

Touchefeu, O. 1981. "Aias II." *LIMC* I: 336–80.

Touchefeu, O. 1984. "Astyanax." *LIMC* II: 921–37.

Touchefeu, O. 1988. "Hektor." *LIMC* IV: 482–98.

Touchefeu-Meynier, O. 1994. "Polyxene." *LIMC* VII: 431–5.

Toynbee, J. 1944. *Roman Medallions.* New York.

Travlos, J. 1971. *Pictorial Dictionary of Ancient Athens.* New York.

Treister, M. 1996. "Bronze Matrices from the George Ortiz Collection." In *Ancient Jewellery and Archaeology,* edited by A. Calinescu, 172–84. Bloomington, Ind.

Trendall, A.D., and A. Cambitoglou. 1982. *The Red Figure Vases of Apulia.* Oxford.

Triantis, I. 1994. "Pelops." *LIMC* VII: 282–7.

Trillmich, W. 1978. *Familienpropaganda der Kaiser Caligula und Claudius: Agrippina Maior u. Antonia Augusta auf Münzen.* Berlin.

Tritsch, F.J. 1942. "The Harpy Tomb at Xanthus." *JHS* 62: 39–50.

Tsetskhladze, G.R. 2008. "'Grain for Athens': The View from the Black Sea." In *Feeding the Ancient Greek City,* edited by R. Alston and O. van Nijf, 47–62. Leuven.

Tsetskhladze, G.R., and A.M. Snodgrass. 2002. *Greek Settlements in the Eastern Mediterranean and the Black Sea.* BAR-IS 1062. Oxford.

Tuchelt, K. 1979. *Frühe Denkmäler Roms in Kleinasien: Beiträge zur archäologischen Überlieferung aus der Zeit der Republik und des Augustus.* Tübingen.

Tudor, D. 1976. *Corpus Monumentorum Religionis Equitum Danuvinorum II: The Analysis.* Leiden.

Tuna-Nörling, Y. 1997. "Attic Black Figure Exports to the East: The Tyrrhenian Group in Ionia." In *Athenian Potters and Painters: The Conference Proceedings,* edited by J.H. Oakley, W.D.E. Coulson, and O. Palagia, 435–46. Oxford.

Tuna-Nörling, Y. 1999. "Daskyleion I: Die attische Keramik." *ADerg* 6: 1–92.

Tuna-Nörling, Y. 2001. "Attic Pottery from Dascylium." In *Achaemenid Anatolia. Proceedings of the First International Symposium on Anatolia in the Achaemenid Period,* edited by T. Bakır, H. Sancisi-Weerdenburg, G. Gürtekin, P. Briant, and W. Henkelman, 109–22. Leiden.

Tür, H. 2002. "Die Bauphasen der Wohneinheit 4." In *Das Hanghaus 2 von Ephesos: Studien zu Baugeschichte und Chronologie,* edited by F. Krinzinger, 41–66. Vienna.

Tybout, R. 1992. "Barbarians in Phrygia: A New Grave Stele." *EpigAnat* 20: 35–41.

Tyldesley, J. 1996. *Hatchepsut: The Female Pharaoh.* London.

Uerpmann, M., and W. Van Neer. 2000. Fischreste aus den Grabungen in Troia (1989–1999)." *Studia Troica* 10: 145–79.

Ulf, C. 1996. "Griechische Ethnogenese versus Wanderungen von Stämmen und Stammstaaten." In *Wege zur Genese griechischer Identität. Die Bedeutung der frürharchaischen Zeit,* edited by C. Ulf, 240–80. Berlin.

Ulf, C. 2004. "Die Instrumentalisierung der griechischen Frühzeit: Interdependenzen zwischen Epochencharakteristik und politischer Überzeugung bei Ernst Curtius und Jakob Burckhardt." In *Griechische Archaik: Interne Entwicklungen, externe Impulse,* edited by R. Rollinger and C. Ulf, 51–103. Berlin.

Ünal, A., A. Ertekin, and I. Ediz. 1991. "The Hittite Sword from Boghazköy-Hattusa, Found in 1991 and Its Akkadian Inscription." *Museum* 4: 46–52.

Ünlüsöy, S. 2006. "Vom Reihenhaus zum Megaron: Troia I bis Troia III." In *Troia: Archäologie eines Siedlungshügels und seiner Landschaft,* edited by M. Korfmann, 133–44. Mainz am Rhein.

Utili, F. 1999. *Die archaische Nekropole von Assos.* Asia Minor Studien 31. Bonn.

Utili, F. 2002. "Graue Keramik aus Pyrrha auf Lesbos im Archäologischen Institut Göttingen." *AA*: 35–159.

Van Dam, R. 2007. *The Roman Revolution of Constantine.* Cambridge.

Van den Hout, T. 1995. *Der Ulmiteåub-Vertrag: Eine prosopographische Untersuchung.* Wiesbaden.

van der Vin, J.P.A. 1980. *Travellers to Greece and Constantinople: Ancient Monuments and Old Traditions in Medieval Travellers' Tales.* Leiden.

Van Straten, F.T. 1995. *Hiera Kala: Images of Animal Sacrifice in Archaic and Classical Greece.* Leiden.

van Wees, H. 1998. "A Brief History of Tears: Gender Differentiation in Archaic Greece." In *When Men Were Men: Masculinity, Power and Identity in Classical Antiquity,* edited by L. Foxhall, and J. Salmon, 10–53. London.

Vandeput, L. 1997. *The Architectural Decoration in Roman Asia Minor. Sagalassos: A Case Study.* Leuven.

Vandiver, E. 2010. *Stand in the Trench, Achilles: Classical Receptions in British Poetry of the Great War.* Oxford.

Vanschoonwinkel, J. 1991. *L'Egée et la Méditerranée orientale à la fin du deuxième millénaire: Témoignages archéologiques et sources écrites.* Louvain.

Vassileva, M. 2005. "Phrygia, Troy and Thrace." In *Anatolian Iron Ages* 5, edited by A. Çilingiroglu and G. Darbyshire, 227–34. London.

Vassiliev, A. 1959. *Das antike Grabmal bei Kazanlak.* Sofia.

Verkinderen, F. 1987. "The Honorary Decree for Malousios of Gargara and the koinon of Athena Ilias." *Tyche* 2: 247–69.

Vermaseren, M.J. 1977a. *Corpus Cultus Cybele Attidisque* III. Italia-Latium. Leiden.

Vermaseren, M.J. 1977b. *Cybele and Attis: The Myth and the Cult.* London.

Vermaseren, M.J., and M. De Boer. 1986. "Attis." *LIMC* III: 22–44.

Vermeule, C. 1968. *Roman Imperial Art in Greece and Asia Minor.* Cambridge, Mass.

Vermeule, C. 1995. "Neon Ilion and Ilium Novum: Kings, Soldiers, Citizens, and Tourists at Classical Troy." In *The Ages of Homer: A Tribute to Emily Townsend Vermeule*, edited by J.B Carter and S.P. Morris, 467–82. Austin, Tex.

Vermeule, E.T., and S. Chapman. 1971. "A Protoattic Human Sacrifice?" *AJA* 75: 285–93.

Vian, F. and M.B. Moore. 1988. "Gigantes." *LIMC* IV: 191–270.

Vierneisel-Schlörb, B. 1964. "Zwei klassischer Kindergräber um Kerameikos." *AM* 79: 85–104.

Vikan, G. 1990. "Pilgrims in Magi's Clothing: The Impact of Mimesis on Early Byzantine Pilgrim's Art." In *The Blessings of Pilgrimage*, edited by R. Ousterhout, 97–107. Urbana, Ill.

Vittinghoff, F. 1936. *Der Staatsfeind in der römischen Kaiserzeit.* Berlin.

Viviers, D. 1987. "La conquete de Sigée par Pisistrate." *AntCl* 56: 5–25.

Vogel, L. 1973. *The Column of Antoninus Pius.* Cambridge, Mass.

Voigt, M.M. 2003. "Celts at Gordion: The Late Hellenistic Settlement." *Expedition* 45: 14–19.

Voigt, M.M., and R.C. Henrickson. 2000. "Formation of the Phrygian State: The Early Iron Age at Gordion." *AnatSt* 50: 37–54.

Vollkommer-Glökler, D. 1997. "Megaloi Theoi." *LIMC* VIII: 820–8.

Von Bothmer, D. 1957. *Amazons in Greek Art.* Oxford.

Von Bothmer, D. 1984. *A Greek and Roman Treasury.* New York.

Von Bothmer, D. 1994. "Sarpedon." *LIMC* VII: 696–700.

Von Gerkan, A., and F. Krischen. 1928. *Thermen und Palaestren. Milet 1.9.* Berlin.

Von Graeve, V. 1970. *Der Alexandersarkophag und seine Werkstatt.* Berlin.

Von Mehren, M. 2002. "The Trojan Cycle on Amphorae." In *Pots for the Living, Pots for the Dead*, edited by A. Rathje, M. Nielsen, B. Bundgard Rasmussen, 33–58. Copenhagen.

Waal, W. 2011. "They Wrote on Wood: The Case for a Hieroglyphic Scribal Tradition on Wooden Writing Boards in Hittite Anatolia." *AnatSt* 61: 21–34.

Walbank, F.W. 1967. *Historical Commetary on Polybius II.* Oxford.

Walbank, F.W., A.E. Astin, M.W. Fredericksen, and R.M. Ogilvie. 1984. *The Cambridge Ancient History VII.1. The Hellenistic World.* Cambridge.

Waldbaum, J.C. 1983. *Metalwork from Sardis: The Finds through 1974.* Cambridge, Mass.

Waldbaum, J.C. 1997. "Greeks in the East or Greeks and the East? Problems in the Definition and Recognition of Presence." *BASOR* 305: 1–17.

Walker, S. 1985. "The Marble Quarries of Proconnesus: Isotopic Evidence for the Age of the Quarries and for Lenos-Sarcophagi Carved at Rome." In *Marmi antichi: problemi d'impiego, di restauro e d'identificazione*, edited by P. Pensabene, 57–68. Rome.

Wallace, S. 2003. "The Perpetuated Past: Re-use or Continuity in Material Culture and the Structuring of Identity in Early Iron Age Crete." *BSA* 98: 251–77.

Wallace-Hadrill, J.M. 1960. *The Fourth Book of the Chronicle of Fredegar.* London.

Wallert, A. 1995. "Unusual Pigments on a Greek Marble Basin." *Studies in Conservation* 40: 177–88.

Wallrodt, S. 2002. "Ritual Activity in Late Classical Ilion: The Evidence from a Fourth Century B.C. Deposit of Loomweights and Spindlewhorls." *Studia Troica* 12: 179–96.

Walter, H. 1962. "Amazonen oder Achäer?" *AM* 77: 193–6.

Walter-Karydi, E. 1985. "Geneleos." *AM* 100: 91–104.

Wandruszka, A. 1964. *House of Habsburg: 600 Years of a European Dynasty.* Garden City, N.Y.

Warner, J. 1979. "The Megaron and Apsidal House in Early Bronze Age Western Anatolia: New Evidence from Karataş." *AJA* 83: 133–47.

Wartke, R.-B. 2005. *Sam'al: Ein aramäischer Stadtstaat des 10. bis 8. Jhs. v. Chr. und die Geschichte seiner Erforschung.* Mainz am Rhein.

Watkins, C. 1986. "The Language of the Trojans." In *Troy and the Trojan War*, edited by M.J. Mellink, 45–62. Bryn Mawr, Pa.

Watzinger, C. 1905. *Die griechischen Holzsarkophage aus der Zeit Alexanders des Grossen.* Leipzig.

Webb, P. 1996. *Hellenistic •Architectural Sculpture: Figural Motifs in Western Anatolia and the Aegean Islands.* Madison, Wis.

Weber, B.F. 1999. "Die Bauteile des Athenatempels in Milet." *AA*: 415–38.

Weber, M. 1993. "Zur Überlieferung der Goldelfenbeinstatue des Phidias im Parthenon." *JdI* 108: 83–122.

Weber-Lehmann, C. 2005. "Trauergesten in Ionien und Etrurien." In *Otium: Festschrift fur Volker Michael Strocka*, edited by T. Ganschow and M. Steinhard, 445–50. Remshalden.

Wegener, S. 1985. *Funktion und Bedeutung landschaftlicher Elemente in der griechischen Reliefkunst archaischer bis hellenistischer Zeit.* New York.

Wegner, M. 1956. *Hadrian, Plotina, Marciana, Matidia, Sabina.* Berlin.

Wegner, M. 1963. *Musikgeschichte in Bildern II.4: Griechenland.* Leipzig.

Weigel, R. 1992. "Lupa Romana." *LIMC* VI: 292–6.

Weilhartner, Jörg. 2000. "Ober- und Unterstadt von Troia im archäologischen Befund und in den homerischen Epen." *Studia Troica* 10: 199–210.

Weinberg, G. 1952. *Corinth XII: The Minor Objects.* Princeton, N.J.

Weinstock, S. 1971. *Divus Julius.* Oxford.

Weiskopf, M. 1989. *The So-Called "Great Satraps' Revolt." 366–360 B.C.* Stuttgart.

Weitzmann, K. 1979. *Age of Spirituality: Late Antique and Early Christian Art, Third to Seventh Century.* New York.

Welles, C.B. 1934. *Royal Correspondence in the Hellenistic Period: A Study in Greek Epigraphy.* New Haven, Conn.

Wenger, M. 1949. *Das Musikleben der Griechen.* Berlin.

Wescoat, B. 1987. "Designing the Temple of Athena at Assos: Some Evidence from the Capitals." *AJA* 91: 553–68.

Wescoat, B. 1989. *Syracuse, the Fairest Greek City: Ancient Art from the Museo archeologico regionale "Paolo Orsi."* Rome.

Wescoat, B. 2012a. *The Temple of Athena at Assos.* Oxford.

Wescoat, B. 2012b. "Insola Sacra: Samothrace between Troy and Rome." In *Tripodes. Religione come sistema di comunicazione: networks e rituali nei santuari tradizionali greci di età romana*, edited by M. Galli. Rome.

Wesenberg, B. 1996. "Die Entstehung der griechischen Säulen- und Gebälkformen in der literarischen Überlieferung der Antike." In *Säule und Gebalk. Zu Strukur und Wandlungsprozess griechisch-römischer Architektur*, edited by E.-L. Schwander, 1–15. Mainz am Rhein.

Wessel, K. 1966. "Daniel." *Reallexikon zur Byzantinische Kunst* I: 1113–20.

West, A.B., and B.D. Meritt. 1925. "Cleon's Amphipolitan Campaign and the Assessment List of 421." *AJA* 29: 59–69.

West, M.L., ed. 1978. *Hesiod: Works and Days.* Oxford.

West, M.L. 1985. *The Hesiodic Catalogue of Women: Its Nature, Structure, and Origins.* Oxford.

West, M.L. 1988. "The Rise of the Greek Epic." *JHS* 108: 151–72.

West, M.L., ed. 1992. *Iambi et elegi Graeci ante Alexandrum cantata.* Oxford.

West, M.L. 1995. "The Date of the Iliad." *MusHelv* 52: 203–19.

West, M.L. 2001a. "Atreus and Attarassiyaas." *Glotta* 77: 262–6.

West, M.L. 2001b. *Studies in the Text and Transmission of the Iliad*. Munich.

Whitehead, D. 1993. "Cardinal Virtues: The Language of Public Approbation in Democratic Athens." *ClMed* 44: 37–75.

Whitley, J. 1988. "Early States and Hero Cults: A Re-appraisal." *JHS* 108: 173–82.

Wiegand, T. 1904. "Reisen in Mysien." *AM* 29: 254–339.

Wiegartz, H. 1994. "Äolische Kapitelle: Neufunde 1992 und ihr Verhältnis zu den bekannten Stücken." In *Neue Forschungen zu Neandria und Alexandria Troas*, edited by E. Schwertheim and H. Wiegartz, 117–32. Bonn.

Wiencke, Martha. 2010. "Lerna." In *The Oxford Handbook of the Bronze Age Aegean*, edited by E.H. Cline, 660–70. Oxford.

Wiencke, Matthew. 1954. "An Epic Theme in Greek Art." *AJA* 58: 285–306.

Wiener, M. 2007. "Homer and History: Old Questions, New Evidence." In *Epos: Reconsidering Greek Epic and Aegean Bronze Age Archaeology. Proceedings of the 11th International Aegean Conference, Los Angeles, UCLA, the J. Paul Getty Villa, 20–23 April 2006*, edited by S.P. Morris and R. Laffineur, 3–34. Aegaeum 28. Liège.

Wilhelm, A. 1911. "Die Lokrische Mädcheninschrift." *Jahreshefte des Österreichischen Archäologischen Institutes in Wien* 14: 163–256.

Willers, D. 1990. *Hadrians panhellenisches Programm: archäologische Beiträge zur Neugestaltung Athens durch Hadrian*. Basel.

Williams, D., and J. Ogden. 1994. *Greek Gold: Jewellery of the Classical World*. London.

Williams, R.D., ed. 1960. *Virgil. Aeneidos. Liber quintus*. Oxford.

Williams-Thorpe, O. 2008. "A Thousand and One Columns: Observations on the Roman Granite Trade in the Mediterranean Area." *OJA* 27: 73–89.

Winter, E. 1996a. *Staatliche Baupolitik und Baufürsorge in den römischen Provinzen des kaiserzeitlichen Kleinasien*. Bonn.

Winter, E. 1996b. "Stadt und Herrschaft in spätrepublikanischer Zeit: eine neue Pompeius-Inschrift aus Ilion." In *Die Troas: neue Forschungen zu Neandria und Alexandria Troas II*, edited by E. Schwertheim and H. Wiegartz, 175–94. Bonn.

Winter, I. 1995. "Homer's Phoenicians: History, Ethnography, or Literary Trope? A Perspective on Early Orientalism." In *The Ages of Homer: A Tribute to Emily Townsend Vermeule*, edited by J. Carter and S. Morris, 247–71. Austin, Tex.

Winter, N. 1993. *Greek Architectural Terracottas*. Oxford.

Wiseman, J. 1973. *Stobi: A Guide to the Excavations*. Belgrade.

Wiseman, T.P. 1982. "Philodemus 26.3 G-P." *CQ* 32: 475–6.

Wiseman, T.P. 1984. "Cybele, Virgil, and Augustus." In *Poetry and Politics in the Age of Augustus*, edited by T. Woodman and D. West, 117–28. Cambridge.

Wiseman, T.P. 1995. *Remus: A Roman Myth*. Cambridge.

Wittke, A.-M. 2006. "Phrygische Vorherrschaft in der Troas, Mysien und der Äolis?" In *Tekmeria: Archäologische Zeugnisse in ihrer kulturhistorischen und politischen Dimension. Beiträge für Werner Gauer*, edited by N. Kreutz and B. Schweizer, 389–400. Münster.

Wittwer-Backofen, U., and H. Kiesewetter. 1997. "Menschliche Überreste aus den Ausgrabungen in Troia: Funde der Kampagnen 1989–1995." *Studia Troica* 7: 509–38.

Wolkersdorfer, C., and J. Göbel. 2004. "Hydrogeologie der troianischen Landschaft: eine Bestandsaufnahme." *Studia Troica* 14: 157–67.

Wolska, W. 1992. "Pathologische Beobachtungen am Skelettmaterial." In *Ausgrabungen in Assos 1990*, edited by Ü. Serdaroğlu and R. Stupperich, 173–82. Bonn

Wolska, W. 2006. "Die archaische Körpergräber in der Nekropole von Assos." In *Ausgrabungen in Assos 1993*, edited by R. Stupperich, 251–91. Bonn.

Wolska, W., and Wolski, W. 1996. "Hyperostosis porotica bei Kindern in der Nekropole von

Assos." In *Ausgrabungen in Assos 1992*, edited by Ü. Serdaroğlu and R. Stupperich, 167–90. Bonn.

Wood, M. 1998. *In Search of the Trojan War.* Berkeley, Calif.

Woodford, S. 1993. *The Trojan War in Ancient Art.* London.

Woolf, G. 1998. *Becoming Roman: The Origins of Provincial Civilization in Gaul.* Cambridge.

Wright, D.H. 1984. *Vergilius Vaticanus: vollständige Faksimile-Ausgabe im Originalformat des Codex Vaticanus Latinus 3225 der Biblioteca Apostolica Vaticana: Commentarium.* Graz.

Wright, D.H. 1992. *Codicological Notes on the Vergilius Romanus (Vat. Lat. 3867).* Rome.

Wright, D.H. 1993. *The Vatican Vergil: A Masterpiece of Late Antique Art.* Berkeley, Calif.

Wright, J.C. 2005. "Offsets in Mycenaean Architecture." In *Autochthon: Papers Presented to O.T.P.K. Dickinson on the Occasion of His Retirement*, edited by A. Dakouri-Hild and E.S. Sherratt, 191–9. Oxford.

Wroth, W. 1892. *Catalogue of the Greek Coins of Mysia in the British Museum.* London.

Wroth, W. 1894. *Catalogue of the Greek Coins of Troas, Aeolis, and Lesbos in the British Museum.* London.

Wroth, W. 1899. *Catalogue of the Greek Coins of Galatia, Cappadocia and Syria in the British Museum.* London.

Wulf, U. 1999. *Die hellenistischen und römischen Wohnhäuser von Pergamon: die Stadtgrabung.* Altertümer von Pergamon 15.3. Berlin.

Wulf-Rheidt, U. 1998. "The Hellenistic and Roman Houses of Pergamon." In *Pergamon, Citadel of the Gods: Archaeological Record, Literary Description, and Religious Development*, edited by H. Koester, 299–330. Harrisburg, Pa.

Yakar, J. 2003. "Identifying Migrations in the Archaeological Records of Anatolia." In *Identifying Changes: The Transition from Bronze to Iron Ages in Anatolia and Its Neighbouring Regions: Proceedings of the International Workshop Istanbul, November 8–9, 2002*, edited by B. Fischer, H. Genz, É. Jean, and K. Köroglu, 11–19. Istanbul.

Yalçın, Ü. 1999. "Early Iron Metallurgy in Anatolia." *AnatSt* 49: 177–87.

Yalouris, N. 1982. "Painting in the Age of Alexander the Great and the Successors." In *Macedonia and Greece in Late Classical and Early Hellenistic Times*, edited by B. Barr-Sharrar and E.N. Borza, 263–8. Washington, D.C.

Yalouris, N. 1990. "Helios." *LIMC* V: 1005–34.

Yates, F. 1975. *Astraea: The Imperial Theme in the 16th Century.* London.

Yavuz, F., and R. Körpe. 2006. "Archaeological Support of Lysandros' Expulsion of the Athenians from the Chersonese after Aigospotamoi." Paper read at the 2006 Annual Meeting of the Archaeological Institute of America, January, Montreal.

Yegül, F. 1992. *Baths and Bathing in Classical Antiquity.* Cambridge, Mass.

Young, R.S. 1956. "Discoveries at Gordion 1956." *Archaeology* 9: 263–7.

Young, R.S. 1981. *Three Great Early Tumuli.* Philadelphia.

Young, W., and B. Ashmole. 1968. "The Boston Relief and the Ludovisi Throne." *BMFA* 346: 124–66.

Zachos, K. 2001. *To Mnemeio tou Oktavianou Augoustou ste Nikopole.* Athens.

Zahle, J. 1979. "Lykische Felsgräber mit Reliefs aus dem 4. Jahrhundert v. Chr." *JdI* 94: 245–346.

Zahle, J. 1982. "Persian Satraps and Lycian Dynasts: The Evidence of the Diadems." In *Proceedings of the 9th International Congress of Numismatics*, edited by T. Hackens and R. Weiller, 101–12. Louvain-la-Neuve.

Zahle, J. 1991. "Achaemenid Influences in Lycia (Coinage, Sculpture, Architecture). Evidence for Political Changes during the 5th Century B.C." In *Achaemenid History VI. Asia Minor and Egypt: Old Cultures in a New Empire*, edited by H. Sancisi-Weerdenburg and A. Kuhrt, 145–60. Leiden.

Zancani Montuoro, P. 1960. "Il corredo della sposa." *ArchCl* 12: 37–50.

Zangger, E. 1994. *Ein neuer Kampf um Troia: Archäologie in der Krise.* Munich.

Zavadil, M. 2009. *Ein trojanischer Federkrieg: die Auseinandersetzungen zwischen Ernst Boetticher und Heinrich Schliemann.* Vienna.

Zimmer, G. 1990. *Griechische Bronzegusswerkstätten: zur Technologieentwicklung eines antiken Kunsthandwerkes.* Mainz am Rhein.

Zimmermann, N. 2002. "Ausstattungen von Haupt- und Nebenräumen. Zur Datierung der Wandmalerein des Hanghauses 2 in Ephesos." In *Das Hanghaus 2 von Ephesos: Studien zu Baugeschichte und Chronologie*, edited by F. Krinzinger, 101–17. Vienna.

Zöldföldi, J., and M. Satır. 2003. "Provenance of White Marble Building Stones in the Monuments of Ancient Troia." In *Troia and the Troad: Scientific Approaches*, edited by G.A. Wagner, E. Pernicka, and H.-P. Uerpmann, 203–22. Berlin.

Zschietzschmann, W. 1928. "Die Darstellungen der Prothesis in der griechischen Kunst." *AM* 53: 17–47.

Zwierlein-Diehl, E. 1969. *Antike Gemmen in deutschen Sammlungen. Berlin.* Munich.

INDEX